Izzy

Izzy

A Biography of I. F. Stone

ROBERT C. COTTRELL

Rutgers University Press   *New Brunswick, New Jersey*

First paperback printing/second cloth printing, March 1993

Library of Congress Cataloging-in-Publication Data

Cottrell, Robert C., 1950–
    Izzy : a biography of I.F. Stone / Robert C. Cottrell.
        p.   cm.
    Includes bibliographical references and index.
    ISBN 0-8135-1847-4 (cloth)—ISBN 0-8135-2008-8 (pbk)
    1. Stone, I. F. (Isidor F.), 1907–   —Biography.   2. Journalists—
United States—Biography.   I. Title.
PN4874.S69C67   1992
070'.92—dc20
    [B]   91-45763
                                                                                                    CIP

British Cataloging-in-Publication information available

To Sue and Adrienne

Contents

Acknowledgments

This book is the product of a decade-long examination of the life and times of I. F. "Izzy" Stone. By weaving together material from interviews, letters, archival materials, and government documents, as well as Stone's own writings, it seeks to tell the tale of one of this nation's most significant journalists, intellectuals, and political mavericks of the twentieth century. Invaluable to that end was the assistance I received from Stone himself, from members of his family, and from certain of his colleagues, friends, and antagonists. And yet, *Izzy* is in no way an "authorized" biography.

Of greatest help was the access that Izzy afforded me, through a series of personal interviews, including a pair of day-long bouts at the Library of Congress and in his home on October 15–16, 1981, and a number carried out over the telephone in 1981, 1983, and 1984. In addition, I briefly spoke with Stone at a reception held in his honor in San Francisco on February 5, 1988, and listened while he expressed great satisfaction that he was "still extant."

I conducted additional interviews, either in person or by way of telephone, that still magical medium for researchers, with Sidney Hook, Victor Navasky, Peter Osnos, Lee Webb, Izzy's brother-in-law Leonard Boudin, his son Chris Stone, his sister Judy Stone, and his brothers Lou and Marc Stone. Highly revealing were lengthy telephone interviews I completed with Lou and Marc Stone in the fall of 1987, a pair of telephone interviews with Osnos in the summer of 1989, and a series of conversations by telephone with Lou Stone from 1990 to 1992. Particularly enlightening were interviews I undertook with Boudin and Navasky in New York City, a full-day interview with Lou Stone at his apartment in Glenside, Pennsylvania, located just outside of Philadelphia—all undertaken in the summer of 1989—a three-hour interview with Chris Stone at his home in Los Angeles in early January 1992, and a two-hour interview with Judy Stone at her residence in San Francisco that February.

After much digging, I uncovered a wealth of archival materials on Stone, comprising letters and other documents of a personal nature, scattered across the country. This was no easy undertaking, for Izzy, writing as he did on a virtually everyday basis, seldom had the luxury to correspond with others. And yet, thanks to various research collections and innumerable research librarians, I was able to discover scores of such writings. Most revealing were the following holdings: the Michael Blankfort Collection, the Ralph Ingersoll Collection, the Martin Luther King, Jr., Collection, and the Shepard Traube Collection at Boston University's Mugar Memorial Library; *The Nation* Collection at Harvard University's Houghton Library; the Freda Kirchwey Papers at the Arthur and Elizabeth Schlesinger Library at Radcliffe College; the V. F. Calverton Papers and the Norman Thomas Papers at the New York Public Library; the SDS Papers, the Alexander Meiklejohn Papers, the James Kutcher Civil Rights Committee Papers, and the Irving Caesar Papers at the Wisconsin State Historical Society; the Malcolm Cowley Papers at the Newberry Library; the Jerome Frank Papers, the Victor Jerome Papers, the Max Lerner Papers, and the Dwight Macdonald Papers at Yale University's Sterling Library; the Matthew Josephson Papers at Yale University's Beinecke Library; the Presidential Personal File and the Post-Presidential General File at the Harry S Truman Library; the Presidential General File at the Dwight D. Eisenhower Library; the White House Central Name File at the Lyndon Baines Johnson Library; and the Presidential General File at the John Fitzgerald Kennedy Library.

In the process of conducting my study, I compiled my own supply of I. F. Stone materials. I have in my home tapes of various interviews I held as well as a file of my correspondence with Malcolm Cowley, Howard Fast, W. H. Ferry, Todd Gitlin, Tom Hayden, Irving Howe, Corliss Lamont, Max Lerner, Kirkpatrick Sale, George Seldes, Chris Stone, Jeremy Stone, Lou Stone, and George C. Vournas.

The work of others also proved instructive, especially Lou Stone's "The Family (Where and When It Began)" and Marc Stone's "Max," the first two chapters in what was once projected as a family history. Testimonials and anecdotes sent to B. J. Stone for "I. F. Stone Memories" were made available to me by Jeremy Stone, various materials from Izzy's childhood and early adulthood as well as photographs were obtained from Lou Stone, and a look at personal and professional memorabilia was afforded by Celia Gilbert and Esther Stone.

A good number of documents acquired under the Freedom of Information Act, particularly those released by the Department of State and its Passport Division and the Central Intelligence Agency, proved useful. So did materials let out into the public purview by the the United States Postal Service, the Department of the Army, the Department of the Air Force, and the Department of Agriculture, originally housed in an FBI file of some twenty-six hundred pages altogether. At the time of the completion of this manuscript, the FBI had itself opted to release or to withhold several hundred of those documents, but the heavily edited nature of the material made it all but worthless to this researcher at least.

Fortunately, I. F. Stone's voice and his image are frozen in time, thanks to the wonders of audiovisual materials. These range from Jerry Bruck, Jr.'s, 1973 documentary, *I. F. Stone's Weekly,* to Izzy's appearances on various talk shows and at public gatherings, to the collection of "Meet the Press" radio and television programs from the 1940s, housed at the Library of Congress. All help to reveal something of the essence of the man and his era.

So too did the twin memorial services held in New York City on July 12, and in Washington, D.C., on July 18, 1989, which provided some kind of closure for this study. Speaking on the many sides of I. F. Stone were Peter Osnos, Christopher Stone, Leonard Boudin, Murray Kempton, Judith Miller, Robert B. Silvers, Victor Navasky, Celia Gilbert, Richard Dudman, Felicity Bryan, Robert G. Kaiser, and Bernard Knox.

I wish to thank the editors for permission to reprint from articles contained in the *South Atlantic Quarterly* (Spring 1987), *Mid-Atlantic* (January 1984) and *Journalism History* (Summer 1985), albeit in very different form.

Given the voluminous nature of his writings (discussed in the first section of the Selected Bibliography) and the length and breadth of his career, preparing a biography of I. F. Stone was a sometimes taxing but ultimately invigorating endeavor. The frequent delight I felt in making some new discovery, in believing that I had come to know him a little better, in simply shaping *Izzy,* could not have been possible without the help of all sorts of good people. I thank my fellow historians, including Sara Alpern, Joseph Conlin, Paul Glad, Robert Griswold, Maurice Isserman, Alan Lawson, David Levy, H. Wayne Morgan, Richard Pells, Dale Steiner, David Thelen, and Frank Warren, some of whom were far more critical of various versions of the book than I might have liked, but whose analyses ultimately made for a much richer work. Professor Steiner, in particular, goaded me into completing *Izzy* at long last and served as a good friend. Dr. Victor Mlotok, a politically kindred soul and another close friend of mine, brought his psychiatrically trained ear and sensitive nature to bear on the project. Archivists and librarians from coast to coast opened up manuscript materials to me. Administrative personnel at my home campus, California State University, Chico, at various points provided funding which enabled me to continue with my research. Lou Stone, looking uncannily like Izzy, deserves a special word of thanks, for his good cheer, encouragement, and vast store of information. Copyeditor Victoria Haire lovingly graced *Izzy* with her deft pen. The folk at Rutgers University Press, including Anne Bentley, Marilyn Campbell, Steve Maikowski, and above all else, Marlie Wasserman, continually coaxed me to turn in necessary papers, photographs, releases, and the book itself. Marlie, the editor-in-chief at Rutgers, is the very model of what an editor should be—at turns demanding and encouraging, but always acutely perceptive and wonderfully supportive.

And finally, I am grateful for the support of my family, who at times must have wondered if I would ever complete this project. Steve and Sharon (Cottrell) Gerson, in particular, readily swapped author tales with me. Most of all, Sue was an author's ideal wife; she pored through archives herself in New York City, Washington, D.C., and Boston, and was simply always there for me.

Izzy

Introduction

He was an American original who demonstrated that one individual, even one without the influence and connections that more respectable sorts had attained, could indeed make a difference. He pointed the way for one to participate in many of the great events of one's time while remaining outside the confines of established truths, ideals, and institutions. He demonstrated that the journalist could stand as an intellectual, the intellectual as a political activist, and the political activist as the conscience of his chosen profession. He employed the power of his pen, wielding it as a warrior might a sword, to criticize the failings of his own land, of other nations, and of the movements of which he was a major actor, as well. He remained ever true to a radical perspective, even as the American left suffered through sectarianism, heavy-handed repression, and resulting near extinction. He helped to usher in the rebirth of home-brewed radicalism, serving as an exemplar for younger rebels who saw him as having avoided the turn toward cynicism, chameleonlike political reconfigurations, and hard-core anticommunism, characteristic of so many of his generational fellows.

I. F. "Izzy" Stone, born in Philadelphia on Christmas Eve 1907, was the oldest child of Russian Jewish immigrants who were determined to experience their own version of the American Dream of economic bounty and political liberty. Rather than follow the "bourgeois" path of his storekeeper father, however, Izzy opted for what he considered to be a life of principle and commitment to liberal and radical tenets. In an era when an academic career seemed beyond the reach of most American Jews, whether first generation or not, the intellectually precocious Izzy chose journalism as his profession. For six and a half decades, until his death in a Boston hospital room in mid-1989, he sought nevertheless to educate his audience as a professor might, employing rare investigative skills; an impressive knowledge of history, literature, philosophy, and current affairs; and an unwavering determination to uncover his version of the truth. Simultaneously, he refused to stand apart from the seminal issues of his times and instead became a key participant in leading political movements associated with

American radicalism. As a result, depending to a large degree on the reception then accorded activists of a progressive stripe, Stone was alternately praised and condemned, ostracized and "rehabilitated" in his own fashion.

The story of I. F. Stone is the tale of the American left over the course of his lifetime, of liberal and radical ideals which carried such weight throughout the twentieth century, and of journalism of the politically committed variety. It is also an account of the intellectual as activist, of the natural maverick in an increasingly insider-oriented world, and of the political rebel as successful capitalist. It is the chronicle of a true believer of a kind, who drew sustenance from his country's finest principles, from Old Testament traditions, and from the socialist vision, but who came to question American domestic and foreign policies, those of the state of Israel too, and socialism as conducted by the Soviet Union, Eastern Europe, and Third World nations. It involves one man's odyssey through the sectarian-riddled ranks of American radicalism; his immersion in liberalism, progressivism, socialism, and communism; and his gravitation to editorially charged and investigative reportage. It demonstrates his determined involvement in campaigns and crusades, both of the not-so-standard political sort and of the seemingly illegal variety, and his personal sense of integrity which often demanded that he go his own way, regardless of what that cost him in terms of jobs, readers, acclaim, and respectability. An examination of the life and career of that ofttimes gregarious, frequently grumpy loner who became his nation's foremost radical commentator thus provides a window through which to examine American radicalism, left-wing journalism, and the evolution of important strands of Western intellectual thought in the twentieth century. It is a means to view the activist intellectual, the place of the outsider in a postindustrial society, the employment of entrepreneurial skills to further progressive ideals, and the erstwhile true believer who came to question certain of his basic beliefs.

Because of Stone's sustained faith in the ideals of socialism and democracy, his devotion to his craft, and his determination to remain true to himself, his is a unique and revealing history. Biographers, of course, are wont to claim uniqueness for their subjects; in I. F. Stone's case, the record, as is often said, speaks for itself. His life and times provide a means to examine something of the intersection between commitment, professionalism, and ideology.

This was an individual, after all, who had inherited a pro-Wilsonian bent from his father, discarded it for La Follette progressivism in the early twenties, moved from a fascination with Kropotkin-styled anarchocommunism later in the same decade to the democratic socialist camp of Norman Thomas, temporarily abandoned that for a flirtation with depression-era communism, shifted to a pro–New Deal and Popular Front stance, supported Henry Wallace's own Progressive Party bid, critically backed the New Left, and held the radical banner aloft into the age of the Great Communicator. He did so in spite of professional setbacks which resulted at least in part from his political bent, increasingly uncongenial times for an Old Lefty, disagreements with younger radicals, and a bank account that grew more and more substantial over time.

He was able to do so, one is compelled to conjecture, because his radicalism was not theoretically based, explicitly formulated, or doctrinaire in any fashion whatsoever. True, he had devoured radical classics from Kropotkin to Marx, from Lenin to Che Guevara, but he was equally versed in the works of the biblical prophets and the writings of Thomas Jefferson, Jack London, and Upton Sinclair. His radicalism took more from *The Communist Manifesto* than from *Das Kapital*, but still more from Amos and Isaiah and the Declaration of Independence than from Marx. Like Eugene Debs before him, and similar to A. J. Muste and Norman Thomas, his elder contemporaries, Stone embraced a brand of radicalism of the generally unsystematic sort. His radicalism, even more so than theirs, was shaped by developments in other lands, particularly those in the so-called socialist states. But while his radical faith led him to insist on the need to promote an appreciation of the historical forces that had resulted in socialist regimes in Russia, Eastern Europe, China, Cuba, or Vietnam, he never—other than for a fleeting moment at the height of the Great Depression—favored anything approximating revolutionary change in the United States. He seemed to believe as Marx had during the previous century, as Muste and Thomas did throughout most of their careers, that a peaceful road to socialism could be attained in this country. The liberal heritage was too rich and still too fertile, he reasoned, to be cavalierly tossed aside in the search for some kind of fantasized utopia.

He was, then, a lifelong American radical, American to the core and radical to the very end. He had lined up with the Old Left during the 1930s and continued to adhere to the depression-era ideals of socialism and antifascist unity throughout his career. Because he had remained true to a radical perspective but in a nondoctrinaire manner, he later came to serve as a model for the New Leftists of the 1960s. Stone, along with A. J. Muste, was virtually alone in this regard and like the pacifist leader thereby served as a bridge between two generations of American radicals. Perhaps this was possible because both men seemed to have learned hard lessons about the excesses and shortsightedness of the early movement from their intimate involvement with it. And perhaps it was due to the moral outrage these two radicals continued to exhibit, whether in print or at the podium, as they caustically analyzed the arms race, U.S. policy toward Castro's Cuba, and the war in Indochina. As a consequence, of the elder statesmen of the American left, none had more impact on the antiwar movement than did Izzy Stone and A. J. Muste.

In fact, Stone's journalistic career and political involvement spanned the heyday of the Old Left and the New Left and beyond. Back in 1922 in Haddonfield, New Jersey, at the advanced age of fourteen, he put out his first little newspaper, entitled, fittingly enough, *The Progress*. After working for a number of local papers, he got a job with liberal publisher J. David Stern's *Philadelphia Record* in 1931, reputedly becoming in the process the youngest editorial writer in the country then working for a major metropolitan newspaper. Two years later, he was hired as a top editorialist at the *New York Post*, which was being converted by Stern into a pro-New Deal vehicle. During the same time period, he began writing, at first under a pseudonym, for important left-of-center publications. At the height of the Great Depression, he wrote a number of scathing essays for *Modern Monthly*, which was edited by V. F. Calverton, a famed unaffiliated radical. After moving to New York, he became a contributor to *The New Republic* and *The Nation*, the top left-liberal journals of the period. A dispute with Stern led to his full-time involvement with *The Nation* and his writing of a regular column for the New York newspaper *PM*, itself an experiment in independent radical journalism. His decision in 1946 to undertake the dangerous underground passage with Jewish refugees from postwar Europe, past the British blockade, and on to Palestine resulted in a severing of his ties to the *The Nation*. He continued writing first for *PM* and then for the *New York Star* and the *New York Daily Compass*, its unhappy successors.

The shutting down of the *Compass* in late 1952 compelled him to begin publication of his own little newsletter. Nineteen years later, of course, he printed the final issue of the now thriving and increasingly influential *I. F. Stone's Weekly*, which had attained a subscription total of some sixty-six thousand. In the years to follow, he joined the staff of the *New York Review of Books* before resigning in protest over a review he saw as dredging up the Cold War mania of the immediate postwar era. He went on to produce a series of op-ed pieces for leading American newspapers before returning to a semi-regular appearance on the pages of *The Nation*.

In his final years, Stone—who saw himself as both a Jeffersonian and a Marxist—concentrated on what he considered to be the most important intellectual and political task of the modern era: to somehow fit socialism and freedom together. Determined to examine the historical roots of the concept of individual liberty, he undertook a study of classical Greece that resulted in, as he saw it, his latest journalistic coup, which eventually led to the publication of *The Trial of Socrates*, his first nationwide bestseller.

Thus, I. F. Stone was a key figure on liberal and left-wing publications from the early 1930s until his death in 1989, an era that witnessed the growing prominence of syndicated columnists, major newspaper chains, and investigative reportage, and generally hard times for independent journalism. He became an editor and bylined columnist for top left-wing journals and newspapers, which afforded him the kind of editorial freedom experienced by few of his contemporaries. He witnessed that editorial freedom disappear at one point because of financial troubles encountered by the newspaper chain of his boss, J. David Stern, perhaps American's top liberal publisher during the period of the New Deal of Franklin Delano Roosevelt. He read thoroughly and widely and developed his own brand of investigative journalism, because of a hearing loss and his own determinedly individualistic inclinations. He participated in a series of experiments in independent radical journalism, including the eagerly awaited *PM*, and of course, his own newsletter. In so doing, he helped to sustain a tradition that reached back to John Peter Zenger, Thomas Paine, Oscar Ameringer, Lincoln Steffens, Upton Sinclair, and George Seldes, and beyond to the Liberation News Service of the 1960s.

I. F. Stone's Weekly, even more than Ameringer's *Appeal to Reason* or Seldes's *In Fact*, was a remarkable journalistic endeavor that succeeded beyond its editor's wildest hopes and served as a voice of radical dissent, both in times when radicalism and dissent were little popular and when they were perceived as somewhat more reputable once again. Its success encouraged others to follow suit, and publications as diverse as *Dissent*, the *Village Voice*, *Liberation*, and the underground newspapers of the 1960s were soon forthcoming.

What readers of the *Weekly* most admired was Stone's determination to ferret out the facts, to uncover that which the establishment press had failed to, and to offer systematic analyses of U.S. governmental policies, both here and elsewhere. Because of his hearing difficulties, apparent as early as 1937 and corrected nearly three decades later but only temporarily, Stone had turned to official, written sources, in addition to any number of writings, both foreign and domestic, to conduct his investigative work. Consequently, he read what others failed or refused to examine, and came up with occasional scoops, as when he caught the Atomic Energy Commission falsifying reports that underground testing was undetectable beyond a certain and quite limited range. Then there was the time he quickly dissected the government rationale for the Tonkin Gulf resolution, which seemed to give President Lyndon Johnson something of a blank check to wage the war in Indochina. And it was Izzy Stone in 1965 who caught the State Department playing fast and loose with statistics in order to produce a White Paper that professed to discuss enemy war material. By setting such a clear example, the *Weekly* encouraged reporters for the establishment press to return to the muckraking and the investigative practices adopted by Steffens and Sinclair during the first part of the twentieth century, which few journals besides *The Nation, The New Republic,* and *In Fact* had featured in the interim.

But it was not simply investigative work or his biting and incisive essays that built the legend of I. F. Stone but his readiness to take a stand when it was not politically expedient to do so or to literally put his body on the line for a cause he believed in. Thus, like John Reed, Upton Sinclair, Norman Thomas, and A. J. Muste, he participated directly at the barricades, in a manner of speaking. He displayed again and again a determination to serve as both intellectual and activist, to appear in his own way as a twentieth-century version of the Winter Soldier. Consequently, he was one of a small band of Old Leftists who attempted to put the Popular Front back together following the signing of the Nazi-Soviet nonaggression pact. He was the first journalist to undertake the illegal and hazardous voyage alongside refugees from Hitler's Europe and members of the Haganah, the Jewish underground, past British ships and on into Palestine. Among those in the Old Left who had made something of a name for themselves, he was one of the few willing to take to the hustings and condemn the red scare mania during the darkest days of McCarthyism. He, along with his friend A. J. Muste, was determined to usher in some kind of a new left following the disintegration of the older movement, and the two men were among the handful who spoke at the initial demonstrations against U.S. actions in Indochina. He was there in Washington in the springtime of 1965 at the first major rally to condemn Lyndon Johnson's dramatic escalation of the war, in Berkeley for the leading teach-in of the era, back in the capital for the rallies of the late sixties and early seventies when the crowds had swelled to the hundreds of thousands, and at university campuses across the land speaking out in opposition to the conflict in Indochina. At many of these rallies, he was there as the voice of reason, urging the same New Left that had come to view him as a kind of patron saint not to act as his own generation had done and to avoid sectarianism, a holier-than-thou attitude, and an inevitable withdrawal from the movement. He was there lecturing at a syngogue after an absence of nearly twenty years, chastising his beloved state of Israel and his fellow Jews in general for refusing to display greater empathy toward the Palestinians. And, near the end of his life, he was there, marching in lonely procession in front of the White House, protesting the crackdown on dissident forces in China.

He was determined to take such stands for the same reason his journalistic work always exuded a sense of commitment. He was the instinctive maverick, the committed iconoclast, who did things his own way and at his own pace, whether that involved any of the aforementioned actions or a necessary resignation over a matter of principle from a publication he had long been associated with. When J. David Stern opted to push the *Philadelphia Record* rightward, he refused to go along with the ensuing change in editorial policy and soon left behind a secure, well-paying job in the midst of the Great Depression. Because he believed so strongly in the Haganah mission, he risked his longtime position with *The Nation*. And later, upset over the decision to print a piece that stirred up once again the controversies surrounding the case of Alger Hiss, he resigned from the highly influential *New York Review of Books*.

But then it seems that he was happiest when he was working alone or with his beloved wife, Esther, close by his side. When he put out the *Weekly*, he did so out of his home in the northwest sector of Washington, always insisting that his research and writing had to come first, yet always supported by an ever gracious Esther and by their sometimes suffering progeny, Celia, Jeremy, and Christopher. Annoyed by distractions of any kind which pulled him away from his work, Izzy could be a difficult, even unreasonable man, as attested to by both colleagues and family members. He could be gracious and giving too, particularly when his work was going well, as his reputation grew, when accolades and applause mounted.

Perhaps his journalistic endeavors, his intellectual quest, and his personal makeup all combined to produce such results. He was faced with the kinds of demands that journalists and intellectuals often encounter, including the need to produce quality work despite having limited resources at their disposal, and the pressure to meet deadlines and keep articles to a prescribed length. He could be his own harshest critic but an incredible self-promoter as well. He was a moody, temperamental man with a considerable ego. He was also enormously gifted, intellectually and at times lyrically, and was befriended by other great men of his time, including Albert Einstein, Felix Frankfurter, Alexander Meiklejohn, Clarence E. Pickett, Bertrand Russell, and Norman Thomas.

Ironically, this gregarious loner and lifelong radical had also proven to be a remarkable entrepreneur, in a way his immigrant father, a dry goods salesman and would-be real estate baron, never could have imagined. He had demonstrated that in the United States, even radical ideas and analyses could be packaged if decorated attractively enough. He had shown that radical journalism, intelligently and "soberly presented," could garner an audience that included not only colleagues and other intellectuals, but also people on Capitol Hill, the White House staff, the FBI, the CIA, and other government agencies. He had indicated, however ironically in his own fashion, the viability of a left-wing version of the late nineteenth-century fables of Horatio Alger. He had displayed the tenacity necessary to indicate that a radical could succeed, even thrive as a capitalist, and that a capitalist could retain his radical ideals, regardless of the bottom line.

This further underscored his uniqueness in relation even to his intellectual compatriots and fellow adventurers in the world of independent radical journalism. He well understood the precariousness of such journalistic ventures, for he was fully aware of the fate that had befallen publications as diverse as *Appeal to Reason, The Masses, Liberation, In Fact,* Dwight Macdonald's *Politics,* and the *PM-New York Star-New York Daily Compass* triad he had himself worked for. He recognized that even well-regarded left-liberal journals like *The Nation* and *The New Republic,* no matter their lofty reputations, were always perched on the economic edge, just a short fall from financial disaster.

Nevertheless, in January 1953 (the *Daily Compass* having closed its doors, with no publications knocking on his door as Joseph McCarthy still dominated national headlines), the now apparently unemployable Izzy Stone felt compelled to put out his own newsletter. At the time, he hoped to keep alive the spirit of independent radical journalism, of which he had so long been a part, and to provide a means of income for his family. But his fierce independence, feistiness, and dedication to his craft served Izzy well, enabling him to succeed with his own experiment in personal journalism as perhaps no other American reporter or essayist before him.

In 1953, fifty-three hundred loyal readers, most of whom were quite familiar with his work, paid five dollars to receive a year's supply of the newsletter. Among the subscribers were Albert Einstein, Eleanor Roosevelt, and Bertrand Russell. By the time concerns about his health compelled him to shut down the *Weekly* in December 1971, a bare year shy of a two-decade run, it had come to boast fanatically devoted subscribers, accolades of all sorts, and near legendary stature. Because of his financial acumen and owing to the fact that printing and mailing costs remained virtually constant during this period, the *Weekly* had enabled Izzy to establish a trust fund for his family, to move with Esther to a more comfortable home in the northwest sector of Washington, D.C., and to ease on into comfortable semiretirement. He became a contributing editor for the *New York Review of Books* and later self-syndicated a number of editorials he had written for the likes of the *New York Times,* the *Washington Post,* the *Los Angeles Times,* and the *Chicago Tribune.*

Stone's opposition to McCarthyism, Stalinism, and superpower machinations; his championing of the movement to fell Jim Crow; and his provision of intellectual firepower for those opposed to the war in Indochina helped to build the reputation of the *Weekly.* So too did his questioning of his own and the American left's most cherished beliefs and assumptions, an ideological stance he had, at the outset, promised the readers of the newsletter he would take. In the pages of the *Weekly* and in the *New York Review,* where many of his longer pieces appeared from the mid-1960s onward, Stone wondered why his own country so often seemed ready to discard Jeffersonian precepts, why the Soviet Union had disgraced the good name of socialism, why Israel failed to display more humanity toward Arab refugees.

These were the three lands that influenced and dismayed Stone—along with much of the American left—more than any others, from the 1930s until the end of his life. He was repeatedly annoyed by the obtuseness or crass cynicism of U.S. governmental leaders during the early years of the Great Depression, throughout the postwar red scare, as the civil rights revolution unfolded, and over the course of the lengthy conflict in Indochina. He was perplexed by the Stalinist hunt for enemies of the Soviet state which resulted in the Moscow Trials of the 1930s, by the stunning announcement of the Nazi-Soviet pact, by the quashing of Popular Front and would-be democratic socialist approaches in Eastern Europe, and by the "New Class" pretensions of the apparatchiks. He was disturbed by the early divisions between Sephardic and Ashkenazic Jews in Israel, by the militarism and xenophobia which he saw as emerging there, and by the lack of concern displayed for the plight of the Palestinians, now stateless as his coreligionists had been during good parts of their own diaspora.

The life and career of I. F. Stone thus serves as a microcosm through which to view the state of the American left, political journalism, and the intellectual experience over the course of the better part of the twentieth century. Stone's ability to maintain his allegiance to progressive causes and movements, to investigative journalism, to his intellectual pursuits, and ultimately to thrive through it all, suggests much about the fate of left-wing ideals, radical news coverage, and the American intelligentsia during that eight-decade period. Yet the life and times of Izzy Stone demonstrate that his very personal successes in no way indicate that the American left, journalism of a radical stripe, or iconoclastic intellectuals fared equally well.

Perhaps this was so because Stone truly was an American original. Like others whose political moorings were rooted in the Old Left, Stone was not unscarred, professionally or intellectually, by the sectarian quarrels of the thirties and forties. He was, after all, a committed Popular Fronter who long afforded the communist states the benefit of the doubt he never allowed right-of-center regimes. Moreover, it was true that as the Cold War evolved and the Old Left all but disappeared, Stone and others like him appeared at various points as if caught in a time warp. They continued to fight the battles they had waged since the 1930s, using the same unchanged rhetoric, so that at times they seemed to be a small band of Don Quixotes tilting at political windmills. Even later, Stone remained capable of romanticizing new socialist states and of failing to criticize them perhaps as fully as he would have denounced rightist governments.

And yet, because of a remarkably stubborn bent which compelled him to question even left-wing shibboleths, Stone nevertheless came to display an independence and a prescience that few of his generational cohorts exhibited. This enabled him to overcome the immediate postwar era, the harshest and hardest time for the post-Debsian American left, and to stake out his own uniquely independent but determinedly radical position on the major issues of the period. As a consequence, he proved able to condemn super-power misdeeds, both in the East and West, and to continue to insist on the need for change at home and abroad: in Cold War America, in Soviet Russia, in Israel, and throughout the Third World, where the political climate was often volatile. Thus, he avoided the dogmatism that doomed some to irrelevance and the rightward turn that led others into the arms of diehard Cold Warriors. Then, as the civil rights revolution in the United States and American involvement in Southeast Asia seemed to bear out his consistently articulated analyses, Stone, long considered outside the pale, was able to reach beyond the left, beyond his chosen field of journalism, and to touch even certain establishment insiders. More and more, he came to be seen as an oracle of sorts, as an astute commentator on the national scene whose alternative vision had something to offer and who, in many ways, reflected the best of twentieth-century American radicalism.

Nevertheless, there were those who continued to view Stone as they had all along: as an apologist for Old Left-tinged Popular Frontism and as a champion of Stalinism and anticapitalist upheavals. Furthermore, such anti-Stalinists, along with younger members of the New Right and neoconservative movements, despised and distrusted Stone for the very reason many in the New Left looked up to him. As others of his generation abandoned the ideals of their youth and early adulthood, Izzy steadfastly supported the causes of reform at home and revolution in other lands. But he did so critically, thus engendering the displeasure of self-proclaimed American revolutionaries, who saw him as just a wrongheaded liberal.

While conservatives denounced Izzy as a cynical and disingenuous un-American and far leftists considered him to be well-meaning but too soft-hearted, many of his fellow American Jews believed this early champion of the state of Israel to be a supporter no more. His radical ideological perspective, they argued, had fatally colored his reading of Israeli policy toward the Arab nations and Palestinian refugees and hinted of anti-Semitism. Furthermore, neoconservatives and neoliberals alike distrusted Stone, challenging his reputation as a cogent chronicler of contemporary America, arguing that he manipulated facts and analyses, shaping or recasting them as he saw fit.

Such charges and accusations amused and angered Izzy, who proclaimed himself a lifelong radical, a religious Jewish atheist, a friend of Israel to the very end, and a journalist who prided himself on his professionalism. But this was a politically committed intellectual who had come to stake out his own ideological posture, free from dogma or inflexibility; a self-professed unbeliever who constantly referred back to the holy scriptures; a critic of Israeli actions who held a special place in his heart for that nation-state; and a scribe who felt obliged to cry out in Jeremiah-like fashion regarding the sins and failings of his own nation.

Notwithstanding the criticisms that came his way, I. F. Stone was a truly remarkable figure. He melded sustained allegiance to the left and to radical tenets, stood as a politically committed journalist and an activist intellectual, ever remained the maverick while becoming a successful businessman, and demonstrated that a true believer in both Jeffersonian and Marxist ideals could come to question how his country and other favored lands violated what he thought to be sacred principles. He was one of a kind, and perhaps the last of the great American radical pamphleteers, following in the tradition of Revolutionary War scribes, antebellum abolitionists, Populist critics of big business, and socialist foes of war, militarism, and imperialism. Indeed, along with Michael Harrington, Izzy Stone was possibly the last of the great American radicals, in a line that reached back to Thomas Jefferson, William Lloyd Garrison, Eugene V. Debs, and Norman Thomas.

1 Izzy, the Icon

S ilver-haired Old Lefties, reminiscing at the passing of yet another one of their own, filled the memorial hall in mid-Manhattan. They had come to pay homage to an icon from days present and past. While their own wizened faces were mostly unrecognizable, his had recently graced the cover of *People* magazine, his latest book had appeared on the *New York Times*'s bestseller list, and auditoriums at august universities throughout the land had overflowed in eager anticipation of his visits. At the time of his death on June 18, 1989, Izzy Stone had seemingly completed the passage he had long ago predicted to Esther, his wife of sixty years: "from a pariah to a character and then . . . a national institution." This was no small accomplishment for a man who had deemed himself an "anarchocommunist" in his youth, heralded "a workers party" at the height of the Great Depression, fellow-traveled with the antifascist Popular Front, championed Henry Wallace as the Cold War unfolded, and been considered outside the pale during the heyday of McCarthyism.[1]

But the determined independence as well as the unwavering belief in himself and his work attested to by one speaker after another at the memorial gathering had served Stone well, enabling him to carry on in his chosen field of journalism as few others before him had. He had managed to carve out a very special niche for himself in both journalistic and left-of-center circles with the publication of his celebrated newsletter, *I. F. Stone Weekly*, which spanned the Eisenhower and Vietnam eras and garnered international acclaim for this veteran of the *New York Post, The Nation, PM,* and the Old Left. His celebrity had only continued to grow when he finally put the *Weekly* to rest and subsequently increased the volume of essays he published in the *New York Review of Books*, considered by the end of the 1960s to be the most influential magazine in the eyes of the American intelligentsia. Stone penned the first article on the Vietnam War to appear in the *New York Review*, helped to tilt it in a New Leftward direction, and served as contributing editor during the very time it became something of an intellectual barometer.

So, it came as no surprise that journalistic heavyweights were prominent among the six hundred people who showed up at noon on Wednesday, July 12, 1989, for the memorial tribute to I. F. Stone in the Big Apple. At the building of the New York Society for Ethical Culture, the gathered throng included political cartoonist Jules Feiffer, George Kryle from "Sixty Minutes," the *New York Post*'s Murray Kempton, the *Village Voice*'s Jack Newfield, the *New York Review of Books*' Robert B. Silvers, and Nicholas von Hoffman, formerly with the *Washington Post*. Also present were old friends and workmates such as Jean Boudin, W. H. Ferry, Mildred Traube, and Sam Grafton.[2]

Lanky and dapper Peter Osnos, Izzy's onetime assistant, served as host and program coordinator for the occasion, as he would for the one to follow a half-dozen days later in the nation's capital. Osnos, formerly a *New York Times* reporter and regular on PBS's "Washington Week in Review" and now a Random House associate editor, carefully devised the speakers' list to include family members, journalistic brethren, and longtime friends like himself. As people continued to pour into the New York City gathering located on the outer edges of Central Park, thereby taxing the building's air-conditioning unmercifully, Osnos remarked that "Izzy would have preferred that you all be a little bit uncomfortable."[3]

Upon reaching the podium, Izzy's journalistic colleague Murray Kempton, now frail and white-haired himself, called him "unique amongst us" and a writer to be compared with someone such as André Malraux, the great French novelist and essayist. What Kempton remembered was "the pure joy he took from the hunt" and how he loved to catch liars, particularly those in the service of their government.[4]

Leonard Boudin, his brother-in-law and a figure of some standing himself in the eyes of the American left, referred to another side of Izzy Stone. The rough-hewn but patriarchal Boudin, a Fifth Avenue attorney identified with leading civil liberties cases over the course of the past half-century, recalled that Izzy was "no respecter of countries, persons, or even friends." But this was a man who had "prescience" and "extraordinary physical and moral courage" also, as demonstrated by his underground journey to Palestine.[5]

Relatives, friends, and colleagues at the memorial service in New York thus spoke of Izzy Stone with warmth, respect, even awe. His passing was likewise noted by leading members of his own profession and by the national television and print media. Many attested to the fact that Stone was no organization man but rather a journalistic lone wolf of sorts, a reportorial maverick who had necessarily staked out his own path. If the truth be known, Mary McGrory of the *Washington Post* suggested, the now "entirely respectable" Stone had in fact been the "quintessential outsider" who "spent his life with his face pressed against the window." No matter; he demonstrated "that outside was the place to be if you really want to know what is happening on the inside." The *Times*'s Anthony Lewis reminded his readers that Stone's early condemnation of U.S. policy in Vietnam had been so sharply at odds with the standard line. Lewis also recalled that Izzy demonstrated that the chief purpose of journalism "is not to get close to power but to speak truth to power." Studs Terkel—who was himself seen in the same light by others—remembered Stone as a journalistic model who spoke the truth, suffered "no crap," and "shone like a beacon light."[6]

For the most part, then, the eulogies painted the picture of a man who had indeed become a legend in his own lifetime. Yet the very response to the death of I. F. Stone said a great deal not only about the man but about both his chosen field of journalism and the American left of which he was such an integral part. While journalistic giants appeared in droves at the public celebrations, sang his praises in syndicated essays, on radio talk shows, and on national television, there were few well-known leftists who did the same. Moreover, the audience in New York, like the one to follow in Washington, was markedly aged, white, and affluent. The Old Lefties and journalists, although "wonderful audiences in terms of the quality of the people," in Peter Osnos's estimation, had not been joined by blacks and browns, by the young or even the middle-aged for the most part (other than the celebrity journalists), or by the indigent. Centered visibly in the middle of the New York crowd was thirty-two-year-old Gregory Lee Johnson of the Revolutionary Communist Youth Brigade, dressed in the same attire he had fashioned during the controversial Supreme Court case involving his burning of Old Glory. But Johnson's presence merely stood out as some kind of aberrational force in the midst of a remarkably homogeneous lot. Not to be seen were many of the leading New Left or antiwar movement figures of the recent past, the same New Left and antiwar movement that Izzy Stone was so intimately involved with. Once again, at least in symbolic manner, a chasm was in place, separating the Old Left of Stone's early career from the radical ferment that followed. Therefore, the turnouts were, as Peter Osnos suggested, fairly predictable, composed for the most part of those who had read Izzy for decades and a highly distinguished group of journalists to whom he had become "a huge figure in the sixties." Yet that too said so much about the state of the American left at the end of his days.[7]

Not all, of course, viewed I. F. Stone in the way those in attendance for the ceremony in New York did. He had been a controversial figure since the ideologically charged decade of the thirties when foes on the left categorized him as a Stalinist or, at best, an apologist for the Soviet Union. There were those who continued to so view him until the very end, while some on the left, who dreamed dreams of revolution in America, came to regard him as simply out of step with the times. And among his bitterest critics were those who saw Stone, once considered a great friend of Israel, as pro-Palestinian and thus a self-hating Jew who desired the destruction of the lone Jewish state. Finally, upon his death, some adopted the familiar litany that Stone was un-American and had wished his own country only harm.[8]

His old friend Marcus Raskin, cofounder of the Institute for Policy Studies, the left-wing think tank based in the capital, dismissed such charges at the second memorial gathering for I. F. Stone, held on Tuesday, July 18, 1989, at the Friends Meeting Hall in Washington. Eloquently, Raskin insisted that his friend—the IPS's initial honorary fellow—had been appalled by U.S. actions in Vietnam precisely because they contradicted his sense of justice and his idealized vision of the American nation. Izzy had been one of the very few, Raskin noted, who were not taken in by the lies of the best-and-the-brightest of the Kennedy-Johnson administrations which he had seen as a mere "cover story for imperial arrogance." Subsequently Izzy had, in Raskin's words, "shared his rage and his knowledge with a generation who took him . . . as a beacon. He enabled a generation to use fact and moral outrage as a path for dissent and resistance."[9]

2 Early Progress and Greater Philadelphia

What a bunch of crap! he undoubtedly thought to himself. Sometime in the spring of 1927, the young reporter was ordered by the city editor of the *Camden Courier-Post* to cover a Rotary Club function. A simple enough assignment on the face of it, he thought. But what this actually entailed was hearing a professor from the University of Pennsylvania, just returned from the Mediterranean, sing the praises of Fascist Italy. It was bad enough that the local Italian community was enthralled with Benito Mussolini; but being forced to listen to some pompous asshole salute Il Duce for having gotten the trains to run on time was something else again. And now, this academic pygmy was lauding that squirt of a dictator for having brought "law and order" to the Italian repubic. Thinking about his Italian anti-Fascist friends and Gaetano Salvemini's recent tour of the United States and indictment in *The Nation*, both of which urged resistance against Mussolini, Izzy could simply stand no more. He was "so goddamned mad" that he jumped up from the press table and fired question after question in the direction of the guest of honor. Why hadn't the good professor mentioned a word about fascism's ugly underside? What about the Fascists' role in the murder of the Socialist legislator Giacomo Matteotti? How about Mussolini's shock troops, the squadristi, which terrorized any and all of the dictator's opponents? Why no mention of the plight of the formerly independent Italian trade unions, now themselves part of the Fascist corporate state?[1]

The more than slightly taken aback Penn professor had just met up with the nineteen-year-old version of Izzy Stone. Already, Izzy had begun to acquire something of a reputation among his friends and colleagues as one who readily spoke his mind, particularly when the topic at hand involved such charged subjects as the rise of fascism in Europe and the appearance of Ku Klux Klan legions in the streets of his hometown. This outspokenness was apparent to the professor from Izzy's alma mater, much to his chagrin. Perhaps the professor could also see the young man's delight in embarrassing an academic from the very institution he had recently unceremoniously departed from.

His determination to challenge profascist ideas so forthrightly was very much in keeping with Izzy's concerns about right-wing thought and his own rebellious inclinations. It also underscored that he was something of a young man apart, who was willing to do what few on the American left then were: to condemn the authoritarianism becoming more and more entrenched in Fascist Italy. The left in the United States and elsewhere was slow to respond to the Fascist threat, but not Izzy, who said he was "very much aware of what was happening in Italy."[2]

R adical journalists, of course, do not come bounding out of the wombs of their mothers. Yet from all indications, Izzy Stone exhibited early, remarkably early, both a radical bent and a determination to make his mark as a journalist. Izzy, for his part, always believed that he "was sort of born a radical." He later referred to the old Gilbert and Sullivan ditty from *Iolanthe* when stating that "every Englishman alive is either a liberal or a conservatype [sic]." And he himself reasoned that "what you are, you're born. Your political attitudes are pretty much born with you."[3]

Izzy reflected upon a dream he had as a young boy about slum dwellers residing along the Philadelphia waterfront. He had awakened from his nightmare with such a deep sadness that he still vividly remembered it seventy or so years later. He pointed to that dream as the beginning of his feeling that a newspaperman should act as "sort of crusader to help the victimized" and aspire to reach as many readers as possible.[4]

Barely into his teens, he had put out his first little newspaper, called *The Progress,* which championed the League of Nations, while condemning William Randolph Hearst's yellow peril campaign and the fundamentalist stance of William Jennings Bryan. While in high school, he supported the 1924 presidential bid of Wisconsin senator Robert La Follette. A short time later, he began reading treatises by Kropotkin, Marx, Lenin, and Bukharin, and fancied himself an anarchocommunist before joining a Socialist Party local in Camden, New Jersey.

There was, then, a certain precocious quality to Izzy Stone's early identification with the craft of journalism, liberal and radical ideals, and the left side of the American political spectrum. He also came to feel very early in his career that intellectuals and journalists should take a stand on controversial issues of their times, and not remain shielded behind the cover of objectivity. The fact that he was an instinctive maverick meant that his actions at the Rotary Club gathering came naturally to him, led to considerable turmoil with his parents and siblings, resulted in his apparent rejection of the Jewish faith, and propelled him to attempt that early experiment in independent journalism.

Evidently, Izzy saw the field of journalism as a means of escaping the boosterism, speculative mania, and small-town Babbittry so common during the 1920s. This was the period when he, born Isadore Feinstein in a Philadelphia hospital on December 24, 1907, began to come of age. Above all else, Isidor—the spelling of his name would be changed more than once—seemed determined to avoid following the road taken by his parents.

Bernard and Katy Feinstein were Russian Jewish immigrants who prospered mightily during this somewhat gilded decade. It seemed so long ago now that Bernard had first come to the United States and begun to make a living peddling his wares by way of horse and buggy. It was in April 1903, in fact, when this émigré from Ukrainian anti-Semitism, Russian pogroms, and the czar's army had migrated across the Atlantic. He had been forced to undertake an odyssey that involved the illegal crossing of borders, driven on by some of the same factors that compelled his eldest son to complete his own underground voyage two generations later. Bernard had escaped from Russia, heading west, before reaching Hamburg, Germany, from where he bordered a ship for England. He had stopped in Cardiff, Wales to visit his brother Ithamar, and then departed for the United States. In this new land of seemingly boundless opportunities, the finely chiseled Bernard met and married pretty Katherine Novack of South Philadelphia, who worked in a women's shirtwaist factory and whose family hailed from the city of Odessa, a Black Sea port. Katy, as she was known, had come to the States in July 1904. In March 1907, Bernard and Katy exchanged their wedding vows, and nine months later, their first son was born. For a spell, Isidor was raised by his maternal grandparents as Katy, experiencing postpartum depression, suffered the first of a series of breakdowns. Consequently, his first language was the Yiddish spoken by the Novacks, while Katy, who hardly knew English herself, taught him the ABCs by reading aloud the manufacturer's name on the kitchen stove.[5]

There existed, however, tension between Bernard and his in-laws, whom the Feinsteins visited almost every Sunday. Much of that centered on the "agnostic feel" Bernard seemed determined to cultivate in his own abode. Katy, in maintaining a kosher home, attempted to assuage the feelings of her parents. But Bernard refused to take religious matters seriously and was skeptical about the worth of even attending services at the synagogue the Novacks frequented. Eventually, in an effort to get away from his in-laws, Bernard took Katy and young Isidor and settled temporarily in Richmond, Indiana, of all places. There, Isidor—known to family and friends alike as Izzy—began kindergarten and a second son, Marcus, was born in September 1912. In January of the following year, Bernard became a naturalized citizen. Family legend has it that shortly thereafter, the rising waters of the Wabash River flooded the Feinsteins out of their home and brought about a return to the Eastern Seaboard.[6]

Following an aborted attempt to set up a butcher shop in Camden, the family ended up in nearby Haddonfield, a small, largely Quaker community perched just outside Philadelphia. Haddonfield, for the most part, retained a countrylike atmosphere. There, on East Kings Highway—an important roadway during the American Revolution—at Haddon Avenue, Bernard and Katy, having saved money from his peddling operations and conceivably with the aid of a bank loan, opened the Philadelphia Bargain Store in 1914. Customers could purchase everything at the Feinsteins' general store from shoes and boots to long johns and B.V.D.s to shirts and dresses. The family, soon expanded by two—a third son, Louis, was born in November 1917 and daughter Judith arrived in May 1924—resided in the same building. Downstairs, at the back of the rather spacious store, was the kitchen and a good-sized dining room. Upstairs, in the rear of the building, there was a library-playroom, a closed-in porch where the children often slept away the hot summer nights, a very large living room complete with a baby-grand piano and radio, a bathroom, a pair of substantial bedrooms which boasted bay windows that faced the main avenue in town, the live-in maid's quarters which lacked the airiness of the Feinsteins', and a small room where Bernard, in the fashion of the times, made his own brandy. Across from the bathroom, a locked door led to an apartment Bernard and Katy rented out to a local dentist.[7]

By the mid-1920s, the Feinsteins had prospered nicely. At one point, on the strength of his signature alone, Bernard was able to borrow 125,000 dollars from the Haddonfield National Bank on a ninety-day note. He bought stock with the money, turned it over, and quickly paid off the loan. He also benefited from a real-estate boom in the area, joining in with the hardware man across the street and the proprietor of a local ice-cream store to purchase one building after another in Haddonfield and nearby Clementon. In addition, Bernard built six stores on Kings Highway—three-story commercial and residential operations—four or five cottages, and a large, brick, showcase home for the family in Haddon Estates, a new and affluent section of town. Along with his partners, he bought up ten additional stores and a theater in Clementon, a good amount of land, and a number of other houses.[8]

Because of his business ventures, Bernard, much to the dismay of his wife, began to pay less attention to the dry goods store. This meant that more and more of the everyday operations of the store fell upon the shoulders of the increasingly displeased Katy. It was she who was compelled to venture into Philadelphia to deal with wholesalers and then return from her treks, heavy packages in hands and thoroughly exhausted. These responsibilities did little to improve her mood or her nerves, and she quarreled frequently with Bernard about how the store should be run.[9]

Consequently, tension riddled the Feinsteins' home. In addition, ongoing, "very bitter" conflicts between Bernard and Izzy, his would-be heir apparent, and between the two oldest boys, did not help matters. Bernard dreamed of owning a chain of stores throughout South Jersey, which Izzy, with some experience behind him, would eventually help to run. But the bookish, introspective, and always independent-minded Izzy, in the words of his brother Lou, "didn't want to have anything to do with the damn business. He didn't like the business. [In fact, he] didn't like anything that had to do with such a lowly thing as selling." Instead, from as early on as anyone could recall, Izzy was, Lou recalled, "in another world . . . the world of intellect." Izzy preferred spending his time upstairs in the family library, surrounded by all sorts of literary and historical works, including Heinrich Graetz's *History of the Jews.* By the age of twelve, he was reading such books as Jack London's *Martin Eden* and Herbert Spencer's *First Principles.*[10]

Drawn to the world of books and ideas, Izzy felt distant from his immigrant parents, who managed English only with heavy "Jewish accents" and conversed with each other in Yiddish. His attitude toward his family in general "was sort of standoffish, if not contemptuous," according to Lou. Izzy simply did not care to be troubled by what he seemed to view as their pedestrian pursuits. Lou later confirmed that he was "not a close family man . . . I scarcely knew him." And because of his constant refusal to attend family functions, other relatives outside the Feinstein household considered him somewhat standoffish.[11]

The strain between Bernard and his first-born, like that involving Izzy and Marcus, was genuine. Izzy continued to display no interest in the store and seemed to go out of his way to antagonize his father. On one occasion, he purchased a big necktie with a very large knot—considered very spiffy during the Roaring Twenties—from Wanamaker's, the great department store in Philadelphia and one of Bernard's competitors. The ties in his store, Bernard bitterly exclaimed, "were not good enough for Izzy!"[12] His brother, Marcus, or Max as he was called (he later went by Marc), was infuriated that Izzy treated his father's business enterprise so disdainfully; their wildly contrasting attitudes toward the family store only deepened the chasm between the two boys. Max, as matters turned out, was his father's favorite, willingly helping out in the store, striving to be the good salesman Bernard so wanted Izzy to become. Furthermore, Max, so unlike Izzy, wanted very much to be "the regular fellow." Somewhat embarrassed by the taunts of "Bookworm" and "Four Eyes" directed at his small, bespectacled older brother, Max hung out with the kids in town, shot pool, played sports of all kinds. At home, he and Izzy had "real knock-down, drag-out fights," the two angrily wrestling to the floor. Both younger brothers, moreover, saw Izzy as "very self-centered" and "a great egotist." Max, in fact, believed that Izzy—whom he looked at as something of "a shadowy figure"—was "not much of a brother in the usual sense."[13]

Lou—more easygoing than either Izzy or Max—later spoke, somewhat wistfully, of a lone occasion when his oldest brother saw fit to give him a ride through the Jersey countryside in his new Dodge.[14]

Undoubtedly a need to vie for their parents' attention, with Max becoming Bernard's favorite and Izzy, Katy's, intensified the ongoing sibling rivalry. While Lou remembered being "hugged, kissed and petted" by his folks, not so Max, who recalled that outward displays of love and affection were never easily made in the home of Bernard and Katy Feinstein. Consequently, as he neared the end of his life, Max reflected on the fact that Katy had invariably set aside the juiciest parts of the sabbath-eve chicken dinner for Izzy.[15]

His parents chastised Izzy in almost identical terms as his brothers would, criticizing his "egotistical and selfish bent," particularly how self-centered he was with regard to "his studies and readings and desires." Nevertheless, to a certain degree, both parents encouraged him in that regard, his father building up an impressive library for a teenage boy and his mother slipping him money when Bernard refused to do so in order that he might head over to Philadelphia. On occasion Katy took Izzy to Leary's, an old used bookstore in the city, where he purchased copies of *The Nation*.[16]

In Philadelphia, Izzy often stopped off to visit the family members he evidently felt closest to, including Grandma and Grandpa Novack, toward whom he was "very sweet and very warm," and Uncle Shumer Feinstein, his particular favorite. Izzy later fondly recalled the home of Uncle Shumer and "lovable Tante Elka," where the smell of freshly baked goods was always in the air and books of all kinds were to be discovered. It was Shumer who taught the self-proclaimed atheistic Izzy and brother Max enough Hebrew so that they might be bar mitzvahed. And it was the uncle Izzy adored who represented a very old scholarly tradition important on both sides of the family, a tradition that saw one male figure serve as scholar only, devote his time to the daily study of the Talmud, and never toil outside the home. This was an ideal that Izzy obviously revered and one that only heightened the tensions within the Feinstein household.[17]

Evidently, Izzy saw Shumer, whom he described as "framed always in a certain majesty, calm, dignified, patient—a veritable Jove of an uncle," in a different light than he did his own father. It was Shumer who was ever ready with the most wonderful tales and always available to answer any questions tossed his way by an enthralled young fellow. It was Shumer who represented, in Izzy's eyes, a "spiritually beautiful" figure—"scholar, philosopher, gentleman, learned yet kind and simple, without bitterness or rancor or envy, Human." Izzy believed that "when God walked with the sons of men, He must have walked with such as my Uncle Shumer."[18]

In a sense, Shumer stood as a kind of substitute father figure, as would a number of other distinguished gentlemen well into the period of Izzy's adulthood. Izzy was invariably drawn to intellectually powerful and accomplished older men who stood as exemplars in a manner Bernard never was able to.

By the time he entered high school, Izzy, with Uncle Shumer as a model, proceeded to bury himself in his books, especially political tracts, philosophical works, and historical studies. He read the two papers his parents subscribed to, J. David Stern's *Camden Courier-Post* and *Der Tag*, a Yiddish publication put out by William Edlin, a Socialist who had backed Woodrow Wilson's call for U.S. intervention in World War I. Back when he was, in his own words, "a politically conscious schoolboy of nine," Izzy and a friend had been the only students in their class to oppose American involvement, but now he too was swept up in the patriotic revelry of the period. At the age of fourteen, he had first come across copies of *The New Republic* and *The Nation*, the leading liberal journals of the era. These were "the serious magazines of opinion," whose regular contributors included Charles Beard, Bruce Bliven, Heywood Broun, Herbert Croly, H. L. Mencken, Raymond Gram Swing, and Norman Thomas, among others. Throughout the 1920s, *The New Republic* and *The Nation* maintained the tradition of politically committed journalism, a tradition threatened by the demise of *The Masses-Liberation* school of publications and only somewhat sustained by the appearance of *The New Masses*, soon to be so ideologically dogmatic. These journals also helped to keep alive something of the muckraking spirit of the early Progressive era, best exemplified by the work of a young William Randolph Hearst, Upton Sinclair, and Lincoln Steffens, all of whom were viewed by Izzy as practitioners of the kind of reporting he aspired to.[19]

During this period, Izzy discovered, too, the essays of Ralph Waldo Emerson and Henry David Thoreau, the poetry of Carl Sandburg, Walt Whitman, and Emily Dickinson, and *Moby Dick*, Herman Melville's epic novel. He read Christopher Marlowe, John Keats, Percy Shelley, William Wordsworth, Thomas Hardy, John Milton (including "Paradise Lost" and "Samson Agonistes"), and *Don Quixote* by Miguel Cervantes. Thanks to George Gissing's "Private Papers of Henry Ryecroft," he began a lifelong love affair with the poets of classical times, including Heraclitus, Lucretius, and Sappho. He became enamored with Charles Beard's *Economic Interpretation of the Constitution* and Louis Boudin's "Government by Judiciary."[20]

It was during the same period that Izzy first thought of becoming a reporter. It might have been the discovery of those issues of *The New Republic* and *The Nation* that led him to begin putting out his own little newspaper, *The*

Progress, in February 1922. Now entranced with the idea of becoming a jour-nalist, Izzy believed that a newspaperman should be "a kind of cross between Galahad and William Randolph Hearst," that is, the "populist and . . . radical" Hearst of earlier days. Establishing a pattern of operations he would return to once again, one Isidor Feinstein was said to be the owner and publisher of *The Progress,* and a kind of journalistic jack-of-all-trades—editor-in-chief, busi-ness manager, and advertising manager. The local print shop ran off several hundred copies of each edition, which were then distributed by Izzy on his bicycle, two staff members, and brother Max, who attempted to sell copies of *The Progress* to commuters on their way home from work.[21]

A remarkably precocious publication, *The Progress* and its editor obviously identified with the reform movement that had withered on the vine of mar-tially induced repression and the postwar disillusionment that followed. It supported Woodrow Wilson's call for the United States to enter the League of Nations and urged that reparation payments be halted in return for a twenty-five-year suspension of the arms race. The ailing former president served as a particular hero—and undoubtedly, another paternal surrogate—for Izzy, who applauded "the man who worked for what he believed to be right . . . who struggled for a high ideal." To the "scouts of civilization"—"Socrates, Aris-totle, Copernicus, Descartes, Spencer, Darwin"—Izzy declared, the name of Woodrow Wilson should be added.[22]

Just as strongly, he blasted onetime presidential hopefuls, newspaper tycoon William Randolph Hearst and William Jennings Bryan. *The Progress* attacked the attempt by Hearst to stir up anti-Asian sentiment and dismissed Bryan as "a modern Torquemada," thus likening the former Nebraska con-gressman to the inquisitor-general who had helped to ensure that Jews were expelled from Spain during the fifteenth century. The antievolutionary stance of the Great Commoner, *The Progress* charged, flew in the face of "the immutable law of progress." Bryan and those of like mind were said to be a millennium behind the times. They more properly fit in the so-called Dark Ages, Izzy declared, "when free thinkers, philosophers and Jews were consid-ered the best fuel for bonfires." They had no place whatsoever, he believed, in a more rational era.[23]

Given the nature of the editorials that filled the pages of his little paper, it was not surprising that the local linotypist predicted that young Izzy "would come to a bad end." It was not the editorial content of *The Progress,* however, but rather Izzy's academic standing—always mediocre at best—that induced his father to put a halt to his journalistic endeavor. After all, Bernard was a Wilsonian Democrat and a free thinker himself who was often heard to remark that politicians were always around when election day approached, but afterward were nowhere to be found. What seemed to upset Bernard was the fact that the paper had ever been put out in the first place. The three issues of *The Progress* were produced while he was away from home convalescing after a recent illness. Bernard evidently feared (and for good reason, as matters turned out) that Izzy's journalistic endeavor was yet another sign that his eldest would never become that right-hand man he desperately wanted.[24]

What troubled Bernard was that it was increasingly clear that journalism, not commerce, appealed to his son's heart. "No way was he going to be a storekeeper" in the not-so-distant-future, Lou later recalled; no way was Izzy going to be a willing helper at the Feinsteins' general store at present. Instead, he became a cub reporter for the *Haddonfield Gazette* and tracked sports— about which he knew next to nothing—for the *Camden Post-Telegram*. His initial assignment involved covering a basketball game at the local high school. Unfortunately, Izzy arrived at halftime to report on a sport he knew nothing about. But having been briefed on everything from the purpose of the game to the number of players to the action in the first half, he wrote a lengthy piece that the *Post-Telegram* ran and for which he received ten cents an inch.[25]

Ironically, he got his first real break because of time he spent so begrudgingly in his parents' store. While working there, he happened to meet a woman by the name of Jill Stern with whom he immediately began to banter. Izzy particularly enjoyed giving this German-American Jew, who, along with her family, had joined the Quakers, hell for being "an assimilationist." He scolded her, insisting she should be proud of her Jewish heritage in the same way that he was, notwithstanding the fact that he considered himself largely an atheist. No matter, she was much taken with him, the two became fast friends and she a type of mentor for young Isidor. She was impressed that Izzy headed off for the woods whenever he could, to read Keats, Shelley, Wordsworth, and the Elizabethan poets. Furthermore, as it turned out, Jill Stern was the wife of one J. David Stern, who would soon head a newspaper chain on the East Coast. Having heard his wife speak fondly of Izzy, Stern stoppped off at the Feinstein store one Saturday evening and offered the high school junior a job as Haddonfield correspondent for the *Camden Evening-Courier*. For the next decade and longer, the liberal publisher served as yet another role model for Izzy.[26]

Harry Saylor, the saucy managing editor of the *Courier*, was less than thrilled that Izzy had been hired because he wanted a full-time man, not some kid, in that position. Izzy's second day on the job, however, he managed to win the hard-nosed newsman over. Rummaging about for news and finding none, Izzy determined to do a tongue-in-cheek story about the ghost of city founder Elizabeth Haddon, which reportedly had been spotted by one of the older members of the community. The ghost desired, or so Izzy indicated, that the plaque dedicated to her—and now fallen upon hard times—be cleaned up. Fearing he might get fired for his "creative" work, Izzy was instead rewarded with a two-column headline, a byline on the front page, and a bonus of forty-five cents per inch of copy. More important, he won the approval of Harry Saylor, who saw the young reporter as "a real bird-dog right from the beginning."[27]

Unfortunately, Izzy's reportorial accomplishments continued to overshadow his performance in the classroom. Yet he did make a mark of sorts at Haddonfield High, serving as president of the chess club in his sophomore year, participating in the school's extemporaneous speaking contest, and appearing in the senior play. He was later remembered by a classmate as "eloquent," "astute," and the most widely read and politically aware student to be found. The youngest member of his class, "Issy" was proclaimed "our philosopher!" in the high school yearbook: "It doesn't seem believable that one head could hold so many theories, ideas, etc. The sad part about his 'wisdom' is that we Seniors find it too profound for our mental capacity to grasp." But Izzy, who so wanted to attend Harvard, managed to finish only forty-ninth in a high school class of fifty-two. As a result, he had to settle for the Philadelphia-based University of Pennsylvania, which was obliged to accept high school graduates from nearby communities.[28]

At the time, Penn was little more than a commuter school that accepted students from all ethnic and racial groups and consequently was known for favoring "the democracy of the street car." Still, discrimination in campus social affairs prevailed for the most part, with Jews separated from Gentiles and fraternity brothers from their less well-heeled classmates. The football team was off-limits to Jews, as was the *Daily Pennsylvanian*, the campus newspaper.[29]

One publication, *Junto,* appeared more receptive to all comers. Youthful would-be intellectuals were drawn to this journal of literature, poetry, and anguished essays and to the organization that sponsored it, the Philomathean Society. Having been on the receiving end of taunts of "Kike" and "Christ Killer" back in his hometown of Haddonfield—something all the Feinstein boys encountered—Izzy welcomed the opportunity to meet up with the small band of "elite thinkers" at Penn who seemed to be somewhat more open-minded.[30]

Consequently, soon after his arrival on campus, Izzy sought membership in the Philomathean Society, which harbored Michael "Sy" Blankfort and Seymour N. Siegel, both Jews themselves. As was the custom, Izzy was obliged to deliver a public talk before the members of the society, who would then vote on his application. Blankfort was pleased that the candidate had opted to talk about the stormy, disillusioned verse of the California poet Robinson Jeffers. Notwithstanding his own enthusiastic response, however, he worried about the reception this short, pudgy, round-faced, and dimpled earnest soul was receiving. The thick glasses Izzy wore over his incredibly nearsighted eyes, his disheveled hair, and his rumpled clothes did not help matters any. Nor, Blankfort feared, did possible anti-Semitism lurking in the ranks of the society.[31]

Nervous and hesitant, the little-known day student spoke at some length until all but three in the crowd, including Blankfort and Siegel, held the dreaded black balls. A distraught Blankfort offered to inform Izzy of the group's decision and met up with him in College Hall, the oldest building on campus. He, for one, had enjoyed the speech and admired Jeffers himself, Blankfort told Izzy. But the other members of the Philomathean Society had never even heard of the poet. Seeing how devastated the young man standing before him appeared to be, Blankfort offered the use of his dormitory room whenever Izzy might want to avail himself of it.[32]

At eight o'clock the following Sunday morning, Blankfort was awakened by a knock on the door of his dorm room. It was Izzy, come to ask Blankfort to breakfast at Horn and Hardart on Broad Street, a haven for politically conscious and budding Jewish intellectuals. Still half-asleep but flattered that Izzy had come in from Camden to deliver the invitation, Blankfort agreed and thus began a lifelong friendship. That initial walk was one of the richest Blankfort had ever had, he later recalled, "for Izzy was the fullest alive person I'd met up to then." Izzy expressed delight over each and every bird call made as they passed alongside the Schuylkill River. He spoke of what he had been reading, including the poetry of Thomas Hardy, Jeffers, Livy, and particularly Horace, and *The History of the Decline and Fall of the Roman Empire* by Edward Gibbon. Izzy pointed out that he had learned Latin by placing pieces of paper with the Latin version in one pocket and the English translation in the other. The two talked politics as well, and it was clearly apparent that Izzy was "a confirmed Socialist who had read Hegel and Marx." To Blankfort, Izzy's "great spirit and vast reading" were most impressive; he appeared to have "an independent and stubborn point of view about everything."[33]

Thanks in good measure to Mike Blankfort, Izzy soon became part of a rather remarkable small circle of friends at Penn—all Jews, ranging from Orthodox to agnostic—including Sidney Cohn, Samuel Grafton (Lifshutz), Walter Hart, Chester Roberts (Rabinowitz), Seymour N. Siegel, and Shepard Traube. Many had dreams of becoming writers, and later realized them. Blankfort turned out to be a well-known novelist and screenwriter; Cohn, a labor and entertainment attorney and a leading figure in the American Jewish Congress; Grafton, a top-flight columnist, editor, and longtime colleague of Izzy's; Hart and Traube, theater directors and playwrights; Roberts, a successful businessman; Siegel, a key figure in public broadcasting in New York City. While in college, they tended to devour the same literature, see the same movies, attend the same theater and concert performances, and swap "tall tales of romance" to the delight and skepticism of all parties.[34]

Mightily displeased, Bernard Feinstein saw his son's friends as bohemians, for they sported loud ties, wore their hair flowing, and played the part of undergraduate intellectuals. During this period, Izzy read *The Dial,* a seminal journal for the pre–World War I lyrical left which now published T. S. Eliot, Henry Miller, Ezra Pound, and William Carlos Williams, among others; tried his own hand at poetry; and favored Irish, Chinese, Latin, French, and German poets.[35]

In addition, Izzy and his friends at Penn were increasingly drawn to radical treatises and radical politics, because they no longer saw fit to identify with the Progressive movement. After all, progressivism, which had dominated the American political scene during the first two decades of the still new century, had dissipated dramatically following World War I. In addition, the Progressive movement, with its largely middle-class, WASPish leadership, was simply a way station for young, Jewish, first-generation Americans such as these. While Izzy was viewed as "a militant Socialist" by Mike Blankfort, his compatriots became radicals of a sort as they protested the incarceration of labor militants Tom Mooney and Warren Billings and the immigrant anarchists Nicola Sacco and Bartolomeo Vanzetti. They viewed President Calvin Coolidge with contempt, looked to *The Nation* and *The New Republic* for the most up-to-the-date information on contemporary matters, and read *Ten Days That Shook the World,* John Reed's classic. Their "day dreams about the great new world of the Kremlin," Blankfort acknowledged, provided "the seeds" that would germinate, for some of the group, into a highly politicized reading of international events in the decade ahead.[36]

For his part, Izzy was particularly fascinated with *The Conquest of Bread,* Peter Kropotkin's anarchist classic, and its "vision of a non-coercive, non-police state, voluntary free community society." Indeed, Izzy, who had so recently backed Robert La Follette's Progressive Party bid in the 1924 presidential campaign, now fancied himself, no matter how temporarily, as an anarchocommunist. But he, Blankfort, and other of their friends delved into Marxist critiques too, including those of the founders themselves, such as Friedrich Engels's *Socialism Scientific and Utopian,* Engels and Karl Marx's *Communist Manifesto,* Nikolai Bukharin's *Historical Materialism,* Vladimir Lenin's "Three Sources and Three Constituent Parts of Marxism." Determined not to give into "those stale surrenders which are called the practical realities of the world," Izzy joined a Socialist Party local in Camden and was placed on the New Jersey State Executive Committee before becoming eligible to vote.[37]

In Philadelphia, as in New York City, young Jewish intellectuals like Izzy and many of his friends were first attracted to socialist analyses because of the presence of a thriving radical subculture. Parents, older siblings, or perhaps a favorite uncle—as in Izzy's case—had first acquainted them with radical thought, while secular academic institutions provided something of a fertile environment. Now, small bands of like-minded young men and women might come together and help to sustain an emerging radical bent. Certainly that appeared to be the case with the Penn gang, which thereby found some protection against the anti-Semitic barbs that came their way courtesy of certain of their classmates.[38]

Also, the radical movement undoubtedly appeared more inviting to these first-generation Americans, caught between the Old World of their parents and the bright new day socialism promised to bring about. Many, after all, were striving to escape from the world of their fathers. Moreover, in the movement, they could compete on more equal terms with their WASPish fellows. There, commitment and learning, not breeding and family lineage, enabled one to make his or her mark. There, Jews such as themselves no longer seemed to be outsiders. And there, a kind of home was provided for some who felt they had none, emotionally at least. This appeal of the movement extended even to those who were not card-carrying members of one sect or another, but rather identified in some more subtle way with one radical group or school of thought.

Not surprisingly, radical philosophy and the radical movement appealed to someone such as Izzy, who was sensitive, intellectually driven, discontented with the middle-class ways of his family, and something of an outsider. But his irascible nature and highly individualistic bent made him the most unnatural of camp followers; he disliked organizations of any kind and attempts to instruct him on the politically correct way to behave or think, something that invariably seems to happen within the confines of political parties and mass movements.

A pair of letters Izzy wrote during his years at Penn demonstrate both his concern with the world of ideas and his fascination with current events, as well as the slightly unconventional side that so troubled his father. Writing on July 21, 1925, to Mike Blankfort, then an aspiring poet temporarily residing in Europe, Izzy noted that he had heard talk of anti-American sentiment in France and would happily have joined "in one of those fist-fights between students American and French holigans [sic]." He reported that President Coolidge was encountering political setbacks, with insurgency presently gaining ground in Congress. But he dismissed Gifford Pinchot, whom he had just interviewed the previous week in Camden, as "the old Roosevelt progressive type—dead, dead, dead." Already friends with several Italian anti-Fascists in the Philadelphia metropolitan area, Izzy asked Blankfort if he had any observations to make regarding Italy, a land which few on the American left then demonstrated much concern about; one who was displaying such an interest was political journalist George Seldes, later a friend of Izzy's and already a bitter foe of Mussolini's.[39]

More flippantly, Izzy suggested that his buddy interview Romain Rolland, the great French novelist and pacifist. He also noted that his work schedule left little time for his own reading, which lately had been limited to Gilbert Canaan's "Round the Corner," a Thomas Hardy poem, and several pieces by George Bernard Shaw, the great English playwright. He was most struck, Izzy pointed out, by Shaw's preface to *Getting Married,* which he urged Blankfort to read before the latter took the vow of marriage, for it contained a "wow of a lot of sense." That 1908 work included a call for a revolt against supposed nuptial bliss, which Shaw associated with sex slavery, hypocrisy, and pathological behavior.[40]

In addition, Izzy informed his friend about a recent weekend excursion he had made to Atlantic City. Among those he had traveled with was "a sweet little brunette" who worked at the *Camden Courier-Post* and had "a deuced lot of sound sense," but who lived "utterly out of my world—beauty, dizziness, etc." She had, he continued, "a lovely body" and was "hot as hell," but Izzy was about to dump her, fearing as he did that matters were getting too serious. He would not mind having her for a mistress, but unfortunately, she was "not the kind who was made for it (not enough intellect, independence) [but] born to be a wife and mother." Izzy also spoke of "a grand booze party" he had recently attended in this era of prohibition where he had encountered "a nymphomaniac restauranteure."[41]

The next summer, in a brief note to Blankfort, Izzy again declared himself to be "busy as hell," covering radio, business, and church news; editing the theatrical pages; handling the assignment book; copyediting the suburban edition; and taking care of rewrites. He also reported on a meeting with Benjamin De Casseres, the poet, journalist, and *New York Times* columnist, who had informed Izzy that a letter he had written some two and a half years earlier would be included in his latest book, along with writings by James Branch Cabell, Havelock Ellis, and Thomas Hardy, among others. A footnote by De Casseres would reportedly indicate that Izzy's letter demonstrated "American youth not only give a charleston." Izzy seemed to take what De Casseres evidently said in jest to heart, but *Forty Immortals* contained no such reference to him.[42]

Along with his occasional ventures to the boardwalk or prohibition-busting outings and his meetings with members of the American intelligentsia, Izzy spent most of his time during this period in ivory-towered classrooms or smoke-filled newsrooms; and whenever he had anything to say about it, he would opt for the latter. He briefly covered the campus for the *Philadelphia Record* but dropped out of school for a short while. He returned to work at the *Courier* as a special correspondent and was assigned the task of boosting the paper's circulation. He traveled to a different town in South Jersey each day, attempting to dig up enough news to attract more readers. By his junior year, he was pulling down ten-hour shifts for the *Philadelphia Inquirer*. After classes, he would head over to the *Inquirer*'s Camden office in the early afternoon to do rewrite assignments. Then he would return to Philadelphia to work the copy desk in the evenings, editing and writing headlines for the Jersey edition until the midnight hour beckoned. By 1927, he was pocketing the tidy sum of forty dollars a week, had switched back to the *Courier,* and withdrew from the university, a decision not well received by his parents.43

Nothwithstanding the hurt feelings never veiled back in Haddonfield, Izzy was convinced he knew what he was doing. He had had it with school, what with all those boring classes and stuffy professors. Although he was in fact drawn to a pair of instructors in his own field of philosophy, the Penn faculty in general simply repelled him. As he later recalled, "the few islands of greatness seemed to be washed by seas of pettiness and mediocrity." Thus, by now, the short-lived dream he once had of becoming a university professor had long since vanished. In its stead, he saw himself as a newsman for the duration. After all, "the smell of a newsroom" seemed eminently more appealing.44

The summer of 1927, Izzy was working once more for the *Camden Courier* when the staff was informed about the impending executions of Nicola Sacco and Bartolomeo Vanzetti. The case of the two Italian immigrant-anarchists, indicted back in 1920 on charges of robbery and murder, had become a cause célèbre for intellectuals throughout the Western world who were deeply distressed that the evidence against them was only circumstantial. Upset by the news that the two men were about to be electrocuted, Izzy asked himself what his grandchildren would think if he failed to protest. After all, he desired to become an activist journalist who would combine dedication to his trade with a sense of political commitment. But owing to a recent flu epidemic, the paper was shorthanded and the city editor turned down Izzy's request that he be assigned to cover the executions.45

There is no consensus on what happened next. Lou Stone recalled that Izzy ran away from home at this point, intending to wind up in Boston where he planned to picket. Their father, however, purportedly cut Izzy off at the ferry and brought him back to Haddonfield. Izzy, for his part, remembered things differently. As he recalled, the city editor's refusal to deliver the assignment he wanted caused him to storm out of the *Courier* office, cram an extra pair of socks in his back pocket, and hitchhike to New York City. There he was informed that a stay of execution had been granted, so he stuck his thumb out once again and landed in Bellows Falls, Vermont, where a friend of his resided. He wired the paper that he was tendering his resignation so that he might get a job out in the countryside. No jobs were to be found, however, so he eventually headed back to Haddonfield. He stopped off to see the Jersey editor of the *Philadelphia Inquirer* and asked him, "Could you use a good man?" The editor bristled, "I could use a half dozen." Izzy retorted, "Well, here's one," and he was immediately hired.[46]

Shortly thereafter, Izzy returned to work at the *Courier* and was placed on rewrite, an assignment normally handed to an experienced newsman. He "worked like hell" to produce fresh leads for stories that had already appeared in the morning paper in order to boost the sales of the evening edition. He also began dabbling in editorial writing on the side, even substituting for the paper's vacationing editorialist at one point.[47]

As the 1920s neared a close, Izzy determined that a raise of five dollars a week was in order and delivered an ultimatum to that effect to the *Courier*'s managing editor. He was so insistent because the same fellow who had forewarned his friend Mike Blankfort about the pitfalls of marriage now planned to take the plunge himself. The object of his affections was one Esther Roisman, whom Izzy had met two years earlier "on a blind date and a borrowed dollar." His blind date had "shagged" him, but the evening, nevertheless, had been a memorable one. For sparks immediately flew between the impish, somewhat portly, five-foot, seven-inch Izzy and the diminutive Esther, who was out on the town with a friend of his. The two couples were double-dating, and Izzy was drawn to both Esther's looks and her lively intelligence, while she "saw those dimples" and immediately thought, "This is it!" Not even the fact that Esther was—at least in Izzy's eyes—a West Philadelphia Republican, and he, a backer of Socialist Party presidential candidate Norman Thomas, could dampen the romantic ardor they felt for each other. Now, having dated for the past two years, Izzy and Esther decided to get married. On their wedding day, Izzy appeared properly splendid in black tux, French-cuffed shirt, and boutonniere; Esther looked lovely with her long veil, swept to the side, and an armful of orchids.[48]

For the next sixty years, the two were all but inseparable, with Esther proving to be completely devoted to Izzy. In a very real sense, she submerged herself in her husband and their soon-to-appear brood of three, sons Jeremy and Christopher and daughter Celia. To Marc Stone, this was still more evidence of Izzy's self-centered nature: "Esther always totally subordinated her life to Izzy. If Izzy wanted to go to the movies, they went to the movies. If he wanted to go for a walk, they went for a walk. If he wanted to eat, they ate. . . . And whatever Izzy wanted, that's what was done. He had a charmed life that way. Like very few men."[49]

Yet Esther never seemed to be troubled by what others would later consider to be her husband's chauvinism. Their marriage, for one thing, was no different from that of most other American couples of the day, whether involving members of the left are not. And as she later indicated, Esther felt "completely fulfilled in Izzy's life. His energies and enthusiasms and excitements are just so great." This was fortunate indeed, for Izzy, determined as he was to make a name for himself, seemed to require such a mate. As Esther acknowledged, "Some people need complete attention and Izzy is one. Complete attention, complete devotion, a complete feeling of being the creative person."[50]

In many ways, then, the Stones' marriage was a traditional one. Izzy served as the breadwinner and Esther created a nurturing home and a haven of sorts, free from the demands of her husband's profession. But Izzy was so involved in his craft and with political matters in general that they were never completely absent from the home front. Indeed, Izzy was one who lived and breathed his work, often bringing it, along with colleagues and political compatriots, home.

But while their relationship might have seemed as if out of an earlier age and "Esther's job" later appeared to be "raising the children," her influence on Izzy was always considerable. Even though he could not quite put his finger on it, Esther, Marc Stone later acknowledged, was not simply "a helpmate."[51]

One welcome by-product of Izzy's marriage to Esther would be improved relations with his father, at least for a spell. He now became a good bit closer to both his parents, his brother Lou later recalled, and Bernard took increasingly great pride in his son's professional accomplishments. But what further strengthened the relationship between father and son was the economic calamity that soon befell the Feinstein household. Until the very end of the 1920s, Bernard had continued to add to his real-estate holdings. The showcase home he was building for the family had neared completion. And then, the economy plummeted.[52]

As the stock market crash of October 1929 triggered a collapse in the American economy, all that Bernard Feinstein had acquired during this speculation-fueled era was lost. A survey undertaken in early 1931 indicated that Philadelphia, along with Detroit and Cleveland, was the hardest hit of some nineteen major metropolitan areas that had been examined. Scores of breadlines and soup kitchens filled downtown streets, while lines of the unemployed congregated in front of the mayor's office. The Feinsteins' financial uncertainty paralleled that of thousands of Philadelphians and triggered another round of nervous breakdowns by Katy, whose bouts of manic depression returned once more. Again and again, she was institutionalized at the Pennsylvania Hospital for Nervous Diseases in Philadelphia, and on one particularly horrific occasion, drank some cleaning fluid before awakening Lou in the middle of the night. Her youngest son induced his mother to throw up, all the while she cried hysterically. She begged for Lou's forgiveness before Bernard was awakened to rush her off to a nearby hospital in Camden. Both Lou and Judy stayed up that night, praying so "Mom wouldn't die." She survived and was again admitted to the state hospital. During her hospital stays, she was often treated much like an outpatient and allowed to make home-visits. In the passage between the hospital in Philadelphia and the Feinstein home in Haddonfield—Lou was assigned the somewhat arduous task of transporting her by trolley car, ferry, subway, and on foot—she frequently broke out in tears.[53]

Adding to Katy's distress, Bernard's financial fortunes continued to worsen. Throughout this period, Izzy generously provided what assistance he could, thus helping, as Lou remembered, "to keep the family." Emotionally, however, Izzy was, at best, "in the wings." Lou, on the other hand, living at home, was intimately involved in the ongoing struggle, while Marc, who had gone off to study at the University of North Carolina, soon returned from Chapel Hill. By early 1933, however, the Feinsteins were compelled to leave Haddonfield, their home for nearly a quarter of a century, for a small, spare house in north Philadelphia. The now fifty-eight-year-old Bernard, who refused to declare bankruptcy, was reduced to peddling silk stockings once again, now in the city, where he targeted relatives and friends or went door to door. But Bernard, Lou later recalled, "had the guts to never say die" and eventually paid off all his debts. Eventually, Izzy pulled what political strings he had in order to help Bernard secure a job at the U.S. Mint building in Philadelphia; Bernard worked there until his retirement during World War II.[54]

The marriage of Bernard and Katy Feinstein remained a troubled one until his death on August 10, 1947, and Izzy sought to avoid having much contact with their "very tense" household. He grew distant from his father once again and returned to Philadelphia only to make the obligatory visit during Passover which entailed stops at the homes of both the Roismans and, very secondarily, his own parents. Katy, nothwithstanding her recurrent bouts of depression, stood as the stronger force in the Feinstein household, appeared "funny, witty, quick" to her grandchildren, and continued to dote on her youngest.[55]

Katy's mental illness and the asthma and bronchitis with which he was afflicted, and which steadily grew worse over time, wore heavily on Bernard. Nevertheless, in spite of all of his troubles, he avoided becoming embittered, remained something of a raconteur, a practical joker, and "the life of . . . family parties." The eldest son he both loved and frequently fought with likewise became a great storyteller and a man inclined to dominate family gatherings.[56]

I zzy Stone was obliged to begin his own family and help care for his parents precisely when he was first striving to make something of a reputation for himself in his chosen field of journalism. Moreover, all of this was occurring as the American economy was starting to unravel. It hardly seemed an auspicious time for a socially committed young journalist to attempt to make his mark, just when papers nationwide were being hit by the disintegration of the economy. Job cuts loomed ahead, not promotions of the kind the ever ambitious Izzy sought.

And yet, Izzy's radical bent and determination to stand as a politically committed journalist and intellectual actually served him well, for both he and a certain portion of the American intelligentsia were about to become more receptive to embittered analyses of capitalism, the kind that had been little listened to for a good while now. His own temperament and ready examination of prevailing conditions led Izzy in that direction and enabled him for the first time to meet up with a number of influential American intellectuals.

Furthermore, although the economic hardships of Bernard and Katy both troubled him deeply and required certain sacrifices on his and Esther's part, they perhaps enabled him to redefine relations with his parents somewhat more along the lines of his own choosing. This was of no little importance for one who sought to govern his environment and closest relationships in the manner that Izzy inevitably did. That very desire to control both his home life and workplace, however, had caused problems for him in the past and would do so again in the future.

3 On the Record

Although the depression soon ravaged Philadelphia, tearing at the very fabric of his parents' home, Izzy's own fortunes had never appeared brighter. In 1931, he joined the staff of the *Philadelphia Record*, which had fallen on hard times at the outset of the previous decade and had recently been purchased by his boss, J. David Stern, now renowned as a liberal publisher. Shortly thereafter, Izzy, who was determined to make a name for himself, became the youngest editorial writer in the country working for a major metropolitan paper. The *Record*'s liberal editorial policy and link to the Rooseveltian wing of the Democratic Party eventually enabled the paper to thrive in a city where Republican publications had long been ascendant.[1]

Desirous of helping to orchestrate the paper's editorial policy, Izzy had sauntered into the office building of the *Record* early one Saturday morning in 1931, carefully crafted an editorial, and then placed it on top of the publisher's desk where Stern could not avoid spotting it. Stern arrived at the office around nine o'clock that morning, discovered Izzy's piece, and angrily read it. He had just brought Izzy on board the *Record* because the youngster seemed unable to get along with the city editor of the *Camden Courier*, another one of his papers. Now, Izzy appeared to be "muscling in" on his own turf. Consequently, Stern proved to be "very nasty about it," and Izzy went away, more than a little shaken up. But he also left thinking, "You son-of-a-bitch, I'm going to keep pestering you until you make me an editorial writer."[2]

And when he arrived at work the next day, Izzy was "really thrilled" to discover that a magnified copy of his editorial—in the custom of the paper—had been placed in the front window of the offices of the *Philadelphia Record*.[3]

As the path cut by the depression widened, however, creditors threatened to initiate bankruptcy proceedings against the *Record*. Desperately attempting to keep the paper afloat, Stern felt it necessary to slice salaries as well as the size of his staff. Among those he had to let go was his chief editorialist. With a spot on the editorial page now open, Stern turned to his feisty but favorite junior reporter. By the time Izzy left the

Record less than three years later, his salary had jumped to eighty-five dollars a week.[4]

Notwithstanding his own relative good fortune, however, Izzy was well aware that many of his journalistic brethren suffered the "payless paydays," smaller paychecks, and job layoffs that the *Record* had itself experienced. Consequently, along with Heywood Broun, the famed columnist for *The New Republic*, free-lance reporter George Seldes, and A. J. Liebling of the *New Yorker*, he became a charter member of the American Newspaper Guild.[5]

Career and intellectual aspirations now came into play for Izzy. The receipt of a key journalistic assignment merely whetted his appetite for still choicer ones. In addition, he was about to be befriended by certain leading members of the East Coast intelligentsia. Izzy's large ambition, his determination to be seen as both a top-notch reporter and an intellectual, his growing involvement with the 1930s' left, and his independent nature all combined to produce considerable conflict for Izzy in what was to become the most ideologically charged period of his career. While he had previously managed to avoid choosing between liberal and radical ideals, for a time he felt compelled to do so, resulting in his lining up, however temporarily, with the American Communists. This was no easy marriage for Stone, given his instinctive distaste for sectarianism. But it was in keeping with his readiness to challenge his own beliefs and what was going on in his own land.

Stone's attention, like that of many of his fellow journalists and intellectuals, now turned to the state of the economy and eventually led him to depart from the ranks of Norman Thomas's Socialist Party, if not officially, then philosophically at least. Stone, along with a fair number of largely unaligned radicals, including Malcolm Cowley, Matthew Jackson, and Edmund Wilson, ended up demanding a wholesale transformation of the American economic system. The faltering actions of President Hoover, formerly viewed as a model progressive, and the early proposals of the administration of Franklin Delano Roosevelt both troubled and angered Stone and his intellectual compatriots. They feared, for a while at least, that an American brand of fascism might be in the offing. Consequently, they came to believe that communism and the Communist Party alone could prevent that occurrence and improve the sorry lot of the American worker, farmer, and consumer. They considered it necessary for intellectuals to take a stand now, given the severity of the economic collapse and the pain that resulted.

Stone's move toward the Communist path was gradual and, as matters turned out, only temporary. But from the outset, he found it difficult to understand why President Hoover, acclaimed for his food relief program for Europe after World War I, offered only a "very callous and hard-hearted" face to the down-and-outers in his own land. Why was the Great Engineer willing to provide a "huge soup kitchen" in the form of the Reconstruction

Finance Corporation to bail out big business alone? The modified laissez-faire approach and the trickle-down economic theory that guided the Hoover administration simply appalled him.[6]

Furthermore, "the hopelessness" of Mr. Hoover and the "disquieting" absence of national leadership were equally troubling. On New Year's Eve, the *Philadelphia Record* declared the nation to be facing its greatest trauma since the Civil War.[7]

Hoover, Stone believed, had now proven to be a hopeless throwback, whose political career happily appeared certain to end soon. So too did the president's social Darwinistic approach, in a time when the nation desperately required action by government at all levels. The ideals that had fueled the speculative practices of the previous decade were, he felt certain, mercifully about to become history.

What was demanded, the *Record* declared, with Stone helping to shape editorial policy, was direct federal assistance for the unemployed, now numbering ten million. The American people, the paper insisted, had to "rehabilitate the destitute." Americans who were economically crippled had to be treated as "economically incapacitated soldiers of our industrial systems," the paper cried as conditions deteriorated in the metropolitan area, and not as "bums." Stone, publisher J. David Stern, and Sam Grafton, the other top editorial writer on the *Record* and a member of the old gang at Penn, repeatedly insisted that the nation must "fight the depression as we fought the war."[8]

After visiting the White House, where he encountered a depressed and clearly overwhelmed chief executive, Stern became convinced that Hoover simply had to go. The *Record* subsequently became the first major urban newspaper to back the presidential candidacy of New York governor Franklin Delano Roosevelt. This required no small amount of courage, for business associates of Stern cuttingly warned that the *Record*—already referred to as "that paper" by Philadelphia's upper crust—would be made to pay dearly for supporting "that Socialist."[9]

The *Record* editorialists, evidently pleased that the Democratic Party nominee had saluted "the forgotten man" perched at the bottom of the economic ladder, acclaimed the 1932 race as the most important one yet held in this century. Roosevelt-styled liberalism, they declared, "MUST become the official governmental economics of our nation, if we are to avoid national decay."[10]

Despite his part in composing such editorials, however, Stone—like many on the left—remained unsure about the Hyde Park aristocrat. True, Roosevelt's cheery nature was in happy contrast to the gloomy visage of Hoover; moreover, the New York Democrat, unlike the Republican president, acknowledged federal responsibility for the welfare of the nation as a whole.

But Roosevelt's platform, while placing "human rights above property rights," remained "spotty" at best, failed to endorse federal aid for the unemployed, and emphasized such old standards as a sound currency and a balanced budget.[11]

All of this caused Stone, along with the editorialists at *The Nation* and *The New Republic*—the era's top left-liberal journals whose philosophy was close to his own during the depression decade—to worry about the genuineness of Roosevelt's liberalism, the depth of his concern for the forgotten man, and his leadership qualities. In the months ahead, both journals and the *Philadelphia Record*, although perhaps less clearly in the case of the paper, saw the Democratic nominee edging "left and right." *The Nation* viewed the forthcoming election as another case of "Tweedledum and Tweedledee" and, along with *The New Republic*, considered the only vote that made any sense to be one cast for Norman Thomas, the Socialist Party candidate. Stone also opted to vote for Thomas once again, notwithstanding the editorial position of the *Record*, which remained staunchly supportive of Franklin Delano Roosevelt.[12]

Izzy's ideology and ambition were now at loggerheads. He was not, at this point, the celebrated figure he would later become, but rather a twenty-four-year-old reporter and husband with a brand-new baby on the way. Moreover, he had a job as a top editorialist with a leading liberal newspaper and was just beginning to acquire something of a reputation for himself. The possibility of working for sectarian publications obviously held little appeal for him, undoubtedly because of their tunnel vision and due to the fact that they promised little in the way of professional advancement.

Thus, although Stone considered Roosevelt's campaign to be something of a "flopperoo," the editorial page of the *Record*, with full encouragement from publisher J. David Stern and shaped in part by Izzy, praised Roosevelt as a great American progressive and asserted that the campaign pitted "liberalism vs. reaction." Not surprisingly, then, the paper predicted on election day that "a peaceful revolution" was in the making, which the *Record* soon suggested could well prevent American institutions from going under. That was precisely what troubled them, *The Nation* and *The New Republic* indicated, for Roosevelt did not promise any radical restructuring of the American capitalist system; just such a shakeup was needed, *The Nation* insisted, while recalling the reformist zeal once displayed by Woodrow Wilson, Izzy's boyhood hero. For now, both journals, like the *New York Post*, applauded the overwhelming defeat handed Herbert Hoover, who was seen as "a complete failure."[13]

As the interregnum wound on in seemingly interminable fashion, the American economy and social order threatened to unravel. Thirteen to fifteen million were without work. Runs on banks mounted, and bank doors were boarded up. Already sparse relief funds of local and state agencies dried up. Hoovervilles, bread lines, and soup kitchens spread across the land. The farming community fared no better, as family after family experienced hard times leading to foreclosure and the increasingly common phenomenon of "going down that road feelin' bad."[14]

The deteriorating economy and the apparent failure of the chief executive and the president-elect to agree on what might be done about it troubled Stone more and more and led him to veer sharply leftward. On January 3, 1933, he sketched a tale about one individual who had failed to act during an earlier crisis. As a consequence, that man, King Louis XVI of France, and other members of the French aristocracy lost everything—their titles, their wealth, even their heads. Stone suggested that attention had better be paid to the report of the President's Research Committee on Social Trends which warned that a similar policy of drift might presently be afoot in America. The study declared that should this country remain riddled by the presence of want amid plenty, "there can be no assurance that these alternatives with their accompaniments of violent revolution, dark periods of serious repression of libertarian and democratic forms, the proscription and loss of many useful elements in the present productive system can be averted.[15]

To avoid such a scenario, Stone wrote, American Bourbons had better heed the report's call for such "socialistic" measures as redistributive income policies; soak-the-rich taxes; old age, unemployment, and health insurance; and industrial planning—his particular favorite. Yet such proposals were "capitalistic" as well, he pointed out, for they merely promised to "curb the abuses of individualism without destroying its benefits" and to "preserve property rights while subordinating them to human rights." They well might prevent American capitalism, he continued, from blindly and foolishly destroying itself.[16]

The Nation and *The New Republic* both underscored the fact that the presidential committee's report was inherently "a revolutionary document" that highlighted the need for industrial planning. This emphasis on planning pleased Stone, who continued to view the scene at this point as a socialist and thus condemned the chaos and the boom-and-bust cycles capitalism seemed inevitably to experience.[17]

For the American left at this stage, planning appeared to be a kind of panacea that would allow for both the curbing of the excesses of capitalism and the introduction of some of that which socialism purportedly had to offer. Stone long remained convinced that planning could help spur productivity and efficiency in both advanced and less developed lands, including the United States and the Soviet Union. Planning, at the very least, he believed, could prevent the U.S. economy from crumbling altogether, thereby avoiding the political chaos that was sure to follow.

Such chaos could lead to an even worse state of affairs. With the disintegration of German democracy, Stone recognized that the withering of a capitalist state could result in fascist terror. That worried him most of all, because fascism endangered the best the West had to offer—political democracy, respect for individual liberties, and the possibility of a more egalitarian society.

Fascism, he reasoned, was irrational and inhumane and threatened to further shackle the already economically downtrodden. He viewed it as little more than a means by which reactionary property holders sought to ward off the inevitable advance of socialism. Fascism he considered to be a vestige of a decayed past, socialism "the common-sense solution of the paradox that puts want amid plenty, idle men beside idle factories, underfed children in a land of rotting crops." Fascism, he believed, involved a particularly reprehensible stage of the very capitalistic decay that continued to push him, however temporarily, into the ranks of the Sovietphiles.[18]

The previous July, Stone and the other *Record* editorialists had worried that Junker, Communist, or Nazi forces might destroy the Weimar Republic which Socialists and centrists struggled to uphold in what threatened to become Germany's "darkest" hour. In August 1932, they warned that should Adolf Hitler, that "self-deluded demagogue," come to power, war would soon follow. They viewed the onetime army corporal as lacking even the character and purpose other contemporary dictators, such as Benito Mussolini and Joseph Stalin, seemed to possess. And they declared that behind Hitler were the most reactionary German forces—"Junker militarists," large landowners, and powerful industrialists.[19]

But Hitler's subsequent appointment as chancellor in January 1933 and the emergence of the Nazi reign of terror startled the *Record* editorialists, who declared that capitalism and democracy were both disintegrating in Germany. Only a general strike—which *The Nation* believed was not about to come off—supported by trade unions and by the Social Democratic, centrist, and Communist parties, they reasoned, could now stave off the likelihood of a "giant Fascist State." *The New Republic,* in its issue of March 29, insisted that the Hitler takeover would never have been pulled off if the forces on the left had united earlier. It noted that both the Socialist Second International and the Communist Third International appeared to be hinting that a genuine united front might be forthcoming.[20]

By this point, Stone was no longer what he had been in the mid-1920s, a kind of "premature anti-Fascist" only, but rather a type of "premature popular fronter" as well. This approach came somewhat naturally to Izzy, who had grown up, after all, in small towns such as Haddonfield and Camden where radicals were few in number and tended to consider one another as friends, whether they held themselves out to be anarchists, communists, or socialists. As Izzy later recalled, "You regarded these other people all as comrades."[21]

This united front approach was also encouraged by Dr. Morris Vladimir Leof, who served as a kind of exemplar and surrogate father for Izzy and other intellectuals and activists in the Philadelphia area. At his four-story brownstone at 322 South 16th Street in the city, M. V. Leof, as he was known, held court to such individuals as Yiddish writer Sholem Asch, Jewish tragedian Jacob Adler, composer Marc Blitzstein, playwright Clifford Odets, and Izzy Stone. Poppa Leof was a nondoctrinaire humanist and longtime Socialist, who was forever viewed by other party members as too independently minded. On several instances, the party hierarchy, beside itself because of his heretical ways, even threatened to deny him his burial plot. But for concerned young folk like Blitzstein, Odets, and Stone, Leof represented the kind of model they failed to see in their own fathers. Moreover, the great issues of the time were debated in the somewhat rarified atmosphere of the Leof home, where, as Odets later remembered, "you could breathe freely."[22]

By early 1933, Stone still considered himself a socialist like his good friend Poppa Leof. But he was enraged by what he considered to be the decision of the "fake Socialists" of the German Social Democratic Party to withdraw from the Second International and apparently strive for some type of rapprochement with Hitler; he now came to see communism as the only force that could hold back the Black- and Brownshirts. In the first article he wrote for V. F. Calverton's *Modern Monthly,* published that April, Stone reviewed Oswald Garrison Villard's *German Phoenix* and Edgar Ansel Mowrer's *Germany Puts Back the Clock.* He saw both works as adopting the standard liberal line on Germany: an "unjust" peace coupled with "unjust reparations" had infuriated the German people, weakened the hold of the Republic on their allegiance, and driven them into the arms of the Nazis. The failure to go much beyond standard liberal analyses, he declared, was due to the "liberal limitations" of *The Nation* editor and to Mowrer's position on the staff of a paper like the *Chicago Daily News.*[23]

Consciously or not, Izzy certainly must have identified with Mowrer's dilemma, so like his own, for he too worked for a liberal publisher and newspaper. But the handful of articles he now produced for *Modern Monthly* enabled him to deliver unrestrained critiques of capitalism as he saw fit.

Villard, Stone reported, all but acknowledged that which now seemed so clear—the German working class had been betrayed by the Social Democratic Party. Apparently recognizing this, Villard had asserted that the SDP had not moved forcefully enough against the great landbarons and industrial magnates. It might have employed "the weapon of socialization" but had failed to do so. The Social Democrats might have learned from the Russian experience, Villard continued, "*without, however, resorting to the cruel and bloody ruthlessness of the Soviets.*"[24]

The italics were Izzy Stone's own as he wondered just how this could have taken place. Implicit, of course, was his assumption that Germany would have been fortunate had the Socialists learned from the Bolsheviks.

Stone's editorials that appeared in the *Philadelphia Record* during this period were only a bit more tempered and indicate that he was engaged in something of a delicate balancing act. On April 15, the *Record* declared that either the purchasing power of the American public had to be increased or State Capitalism might result. But in another article published the same month in *Modern Monthly*, Stone warned that inflation was merely a temporary Band-Aid which left "the fundamental contradictions of capitalism" intact.[25]

Stone's *Modern Monthly* pieces, four in all, were written during Roosevelt's First Hundred Days, a period when many on the left continued to view the new administration with more than a little concern and skepticism. Now, for a brief while, he had parted company with those at *The Nation* and *The New Republic* who saw Roosevelt as a courageous and forthright progressive determined to end laissez-faire practices. The volume of reform legislation that Roosevelt quickly shepherded through Congress was said by *The New Republic* to be "the marvel of the world." By contrast, Communist Party members and fellow travelers denounced the president for setting the stage for an American brand of fascism. Many worried that Roosevelt might be heading in the direction certain legal and financial tycoons had been urging for some time now—toward cartelization as a means to right the national economy, bring stability to the marketplace, and rope in increasingly disgruntled workers. Izzy Stone, for his part, was furious that Roosevelt seemed to be adopting a deflationary policy in line with the thinking of the "goddamnest bunch of Wall Streeters." Troubled by the apparent thrust of much of the early New Deal and trying like so many others to discover "what the hell was going on," Stone completed his most embittered works yet, "Roosevelt Moves Toward Fascism" and "Morgan & Co.: A House of Ill Fame." As he later admitted, "It was agony to live through that period."[26]

In sharp contrast to many others, particularly members of the sectarian left, Izzy did not view with satisfaction the economic calamity that had befallen the American nation. He took no comfort from the fact that radical critiques of capitalism had seemingly been borne out. His articles in *Modern Monthly* characteristically were embittered analyses, not celebrations of capitalism's failures or paeans to the bright promise of socialism.

Izzy's *Modern Monthly* pieces all appeared under the pseudonym of Abelard Stone. He adopted such a byline because Peter Abelard, the medieval philosopher noted for his dialectical and rationalist approach, was an old favorite of his. But more significant, Izzy employed the pseudonym because the four articles were published in V. F. Calverton's journal and because of the arguments they contained; he undoubtedly recognized that they would have exasperated J. David Stern, a staunch Roosevelt supporter, to no end and very well might have cost him his job at the *Philadelphia Record*.[27]

Mike Blankfort, at the time an associate editor with *Modern Monthly*, had introduced Izzy to Calverton in early January, and discussions had taken place about the possibility of Izzy contributing to the journal. Izzy was quite thrilled that Calverton—who was host to a veritable "who's who of the best radical minds" of the period—displayed such an interest in him and his work.[28]

Calverton, like Stone, favored a united front against capitalism and fascism, but had become a pariah to Stalinists who denounced his publication as "a 'Trotskyite' organ" and dismissed him as a fascist. In January 1933, *The New Masses* had delivered a blistering attack against Calverton, who continued, nevertheless, to consider himself a communist.[29]

It was during this period that Izzy was beginning to establish something of a reputation for himself, attracting attention from journalists as diverse and as noteworthy as V. F. Calverton, J. David Stern, and H. L. Mencken. Mencken, the iconoclastic editor of the *American Mercury*, published a piece of his attacking Pennsylvania governor Gifford Pinchot as "a Great Liberal in a Tight Corner" who had fallen victim to a Hooverlike "doleophobia." Stern had made Stone the top editorial writer on the *Philadelphia Record* and afforded him and Sam Grafton considerable latitude in establishing the paper's editorial policy.[30]

But no matter how enlightened that policy might be, the *Record* remained a liberal newspaper at best and its publisher one of Roosevelt's staunchest supporters and something of an unofficial adviser. Although not uncritical of the new administration, J. David Stern was not about to lend his newspaper as a forum for the kinds of analyses employed in "Roosevelt Moves Toward Fascism" and "Morgan & Co."

Not wanting to jeopardize his position on the *Record* but increasingly drawn to a more radical perspective, Stone passed these articles along to Blankfort and Calverton, who published them in *Modern Monthly* under the nom de plume of Abelard Stone. At this point, the late spring and early summer of 1933, Izzy Stone, like certain other American intellectuals, determined to move beyond the "near-beer" aroma of the Socialist Party. He now considered the charge of certain members of America's intelligentsia, ranging from Malcolm Cowley to John Dos Passos to Edmund Wilson, to "take Communism away from the Communists" to be a reasonable one.[31]

Consequently, in June 1933, "Roosevelt Moved Toward Fascism" appeared in *Modern Monthly*. There Stone reflected on the recently concluded presidential election, declaring it to have involved nothing more than a choice between "Tweedledum" and "Tweedledee." The triumph of the smiling, seductive-sounding Tweedledee, who hinted about a "new deal" and spoke of the forgotten man and the need for experimentation, he continued, had determined the immediate fate of the American people. Foreclosed for now at least was the option of carving a path to "a Soviet America," which Stone declared to be "the one way out that could make a real difference to the working classes." Two other possible roads lay ahead, the first pointing toward governmental action to boost the purchasing power of the masses, the second, in the direction of fascism.[32]

Unknowingly, Stone continued, President Hoover had already begun to take the nation down that last avenue with the Reconstruction Finance Corporation, his "two billion dollar soup kitchen." Designed to benefit big banking and giant corporate interests, the RFC threatened to become the cornerstone for "an American State Capitalism." It was now readily apparent, Stone wrote, that Roosevelt, like Hoover before him, did not intend to increase the purchasing power of the masses to any great extent. Instead, he called for "a reforestation labor army" that would be paid at the rate of one dollar a day and placed under military control at a time when fascist dictators were gaining ground. He maintained his predecessor's policy, as demonstrated by his farm and home mortgage proposals, of underwriting private investments with public funds. He cut government expenditures when an inflationary boost was desperately needed. He did, in other words, "exactly what Mr. Hoover would have liked to do."[33]

All of this led Stone to believe that "Mr. Roosevelt intends to move toward Fascism," something the American comrades were warning against, as well as Norman Thomas and Reinhold Niebuhr, the eminent theologian. Higher prices were to be fixed, antitrust laws suspended, American industry "cartelized" under the watchful eye of a government dominated by big business. And talk of the planned economy characteristic of *New Republic* editorials, Stone declared, was simply setting the stage for an American fascism. True, "it will be a more refined and better-smelling specimen than Hitler's or Mussolini's." But nevertheless, "there will be the same organization of industry at the expense of worker and consumer, government-based monopolies, and 'regulation' by a government which is only an instrument of the finance capital it pretends to regulate."[34]

Izzy's charged rhetoric, at this point, might easily have fitted into the pages of *The New Masses* or even the *Daily Worker*. He saw the Communist route as the only one that would have bettered the lot of the average American citizen, considered greater government spending to be a mere palliative, and viewed Roosevelt as no reformer but rather a cryptofascist, however smooth-talking.

No longer was Stone willing to give Roosevelt the benefit of the doubt as he had earlier felt compelled to do while covering the presidential campaign for the *Record*. Now, all of the reservations and misgivings he had felt about the then Democratic Party candidate, and his fears regarding the new administration's programs, combined to produce stinging analyses of this sort. This was a period when he saw Roosevelt as endangering the American democratic system, something those on both the far left and right agreed was taking place. But in contrast to the sectarians, Stone scarcely seemed to believe that "after him, our time will come." Rather, his own nation and compatriots appeared headed for still more difficult times, while the possibility of the good society appeared more distant than ever.

It should not have been all that surprising, then, that in the following issue of *Modern Monthly*, Stone continued his assault on Roosevelt, whose chief talents, he suggested, were those of "a slick salesman." But this time around, he saved his heaviest ammunition for American corporate moguls. A congressional inquiry into the operations of the Morgan banking trust, he argued, demonstrated that the new administration was as strongly tied to finance capital as was the one it replaced. Moreover, the investigation again pointed out the futility of the seemingly perennial battle waged by the lower middle class against "moneyed interests." The Jacksonians, greenbackers, Populists, grangers, and progressives had all proven incapable of preventing the growth of a financial oligarchy. This was due to the fact that the lower middle class, no matter its political prominence and the influence it wielded over the working class, was just "as much a victim of the democratic myth as the proletariat whom that myth was intended to deceive." Because the lower middle class itself "had something to lose," it did not favor "revolutionary action," opting for halfhearted regulation instead.[35]

However, the American lower middle class failed to recognize that "the state is in every way an instrument of the ruling class"—an analysis the sectarians wholeheartedly agreed with. That would remain the case, Stone charged, even if the Socialists came to power so long as they proposed to work within the capitalist system. The Morgan probe thus demonstrated that the proletariat alone was "a really revolutionary class" and that "only a workers party and a Communist party" could curb the power of the financial oligarchy.[36]

Thus Stone, implicitly at least, now stood with those who argued that a total transformation of the U.S. economic system was in order. He dismissed reformers as well-intentioned, but largely impotent actors and seemed to suggest that the socialists were little better. Communism alone, he now believed, promised to serve the interests of the people.

On July 12, Bruce Bliven of *The New Republic* agreed that many of the criticisms "the revolutionists" directed at the New Deal rang true. It was not yet clear, he admitted, if the outpouring of legislation passed in the First Hundred Days would do more than simply "patch up" the starkest failings of industrial capitalism. But he denied the charges that Roosevelt was any kind of "Fascist dictator," pointing out how sympathetic the president was to labor unions, something Izzy Stone too would shortly come to appreciate.[37]

"Morgan & Co." was the last article I. F. Stone wrote that accused Roosevelt of dictatorial intentions. It was also the final piece he published in *Modern Monthly*. Michael Blankfort resigned from the journal the same summer, following the increasingly doctrinaire stance adopted toward V. F. Calverton by those close to the American Communist Party. Mike Gold, who had defended Calverton prior to *The New Masses'* onslaught, now determined that his former friend was in league with discredited Lovestonites and Trotskyists. Newton Arvin and Granville Hicks refused to contribute to *Modern Monthly* any longer, as did Stanley Burnshaw, Kyle Crichton, and Edwin Seaver, among others.[38]

Exactly why Stone never wrote again for Calverton is difficult to ascertain. Perhaps this simply indicated solidarity with Mike Blankfort. Perhaps it demonstrated how far Calverton's standing with certain elements of the left had fallen. Perhaps it signified how closely Stone was lined up, no matter for how brief a time, with the American comrades.

Izzy Stone, unlike Granville Hicks, but in the manner of Lincoln Steffens and Malcolm Cowley, never made the decision to join the Communist Party. Nevertheless, he, along with a good number of other American intellectuals of the time, ranging from Steffens to Cowley to Hicks, harbored certain romantic notions about communism. After visiting the new communist state where the future was supposedly to be found, Steffens, in his own fashion, thereafter supported the revolution. Appalled by the waste and misery resulting from a capitalist economy, Cowley applauded the revolutionary fire of party comrades. For Hicks, with economic chaos all about, communism appeared to be the only rational solution. In the 1920s, Izzy Stone had been temporarily spellbound by Kropotkin's vision of an unbounded society. And while he acknowledged that Lenin's Soviets exhibited "cruel and bloody ruthlessness," he saluted the Russian Communist Party for having presented Europe's least industrially advanced state with new turbines, railroads, factories.[39]

Yet he never viewed the Soviet Union as any kind of utopia or, ultimately, as a model for his own nation. While acknowledging that remarkable progress had been made by "the dictators of Moscow," he characterized them as "fanatics of the blueprint, idealists in steel and concrete." However, "human nature," he pointed out, was as yet "unconvinced." The pace of the first Five-Year Plan was slower than expected, inefficiency more widespread, and the masses were riddled with apathy and dissatisfaction. This was not surprising, Stone had indicated in early January 1933, for the Russian peasant had been just as thoroughly exploited by the Soviets as by the czars they had come to replace.[40]

What Stone did believe was that communism had something to offer, that its emphasis on planning and public control, if applied in the United States, could prevent the cyclical downturns and vast human waste that capitalism inevitably experienced. What he also recognized was that the communist route was a difficult, even brutal one, and that political and economic democracy had not been joined in the Soviet Union. He made no claim that greater political rights had come the way of the Russian people, only that capitalistic abuses and excesses had been terminated.

Bruce Bliven of *The New Republic* was one who then viewed the Soviet Union in much the same light. "Almost unbelievable advances" had unfolded there, he wrote, but no paradise. For consumer goods and food were still in short supply, and individual freedom was lacking, which he refused to dismiss in the manner of party folk as "a bourgeois delusion."[41]

I. F. Stone's attraction to communism during this period, of course, was in no way unique. The first several months of 1933 were the bleakest of the already prolonged Great Depression, while Soviet Russia appeared to have avoided the economic chaos that had befallen the capitalist nations. Indeed, as an editorial in the *Record* on June 25 indicated, the "real Red menace" seemed to lie in the apparent successes of the Five-Year Plan. Social democracy, for its part, having collapsed before the Nazi putsch, appeared more impotent than ever.[42]

Furthermore, the true costs of Soviet collectivization were at the time carefully hidden, at least for those who wanted them to remain hidden. Still to come were the bloodiest of the Stalinist purges and the pact with Hitler's Germany. Instead, in the early thirties, communism, no matter its failings, was considered to be on the right side of progress. Those associated with it were viewed as well-intentioned sorts, no matter how wrongheaded, who battled on behalf of the lumpenproletariat. And overriding all else was the belief that in the Soviet Union, despite its excesses, the great socialist experiment was being played out.

In the period ahead, Stone would continue to view communism, the American sectarians, and the USSR in just such a light. He would continue to support a united front approach. But he would never again advocate—however implicitly—communism for his own land or hold the banner aloft for an American Communist or workers party.

Why this was so cannot be pinpointed precisely. It seems likely that ideology, temperament, ambition, employment, and family considerations were at work once again. Fears about where his own country might be heading had led this naturally left-inclined journalist to position himself temporarily with the advocates of another American revolution. But he expressed no delight or assurance that a new day would be coming. He recognized then, as he would later, that revolutionary change was always chaotic and brutal, albeit sometimes necessary. And he believed that violent social upheaval threatened to undo the liberal, rational, and humanistic tradition he associated with the West and which he revered more than anything.

At times he also worried about the very nature of the American Communist Party, which was riddled by sectarianism, its followers compelled to toe the line and to do so rigidly. A natural maverick, Stone was repelled by "the very stuffiness . . . thought control . . . conformity . . . yesmanship . . . parrot-like obeisance, and . . . arrogance" of the CPUSA. He was particularly put off by the notion of "being subject to party discipline and told what to do, or what to think, or what to write." Thus, even though he had declared a Communist or workers party to be in the best interest of the general populace, he never considered joining the CPUSA himself.[43]

Perhaps he refused to do so as well because of his recognition that party membership would likely result in certain doors being closed to him. Even liberal newspapers and journals would have found it difficult to hire a card-carrying member, and these were precisely the kinds of publications that provided the best opportunity for a young journalist like Izzy Stone to get a start in his professional career.

Then there were familial responsibilities which had to be considered. For one thing, Izzy and Esther's first child, Celia Mary, had been born on September 9, 1932. For another, Bernard and Katy, during this sad economic time for so many, eventually lost all of their hard-earned holdings. As noted, their economic plight induced or contributed to another round of breakdowns by Katy and the Feinstein household itself had a feel of desperation about it. So it was not ambition and ideology alone that had compelled Izzy to write off the *Record*—both literally and otherwise; financial considerations, both his own and those of his parents, led him to do so as well. By mid-1933, it could be argued, he simply determined not to put his job with the *Record*, now paying eighty-five dollars a week, at risk any longer.[44]

And at risk it certainly must have been while he continued to publish the type of articles he did in *Modern Monthly*. J. David Stern was, after all, a staunch liberal and "a wonderful boss" who allowed Stone and Sam Grafton remarkable leeway on the editorial page of the *Philadelphia Record*. But Stern would never have allowed the kind of language and the running commentary Abelard Stone had employed in Calverton's journal. Stern welcomed, even expected, a liberal slant but not the kind of verbiage that had appeared in articles like "Roosevelt Moves Toward Fascism" and "Morgan & Co."[45]

Then again, perhaps Stone simply recognized how much of a free hand he had on the *Philadelphia Record*. Very seldom did Stern push him to deliver an editorial he did not want to write, and the *Record* so often stood on the right side of crucial issues during these troubled yet exciting times. It had insisted, after all, that the federal government own up to its responsibility for righting the economic state of the nation and agree to provide for those forgotten men. It had supported old age pensions, minimum wage laws, the abolition of sweatshops, and unemployment insurance.

Furthermore, the worsening state of affairs in Germany, which had compelled Stone to view communism more favorably, now led him in another direction. German Communists, following the Comintern line, had done little to oppose Hitler's growing stranglehold on power, believing that after the Nazis, it would be their turn. Such reasoning was incomprehensible to Stone, a united front champion. Consequently, by June of 1933, he and Grafton had come to blame not only the Social Democratic Party for having failed to use "the weapon of the general strike" against Hitler, but Catholic centrists and Communists too.[46]

In September, the *Record*—to Stone's obvious delight—condemned Hitler's fascism still more forcefully, with Stern linking up with an anti-Nazi league in urging a boycott by leading department stores of German products in the Philadelphia area. On September 13, the paper—in language Stone regularly employed—warned that the goosestepping Nazi was "of a different order" than liberals, conservatives, capitalists, or communists. Alone among them, the *Record* charged (as did Oswald Garrison Villard in *The Nation*), "[the Nazi] represents a revolt against reason itself, against the whole rationalistic tradition of the West."[47]

That was precisely the problem as Stone saw it and the reason that fascism had to be held back. Feeling so strongly about the threat poised by right-wing totalitarianism, he moved away from his general anti-interventionist stance, which led him to oppose American practices in Latin America and to warn about possible U.S. entanglement in a war in the Pacific. Fascism, Stone repeated again and again over the course of the decade, had to stopped by any means necessary.

On September 14, 1933, the *Record* editorialists declared the establishment of an economic boycott to be the quickest way to confront "these sinister forces of social degeneracy." They charged that the Nazis had rekindled "the age-old struggle of barbarism against civilization." They went on to proclaim that Nazi terrors had threatened the "concepts of individual liberty and human brotherhood which are the very bases of modern civilization."[48]

On October 8, the *Record* editorialists demanded that Germany not be allowed to rearm. Hitler's regime, they declared, would inevitably turn out-ward to deflect attention from its failed domestic program, which had been based on sharply reduced wages and had resulted in hunger for the German masses. Consequently, a united front bringing together France, Great Brit-ain, the United States, and even Mussolini's Italy was "the last chance of bringing Hitler to book, and forestalling if not preventing catastrophe."[49]

The interplay between German fascism and communism, coupled with developments on the home front, now led Stone to view piecemeal reform more favorably than he had for a while. By the close of 1933, his analysis again came close to paralleling that of *The New Republic* and *The Nation*, which began to argue that "a mental revolution" had unfolded and remarkable advances carried out under the auspices of the New Deal of Franklin D. Roosevelt. The disintegration of democracy in Germany along with reform in the United States helped to bring about this change in perspective. Stone was particularly pleased by the president's apparent acknowledgment of the right of workers to organize and bargain collectively, as demonstrated by Roosevelt's backing of Section 7-A of the National Industrial Recovery Act. While originally distrustful and skeptical about that measure, Stone wit-nessed the way it was received in the coal mines, steel mills, and captive fields as the president's call to organize. To his delight, Roosevelt proved "resilient and sympathetic . . . and empathetic enough" to "go with tide." Stone, in turn, no longer dismissed the New Deal as nothing more than "a phony gesture," but began to see it as something of "a considerable reality."[50]

Stone's caustic analyses of Roosevelt's policies and intentions were now replaced by the feeling that perhaps reform still had a role to play in this country. Disillusionment with communist practices, fear of fascism, personal and professional concerns, and recognition that revolution made little sense at present undoubtedly made FDR look still more attractive to Stone. After all, those who had awaited the revolution in Germany, it was increasingly clear, had helped open the door to Nazi terrors instead. And New Deal reforms and Rooseveltian optimism seemed to ensure that the darkest days of the Great Depression had now passed, having taken with them the illusion that revolution might be in store for the United States.

Izzy Stone's new perspective on the Roosevelt administration was fortu-nate because he was about to begin a new chapter in his life, one that would take him, Esther, and daughter Celia to the nation's intellectual and cultural center. In December 1933, his boss, J. David Stern, transferred Izzy to the editorial staff of the historic *New York Post*, which the publisher intended to turn into a pro–New Deal vehicle. Thus, in a span of three years, Izzy had come full circle, in a manner of speaking. He had begun the decade as a follower of Norman Thomas and a believer in the possibility of evolutionary change. He had shifted leftward as the depression deepened and fascism reared its ugly head in Central Europe. For a brief time, he had ended up in the procommunist camp, although never in the more narrow confines of the party. As Rooseveltian reform began to make a difference, he had once again determined that American society could be peacefully reordered.

Writing for the *Philadelphia Record,* Izzy had made his name well-known among journalists and intellectuals on the East Coast, as well as among certain members of the American left, as witnessed by his work for individuals as disparate as H. L. Mencken and V. F. Calverton and his continuing friendship with Mike Blankfort. His appointment to the *New York Post* seemed only to ensure that he was destined to become even more of a figure to be reckoned with, something that undoubtedly pleased the ever ambitious and self-assured young reporter.

4 A New Deal and the Popular Front at the Post

"Gagging with excitement like a pregnant woman," Izzy headed for the office building of the *New York Post* at 75 West Street early one morning in December 1933. After all, he was about to begin work in the city where the American artistic, cultural, literary, and journalistic worlds were molded as in no other. New York City also remained the home base of the nation's most powerful corporations and of Wall Street, that archetypal symbol of capitalism in the United States. Here the extremes of wealth and poverty wrought by that economic system were clearly on display, as Izzy readily witnessed while carrying out his investigative work or simply strolling about the city. For the next five years, he did so as chief editorial writer for the famed *Post*, America's oldest newspaper. This was the same publication that had been founded by Alexander Hamilton and edited at one time or another by the likes of William Cullen Bryant, Carl Schurz, Edwin Lawrence Godkin, and Oswald Garrison Villard. Furthermore, the *Post*'s association with reform movements from abolitionism to unionism and its independent political stance were the stuff of legend.[1]

As he approached the headquarters of the *New York Post*, the young reporter strutted a bit, feeling now that he had made it. Nevertheless, he was determined to prove to his boss, J. David Stern, that the decision to transfer him to the *Post* was a good call. He was somewhat familiar with New York City politics, having done publicity work for Norman Thomas during the 1928 presidential campaign. But as was his custom, he diligently prepared for that inevitable first meeting with the paper's brass, boning up by reading Allan Nevins's *Evening Post* and everything else he could get his hands on that dealt with politics in New York City. One of the key issues to be discussed at the editorial meeting was whether the *Post* should throw its weight behind a Tammany Hall politico seeking reappointment to public office. Fiorello LaGuardia, a hero to both Stone and Stern, was about to begin his first term as mayor. Not surprisingly, the twenty-five-year-old Stone was the youngest staff member invited to the conference, the only one besides Stern not a native New Yorker, and the last person called on to express an opinion about the options that LaGuardia had. But Izzy was also the only one who had really done his homework, having pored over newspaper clippings on the political hack at the New York Public Library. Consequently, he alone provided a thorough review of the man's career, then proceeded to analyze his positions and point out what issues were involved for both the paper and the city. He concluded by calling for the *Post* to get "the son-of-a-bitch." Stern sat back, taking it all in, but was obviously delighted that "this kid he brought up from Philadelphia" had turned out to be more knowledgeable about the subject at hand than had any of the high-powered executives. That incident, as Izzy later recalled, "solidified me."[2]

F ranklin Delano Roosevelt's first term as president coincided with Stone's happiest times at the *Post*. These were heady times for the young journalist and for the American left of which he was soon to become a key part. There was a sense of excitement in the air as the New Dealers devised one program after another that at least harked back to the Progressive movement of the early twentieth century and at times beyond that to the Populist and Socialist platforms as well. Long-standing calls by American reformers and radicals for greater government control over business operations, for support of labor unionization, for social welfare measures, for public works projects, for planning, and for a discarding of laissez-faire approaches appeared to be heeded to some degree or another by the Roosevelt Brain Trusters. While it was clear, after a brief spell, that the New Deal was not ushering in a hoped-for revolution of the left or a feared one spearheaded by the right, it was also evident that the influence of progressive intellectuals and activists on government policy was greater than ever. This development was possible not simply because the economic collapse had thoroughly discredited conservative panaceas, but also because many radicals had discarded their early insistence on the need for drastic change in the United States. And fearing the growing threat of fascist aggression, the Soviet Union—that "model" socialist state—began, in the middle of the decade, to urge an antifascist alliance of liberal and radical forces. That development, coupled with apparent New Deal successes at home, made peaceful reform appear increasingly attractive.

Never before had the American left, having helped to shape governmental policy, union drives, and the perceptions and hopes of intellectuals, appeared as respectable as it did throughout much of the depression era. The Old Left, as the movement of the 1930s came to be referred to, particularly encompassed Popular Front organizations and the American Communist Party. The CPUSA, following the Comintern's lead, had muted its calls for revolutionary action and subsequently acquired a measure of legitimacy. This proved to be short-lived, as did the prominence of the left in American political, intellectual, and labor quarters. But for a time, the Old Left was positioned as if on the far side of the broad New Deal coalition. An analogous development occurred a half-century later, when many members of the New Right backed the Reagan administration, which was determined to whittle away at the American welfare state, largely shaped in its infancy by the same New Deal many associated with the Old Left had once critically supported.

During the heyday of the New Deal, I. F. Stone became an increasingly influential member of the Old Left, thanks to his job at the *Post;* the growing number of articles he contributed to *The Nation* and *The New Republic,* still the top left-liberal publications around; and his friendships with well-known intellectuals and political activists. More than ever before, he was able to combine his commitment to the left, to progressive ideals, to critical journalism, and to the notion that the intellectual should demonstrate a greater sense of commitment. For a while, Izzy, like a certain portion of the Old Left, was able to bridge the sometimes cavernous gap between the world of liberal "pragmatists" and radical "idealists," between support for liberal reform and the hoped-for bright socialist world to come. But such an approach never lasted for very long, with the always temperamental Izzy consequently compelled to throw in with the Old Left more fully than ever. Nevertheless, having become a New Deal supporter in mid-1933, he remained one for the duration of Roosevelt's tenure.

This allegiance was possible because Izzy, much like Oswald Garrison Villard of *The Nation,* had come, by late 1933, to view the New Deal as "history in the making." Feeling as strongly as he did, he believed that it must not be allowed "to go down the drain." At the same time, he did not want to get "suckered" and desired to speak his mind about contemporary events as he saw them. Fortunately, for a good long while, publisher Stern did not intend to mute his own misgivings about Roosevelt's programs and seemed to recognize that "it was our duty to pull for the left and hard."[3]

Naturally, Izzy was pleased by Stern's plan to convert the *Post* into a pro– New Deal forum, as was President Roosevelt, who mailed a congratulatory note to the publisher. Izzy well recognized that Stern was an adviser of sorts to the man who was reshaping the makeup of the American political order. In the first editorial appearing in the new *Post,* Stone had little difficulty in announcing the rebirth of "a fighting, independent, liberal newspaper" that would support the New Deal, provided it promised to rectify the issue of maldistribution of wealth, "our fundamental ill," and bring about social justice and economic recovery. But it would have no truck with Tories shielding economic autocracy through self-serving rhetoric, he went on to say, with union-busting industrialists, with irresponsible labor chieftains, or with the "pullbacks" who failed to appreciate that the "profiteering debauch" of the Roaring Twenties was now history.[4]

For the next six months, Stone all but single-handedly took care of the entire editorial page, including makeup duties and letters to the editor. In the process, he quickly helped convert the *Post*, which had become the most conservative paper in the New York area, into the most radical one around, other than the sectarian papers. At the end of that stretch of time, he was joined on the *Post* by Sam Grafton, his old colleague from the *Philadelphia Record*, and the two constructed what one correspondent would soon acclaim as "the most intelligent and independent editorial policy any big metropolitan newspaper had displayed in recent years."[5]

The new *Post* proved to be staunchly, though not uncritically, supportive of the New Deal. Early in the first month of Stern's tenure on the *Post*, Stone helped to establish the editorial slant of the paper. He termed Roosevelt a liberal chief executive who was going to push for "a permanent New Deal" and an "ordered liberal national economy." But he proceeded to urge Roosevelt and Congress to shift even farther leftward in the direction of industrial democracy. He asserted that Roosevelt was "the man of the hour" who was trying—in the manner of the *New York Post*—"to save capitalism from itself" and American democracy "from pillagers and exploiters."[6]

Because of his changed perspective on Roosevelt, writing such editorials came easily to Stone, who now happily viewed the president as stationed on the side of the people in decidedly Jacksonian fashion. He believed that Roosevelt was moving, however haltingly, in the direction of economic democracy. Consequently, from this point forth, FDR stood as a still more distant type of surrogate father for Izzy, as he did for many Americans. Roosevelt had joined Stone's personal hall of heroes, where he would remain comfortably ensconced for the next half-century.

Two periodicals Izzy continued to read at the close of Roosevelt's first year in office provided a harsher analysis of the early New Deal. Both *The Nation* and *The New Republic* insisted that while the president desired to preserve American capitalism, the capitalists were not doing their part, exhibiting little of the "enlightened unselfishness" that he hoped to encourage.[7]

Izzy was well aware of such criticisms—with which he largely agreed—having maintained and strengthened his connections on the intellectual and political left. Copies of *The Nation*, *The New Republic*, and *The New Masses* could be discovered on the coffee table of his home at 1 West 68th Street in mid-Manhattan. And within a short while, Izzy was contributing articles to both *The New Republic* and *The Nation*, which continued to be viewed as the most influential magazines among politically conscious members of the American intelligentsia. *The Nation*, with an editorial staff that included Freda Kirchwey and Oswald Garrison Villard, thus retained a distinguished historical lineage that dated back to the editorship of E. L. Godkin in the immediate post–Civil War period; *The New Republic*, begun in 1914 by Herbert Croly, Walter Lippmann, and Willard Straight, now boasted names such as Bruce Bliven, Heywood Broun, and George Soule.[8]

During this period of their stay in the nation's intellectual center, Izzy and Esther Stone's dwelling served as a type of salon for literary, artistic, legal, and political folk of a progressive nature. Radicals of all shades showed up, including representatives of the old intellectual left such as Ben Stolberg and Ben Gitlow, but so too did liberals and Rooseveltian Democrats in good standing. Writers Mike Blankfort, Henry Hart, John Strachey, and Shepard Traube frequently came by, as did Alabama senator Hugo Black and New Deal attorney David Moskowitz. As the chief editorial writer on the *New York Post*, Izzy attracted all kinds of people who attempted to influence him in some fashion or another. They recognized that throughout much of the New Deal era, the *Post* stood as the nation's most prominent liberal newspaper. By 1937, the paper's subscription totals mushroomed fourfold to over a quarter of a million, to Stone's and Stern's delight. Not surprisingly, then, like-minded individuals were happy to have a man who was "sympathetic, left-liberal-radical sympathetic" occupying the position he now did. That was fine with Izzy, never the modest sort, who undoubtedly welcomed the attention and greater acclaim. He also reveled in the give-and-take, which must have reminded him of Papa Leof's place in Philadelphia, and he retained good friends across the left side of the political spectrum—including communists, Trotskyists, Lovestonites, socialists, and liberals. Such an approach led some more doctrinaire sorts to dismiss him derisively as "a goddamned liberal."[9]

His brother Marc stayed with Esther and Izzy for a short while during this period and was fascinated by the well-known liberal and radical figures who dropped in from time to time to discuss the latest administration moves or the Comintern's most recent pronouncements. Marc eventually went to work for a succession of left-wing journals, such as *Fight* magazine (Fight Against Fascism and for Democracy), and wrote for the Federated Press, the labor news service; later, younger brother Lou temporarily joined Marc at the Federated Press. Considering himself a radical—he "went for it hook-line-and-sinker"—Marc joined the Communist Party, which only intensified a still strong sibling rivalry with his older brother. Izzy, for his part, as Marc later recalled, was "never a communist" of the party variety or any other. Now believing more firmly than ever that a newspaperman must not allow himself to become a party sycophant, Izzy undoubtedly did not hesitate to indicate as much to his brother. Indeed, the very idea of "being subject to party discipline and told what to do, or what to think, or what to write" was wholly "repugnant" to him.[10]

Like his friend Matthew Josephson, Stone had considerable reservations about the American comrades. He continued to believe that the American

Communists, like their Socialist rivals, performed a constructive role in the depression era. He credited them with helping to organize sharecroppers and tenant farmers and with fighting the good fight to bring about social justice. But the Stalinist nature of the party greatly disturbed him. In New York City, the somewhat relaxed attitude of the Philadelphia crowd was nowhere to be found. Instead, he discovered that the radicals in the great metropolis were divided by the ugliest, nastiest sectarian squabbles he had yet encountered. They battled one another even within their own parties "for lousy little $50 a week jobs, and for prestige, and for egoism." And the American Communist Party appeared particularly riddled with its own "little Stalins . . . some pretty horrible people. And they acted like little Stalins, right in New York."[11]

He believed as *The New Republic* did that sectarianism was "the heaviest handicap of those who want to change the world." Consequently, he was favorably disposed to the decision by the *Post*'s editorial board as the 1936 presidential campaign rolled around to defend the Roosevelt administration from attacks emanating from both the far left and the far right.[12]

In a pair of editorials, he once again drew analogies between present-day America and France, before its revolution. This time, he portrayed Louis XVI's minister Turgot and President Roosevelt as reformers who were castigated by both the conservatives and the Norman Thomases of their day, the first of whom denounced them as revolutionaries while the latter dismissed them as "stick-in-the-mud, shortsighted" liberals. Stone readily acknowledged that the revolutionary call for a "clean sweep of capitalism" now held little attraction for him. The bloodletting of the French Revolution had, after all, caused a wearied people to look first to Napoleon and then back to the Bourbons. In the same period, as the clock was turned back in France, democratic norms took hold in England. The stark contrast between French and English history thus shed a great deal of light on the worth "of peaceful, even halfway, reform and revolution." Keeping this in mind, the *Post* would bank on the New Deal, Stone wrote, in spite of its all too surely "exasperating" pace.[13]

Those who attacked necessary reforms as revolutionary, he charged, were "playing with dynamite." For should reform not be forthcoming, pent-up frustrations and anger might touch off a genuine explosion. But those who viewed " 'bourgeois' reforms" contemptuously and insisted on a clean sweep were equally mistaken, according to Stone. Just such an approach often resulted in "black reaction."[14]

Not so long ago, of course, Stone had dismissed anything other than a revolutionary party. Now, three years into the New Deal, he considered the United States fortunate to have a statesman such as Franklin Roosevelt presiding in the Oval Office. With fascism quickening its march overseas, he continued to believe that wholesale transformation had to be avoided. New Deal reformism, which Stone often criticized as halfhearted, nevertheless seemed to be a better bet.

As the 1936 presidential campaign unfolded, *The Nation* and *The New Republic* came around to the position of the *New York Post* that Franklin Delano Roosevelt had earned another four years in the White House. Roosevelt had, after all, supported passage of the Social Security Act and the Wagner Labor Relations Act, which upheld the right of workers to bargain collectively, and had induced a new, militant labor organization, the CIO, to back him.[15]

Following Roosevelt's landslide victory over Kansas governor Alfred Landon, the Republic Party candidate, Stone and editorial partner Sam Grafton immediately proclaimed that democracy had won out; *The New Republic* soon called it the greatest triumph to date for liberalism in the United States. The vote cast for the greatest liberal president since Abe Lincoln, the *Post* editorialists suggested, indicated that the "peaceful revolution" begun in the age of Jackson had finally ended. Now the struggle to bring about economic democracy was in place and the doctrine of rugged individualism thoroughly discredited.[16]

A new wave of reform activity lay just ahead, Stone and Grafton reasoned, as did the president. One possible stumbling block, however, was the U.S. Supreme Court, which had already declared key New Deal measures to be unconstitutional. Roosevelt was deeply distressed by such decisions and worried about the fate of the Wagner Labor Relations Act and the Social Security Act, the second New Deal's centerpieces. Consequently, he sought presidential authority to appoint an additional member of the Court, up to a maximum of six, for each jurist who reached the age of seventy but remained on the bench. New Deal critics and many supporters alike charged that Roosevelt was out to pack the Supreme Court. Progressive senators Hiram Johnson of California and Burton K. Wheeler of Montana and Oswald Garrison Villard of *The Nation* were among those who came out in opposition.[17]

By contrast, Congressman Maury Maverick of Texas, Republican senator Robert La Follette of Wisconsin, J. David Stern of the *New York Post*, Freda Kirchwey of *The Nation*, and Bruce Bliven of *The New Republic* all strongly backed Roosevelt's call to reorganize the Court. Stern, in fact, had recently supported a constitutional amendment that would clarify congressional authority "to legislate for human rights as well as property rights" and thereby check arbitrary judicial might.[18]

Since 1932, Izzy Stone had been assigned by Stern to cover the Court for the *New York Post;* the law, in fact, had become a special interest of his.

To better understand the workings of the final appellate court in the land, he had studied the legal treatises of Roscoe Pound and the decisions of Benjamin Cardozo and had talked about judicial preconceptions with lawyer friends Louis Boudin and Sid Cohn. Now, he and his boss both agreed with the analysis made by other friends such as Max Lerner of *The Nation* and Edwin Corwin of Princeton University Politics Department that Roosevelt was attempting "to unpack the Court." For all too long, Stone asserted in an editorial in the *Post*, the Supreme Court had been " 'packed' with safe, conservative majorities." The very same majorities had brought about the Civil War, opposed one piece of significant social legislation after another, "twisted" both the Constitution and constitutional amendments beyond recognition of the Framers, and, most recently, brought about a four-year "wholesale, systematic and unparalleled *destruction* of a broad program of national *construction*."[19]

Consequently, Stone was favorably disposed to Roosevelt's plan to transform the Court. Like the president, he seemed to believe that the possibility of peaceful reform and democracy itself were endangered by the reversal of New Deal measures. If the Court could act in such a manner, he believed, the arguments of would-be revolutionaries that capitalist democracy was incapable of righting social and economic ills would be borne out.

A short time later, Izzy went down to the capital and stopped in to see someone he greatly admired, Brain Truster Tom Corcoran, who happened to be meeting with Ben Cohen, another key New Dealer. Corcoran showed Izzy an outline he had sketched concerning a possible book on the controversy surrounding the Supreme Court. Izzy indicated that he didn't think much of it, and Corcoran was somewhat put out. Corcoran asked him, "Can you do better?"—to which Izzy replied, "Sure!" The New Deal adviser proceeded to loan Izzy his office for the weekend, whereupon he pored through volume after volume of *U.S. Reports*. Izzy determined to send his own outline to Felix Frankfurter and was thrilled that the Harvard law professor seemingly gave his blessing to the project. Consequently, he took a couple of weeks off work, went back down to Washington, and labored well into the night, happily aided at times by brother-in-law Leonard Boudin, who was married to Esther's sister Jean. Corcoran, not surprisingly, thought the manuscript did not measure up, but Covici Friede, a small left-wing outfit, published *The Court Never Disposes*, which received favorable reviews in the left-of-center press. Mattie Josephson, writing in *The New Masses*, termed Izzy "one of our ablest young journalists" and his book "the most sensible and most lucid tract" on the Court controversy. *The Nation* declared that *The Court Never Disposes* was filled with "pungent, effective, and even brilliant political argumentation," the *Saturday Review of*

Literature proclaimed it "an effective lethal instrument," while *The New Republic* noted its author's "exceptional talents." Despite the accolades, the book's sales did not amount to much.[20]

The little book, Stone's first, argued that the High Court, since the turn of the century, had carried out "a third American Revolution," a judicial revolution whose significance was little understood. Serving as "a citadel of privilege," the "American House of Lords" was able to reign supreme over the entire nation. Either the power of these "medicinemen" with their legalistic "mumbo jumbo" had to be curbed, Stone exclaimed, or American democracy would be.[21]

Despite such fiery analyses and notwithstanding his condemnation of "our judicial Robespierres," Stone was uncomfortable about the Court-packing plan. The Court had been attacked before, he recognized, and Roosevelt's proposal might very well establish a dangerous precedent. Nevertheless, he now believed so strongly that New Deal reforms, at a bare minimum, had to be enacted that he supported the president's package. As matters turned out, of course, Congress denied Roosevelt's request. Furthermore, this setback and the furor it resulted in helped to halt the momentum of the New Deal, much to Roosevelt's chagrin and Izzy Stone's dismay—no matter that both soon declared Court reversals and resignations to have brought about a constitutional revolution.[22]

This pleased Stone, who had feared that reactionary jurists might prevent needed reform from being enacted, which would ensure that the New Deal would be grounded. That possibility deeply disturbed him because he believed, along with the editors of *The New Republic*, that the Roosevelt administration had "made more progress toward a socialized economy" than had any other. And in a sense, Stone seemed to believe that the New Deal represented the last opportunity to demonstrate that FDR was correct in reasoning that the nation's economic and social ills could "be peacefully and democratically solved within the framework of capitalist democracy."[23]

In a series of articles published in *The New Republic* in the fall of 1937—by now, something of an ideological partner of the *New York Post*—Stone contended that Roosevelt represented the present-day struggle for social democracy, just as Jackson had earlier symbolized the fight for political democracy. And the contemporary battle was all the more necessary, Stone argued, because of "the irreconcilable conflict of our age": "a sense of the impotence to which political democracy is reduced by economic inequality, of the incongruity between the free citizen at the ballot box and the anxious creature at the paymaster's window, of the existence of economic sovereignties so vast that they overawe the State."[24]

It was vitally important to prove the worth of democratic reform, Stone also reasoned, because of the seemingly omnipresent threat posed by fascism, which he saw as a bastardized form of capitalism. Here, ideological considerations certainly shaped his perception of events, including his disdain for right-wing totalitarianism, his faith in the democratic and socialist visions, and his understanding that fascism endangered both. Such concerns, along with the state of domestic affairs, led him, along with his colleagues at the *New York Post, The New Republic,* and *The Nation,* to line up on the left side of the New Deal coalition. What they all now agreed on was that the Roosevelt administration had to be supported and an international, antifascist alliance put together.

Such an alliance was necessary, Stone fervently believed, for fascism was capitalism's misbegotten offspring, crushing individual freedom, gagging the press, extending the method of a Pennsylvania coal-company town to whole nations, treating whites in European nations as "imperialists have been accustomed to treat black, brown, red, and yellow men in 'backward countries,'" destroying the labor unions, bringing labor and capital both under the sway of a war machine run by demagogic adventurers who plunder the capitalism they protect as a gangster plunders the merchants he forces into a 'protective association.' "[25]

So it was not surprising that Bruce Bliven of *The New Republic,* Freda Kirchwey of *The Nation,* and Izzy Stone applauded the call by Georgi Dimitrov, secretary-general of the Comintern in August 1935, for a "people's anti-Fascist front." Since Hitler had come to power in Germany, *The New Republic* and *The Nation* had condemned fratricidal developments in general; *The Nation* had also castigated the Communist Party in particular for having blunted earlier united front efforts in the United States, while *The New Republic* had been cheered by prior word that French socialists and communists were linking up in a fight against fascism and in support of workers' and democratic rights. Long aware of the suicidal propensity of leftists to squabble among themselves rather than to contest "the Fascist enemy," Stone had likened the "dangers of sectarianism and sectarian fanaticism and semanticism, the various strands of Marxism," to "the various strands of Christianity whereby people killed themselves over hair-splitting words."[26]

The *Post,* like *The Nation* and *The New Republic,* repeatedly decried the "fatal hesitations" supposedly characteristic of the democracies. These three publications cheered the establishment of Popular Front governments in both Spain and France. The rise of Hitler, possible only because of divisions among German liberals and radicals, all seemed to believe, had evidently "taught the Left a lesson." The USSR too had changed its tune, the *Post* indicated, and was muting revolutionary aims and supporting capitalist parties in the fight against war and fascism. In addition, the fate of the People's Front in France, the newspaper suggested, might provide the people of Europe with a means to usher in reform "while avoiding bloody extremes of either Right or Left."[27]

The advent of the Popular Front delighted Izzy Stone, who had long supported the idea of a confederation of antifascist forces. He had earlier called for "a broad united front" of both Austrian and German workers, arguing that it was better "to die on the barricades" than in Nazi concentration camps. For the remainder of the decade, Stone stood as a confirmed Popular Fronter who believed that the Iron Heel simply had to be warded off. The Popular Front approach with its emphasis on a supposed merger of all left-of-center groups greatly appealed to him, as did its purportedly nonsectarian makeup. He saw it as a means to shield the democracies and defend the lone socialist state, while preventing the spread of the lethal virus of fascism.[28]

The Popular Front, Stone also believed, stood on the side of reform but in opposition to revolutionary change in industrial lands, at least for the present. Given the results of cataclysmic upheaval in Italy and Germany and the success of the New Deal at home, Stone and many other radicals had come to appreciate the uncertain course of modern-day revolutions and to look at gradual reform more favorably. They followed the establishment of coalition, left-of-center governments in France and Spain with great expectations.

But if Popular Fronters like Bliven, Kirchwey, and Stone identified with Léon Blum's Popular Front government, they invested a good deal more, emotionally speaking, in the Spanish Republican government. And, as Generalissimo Francisco Franco moved to overthrow the Republicans, *The Nation* proclaimed Spain to be the front line in the fight against fascist aggression. The journal went on to insist that "the supreme test of an anti-Fascist today is not what he says but what he does for Spain." The editorial staff of the *Post* felt much the same way, insisting that in Spain "democracy is fighting for its life."[29]

What this meant was that the stakes in the outcome of the Spanish Civil War were perceived to be enormous. The Loyalist government, consequently, had to be supported, notwithstanding certain deplorable excesses. Those excesses, nevertheless, were said to be nothing compared with what a fascist-backed victory by Franco's Falangists would invariably result in.[30]

Continuing to condemn the "rape of Spain," Stone and Grafton at the *Post* criticized the failure of the European democracies to come to the aid of the Republic. They noted, however, that there was one country that refused to honor the pledge of nonintervention in Spain—the Union of Soviet Socialist Republics.[31]

It was that very fact which troubled so many on the left. For Russian aid poured into Madrid and Barcelona, bringing with it heightened Communist influence which threatened to tear apart both the Loyalist government and the Popular Front. The Republic's struggle, as a result, was increasingly beset by sectarianism, with the Communists moving to repress the anarchists and the POUM, a dissident Marxist group befriended by the English author George Orwell but dismissed as Trotskyist by party members. The *Post,* however, saw the Spanish government as becoming more democratic in Popular Front fashion, since it seemed to be heading away from a hard left line. But because it was true that churches had been burned and priests murdered, the paper acknowledged, the Spanish government was compelled to put a halt to "mob disorders."[32]

In the manner of most Popular Fronters, Izzy Stone of the *Post,* like the editorialists at *The Nation* and *The New Republic,* claimed that the government simply was forced "to deal with the mob and to discipline it." What all of this involved, he admitted, was a choice between "lesser evils and worse evils." But he for one believed that something had to be done, that the Spanish government had been forced to act. Anarchy and random bloodletting had to be curtailed, or the Loyalist regime would have been thoroughly discredited.[33]

Perhaps a bit of disingenuousness was involved here. Stone seemed more concerned with the violent actions of the non-Communist forces than with those committed by the Spanish government. At the very least, this was not the first time he proved willing to give those positioned to his left the benefit of the doubt. He continued to view Communist Party members as lined up on the correct side of historical developments, unlike fascists or even members of the smaller left-wing sects.

As matters turned out, Spain served as something of "the ultimate test of the Popular Front." For some, including George Orwell who fought in defense of the Republic and John Dos Passos who reported on the war, Stalinist practices in Spain shook their very faith that an alliance of all forces on the left was either possible or desirable. For others, such as Izzy Stone, the lesson of Spain was that the Popular Front had to be maintained in place. He indicated as much upon joining the League of American Writers, and he served as a delegate to the organization's Second Writers' Congress held in New York City in June 1937 which turned out to be a festival celebrating the Spanish Republic. There he heard Archibald MacLeish ask how support could be withheld from "those who fight our battles . . . who truly fight our battles *now—now,* not in the some future war—*now:* now in Spain." Among the literary stars presently attracted to the League—which was unquestionably Communist-dominated—were Van Wyck Brooks, Erskine Caldwell, Malcolm Cowley, Ernest Hemingway, and Upton Sinclair. Among those not invited to attend the Second Writers' Congress were V. F. Calverton, Joseph Wood Krutch, James T. Farrell, Dwight Macdonald, and Edmund Wilson, anti-Stalinists all.[34]

Thus, Izzy was determined, as were so many other writers, journalists, and artists of this era, to stand as both an intellectual and an activist. Such a desire was in line with a time-honored tradition, as carved out by individuals as disparate as Sinclair, Lincoln Steffens, John Reed, and Max Eastman, and followed by a host of leading intellectual figures of the 1930s. The intellectual, all believed, could in no way be removed from the great events of one's time, particularly when the times were as charged as they were at present.

In response to a query from league president Donald Ogden Stewart, Stone wrote that the fall of the Spanish Republic would be a catastrophe for democracy worldwide. For in its wake would come "a tidal wave of reaction, obscurantism, race hatred and thuggery, menacing our lives and our homes." Nearly four hundred leading American intellectuals agreed with striking near-unanimity.[35]

There existed no meeting of the minds, however, regarding the one nation that had continued to stand as a solid ally of the Spanish Loyalists. Even more than Spain, the Soviet Union represented a state of mind for Popular Fronters like Izzy Stone. They considered Russia to be the leading bulwark against fascism and the scene of an ongoing experiment in socialism. Fascism remained the evil to be contested and socialism the ideal for the good society to come. The USSR's seemingly determined opposition to the fascist regimes contrasted favorably with the inadequate, halfhearted responses of the capitalist democracies. Its image as the linchpin of the antifascist front cemented that nation's reputation in the minds of many radicals in the West. Admittedly, equally important in their eyes was its socialist makeup, seemingly so solitary and yet so promising.

With the passage of time, however, increased misgivings began to develop concerning "a lot of . . . evils" in the Communist heartland, as Stone later acknowledged. And yet, as he contended, nobody was fully cognizant of the horrors behind "the Soviet facade," and he and other Popular Fronters considered Communist Russia an imperfect version of socialism, but a socialist state nevertheless. Given these sentiments, he and many other intellectuals in Europe and the United States, including the editors of *The Nation* and *The New Republic*, did indeed behave during this period as they later were accused of having behaved, as apologists for Soviet and Communist practices.[36]

This is all the more striking in the case of Izzy Stone for he—like Freda Kirchwey at *The Nation* and Bruce Bliven with *The New Republic*—refused to view the Soviet Union with blinders. Unlike many party members or fellow travelers, he acknowledged that Communist Russia was a dictatorial state, not much of a socialist model. He believed, after all, that Lenin and Trotsky had brought communism to the land of the czars by way of "the cruel and bloody ruthlessness of the Soviets." On December 7, 1934, in an editorial in the *New York Post*, Stone decried the execution of sixty-six Soviet citizens who had been denounced by Stalin as White Guardists, which followed the assassination of Sergei Kirov, the Leningrad Communist Party chief. He likened the Russian showtrials to those being carried out in Nazi Germany. Employing precisely the same argument he would use again and again over the course of his career and one that Kirchwey and Oswald Garrison Villard were also delivering in the pages of *The Nation*, he insisted that the Soviet state was certainly "strong enough today not to stoop to such tactics." And he, like Villard, implied that while the Russian Revolution had been the product of intellectuals, the present Soviet regime was now adopting the tactics of "Fascist thugs and racketeers." Was there any justification whatsoever for this assault on basic human rights, he asked, or were the Bolsheviks "nervously see[ing] a 'counter-revolutionary' behind every tree as the reactionaries of the capitalist world see a 'Communist' behind every bush?" Terror, he warned, inevitably corrupted those who wielded it.[37]

Thus, Stone refused, at this stage, to sweep away charges regarding Stalinist practices. Repression in the Soviet Union, he believed, was a perversion of the socialist society he envisioned and, at times, a frightening reminder of the horrors unfolding in Central Europe.

Other Popular Fronters, including Louis Fischer, Villard's colleague at *The Nation*, and the editors of *The New Republic*, responded somewhat differently to what seemed to be going on in Russia. Fischer acknowledged the heavy hand of Stalinist repression there but still believed socialism to be emerging. While *The New Republic* initially declared that the executions in the Soviet Union brought to mind Hitler-style terrorism and the star chamber, the journal soon called for judgments to be suspended until all the evidence was in. But like Stone, Kirchwey, and Garrison, *The New Republic* warned that terrorist practices merely bred more of the same.[38]

A short time later, new trials involving Grigori Zinoviev, Lev Kamenev, and other Old Bolsheviks again led Stone to question just what it was that Joseph Stalin was up to. For "no government, no matter what its principles, can shut off free speech and deny legal processes without suffering from it. The checks and balances of free discussion can alone keep government efficient and the servant rather than the ruler of its people."[39]

But in a way, Stone suggested, all this should not have been unexpected. After all, no one was more paranoid than a dictator. And Comrade Stalin appeared to "be suffering from the usual hobgoblins that go with absolute power."[40]

As a new round of purge trials unfolded in mid-1936, trials which eventually culminated in the mass execution of thousands of Old Bolsheviks, Stone again condemned the proceedings on the editorial page of the *Post*. He dismissed charges of a terrorist plot purportedly concocted by heroes of the October Revolution and of a reputed Hitler-Trotsky cabal as all too "fantastic." He warned that the favorable impression cast by the new Soviet constitution and by the supposed introduction of more democratic proceedings was called into question by the plot tales. And he declared that if the most recent trials were not carried out for all eyes to see, suspicions could not be allayed. Finally, Stone pointed out that infighting between leaders of the French Revolution had resulted in Bonapartist reaction and insisted that "summary executions . . . would be disgraceful."[41]

In contrast, *The New Republic* proved willing to accept at "face value" the word of the Soviet government which was carrying out the political trials, while *The Nation* did not know what to believe. After all, conducting the proceedings without hard evidence made no sense whatsoever. But then neither did accusations that Lenin's onetime heir apparent had conspired against his homeland.[42]

While still holding to his belief that Russia was involved in a massive and long-term program of social reconstruction, Stone also remained deeply troubled and perplexed by the onrush of events in the Soviet Union. In his *Post* editorial of January 26, 1937, entitled "?????????," an obviously anguished Izzy Stone—as were fellow Russian sympathizers Kirchwey and Bliven—now acknowledged that either Leon Trotsky or Joseph Stalin had to be some kind of "monster." He found it troubling, he admitted, that none of the condemned Old Bolsheviks had recanted their confessions. Still, he was as yet unconvinced that the former Red Army commander had engaged in intrigue against his homeland. Furthermore, the delivery of such confessions in a land like Stalinist Russia, he wrote, could only breed mistrust. Closing the editorial, Stone absolved neither Trotsky nor Stalin of conspiratorial actions. "Revolutions do not take place according to Emily Post. The birth of a new social order, like the birth of a human being, is a painful process. Revolutions tend to destroy their makers. The French Revolution culminated in Thermidor, when Robespierre himself was devoured by the Terror he had fostered. Perhaps, as Trotsky contends, Thermidor approaches in Russia. Perhaps, as Stalin contends, a vast counterrevolutionary conspiracy has been uncovered. We don't know."[43]

As "?????????" indicated, Stone, unlike many anti-Stalinists who saw Leon Trotsky as the most legitimate claimant to Lenin's mantle, considered him little different from Joseph Stalin. True, Trotsky seemed brilliant, so unlike the Georgian, but "very draconian" as well, and thus in Stone's estimation did not offer much of an alternative.[44]

But what is most significant about this editorial is that for the first time,

Stone appeared to be backing away from his earlier, unequivocal denunciations of the purges. Now he had inferred that there might be something behind the charges of Stalin's judicial henchmen. Like so many Popular Fronters, Stone seemed incapable of believing that the trials could have been entirely fabricated, the handiwork of a different kind of fiendish plot. In one sense, this was understandable, because to think otherwise would have indicated that Stalin's government was every bit as maniacal as Adolf Hitler's. And that would have threatened even the possibility of collective action, given the undoubted prominence of the Soviet Union within any kind of antifascist alliance. Meanwhile, the part played by the USSR in the Popular Front would have ensured that the very ideal of socialism was imperiled.

It was in fact the prominence of the Soviet Union within the antifascist camp that now led Stone to begin to soften his critiques of what appeared to be taking place inside that nation. The battle against fascism was of paramount importance in his estimation, even if that required one to line up alongside allies who were not without rather large failings themselves. But again, ideology undoubtedly played a part in the shaping of his thinking. Soviet Russia he still viewed as a progressive nation, in spite of the Moscow Trials, purges, and mass executions. That was owing to the supposed socialist composition of that country, which contrasted so starkly in his eyes with the imperfect and seemingly decayed democracies boasted by England and France.

His colleagues at *The Nation* and *The New Republic* now suggested more and more that conspiracies were being concocted in the Soviet Union, while admitting that the closed nature of the Communist system allowed little room for either open discussion or dissenting viewpoints. Examining "the riddle of Russia" in *The New Republic*, Walter Duranty of the *New York Times* went a good deal farther, explicitly condemning the accused Old Bolsheviks for being part of a treasonous "Trojan horse."[45]

The Moscow Trials, along with the war in Spain, eventually helped to tear at the very fabric of the Popular Front. Izzy Stone, along with Kirchwey and Bliven, continued to believe that an international alliance against Hitler had to be put together, even if that made one an apologist for Stalinist terrors to one extent or another. True, as the purges wound on, Stone and his ideological soulmates felt more anguish than ever concerning the Soviet state. They recognized that the Soviet system was deeply flawed in many ways—"we were far from being taken in," he later insisted—but reasoned that while "this may be a distortion of socialism . . . it's still socialism."[46]

This being the case, there was all the more reason, Stone thought, for attacks against the USSR not to be undertaken lightly. In an article that appeared in the November 6, 1937 issue of *The Nation* and that acknowledged the continuation of the "bewildering" purge trials, he seemed to suggest still more strongly that perhaps there really was something behind the charges of the Soviet prosecutors. The search for and execution of supposed foes of the Communist state, after all, had come on the heels of the Kirov assassination, he now pointed out.[47]

There remained, he readily admitted, problems in making over a land such as Russia—a shortage of capital, widespread illiteracy, and international tension. But in spite of such obstacles, he noted, the Soviet Communist Party was striving to convert "the most backward of the great European nations into the most advanced." Furthermore, Stone, like Freda Kirchwey of *The Nation* and Malcolm Cowley of *The New Republic*, continued to believe that the USSR was "the scene of the greatest social experiment of our time." Because this was so, even the attendant failures as well as the successes of the Soviet experiment were of vital importance. For "there we can see the defects of Socialism as here we can see the defects of capitalism."[48]

The willingness of the *New York Post-The Nation-The New Republic* Popular Fronters to continue to view the Soviet Union hopefully and their seeming inability to condemn Stalinist terrors more forthrightly led some to accuse them of dishonesty, of remaining mired in "People's Front Communism," of serving as "the most effective amateur propaganda adjuncts to the American Communist movement," as a contributor to the *American Mercury* charged. They were denounced for their reputed "pro-Stalinism" and for continuing to "goosestep toward the Kremlin."[49]

Such accusations were undoubtedly unfair when applied to someone like Izzy Stone. He did not view the Soviet Union uncritically, acknowledged that there was a stench behind the judicial proceedings in place there, had little liking for the American Communist Party, was no celebrant of any brand of totalitarianism, and certainly did not genuflect toward Moscow. Nevertheless, there was something disingenuous in his willingness to suspend judgment or to refuse to criticize still more forcefully the terror that was being played out in Soviet Russia. It is difficult to imagine Stone and so many other Western progressives allowing any right-of-center state to escape hard questions regarding authoritarian behavior. What could not be denied was that Stone, like many of his political and intellectual counterparts, continued to afford Russia and even Stalinist communism something of a double standard, fearing that to do otherwise would endanger the Popular Front and the very possibility of socialism.

By early 1938, Stone's determined defense of the Popular Front and the Soviet Union had brought him into open conflict with his boss, J. David Stern, at the very time he was having to suffer through a series of personal and professional changes. For some time, he had experienced some degree of deafness and now felt compelled to make use of a hearing aid. Upon discovering official briefings—which he still attended—to be unenlightening for other than the usual reasons, he initiated a practice of turning to public documents instead. As he began to do so, he found that reporters generally did not uncover all that could be unearthed in the public record. To further compensate for his physical disability, he determined to read even more extensively than ever. Thus began a new stage in the investigative career of Izzy Stone, which would later acquire something of a mythical quality.[50]

During the same period Izzy officially adopted Stone as his surname. Because of the appearance of groups like the Black Legion and the Silver Shirts on the home front, he worried about the fate of his (soon to be) three children—Celia, Jeremy Judah (born November 23, 1935), and Christopher David (born October 2, 1937)—should a lethal strain of anti-Semitism spread on this side of the Atlantic. Furthermore, he was pressured by Stern, who had long sought to make the *Post* seem somehow "less Jewish." Sam Grafton, his fellow editorialist on the *Post,* had already changed his name from Lifshutz back in 1932. Now, as Izzy explained to younger brother Lou while the two walked along Roosevelt Boulevard in Philadelphia, perhaps Stern was right, perhaps in confronting fascism "he could be more effective if the name didn't stand out as . . . obviously Jewish." In the fall of 1937, Izzy initially considered employing the romantic-sounding Geoffrey Duprion before deciding upon Geoffrey Stone instead. But almost as soon as that byline made an appearance, it was replaced both in print and official courthouse records by yet another, I. F. Stone.[51]

It was his old friend Mike Blankfort who suggested that Izzy "think of himself as . . . I. F. Stone." Trying to come up with a way to both change Izzy's name and maintain the reputation he had already acquired, Blankfort tossed out any number of possibilities, including "Fein-stone, Fine-Stone, Stone." Then Blankfort hit upon a solution. "Call yourself Isadore Feinstein," he suggested, "then reduce it to the initials I. F. Stone. With that, you can have it both ways." On December 28, 1937, a New York superior court issued the decree officially changing his name. Later, Stone acknowledged feeling troubled by his decision to make the change.[52]

Although Izzy acceded to Stern's request, his relationship with his boss now soured. This was due largely, although not entirely, to a dramatic shift in the editorial policy of the *New York Post.* Throughout much of the thirties, the *Post* had stood as "a real, fighting liberal paper," and Izzy was afforded a good deal of freedom and thoroughly enjoyed his work. Others in the journalistic trade appeared envious of his position as demonstrated by a study undertaken during this period which indicated that correspondents ranked the *New York Post* or the *Philadelphia Record* as the sixth most desirable newspapers in the nation to work for, thereby placing them behind only the *New York*

Times, the Baltimore Sun, the St. Louis Post-Dispatch, the New York Herald Tribune, and the Scripps-Howard Alliance. Stern was himself well-respected and was viewed as a prolabor, prounion employer. But the recession of 1937–38 imperiled the financial standing of the newspaper, and the possibility of a red smear threatened ruin. Upset by the Post-Record's editorial line on Spain, priests in the Philadelphia area denounced Stern's papers, which they forbade their parishioners from reading. Pamphlets appeared in Philadelphia declaring that "J. David Stern applauds murder of priests and rape of nuns."53

The chain makeup of the Stern newspaper empire, which had enabled the publisher to thrive financially and his publications to exhibit the kind of hard-edged editorial position that many praised and others despised, now threatened the very viability of both the New York Post and the Philadelphia Record. More and more, chain ownership had come to prevail in many American cities, resulting in a quasi monopoly that at times threatened to stifle creative journalism and prevent the reappearance of muckraking works. Furthermore, newspaper publishers tended to be politically conservative as evidenced by their hostility to the New Deal and Franklin Roosevelt. Stern was an exception, of course, with his papers exhibiting a decidedly liberal viewpoint.54

But now, beset from all sides, Stern decided to give ground; he adopted a more critical stance toward radicals, the USSR, the Spanish Republicans, and the Popular Front. On February 15, 1938, a page-one editorial orchestrated by the publisher denounced in no uncertain terms both Joseph Stalin and the very idea of a united front. It proclaimed that communists, like fascists, sought class war and dictatorship and would settle for nothing less. Thus, liberals must avoid entangling alliances with the reds, the Post insisted: "There can be no united front for democracy with enemies of democracy."55

With the publication of this editorial, relations between Stern and his former fair-haired boy proceeded to deteriorate rapidly. Furthermore, bitter fights now riddled a deeply divided editorial board. Stone's long-standing propensity to argue with his boss and anyone else on the paper, for that matter, did not help the situation either. What followed was his removal from the editorial staff, a dearth of subsequent assignments, and the instituting of unsuccessful legal action on his behalf by the American Newspaper Guild.56

While the loss of his position at the Post was certainly not welcomed, it proved to have something of a liberating effect on I. F. Stone. He had made a break, whether forced or not, with another of those surrogate fathers and was about to become a still more influential figure in journalistic and left-of-center circles.

Personal and professional connections Izzy had established with Mattie Josephson, Mike Blankfort, Bruce Bliven, and Malcolm Cowley of The New

Republic, and Max Lerner and Freda Kirchwey of *The Nation,* now came in handy. At this point, Hannah and Mattie Josephson were close enough to the Stones that they occasionally stayed with Izzy and Esther when they came to New York City. Cowley, for his part, sought Izzy's help in getting his younger cousin a job as a cub reporter on the *Post,* both imploring and ribbing him as only a good friend could. But it was thanks to a recommendation by Lerner that Izzy joined the staff of *The Nation,* which had recently placed itself in the camp of "militant liberalism." The influence of *The Nation,* like that of its sister publication, *The New Republic,* remained considerable throughout this period, with newspaper correspondents, for example, proclaiming it, along with *Harper's* and the *Saturday Evening Post,* the magazine they turned to the most after Henry Luce's *Time;* they read *The Nation* far more frequently than they did the *New Yorker,* the *Atlantic Monthly, Fortune, Reader's Digest,* and *Scribner's; The New Republic* came in sixth in the poll, right behind *Collier's.* Intellectuals in general were even more likely to be influenced by both *The Nation* and *The New Republic.*[57]

Izzy had made his first contribution to *The New Republic* in mid-1934, and his initial article in *The Nation* appeared a year later. Through the remainder of the decade, a small number of his writings were published by *The New Republic,* but the vast majority of his journal entries could be found in the pages of its major competitor. In *The Nation,* that "representative of radical democratic thought," Izzy contributed any number of signed articles and editorials and unsigned editorial paragraphs as well; the latter were occasionally farmed out to writers and journalists whose ideological slant closely resembled that of *The Nation's* editors. In the summer of 1938, he had an earlier trial run of sorts, temporarily filling in for the vacationing Lerner. Now, as Izzy informed the Blankforts in a letter dated September 11, shortly before he left the *Post,* he was "taking the jump." He would be responsible for the journal's most important domestic editorials and was about to take on the title of associate editor "unless the *Post* kicks like hell."[58]

The year 1938 had been "a terribly unhappy" one for Izzy at the *Post,* which was "going Right fast" and whose financial straits had necessitated a twenty-five percent cut in pay. *The Nation,* after a tough bout of negotiations, now gave him "a substantial oar to windward." Furthermore, "the editor's title and job" were promised once the journal was able to hire someone full-time.[59]

What this meant was that for once he was drawing "a WHOPPING big combined salary," had actually been able to place one hundred dollars in a savings account, and had just purchased a 1932 Dodge, appropriately enough named Rin Tin Tin. In addition, the summer had been lucrative financially, thanks to his work on *The Nation,* his filling in at the *Post* for the vacationing Sam Grafton, and the fact that he had sold a considerable amount of material on the side. Thus, as was so often the case, Izzy had "been busier than all hell." The family had sublet its apartment and rented a large, old, isolated house outside the city in Northport, Long Island, and were soon to be joined by Chester Roberts in a nearby bungalow. Walter Hart and his wife came to visit, and three-quarters of "the jolliest quartette" of the Penn years were back together again; only Mike Blankfort, now out in Hollywood, was missing.[60]

The countryside seemed to agree with the entire Stone clan generally, although Izzy suffered from a bout of asthma. Still, his tone was cheery, he had taken up roller-skating once again, and promised that he was now "REFORMED." Although admittedly an "old reprobate" and "a dog of a dog of a dog" who often neglected to correspond as promised, he did indeed plan to write Mattie Josephson on behalf of Blankfort, who was seeking a fellowship from the Guggenheim Foundation. Each morning, Izzy took the train into Manhattan and seemed to get more work done that way. He was able to plow through the *New York Times* and the *Tribune* while riding into the city and consequently started writing at the *Post* early in the day rather than in midafternoon as was his custom. Returning home, he pored over documents of all kinds, thereby conducting research for his editorials at *The Nation*. Esther, too, was enthralled with the countryside. Celia was attending school there, Mike's godson "Jay Jay" was about to turn three, and Izzy had just brought "fat faced, pug nosed Chriffy"—that "most benign little guy"— downstairs so that he could watch his dad compose the letter. As Izzy put it, "They have all thrived out here."[61]

At this stage, Izzy seemed to dote on Jay, Chris, and Celia. In another letter to Blankfort written the following fall, he expressed delight that the three kids were all bunched together in a front bedroom of the house in Forest Hills where his family was now residing. The neighborhood school was nearby, friends were made easily, and great fun was had by all. Only Jay appeared "a little disappointed in his fate." After all, the boy next door could boast that his father was a policeman, but Jay "seemed resigned when he asked Esther about my not being one." In follow-up correspondence, Izzy remarked that his daughter was growing up, and he proudly noted that his two boys were "awfully sweet."[62]

With the position at *The Nation* firmed up, Izzy proceeded to turn down a subsequent offer to serve simultaneously as an editor at the journal and press secretary for the New Deal National Housing Administration. Despite his pro-Roosevelt slant, he believed it would be unethical to take on a government job while working for a publication like *The Nation*. Nevertheless, Izzy proceeded to run himself "ragged."[63]

Stone's writings immediately took on a more radical coloring once again, although never approaching the ideological stance of those *Modern Monthly* pieces of the early New Deal period. No longer did he have to appease, in whatever fashion, the liberal bent of J. David Stern or the relatively mainstream audience that was the *New York Post*'s. Throughout this period, Izzy had displayed a striking ability to tailor his writings for the particular publication he was writing for. But now he seemed to speak his mind more freely and to pull fewer punches. Working for *The Nation*, itself a major vehicle for the Popular Front, Izzy was reaching out, for the most part, to the left-oriented intellectual crowd, the same audience that would most loyally follow him for the remainder of his career.

Soon to appear were more critical, although not unsympathetic, analyses of the New Deal and a more open advocacy of socialism. Once again, both ambition and ideology undoubtedly influenced his analyses. In a series of articles in *The Nation* and *Current History*, Stone now began to argue more consistently and more forcefully that the Roosevelt administration had not lived up to its billing; this was in contrast to the position adopted by *The New Republic*, which became more decidedly pro-Roosevelt as the 1930s neared an end. Yes, the New Deal and President Roosevelt had accomplished much, Stone admitted, and that in the face of powerful opposition. In the Harlan coal country, for example, where "espionage . . . the blacklist and the company-paid deputy" had long prevailed, near revolutionary change had resulted, regardless of all the twists and turns of the Roosevelt administration. And no contemporary democratic leader, Stone wrote, better appreciated the lot of the truly disadvantaged than the president himself. But the New Deal had not solved the problem of the ill-fed, ill-clothed, ill-housed. It had not brought about any major redistribution of income. Moreover, simply redividing the existing pie, Stone insisted, was an idea whose time seemed to have come and gone. Production levels simply had to be augmented. In fact the better solution, he indicated, would involve direct government action to "bring idle men and idle materials together" to "end the paradox of want amid plenty"—a standard line of the American left during the 1930s.[64]

But the New Deal middle way, Stone declared, mistakenly sought public control in the midst of "private irresponsibility." Rather, more planning was needed, although "that way lies Socialism, the horrid word." At times, public ownership was called for, he suggested, but only where competition and regulation had proved unavailing. The Scandinavian states, with their mixed economies, served as appropriate models.[65]

In the spring 1939 edition of the *Southern Review*—then welcoming stories and articles from Kay Boyle, Kenneth Burke, James Farrell, F. O. Matthiessen, Mary McCarthy, and Philip Rahv—Stone singled out American liberals for criticism. By implication at least, he seemed to be speaking to J. David Stern and Franklin Roosevelt, something of a political godfather by this point, among others. Liberals, like his author-friend Max Lerner, Stone insisted in reviewing *It Is Later Than You Think,* failed to appreciate that capitalism was destined to fail because of a lack of planning. Indeed, efforts to produce "a planned capitalism," which Lerner appeared to be calling for, would more likely result in "a planned Fascism than . . . a planned Socialism."[66]

Liberals, in Stone's eyes, thus continued to be well intentioned but all too clearly inadequate, just as they had seemed to be during the worst days of the depression. Comparing Lerner with Oswald Garrison Villard, the former editor of *The Nation,* Stone indicated that both sought planning without the pain evidently required. Villard wished that a bloodless revolution had been carried out by the German Social Democrats before Hitler had come to power. Lerner also wanted "to take capitalism from the capitalists—but peacefully." However, revolutions, Stone reminded his readers, were in no way "pretty affairs." Liberals, he declared, were unwilling to acknowledge this. But like it or not, the contemporary age was a time "of gigantic revolution and counterrevolution."[67]

And yet Stone had acknowledged in an earlier essay in the *Southern Review* that revolution was but "a last resort, not a good in itself." The ugly specter of fascism, this good Popular Fronter reflected, again called into question the self-assuredness with which the left had earlier awaited the revolution. Given the all too clear-and-present danger of fascist aggression, civil strife inside the democracies now could only be disastrous. Therefore, a way to meld the best of democracy and socialism and a means to ease the passage from capitalism to socialism had to be discovered. Stone noted that Marx himself had once indicated that the possibility of devising such a middle course appeared brightest in England and the United States.[68]

One theme Stone returned to again and again over the course of his career involved the need to blend democracy and socialism. The good society, he believed, required something of both. Political liberty without economic democracy was precarious at best, while authoritarian socialism was simply inadequate, particularly for those who believed in "the rights of man." What Stone envisioned as socialism he never explicitly indicated. Notwithstanding his reading of Marx, Engels, and Lenin, and his familiarity with seminal Marxist tenets, he devised no grand theoretical framework on which his belief in socialism was based. Instead, his ideology appeared to have derived from a fusing of La Follette progressivism, Thomas's democratic socialism, a study of radical classics, and Popular Frontism. Indeed, Izzy's socialism seemed to encompass the left side of the ideological spectrum, at least from Swedish social democracy to Soviet communism. It was more hopeful than systematic, and every bit as grounded in romanticism as Marxism was itself. It enabled him to champion both democratic reform and the Popular Front, in keeping with much of the American Old Left.

By early 1939, the Popular Front ideal—which Stone believed to be necessary to safeguard the possibilities of both democratic reform and socialism—appeared more tenuous than ever. After all, that Popular Front frontier, the Spanish Civil War, had ended so disastrously. Just before that calamity took place, Stone, in the manner of so many members of his generation, including his friend Mattie Josephson, had ominously warned that Spain's fight was democracy's too: "It is not too much to say that in the mountain vastnesses of Catalonia the destiny of our century is being decided."[69]

For many, both at the time and later, such rhetoric would appear over-heated, the product of a feverish imagination. But to Izzy and to his compatriots, the battle in Spain had been the first stage in the Second World War, the testing ground for the ability of the Popular Front to withstand an assault by fascist-led forces. They saw the refusal of the Western democracies to back the Spanish Loyalists as a potentially fatal failure of will, which would only further whet the appetite of right-wing aggressors.

Following the Falangist victory and the takeover of Czechoslovakia by Nazi Brownshirts, both that destiny and the fate of the Popular Front appeared bleaker and bleaker. For some, like Stone and Josephson, the crushing of the Spanish Republic only heightened their belief that the Popular Front in which they had invested so much was more necessary than ever. But Communist repression in Spain and the Moscow Trials fragmented the ranks left-of-center; as early as March of the previous year, *The Nation* had acknowledged that the trial of the Old Bolsheviks was dissolving "the dream of anti-Fascist unity." Now such leading lights as V. F. Calverton, John Dewey, John Dos Passos, Max Eastman, Sidney Hook, and Norman Thomas formed the Committee for Cultural Freedom, which demanded an end to the Popular Front and implicitly condemned those who attacked German totalitarianism but acted as apologists for Soviet oppression.[70]

Some four hundred noted intellectuals who remained wedded to the Popular Front, including Roger Baldwin, Dashiell Hammett, Ernest Hemingway, Granville Hicks, Matthew Josephson, Corliss Lamont, Max Lerner, and I. F. Stone, responded with a vengeance. Insisting that antifascist solidarity had to be maintained, they charged in a heated response to the CCF that those cut from a profascist mold spewed forth with "the fantastic falsehood that the U.S.S.R. and the totalitarian states are basically alike." They proceeded to praise the evolution inside the Soviet Union toward "steadily expanding democracy in every sphere," termed the Stalinist dictatorship temporary, and lauded "the epoch-making" Soviet constitution.[71]

Viewing the document as too unabashedly uncritical of the Soviet Union, Freda Kirchwey and the majority of the editorial board of *The Nation* refused to support it. Only Izzy and Maxwell Stewart agreed to do so.[72]

Unquestionably, Stone signed this manifesto for the same reasons so many of his intellectual brethren did. For one thing, he continued to view the Soviet Union as the bulwark of the fight against fascism. Socialist Russia had been the one great power to support both the Spanish Republican government and Czechoslovakia against fascist encroachments. The democracies of France and England, in seemingly stark contrast, had failed to come to the aid of the Spanish Loyalists and had allowed Germany to take over Czechoslovakia. Hoping that the policy of appeasement might be abandoned in favor of one supporting collective security, Stone had "wanted to see Russia in alliance with the West." And in spite of his considerable qualms about Stalinist practices, Soviet Russia remained for him what it was for so many, "ultimately not a country but a state of mind."[73]

He continued, despite more and more misgivings, to view the Soviet Communist experiment with sympathy. He still believed, as he had indicated earlier, that "revolutions are the surgery of history. Surgery means bloodshed and horror and mistake and you don't do it unless you're in such a bad way that nothing could be worse." Those fortunate enough to live in more favored lands, he reasoned, had to display compassion and understanding toward revolutionary societies.[74]

Consequently, he proved willing in this one instance to cast aside all his concerns regarding the terrors being played out inside the Soviet Union. Those concerns were long held and deeply felt, which makes his behavior at this stage all the more remarkable.

His willingness to affix his name to the Sovietphile manifesto and his dogged commitment to the Popular Front led some at the time, such as Sidney Hook, and others afterward, to claim that Stone was an apologist for the hammer-and-sickle. The novelist James T. Farrell, a Trotskyist himself, in a letter to Freda Kirchwey would soon demand a public explanation from Stone and Stewart regarding why they had signed the document; Farrell then went on to denounce the presence of the same "two Stalinists" on the journal's editorial board. Richard Rovere, at the time a writer with *The New Masses,* likewise came to view Izzy Stone as a Stalinist who employed "their polemical techniques," while playing fast and loose with the facts. James Wechsler, a staffer on *The Nation,* later suggested that Stone was one of two on the journal who "at times . . . were so defensive about not being Communists" themselves. During this period, Wechsler went on to say, "the Communist underground seemed to have a mysterious attraction for those who had never entered it."

This, he declared, was especially the case with Izzy Stone. Wechsler continued: "In the years I knew him I always had the feeling Stone could remain a fairly regular apologist for the Communists, with intermittent stories to to the left and right, only by staying out of the organized movement; like other instinctive mavericks, he would not have lasted very long inside."[75]

Later, Izzy acknowledged that he, like other Popular Fronters, was "something of an apologist . . . not being as outspoken . . . as . . . later." His readiness, like that of others—no matter how short-lived—to veil very real concerns about Soviet practices was certainly not without significance. By this point, after all, he had read transcripts of the Moscow Trials and was convinced that they had been "a lot of hot air, not hot air . . . phony. I could just feel the texture was a typical governmental frame-up, taking a little bit of truth and building a lot of lies out of it." Given that this was the case, I. F. Stone's decision to allow his name to be connected to a tract so obviously designed to paper over the purge trials and Stalinism in general was unquestionably the most foolish and dishonest action of his entire career. It resulted above all else from his determination to keep alive the Popular Front, that antifascist combination.[76]

But the world of the Popular Fronters, along with many of the dreams of the 1930s, was shaken by the announcement on August 23, 1939, that the Soviet Union and Nazi Germany had signed a nonaggression pact. American progressives of all sorts, other than perhaps the growing number of "premature anti-Stalinists," were thrown into a state of disbelief and bewilderment. For many, knowledge of the pact, coupled with the dismay induced by the purge trials and the Spanish Civil War, ensured that "the masquerade . . . [was] over." As a consequence, neither the USSR nor the CPUSA would ever again be seen in quite the same light by longtime Popular Fronters such as Heywood Broun, Matthew Josephson, Freda Kirchwey, Max Lerner, Louis Fischer of *The Nation*, and Malcolm Cowley of *The New Republic*. Indeed, the dismay and disgust experienced by so many soon culminated in a militant, anti-communist posture, one so heartfelt that even wartime exigencies proved incapable of fully abating it.[77]

The journalist Richard Rovere later remembered "no one from the period [. . .] more outraged by the outrageous document" than was Izzy. Perhaps that was because it had called into question three of his and the American left's major touchstones of the time—Socialist Russia, socialism in general, and the Popular Front. In the first several months following the revelation of the Nazi-Soviet accords, a series of unsigned editorials and editorial paragraphs in *The Nation* demonstrated the anger and anguish of this longtime Popular Fronter, who acknowledged in a note to Freda Kirchwey that "we may all have to make our peccavi's some day." He now castigated American Communist Party members, said to be jumping once again "at the pull of Stalin's string." But he acknowledged that all who had considered the USSR as the backbone of the antifascist fight—and he was obviously speaking for himself—had shared "their indignation and contemptuous disbelief" that such an agreement could be in the making. For such a pact could only serve to "discredit the Soviet Union."[78]

Yet the pact had been drawn, he indicated, so that Russian strategists could both avoid war with Germany and grab Polish territory. Nevertheless, Stalin's hopes of turning Hitler westward, he predicted, would prove as unavailing as had the appeasement policy of Britain's Neville Chamberlain. He warned that more surprises might be in store from the German despot and "the Moscow Machiavelli." While it was true that the pact heightened the likelihood of a Nazi blitzkrieg to the west, Stone pointed out, only Alice in Wonderland "could do justice to Hitler's faith in Stalin." But the new editorial policy laid out in *Izvestia,* he admitted, indicated that such faith might not be completely misplaced. For now, the same regime that dealt so brutally with the slightest ideological deviations at home was comparing the battle against Nazism to the witch-hunts of the Middle Ages.[79]

Although Stone had never viewed that Soviet Union in the manner certain starry-eyed Western intellectuals did, he had considered it to be in the forefront of progressive nations, the lone socialist state, and the cornerstone of antifascist unity. But no longer did he consider Communist Russia to be engaged in some kind of grand social experiment. And never again did he have quite the same illusions about Soviet intentions.

In mid-October, Stone wrote a pair of letters to Mike Blankfort, in which he discussed the pact. Now, he declared, "I'm off the Moscow axis." The Russians, he admitted, were not "playing a bad game for themselves," and both the Ukraine and White Russia were "better off under them." But he was disgusted with recent editorials in *Pravda* that blamed the Poles for the outbreak of the war and in *Izvestia* that declared one's attitude toward Nazism to be a matter of taste only. He wrote, "Thus Marx is wedded to Savarin." All of this had "turned my stomach." Moreover, "the party and its organs here have stunk pretty badly in their efforts at explanation."[80]

Izzy proceeded to ask Blankfort if the two had ever talked about an Italian labor leader and syndicalist by the name of Armando Borghi, whom he had recently lunched with. Borghi, a contemporary of Lenin, had quoted from Karl Radek that "every Marxist ought to read Macchiavelli." In Izzy's estimation, Broghi had nicely summed up the situation: "Macchiavelli—all right for Caesar—no good for Brutus."[81]

What was most unfortunate, Stone suggested, was that "a new Jesuitry is visible in these interminable and contradictory 'explanations.' " There appeared to be "a new Catholicism . . . growing up in Communism and directed from Moscow, with its own Pope and its own heretics, bitterly persecuted and pursued. The ease with which party members flip-flop on instruction and are all against Nazism one day and British imperialism the next is indicative of the robot quality the party creates."[82]

Despite his scathing analysis, Izzy wrote Blankfort less than a week later, asking where his friend had heard "that I felt a sense of 'personal betrayal.' " Such a notion was absurd, he insisted, but then admitted that there might be something to it, after all. He had "recovered" but was ready for "no more fellow-travelling." The American Communist Party, he asserted, became more Jesuitical day by day. He considered it particularly reprehensible that the party was demanding peace in the fashion of German-American Bundists.[83]

In the latter stages of 1939, Stone, in a series of unsigned editorials that appeared in *The Nation*, repeatedly suggested that a Soviet drive westward, carried out as it would be behind the cover of another world war, might transform Stalin into the "master of the Eastern Hemisphere." Such a development could very well hold a certain appeal for land-starved peasants in the Balkans, he admitted. But revolutionary rhetoric justifying such a move would simply be designed to ensure Comintern control of any indigenous uprising, Comintern control of "the orthodox Stalinist variety." To date, Stalin had already grabbed Latvia, Estonia, and Lithuania, and, with his partner-in-crime, was presently threatening Poland and Romania.[84]

Caustically, in another editorial in *The Nation*, Stone compared Soviet incursions into Finland with Franco's rape of Republican Spain; *The New Republic* also condemned what it saw to be Stalin's "criminal folly." But this time, the Russians had quite possibly overextended themselves, Stone hinted, and, at the very least, had made the brandishing of the red bogy they so feared more likely than ever. Their actions also ensured that the American left, which had at times appeared so potent during the depression decade, would remain splintered for some time to come.[85]

I. F. Stone was very much a part of that now increasingly fragmented left. First as an editorial writer with the *New York Post* and later as a member of *The Nation* staff, he had become a figure of some importance in liberal, radical, and journalistic haunts. This no doubt pleased Stone, who was a proponent of the two leading left-of-center movements of the decade—Franklin Delano Roosevelt's New Deal and the Soviet-backed Popular Front—both of which seemed to support broadly based reform efforts to head off the threat posed by economic and political collapse. While New Deal reformism and the anti-fascist Popular Front were said to be deliberately nondoctrinaire, Stone believed in them as would a committed ideologue. And that very level of commitment eventually led him on a reportorial path that involved more investigative journalism and a position on the editorial board of *The Nation*.

But what Stone and those of like mind could in no way anticipate was that the prevailing political climate would, in a sense, never again be as supportive for radical Popular Fronters as it had been for a brief spell during the soon-to-be-departed decade. Although few recognized it at the time and many would have disputed the notion in the period just ahead, the glory days of the American Old Left were now past. Yes, a second Popular Front soon emerged that involved a wartime alliance with the Communist behemoth itself. But the prosocialist coloring, even the reformist thrust of the earlier united front, was discarded for homilies concerning Uncle Joe, the glorious Red Army, and the Grand Alliance. Moreover, the celebration of the United States was beginning as well, something which would not be easily tossed aside when the postwar era arrived.

Perhaps the fate of the Old Left might have been different had more been learned from the sectarian squabbles and seemingly inevitable ideological disillusionment which so many experienced—and which led to their determination to discard politics altogether, reject radical thought, and disassociate themselves from former colleagues. The Old Left did make some egregious errors, foremost among them the all-too-familiar acceptance of the word of the Soviet Communist Party as gospel; the papering over of terrible excesses and real misgivings; the willingness, in other words, to entirely suspend critical judgment—which both political activists and intellectuals must possess to carry out their proper functions.

One of the saddest results of the departure of so many depression-era radicals from the path of the revolution was the tendency of some to find new ideological gods to parrot blindly; another was their all-too-easy discarding of what was best in the radical tradition—the search for a brotherhood and sisterhood of humankind—in the name of greater "objectivity" and "rationality." Thus, some would soon line up with the hardcore anti-Communists, while others became apologists in their own fashion for the national security state, soon to make its appearance.

There were, of course, those who held on to their radical tenets, some continuing down the same blind route they had followed all along. A much smaller number of others, such as Izzy Stone, attempted to sustain the radical tradition and the role of intellectuals as social critics by learning from the internecine battles of the 1930s, which they were determined to avoid in the future. But even they often refused to examine their own activities during the period and how they too had participated in the general failure of left-wing intellectuals and activists to remain true to the radical vision. That refusal only ensured still more rocky and sometimes disastrous ideological times ahead.

5 The American Left, Interventionism, and Civil Liberties

I F. Stone's strong-willed nature and that of other leading Old Leftists ensured that American radicalism remained divided in the immediate
postpact period. The events of 1939, particularly the signing of the Nazi-
Soviet accords and the opening stages of World War II, had thrown the
American left into a state of disarray. The ensuing disintegration of the Popular Front ideal, which had ushered in everything from the League of American Writers on the home front to the International Brigades battling in
defense of the Republic in Spanish towns, villages, and mountain passes, had
resulted in a vacuum a handful of intellectuals did their best to fill. Granville
Hicks, a former instructor at Harvard and editor of *The New Masses* and one of
the growing ranks of party-exes, wondered if the time might not be ripe to put
together "an independent Left Wing party" and reconstruct "a new non-
Communist united front." This would be, as Hicks put it, "an American
Popular Front," or, in the words of Richard Rovere, "a neo-Marxist movement." On October 15, Hicks gathered with other interested parties—all of
whom remained socialists and dedicated antifascists—including Leo Huberman, Joseph Lash, Robert Lynd, Rovere, Paul Sweezy, Jimmy Wechsler, and
Izzy Stone, at the home of Max Lerner to hash matters out. In the months
ahead, a handful of other left-of-center intellectuals, such as Malcolm Cowley,
Kyle Crichton, Robert Graham Davis, Louis Fischer, and Mattie Josephson,
were included in discussions about the advisability of establishing a new organization, intended to be largely educational in nature, of progressive forces
left-of-center. All appeared to agree that the American Communist Party had
at long last been "exposed as a branch of the Soviet Foreign Office" and that
factionalism relegated both the American Socialist Party and the Trotskyists to
the ranks of historical also-rans.[1]

Stone's involvement in the effort to construct a new, non-Communist
American left made a good deal of sense, given his growing antipathy to
party members at home and displeasure regarding the pact and Soviet incursions into Eastern Europe. Moreover, Stone was far more comfortable in

questioning even those he generally agreed with than in keeping silent on issues that tore at his inner conscience.

However, personal and ideological considerations prevented this American version of a "New Beginnings" from getting very far. While there were those who condemned the USSR unequivocally, others continued to see it as a socialist state which had to be defended. And in general, it appeared as though the American left had divided "a dozen different ways." After the initial meetings had resulted in no single plan of action, Hicks attempted a different tack, putting out a bulletin sheet that served as a kind "of correspondence committee among former sympathizers of Russia who were sympathizers no longer." There were those who now likened Soviet communism to German Nazism, others who condemned Stalinism from a Marxist vantage point, some who wanted nothing further to do with Marxism, many who wanted to move beyond the New Deal in a socialist direction, a number who saw World War II as an antifascist fight, and still others who viewed it simply as a battle involving imperialistic competitors. Following the collapse of France, the Independent Left splintered irrevocably into interventionist and noninterventionist camps, which lined up behind either President Roosevelt or Norman Thomas. Eventually the "Lonely Hearts," as James Farrell so aptly named them, determined to go their own ways. Cowley, for example, one of the dominant figures on the left in the thirties because of his politically charged literary editorship of *The New Republic*, opted to abandon politics entirely. Wechsler chalked up the failure of the Independent Left to the "ambiguity and disagreement about what is to be done next." He also pointed to the practical matter that so many of the short-term participants were obliged to fulfill book contracts and were, anyway, among the "perennially unaffiliated." Among the latter, of course, was Izzy Stone, who continued to view organizations of any sort, no matter how well intentioned, with more than a little discomfort.[2]

Nevertheless, Stone, unlike certain other members of the aborted Independent Left, remained determined to stand as both an intellectual and an activist. As was the case during the Great Depression, the times demanded this stance, he reasoned, what with another international conflagration pending. And as a journalist, he felt further bound to display commitment, unlike many members of his profession who trumpeted their self-proclaimed objectivity. The intellectual and the journalist could in no way be disinterested about the great events of the era, he believed, but were obliged to call to the public's attention both the failings of one's own nation and the troubles looming ahead in international waters.

To that end, Stone still hoped that the Popular Front might somehow be patched together again. Consequently, he joined with a group of sixteen other self-proclaimed liberals, among them Franz Boas, Theodore Dreiser,

Robert Morss Lovett, Robert Lynd, Carey McWilliams, and Jimmy Wechsler, in what proved to be a futile attempt to have Elizabeth Gurley Flynn readmitted to the American Civil Liberties Union. Lovett, in fact, later reported that Stone had been the one to solicit his signature on a petititon on Flynn's behalf. In February 1940, on the heels of the outbreak of World War II, board members, including Roger Baldwin, John Haynes, and Norman Thomas, had determined to oust Flynn, a former Wobbly and presently a Communist Party activist, from the ACLU on the grounds that she was affiliated with a totalitarian political organization. Thus, the divisions on the American left only continued to widen.[3]

P erhaps, as historian David Shi has noted, divergent attitudes on U.S. involvement in the war that had broken out in Europe were what best accounted for the failure of the Independent Left. While the final days of the Red Decade caused some to discard politics altogether, others struggled in their own way to make sense of global developments in particular. Competing for their allegiance were the tenets of internationalism and anti-interventionism. So too were the conflicting beliefs that the intellectual, like the journalist, should adopt a posture of objectivity, or should rush in to enter the battle wherever it was taking place. From John Reed to Ernest Hemingway, left-leaning American intellectuals had often chosen to follow the latter course, refusing to stand on the sidelines when the great conflicts of the first part of the twentieth century had broken out. They had been there at the barricades, with pen or gun in hand, in Chihuahua City, in Verdun, in Petrograd, and in Madrid. There were those among them who had supported the Zapatistas, the Allied powers, the Red Army, or the Abraham Lincoln Brigade. They had battled against the Federales, the kaiser's forces, the White Russians, and Franco's Blueshirts. They had done so in the name of anticolonialism, democracy, socialism, and antifascism.

On the very same grounds, a number of American intellectuals, including Roger Baldwin and Norman Thomas, had adopted an anti-interventionist stance. They had argued that the United States should remain outside of other nation's fights, that military escapades inevitably resulted in militarism and a curbing of civil liberties on the home front. Empire and democracy, they believed, simply did not mix. They had encouraged conscripts to proclaim themselves as conscientious objectors, urged soldiers to lay down their arms, beseeched statesmen to carry out disarmament pacts or to outlaw war altogether, condemned the merchants of death, and favored the taking of pledges to allow war no more. They had formed organizations like the War Resisters League, the American Civil Liberties Union, and the Student Peace Union. They had opposed the entrance of the United States into the First World War and its neocolonial excursions involving the Far East and Latin America. They championed the right of self-determination and the ability of a people to revolutionize their own social, political, and economic orders without outside interference. But even Baldwin and Thomas would be at odds when it came to the question of defending revolutionary regimes and staving off the threat of right-wing aggressor states.

By the end of the 1930s, I. F. Stone had moved back and forth between the two camps, while always retaining his belief that the intellectual and journalist often were compelled to take a stand, both in print and sometimes otherwise. He had been that politically precocious schoolboy who had supported President Wilson's call for a League of Nations. He had opposed U.S. involvement in Far Eastern affairs in the early thirties, when Japanese militarists began their own outward march. He had supported a Good Neighbor Policy for Latin America, condemning the sending of marines and ambassadors who sought to sustain conservative regimes that allowed for the exploitation of peasant and urban masses. He had exhorted the European states and his own government to construct antifascist alliances to restrain Hitler so that war might be avoided altogether.

As early as September 1937, he had wrestled with the question of possible U.S. involvement in a second world war. He acknowledged in an article in *The Nation* that if the United States could be insulated, he would support "isolationist neutrality legislation," for this country had not been intended "to set the universe aright" and war was atrocious. But should the nation "arm to the teeth," he warned, an unprecedented "militaristic, regimented, goosestep influence" would soon be present. Consequently, only international cooperation, he believed, backed by the might of the United States might stem aggression and stave off a worldwide conflagration. Freda Kirchwey of *The Nation* also saw isolationism as illusory, arguing that the United States would inevitably get caught up in "the vortex of war" the fascist states were creating.[4]

He remained somewhat more conflicted about his country's own role in such a movement. Once more, ideological considerations—his hatred of fascism, his hopes for socialism, and his recognition of the horrors war resulted in—helped to shape his reading of events. In the summer of 1939, shortly before the German and Russian foreign ministers affixed their names to the pact, Stone again warned, as he responded to a query by *The New Republic*, about the dangers of adopting the same isolationist line that that journal did. Adolf Hitler, he pointed out, just might conquer the world unless Americans understood security to be "indivisible." Appeasement, he had no doubt, would surely result in war or something worse. Still, Stone insisted that Uncle Sam not hand over "a blank check . . . to the umbrella man from Birmingham." Stone, like fellow Popular Fronter Max Lerner, condemned the "pro-Fascist elements" perched at the top of the British and French governments, whom he saw as so unlike the genuine democrat sitting in the White House.[5]

When the guns of war sounded once more, Stone seemed determined that the United States remain outside the fray; aid to the Allies, he believed, as did Freda Kirchwey, could best ensure that result. In November 1939, in an unsigned editorial paragraph that appeared in *The Nation*, he condemned not only "the hammer-and-sickle" and "the swastika," but also "the umbrella" for the carving up of Poland. Shortly thereafter, in the middle of a review of *The British War Blue Book*, he went on to blame British and French imperialism for Hitler's rise to power. Nevertheless, he urged that neutrality legislation be repealed and supported the granting of aid to the Allies, while insisting that U.S. intervention need not necessarily follow. Still, in March 1940, he charged in a book review essay that the British aristocracy had no intention of carrying out another crusade for democracy. He had come to view the war in Europe not as a great ideological struggle, but rather as a clash between imperialistic rivals; Communists and anti-Stalinists alike were delivering similar analyses.[6]

Izzy Stone was walking something of a tightrope in declining to adopt fully either an isolationist or an interventionist viewpoint. The Soviet role in the outbreak of the war, which he had so roundly denounced, nevertheless had temporarily induced him no longer to view it as a battle of rival ideologies. He feared that the war might result in the unleashing of another anti-Communist crusade and play into the hands of reactionaries in both Europe and the United States. Thus, at present, he saw nothing that cried out for direct American involvement. And little was likely to come of the conflict, he indicated, that could make up for the casualties, along with "the bigotry, madness, and folly inevitably unchained by war."[7]

At this point, Izzy and his brother Lou began researching a book intended to be a "kind of anti-war theatre." Lou had joined Izzy in New York City in mid-1939, when the two participated in the campaign by Sam Leibowitz, the noted defense attorney for the Scottsboro Boys, for the post of Kings County district attorney. Izzy, with Lou's assistance, had served as a researcher and speechwriter for Leibowitz, before their candidate decided to withdraw from the race. They now planned to write a book on man's warlike nature and spent long hours at the New York Public Library. The proposed manuscript was to focus on the seemingly perpetual struggle between men—those on "our side"—and the monsters who inevitably gave in to primal, martial urges. As the German blitzkrieg continued to sweep across Europe, however, Izzy decided to abandon the project, reasoning that the fight against fascism was of far greater importance.[8]

The fall of France in June 1940 made that struggle appear even more necessary. As Stone soon acknowledged in an editorial in *The Nation,* the French collapse had converted him into "a war-monger." Of immediate concern to him was the plight of antifascists presently mired in French-occupied territories. They—the Matteottis, the Ossietzkys, the Viennese workers, the fighters of the Asturias, and the veterans of the International Brigade—had been the first combatants in the struggle against fascism, and its first victims as well. What the United States did for these brave souls, many of whom were now residing in concentration camps outside Paris, he declared, "will be a test of our democracy's power to act and will to win."9

Notwithstanding the Nazi takeover of France, the American left remained deeply divided about what course of action the U.S. government should follow now. Communist Party members, of course, continued to adhere to the Comintern line, which since the signing of the nonaggression pact had condemned "the imperialist war." Socialists who looked to Norman Thomas for guidance opposed intervention of any kind. *The New Republic* maintained a largely anti-interventionist stance. Malcolm Cowley, who now believed that the United States should act otherwise, resigned from the journal by year's end. Oswald Garrison Villard, responding to Freda Kirchwey's championing of universal military training, terminated a near half-century association with *The Nation.*10

I n the same period when he wrote for the *The Nation,* which he happily saw as "anti-Munich" and "pro-collective security" thanks to the likes of Robert Bendiner, Freda Kirchwey, and Maxwell Stewart, Izzy found it necessary to take on any number of odd jobs. In the summer of 1939, Izzy had accepted an assignment from the Institute for Propaganda Analysis to tour the nation and report on the activities of the Associated Farmers, an antiunion agribusiness organization. The Columbia University-affiliated institute had been established in 1937 with the explicit charge to analyze propaganda of all sorts and then disseminate such information to both educational institutions and the general public. In October 1939, his contract with the institute had just about run its course; the institute was itself in dire financial straits. The Stones had then moved from a house in Richmond Hills to one in Forest Hills that cost only fifty dollars a month, required far less fuel, and was easier to manage. Consequently, Izzy and Esther were able to let their German maid go and reduce their monthly expenses by some one hundred dollars. Izzy proceeded to take care of his debts, and the Stones had more money saved up than ever before, enough to tide them over for a six-month period.11

That being the case, Izzy had decided "to try and become a writer." He had his half-time job with *The Nation* to fall back on and figured he could make enough free-lancing to cover the family's expenses. He had received five hundred dollars up front from the left-wing publishing house Modern Age Books to complete a history of the Associated Farmers; this was a project that he evidently never completed. But he was determined not to get saddled with a regular job if he could help it and felt more confidence in his ability as a writer than he had before. "So here goes," he informed Mike Blankfort. "I hope I can stick it out." He was obliged to write one last five-thousand-word bulletin for the institute, continued his association with *The Nation,* and had a hundred dollars coming to him for work already carried out.[12]

The following July, he undertook the task of writing and editing three complete issues of *Your Investments,* the American Investors Union journal. The AIU, which had been established in late 1939 with the blessing of John T. Flynn, Robert Lynd, and George Seldes, among others, considered itself the champion of the little guy, particularly the small investor and the less well heeled depositor. In the fall, Izzy received the most lucrative appointment he had had to date. He was named speech writer and publicist for Lawrence Tibbett, head of the American Guild of Musical Artists, who was warding off an attempted mob takeover of the union. His weekly salary would be two hundred and fifty dollars.[13]

But in his third week on the job, Freda Kirchwey offered Izzy the post of Washington editor of *The Nation,* the same journal *Time* had recently declared was given to a "devout and single-minded Leftism." The pay was to be ninety dollars a week with a fifteen-dollar expense allowance, the base salary to be reduced to seventy-five dollars after a six-month period in which he could acquire a steady supply of outside writing assignments. Such a salary was considerably lower than that of the standard Washington correspondent but was in keeping with the tradition of both *The Nation* and *The New Republic,* seemingly always strapped financially. Izzy accepted immediately, and the Stones packed up and headed off to the nation's capital. They bought a three-bedroom house at 5618 Nebraska Avenue, acquiring in the process a monthly mortgage of seventy-five dollars.[14]

Just as he had been elated with his move to Manhattan to join the staff of the *New York Post* back in 1933, Izzy was now delighted with Kirchwey's decision to send him to Washington. After all, that city, since the start of the New Deal, had become both the power center and "the year-round news capital" of the American nation. It was also the place where insider information prevailed, where correspondents had come to rely on press conferences, official handouts, press releases, and a near-incestuous relationship between themselves and politicians. Izzy too had his sources within the Washington bureaucracy and would, on occasion, attend important press conferences, while at other times he would be denied entrance. He worked out of the

Kellogg building in downtown Washington, alongside colleagues from the *Chicago Tribune*, the *Philadelphia Inquirer*, and the *St. Louis Post-Dispatch*. But unlike so many other Washington reporters, he refused to be "taken in" by smooth-talking, glib government officials who came bearing information in hand. This was all the more noteworthy for Izzy, unlike most correspondents in Washington, never opted to move on to another assignment except for a brief spell when he was temporarily stationed or had temporarily stationed himself overseas during the worst days of McCarthyism. Among his fellow journalists in Washington, Izzy was unique in other ways as well: he continued to read widely and extensively and to retain his association with both the left and leading American intellectuals.[15]

For a while, the Stones' finances were tight once again, so Izzy did a bit of additional writing on the side for the *Washington Post*. He did so off and on throughout the war years, albeit not always happily because he sometimes disagreed with the editorial positions of the paper. More important, though, he began contributing to another paper, *PM*, which had acquired somewhat legendary stature even before it first reached the newsstands in mid-June 1940. The journalistic genius behind *PM* was publisher and editor Ralph Ingersoll, formerly with the *New Yorker* and Henry Luce's *Fortune* and *Time* magazines. Ingersoll sought to make a go of a newspaper that would be run by journalists, not "men of property," and would be sustained by an ever-growing number of readers willing to hand over a nickel for an afternoon paper that was competing in the already crowded New York City market. The credo of *PM*, Ingersoll conveyed to staffers and the public alike: "We are against people who push other people around, just for the fun of pushing, whether they flourish in this country or abroad."[16]

Although Ingersoll denied allegiance to any ism and declared democracy to be the best form of government, *PM* proved to be a highly controversial undertaking. Some were opposed to the fact that the paper had initially been intended to serve "as an organ of the United Front"; others, to its obvious pro–Popular Front slant. But most of all, charges of Communist influence hung heavily over *PM*, even though its financial angels included Marshall Field, Eleanor Gimbel, M. Lincoln Schuster, and Philip A. Wrigley. The staff of *PM* was admittedly first-rate and very selectively drawn; names such as Margaret Bourke-White, Kenneth Crawford, Leo Huberman, Max Lerner, Tom Meany, Jimmy Wechsler, and Izzy Stone appeared in bylines or photographic credits. In addition, *PM* attracted contributors on the order of Ernest Hemingway, Eric Sevareid, Dr. Benjamin Spock, James Thurber, and Dalton Trumbo. President Roosevelt was one who welcomed *PM* to New York City, predicting that it would "add a notable chapter to the history of our free press."[17]

Others, however, did not view either *PM* or the *PM* staff quite so charitably. Victor Riesel, managing editor of the anti-Communist *New Leader,* accused the paper of "a clear and blatant pro-Stalin bias." Eugene Lyons listed the Communist and fellow-traveling ties of *PM* staffers, while Ferdinand Lundberg dismissed it as "a daily pro-Soviet hybrid of *Time* and *Life* with overtones of the *New Yorker.*"[18]

But as Richard Rovere pointed out in *The Nation* even before the first issue of *PM* rolled off the presses, publisher Ingersoll was decidedly "anti-isolationist" and thus sharply at odds with the current line of the American Communist Party. Ingersoll was also staunchly pro-Roosevelt, placing the paper "150 percent" behind the president's call for lend-lease aid to the Allies. That resulted in Communists damning him as "a Fascist son of a bitch," the same Communists who denounced *The Nation* and the *The New Republic*—which was now changing its tune—as "idealistic whitewashers of the imperialist war."[19]

In late 1940, another anti-isolationist, I. F. Stone, began writing for *PM* and soon was named Washington correspondent of the paper; later he became a regular columnist. As much as anyone, Izzy and Max Lerner helped to shape *PM*'s "Left–New Deal philosophy." But this should not have been all that surprising, for Freda Kirchwey of *The Nation* appeared to see the journal as occupying the left side of the New Deal coalition. Stone's and Lerner's regular columns, which the leaders of *PM* now turned to eagerly, also helped to sustain "the old tradition of personal journalism," as did the syndicated work during this period of such noteworthy scribes as Walter Lippmann and Drew Pearson and Robert Allen.[20]

A good deal of Izzy Stone's work at this point was of the investigative variety. Like Sinclair and Steffens before him and somewhat in the fashion of his friend George Seldes, Stone employed "the journalism of outrage," as David Protess has so aptly put it, to compel his readers to question both the state of international affairs and domestic policies. Like other practitioners of investigative journalism, he believed that the individual reporter or story could make a difference. In the fashion of Lerner and the rest of the *PM* staff, he refused to consider objective reporting as the noblest ideal for his profession or even much of a possibility. Nevertheless, he was determined to get his facts straight to back up his own biting analyses.[21]

I t was a recommendation from Max Lerner, in fact, that had again enabled Izzy to receive a prized appointment on a key left-of-center publication. But in thanking Lerner for his vote of confidence, Izzy declared, "I know I will enjoy working with you. I want you to enjoy working with me. You can count on my honesty and sincerity. But I am sometimes gauche, tactless, overeager. If I should sometimes offend or rub you the wrong way, I will appreciate it and take it in good part if you tell me so frankly." Thus, Izzy acknowledged something his journalistic intimates inevitably discovered, that he was never the easiest man to work alongside of. His fiery temperament and determination to go it alone, which occasionally bordered on self-righteousness, helped to keep matters lively at both *PM* and *The Nation*.[22]

On more than one occasion, Freda Kirchwey, his boss at *The Nation*, found it necessary to attempt to call Izzy on the carpet. To avoid libel charges at one point, she reworked an article of his dealing with wartime corporate maneuvers and warned him not to call others "traitors" without being able to back up such accusations on both legal and ethical grounds. Later she felt obliged to advise him to employ "due tact and discretion" in shaping his editorials in general and pointed out that she shared the concerns of other staff members about "the violence of your language."[23]

Another colleague on the staff of *The Nation*, evidently either Robert Bendiner or Keith Hutchinson, discussed "a cat-and-dog fight" he had suffered through with Izzy. This individual informed Izzy that he was too temperamental himself to be subjected "to the second abusive display of yours within a few months."[24]

While his colleagues at times had reason to question Izzy's judgment, others he came in contact with in the course of his work did so as well. On September 15, 1941, R. W. Flournoy, a legal adviser at the Department of State, wrote to Assistant Secretary Dean Acheson concerning a series of telephone conversations he had had with Izzy Stone. Flournoy reported that Izzy appeared particularly interested in uncovering the history of State's employment of the term "United Kingdom" because of concerns about its possible application to the 1939 Neutrality Act. Izzy was apparently annoyed by attempts to reroute him to the Department of Justice. When he was then referred to Assistant Secretary Acheson, Izzy sought to "pin [Flournoy] . . . down," adopted a highly sarcastic tone, and asked if he needed to deal with "one of the watchmen at the doors of this building or . . . the janitor." The harried State Department attorney, considering Izzy's behavior "entirely unreasonable and impertinent," abruptly terminated the conversation.[25]

But while others might have been displeased with some of Izzy's antics, he for one was "busier than hell covering this 30-ring circus but having such fun!" Writing to Mike Blankfort in Janurary 1941, he expressed dissatisfaction with the quality of his own work, while acknowledging that others, happily, were not so discriminating. He did not deserve the kudos that came his way, Izzy insisted, for "God knows I haven't yet learned how to write English and the New York office [of *The Nation*] is always futzing around with my prose as is." And yet, he admitted, "I seem to be getting a reputation." And he was, he knew, "a good reporter."[26]

Perhaps this was owing to the diligence, competitiveness, and single-mindedness that Izzy brought to the journalistic trade. These qualities helped to make him a first-rate investigative journalist who was wholly immersed in his work. Whether he was working in his downtown office or at home, Izzy's typewriter rang loud and clear. For young Chris Stone, "Dad really pounded his typewriter; we knew we had to stay out of his way." Nevertheless, it "was a reassuring clamor," indicating that all was as it should have been in the family household. Moreover, because Izzy "had this absorbing career" which he clearly loved, it "was really wonderful to watch" him at work.[27]

But the same driven quality that exasperated colleagues and the subjects of his exposés affected the tenor of family life at 5618 Nebraska Avenue, situated in the northwest sector of Washington. With virtually everything revolving around Izzy and his need to get out daily copy, there was little in the way of a "*Saturday Evening Post* sort of style" of family existence. In fact, owing to the constant barrage of assignments from both *The Nation* and *PM*, "the house was," according to Chris, "always rich with tension."[28]

Izzy operated on a type of "internal schedule" that enabled him to produce the steady stream of editorials and articles demanded by these publications. The pace was punishing, but Izzy thrived on it. Perhaps the urgency of the times, the felt need to follow the global threat posed by fascist aggression, the belief that *The Nation* and *PM* were linked to the great events of the era, served to sustain him. Even the noise from other typewriters and teletype machines clanging in his office at the Kellogg building, reporting on the Nazi push throughout the continent of Europe and the early, largely ineffective American response, further heightened the sense that momentous happenings were taking place.[29]

Like one requiring an adrenaline fix, Izzy reveled in all of this. "He loved it," Chris noted, "he wouldn't have wanted it any other way." For he functioned as a journalist, Chris continued, in the same manner that he handled the family car. "Dad pulsed. He pushed the accelerator down and let up. Pushed it down and let it up." He drove himself in the same manner, working until near exhaustion, or at the least, a welcomed and much needed nap.[30]

Consequently, there was little time for picnics or ball games or social gatherings with friends. Indeed, Izzy seemed to prefer watching movies in his spare time to dinner parties and the like. Perhaps this was the case because in certain regards he "wasn't a sociable guy," inasmuch as "he had other things to occupy him than polite conversation." Besides, most of Izzy's old friends were still in New York City or like Mike Blankfort now or soon to be in the armed forces. And for his part, Izzy was unwilling "to make adjustments in his own pace" to accommodate others. Owing to his grinding schedule, he simply had no time "to add any other obligations."[31]

T hus, Izzy reserved his considerable store of energy for his work. His reports on the American defense program now served to add to an already growing reputation. In a series of articles that appeared in *PM* and *The Nation,* he continued to lay out the argument that he had first articulated in August 1940, that defense preparedness simply had to be speeded up. He insisted that "business-as-usual"—which impeded the mobilization effort—be brought to a halt. Big business, so used to treating labor heavy-handedly, seldom even gave a thought to improving wages or working conditions. Big business, accustomed to the game of monopoly, tried to grab all the defense contracts for itself. Big business, antagonistic to the very idea of competition, attempted to maintain prewar cartels in place, even those with links to the fascist states. Big business, spoiling for every penny, held out an economic lifeline to the Axis powers. But all of this was less acceptable than ever, Stone believed, with war now on the horizon.[32]

In fact, as Congress passed the Lend-Lease Bill in January 1941, he declared in another article in *The Nation* that the American people might soon be forced to take part in humankind's greatest war ever. And in classic Wilsonian fashion, he proclaimed that the United States was striving "for imperial responsibilities" and was seeking to determine "the destiny of the world."[33]

Far from troubling Stone, all of this proved reassuring. He believed once again that the United States must take a stand to stop the fascist states and chart a course for transformed international relations in the postwar period. U.S. intervention must proceed, he reasoned, in order that internationalism might have a chance. By mid-February, *The New Republic,* influenced by Michael Straight, its new Washington editor, had come around to the editorial position of *The Nation,* insisting that the Axis powers sought neither friends nor compromise, but reveled in war and desired their own world order.[34]

I. F. Stone maintained his missionary zeal in discussing the plight of Benito Mussolini. It was high time, he insisted in a *PM* editorial in February, that the United States establish an Italian government-in-exile and inform the people of Italy that "we are going to set them free."[35]

In April, Stone demanded that an embargo be placed on oil deliveries to the Far Eastern member of the Axis, while continuing to castigate "*Pravda*'s belly-crawling assurances" to the fascist states. He denounced the "rancid" unwillingness of U.S. oil companies to contribute to the national defense and declared that a government "too flabby" to curb their operations was incapable of winning the war. The following month he wrote that a government unable to organize industrially could not "organize the world for freedom." At the beginning of the month of June, he acknowledged that he now saw U.S. involvement in the war as inevitable.[36]

Certainly, Ralph Ingersoll, to Izzy's satisfaction, thought this was the case. As early as midspring, Ingersoll had called a staff meeting at which he announced "that *PM* was about to go to war." Soon boldfaced headlines in *PM* read "FASCISTS ARE WINNING: WHAT ARE WE GOING TO DO ABOUT IT?" and "Our Conclusion: WE'RE IN IT." Ingersoll wrote that "the total war" threatened by the fascists had already begun. And he insisted that if war alone could extinguish fascist aggression, "then war it will be."[37]

Izzy, at this point, determined to take some time off work and complete an in-depth study of the defense program. He turned to a friend of his, Archibald MacLeish, the poet and librarian of Congress, who provided special facilities for Izzy to work on his manuscript. The research he and his brother Lou had carried out the previous spring now came in handy, with Izzy acknowledging in his new book that humankind appeared to be instinctually "quarrelsome." Thus, the German people, he wrote, must not be perceived as "monsters"; nor should Nazism be seen as racially induced. Nevertheless, in *Business as Usual,* which came out at the end of the summer, Stone affirmed that this was "an anti-Fascist war." He was able to do so unequivocally now that the Communist state was back on the side of the angels—a far happier circumstance for this perennial Popular Fronter— following the German invasion of the Soviet Union.[38]

A united front of capitalists, workers, and engineers, Stone believed, must come together on behalf of the defense effort and discover how the United States might be reordered. Happily, through "co-operative industrial democracy," Americans could then experience "central planning without central despotism," while avoiding exploitation and retaining needed incentives for private initiative.[39]

Lewis Corey in *The Nation* proclaimed *Business as Usual* "timely" and a tale told "with superb journalistic skill." Michael Straight in *The New Republic* called it "an admirable analysis" of the defense program. A brief note in the *Management Review,* on the other hand, declared that notwithstanding Stone's occasional "bull's eye . . . his position well to the left of center sometimes distorts his aim." And Dwight Macdonald, writing in the *Partisan Review,* termed him "an American left New Dealer" who failed to appreciate that it was Roosevelt who had turned the defense program over to big businessmen. Still, Macdonald praised Stone as "an excellent reporter" whose Washington reports had for some time now provided "the only bit of journalistic *terra firma* in that slushy mushy quagmire of liberal yearnings the *Nation* has become." Thus, at the very least, *Business as Usual* seemed to have partly escaped the fate of other works published by Modern Age Books—being ignored by reviewers altogether.[40]

In spite of the generally favorable reviews it received and although it made the *New York Times*'s bestseller list for the capital, *Business as Usual* proved to be no financial windfall for I. F. Stone. As he indicated in a letter to Freda

Kirchwey dated September 25, fiscal problems hit home yet again. He was several hundred dollars in arrears following a vacation that might well have involved a visit to Philadelphia to see Katy, once more suffering from bouts of depression. Household expenses had eaten up the three hundred dollars he had received from *PM* for a series of special reports on the defense program. And now, for a time, owing to financial constraints, *PM* was unable to accept any more of his work. That was unfortunate because he had often been able to pick up an easy twenty or thirty dollars by knocking out a quick story that was inappropriate for *The Nation* but welcomed by the New York tabloid. Consequently, he attempted to sell an article on the financing of small business enterprises outside of his usual journalistic haunts. Despite Kirchwey's suggestion that Izzy remove "all unkind remarks about everybody and any hint of leftness from his work," *Reader's Digest* declined to publish it. But Izzy did collaborate with Philip Murray, John Brophy, and James Carey on *The C.I.O. and National Defense,* a pamphlet that laid out the union's position on the mobilization effort.[41]

W hile Stone now lined up as an ardent interventionist, he remained concerned about the possible domestic repercussions of U.S. involvement in another world war. He worried that repression might follow, as it so often did in the midst of martial endeavors. This was a matter of great concern for Izzy, who had frequently articulated that the rights of all—including despised far leftists and far rightists—must be protected. In the twenties, he had spoken out in the case of Sacco and Vanzetti, whom he saw as being persecuted because of their prounion and anarchist beliefs. In the thirties, he had argued that the Bill of Rights must extend even to those viewed as political pariahs, such as Communists and fascists. While on the *Philadelphia Record,* he and Sam Grafton had insisted that the Constitution must be applied "to those with whom we disagree. Exceptions are the first step toward tyranny." After all, even Hitler, Mussolini, and Stalin, he had written, allowed gladhanders to agree with what they had to say.[42]

Upon switching to the *New York Post,* Stone had proceeded to support broad constitutional protections for unpopular American far rightists. The right-wing "lunatic fringe," he had admitted, was annoying and perhaps even dangerous, but he declared it to be "part of the price we pay for democracy." Anti-Nazi legislation, he had insisted, would both demonstrate a lack of faith in American ideals and institutions and establish dangerous precedents.[43]

His belief in an expansive civil libertarian approach was one that Izzy adhered to during the greater part of his career. In this area in particular, his stance was virtually unique among his fellow intellectuals and those positioned on the American political left. And yet, for a time at least, he started to make exceptions (albeit fewer of them than did his colleagues and compatriots) regarding the activities, associations, and even the speech of the far right. Such a stance might have been somewhat understandable given the charged nature of the times but was no less inexcusable for one who understood so well that political liberty could not be divisible.

After working for the Institute for Propaganda Analysis, Stone, in a series of unsigned editorial paragraphs in *The Nation,* had urged that the "Fascist overtones" of an organization such as the Associated Farmers should be highlighted by both the U.S. Congress and the members of the journalistic profession. Angered that Roosevelt had been accused of dictatorial designs in the midst of the Court-packing controversy, Stone had beseeched Congress to shed light on "all of the dark corners of the campaign." In discussing an attack by veterans of the First World War upon a meeting of the German-American Bund, he had insisted that legislation and exposure, not vigilantism, must be wielded against political armies. Believing as he did that the House Committee on Un-American Activities chaired by Martin Dies was little inclined to take up such a task, he had called instead for a reputable, liberal examination of fascist activities. He was particularly insistent that accusations of ties between U.S. big business interests and the German Nazis be looked into.[44]

The bitterly anti-Communist and anti–New Deal HCUAC was itself an investigative committee of the sort Stone was calling for. HCUAC had come into existence with the support of liberal congressman Samuel Dickstein, who sought to unveil the practices of race-baiting, hate-mongering groups. Dickstein had joined forces with the right-wing Dies, who planned to search for "subversive and un-American propaganda." As matters turned out, of course, HCUAC sought reds in places both high and low, while affording little attention to the far right. HCUAC involved itself in a search for leftists of all kinds and eventually helped to narrow the political spectrum, while destroying reputations and lives and doing great damage to the country as a whole.[45]

The worsening state of international affairs and his hatred of fascism now compelled Stone to support a congressional investigation of fanatical rightists. War appeared increasingly imminent, war brought on by the rightwing agressor states. Guiding those nations was fascist ideology, which, like a plague, threatened to wipe out everything it touched. The democracies and socialist Russia, as well as rationality, liberal values, and the possibility of socialism all seemed to be in a more precarious position than ever. Thus, Stone agreed that for a limited time, certain restraints should be placed on those who subscribed to fascist thought at home. As he saw it, all of the advances the Western world had made since the Middle Ages were at stake.

Nevertheless, when the American mobilization began, Stone worried that war might usher in repression, as was frequently the case; repression, he feared, that would be targeted against the political left. He was particularly troubled by the actions of certain government operatives and agencies that promised to amass power in their hands as had Woodrow Wilson's Committee on Public Information during World War I. The governmental bodies he distrusted most of all were J. Edgar Hoover's FBI and Martin Dies's HCUAC. The Federal Bureau of Investigation responded in kind, keeping a close watch on I. F. Stone, as well as on Freda Kirchwey and undoubtedly other colleagues of theirs at *The Nation*. In fact, the FBI, which had a file on Izzy in the mid-1930s in response to his editorials critical of the agency, continued to compile what later became a massive dossier on Izzy—eventually some twenty-six hundred pages in all. Indeed, it dwarfed the files held on World War II literary contemporaries such as Dashiell Hammett, Lillian Hellman, Ernest Hemingway, Archibald Mac-Leish, Dorothy Parker, and John Steinbeck.[46]

In an unsigned editorial in *The Nation* that appeared in early 1940, Stone complained about "our lawless G-men" who held files on Herbert Hoover, labor boss John L. Lewis, Supreme Court Justice Harlan Stone, and Senator Burton Wheeler. Did J. Edgar Hoover, Stone asked, aspire to become "an American Himmler?" The FBI, with its apparent disdain for the rule of law, he charged, was starting to behave like Hitler's Gestapo and the OGPU, Stalin's secret police.[47]

Freda Kirchwey, editor-in-chief of *The Nation*, seemed to encourage the very kinds of analyses that had resulted in FBI surveillance of Izzy, herself, and the journal. Her letter to Izzy on February 11, 1941, opened with the observation that he had invariably "pretended to be interested in the Constitution and all its guarantees. . . . Here is your chance to prove it!"[48]

Izzy proceeded to discuss "the peculiar kind of Americanism" displayed by HCUAC and the FBI. In Germany, he noted, one dared not question Hitler. In Russia, Stalin was above criticism. In Italy, Mussolini's word was law. In the United States, Martin Dies's committee, in "smearing, terrorizing and pillorying" its opponents, practiced its own brand of "*lèse majesté*." But it was the FBI, Stone feared, that remained the bastion of rabid anti–New Dealers who might someday perform "a sinister role" in the United States.[49]

While others on the left viewed the FBI and HCUAC with equal disdain, Izzy's position on governmental prosecution of the Trotskyist Socialist Workers Party was lonely and prophetic. On July 26, barely a month into the German invasion of Soviet Russia, Stone condemned the indictment handed down against leaders of the SWP for purportedly having violated provisions of the 1940 Smith Alien and Sedition Act. The Smith Act made it illegal to "advocate, abet, advise, or teach the duty, necessity, desirability, or propriety of overthrowing or destroying any government" through violent means. While the American Communist Party applauded the governmental action against its sectarian rival, Stone warned, "You cannot kill an idea by putting its spokesmen in jail."⁵⁰

In an ensuing piece in *The Nation,* Stone did not dispute the fact that a government had the right to defend itself against both overt acts and the expression of ideas that might result in disorder or revolution. He was willing—although not without certain misgivings—to accept the "clear and present danger" formula devised by Justices Oliver Wendell Holmes, Jr., and Louis D. Brandeis. But "this political gnat," he insisted, hardly threatened the viability of the U.S. government. Rather, its leaders had been imprisoned for words alone, much as their compatriots were being jailed in the Soviet Union.⁵¹

Stone later agreed in his column in *PM* that greater restrictions on freedom of speech and freedom of press could be made in wartime. Nevertheless, the test of the Supreme Court, he wrote, remained its willingness to defend the constitutional prerogatives of "the tiniest minority." And the prosecution of the Trotskyists, "the Ishmaelites of the Left," was simply unworthy of the U.S. government.⁵²

Throughout the war, Stone frequently and often admirably continued to condemn infringements on the constitutional rights of unpopular left-wing groups or individuals, such as Harry Bridges of the International Longshoreman's Union. In fact, Stone evidently helped sponsor the Citizens Committee and the Citizens Victory Committee for Bridges.⁵³

And yet there was, curiously, a blind side to Stone's reading of wartime civil liberties. In May 1942, for example, notwithstanding the herding of tens of thousands of Japanese-Americans and Japanese aliens into relocation camps, he proclaimed in the "Washington Notes" column of *The Nation* that the case against the Trotskyists was the only issue that "haunt[ed] our speeches about free government." At the tail end of the following year, he again condemned the government case against the sectarian leftists, arguing that the United States had never waged a war with fewer restrictions on personal freedoms. It was not until a full year later that Stone even addressed in print the issue of the internment of over 100,000. At that point, in an unsigned editorial examining Justice Black's opinion in the Korematsu case upholding the placement of Japanese-Americans in relocation centers, Stone did express concern over his old friend's declaration that "pressing public necessity" might allow for the curbing of the free movement of a particular racial group.⁵⁴

Stone's analysis of the issue of wartime civil liberties and that of Freda

Kirchwey were on still shakier grounds when it came to discussion of the supposedly milder treatment afforded American far rightists. In fact, as historian Sara Alpern has noted, Kirchwey, with the guns of war having been sounded once again, reasoned that the Constitution must not be employed "for the wiping out of the very rights it aimed to protect and our devotion to it should not lead us to commit national suicide."[55]

This was precisely the same argument others would make when the post-war red scare unfolded. The difference was that Kirchwey was speaking of those she saw as home-grown fascists, whereas anti-Communists applied that rationale to groups and individuals positioned on the left. Significantly, Izzy seemed to share his editor's perspective at least for a while; he did not appear to be merely dutifully following her lead, however reluctantly.

In an unsigned editorial published twenty-two months before the Japanese attack on Pearl Harbor, he followed up on Kirchwey's demand that legal shackles be placed on American fascists. Stone called not only for a "proper and constitutional" handling of paramilitary forces that were patterned after fascist troops but for legislation that would preclude racial or religious slander. In addition, he urged full exposure of the financial ties of all publications and organizations engaged in propaganda.[56]

The proposed measures were precisely the kind he would later oppose so bitterly when they came to be targeted against the activities, the associations, and the beliefs of individuals and groups on the left. What he again failed to appreciate was that dangerous precedents for the postwar period were being established, precedents which were, of course, very much in the American vein.

Freda Kirchwey, in another unsigned editorial dated March 28, 1942, went on to demand that the fascist press in the United States be suppressed. Pro-Nazi newspapers had to be curbed, *The Nation* insisted in a follow-up editorial note, regardless of whether they were sustained by Adolf Hitler or by Father Charles Coughlin, William Pelley, or Edward James Smythe—the latter three all considered to be "native fascists." And in response to a letter from ACLU founder Roger Baldwin that accused the journal of lacking faith in democracy, the editors of *The Nation* fervently supported Kirchwey's position.[57]

PM, with Ralph Ingersoll orchestrating a massive write-in campaign directed at the Department of Justice, also demanded the censoring of *Social Justice,* put out by Father Coughlin. Quoting from Abraham Lincoln, who had justified the suspension of constitutional rights during another wartime era, Ingersoll declared that the Radio Priest was slandering the U.S. commander-in-chief.[58]

Earlier in his career and later again, Izzy tendered his resignation following a dispute over an editorial position staked out by the publication for which he was working. There is no indication, however, that he ever considered doing so because of either the *The Nation*'s or *PM*'s attitude toward the right-wing press or because of Kirchwey's and Ingersoll's belief that, for a time at least, there should be a curbing of "civil-liberties-as-usual."[59]

That says a great deal, given Stone's concern about the state of political liberties in the United States. It indicates, once again, how much emotional capital he had invested in the antifascist struggle. It was a fight, he believed, that needed to be waged on all levels. In the period ahead, others would also argue for a concerted domestic and international campaign against an ideological menace perceived as diametrically opposed to fundamental American precepts. That ideology, of course, was not fascism but rather communism, the chief proponent of which was soon to be temporarily allied with the U.S. government.

But at this point, Stone appeared determined that the prosecution of "33 seditionists"—whom he dismissed as "pro-Axis termites"—be continued. Among the native fascists accused of conspiring on behalf of Adolf Hitler to cripple American military morale were right-wing ideologue Lawrence Dennis; anti-Semitic demagogue Gerald L. K. Smith; Elizabeth Dilling of *The Red Network* fame; German-American Bund leader William Kunze; and James True, creator of the "kike killer," a billy club that came in a special size for women. Stone's passion for the case was considered so great that Kirchwey felt it necessary to point out that conspiracy charges would not likely stand up against defendants who were not even tied to the German-American Bund or a like-mannered organization. Undaunted, Stone, in an unsigned editorial in *The Nation*, wondered aloud near the end of the war why "termites" such as Edward A. Rumely had been allowed to operate freely. Rumely was, after all, "a convicted German agent" who had done time for receiving funds from Kaiser Wilhelm in order to soil U.S. newspapers with "pro-German propaganda" during World War I. Presently, Rumely, in his position as executive secretary of Frank Gannett's Committee for Constitutional Government, was hurling scurrilous invectives against President Roosevelt, hated even more by the Nazis than Wilson had been by the German monarch. Was it so surprising, then, Stone asked, that the Nazis refused to take seriously the possibility of resistance by the democracies?[60]

After a mistrial, the government determined to retry the American fascists, but when Assistant Attorney General John Rogge was removed from the case as William Power Maloney had been earlier, Stone exploded. With the Supreme Court indicating that a conviction would invariably be overturned, he asked why classic civil libertarian arguments were being used to free these fanatics, while the sedition convictions of the Trotskyists were allowed to stand?[61]

I. F. Stone's attitude toward the defendants marred a civil libertarian record that remained noteworthy still. The ACLU, for its part, strongly condemned the government action against the far rightists from its inception, while historians have determined that neither a conspiracy nor an intent to disrupt the military was ever proven. But most significant of all, the case involved the prosecution of a despised political group by means of sweeping conspiratorial charges, the kind of governmental action Stone had so often denounced in the past and would again in the future. In fact, the accused were being tried for Nazi-styled views aired before the United States officially became a combatant. Eventually, a dismissal was granted, with the appellate court determining that the indictment itself was a travesty of justice.[62]

But generally, the warnings Stone delivered during the war years regarding the indivisibility of civil liberties proved acutely prophetic. On March 3, 1945, in an article in *The Nation*, he discussed the decision by the Department of War to discriminate no longer against soldiers considered to be Communists. Such a practice had been especially absurd, he believed, for Communist fighters everywhere had honored themselves in the battle against fascism. "Discrimination on the basis of political beliefs—unless they were the same as "an enemy's in war time"—he believed, would weaken the very fabric of a free society. Anti-Communist leftists who thought differently and determined to go after their progressive rivals, he warned, were only foolhardy. For should such practices be allowed, "the right will set the standards, and the standards will be broad enough to encompass leftists of many varieties."[63]

Just as the threat of fascism compelled I. F. Stone to adopt an unfamiliar position regarding a military buildup and U.S. intervention, that same peril and then the reality of war caused him to shift ground on occasion where civil liberties were concerned. This was a matter of no small import, for Izzy's record concerning freedom of speech, freedom of the press, and political association was a long one already and one for which he would later be much applauded. To his credit and unlike American Communists, his defense of civil liberties did extend leftward, to include the unpopular Trotskyists. But for a time, Stone, like Freda Kirchwey, Ralph Ingersoll, and the other editors of both *The Nation* and *PM*, appeared willing to accept something of an abridgement of protection under the Bill of Rights for those he saw as stationed on the far right side of the political spectrum.

When left-wingers of any stripe were involved, Izzy was a stalwart civil libertarian, something of an absolutist. Where political liberties were concerned, he apparently subscribed to the notion of "no enemies to one's left." His record regarding right-wingers was admittedly a good deal more complex. He appeared to feel that the viewpoint of the far right, delivered in the middle of an antifascist struggle, could simply not be tolerated. Consequently, whether through legislative exposure, court proceedings, or congressional action, the American right, he believed, had to be silenced. What Izzy seemed unable to appreciate was that such a call did itself establish a dangerous precedent that could and would return to haunt the left and the American nation in the future.

6 Fighting the Good War

T he war years brought greater respectability to *The Nation* and *PM*, both of which appeared to be lined up on the left side of the often-shifting New Deal coalition. Eleanor Roosevelt subscribed to both publications and invited staff members from *PM*, including Izzy Stone, to the White House one evening. In her newspaper column, "My Day," she asked her readers: "I wonder if *PM* is becoming to you as interesting a paper as I find it?" There was hardly a day, Mrs. Roosevelt indicated, when she failed to encounter something in *PM* worth reading. The president considered *PM* publisher Ralph Ingersoll a confidant and even attempted, albeit unsuccessfully, to dissuade him from entering the armed forces. As FDR saw it—and Ingersoll for a time did as well—the newsman could do more for the war effort out of his *PM* offices than in uniform. Along with the First Family, other readers of *PM* included Vice-President Henry Wallace; Secretary of the Interior Harold Ickes; Secretary of War Frank Knox; Senator Harry Truman; Wendell Willkie, FDR's 1940 Republican opponent; Albert Einstein; J. Edgar Hoover; and Thomas Mann, the great German novelist.[1]

At war's end, the circulation of *The Nation*, like that of *The New Republic*, passed the forty-thousand mark. More significant, those who subscribed to the journals tended to be well-educated urban professionals who carried a certain amount of weight in their respective communities. And among the American intelligentsia in general, the two magazines were perceived as particularly influential.[2]

President Roosevelt, Charles de Gaulle, head of the French Committee of National Liberation, and Eduard Beneš, president of the now interred Czechoslovakian republic, all saw fit to mail warm letters to Freda Kirchwey, editor of *The Nation*, on the occasion of a twenty-five-year testimonial dinner held in her honor. Among those who sponsored the tribute to Kirchwey were Hugo Black, John Dewey, John Dos Passos, Albert Einstein, Lillian Hellman, Walter Lippmann, and Thomas Mann. Singing her praises to the gathered throng of twelve hundred at New York's Commodore Hotel were former presidential adviser Thurman Arnold; Dorothy Thompson, columnist for the *New York Post;* and Reinhold Niebuhr, chairman of the liberal Union for Democratic Action.[3]

Leading New Dealers such as Tom Corcoran and Ben Cohen reportedly considered the pressure which *The Nation* had executed against "the defense profiteers"—much of that the result of investigative work by Izzy Stone—to be taken seriously in administration circles. Not surprisingly, then, the inner Brain Trust often provided invaluable information, frequently off-the-record, for *The Nation's* reporters, including Stone. Among those who readily spoke with him behind closed doors in the sanctity of their own offices were Corcoran, Cohen, Felix Frankfurter, Archibald MacLeish, and Secretary of the Interior Ickes (until the two had a falling out). Thus, during the latter Roosevelt years, *The Nation, PM,* and staffers such as Stone were "sort of, in a way, part of the establishment," a novel and, as matters turned out, short-lived experience for him.[4]

And yet even during this period he was heard to complain about lack of access to the White House. Reporters from *Newsweek* and *Time* were freely admitted, as were "journalistic sightseers," he complained to Freda Kirchwey, so "why in hell can't [the] *Nation* get in?" He found it ironic that Kirchwey was "good enuff and important enough" to elicit progressive support for the president, but wondered "why in hell can't your representative get credentials?" Stephen Early, Roosevelt's press secretary, informed Kirchwey that Stone had been welcomed on several occasions but that presidential conferences were restricted to Washington correspondents from the daily newspapers.[5]

Izzy later reflected that even in the midst of the world war, government officials, including members of the president's own cabinet, were afraid to be seen in public with reporters such as himself. This was not surprising, for many government agencies had "their own little gestapos" which sought to find out which employees were leaking inside information to journalists. Thus, there was the need for a type of underground comprising left-of-center journalists and government operatives. A liberal reporter in wartime Washington, Izzy believed, had to function as "a kind of guerrilla warrior, watching for a chance to get at the truth, making a foray when opportunity offers, succeeding, despite the efforts to keep certain kinds of information secret." Nearly two decades later, Stone employed almost identical language in describing the plight of the independent journalist in Cold War America.[6]

But for now, despite their still vaguely netherworld status, reporters for publications like *The Nation* and *PM,* Izzy believed, had to use every means at their disposal to support the war effort. At the same time, as persistent advocates of an antifascist united front, as proponents of an American Middle Way, and as intellectuals who believed in political commitment, *The Nation-PM* editors and columnists were determined that the war be waged as an ideological battle. Feeling as strongly as he did about this, and very much in character, Izzy consequently clashed with less ideologically driven administration officials on more than one occasion.

T o Stone's delight, *The Nation* by the fall of 1941 became more overtly antifascist than ever. In early September, Freda Kirchwey named Norman Angell, Jonathan Daniels, Louis Fischer, Reinhold Niebuhr, and Julio Alvarez Del Vayo as contributing editors. These men were not merely well-known writers, she indicated, but also active participants in the many-sided struggle to preserve freedom and create a democratic world, a fight to which *The Nation* was unequivocally committed.[7]

Stone was perfectly comfortable with the editorial position of the journal, since he viewed the war as a means to erect a new international order that would be guided by Wilsonian ideals such as political democracy, constitutionalism, antimilitarism, and anticolonialism. But none of this would be possible, he believed, if the Axis states continued their expansionist drives in Europe, Asia, and the Middle East. At some point, he was certain, the United States would have to join up with both England and Russia in an antifascist alliance. Thus, he envisioned the Popular Front as resurfacing, fighting the good fight, and leading the way for the global transformation he saw as so necessary.

Publisher Kirchwey of *The Nation*, happily in Stone's eyes, appeared to be following the lead of *The New Republic*, which had recently urged the U.S. government to issue an official declaration of war. Izzy, the Washington editor of *The Nation*, again expressed concerns about the pace and direction of U.S. foreign policy. Worrying about the possible appeasement of Japan, Stone asked how could "the common people" around the globe take to heart President Roosevelt's pronouncement of the Four Freedoms—of speech, of worship, from want, and from fear—and how much stock could they place in the ability of the United States to shape a better world, if "blundering, old-style politics" were not discarded.[8]

Troubled by the "Washington Zigzag," Stone also condemned the oil deliveries still being made to Franco's Spain and the unwillingness of some to assist the Soviets. A different Spanish policy, he suggested, offered a chance to prove that the United States really intended to establish a new democratic world order. Moreover, he worried that many Americans failed to recognize that if Russia were to fall, an avalanche of appeasement in Western Europe might even endanger democracy at home.[9]

Colonel William J. Donovan's secret agents in the Office of Strategic Services could help the cause too, Stone argued, by carrying out the type of "revolutionary, democratic fifth-column work" the United States had done during World War I in Central Europe. Operations of that sort, he wrote, would help to construct an anti-Nazi network. Intelligence gathering or covert operations thus troubled him not at all, provided that they helped to win the war and were directed at fascist elements, self-professed or not.[10]

The official declaration of war by the United States which followed the Japanese attack on Pearl Harbor therefore came as something of a relief to him. Another world war was at hand, Stone declared, and was "better fought now when we still have allies left." He expressed gratitude that President Roosevelt was lined up with democratic and progressive forces.[11]

Izzy appeared certain that an antifascist crusade lay ahead. What he hoped for was that fascism would be eradicated entirely, the seeds of reform planted both at home and abroad, and international relations reordered. At the time, none of these notions seemed particularly fanciful. Later, they would appear more than a little utopian, part of the failed legacy of the American Old Left.

R ecognizing that wartime policies not only affected the fight against fascism but also the possible future course of world events, Izzy remained troubled by any number of administration officials and actions. He was regularly exercised by the apparent disinclination of the State Department, the OSS, and U.S. corporations to adopt more of a hardline stance against fascist and collaborationist elements. He decried State's "incorrigible determination to play pat-a-cake with Vichy" and its unwillingness to recognize Charles de Gaulle's Free French forces. This suggested to him that the Department of State remained the final bastion of appeasement. He urged the firing of Secretary of State Cordell Hull and insisted that the "undemocratic little clique of decayed pseudo-aristocrats and backsliding liberals" at the helm of State were not up to leading "a democratic crusade."[12]

In November 1942, Stone warned that the fight to reshape Europe was already in its infancy. Unfortunately, there were those in the State Department and the OSS who championed "new regimes far enough to the right" to shield corporate interests. Most big businessmen now recognized that Adolf Hitler had to be deposed, Stone maintained, but still wanted the trains to run on time. The Resistance, he warned, desired something else again.[13]

So too did Izzy Stone, who believed that the roots of right-wing totalitarianism had to be eradicated from fascist-controlled lands. Were this not to happen, he feared, all the pain and suffering, all the anguish and loss caused by the war would be for nought. Yes, Der Fuhrer and Il Duce had to be removed from power, but even that was not enough. For unless the source of their support were attacked "root and branch," it could reappear once again. And at the very least, the possibility of remaking the fascist-afflicted lands as well as the remaining democracies would be all the more difficult.

Thus, at a Washington press conference in January 1943, Izzy took advantage of the occasion to confront Secretary Hull about U.S. dealings with

Vichy France. Was the State Department, he asked, following up on President Roosevelt's request that Nazi-inspired laws be repealed in North Africa? Rather than responding to the question, however, an angry Cordell Hull demanded to know the name of the reporter. When Izzy replied, "Stone," Hull retorted: "You have some other name, too, have you not?" That provoked Representative John Rankin of Mississippi to take to the floor of the House on February 1 to denounce Izzy roundly. Were his colleagues aware, Rankin began, that "a man by the name of I. F. Stone of *PM*, I think his name is Feinstein," was inciting the "crackpots" who were going after the secretary of state? The "crackpots" Rankin referred to were, in the words of his colleague Martin Dies of Texas, attempting to produce hard feelings between "the white and colored races." The following day, Rankin again laid into this "Bernstein or Feinstein" whom he damned as "one of the pen pushers on this communistic publication known as *PM*."[14]

Robert Bendiner, Izzy's colleague at *The Nation*, recognized "how hot under the collar" he must have been following the attack by Secretary Hull which had spurred Rankin on. Izzy, acting on Bendiner's suggestion, condemned Hull in an unsigned editorial for his "petty attack" which played into the hands of "Congressional Jew-baiters" such as John Rankin. It was disgusting, the editorial declared, that a high government official would resort to "a cheap and childish retort" to avoid genuine journalistic queries.[15]

While *The Nation* quite naturally defended one of its own from such scurrilous attacks, Freda Kirchwey was herself more than a little perturbed by Izzy's lack of tact and discretion in handling certain assignments. She was also somewhat put off by the fact that his reading of administration policies often appeared to be at odds with that of other editorial board members. Thus, once again, both his ideological slant and his volatile temperament made him a controversial figure, even among those he worked most closely with. "You are much more anti–New Deal in general," she wrote to Izzy, than the rest of *The Nation* staff. At one point, she indicated that she had deleted his concluding remarks from an article discussing Attorney General Francis Biddle's handling of the Bridges case. True, she admitted, *The Nation* naturally demanded far more of those few government officials it regarded as liberals. Nevertheless, "I do think . . . that we should give the guy a chance." In another instance, she warned Izzy not to turn Secretary of the Interior Harold Ickes "into the opposite of a sacred cow, whatever that would be—a sacrificial goat perhaps. Don't make him into one of those little images that primitive people stick pins into to express their hatred of somebody." Like Biddle, Ickes *was* a liberal and thus Izzy was prone to criticize him more harshly when he went "off the track." While this was perfectly natural, Kirchwey continued, it was simply not politic. "Abuse or even extreme moralizing," she declared, did not help matters. The bottom line, she indicated, was that "we cannot afford to throw overboard too lightly the few progressives we have in high office."[16]

On another occasion, Izzy, deeply upset about the way Keith Hutchinson had edited his work, insisted that he had proved willing "to meet the desk halfway on things like that" in the past. But the removal of his concluding passage made him appear, he worried, like "another of those cowardly correspondents" fearful of Harold Ickes.[17]

Editors, the subjects of his pointed interviews, and readers alike were all annoyed, exasperated, and infuriated at various points with Izzy's work. This was due to the fact there was often such an ideologically charged cast to his writings and because it so often seemed that Izzy was simply spoiling for a fight. He seemed to enjoy provoking others, whether that involved an attempt to get them to rethink their positions, question public policy, or just accede to his wishes. He was capable of being quite charming when he chose to be, but he could just as easily be stubborn, irascible, and ill-tempered.

In the summer of 1943, an obviously agitated Stone expressed dismay over the strangely subdued reaction displayed by Secretary Hull and President Roosevelt to the fall of Benito Mussolini. Stone was troubled by the apparent American unwillingness to push for broad-scale reform in Italy or anywhere else. Instead, the United States appeared ready to deal "with any of crooks at the top except the full-fledged, fully labeled Nazis and Fascists"; *The New Republic* soon delivered a similarly embittered analysis. Certain State Department officials, Stone complained, were now arguing that Europeans must choose "between reaction and Communism," a message heard earlier in Italy, Germany, and Spain. He worried that the lessons of history had not been learned and wondered what that might portend for the future.[18]

As the war in Europe wound to a close, Stone warned even more forcefully that the fascist-marred lands had to be completely recast. At the tail end of 1944, he insisted that the power of the great German industrialists and landowners had to be broken and Germany disarmed. In January 1945, he discussed the fate of *Il Messagero*, a "Fascist and pro-Nazi" newspaper owned by the Perrone brothers, who just happened to be the "loyal supporters, servants and collaborators of our enemies." Members of the Italian underground and German anti-Nazis were in no mood to trouble themselves, he pointed out, about " 'freedom of the press' or 'property rights' for those who supported the . . . terror, shared its profits, and spread its propaganda poisons." Stone dismissed out of hand the notion that the murderers of Matteotti were in some way less guilty than the assassins of Carl von Ossietzky, the German pacifist, editor, and 1935 Nobel Peace Prize recipient. He considered equally absurd the contention that big businessmen like the Perrones—who claimed that the bottom line on the lira had compelled them to back Mussolini—should be treated more leniently than the fascist true believers. Such talk was "treason" to future generations, exploded Stone, for "the upper middle class canaille like the Perrones . . . [which] egged Fascism and Nazism on to power, secretly subsidizing its leaders and then openly profiting from their success, will do it all over again if they get the chance." The Perrones must be jailed and immediately, Stone indicated, but if the European underground should determine it was "safest to shoot the Perrones, we won't send flowers."[19]

This was strong language indeed and indicated how deeply Izzy felt about the necessity of fully extinguishing all vestiges of fascism. Fascism was like a cancer, he believed, against which society had to be inoculated. Anyone who had been tainted by the ideological disease had to be dealt with or it would reappear. The kinds of protections against abuse of government authority which liberal democracies could afford in peacetime, he seemed to reason, war-torn and fascist-plagued lands could not.

During the month of February, Stone, in addressing the question of war criminality, repeatedly indicated just how strongly he felt about the issue. "The Hitler Gang," he insisted, must not be allowed to go scot free as had the Junker aggressors a generation earlier. Both justice, pure and simple, and the fate of millions still under the yoke of the German Third Reich and of future generations, he wrote, very well might be at stake. A determined stand by the Allies could discourage the most diehard Nazis and Japanese from heading underground to make plans to do it all over again.[20]

I. F. Stone thus belived that World War II *was* the Good War, a righteous battle, the vehicle through which fascism could be obliterated. Consequently, at times his work took on a crusading tone, which could be biting and caustic, angry and impassioned. Moreover, like an ideologically driven crusader, he was inclined to cast aspersions on those he considered not as true to the cause of antifascism as himself. He was given to accusing isolationists of aiding the enemy and of being cryptofascists themselves. He continued to view the war as a fight pitting nations that represented the best humankind had to offer against countries in which the forces of darkness had come to predominate. Consequently, words were a weapon, Stone argued, that could be employed by intellectuals to sustain the Grand Alliance and besmirch its opponents.

Soon others demonstrated their agreement with such a notion, hurling abuse on those seen as not zealous enough in their determination to rid the

United States and the world of another kind of totalitarian menace. They too viewed critics of U.S. foreign policy as giving comfort to this nation's greatest foe and were angered that such covert "subversives" were allowed to remain as unindicted coconspirators. They too argued that intellectuals must join in a new ideological crusade.

Although Izzy's ideological perspective sometimes marred his editorial analyses, a number of his wartime writings, no matter how heated, proved to be remarkably prescient. Certainly that was the case concerning the Grand Alliance, which was ever so controversial. He feared that British and American reluctance to aid their Soviet ally could cripple the war effort and plant the seeds of distrust that would destroy the possibility of international cooperation in the postwar period.

Stone was nearly beside himself that a second military front on the European continent was so long in coming. It was appalling, he indicated, that while Russian soldiers "heroically" fought for the United States as well as their homeland, his own countrymen "haggled over . . . patents," thus denying the Soviet Union crucial oil processing and refining techniques. He found still more disturbing suggestions that the Red and German armies be allowed to bleed each other dry.[21]

But most troubling of all was what he feared to be the opening stages of yet another anti-Communist campaign. This was something he had worried about since World War II had begun, for he recognized that just such a phenomenon had destroyed Wilson's quest for a peaceful world order and provided fertile ground on which fascism could grow. Concerned about postwar Eastern Europe, certain State Department officials, he recognized, evidently believed in "old-fashioned power politics" and sought buffer states to separate Russia from the West. Others seemed determined to erect "a new *cordon sanitaire* against Bolshevism, through restoration of the Hapsburg monarchy." Then there were those in the boardrooms of corporate America who envisioned an open-door policy for U.S. trade and commerce. What everybody wanted, Stone wrote, was Russia's abandonment of its claim to the Baltics and Eastern Poland, a position Stalin had indicated was in no way negotiable.[22]

Like the editors of both *The Nation* and *The New Republic*, Stone seemed to consider the Soviet Union's insistence on secure borders to be a reasonable one. No longer did he warn of Stalin's designs on Eastern Europe or liken him to Hitler, but instead now accepted Russian demands for friendly neighbors to the west, in place of the profascist governments that had come to power in the interwar period. Perhaps Izzy's change of heart was due in part to Russia's role in liberating much of Eastern Europe.

Believing in the need to wipe out fascism completely and the progressive nature of the Soviet Union—it had "made Communism work"—Stone consequently welcomed the early appearance of the Red Army in the war-torn streets of Germany. "The Red Army, like an avenging juggernaut," he exulted, was ushering in the final days of Adolf Hitler, the Third Reich, and Nazism. There must be millions in Eastern and Central Europe, he declared, who "can hear a music sweeter than our most ecstatic imaginings in the roar and clatter, and tramp of the Red Army's advance." And he suggested that it might well prove fortunate that Berlin had first been liberated by those who did not view Nazism as a theoretical matter only. Moscow, fortunately, was not given to that strange brand of "legalism" evidently afflicting British and U.S. policymakers.[23]

Again, Stone believed that legal niceties were not necessary when it came to dealing with fascists. Swift and certain punishment should be their lot, he reasoned, rather than convoluted trials which would prevent justice from being carried out. And who better to ensure that the fascists were dealt with as they should be, he argued, than the Soviets.

To that end, in an unsigned editorial in *The Nation*, he appeared to justify a Russian takeover of Eastern Europe. He argued that the placement of non-Polish peoples behind Russian lines was to their advantage. No longer would they experience racial discrimination—and neither would the Poles, he insisted—while the peasants in the Baltics would be afforded greater opportunities than they had been.[24]

Following the incarceration of sixteen leaders of the Polish underground in a Soviet prison, Stone, with apparent encouragement from Freda Kirchwey, urged American progressives "to keep their shirts on." After all, he pointed out, the sixteen were considered responsible for the deaths of over a hundred members of the Red Army; furthermore, at least two were "anti-Semites and Fascists," or so the Lublin government had claimed.[25]

The handing out of relatively "light" sentences appeared to satisfy him, Max Lerner of *PM,* and the editors of *The New Republic*. How much "justice" was afforded the defendants or the nature of their "guilt," however, was certainly questionable. And the language Stone employed in defending the arrests of the sixteen Poles—there was that twin pair of "anti-Semites and Fascists," he emphasized—was fairly remarkable. Never before and never again would Izzy display such a seemingly cavalier attitude about elementary matters of justice or defend the prosecution of a group of individuals because of the political perspective of some of the accused alone.[26]

Thus, like so many others, including Freda Kirchwey, Michael Straight of *The New Republic,* Henry Luce of *Life* magazine, and Vice-President Henry Wallace, Stone not only championed the Grand Alliance but was caught up in the Sovietmania of the period. He worried that negative press concerning the Russian ally might endanger the entire war effort. But his rose-colored reading of Soviet actions enabled others to dismiss his reports completely. At the very least, it led critics to accuse him and others sympathetic to the Soviet Union of employing double standards when it came to evaluating Communist and non-Communist actions.

This was unfortunate because I. F. Stone's concern that anticommunism might guide U.S. and British foreign policymakers did indeed come to pass. The Soviet Union quickly supplanted Nazi Germany as the major antagonist of the leading Western nations, with communism now viewed as little more than "red fascism." And American strategists in particular became determined to thwart what they perceived as the international red menace.

The soon-to-emerge anti-Communist fixation ensured that the kind of world order that Woodrow Wilson, Izzy's old hero, had once hoped for remained quixotic. Along with Freda Kirchwey, Michael Straight, and Henry Wallace, once again, Stone favored a concert of nations, with the great Allied powers bound to serve as policing agents. He did so despite recognizing that any international organization employing collective security of this kind was hardly egalitarian. Although he believed that it was easy to wax sentimental about less powerful states, he asked his readers to consider, for example, how the United States would respond should Panama insist on a return of the Canal or should a Cuban-German entente result, a striking analysis in view of what lay ahead.[27]

Stone did warn that the failure of the United Nations, whose opening sessions he attended in San Francisco along with Alexander Uhl of *PM* and Bruce Bliven of *The New Republic,* would transform small nations into pawns in a kind of global chess game. Moreover, he recognized that the war was reshaping international relations, bringing to a halt more than a century of European imperialism, and stoking the flames of anticolonialism.

Heavily outnumbered white Europeans, he agreed, could not permanently rule "hundreds of millions of brown and yellow people." And he pointed out that neither a return of "the prewar *status quo*"—"The *status quo ante* wasn't good enough"—nor the displacing of the old white rulers with "new yellow Tuans" would do in the end. What had to be realized, he insisted, was that the obliteration of fascism was resulting in demands for freedom worldwide. And on "inflated expectations and morning-after disillusionment," revolutionary fires were fed.[28]

Stone seemed to have mixed feelings about that very possibility. He had long worried about the effects of revolutionary action in depression-stricken industrial lands but recognized the immensity of social, economic, and political problems in Asia, Africa, the Middle East, and Latin America. He did frequently reason that revolution was sometimes a necessary last resort, when the possibility of peaceful reform was absent.

He saw "a people's war" and "a rural New Deal rather than Sovietism" being conducted by the Chinese Communists, whom he compared with

American Revolutionary War heroes. But he warned that should the Indian anticolonialist Mahatma Gandhi—"their Lenin, their George Washington, and something more besides, something of an Indian Jesus"—die in jail, belief in his principle of nonviolence might also perish in that land. And a "sword in the hands of 400,000,000 people," he prophesied, would pose something of a problem.[29]

According to Stone, the world powers had two options in dealing with the colonial problem. One involved the invoking of "prejudice and race hatred, Fascist style"; the other, the inclusion "of the colonial and colored peoples into full equality and partnership." If the wrong choice were made, the rift between Russia and the West would widen and the United States itself be condemned as imperialistic and reactionary.[30]

What I. F. Stone rightfully feared, of course, did indeed take place. As the postwar era wound on, many in the developing world came to view the United States as the leading counterrevolutionary nation. The all-too-apparent hostility exhibited by Third Worlders, in turn, only further convinced U.S. policymakers that such "inimical" sorts were determined to do America harm. As the Grand Alliance came apart, the United Nations failed to stand as the embodiment of internationalism which Stone had hoped it might become. Instead, the UN was soon ensnared in the Cold War antics of East and West, while the smaller countries were alternately seen as fertile territory for Soviet-sponsored communism or American-backed reaction.

On the domestic scene, the antifascist fervor of the World War II era gave way to an equally strong passion, shared by American policymakers and the public alike, to eradicate yet another authoritarian peril. That passion fueled the bitter anti-Communist campaigns of the late 1940s and the 1950s.

When this ideological shift took place, the standing of former supporters of the Grand Alliance and opponents of the Cold War plummeted. No longer was someone like Izzy Stone able to consider himself, in whatever fashion, as "part of the establishment"; nor were publications like *The Nation* and *PM* viewed as somewhat politically respectable. The left, of which Stone and these publications were intimately a part, suffered grievously. And so too did the left-wing ideals they subscribed to.

7 Going Underground

Although the Japanese surrender in September 1945 brought to an official close the Second World War, the fight against fascism, as I. F. Stone saw it, had yet to be successfully concluded. Franco's Spain, he believed, remained infected with the virus of fascism, and, consequently, a threat to world peace. And even more strikingly, the ghostly presence of the survivors of Auschwitz, Buchenwald, and Treblinka stood as a reminder of the evil of right-wing totalitarianism.[1]

Hitler's Final Solution had kindled the spirit of Zionism in I. F. Stone, who had long considered himself to be something of a Jewish unbeliever. Throughout the war years, he had written a number of perceptive pieces warning about the plight of Europe's "forgotten man," so infinitely more tragic than America's own. With the liberation in Europe, he had come to focus on the displaced persons in Hitler's death camps and became friends with members of the Haganah, the Jewish self-defense organization that demanded an open-door policy to Palestine, a policy the British bitterly fought against.

In the spring of 1946, a Haganah fighter whom Izzy met in Manhattan asked if he would care to go along on a mission that involved the transporting of European refugees past the British blockade and on to Palestine. She took him over to Staten Island to a secret shipbuilding yard where one of the boats to be used stood in waiting. Izzy was ready to take off immediately but was told, "No, we'll arrange for it."[2]

In the meantime, he was urged to maintain complete discretion. He was, after all, about to become the first journalist to travel with the Jewish underground to the Holy Land. Consequently, he told only Esther and Ralph Ingersoll and John P. Lewis of *PM*—who were destined to foot the bill—about his impending venture. However, he failed to inform Freda Kirchwey, his boss at *The Nation*, who was soon to take off for Palestine herself, or anyone else at the journal about his upcoming trip. Word had it that there was one "very pro-British" member of *The Nation*'s staff who simply could not be allowed to get wind of his plans.[3]

When Kirchwey finally discovered what Izzy was up to, she was, needless to say, quite put out and fired him on the spot. Within a number of months, however, the two were negotiating his price for an occasional article and by January 1949, his return as a regular contributor.[4]

But as matters turned out, Izzy had cast his lot with *PM*. His series of reports on his Middle Eastern odyssey proved compelling reading and temporarily boosted the paper's circulation to 250,000, always considered its break-even point, though seldom attainable.[5]

Izzy's determination to document the Haganah trip to Palestine demonstrated his faith in committed journalism and his belief in the need for intellectuals to take a stand. On a less ethereal note, his joining up with the Haganah also demonstrated his continued propensity to squabble with his employers, no matter how close they were to him both ideologically and personally. There were few individuals, aside from Esther and the children, who felt more like family to Izzy than did Freda Kirchwey. But having determined to act as he had, Izzy ensured that his relationship with Kirchwey and *The Nation* would never be quite the same again.

I zzy Stone had been calling attention to the Jews in Nazi concentration camps as early as December 1942; in an unsigned editorial in *The Nation*, he had discussed the "murder of a people," the nightmare "so appalling . . . that men will shudder at its horrors for centuries to come." Only the complete obliteration of the top Nazis, he suggested, would save Europe's Jews from extinction. In another unsigned editorial in the magazine dated February 27, 1943, he insisted that silence and indifference in the face of evil had a corrosive effect which diminished the "will to resist the despot and the tyrant." The appeal of Zionism, *The Nation* indicated later in the year, was growing among American Jews who saw Palestine as a different kind of "final solution."[6]

By the time the war in Europe finally ended in the spring of 1945, Izzy joined *The New Republic, The Nation,* and *PM* in supporting the idea of Zionism. He viewed himself as a kind of irreligious Jew or as something of "a religious atheist." But he had early recognized Nazism's anti-Semitism, which gave him even more reason to despise that racist strain of fascism. Moreover, he had viewed Palestine as a potential homeland for dispossessed Jews for some time now, reasoning that they could peacefully coexist there with Christians and Moslems. He saw the latest Jewish immigrants as having transformed desert and swamp land in the Middle East into fertile soil, which he believed could only help to raise the living standards for both Jews and Arabs. Zionism, then, provided a means to continue the battle against fascism and to provide a haven for his unwanted brethren. Leavened by socialism, Zionism would provide, he hoped, a model society for others.[7]

Given the gravity of the situation facing Jews under the yoke of Naxi control, Stone and Freda Kirchwey were appalled by the continuation of business-as-usual practices by American corporations and the U.S. government. He condemned those who seemed more concerned about commercial interests, particularly as they related to Middle Eastern oil, and the bureaucratic mazes that had helped pave the way for the murder of millions.[8]

Once again, he failed to understand why his own government was unable or unwilling to concern itself more fully with such moral issues. In his eyes, there was a connection between the State Department's refusal to move more forcefully against fascist forces and its disinclination to do much at all to aid the Jews in Eastern and Central Europe. This made no sense at all to him if the goal really was the eradication of fascism, something both *The Nation* and *PM* demanded.

The Nation highlighted the dismissive and often prejudiced attitude displayed by the Allies toward those they had liberated. In a *PM* editorial, Stone cited a government report that accused the Allies of affording the Jews the same treatment their Nazi captors had, "except that we do not exterminate them." Either a remarkable indifference or incalculable insensitivity, he pointed out, had reduced former concentration camp inmates to "the final ignominy" of donning SS apparel. Politically and morally, this was a self-defeating position for the United States to take, Stone argued, for the fate of the displaced persons would demonstrate the extent of America's resolve to extinguish Nazism. And if every vestige of Nazism were not destroyed, he feared, the pain and suffering engendered by the war would have been for nought, with Jews worldwide always remaining at risk.[9]

This was the case because the plague of anti-Semitism had in no way disappeared. Because European Jews were aware of this hostile climate, few sought a return to their own nation-states. They, like others, wanted to return home, Stone reported, but this involved moving on to British Palestine, whose borders necessarily had to be opened up to "the No. 1 victims of Nazi fury." They had attempted to live as European nationals but had been persecuted as Jews. Now they wished "to live as Jews, to hold their heads up as Jews," and sought to settle in Palestine; for them, *The Nation* declared, that land represented security and justice. Furthermore, the remnants of the once-thriving European Jewish community, Stone acknowledged, had nowhere else to turn to.[10]

In late October 1945, Izzy—more and more drawn to Zionism—traveled to the Middle East on assignment from *PM* and *The Nation*. The White House staff forwarded the request for a passport, following solicitations by the two publications. While in Palestine, he movingly acknowledged that he too had experienced "a sense of homecoming" and a sparking of "filial memories." He came away appreciating more than ever what the Holy Land meant to Jews from Eastern and Central Europe. There, he wrote, "a Jew is a

Jew" and need not be apologetic or defensive about what was meant by that. No lengthy discourses about whether Jews comprised a race, a religion, or simply a myth were required.[11]

Nevertheless, Stone indicated that he did not favor the creation of a Jewish nation. Like American Socialist Party leader Norman Thomas, he advocated instead the establishment of a binational state, which would be "nobler and politically sounder"; others on the editorial board of *The Nation*, including Freda Kirchwey, disagreed. The Palestinian Arabs, "a great people with great potentialities," Stone declared, had history on their side every bit as much as the Jews did; they would not easily accept second-class status in a Jewish state.[12]

Izzy's support for a binational land was unusual among American leftists. But he saw no reason that the two peoples could not live as one, believing as he did that the inspiration of Jewish immigration had already helped Palestine begin to bloom. The democratic and socialist principles that many of the European Jews brought with them to the Middle East, he hoped, would benefit the Arabs too.

I zzy's six-week trip abroad was his first; he reported on it in "Palestine Pilgrimage," which appeared in *The Nation*. After flying over from New York, he landed in London, where he spent five full days, then headed off for two days in Paris. He stayed over in Rome before arriving in Athens, where this longtime lover of the classics was able to climb the Acropolis. He then went on to Cairo for five days before departing for the Middle East. On the return trip, he visited Lebanon for two days, then Cairo and London for three days each, with shorter layovers in Cyrenaica, Malta, southern France, Ireland, and Newfoundland.[13]

He felt, upon returning home at the end of November, a bit like the lead character in Jules Verne's *Around the World in Eighty Days*. And he came back to the United States "drunk on the beauties of the world"—the Manhattan skyline; St. Paul's Cathedral, standing so clearly amid the bombed ruins of London; Paris, which had escaped the physical destruction that many other European cities had experienced; Jerusalem, which appeared immaculate and glorious, and the Wailing Wall.[14]

B y late 1945, Stone and *The Nation* indicated that the European Jews and their Palestinian counterparts were running out of patience. In Palestine, he pointed out, the Jews were constructing a nation and considered illegal immigration "a Jewish Dunkirk across the Mediterranean, an urgent and inescapable duty." Thus, the alignment by the British Foreign

Office with the most reactionary of Arab potentates, a move reminiscent of "disingenuous power politics, nineteenth-century style," was simply not good enough.[15]

In January 1946, he praised the Haganah, "the People's Army of Palestinian Jewry," for remaining a disciplined military force in the face of mounting provocations. This "democratic militia," Stone declared, unlike the Stern Gang and the "quasi-Fascist" Irgun, was no irresponsible terrorist organization, its members "no more gangsters" than George Washington and Thomas Jefferson had been. Indeed, the Haganah had condemned the recent bombings of British offices in Palestine, which were said to have strengthened the hand of those who opposed the illegal immigration.[16]

In the spring of 1946, the Haganah—obviously pleased with his analysis of the organization—informed Izzy that it was time for him to accompany a boat that was about to run the British blockade in the Mediterranean. Both the departments of State and War—which, of course, were not aware of his final destination—now assisted *PM* in obtaining approval for Izzy's overseas venture. Indeed, the acting chief of the Passport Division at State suggested that he apply for accreditation as a correspondent with the War Department. While in Paris on May 20, Izzy petitioned to have his passport amended once more, this time to enable him to head into Belgium, occupied Germany, Czechoslovakia, and Poland. The very day following receipt of such a request, a cable was sent on to Frankfurt, authorizing his entry. The White House, once again, evidently helped to expedite matters, while officially at least, the Joint Chiefs of Staff had to agree as well. On May 24, Izzy received the stamp of approval from the American consular office located in Paris.[17]

Traveling by both legal and extralegal routes through Europe and the Mediterranean, Izzy first passed through the "Germany of destruction, death, and dreadful memories" and Poland, where anti-Semitism remained alive and well. He heard frightful tales of the Holocaust in addition to warnings that more pogroms were possible. He witnessed the devastation unleashed by the war and the pathetic lot and continued mistreatment of the survivors. Then in Italy, Izzy was himself temporarily detained by police officials who were acceding to the British demands that the illegal migration be thwarted. But soon this "religious atheist," along with his religious kinsmen, boarded a ship bound for Palestine.[18]

The ensuing trip to the Middle East proved both difficult and eventful. Near the border of Palestine, the passengers transferred to a small Turkish boat. Stifling heat and unbearable odors awaited the human cargo, soon to be crammed together like animals destined for the slaughterhouse. One incident in particular, Izzy later recalled, enabled him to experience some small part of what residents of concentration camps must have gone through. Although granted special privileges as the chronicler of the journey, he volunteered to take a turn below deck, where conditions were most oppressive. After only two hours, he could no longer stand the deadening heat and lack of ventilation, and gratefully returned up top. The boat finally docked in Palestine and Izzy thought to himself: "These Jews were my own people and I had come to love them on our long trip together."[19]

Izzy's stay in Palestine was hardly uneventful. Following the landing of the "illegal" ship, British authorities wanted him brought in for questioning. Evading the British dragnet, however, he headed into Tel Aviv, then under a state of martial law owing to a concern about terrorism. One evening, Izzy got lost as he attempted to make his way back to his hotel room, and therefore was out on the streets, in violation of the city's strict nighttime curfew. As he wondered what to do next, a British armored car approached, its searchlights glaring. Ducking into a doorway, Izzy instinctively recognized that he had but two choices. He could remain where he was, hoping not to attract attention. But if the soldiers were to spot him, he knew that they might simply fire first and then later attempt to discover the identity of their victim. Consequently, "he made a split second decision," determining to leap out of his hiding spot directly into the path of the oncoming vehicle. Fortunately, the two young soldiers, fearing they had come upon members of the Stern Gang, bolted from their armored car in a show of surrender. Upon being informed that Izzy was an American journalist only, the soldiers happily escorted him back to his hotel, apparently unaware that the British government wanted him interrogated.[20]

His son Chris later pointed to this incident as an example of Izzy's "incredible presence of mind." And it contained still greater symbolic import to Chris, for during the days ahead as the political climate in the United States worsened, Izzy was often heard to say, "it's the guys who hide who get dragged out and shot."[21]

Izzy never did inform Esther of his close call, believing that she had worries enough regarding his overseas travels. Thus, he failed to write any account of this particular adventure. He did, however, relate the tale to Chris, coupling it with a seldom heard admonition "not to pass it along to Mom."[22]

Even without news of this particular episode which could easily have ended in tragedy but instead displayed Izzy's ability to "think on his feet," a friend later told him that his travails had become part of Haganah lore. For if those stopping off at underground stations complained about the quality of the meals they were served, a scolding was sure to follow: "If our food was good enough for Stone, it is good enough for you."[23]

The story of Izzy's trip first appeared in *PM* in the summer of 1946, resulting in the mushrooming of that newspaper's sales figures. The initial report, dated July 5, exclaimed: "I. F. Stone Smuggled into Palestine by Underground; Exclusive Stories on His Experiences to Start Soon." The *PM* accounts compelled Mike Blankfort to proclaim them "fascinating" and "deeply moving" and to liken them to a suspenseful detective story.[24]

As Blankfort suggested, a book recounting Izzy's complete venture, entitled *Underground to Palestine*, soon followed. In that work's epilogue, Stone declared that for his comrades—the Jews waiting in DP camps and their fellows escaping Europe and a possible new wave of persecution—Palestine was more than just a theoretical matter. Simply but eloquently, he asked if there were any other option available to these previously unwanted folk. And he reported that he had been told again and again: "We want to build a Jewish country . . . We are tired of putting out sweat and blood into places where we are not welcome . . . We have wandered enough."[25]

Underground to Palestine closed with Stone's call once again for a binational state and his urging of full support for the Jewish émigrés. He concluded with the following observation: "If those ships were illegal, so was the Boston Tea Party."[26]

A critique in the *New York Times Book Review* heralded *Underground to Palestine* as "a notable journalistic achievement" which possessed "the ring of simple truth" and was the product of "three-dimensional reporting." *The New Republic* declared that Stone's "stirring" tale would "wound the conscience of the civilized reader." Bartley C. Crum, writing in *The Nation*, suggested that no public testimony could equal such a "moving eye-witness account."[27]

Notwithstanding such reviews, *Underground to Palestine* did not sell all that well, a fact which Izzy attributed to a boycott supposedly undertaken against it. The boycott allegedly followed a meeting he had with some Zionist friends who promised a high-powered advertising campaign provided "just one sentence or so" were deleted. The crucial sentence, of course, indicated Stone's support for a binational state, support he naturally refused to withdraw. And yet when war broke out in the Middle East a short while later, the sabras—native-born Palestinian Jews—were handed Hebrew translations of his book so that they might more readily understand just what their European brothers and sisters had experienced.[28]

Izzy himself mailed a copy of *Underground to Palestine* to the White House, with the inscription acknowledging that President Truman had done more to aid "these unfortunate people" than had any of his predecessors.[29]

Stone returned to Palestine in February 1947, only to be detained at the airport by British customs officials who discovered his name among those listed in a special file located in the Control Office. As Izzy put it, "I seem to have arrived the object of great suspicion." A fellow American correspondent informed Izzy that he was suspected of having served as the Irgun's press liaison back in the States.[30]

In March, he accompanied European refugees bound for Cyprus. But although he received clearance and a visa from the British Foreign Office, quarantine officers refused to allow him to set foot on the island. They also denied him permission to wire copy back to *PM*'s home office. When he was finally able to file his report, he bristled that herding refugees into cages "like zoo exhibits" indicated the stupidity and torment of England's Middle Eastern policy. A short while later, he managed to get into Cyprus to see the internment camps, evidently "by air," as *PM* hinted.³¹

Later that year, Stone cheered the UN approval of a Jewish homeland, an action which Freda Kirchwey, his old colleague at *The Nation*, had long been calling for. History, he now declared, would affirm "that the world did make recompense to the new Attila's foremost victims"; "good will and Christian conscience did triumph after all."³²

Now, to all appearances, Izzy seemed to have gone fully over to the camp of the Zionists. He refused to criticize the founding of the Jewish state, evidently viewing it not simply as a fait accompli but rather as an urgent necessity.

While covering the 1948 war for *PM* and *The New Republic*, Izzy—once again aided by the U.S. State Department—passed through customs in Palestine, an enterprise now run by his fellow Jews. He was the first individual to have done so, he was told, in two full millennia. Asked whether he had arms or ammunition in his possession, Izzy replied, in broken Yiddish, "Unfortunately not." In an article published in *The New Republic*, he demanded that the American arms embargo on shipments to the Jews be lifted and recognition of the state of Israel be forthcoming. Freda Kirchwey, his former editor at *The Nation*—for whom Izzy was again contributing essays on a semiregular basis—was making the same demands.³³

While Izzy was in Palestine, his family, which had remained in Washington, D.C., received a pretty bad scare at one point. Esther, who was always supportive of his adventures, went along with his decision to head off to the Middle East. But just before he left, Izzy had declared at the dinner table one night that although he would not be terribly disturbed if felled by an Arab bullet, he "certainly would hate like hell to end up being shot by the Jews." Then, while he was abroad, word went out that a man named Stone was a casualty of the fighting. Esther was extremely upset before discovering this to have been a case of mistaken identity.³⁴

In his short book *This Is Israel*, Stone saluted the results of the war and discussed the future and what he expected from the new Jewish nation. He praised the democratic and socialist composition of the Israeli government, along with the Jewish settlers' tradition of "a cooperative and collectivist way of life." Still, he acknowledged that Israel was "far from being a socialist commonwealth," although he was yet hopeful that strong labor and socialist roots just might allow the nation to become "a laboratory in the building of a new society. Its mixed economy already indicated how Socialist devices and democratic methods could be combined, social justice achieved, without sacrifice of individual freedom."[35]

Once again, laudatory reviews followed. A write-up in the *New York Times* declared that Stone had shaped "history out of isolated dispatches and supplied a yardstick" by which to measure "this new-born, almost-stillborn, state." A reviewer in *The Nation* noted the "moving quality" with which he had penned his "honest, vivid, authoritative" work. But the *New Yorker* remarked that the book's general tone indicated how "even the most seasoned journalist" was evidently unable to write dispassionately about the region.[36]

I n Izzy's reading of the new nation lay the seeds of profound disillusionment. For if Israel did not prove to be that laboratory in the making of the good society, it would lose some of its special appeal for him. But at present it stood as the embodiment of the democratic socialist spirit and as a shining example of what the antifascist struggle had resulted in.

In the period just ahead, fundamentalism, ethnocentrism, and strident nationalism did in fact start to make inroads into the new Jewish state. Izzy expressed outrage over the assassination by Jewish terrorist forces of Swedish Count Folke Bernadotte of Wisborg, the UN mediator. Jews everywhere and Israel's friends too were "shamed" by "this insane and savage act" of terrorism, which, in Izzy's view, only disgraced the Jewish nation.[37]

Groups like the Irgun and the Stern Gang, he admitted, did serve something of a historical purpose—empires, after all, were little inclined to respond to more subtle proddings; such terrorists put pressure on the British and garnered the attention of the United Nations. But now that the state of Israel was a reality, the actions of these "extremist, chauvinistic, supernationalistic" and "deeply anti-democratic" groups had to be terminated. For "their follies serve Israel's enemies. Their example corrupts a section of its youth. Their crimes dishonor a community which was built by patient unglamorous courage and high moral devotion not by arrogant loud mouths hurling bombs and ambushing the defenseless."[38]

Stone was also disturbed by what he considered to be the Irgun's and the Stern Gang's fascist or quasifascist leanings. If such organizations were to gain greater influence, he worried, the possibility of constructing a democratic socialist state would be reduced.

Still, Stone remained hopeful that groups such as the Histadruth, the powerful and idealistic labor organization, would be able to pair workers and farmers, promote both "collective and co-operative life" and individual freedom, and produce a socialism unencumbered by "the often cruel and clumsy hand of an all-powerful centralized state." In fact, for a time, Stone held fast to his vision that within Israel "something of the free society of which Kropotkin dreamed" was being shaped.³⁹

But during another trip to the Middle East, this one undertaken in August 1949, Stone saw something else again. Now he discovered class and ethnic divisions emerging precisely where he had envisioned "a miniature America, a tiny melting pot" evolving that would willingly take in "the best from other lands and cultures." Slums peopled by impoverished, religious, darker-skinned Jews, "the lumpenproletariat" of Israel, who performed so many of the thankless, unskilled tasks, were cropping up. And established Israelis viewed the newest immigrants as a group apart. As a result, familiar and denigrating stereotypes could be heard: these folk did not want to work; they were dirty; they were lazy. Prejudices of this sort, Stone admitted, only demonstrated that Jews were human too. However, he argued, "being human isn't good enough if it means so quickly forgetting all that one has oneself suffered."⁴⁰

What he now witnessed evidently discouraged him and planted the first seeds of doubt that Israel could turn out as he had hoped it might. And yet he continued to view the Jewish homeland as a special place and as a kind of model for democrats and socialists alike.

By the time a second Middle Eastern war beckoned in 1956, Stone, again like Norman Thomas, had come to see Israel as having another problem that needed attending to—the presence of Arab refugee camps. According to Stone, the plain and simple fact was that the refugees were "a moral millstone around our necks as a [Jewish] people." The treatment afforded the Arab refugees, he indicated, would decide "our future as a people and Israel's future as a nation." Moreover, it would be appalling to him if Jews, with their tormented history, exhibited no empathy for these Arabs. And in an eloquent passage, Stone suggested that "a crossroads" was being reached by the Jews: in one direction loomed militarism and ethnocentrism and more pronounced anti-Arab sentiment. Such a course, he prophesied, would despoil Israel because of the presence of Arabs and Sephardic Jews within its very borders. Ultimately, then, the way Jews dealt with the Arabs, he exclaimed, "will determine the spiritual level of Jewry and of Israel. We dare not treat the Arabs as human dirt swept out of the land without dirtying ourselves."⁴¹

The second-class status offered Arabs within the borders of Israel eventually led Stone, following the Six-Day War, to proclaim the need for a Palestinian state. This pronouncement would result in accusations that he was anti-Israeli and anti-Semitic too. But charges of that kind did not come his way now, despite the fact that his analyses after the 1956 conflict were every bit as damning as they would be in the following decade.

Later, Stone was also criticized for his supposed opposition to Zionism, notwithstanding his support for the Jewish refugees and the founding of the state of Israel. What Stone did believe was that Zionism should not be used as a cover for mistreating Arabs inside Israel or the occupied lands, for territorial expansion, or for right-wing nationalism.

Arab-Israeli relations, which so concerned I. F. Stone, proved to be one of many issues that helped to divide the postwar American left. Those who continued to view themselves as socialists, like Thomas and Stone, tended to be among those most troubled by the "Arab question." But many who were part of the anti-Stalinist left now became more and more conscious of their Jewishness, particularly following the revelations of the horrors of the Holocaust and the establishment of the Jewish nation. Consequently, in Irving Howe's words, American Jews experienced "a wave of simple-hearted nationalist sentiment." The two groups were bound to clash and soon did, with the Zionists condemning those who criticized Israeli policies as anti-Jewish and pro-Palestinian.[42]

As Stone had recognized, the problem of the Arab refugees was a particularly vexing one, and so too was the political and racial divide separating the Sephardim and the Ashkenazim. The plight of the growing number of stateless Arabs disturbed many, as did the propensity of Jews of Middle Eastern origin to support a more conservative political stance than that favored by European Jews, who tended to back the Labor Party of Israel's founder, David Ben-Gurion, another one of Izzy's father figures.

Notwithstanding his concerns for the stateless Arabs, accusations that Stone ever adopted an anti-Zionist posture were simply without foundation. Although increasingly disappointed by Israeli policies, he continued to view the Jewish nation in fraternal fashion. He did oppose the idea of a Greater Israel whose boundaries must ever expand at the expense of its Arab brothers and sisters. He envisioned, rather, a coming together of the two peoples. It was hardly anti-Semitism that resulted in his analyses of Israeli actions, but instead his fervent belief in universalism.

Izzy's reports on the state of Israel, similar to his earlier accounts of Palestine, were among his most passionate. Not only did they put into practice his conviction that intellectuals and journalists should take a position on the controversial issues of their times, but they also underscored his growing readiness to challenge even those ideas and preconceptions that he held dear.

8 The Demise of the Old Left

T hroughout the war years, as during the Great Depression, I. F. Stone had repeatedly spoken of the need for the United States to veer leftward. Whether the objective was world peace or economic prosperity and full employment on the home front, success could not be ensured, he had insisted in October 1944, "without some large measure of Socialism. We have to get used to this terrible, dreadful word 'Socialism.' We have to get used to saying it right out loud." Thus, his own country simply had to move beyond the significant but limited reforms of Roosevelt's New Deal and exhibit an open-minded attitude about the need for sweeping change in Europe and elsewhere.[1]

Stone was not alone in believing that socialism—no matter what the variety—remained the wave of the future, not only in the United States and Western Europe, but also in Asia and Eastern Europe. Indeed, many on the left held high hopes that some kind of new order in colonial lands and in the West was possible, particularly where Resistance or reform forces were ascendant. They believed that the wartime creation of the second Popular Front held the promise of happy days for the United States too. After all, front-styled groups such as the National Farmers Union, the CIO-Political Action Committee, the liberal National Citizens Political Action Committee—whose members included Bruce Bliven, Freda Kirchwey, and Max Lerner—and the Communist-dominated Independent Citizens Committee of the Arts, Sciences, and Professions had thrived during the war. The expectation was that the New Deal would be expanded in the United States and a "New Deal for the world" created overseas.[2]

But the dreams of the latest version of Popular Fronters soon became stillborn. As the Grand Alliance came apart and as the political atmosphere at home shifted to the right; as Eastern Europe appeared to be goosestepping to the tune of the authoritarian left; as the quest to ferret out reds replaced the battle to hold back the Brownshirts; as the supportive atmosphere of the Roosevelt years gave way to a resurgence of conservatism, the Grand Old Party, and a new red scare; the visions of socialism and world government faded for many, and belief in liberal anticommunism and a Pax Americana took hold. American radicals who continued to dream the dreams of days gone by proved fair game for their left-of-center competitors—particularly anti-Stalinists, whose ranks were soon to grow so steadily—and right-wing antagonists too. Rather than thriving, the American left, as a consequence, splintered once again, this time between its liberal and radical wings, and the latter, for a time, soon threatened to become all but extinct.

This troubled I. F. Stone and others who continued to comprise the now rapidly dwindling ranks of the Old Left. Such left-wing stalwarts looked no more fondly upon those who had experienced something of an ideological deconversion than former radicals did upon those who were still true believers. Stone appeared to have little respect for onetime Popular Fronters who now seemed determined to disassociate themselves from the left of the 1930s. Stone, in contrast, appeared as devoted as ever to the ideals of socialism and a united front.

Those who remained true to the left, like Izzy Stone and the publications he worked for, eventually paid a price for their ideological forbearance. The respectability that they and certain other individuals and journals had attained would soon vanish. The warm reception that they had enjoyed—even within the inner sanctums of high government circles—would turn cold. More and more doors would be closed to them, doors which might have led to both prestigious appointments and insider information.

This proved to be something of a mixed blessing for Stone. No longer was he a welcome visitor at the White House or the offices of cabinet members. For an individual as concerned about his place in the journalistic profession and as ambitious as Izzy was, this must have been a considerable setback. But it did force him, as had his hearing difficulties a decade earlier, to fall back on his particular reportorial strengths—an intensive reading of public documents and other printed sources, more selective interviewing, and an expansive historical and philosophical grounding.

Moreover, his change in status certainly did not lead him to consider the possibility of muting his criticisms of U.S. foreign and domestic policies or of adopting the supposedly more objective stance of many of his journalistic colleagues. Rather, for Izzy, it undoubtedly made him still more determined to produce biting essays, to support unpopular causes, and to remain the intellectual activist.

To Izzy's and the Old Left's infinite displeasure, the demise of the second Popular Front was all but assured following the death of the man the Old Left never had quite come to terms with. He had alternately been viewed as a would-be fascist, a halfhearted reformer, a great American democrat, a vacillator, a warmonger, and one of the triad of antifascist kingpins. He passed from the scene as the long and bloody war against fascism—waged in the parched deserts of Ethiopia, the mountains of Spain, the frozen Russian tundras, the blood-drenched Warsaw ghetto, and the bomb-pocked capital of the Third Reich—was finally drawing to a close. He had guided the United States through the better part of it all, as he had earlier lifted this land out of the depths of depression, but now he would not be around to savor the fruits of victory. On April 12, 1945, Franklin Delano Roosevelt was felled one final time, by a cerebral hemorrhage that cost him his life.

The death of "our great President" in mid-April 1945 hit I. F. Stone very hard, as it did so many others, including his colleague T.R.B., Richard L. Strout, of *The New Republic*. Tears flowed easily in the *PM* offices as the news rolled off the wire service. No man who had presided over the American republic, not even Abraham Lincoln or Woodrow Wilson, Stone wrote in an editorial for the left-wing tabloid, had had more weight placed on his shoulders. Roosevelt had guided the nation out the depths of the Great Depression and on to now certain victory over the Axis powers. "His humanity . . . quick instinctive sympathy for the oppressed . . . sense of justice . . . masterly sense of politics . . . toughness of fibre," Stone declared, had made all the difference.[3]

FDR's passing appeared only to strengthen Stone's determination that a post–New Deal agenda be carried out; but in reality, his death ensured that nothing of the kind was to come about. Nevertheless, writing in *The Nation* in early August on the eve of the British Labour Party's stunning electoral victory, Stone wondered if the United States would follow the lead of its wartime ally. For the formation of a British Labour government suggested the possibility of ushering in socialism sans "bloodshed and dictatorship, of developing a democratic Socialism suited to the Western European and American peoples, of avoiding the creation of a monolithic state, of preserving elements of economic freedom and enterprise within the framework of Socialist direction and planning."[4]

This is what Izzy hoped for above all else, that socialism and liberty could come together in such a way that the economic inequities so clearly present in the capitalist democracies and the authoritarianism that afflicted Communist Russia could both be avoided. If British Labour were able to chart a middle course, he believed, the future of the postwar era would promise to be a good deal more hopeful.

British Labour's triumph, in Izzy's estimation, underscored the importance of leaving behind the worn and tired rhetoric and economics of the New Deal, of nurturing a new American socialist movement, and of following a nondogmatic, Marxist approach. What he envisioned was a mixed economy that included government ownership where appropriate, full employment brought about through planning, and, in his words, a healthy infusion of "Socialist prodding and Socialist understanding."[5]

Harry Fleischman, national secretary of the American Socialist Party, praised Stone's "thoughtful" essay and its contention that liberals and labor had to move beyond the New Deal. *The New Republic* agreed that British Labor was beginning "a hopeful and exciting experiment" which the United States would be well advised to duplicate. But what Stone and others who held on to economic analyses rooted in the verities of the Old Left failed to take into account was how resilient modern industrial capitalism would prove to be. Welfare, of both the corporate and governmental variety, became a savior of sorts for capitalism in the West. And as economies rebounded and then thrived in Western Europe, Canada, and the United States, it became increasingly apparent that the age of socialism was not to be.[6]

Many willingly accommodated themselves to that fact, an accommodation which reached the point of celebration by the following decade. In contrast and to their credit, Stone, A. J. Muste, and a handful of others who came out of the ideological wars of the thirties refused to abandon their responsibility as intellectuals to take a hard look at the failings of American society. But their inability or unwillingness to appreciate the full dimensions of the economic changes taking place helped to bring about their isolation from the intellectual mainstream.

That, in itself, was hardly insignificant. For notwithstanding such figures as Harvard economist John Kenneth Galbraith and Socialist author Michael Harrington who warned about the presence of mass deprivation in the midst of the affluent society, the realities of an American underclass, decaying cities, and pockets of rural poverty helped to make the social contract in this land a good deal more fragile than it might have been.

In Stone's estimation, the man who succeeded FDR in the Oval Office was not even up to the job of bringing about capitalism with a human face. President Truman and the American people, he wrote in *PM,* rhapsodized about free enterprise, "the great American religion, our own Shintoism." And yet they remembered that the freewheeling twenties had precipitated the collapse of the U.S. economy, which New Deal reforms had proven incapable of revitalizing.[7]

More and more, Stone expressed concerns that Harry Truman was no Franklin Delano Roosevelt. In early 1946, he indicated in an unsigned editorial in *The Nation* that Truman, so unlike his predecessor, displayed no ability to highlight issues of great import. Truman lacked the inspirational leadership that was FDR's, both Stone and *The New Republic*'s T.R.B. agreed, and along with "the little band of mediocrities" advising him, seemed to be in over his head.[8]

This weak leadership had unfortunate implications, Stone believed, not only in the domestic arena but in the international one as well. For a brief time, Stone looked to the British Labour government to provide a model for more conciliatory relations but was quickly disappointed by Foreign Secretary Ernest Bevin's assertion that the new governments of Bulgaria,

Romania, and Hungary were unrepresentative. The Communist-headed governments, Stone admitted in a *PM* editorial, were "hardly democratic in the full sense of the term." After all, they were in no way the products of free elections, nor did they allow for unfettered opposition. Nevertheless, Stone evidently viewed them as Popular Front—like regimes which represented workers, peasants, and small landowners, and consequently insisted that their promise of economic reform and land was unquestionably in line with majority demands.[9]

Furthermore, Stone went on to say, using the same kind of argument that the editors of *The New Republic* did, it made little sense to insist that these former Axis allies immediately establish "democratic regimes of the standard variety." The new Eastern European governments, the product "of defeat and revolution," were necessarily provisional ones that first had to quash all vestiges of fascism.[10]

His belief that fascism had to be thoroughly eradicated led Stone to dismiss accusations concerning the undemocratic nature of the Eastern European states. These were the very kinds of charges he repeatedly delivered when right-of-center regimes were being examined. And he had made many of them himself regarding the onetime communist utopia, the USSR. But once again, his fears of fascism were so great that he was willing to make exceptions, however temporarily, when governments he saw as antifascist were the subject of debate.

The tearing apart of the Grand Alliance, which accompanied the outbreak of the Cold War and the Stalinization of Eastern Europe, troubled him too. He feared Churchill's ringing denunciation in early 1946 of an "iron curtain" which had reputedly fallen across the European continent; he considered it to be a call for an anti-Soviet alliance between England and the United States.[11]

It was true, Stone declared as the Soviet Union insisted on oil concessions from Iran, that the United States should in no way give in "to unlimited expansionist demands" from the Communist giant. But the question to be considered was whether such demands were in fact "unlimited, and where we draw the line."[12]

Thus, Stone was not in favor of granting Soviets a free hand to march outside their own borders or beyond Eastern Europe at least. But he feared the unfolding of an anti-Communist campaign, which he saw as invariably playing into the hand of reactionaries everywhere. In that regard, he was certainly not mistaken, but his concerns about the antipathy directed toward the Soviet sphere did lead him for a while longer to soften his criticisms of the Eastern European states.

As Stone expressed concerns that Americans were becoming tools of the British, who seemed determined to maintain their dominant position in the

Middle East, William Barrett of the *Partisan Review* in turn attacked him and his friend Max Lerner as "apologists" for "the Socialist Fatherland." The anti-Communist journal in the summer of 1946, in a scathing editorial entitled "The 'Liberal' Fifth Column," rather remarkably condemned the "liberals" of *PM, The Nation,* and *The New Republic* for being part of "a powerful vocal lobby willing to override all concerns of international democracy and decency in the interests of a foreign power." Because of their very deceptiveness, these "Russian patriots," the *Partisan Review* believed, were still more dangerous than self-professed Communists. While *PM,* the *Partisan Review* insisted, possessed "Stalinist sympathies" and was "the plebeian wing of the 'liberal' admirers of Russian totalitarianism," *The Nation* and *The New Republic* were said to be "at once more confused and more subtle" yet.[13]

The antagonism flowing from the *Partisan Review* in the direction of *PM, The Nation,* and *The New Republic,* the last three all still members in good standing of the second Popular Front, demonstrated that the ideological divide that had appeared in the thirties continued to separate those who saw themselves as positioned on the left. The growing rift between the former Allied powers and a cooling of hopes for both international cooperation and a domestic policy that reached beyond the New Deal created still more fissures among American liberals and radicals. The removal of Henry Wallace from Truman's cabinet, the adoption by labor unions of anti-Communist provisions, and the disastrous results of the congressional elections of 1946 which returned control of Capital Hill to the Republicans, seemed to portend darker days ahead for the Popular Front left. But then so too did condemnations of Communist practices abroad by historian Arthur M. Schlesinger, Jr., theologian Reinhold Niebuhr, and Eleanor Roosevelt; the Harvard University professor also denounced what he considered to be the conspiratorial practices of American Communists. The left, Schlesinger argued, should insist that "Communists and fellow travelers stand and be counted" and warned that the influence of party members "immobilizes the U.S. left."[14]

In late December 1946, those who continued to champion the ideals of the Popular Front now had the option of joining the newly formed Progressive Citizens of America, which warned against an anti-Soviet foreign policy and envisioned a new spate of reform measures. Anti-Communist liberals, who had previously come together in the wartime Union for Democratic Action, now established Americans for Democratic Action, which adopted a policy of noncooperation with the Communists. While Bartley Crum, Jo Davidson, Philip Murray, and Henry Wallace, the organization's greatest star, were attracted to PCA, prominent liberals such as Joseph and Stuart Alsop, Chester Bowles, John Kenneth Galbraith, Hubert Humphrey, Niebuhr, Joseph Rauh, Eleanor Roosevelt, Walter Reuther, and Schlesinger all lined up with the explicitly anti–Popular Front ADA.[15]

The divisions on the left displeased and troubled Stone, who continued to hew to the Popular Front line. A war with the Soviet Union, he warned in the pages of *PM*, would prove to be humankind's most expensive and deadliest and would inevitably result in the very occupation of the whole European continent that so many worried about. In addition, it would burden the United States, he warned, with a totalitarianism as dark as that attributed to Russia.[16]

By the spring of 1947, the Cold War had begun in earnest. Anticipating revisionist scholars of a later day, Stone fully appreciated the roots of this simmering conflict: marked ideological differences, war-induced power vacuums, the determination of the victors of World War II to carve out spheres of influence, Soviet security concerns, American fears of a Nazi-like aggressor redux, the emergence of national liberation movements, and the presence of a new hard-line administration in Washington.

Stone now worried, as he had before, that his own land was turning into "the citadel of world reaction." In speaking before Congress on March 12, 1947, President Truman proclaimed that the United States was necessarily obliged to back "free peoples" who were warding off armed revolts, either directed from within or from outside their own country. Many on the left were outraged by both the Truman Doctrine, as the president's pronouncement was called, and the administration's decision to send 400 million dollars in military aid to the undemocratic Turkish and Greek governments—both of which were attempting to quell guerrilla insurgencies. ADA members Arthur Schlesinger, Jr., and Hubert Humphrey strongly supported the presidential action, but opposition within the ranks of the organization was considerable. Freda Kirchwey of *The Nation* condemned this expanded version of manifest destiny, and warned that "this is the Great Crusade—the one, you will remember, that Hitler invited us to join long ago." Henry Wallace, now serving as editor of *The New Republic*, called Truman "the best spokesman Communism had." Writing in *PM*, Stone warned that governments like those the United States was rushing to aid would always be able to uncover red plots of one kind or another. The Turks, he admitted, did possess genuine fears of Soviet designs on the Bosporus Strait. But power politics was involved there, he contended, not ideology.[17]

As for the Greek government, with its "coalition of crooks, incompetents, ex-Axis agents and decayed monarchists," Stone viewed it in a far different light. American policy toward Greece, he warned, would soon involve nothing more than "harsh and cynical collaboration" with crooked and dictatorial elements. Greek liberals were being afforded the choice of throwing in with an authoritarian regime or heading for "the hills with the 'bandits.'" Such practices, *The Nation* declared, were "bankrupt . . . inefficient," "suicidal" in fact.[18]

Moreover, the Greek model, Stone pointed out, was being repeated in the Middle East and in Latin America. Sadly, "we seem to have opened a military shopping service for dictators, guns for the asking to anti-democratic regimes from Iran and Turkey to Brazil and Argentina, guns for use against their own peoples, guns marked U.S.A., not the best kind of advertising."[19]

Throwing down the gauntlet as the United States was doing in Greece, Stone charged, was as destructive to world peace as anything the Soviets were up to in Eastern Europe. The United States was starting to draw its own lines and demand that reaction be supported "or else." But such an approach only bred civil war, a scene already being played out with deadly results in both the Far East and the Mediterranean.[20]

Stone's reading of early postwar U.S. foreign policy unfortunately proved to be remarkably prophetic. One American administration after another did opt to back right-of-center military, oligarchical, and dictatorial forces that were determined to crush popular uprisings or prevent necessary change from taking place. Such practices violated basic American precepts concerning the right of a people to chart their own course and to overthrow tyrannical rulers; moreover, they resulted in U.S. involvement in the internal affairs of other states. That inevitably left a sour taste for grandiose American rhetoric among nationalists in Africa, Asia, Latin America, the Middle East, and Europe.

In August 1947, Stone discussed just what it was that the West was up against. Communist Russia, he acknowledged, did seek to appeal to both peasants and workers. To that end, it was able to call on "a new force: an international Communist movement, with all the fervor and fanaticism of a new religion." This movement, "Jesuitical in its tactics and disciplined in its maneuvers," considered the collapse of social democracy before the German and Italian fascists to have validated Leninist tenets. Communism, its true believers intoned, demanded "ruthless dictatorship in the name of the proletariat."[21]

Such a movement was unsettling to many: the Catholic Church, engaged in its own struggle to win more adherents; democratic socialist movements and capitalist classes, equally fearful of Bolshevik-orchestrated extinction; and Western states troubled about the possibility of "a Communist One World." All, in turn, naturally looked to the United States for protection against the Red Bogy. Only the United States possessed sufficient capital to rebuild the war-torn European continent. Only the United States boasted reactionary forces powerful enough to kick off an anti-Communist drive.

Only the United States was still viewed so favorably by the masses in the distant corners of the world, although this too would change.[22]

But what this nation seemed unable to grasp, Stone continued, was that socialism had great appeal outside the boundaries of the Soviet bloc. In England, France, and Italy, the contending forces were not " 'free enterprise' American style" and communism, but rather communism and social democracy. The movement toward socialism was badly misunderstood by U.S. policymakers, who viewed it as a type of "queer mental quirk" on the part of Europeans which could somehow be corrected.[23]

Unfortunately, Stone wrote, matters were further complicated by the displacement of New Dealers by conservative and reactionary elements opposed to any kind of reform at home or abroad and desirous of unrestricted exploitation. It was Franklin Roosevelt, with his American version of the Middle Way, Stone noted, who had instinctively known how to battle communism.[24]

Under Truman, he continued, the rhetoric might be the same but the tune was "Mr. Hoover's." Although "we preach democracy, we practice plutocracy." As a consequence, U.S. policy was increasingly making the country appear to be "hypocritical and untrustworthy." While U.S. policymakers spoke of reform, they backed Greek cryptofascists; while U.S. policymakers spoke of freedom, they supported the restoration in the Far East of Western imperialism. Such actions enabled the Soviet Union to pose as the defender of democracy, notwithstanding its own authoritarianism. And they weakened the United States' understandable condemnations of Soviet despotism in Eastern Europe, by allowing for the same kinds of practices or even worse ones to be carried out in the American sphere, particularly in Greece, Chiang Kai-shek's China, and Franco's Spain.[25]

On August 27, Stone discussed "The ABC of an Effective Foreign Policy." He quoted from Lieutenant General Albert C. Wedemeyer, who, upon leaving China, had forewarned that military force alone would not stamp out communism. Stone readily agreed: "You cannot kill an idea. You cannot substitute bullets for bread. You cannot make misery more palatable by putting it under guard. You cannot build a stable society on exploitation and corruption." When President Truman came to understand this as clearly as President Roosevelt had, Stone continued, U.S. foreign policy would come to represent more than a hopeless bid to block a Soviet advance "on the quicksands of bankrupt ruling classes."[26]

American ranks left of center were still more divided in their response to the administration's program to reconstruct Europe. Like some Popular Fronters but unlike a good many others, I. F. Stone and Max Lerner of *PM* saw the Marshall Plan as possessing the imaginative and humanitarian qualities that they believed should necessarily characterize U.S. foreign policy. It emphasized economic and social reconstruction in order that political stability could be effected. Stone saw nothing wrong with this, fearing how both the United States and the USSR might respond if a revolutionary explosion were to occur on the European continent. Once again, he supported immediate reform rather than holding out for what he considered to be only fanciful wishes.

Stone considered the Marshall Plan, pledged by its architect to be "directed not against country or doctrine, but against hunger, poverty, desperation, and chaos," to be one that people of goodwill simply had to champion. Much to his displeasure, the Soviet Union and the CPUSA disagreed, the latter terming it a "cold-blooded scheme of American monopolists to establish their ruthless domination over harassed world humanity." Henry Wallace and the PCA viewed the Marshall Plan as yet another part of the Truman Doctrine; Michael Straight of *The New Republic* opposed the former vice-president's position. The ADA backed it wholeheartedly, while *The Nation* argued that without foreign aid, the type of austerity that could result would necessitate authoritarianism.[27]

Stone noted that the future of Western Europe, economically devastated by the war, was precarious. The Soviet five-year plans demonstrated how capital might be amassed "under a system harsh, ruthless and single-minded enough to underfeed and underclothe a whole generation for the sake of the future." And if U.S. aid were not forthcoming, Stone charged, Western Europe, already lacking investment capital and soon its empires, would either decay or "adopt a system, like Communism, draconian enough to marshall all national resources and to harness all national energies under a system of virtual forced labor."[28]

Stone discussed the fears American capitalists justifiably held regarding socialism. After all, ideas carried more weight than did the mightiest weapons of war, "and the idea of Socialism, of social ownership and control of the means of production, an idea older than Marx, an idea at least as old as Jesus and his first followers . . . has become the most potent idea of modern times."[29]

Socialism was inevitable, Stone insisted. But if reason and peace were to prevail, national characteristics, traditions, and histories would determine the pace of its arrival. And unless the possibility of a middle way were precluded by the world's greatest power, communism, Soviet-style, was in no way inevitable. Just such a middle way, he believed, could avoid the economic pitfalls of communism—the deadening hands of bureaucratization and overcentralization.[30]

In November 1947, Stone discussed "What Is Going On Behind the Iron Curtain," where recent events had so disturbed both American capitalists and anti-Stalinists. It was not simply terror alone, he suggested, that held the

Soviet Union together or sustained pro-Russian governments in power. Other factors at work included economic planning, the presence of "fanatically devoted" party members, and the considerable gains made by both peasants and workers. While in no way Western-style democracies, the Eastern European governments, Stone argued, were not simply one-party regimes like that in the Soviet Union either. In such countries, which had known so little freedom, the carrying out of "revolutionary methods," in spite of their "dreadful abuses," should not have been surprising.[31]

Nor, Stone argued once more, did such practices demonstrate that these governments were lacking in either popular support or worth. In fact, he viewed them as determinedly antifascist and as laying the path for the socialism certain to come. The strength of his belief in these two tenets led him to accept the temporary absence of that which he most believed in, democratic development. Consequently, once again, Stone appeared to articulate one set of standards for left-wing regimes, another for those right of center.

The communization of Eastern Europe, which resulted in such intellectual paradoxes for some, had dramatic impact on the American political front. It ensured that the left, recently so hopeful and seemingly so potent, continued to come apart, with many liberals and erstwhile radicals beginning to adopt stances vis-à-vis communism of a rather virulent sort. As I. F. Stone feared, anticommunism would come to dominate not only U.S. foreign policy but also the domestic scene. While the worst fears of Stone and other fervent Popular Fronters were never borne out, another postwar red scare did appear, eventually resulting in ruined reputations, curtailed careers, straitjacketed policies, and a diminution of alternative ideas, or, as one historian of the period has put it, the time of "The Great Fear."[32]

To his credit, Stone consistently warned against those who sought to win political points from first the stirrings and then the continuance of the domestic Cold War. Among those he saw as out to do so included government agents, vote-seeking politicians, cynical conservatives, frightened liberals, and dogmatic anti-Communists. But he was no more pleased with the antics of the Communists themselves, who so often appeared to be deliberately provocative.

In October 1946, Stone questioned just what J. Edgar Hoover, in delivering an address on the "Red menace" to a convention of the American Legion, was up to. Why had the FBI boss not spoken out on "the menace of racism, or anti-Semitism, or anti-Negro feeling?" Why was J. Edgar striving so diligently to depict the CPUSA, "which can't elect a dog-catcher outside New York City, into Public Enemy No. 1?" The Communist Party had never fully rebounded from the days of the Nazi-Soviet pact, Stone noted, while "its intellectual antics" deteriorated daily with its continual round of "Moscow-style" purges.[33]

Just what did Hoover intend? he wondered. Was talk of the Red Menace a precursor to some kind of far-right buildup? Were "even the palest pinks" about to be viewed as suspect?[34]

In February 1947, he passionately discussed the HCUAC hearings on the German Communist Gerhart Eisler, said to be the Soviet's top agent in the United States. No one with political acumen believed that the Comintern had been interred, Stone acknowledged, before declaring that "the Russians cannot have the cake of conspiracy and the penny of cooperation at the same time. That is an issue the Kremlin must face."[35]

And in the United States, he warned, "the conspiratorial habits" of a small number of Communists might soon result in a more sweeping red scare than this nation had yet experienced. Thus, the comrades should come "fully into the open," abandoning "all the penny dreadful hole-in-the-wall, playing at revolution" capers.[36]

Already, Stone noted, he could hear the cries from Union Square. But the American Communists simply had to realize that while they were not about to usher in the millennium, they could kick off a counterrevolution that would crush civil liberties and the progressive movement in this country, as well as dampen hopes for world peace.[37]

One lesson Stone had learned from the 1930s was that the American Communist Party, no matter the noble intentions of many of its members, was deservedly a discredited body. The obeisance displayed by party higher-ups toward Moscow had cost it the goodwill and support of a sizeable number of intellectuals, unionists, and other activists, causing some to shift rightward and others to disavow politics altogether. The flip-flops and manipulative practices of the organization that was most closely identified in the public mind with socialism had resulted in the wholesale discrediting of radical ideology. That made the left far more vulnerable than it might otherwise have been.

Following the revelation of a Canadian spy network, President Truman initiated a loyalty program in March 1947 intended to ferret out subversives in the employ of the federal government. The *New Leader,* a stridently anti-Communist social democratic journal, applauded the administration action, while *The Commonweal,* a liberal Catholic publication, supported the intentions but not the means of the president's plan, worrying that party members could become "a universally proscribed group." By contrast, James Wechsler, writing in the *Progressive,* Robert M. La Follette's old magazine, warned that Truman was simply attempting to demonstrate his politically correct colors. *The Nation* charged that the program provided ample "opportunities for malicious gossip, character assassination, and the settlement of private grudges."[38]

By the summer of 1947, with anticommunism becoming the dominant ideological force in the land, I. F. Stone was still more troubled about the nation's political atmosphere. Perhaps that led him to return to a standard libertarian stance in defending free speech for both the anti-Semitic Christian Front and a right-wing, Jew-baiting priest by the name of Arthur W. Terminiello. Or perhaps it had been wartime conditions alone that had led him to adopt a more restrictive reading of the U.S. Constitution. Now Stone painted the Christian Front with a fascist brush but insisted that "the screwballs" must be allowed to speak. What was at stake, he declared, was vitally important. For "it's as easy as rolling off a log to uphold basic rights when our own side is involved. The test of the quality of our thinking and the quality of our faith comes when it's the other fellow's right to speak that's at stake. Especially when the other fellow is selling ideas as repellent as the Christian Front."39

While acknowledging that there were those who might dismiss such reasoning as characteristic of "bankrupt liberalism" and "ostrich tactics," Stone asserted that in this area at least, he was both a liberal and a socialist. And he argued that in spite of revolutionary demands, the socialist states too must eventually either adopt Lockean and Jeffersonian precepts or deteriorate "into the facile falsehoods" of Hitler's national socialism. Those precepts, he wrote, bespoke the notion that freedom of thought possessed as much "absolute value as anything in this finite world," that individual liberties were the cornerstone of change and progress, that such rights must be safeguarded from governmental interference. What it came down to, Stone suggested, was whether a small band of "loudmouth Hitler heilers and Jew-baiters in Queens" could bring about the abandonment of Jeffersonian principles.40

Thus, Izzy took to task the authoritarian bent of both the far left and the far right. Fascist or cryptofascist forces, he believed, did not even bother to make a pretense of showing a regard for civil liberties. Communists, on the other hand, often said the right things, but they did so selectively, and, Stone believed, frequently disingenuously. Fascist regimes had no redeeming qualities, he was certain, because of their antirational, antihumanitarian orientation. By contrast, there was some hope for the communist states, because of their professed support for progressive ideals; but the goodwill they possessed was hardly limitless.

Stone, like James Wechsler, Freda Kirchwey, and Michael Straight, soon became even more concerned about the hysteria that he saw as beginning to envelop Washington, D.C. Wechsler saw a "purge" developing, while Kirchwey termed the loyalty program "an organized system of thought control." *The New Republic* worried about the pattern of covert investigations leading to dismissals which appeared "frighteningly unfamiliar" here. Returning to the capital, Stone noted on July 2, 1947, was like coming back to a land "under the shadow of a terror." More and more, government employees, both grand and small, were afraid to speak openly. There were legitimate security concerns to be considered, he admitted, but "the kernel of fact" was submerged by a groundswell of absurd accusations and "purges for opinions." While individual workers—including ten summarily dismissed from the State Department—were now paying the price, the government itself, he suggested, would eventually. Already, intellectuals were being hounded from government service. Already, honorable sorts able to pass the congressional litmus test were hard to find. If this were to continue, the country threatened to wind up with "a Government of scared yesmen."[41]

Two days later, Stone sadly noted that the signers of the Declaration of Independence would presently be ineligible for government service. They had, after all, invoked the right of revolution. This was embarrassing, Stone charged, and might someday culminate in "a different kind of America" which would "discreetly edit the Declaration, keeping the original in the back room of the library, with other works fit only for mature minds above the ideological age of consent."[42]

As Congress passed the Taft-Hartley Act which mandated that labor officials take an anti-Communist oath, Stone wondered what had happened to the American belief in the average citizen and democracy. Was that not the very essence of Americanism? he asked. Many liberals seemed to agree, and Truman's veto of the measure won him plaudits from Richard L. Strout of *The New Republic*, James Wechsler in the *Progressive*, and *The Nation* magazine.[43]

But *The Nation* was less pleased about the general direction in which it saw the United States as heading. Freda Kirchwey indicated that the absurdities of the post–World War I red scare had not yet been equaled, but, she asserted on August 23, "we are well on the way."[44]

In the fall, as HCUAC began to investigate the film industry, Stone charged that very body with having made it perilous, over the course of its ten-year history, to exercise basic American liberties. HCUAC had destroyed reputations and deprived people of their livelihoods. If allowed to go unchecked, Stone declared, it would infringe upon First Amendment freedoms. Eventually, none would be safe "from the *auto-da-fes* of these new Torquemadas." But those exalting the role of the Communist Party in Tinseltown hardly helped matters, he suggested, for they lacked any sense of "Bolshevik self-criticism."[45]

On October 31, Izzy appeared on "Meet the Press," the nationally syndicated radio program; during the war, his reputation and flirtation with respectability were such that he was invited to make an appearance on the show; by now, he had become something of a regular panelist. The guest was Robert W. Kenny, cochairman of the PCA and chief counsel for the soon-to-be infamous Hollywood Nineteen, people in the industry placed on the congressional hotseat because of past or present affiliations with the Communist Party. Among the panelists peppering him with hostile questions was Jimmy Wechsler, earlier a staffer on both *PM* and *The Nation*. It was Wechsler, a onetime member of the Young Communist League, who had been selected by Ralph Ingersoll to run *PM*'s labor department. Just the previous year, Wechsler had demanded that Ingersoll fire Izzy Stone and Alex Uhl, whom he saw as lined up with the paper's Communist faction. But Wechsler, not Stone or Uhl, was eased out of *PM*, purportedly because publisher Ralph Ingersoll "continuously yielded to Communist pressure."[46]

By the end of 1947, the divisions that had long separated former colleagues like Wechsler and Stone were more clearly drawn than ever. All indications suggested that the star of the PCA, Henry Wallace, FDR's third-term vice-president, was about to initiate a presidential run of his own under the PCA umbrella. Wechsler, stationed firmly in the anti-Stalinist camp for a full decade by this point, worried that a third party would only play into the hands of both Communists and isolationists and make it more difficult to distinguish between "Wallace wonderland and simple-minded Trumanism." Stone, ever hopeful about a resurgence of the Popular Front days, was far more troubled by the drift within the Truman administration toward Cold War hysteria.[47]

Consequently, when Kenny, leader of the liberal wing of the California Democratic Party and the new chair of the PCA, appeared on "Meet the Press," Izzy felt obliged to counter the questions of Wechsler and the other panelists with loaded ones of his own. Would it be better if Mississippian John Rankin still chaired HCUAC? he asked. Did Kenny believe that a congressional committee should be allowed to examine an individual's political beliefs? Why did the recently selected chair of HCUAC, Parnell Thomas, condemn such films as *The Brotherhood of Man?* How would Kenny explain the committee's refusal to investigate the Klan and movies that espoused racial intolerance?[48]

The committee, Stone believed, was accomplishing precisely that which it had set out to. It was feeding fears that the Communists were everywhere; that they imperiled the prize national totem, the atomic bomb; and thus, drastic countermeasures were demanded. What was emerging, Stone wrote, was a type "of plot-and-persecution system akin to paranoid obsession and like paranoia impervious to correction by rational government." Such a state of mind was planting the seeds for a fully blown fascist movement which would come waving Old Glory. Consequently, people of goodwill had to condemn the congressional witch-hunt that was intended to strike fear into the hearts of everyone left of center and progressive intellectuals.[49]

In December, Stone focused on yet another chapter in the loyalty purge,

Attorney General Thomas Clark's listing of purportedly subversive organizations. The publication of the attorney general's list, Stone declared, dangerously widened the scope of the red scare as guilt by association now possessed a governmental seal of approval. At stake, he insisted, was the belief that the free exchange of ideas best served to promote reform and mitigate discontent. The argument that political liberty enabled Communists to advance their cause, he wrote, was simply wrongheaded. For communism had made the fewest inroads precisely in those lands—the United States, England, and Canada—where its cadre had been allowed to operate openly.[50]

Conspiracies and political theories did not overturn existing social orders, he continued, until they had decayed from within. The real subversion "is that which is destroying faith in freedom, faith in free discussion, faith in the power of truth and the ability of ordinary folk to grasp it. This faith is the essence of the American creed; to give it up, the ultimate disloyalty."[51]

What thoroughly appalled Stone was the part liberals played in the anti-Communist mania that threatened to envelop the nation. It was one thing for right-wingers or Communists to be dismissive about civil liberties. It was something else again for liberals to follow suit. To Izzy, it was as though liberals were determined to discard the most sacred tenets of their faith. This, he found to be wholly inexcusable as well as politically foolish. For if liberals thought they could deflect criticisms of themselves by throwing radicals to the red-baiting sharks, he argued, they were sadly mistaken.

B y the end of 1947, Communist as well as many non-Communist members of the Progressive Citizens of America had come to the conclusion that they could in no way support Harry Truman in the upcoming presidential race. Instead, they decided to call for the establishment of a third party, one that could rally in proper united front fashion around Henry Wallace, the man they believed should have followed FDR into the presidential mansion. They were troubled by the Truman administration's seeming departure from the path of Roosevelt. Consequently, they were elated when Wallace announced on December 29 that he was seeking to rally around him a new Gideon's Army; in his own quasi-religious fashion, Wallace was harking back to the ancient Israeli hero. But Wallace's good friends Eleanor Roosevelt and Florida Senator Claude Pepper wanted nothing to do with his campaign, nor did Max Lerner of *PM* or Freda Kirchwey of *The Nation*. Kirchwey considered Wallace's bid, lacking labor support as it did, to be "strategically unwise" and bound to divide progressive ranks; it also would demonstrate, she predicted, how weak the American left really was. Like Kirchwey, Lerner worried that Wallace could throw the election to the GOP, and he felt called upon to point out that the new party was not representative of "American independent progressivism." However, Arthur Schlesinger, Jr., expressed satisfaction that Wallace's Progressive Party had "cleared liberal minds of much confusion."[52]

The obvious influence of Communists within the Wallace movement disturbed many liberals, as did the candidate's view on international affairs, which some saw as blindly pro-Soviet. However, by early 1948 and particularly following the Communist takeover in Czechoslovakia, the Soviet Union had again lost a good deal of its luster. Even I. F. Stone, a dedicated Popular Fronter who viewed Wallace favorably, reported in January that the Soviet way relied "on outlawry, suppression, and terror." With the Communist giant fearing competition from the West, the Soviet satellites had been compelled, he charged, to withdraw from the European recovery program spearheaded by the United States. This was yet another example, Stone believed, of the Communists' insistence upon an unattainable degree of perfectionism. Kirchwey went still farther, declaring Russia to be "an accomplice, at the very least," in the appearance of "two warring camps" on the European continent.[53]

In February, when the Communist coup d'état took place in Czechoslovakia, a type of Popular Front government had been in power; Wallace, to the dismay of many, refused to condemn the takeover. *The Nation* blamed both the USSR and the United States for what had transpired, and Freda Kirchwey unhappily noted that U.S. policy had involved treating the democratically elected Czech government as a Soviet puppet. *The New Republic*—Wallace having resigned as its editor by now—went a good deal farther, declaring that Stalin would accept sycophants only at the head of ruthless communist states. It was obvious, Stone pointed out in *PM* in late March, that the Soviets could take a lesson from Americans where freedom of expression was involved, just as Americans could learn a thing or two from the Soviets when it came to economic planning.[54]

Notwithstanding Wallace's disastrous stance on Czechoslovakia, Izzy, on March 15, cast his lot with the former vice-president. He admitted that he did not dislike Harry Truman, whom he saw as too honest a man for demagoguery and yet no leader in the Roosevelt mold. But now Truman was being pulled, he feared, "by a sinister undertow of fear, suspicion and hate toward a new, a disastrous, an unnecessary, and a criminal war." Standing up for the third party was not without risks, Stone admitted, but he for one—thanks to the freedom he enjoyed in the United States and the privilege of working for a publication such as *PM*—had decided to stand "on my hind legs and thumb my nose at the so-and-so's, and say 'I'm for Wallace too.' "[55]

Stone decided to back Wallace and oppose the reelection of President Truman because he was more and more troubled by administration policies in general. By contrast, the third-party bid seemingly offered the hope of recreating the Popular Front, which could condemn the drift toward war and the deteriorating state of civil liberties in the nation. But above all else, he was simply disgusted with the overall state of affairs as of early 1948, so different from what he had envisioned such a short time before. Not only had the antifascist Grand Alliance terminated and the United States aligned with some unsavory but avowedly anti-Communist types, but the possibility of a socialist America appeared more remote than ever. Yet it was not simply the liberals in the Truman administration, he acknowledged, who were to blame for the Cold War. The Soviets, who had quashed any hopes for democratic reform in Eastern Europe, were at least equally responsible.

Nevertheless, he was particularly disturbed by congressional calls that spring for the registration of the Communist Party and front organizations. Such proposals, he declared on May 2, indicated that "leading American democrats" had too little faith in the free discussion that a democratic society required. Forcing the party underground, he continued, would only make it appear more threatening and add to the hysteria. The Communists, like the Francophiles, anarchists, and abolitionists of earlier days, Stone conceded, did pose a problem. The question of liberty was something that each genera-tion had to contend with in its own fashion, challenging "anew faith in freedom." But a calm reading of present-day America, he insisted, simply did not justify "the panic-stricken adoption of methods which smack of the totalitarianism for which we criticize Moscow."[56]

That summer Stone condemned the indictment of twelve Communist Party members charged under the Smith Act. The party had, after all, discarded its revolutionary thrust some time earlier. In fact, "the zigzags of party line, and the constant adjustments to Moscow's latest, have left the comrades as confused as the FBI."[57]

By the summer of 1948, shortly after the Soviet Union began a blockade of West Berlin, he angrily called for a plague on the houses of both super-powers. He happily noted how disgusted the less powerful states were with the "arrogance . . . egotism and . . . boundless fears" of Russia and the United States. While the fears of the most powerful nation on the face of the earth bordered on the absurd, Soviet paranoia seemed little better. That great nation-state, its strategic borders expanded once more, failed to re-member the heroism so recently displayed by its own people; instead, "an old fashioned Russian orgy of suspicion for foreigners, intellectuals and any kind of dissent" was again taking place.[58]

Consequently, the Israelis, the Scandinavians, the French, and evidently the Yugoslavs as well, all desired to go their own way, to seek out "a little space in the sun." And so would the Poles and the Czechs, Stone suggested, if only they were allowed to.[59]

What Stone recognized so clearly was that neither of the great powers was inclined to allow certain countries in its sphere of influence any large degree of national autonomy. Although one claimed to be the standard bearer of liberal democracy and the other the architect of world communism, both cared little about the desires of other peoples and other lands. Both were determined to maintain an imperialistic or neocolonial stance, an unhappy occurrence in Stone's estimation.

B y the time the Progressive Party gathered in Philadelphia in late July, Cold War tensions and his own foot-in-mouth propensities had caused Henry Wallace's standing in the polls to plummet dramatically. Just back from another jaunt halfway around the world—with stops in Palestine, Cyprus, Athens, Bani, Nice, and Paris—and undoubtedly suffering from jet lag, Izzy refused to go to the convention. It proved to be, in the words of *The Nation,* "half political rally, half religious revival," which was precisely what Izzy had feared. He had thought that if he were to attend, he would be so put off "by a lot of the kooks, that I might lose my bearings because I wanted to be for Wallace because I thought it was the right thing to do." He was lining up with the Progressives regardless of certain of Wallace's "naive ventures into Soviet zone politics" and in spite of the fact that Communists appeared to be running the show. Izzy indicated that he was backing Wallace in the face of any number of reservations:

> I don't like yogis and I don't like commissars. I condemn the way Stalin combs his hair and I disapprove the way Molotov blows his nose. I can't help cheering for Tito, and when Socialism comes I'll fight for the right to spit in the nearest bureaucrat's eye. I own a house in Washington and I don't want proletarians trampling petunias on their way downtown to overthrow the government by force and violence. I wouldn't want my sister to marry a Communist, and force me to maldigest my Sunday morning bagel arguing dialectics with a sectarian brother-in-law.[60]

Izzy admitted that yes, he was "a dupe, or worse," and needed "to have my ideological tires checked at the nearest FBI service station." Moreover, he recognized that if the American comrades ever took over Washington, "I'd soon find myself eating cold *kasha* in a concentration camp in Kansas *gubernya.*"[61]

And yet he had a feeling, Izzy continued, that he was not "as big a dupe" as those who refused to blemish their politically correct records by voting or those who considered a vote for Truman to be one delivered on behalf of peace, reform, and prosperity. Supporting Wallace, at the very least, was "a protest vote against cold war, high prices, and hysteria." Izzy, along with Norman Mailer and some 150,000 others, cast yet another protest ballot in the 1948 election, this one for CP member Si Gerson, who was running to fill the New York City council seat left vacant by the death of Pete Cacchione, his comrade.[62]

Such votes, Stone believed, were simply votes of conscience. Izzy recognized that Wallace in particular had no chance whatsoever, but he had determined that he simply had to back the New Dealer. He also was well aware of how much his support for the Progressive Party candidate was costing him in terms of political respectability, access to the kinds of information reporters thrived upon, and possible professional opportunities. But as the ever-loyal Popular Fronter, he could not bear to do anything else.

Izzy's old employer, *The Nation,* refused to endorse Wallace or any other candidate for that matter, while the *Progressive* chose to back Norman Thomas and *The New Republic* eventually threw in with the president.[63]

Harry Truman, of course, eventually won the 1948 presidential election in a stunning upset over Thomas Dewey, the Republican governor of New York. Henry Wallace, by contrast, garnered barely over a million votes, a mere two percent of the total ballots cast. Rabid red-baiting of Wallace and the Progressive Party had resulted in such a disastrous showing, but so too had liberal concerns about a Republican takeover of the executive branch, Truman's tardy but effective move leftward during the campaign, and repeated faux pas by Wallace. The Wallace presidential bid was so pitiful in fact that, just as Freda Kirchwey had feared, it spelled the end of this third Popular Front. Indeed, in many ways, the Wallace campaign proved to be the last gasp of the Old Left as a whole, and the fate that had befallen it demonstrated the impotence of American radicalism in the early postwar era.

In 1949, Arthur M. Schlesinger, Jr., completed a book whose title came to signify the appearance of a new kind of liberalism, one that was militantly anti-Communist and diametrically opposed to the very notion of the Popular Front. In fact, *The Vital Center,* heavily influenced by the pessimism of Reinhold Niebuhr, lumped fascism and communism together, while calling for a resurgence of American radicalism. But this was to be radicalism of the specifically anti-Communist kind, as represented by Walter Reuther, head of the United Auto Workers. This "non-Communist left," Schlesinger believed, could join hands with "the non-Fascist right" to strengthen American freedom. It would back the Fair Deal at home and the implementation of both the Marshall Plan and the Truman Doctrine overseas.[64]

As historian Richard Pells has noted, what the Vital Center amounted to was the transference of allegiance by American intellectuals "from one set of symbols to another: from Socialism to democracy, from economic justice to political pluralism, from collective action to personal morality, from the Internationale to the American Dream."[65]

The horrors of Stalinism and the manipulative practices of the Communist Party, of course, had helped to bring about this change in perspective. But so too did the altered status of certain members of the American intelligentsia. No longer marginal actors on the periphery of power, they were now increasingly positioned as seminal architects and celebrants of the Pax Americana and the managerial society.[66]

I n contrast, I. F. Stone, with the Wallace campaign having sealed the fate of the third Popular Front, was somewhat cast adrift politically and professionally in a nation that, in spite of Truman's reelection triumph, was about to continue its rightward shift. With the Old Left all but history, the publications Stone wrote for lacked any kind of political connection and, very soon, much of an audience as well. Once again, this was unfortunate because Stone's comments on the political climate in the country were often so perceptive. He rightly recognized that the bourgeoning paranoia boded ill not simply for targeted individuals and despised political groups, but for the American nation as a whole. The state of civil liberties did indeed suffer accordingly, as did the health of liberal and radical movements. Less clearly evident at the time—though not to Stone—was the retreat from New Deal idealism and the stasis and reaction certain to follow.

His easy employment of charged words like "terror" and "fascism," however, coupled with the shift in the political atmosphere, undoubtedly lessened the impact of his essays and that of the publications he continued to write for: *The Nation* (even after his trip underground to Palestine), *The New Republic*, and *PM*. His analyses of events appeared to be colored by his as yet undiminished attachment to certain of the ideals and concerns of the 1930s.

But unlike committed party members, oldtime fellow travelers, and embittered anti-Communist liberals—all of whom viewed the international scene as might the most dedicated of Manichaeans—I. F. Stone had early denounced the Cold War antics of both the United States and the Soviet Union. The crushing of the Czech democracy and the Russo-Yugoslav rift caused Stone to view the presence of the Red Army in Eastern Europe in a different light than he had heretofore. Now he recognized that the stationing of Russian divisions there was intended simply to maintain Soviet hegemony and the "People's Democracies" in place.

Stone's reading of U.S. postwar foreign policy proved remarkably astute, foreshadowing revisionist analyses of a generation later. Very early, he recognized that a new anti-Communist bloc had been constructed, whose emergence helped to ensure the outbreak of international hostilities. Notwithstanding his own earlier Wilsonian bent, Stone was increasingly leery of the notion of an American Century once envisioned by individuals as disparate as Henrys Luce and Wallace, the magazine mogul and Roosevelt's third-term vice-president respectively. Theirs was a notion that he too had once propounded in days past, but would no longer.

Furthermore, as he so astutely recognized, U.S. policymakers, caught up in Cold War machinations, tragically failed to heed the demands for change now sweeping across much of the globe. Instead, the very same strategists chose to link up with conservative, even reactionary figures and forces, while engaging in a simplistic reading of the unrest that was beginning to boil over. They seemingly considered the hammer-and-sickle, stamped with a Soviet insignia, to be orchestrating virtually every Latin American, African, Asian, or Middle Eastern drive of a radical or even reformist sort. That in turn led others to view the United States as Stone had warned it should be seen, as the fortress of reactionaries worldwide.

Thus, Stone's reading of the early Cold War—whose appearance had proven so unhappy for the third Popular Front—left him standing more and more alone as the American nation continued to move to the right. So too did his devoted commitment to the vision of socialism at a time when that very word fed hysteria and hatred in the United States. Still, as 1948 wound down, Stone and the remnants of the American Old Left had no way of knowing that the hardest and harshest times for progressive forces were only about to begin.

9 The Panic Was On

I F. Stone returned to the States in June 1951, having spent the past ten
months overseas. Feeling that he simply could not "stand America any
longer," he had given serious consideration to the possibility of remaining abroad. As Izzy informed a British colleague in Belgrade, he did not see
how he could practice his craft at home and remain "sane and honest."
Fearing that fascism might come to his country, Izzy, more than a little
depressed, gave thought to establishing permanent residence in England
and becoming a political refugee. He attempted to convince his brother
Marc to join him and agreed to serve as head of his newspaper's Paris
bureau.[1]

Esther, Jay, and Chris had come to France following Izzy's visit to Yugoslavia, while Celia continued with her studies at Smith College. Now Esther and
the boys accompanied him back home, their European adventure having
come to an end. It had enabled Jay and Chris to receive something that their
father had long desired for them, a European education, however abbrevi-
ated. While in France, the family had resided at the estate of the widow of
Léon Blum, the former prime minister, which was located in Jouy-en-Josas,
between Paris and Versailles. Their departure, decided upon suddenly by
Izzy, had resulted in "an unpleasant scene" with Madame Blum, who came
rushing out of her house demanding payment for every little trifle.[2]

Izzy, although continuing to feel that the United States "was just too crazy
a place," had opted to come back because of pressure brought to bear by Ted
Thackery, publisher of the *New York Daily Compass*, the last in the line of *PM*
would-have-beens. Thackery had informed Izzy that unless he returned, the
paper was certain to go under. Encouraged by Marc to appeal to his ego,
Corliss Lamont relayed a similar message. So too did Judy Stone, upon
visiting Izzy and his family. More than one impassioned discussion was held
between Izzy and Judy regarding the need for him to return to the United
States to "fight fascism." Eventually all the coaxing did the trick and Izzy and
Esther loaded up the kids and headed back home.[3]

That decision was of immeasurable relief to Esther and the two boys
because Izzy had earlier indicated that he was going to decide whether they
should head back to New York or on to Israel. As Chris, homesick for his
friends in the United States, was later to acknowledge, he at least "was in
terror" that Izzy was planning to move to the Holy Land; typically, the fate of

the Stone four lay in the hands of Izzy alone, whose career always came first. But instead, they boarded the *Liberté,* unsure of what awaited them back in the United States.[4]

When the ship entered New York harbor, a small boat boarded the *Liberté;* shortly thereafter, an announcement came over the address system that I. F. Stone was to come to the foredeck. There was some concern that perhaps Izzy was about to be arrested or the family's passports lifted. Paranoia had been rife among the American expatriate community in Paris, which was not surprising given its largely Hollywood makeup. In Izzy's case, more than paranoia was at stake, as the FBI maintained its security investigation of him. That in turn had brought Izzy's actions overseas to the attention of other government agencies, including the CIA, whose assistant director termed him a "well-known pro-Communist newspaper correspondent." But the call on board the *Liberté* proved to have been made at the request of Thackery, who had sent a reporter out to shoot Izzy's picture upon his reentry into the United States.[5]

Nevertheless, there was yet another scare in store for the Stones, who remained riddled with tension at this point. At passport control on the ship, Izzy was confronted by a big, burly immigration official who looked first at him and then at his passport before asking in thick Brooklynese, "Hey, is you the Stone that used to write for *PM?*"[6] Fearing the worst, Izzy said to himself, "Oh, boy, this is where I lose my passport! He's going to confiscate it!" Nevertheless, he jauntily replied, "Yep, that's me!"[7] To his delight and astonishment, the government official promptly stamped his passport, handed it back, and said in Yiddish, "Sei gesund" (Be well). Given the times, it was "such a nice welcome back."[8]

Having returned to the States, Izzy then chose to reside in New York City, refusing at this point to return to the capital. Although finances were tight yet again, the Stones rented an apartment at 1133 Park Avenue, a mere two blocks from the home of John Foster Dulles, then a high-powered Wall Street attorney and a key figure in the Republican Party.[9]

The late forties and early fifties were not the easiest times for individuals like Izzy Stone, who remained very much a part of the rapidly dwindling progressive ranks. The fate of *PM* and its successors, the *New York Star* and the *New York Daily Compass,* bespoke that of radical journalism and of the American left as a whole. In June 1948, after a run of eight years, *PM* called it a day. Having lost millions on the enterprise, publisher Marshall Field sold his interest in the paper to Bartley Crum, an attorney formerly with the Hearst publishing empire, and Joseph Barnes, a reporter with the *New York Herald Tribune.*[10]

The greater and greater costs of publishing, the still fierce competition for readers in the New York City market, and the attraction of television and radio news programs all had something to do with the demise of *PM*. So too did the changed political atmosphere of the postwar period, so different from what had been envisioned when the newspaper first appeared at the beginning of the decade. The much-awaited early version of *PM* had received support from a still vibrant Old Left, from New Deal supporters, and from those who believed that fascism had to be confronted. Now the Old Left was in tatters, the New Deal and fascism both becoming something of a memory, while communism was increasingly viewed as the greatest threat to the American Way.

In the midst of all this, on June 23, the first issue of *PM*'s immediate successor, the *New York Star*, rolled hot off the presses. The *Star* proclaimed itself "an independent newspaper" which lined up with FDR-Willkie supporters, New Deal reform, and the fight against fascism. But by the first of the year, it was increasingly clear that the *Star*, lacking the deep pockets of *PM*'s publisher Marshall Field, was having a hard time of it. Consequently, Izzy again spoke with Freda Kirchwey about a possible return to *The Nation*. Then on January 27, 1949, Joe Barnes called Izzy at home and forewarned him, "We're going to close down tomorrow." Izzy turned to Esther and said, "This is my chance to write that book" and headed upstairs to take a hot bath and relax. When he came downstairs, Ted Thackery was on the phone, wanting to know if he would transfer his column to the *New York Post*, which had been sold a full decade before by J. David Stern, his former boss at the paper. His editorials were to appear six times a week in the *Post*, (he had been writing three per week for the *Star*); his salary was to be doubled as well.[11]

In his first editorial for the *Post*, Izzy delivered his own farewell to *PM*, praising the paper's bid to abandon "the deadly conveyor belt method" of contemporary journalism and its attempt to give "a break to the poor sucker getting the dirty end of the stick." In fact, for those who worked there, *PM* afforded "a chance to do the kind of newspaper job small boys dream about, mixing it all up with windmills and knights errant." And in spite of never-ending squabbles and the brickbats that came their way, the *PM*ers were proud of what they had accomplished. Yes, regardless of the insults, they considered themselves to be humbly walking in the footsteps of Jefferson and Whitman. A. J. Liebling, the famed columnist for the *New Yorker*, acknowledged that *PM* was "pure of heart."[12]

Izzy jumped when Ted Thackery asked him in May to transfer his column once more, this time to the *New York Daily Compass*, the latest in the *PM-Star* line. Thackery and his wife, Dorothy Schiff, publisher of the *Post*, had just experienced both a marital and political falling-out. She had named Jimmy Wechsler editor of the paper and had announced that the *Post* would now battle "all totalitarianism, whether Fascist or Communist." Thackery, by contrast, envisioned the *Compass* as continuing to uphold the Popular Front banner. There Izzy would come to serve as the "main attraction" for the dwindling band of post-*PM* readers.[13]

But the newest tabloid, like its immediate predecessor, lacked the remarkable cadre of journalists who had made up the *PM* staff, never acquired the respectability and acclaim that had allowed *PM*ers entrance into the White House, and experienced a sharp reduction in subscriptions as befitting the rapidly deteriorating state of the postwar American left. Nevertheless, it did provide Stone with a forum for his editorials, every bit as radical as before. Moreover, the *Compass* did help to maintain a tradition of independent left-wing journalism, whose ranks were about to become still more circumscribed, what with the impending collapse of Dwight Macdonald's *Politics* and George Seldes's *In Fact*. For a time, the *Compass* remained one of the very few vehicles that allowed politically committed journalists and intellectuals to express the kinds of viewpoints that were now heard less and less frequently, even in the left-liberal journals that had been affected by a loss of subscribers, a growing sense of disillusionment concerning socialist "experiments," and, undoubtedly, the pressures of the Cold War itself. The *Compass* remained very much tied to the now increasingly discredited Old Left. That afforded some small comfort to Stone, for he was determined to continue taking a stand on behalf of what he considered to be progressive principles, no matter how little attraction they held for most of his compatriots. He did so both in print and at the podium, to the considerable displeasure of liberal anti-Communists, hard-line conservatives, and government agents.

I n these difficult times, as political and professional frustrations mounted for those who remained situated on the left, the Stone household served as a haven of sorts for its male breadwinner. True, Izzy, as always, faced a constant barrage "of deadlines, pressures, competition, unrelenting hard work," but life at home revolved around him, seemingly absolutely. There "Father and his work were one," daughter Celia later acknowledged, "and to that one we were all of secondary importance."[14]

Thus, when Izzy required a nap, the children were obliged to tiptoe around; when he was ready to eat, the family gathered at the dinner table; occasionally, when he required a break from his toil, they all huddled into the family auto and headed off for the beach in un-air-conditioned discomfort— the children carsick, Esther worn out from making preparations for the excursion, and Izzy contentedly calling out, "Isn't this fun, kids?" When he wanted to go to sleep in the early evening, Esther headed upstairs with him. When he desired to play the piano in the midst of a dinner party, all were expected to gather round to listen. And when his teacup was not properly filled, Izzy exploded.[15]

Izzy's "life pulsed," his son Chris later reflected, "and we pulsed with it or steered out of the way." Izzy was, then, a "rather difficult man," and there was always pressure to produce the daily copy that was the Stones' bread-and-butter. Indeed, the household marched to "the rhythm of creation under the rein of a deadline."[16]

Happily for Izzy, Esther ministered to his every need. True, Celia reported, "she counseled, but always obliquely; governed, but only the Interior." She dismissed Izzy's fits of anger; they were a "necessary" release, she indicated, from work-induced stress. Moreover, Esther heartily supported her husband's dogged commitment to his writing and his ideals, notwithstanding the fact that her own priorities were otherwise: "personal loyalties, love of family, friends, her daily relationship with the people around her." The two appeared as if mirror images of each other: Izzy "could only be happy satisfying himself; she, others." Theirs was a marriage from the previous century. This was a family where "father worked" and "mother mothered."[17]

And yet this truly was a relationship of a very special sort. Perhaps, as Chris acknowledged, not many women could or would have catered to Izzy's every whim as Esther so lovingly did. But the two were bonded like few others, a seemingly perfect fit. Izzy shared with Esther "feelings, shared exchange of ideas about his life" as he did with no one else.[18]

Fortunately, each summer the Stones were able to leave the frenetic pace of Izzy's work schedule and the sweltering heat of Washington, D.C., behind as they headed off for vacation sites on Fire Island, Seaview or Ocean Beach. While still in New York that first time around during the thirties, they had begun to spend summers outside of the city; then, in 1946, they purchased a home on Fire Island, perhaps at the urging of brother-in-law Leonard Boudin. There even Izzy was able to relax a bit while he worked on a book-length manuscript or copy for *The Nation* or *PM*. When necessary, he would take the train into Manhattan or fly to Washington. But Izzy particularly appreciated being outside of the capital, which he considered cold and increasingly hostile, although he remained "addicted" to it. He also enjoyed running into readers and acquaintances from his days in New York City. He took great pleasure in being recognized by old subscribers and compatriots. And as always, he loved taking long walks, which invariably became extended conversations focusing on subjects as diverse as poetry and politics, when another family member joined him.[19]

I zzy also enjoyed the parties he and Esther held at their summer places on occasion. At one such gathering, Charlie Chaplin, long considered the world's greatest cinematic performer, made an appearance.[20]

This was all to the good, for the world outside of his family and circle of friends, both in the United States and abroad, offered less and less comfort as the postwar era continued. Truman's upset victory in the 1948 presidential campaign had stunned Stone as it did so many others, causing him to envision yet another round of New Dealism. *The New Republic, The Nation,* and the *Progressive* all expressed elation about the election results. But they were sadly mistaken in their belief that a new period of reformism lay just ahead.[21]

Very quickly, Stone recognized this and returned to his earlier evaluation of the Truman administration. He was disturbed by the belligerent tone of President Truman's 1949 inaugural address, which spoke of a government with values antithetical to America's own and which "set ourselves up to police the world." The formation that spring of the North Atlantic Treaty Organization, a military alliance involving the United States, ten Western European countries, and Canada, Stone likened to "a new Holy Alliance" intended to hold back the forces of change.[22]

Both the diversion of funds to NATO from the European recovery program and its martial spirit greatly disturbed him. Long-term investments, he acknowledged, would only be possible if certain preconditions were met. The Soviet Union could not engage in military aggression. Communist revolution could not be carried out in the very countries where investments were to be made. And war between the United States and Russia could not take place.[23]

An increase in international tensions also had to be avoided, Stone insisted, but he feared that the administration was gearing the American people up for war. It made sense, he acknowledged, to indicate in writing that the United States would come to the aid of Western Europe in case of an attack; he further admitted that the greatest deterrent to aggression from Russia was "fear of American power." But he refused to accept the notion that the Atlantic pact was the proper vehicle. He worried that the Western nations were creating their own "rival organization" outside the control of the Security Council of the UN.[24]

Monthly Review, a new journal put out by Leo Huberman and Paul Sweezy, two other Old Leftists, agreed with Stone's analysis and warned that NATO was intended to lay the foundation for an anti-Soviet front; that in turn would be used in a war against the Communist state. Freda Kirchwey of *The Nation* believed that NATO had been designed as an anti-Soviet pact which violated the charter of the United Nations; Russia, she declared, would inevitably react by tightening its grip on Eastern Europe and moving to create its own military alliance. Nevertheless, she denied the Russian accusations delivered by the Soviets that NATO possessed "an obviously aggressive character." Like Michael Straight of *The New Republic*, she saw it as a "defensive" arrangement only. Still, Straight recognized that the decision to create NATO was truly monumental.[25]

On April 4, 1949, the very day NATO officially came into being, some twenty-five hundred congregated at the Manhattan Center in New York City to protest Cold War happenings. Among those who spoke at the "Caucus for Peace" sponsored by the Joint Anti-Fascist Refugee Committee—which was prominently located on the attorney general's list—were Julio Alvarez Del Vayo, foreign minister of the Spanish Republican government and the foreign editor of *The Nation*; Henry Wallace; and I. F. Stone. Stone, as a confidential government report indicated, insisted that the attorney general had no authority to compile his list of purportedly subversive organizations. It was HCUAC that was "un-American," Stone proclaimed, and it was Wall Street that employed Franco as "a satellite," Franco, that "former satellite of Hitler." The report underscored the fact that "obscene language" punctuated Stone's address.[26]

On August 14, 1949, in a special supplement to the *New York Daily Compass*, Stone attempted to analyze the early Cold War period. "The Russian Revolution, the biggest event of our time," he declared, had fostered the same kinds of anxieties that the French quest for "Liberty, Fraternity, Equality" once had. In each case, the forces of reaction played upon the horrors that resulted from "the brutalities, fanaticisms, cruelties and stupidities" present in any revolutionary era. No matter; the advance of socialism, Stone declared, remained as certain as had the earlier march of republicanism.[27]

Force, he insisted, could hold back new ideas but only temporarily and only at the cost of later and still more violent change. It was in England, with its heritage of parliamentary government, where socialism was slowly and peacefully taking root. It was in Russia, where the despotic practices of the czars had gone on for centuries, that the bloodiest upheaval had come about. To meet the Communist threat with force, Stone warned, was to usher in its appearance in the most horrific manner imaginable.[28]

Nine days later, Stone insisted that communism would better the economic lot of the Chinese people. Like others, Stone had once viewed the Chinese Communists in somewhat utopian fashion, declaring them to be only agrarian reformers who desired "a rural New Deal rather than Sovietism." Now he warned that intervention intended to overturn the Chinese Revolution—which he and the editors of *The Nation* and *Monthly Review* considered to be the biggest event of the era—would cost the United

States both materially and morally. A better approach, he reasoned, would be to promote the "independent tendencies" of nations in the Soviet zone of influence.[29]

That fall, Stone, in emphasizing the need for coexistence, explained that communism had proven its mettle in "backward peasant" lands like China. It helped to bring about industrialization there but at an admittedly high cost—the creation of an all-powerful state that hampered both progress and efficiency. How to dissolve this state after it had carried out "its historic function," Stone admitted, remained a dilemma.[30]

What such an analysis suggested was that in spite of the brutal collectivization campaign, the Moscow Trials, the Nazi-Soviet pact, the latest quashing of the Czech democracy, and the Stalinist takeover of Eastern Europe, Stone continued to believe that communism was a progressive force, lined up on the correct side of historical events. He remained convinced that something like communism with a human face could yet appear, whether in Russia, Eastern Europe, China, or Yugoslavia.

Furthermore, he cared little for those positioned on the anti-Communist side of Cold War lines, spotting too many fascists, friends of fascists, or opponents of reform in such overseas encampments and too many foes of the New Deal alongside too many "turncoats" in such a grouping at home. Consequently, he ended up among the small number of American intellectuals and activists who determined to adopt an anti-anti-Communist stance.

A determined commitment to socialism and an anti-anti-Communist posture in the face of heightened international tensions, then, were the ideological forces that drove Stone onward during Harry Truman's second term in office. As others who had previously lined up on the left continued their movement out of the progressive camp and the nation as a whole underwent a rightward shift, Stone maintained his belief in socialist ideals and principles. Their implementation, he recognized, required peace and a generous spirit, both of which were threatened by the sharper rhetoric and narrowing of political boundaries his own country was experiencing. Recognizing that the verbal hostilities between East and West threatened to spill over into actual combat and had already resulted in the employment of martial surrogates, he argued for a tolerant view of global events, particularly as they pertained to nationalistic yearnings and demands for change. Political intrigues at home also promised to curb any efforts to bring about New Deal–style reform, let alone anything more wide-ranging.

Thus, by 1949, Izzy had adopted the ideology of anti-anti-communism, which cost him the remaining strands of respectability and political pull he had once had. Ideology, commitment, and his own stubbornness had triumphed over ambition and Stone appeared to be headed for only the footnotes of histories on modern American journalism.

His staking out of such an increasingly unpopular position required no little courage. Yet it demonstrated that he—unlike some other Old Left veterans who had headed politically rightward—failed to appreciate the full costs of first Stalin's and now Mao's brand of communism. But while these former colleagues had departed from the radical ranks altogether, he continued to celebrate the ideals of the Old Left, which caused him more anguish and less certainty than the now disbelievers appeared to be experiencing as they adopted the new verities of hardcore anticommunism. That very anguish and uncertainty, coupled with a still firm belief in socialism, was leading Stone onto the course of a more independent radicalism.

T hroughout 1949, that third year of the Cold War, Stone acknowledged that this conflict was persisting not simply because of the actions of Soviet-baiters and red-haters. Rather, he reserved some of his sharpest barbs for onetime allies in the Popular Front, versions one, two, and three, and for their ideological homeland. In February 1949, he condemned the depiction by the Soviet government of Anna Louise Strong and Agnes Smedley, two perennial supporters of a united front, as spies for the United States. Absolutism, he warned, necessarily bred conspiracy and paranoia. The Soviets appeared "even nuttier" and "more fruity" than their American counterparts, he noted, with the Strong deportation from the USSR calling to mind "pandemic dementia." The officialdom who had expelled Strong, one of the Soviet Union's strongest supporters, demonstrated what became of unbridled stupidity. It resulted in despotism which "the sycophant, the lickspittle, the yes-man, the apple-polisher, the guy who plays safe" did not dare to contest.[31]

Sometime later, Stone contrasted Secretary of State Dean Acheson's defense of Alger Hiss, the former Roosevelt aide accused of having committed espionage for the Soviets, with the *Daily Worker*'s treatment of Strong. She, who had devoted her very life to both the American working class and the great revolutions of this century, had been cruelly excised from "the movement." Her treatment by Soviet bureaucrats again demonstrated that while it was "pretty bad" to be labeled a red in Washington, it was something else again to be denounced as a spy in the Communist heartland.[32]

The Smith Act trial of American Communist Party leaders, Stone reported in March 1949, again underscored the sharp contrast between court proceedings here and "the quick heave-ho" dissidents were afforded in the Soviet Union. And he blasted the decision by the party to respond in agitprop fashion, with the "brave working class advocates spitting manfully in the eye of the capitalist judge as they are dragged off to the counter-revolutionary gallows screaming defiance on their way." This was the same mind-set, he suggested, that had cheered the prosecution of the Minneapolis Trotskyists during the war and demonstrated how "inadequately schooled" the comrades were when it came to the civil liberties of others.[33]

The Communists also declined to lend support in "The Case of the Legless Veteran"—a phrase coined by Stone himself—which involved the firing of James Kutcher, a Trotskyist and World War II vet, removed from a clerical post with the Veterans Administration as the red scare began. Izzy, by contrast, readily joined the Kutcher Civil Rights Defense Committee, along with Warren Billings, Norman Mailer, Carey McWilliams, C. Wright Mills, A. J. Muste, Philip Rahv, and Max Shactman. But few of the leading liberal publications believed as *The Nation* did that the travails of Kutcher warranted attention.[34]

In the midst of that trial of top American Communists held at the federal courthouse in Foley Square in Manhattan, Izzy ran into George Charney and V. J. Jerome, said to be the cultural commissar of the party. Jerome sought to elicit Izzy's help in reaching out to liberals willing to stand by Smith Act defendants such as Charney. Quietly but firmly, Izzy reminded Jerome of the Communist Party's long-standing and dismissive attitude toward liberals of any kind, even Marxist-favored ones. This "devastating" encounter, as Charney later recalled, spoke volumes about the embitteredness and suspicion with which the CPUSA was presently viewed in ranks left of center and how divided those ranks now were.[35]

Morris Ernst, an attorney with the ACLU, and Senator Hubert Humphrey of Minnesota had no qualms about the prosecutions. But Roger Baldwin, the founder of the ACLU, criticized the fact that the government case rested wholly on speeches and writings, not on overt action. Arthur M. Schlesinger, Jr., also argued that "dangerous opinions" must be tolerated, due process provided, and the old Holmes-Brandeis test of clear and present danger returned to. *The New Republic* worried about the conducting of a "political trial" in an atmosphere of "hysteria." Robert Bendiner of *The Nation* refuted the notion that the party, its membership having plummeted dramatically, presented any real threat whatsoever.[36]

After attending the Conference to Defend the Bill of Rights held at the end of June in New York City, which had been orchestrated by the Communist Party, Stone—recently damned by the *Daily Worker* as "disruptive"—blasted the invectives directed at a Socialist Workers Party member who had attempted to address the gathering. This once again demonstrated to Stone how little members of the Communist Party understood. The Communists saw the Trotskyists, he wrote, as the red-baiters saw the reds, thus repeating the propensity of "a hounded faction" to hound its own heretical offshoot. Once again, principle took a back seat to party fanaticism.[37]

On occasion, Stone acknowledged, while refusing to declare this to be the case at present, "single-minded fanatics" were required to bring about sweeping change. Martin Luther and Vladimir Lenin fell into that camp, not the unpopular liberals such as himself who admittedly were not up to such tasks. And when a society could not be reformed peacefully, terrible strife was certain to come. At that point, "mentalities like mine are unsuited. I hate cruelty and injustice too much to accept it without protest even in a 'good' cause."[38]

But history, Stone insisted, required both liberals and fanatics. Moreover, Communists had to be reminded that the law according to Marx depicted revolutionary excesses as unfortunate but temporary necessities, not as the harbingers of "a new way of life." Indeed, the search for the truth could "no more be left to commissars than to Cardinals."[39]

Izzy's pointed criticisms of American Communist Party members underscored the divide that had occurred between him and the sectarians and the ruptures that had rent the latest edition of the Popular Front. The Wallace campaign had attempted to bring together Communists and non-Communists, an alliance that could not hold because of disparate ideological perspectives. While Izzy continued to defend the right of Communists to the protections supposedly afforded them by the first ten amendments to the U.S. Constitution, he denounced the twists and turns of party policy, brought on by its continued genuflecting toward Soviet Russia and the failure of its members to think for themselves.

R egardless of his greater and greater disdain for the American comrades, Stone consistently warned that the rights of the party faithful had to be upheld and the domestic Cold War ended. Izzy Stone found himself moving farther and farther away from the political and journalistic mainstream. He was one of the very few who recognized that any abridgement of the political freedoms of such an unpopular group as the American Communist Party threatened the liberties of all Americans. Thus, he continued to condemn those who helped to kindle the anxieties fed by the domestic Cold War and urged that this "war" be ended immediately.

On June 29, 1949, in the midst of a "Meet the Press" interview with Idaho Senator Glenn Taylor, Henry Wallace's latest running mate, Izzy wondered if the American people had "the red heeby-jeebies." In the *Compass* in mid-October, he expressed concern that the Smith Act conviction of Communist Party leaders might drive their compatriots to disband or to head underground. At that point, he warned, "the real panic, the real terror" would begin. For others would then be wary of possessing volumes of Karl Marx on their bookshelves, of teaching the historical import of revolution, of championing socialism, or of speaking critically of capitalism.[40]

(*Previous page*) I / Bernard and Katy Feinstein posed with young Isidor for this formal portrait, c. 1908–1909. Izzy was long considered his mother's favorite.

(*Above*) 2 / Bernard Feinstein, shown standing in front of the building, ran the Philadelphia Bargain Store from 1914 to 1933 or so. The family lived above the store. Bernard and his eldest son, Izzy, waged innumerable battles over his future, especially in regard to his involvement in his father's commercial enterprise.

(*Opposite, top*) 3 / On the day of his wedding to Esther M. Roisman on July 7, 1929, Izzy appeared properly splendid in black tuxedo, French-cuffed shirt, and boutonniere.

(*Opposite, bottom*) 4 / A well-seasoned journalist by early middle age, I. F. Stone wrote for leading liberal newspapers such as the *Philadelphia Record* and the *New York Post,* top left-liberal journals including *The New Republic* and *The Nation,* and experimental progressive publications on the order of *PM,* the *New York Star,* and the *New York Daily Compass.*

PR

City and State __Washington, D.C.__

DESCRIPTION AND PHOTOGRAPH OF APP

Height __5__ feet, __7__ inches.

Hair __Brown__

Eyes __Blue__

Distinguishing marks or features __mole on right__
(Note any marks or scars on hands or face
__side of nose__
by which applicant may be identified)

Place of birth __Philadelphia, Pa__
(City and State)

Date of birth __Dec 24, 1907,__
(Month, day, and year)

Occupation __Newspaperman__

I solemnly swear that the statements made on both sides of this application
hereto is a likeness of me.

I { ~~have~~ } been naturalized as a citizen of a foreign state: taken an oath or

DESCRIPTION OF APPLICANT

Height: __5__ feet __7__ inches.

Hair __Brown__ Eyes __Blue__

Distinguishing marks or features _____

Place of birth __Philadelphia Pa.__

Date of birth __December 24, 1907__

Occupation __Newspaperman__

EVIDENCE OF CITIZENSHIP AND IDENTIFYING DOCUMENTS

Passport No. __16085__ issued on __October 8, 1945__
by __Department of State at Washington__
{ to applicant,
{ to _____ } SUBMITTED.
(State name and relationship)
State disposition of passport __cancelled - returned to__
__applicant__

Other evidence of citizenship and identifying documents submitted, as
specified below: (Indicate whether sent to the Department, retained

in files of office, or returned to applicant.) _____

The following should be filled in if this application is for a PASSPORT:

MY TRAVEL PLANS ARE AS FOLLOWS:

PASTE PHOTOGRAPH HERE

Port of departure __N.Y.C.__

Approximate date of departure __Early April__

Proposed length of stay abroad __6 weeks__

Means of transportation __Plane__
(Name of ship or air line)

Countries to be visited
__Israel, France, England, Italy__
__(if visa) Soviet Union__

Purpose of trip
__Newspaper work__

I solemnly swear that the statements on both sides of this application
hereto is a likeness of me.

I { ~~have~~ have not } been naturalized as a citizen of a foreign state; taken an
declaration of allegiance to a foreign state; entered or served in the armed fo
the duties of any office, post or employment under the government of a foreign state or political subdivision thereof; voted
in a political election in a foreign state or participated in an election or plebiscite to determine the sovereignty over foreign
territory; made a formal renunciation of nationality before a diplomatic or consular officer of the United States in a foreign

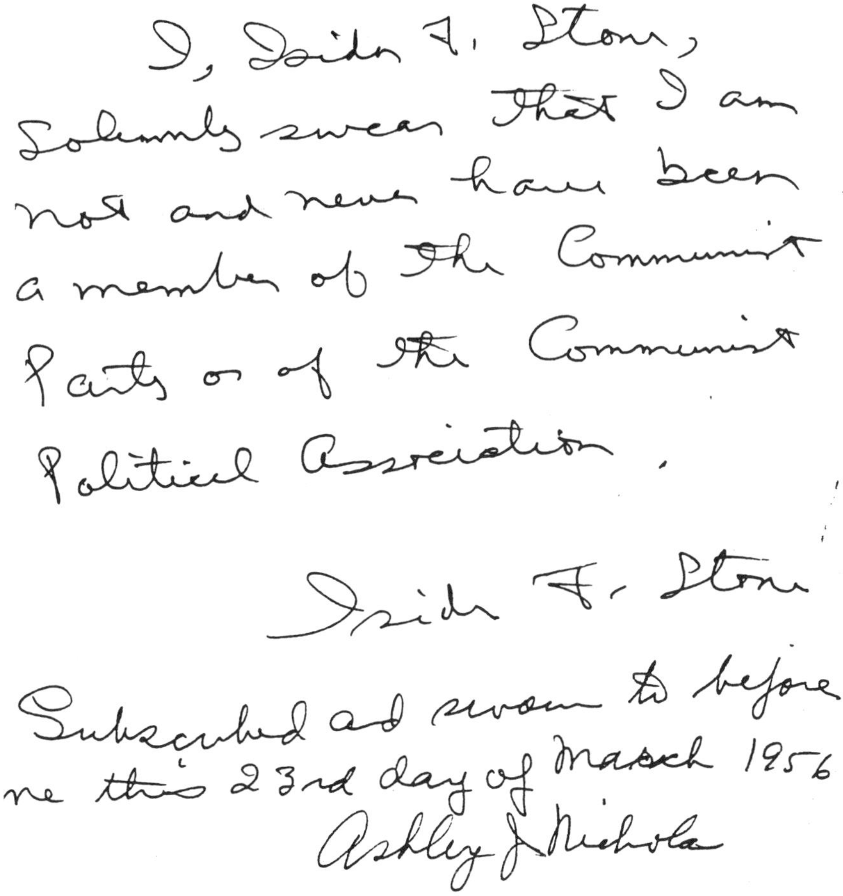

*I, Isidor F. Stone,
solemnly swear that I am
not and never have been
a member of the Communist
Party or of the Communist
Political Association.*

Isidor F. Stone

*Subscribed and sworn to before
me this 23rd day of March 1956
Ashley J. Nichols*

(*Opposite*) 5 / Portions of I. F. Stone's passport applications, in 1945, 1949, and 1956, as he headed off for Europe, the Middle East, and the Soviet Union, respectively. These applications are from his State Department file.

(*Above*) 6 / A letter from I. F. Stone's State Department file.

(*Opposite*) 7 / Having become a dean of American journalism, Izzy enjoyed the pleasures of a comfortable and productive period as he wrote his best-selling book, *The Trial of Socrates*.

(*Above*) 8 / Izzy carries on a typically animated conversation at a party celebrating his and Esther's fiftieth wedding anniversary, in the backyard of his home in the northwest section of Washington, D.C., 1979.

(*Top*) 9 / Izzy and Esther Stone, whose marriage spanned six decades, produced *I. F. Stone's Weekly* side by side. They particularly enjoyed the celebrity of their golden years.

(*Bottom*) 10 / Three of the Stone siblings—Lou, Judy, and Izzy—are seen here at a restaurant outside Norristown, Pennsylvania, on the eve of Lou's seventieth birthday. All the Stones, including brother Marc, not pictured, worked at the journalistic trade.

The CP, it was significant to note, remained legal throughout Western Europe and in occupied Japan and Germany. It had been outlawed in numerous "backward" Arab states, Stone noted, in Greece, and "in the clerical totalitarian regimes of Portugal and Spain." Thus, the United States was going along with some unsavory sorts in "relegating Jefferson to the museum of forgotten pieties."[41]

And all of this was happening at the very time when the CPUSA was more impotent than it had ever been. The party had never rebounded from the "moral blow" it had suffered in the fateful summer of 1939, and radical American intellectuals had never proven less well disposed to the Soviet Communist model. Thus cowardice alone, Stone charged, explained the cheers that followed the convictions of the party upper echelon.[42]

On November 14, Stone expressed dismay over a "Meet the Press" program he had been a panelist on which amounted to a grilling of John Gates, the *Daily Worker* editor. After watching moderator Lawrence Spivak attempt to tear apart the Spanish Civil War and World War II veteran, Stone wondered if this radical-phobe—with whom Izzy had had run-ins in the past—might not have been a grand inquisitor in some other existence.[43]

Izzy wondered, too, what purpose he served as "the 'Hot' radical" of the "Meet the Press" radio and television program. It seemed to him that "whenever some poor Red or near-Red" was to be "barbecued," he was asked to appear to give the show some semblance of fairness. This because no other journalists in Washington remained "willing to stick his neck out in this capital of the land of the free and the home of the brave."[44]

And yet every time he appeared on the show, Izzy reflected, he managed to antagonize somebody. Back in October 1947, in the midst of an interview with George H. Earle, the former governor of Pennsylvania who urged a preemptive strike against the Soviets, Izzy had been denounced for representing the kind of newspaper that Benedict Arnold supposedly would have been comfortable with. Three months before the Gates affair, Major General Patrick Hurley, onetime secretary of war and former ambassador to Kuomintang China, had likewise taken exception to Izzy's line of questioning. At one point, an obviously angry Hurley blurted out, "I know you. You are noted because you are not for the United States. You are for Russia. . . . You just give us your old party-line and it's red." As Izzy persisted in asking why the United States should waste billions more on Chiang Kai-shek, the Kuomintang dictator, Hurley cried out, "Quit following the red line with me" and demanded that the "kid . . . go back to Jerusalem."[45]

At other times, Izzy had been on the receiving end of attacks from the Communist left. The *Daily Worker* no more appreciated his questioning (of Sava N. Kosanovic, the Yugoslav ambassador to the United States, and of a young Communist Party member by the name of Hans Freistadt) than did Governor Earle and General Hurley. When Izzy spoke respectfully to Kosanovic in a 1946 "Meet the Press" interview and when he complimented Freistadt in mid-1949 for having courageously proclaimed himself to be a Communist during such troubled times, the American comrades undoubtedly were not displeased. But when Kosanovic again appeared on the program following the Soviet-Yugoslav break, Izzy's gentle probing about the need for national autonomy must have raised the ire of party members. Their anger must have also flared at his obvious incredulity when Freistadt, a University of North Carolina student, insisted that dissident views were well received in the Soviet Union.[46]

The Gates interview, however, had apparently been the final straw for Izzy. Writing in the *Compass*, he indicated as much. This was an era of competing dogmas, he declared, and the only ones he bought into were his own. Moreover, he relished tossing out troubling queries even to friends and kindred spirits. This made him appear to be either "a stooge or an enemy." Thus, he anticipated receiving Bronx cheers for having failed to expose the Yugoslav ambassador as an Anglo-American puppet "a la the rubbish of the Cominform."[47] What it amounted to, Izzy continued, was that in Washington he was considered to be "a dirty red"; in Union Square, "a dirty counter-revolutionary."[48]

And in his analysis of John Gates as the kind of true believer capable of insisting that democracy was alive and well in the Soviet Union, Stone fed charges of "counter-revolutionary" or worse from the *Daily Worker* crowd. Lenin's followers, he pointed out, refused to acknowledge something that their intellectual master had recognized—that socialism could be brought about only following a transitional stage of dictatorship. Lenin's theory made sense, Stone affirmed, but only if certain conditions were present; the comrades' refusal to own up to this had led to all sorts of unfortunate consequences. It resulted in untruthful assertions which appalled unbelievers. It led the faithful onto the road toward disillusionment when they at last saw the light. Most tragic of all, it caused the nonheretical ones to consider as permanent that which Lenin and Marx had meant to be temporary. Those philosophers, Stone reported, had considered freedom in a classless state to be the highest ideal, not "the repressions, heresy-hunts and purges which afflict revolutionary periods."[49]

Such criticisms undoubtedly riled the rose-hued sectarians, whom Izzy was so wont to antagonize. But his sweeping dismissal of "Meet the Press" itself—the program, he insisted, was about as helpful in clarifying matters "as a dog-fight"—only ensured that he was burning still more bridges behind him. Izzy evidently made but one more appearance on the show, when Representative Walter Judd of Minnesota was interviewed in a television broadcast on November 26, 1949. A staunch supporter of the recently ousted Chiang Kai-shek, Judd verbally fenced with Izzy, who declared that a policy of intervention and blockade would only antagonize the Chinese people. Izzy asked if the United States were not attempting to prop up Chiang's corrupt government. "That line," Judd retorted, was the same one always adopted by "people of your persuasion."[50]

It would be nearly two decades before Stone would again appear on a nationally syndicated radio or television program; even at that point, he would serve no more as a regular panelist on a news show as influential as the one he now angrily departed from. Thus, at the very point when the domestic Cold War was about to undertake a still more dangerous turn, I. F. Stone became persona non grata. Perhaps this was inevitable, given the realities of the Cold War and the paranoia that was such a part of it. Izzy was, after all, an avowed radical, a self-proclaimed socialist, a scathing critic of mainstream Democratic and Republican readings of Soviet designs, national liberation movements, and the U.S. Constitution. Still, it is hard to avoid the conclusion that his exclusion from the national media was, at least in part, self-induced and not the wisest decision he ever made. But now he could really see himself as the outsider, as the true independent cast adrift in "an age of warring dogmas."

Whatever the reasons, Izzy's scathing attack upon the very program that had afforded him a national audience had to have been costly, both in the short run and, ultimately, to "his side." And having been on the receiving end of the invectives Izzy threw their way, the producers of a show such as "Meet the Press" were not about to bring on the air someone of the same ilk, politically or temperamentally. That was indeed tragic, for upon hearing these old programs one is struck by the fact that Izzy so often sounded like a lonely voice of reason crying out in the wilderness. That voice, for some time to come, would now be speaking more and more only to those of like mind. And the number of such folk would be fewer and fewer as the new decade opened.[51]

The year 1950 proved to be a time of considerable danger. In January, Stone likened the victory of the Chinese Communists to a plebiscite, one made possible by wholesale disgust with Chiang's Kuomintang. He presciently warned that a clear demonstration of hostility toward the new regime would prove counterproductive and enormously costly, resulting in the very anti-American bloc U.S. policymakers so worried about. It made far more sense, he suggested, to treat "this newly awakened giant" soberly, intelligently, and graciously.[52]

Unfortunately, Stone recognized, the domestic Cold War had imprisoned the Truman administration, politically and intellectually. Secretary of State Dean Acheson increasingly appeared to subscribe to "the bogeyman theory of history" which proclaimed revolutionary doctrine to be a type of bacteria, and change, the product of conspiracy alone. Such paranoid delusions, Stone exclaimed, had long papered over "the pseudopolitics of stupid rulers and ruling classes." And it had resulted in Washington, D.C., becoming "the capital of world reaction, subsidizing and fostering the exiled men and bankrupt movements which seek a new holy alliance to destroy the hope of backward millions for an end to poverty."[53]

A simplistic reading of events worldwide, Stone believed, would cost the United States dearly—financially, morally, and politically. Even this country was not rich enough to finance anti-Communists across the globe. Nor was the goodwill engendered by the fight against Hitler, Mussolini, and Hirohito inexhaustible. And the anti-Communist frenzy only played into the hands of American far rightists.

As matters turned out, of course, the conspiratorial view of history was now about to acquire a new champion, Senator Joseph McCarthy of Wisconsin. That heretofore unheralded legislator came upon a winning political issue in brandishing charges of Communist infiltration of the State Department. McCarthy's wild accusations rang true, at least true enough, with Asia Firsters, Soviet-haters, and the ever growing number of red-baiters, as well as with conservative politicians out to do in the New and Fair Deals. As a second and more virulent phase of the red scare began, those willing to stand up and condemn McCarthyism outright appeared to be a lonely handful, including *The Nation*'s Freda Kirchwey, the *National Guardian*'s James Aronson and Cedric Belfrage, *Monthly Review*'s Leo Huberman and Paul Sweezy, and I. F. Stone, all still influenced by the ideals and visions of the Old Left of the 1930s.

Political ambition, Kirchwey charged, drove the cynical few who were willing to "subvert the instruments of justice and hold up to contempt the government itself." Those same sorts, imbued as they were with "the lowest type of Fascist mentality," *Monthly Review* insisted, were encouraged in such pursuits by "the most 'respectable' conservative quarters." *The New Republic* warned about the great and ultimately disastrous pressure "to conform, to think and to write for the record, to take the safe point of view," which government officials now had to contend with.[54]

On March 22, Stone flung charges of his own at the new darling of the American far right. McCarthy's irresponsible, undocumented attack on the Department of State and the spreading of "panic and distrust," he claimed, followed the pattern employed by the Nazis. It was Joe McCarthy and not Owen Lattimore, he declared, who should be the subject of congressional investigation. Just what were his ties with German militarists and industrialists and Chiang's Kuomintang? And why was Senator Robert Taft, head of the Republican Party's conservative wing, egging McCarthy on? Taft's insistence that if McCarthy simply talked long enough, people would begin to believe what he said, Stone cried out, was the kind of advice one could uncover in *Mein Kampf*.[55]

In the United States, Stone soon reported, "a mass mental illness" seemed to be spreading; *The Nation* and *The New Republic* were delivering similar warnings. Once this illness reached a certain stage, he declared, it would not be cured easily. What was needed were individuals with enough fortitude to champion "a sane, sober and adult view of politics in a period of change."[56]

On April 6, Stone urged forces on the left to stand together against the red-chasers. He suggested that the Cold War was particularly intended to deal a fatal blow to America's own radicals. Consequently, Stone declared his willingness to be grouped "with the unrespectably red as well as pink."[57]

The following month, he chastised President Truman and the Democratic Party for feeding Cold War paranoia. What had resulted, he declared, was "miasmatic panic and degeneration spreading" in the capital itself, the kind of mass hysteria not seen since the days of Nero and Caligula.[58]

While onetime Popular Fronters like Izzy Stone, Michael Straight, and Freda Kirchwey agreed that McCarthyism had to be contested, they disagreed, along with many who were yet or once had been positioned on the left, about the issue latched on to by the Wisconsin demagogue, the peril posed by communism. Anti-Stalinists had been arguing since the 1930s that communism was indeed little more than red fascism, while postwar liberals now had lined up almost unreservedly in the anti-Soviet and anti-Communist camp.

Stone felt it necessary to respond to one anti-Stalinist, philosopher Sidney Hook, who argued that heretical ideas—even those of the Communists— were permissible under the law of the land but conspiracy, as represented by the Communist movement, was not. Stone saw Hook's argument as "slickly designed" to open the door for "widespread repression." It appeared to Stone that Hook, a former Communist, had discarded, like other exes, every Marxian premise except for the distrust of "bourgeois liberalism." And the main difference between anti-Communists like Hook and the Communists, he continued, was that each group desired to see "a different set of people in jail." The doctrine of conspiracy, Stone went on to say, had served as an instrument of repression to be wielded against workers and reformers for many years now.[59]

Michael Straight's analysis of McCarthy's red scare undoubtedly did not sit much better with Stone. Straight spoke of reform as "the right way to beat

Communism," as Stone had recently done; but the premises *The New Republic* editor now operated under were in no way the same. Straight opened by declaring that other than hard-liners left and right, all understood Soviet communism to be "today the greatest organized evil in the world." Furthermore, liberals now recognized that working with Communists had been a mistake. There simply were no good Communists, he maintained. And the Communist Party was "a recruiting ground for subversion and espionage," declared Straight, once involved in a spy ring himself.[60]

Soft-headed idealism, Straight continued, did not help matters. What needed to be recognized, he declared, was that "America's front lines in this struggle are not on Times Square but in the jungles of Indo-China and the streets of Berlin." And, he soon added, on the battlefields of Korea. On June 25, 1950, Communist forces moved across the thirty-eighth parallel, which separated pro-Soviet North Korea from the American-backed regime in South Korea. Now the concerns of Straight and others about Communist designs appeared less overblown. Straight's own journal, *The New Republic*, denounced the military action by the North Korean "puppet state" and urged the United States to throw its weight behind the United Nations. *The Nation* magazine condemned the North Korean action as "a full-scale invasion, well planned and deliberate" which the UN Security Council had necessarily moved to counter. To not have done so, the journal declared, would have ensured that other examples of aggression would follow.[61]

Even I. F. Stone at first accepted the commonly held belief that it was Kim Il Sung, the North Korean dictator, who had initiated the fighting on orders from the Kremlin. Fearing that another world war might lie ahead, Stone urged Moscow to call a halt to the invasion. This latest reversal of Soviet policy, he further charged, was intended to pull the United States and its allies into a series of fights with Russia's client states.[62]

Soon, however, Stone warned about what might follow if U.S. troops were to get bogged down in a land war in Asia. For one thing, those troops would be positioned on the colonial side in Korea, Formosa, and Indochina. For another, guerrilla bands could more than hold their own against much larger military forces. Why should the United States throw its weight behind "the unpopular side in Asia?" Stone asked, and why must Americans give up their lives for South Korea's Syngman Rhee and Chiang Kai-shek, "our pet puppets." *The Nation*, too, worried that the United States was acting to prop up "willing stooges."[63]

By the beginning of August, Stone's condemnation of U.S. policy in Asia was sharper still. He denounced the Truman Doctrine's call for his country to serve as "policeman of the world"; that he likened to "a 'pax romana.' "[64]

Izzy's analysis of U.S. policy toward Korea and other Southeast Asian lands was pointed and often prophetic too. Western forces could easily move into such a region, he recognized, but departing from there would be considerably more difficult and possibly painful as well. What he worried about the most was that his country was once again throwing in with some pretty despicable sorts, who threatened to spin a spiderlike web that could do damage to the good name and reputation of the United States.

Following a series of meetings held by the *Compass*'s editorial staff, it was agreed that Izzy should venture overseas on a mission that was admittedly a long shot. He was to try to determine whether "a neutral bloc or 'Third Force,' " which Claude Bourdet, Albert Camus, and Jean-Paul Sartre, among others, had been calling for, could bring a halt to the fighting. He was particularly interested in discovering what support might be had in India, the birthplace of Mohandas Gandhi and Jawaharlal Nehru, and Yugoslavia, the dissident Communist state where Marshal Tito held power. In September, he spent two full weeks in India, whose immense poverty and budding "police-state mentality" greatly troubled him.[65]

In mid-October, Izzy began wiring reports out of Belgrade, one of which indicated how thrilled he was to have met with Tito, that "legendary figure" and "hero of the fight against Fascism." He was still more delighted that he had found party members open to discussing Marxist-Leninist doctrine.[66]

But he acknowledged that the Yugoslav government displayed "merciless mendacity" of a Stalinist sort toward so-called deviators. Also familiar was the emergence of a "new privileged class"—composed of members of the party—determined at all costs to preserve its prerogatives.[67]

Still, the self-respect and progress he discovered in a large industrial plant made him feel for the first time during his overseas visit that he was inside the borders of a socialist nation. He remained hopeful that Yugoslavia might someday boast the best of socialism and the West if "force, fraud and terror" could be halted. But for now, there was an electricity in the air and a hopefulness which he had not experienced in either England or France. Consequently, he wished the Yugoslavs well.[68]

For a brief spell, the Eastern European state served as a model of sorts for Stone of what one small country might be able to accomplish under a socialist economy if allowed to chart its own course. Yugoslavia seemed to be constructing its own middle way, which with the passage of time would head, he hoped, in a more democratic direction. Thus, with the Soviet Union long ago having lost its luster and the state of Israel no longer appearing like a surefire democratic socialist bet, Yugoslavia now served as the latest embodiment of revolutionary change for certain radicals in the West. Asian Communists like Kim Il Sung of North Korea and Mao Zedong of China appeared too far removed, historically and culturally, for those like I. F. Stone who were enamored with the Western intellectual tradition. But a Joseph Tito and a Milovan Djilas, then serving as Yugoslavia's vice-premier, because of their service in the Resistance and their attempts to construct a new society out of the ashes of the old, appeared to be tied to that same legacy.

From the vantage point of his cramped Paris hotel room, Stone expressed more apprehension than ever about just what was taking place back home. Prior to his departure for the East European state, he acknowledged—now that he saw "the panic is on"—feeling "like a man trying to shout into a hurricane." While overseas, he was still more disturbed by congressional passage of the McCarran Internal Security Act, which required that all Communist-dominated groups register with the Subversive Activities Control Board.[69]

A "Mad Hatter quality," Stone charged, was increasingly characterizing the United States, headed as it was "toward Fascism and folly." The country was beginning to discard "all the precious faith in freedom," and "all that made [it] a proud name in the eyes of the world is being dirtied and destroyed and degraded." Worst of all, Stone wrote, he was at a loss for imagining how any of this could be prevented.[70]

Izzy's friends at *Monthly Review*, Paul Sweezy and Leo Huberman, disagreed with his analysis. The McCarran Act, they noted, did not seek to usher in a one-party state, a prerequisite for any kind of fascism. Moreover, even if Communists could be deprived of their rights, that would not in and of itself bring about the demise of "bourgeois democracy." What the left could ill afford, Sweezy and Huberman suggested, was an absence of level-headed political analysis. What American radicals had to realize was that politics in a "bourgeois democracy" involved a contest for public opinion. The failure of the left to recognize this was becoming more costly daily, as attested by the passage of the McCarran Act.[71]

In a sense, the editors of *Monthly Review* might have been talking to their friend Izzy Stone. While believing so strongly in the importance of public discourse, he had all but given up hope that such discourse was possible in the United States at present. Stone developed a greater and greater sense of political and professional isolation as the American left virtually disappeared, liberalism settled into an increasingly impotent state, and the right grew in influence.

It was during this dark period that Stone found some kindred spirits in France, where he was stationed for several months. In certain ways, he felt more comfortable with European journalists and intellectuals than he did with their counterparts in the United States; but then this was not surprising since the former looked more kindly on his writings at the time. He was closest to Claude Bourdet, a noted figure in the French Resistance and the editor of *L'Observateur*, a liberal weekly which called for a neutral Europe, and which published a number of Izzy's writings. And a figure as esteemed as Jean-Paul Sartre came to visit Stone at the Blum estate; Sartre also published Izzy's works in *Les Temps Modernes*. In addition, Izzy linked up with fellow American expatriates, such as the sculptor Jo Davidson and author Meyer Levin. On occasion, he saw Stanley Karnow, then writing for the *National Guardian*. *The New Statesman*'s Kingsley Martin, Izzy's British publisher, was yet another confidant.[72]

A short while later, after his return home and following Davidson's death, Izzy reflected upon his friend's stay in Paris, but he could easily have been speaking for himself as well. Izzy expressed satisfaction that the artist had died in France, "his second home, as it has been the second and spiritual home of so many civilized men." Unlike the United States, Stone continued, France remained "a congenial place" for one such as Davidson who had long been "sympathetic with all the revolutionary strivings of his time."[73]

As he worried about developments back home, Stone began reexamining the war in Korea, which put him at odds with his friends and former colleagues on *The Nation* and *The New Republic* and, not surprisingly, with the establishment press in general. Within two months, he was condemning what he saw as the American determination to mete out "terror from the skies"; accusing General Douglas MacArthur, commander of Allied forces, of inflicting "methodical destruction"; and denouncing the Air Force propensity to bomb at will. "To 'devastate,' " Stone charged, "seems to be synonymous with American political argot 'to liberate.' This is terror and total warfare and moral degeneration." Blood, he declared, was on the hands of his compatriots.[74]

At this point, Izzy began to reevalutate whether it was the Politburo and not the Pentagon that had been most taken aback by the initial round of hostilities. He began to detect marked discrepancies between the official communiqués coming out of MacArthur's Far Eastern headquarters and reports by European journalists. His initial articles on the origins of the war appeared in Bourdet's *L'Observateur*. Bourdet proclaimed Izzy's editorials to have caused quite a commotion in diplomatic circles and led him to wonder if "the greatest swindle in military history" were now taking place.[75]

Eventually, Izzy's research culminated in the writing of *The Hidden History of the Korean War*, his most controversial work to date and at the time the lone book of any real distinction to challenge the bipartisan reading of the conflict. *The Hidden History* charged that both sides had repeatedly made forays across the thirty-eighth parallel prior to the start of the war; that an increasingly unpopular Syngman Rhee had encouraged the North Korean attack;

that Chiang Kai-shek, MacArthur, and President Truman had collaborated with Rhee in bringing it about.[76]

Such a work, as might have been expected, held little appeal for publishers in Cold War England or America. Thirty or so publishing firms rejected the manuscript, with some acknowledging, off the record, that it was simply "too hot to handle." However, in the fall of 1951, Izzy ran into Leo Huberman and Paul Sweezy at a restaurant near the Central Park Zoo in Manhattan; the two had recently termed Stone "the outstanding left-wing journalist in America today." Izzy informed them about his manuscript and agreed to send it to their office the very next morning. Upon reading it, Huberman and Sweezy determined that *"this book must be published."*[77]

But reviews, almost without exception, were sharp-edged in their indictment of Izzy's "tendentious" work. *Foreign Affairs* claimed that Stone's thesis "at times verges on the official Soviet line." Michael Straight's critique in *The New Republic*, entitled "A Fictive Report," insisted *The Hidden History* was "not reasoned dissent." Most biting of all, however, was the attack delivered by Richard Rovere, a former party member and a Cold War liberal, in the pages of the *New York Post*, Izzy's old employer. Stone, Rovere acknowledged, had once been "an adroit stylist, a shrewd and thoughtful analyst . . . with an incredible capacity for gathering and storing information." At one time, Rovere continued, Stone had possessed the potential to become a top national journalist and in fact "was as good as the best and perhaps was the best." His earlier writings, Rovere admitted, had been radical but could in no way be associated with the hammer-and-sickle. Now, however, "something unpleasant" had happened. Now Stone was no longer a promising journalist or even an adequate one. Now, although still no red himself, he thought up "good arguments for poor Communist positions." Such diatribes suggested to one of *The Hidden History*'s few favorable reviewers—a Trotskyist no less—that Izzy Stone was "being read out of the world of 'decent'—that is subservient journalism."[78]

The U.S. government, not surprisingly, viewed *The Hidden History* no more favorably. Fraser Wilkins, political counselor at the American Embassy in New Delhi, fired off a dispatch to the State Department reporting that some twelve hundred copies of I. F. Stone's book had been shipped into India. To the chagrin of the government man, every single copy of *The Hidden History* had sold, while excerpts had been published in a magazine that had since folded. The book, Wilkins indicated, was considered "to have done some damage," and he called for "refutatory materials."[79]

In the midst of another American adventure in Asia, *The Hidden History* would be seen in a different light. Nearly a generation after it was first published, *The Hidden History* was looked at as a prescient warning of what American soldiers might have to contend with in a land war in Asia. In

addition, it came to be viewed as a prophetic analysis of the American willingness to back unpopular, dictatorial forces and to wreak devastation upon
other peoples under the guise of liberation. What remained controversial
about *The Hidden History* was its author's emphasis on the "way to war"
plotted by Asian despots, the Pentagon, and an American president. What
remained disturbing was the readiness with which Izzy Stone had accepted
that which he had so often condemned in the past and would again in the
future—a conspiratorial reading of history.

By the time Harry Truman's presidency came to an end, Izzy Stone was
increasingly considered to be one who had drifted outside the pale,
both intellectually and professionally. His backing of Henry Wallace
in 1948, his consistent championing of the rights of political pariahs, and his
fiery temperament had helped to ensure that this would happen. So, too, did
his refusal to cast Stalin and the Soviet Union as the diabolical ones in a Cold
War play, and his more recent condemnation of U.S. practices in Korea. Yet,
if anything, Izzy seemed almost to revel in his loss of respectability, refusing
to soften his charged analyses.[80] For example, shortly after returning to the
States in June 1951, Stone declared that "the land of the brave and the home
of the free" was appearing more and more like "the land of the belly-crawler
and the home of the fearful."[81]

While continuing to use his pen as a weapon, Izzy took to the hustings to
attack the paranoia fed by the Communist-phobes. He joined with Thomas
Emerson, Corliss Lamont, and Carey McWilliams, among others, to found
the Emergency Civil Liberties Committee; the ECLC was intended to do that
which the American Civil Liberties Union no longer seemed willing to do,
namely, defend the rights of political outcasts. He headed off to San Francisco to speak at a mass gathering at the Civic Center that was called to
protest the Smith Act. He denounced McCarthy at a rally held in Carnegie
Hall to bring the East Coast left together. In spite of a protest by the local
American Legion chapter, he showed up in Syracuse to deliver a blistering
attack against the red scare. When informed that Legionnaires were up in
arms about his impending visit, Izzy roared, "You invite them! Call them up
and tell them that if they don't like it, to come to the meeting and speak up in
the discussion period!" Subsequently, upon the close of his address, one of
his critics stood up and cried out, "We believe in the First Amendment too,
just like you do!" But why, he was asked, should constitutional safeguards be
provided to those who opposed the basic principles on which this nation had
been founded? "Why should we let people who are opposed to these principles get the benefit of them?"[82]

Such a view was held by any number of distinguished officers of the legal profession, Izzy retorted, and by one Andrei Vyshinsky, head of the Soviet judicial system. Vyshinsky argued much as the American Legion folk did, insisting that the Soviet constitution did not protect those who were opposed to the very notion of the Communist state. But the American Founding Fathers, Izzy continued, "didn't draw a line." They upheld the right of revolution and put "no ifs and buts" in the First Amendment, a position which both the American Legion and Andrei Vyshinsky obviously disagreed with. The Legionnaire was left speechless.[83]

Others, however, were never at a loss for words in attacking those who attacked the red-baiters, particularly anti-anti-Communists such as Izzy Stone. Irving Kristol of the American Committee for Cultural Freedom dismissed the Emergency Civil Liberties Committee as a Communist front with no real concern about liberty in the United States or anywhere else. He then proceeded to single out Thomas Emerson, Carey McWilliams, and Stone as particularly suspect. Louis Budenz, onetime editor of the *Daily Worker,* charged that Izzy cooperated "in the Communist conspiracy" by seeking to further "the Stalinist game." The *New York Herald Tribune*'s Ogden R. Reid, in a column entitled "The Red Underground," discussed any number of the dozen or so speeches condemning the Smith Act Izzy had delivered since his return from overseas.[84]

And the Passport Division of the State Department, which had assisted Stone in his travels abroad in the past, would do so no longer. In fact, a special agent now came to his office to collect his passport; phone calls and letters demanded the same. When Izzy responded that he could not simply surrender his passport "in so unbusinesslike a way," he was informed of the Passport Division's determination "to give consideration to any future travel which you may contemplate.[85]

I n many ways, this very period proved to be the nadir for the twentieth-century American left. The relinquishment of the ideals of one's youth, the waning of the appeal of socialism, the horrific realities of both Nazism and Stalinism, and the postwar red scare had all served to diminish the number of those willing to line up on the left side of the political spectrum. The Old Left was now reduced to little more than a shell of its former self. For those who remained true to certain of the visions of the thirties—in spite of Spain, the Moscow Trials, the Nazi-Soviet pact, the Stalinization of Eastern Europe, and postwar reaction—the atmosphere surrounding them was not a comfortable one. The old touchstones were more tattered and torn than ever, with no replacements in the offing. Thus, those who held on to their radical tenets appeared as if relics of a bygone era, and increasingly discredited relics at that.

I. F. Stone's stock fell ever farther by the end of 1952, and this well-seasoned and formerly esteemed member of the Fourth Estate found himself out of a job with seemingly no prospects in store. By that point, he had antagonized the American sectarians every bit as much as the red-haters and the Cold War liberals. On the eve of the 1952 presidential election, Ted Thackery called Izzy at home and informed him that the *New York Daily Compass* was about to shut down. There was talk that a series of editorials Izzy had written praising Democratic Party nominee Adlai Stevenson and criticizing the Communists' support of the Progressive Party candidate had angered Corliss Lamont—who held a mortgage on *Daily Compass* property—and ensured that the paper had to close its doors. *Monthly Review* insisted that this was not true, that Lamont had enabled the *Compass* to hold on for as long as it had.[86]

Earlier in the year, Izzy had already riled American left-wing sectarians once again. In March, Dashiell Hammett had invited him to speak at a rally to be held for Izzy's old nemesis, V. J. Jerome, one of sixteen New Yorkers tried under the Smith Act. Izzy obviously did not think much of Hammett's call for a united front against the act. In declining the invitation from "Dash," Izzy called Jerome "a hell of a nice guy personally," but one who had attempted "to ride herd on the intellectuals . . . often in most humiliating ways." Because of this, "I'd feel like a stultified ass to speak at a meeting for Jerome without making clear my own sharp differences with the dogmatic, Talmudic and dictatorial mentality he represents." Although Izzy intended to continue defending Jerome, he was unable to "pretend he's a libertarian, so I'd better stay away."[87]

Believing 1952 was "the year of danger," Izzy urged Progressive Party members to disavow "Communist Party line simplistics," avoid getting ensnared in pro-Russian arguments, and adopt a stance for peace. The Democrats still represented the common man, still served as the party of Roosevelt, and the Popular Front had to lean rightward as well as leftward, Stone insisted. Furthermore, he feared the possible influence that the right wing of the Republican party would have if the GOP came to power; it well might push U.S. foreign policy makers just enough, he worried, so that another world war, fueled by another anti-Soviet crusade, would result.[88]

In reality, Izzy seemed at last to have determined that the Popular Front was not about to reappear; moreover, he saw the now Henry Wallace-less Progressive Party as even more of an impotent actor than it had been previously. In his own way, he seemed to be realizing more fully than before that the Old Left was surely bound for extinction. The continued prominence of the American Communist Party and its members in the ranks of radical organizations, he recognized, resulted in politically suicidal sectarianism and a discrediting of those organizations.

In a three-part series in the *Daily Worker,* Alan Max criticized Izzy's decision, which was said to have occasioned considerable talk in progressive circles. Stone, Max admitted, had long championed the causes of peace and civil liberties, and so his views were to be taken seriously. But in dissecting Izzy's rationale for backing Stevenson, Max declared that he too was helping further the cause of "McCarthyism and Eisenhowerism."[89]

"The possessors of the One True Faith," Izzy responded, always viewed "erring heathen like me" critically. But it was they who had made the mistake of opposing Eugene V. Debs, Robert M. La Follette, and Franklin Delano Roosevelt, the three greatest progressive figures in the United States during the first half of this century. And it was they who had once cried "Social Fascism" in refusing to cooperate with the German Social Democrats, thus laying a clear path for Adolf Hitler's rise to power.[90]

On October 15, Stone discussed the case of Julius and Ethel Rosenberg, charged with having been involved in a World War II–era spy ring, which involved the transmission of atomic secrets to the USSR. Confessions by Allan Nunn May, Klaus Fuchs, David Greenglass, and Harry Gold in Canada, England, and the United States, respectively, indicated that all had engaged in espionage for the Soviet Union. The Russians, then, had employed "ideological sympathies to recruit for scientific espionage." While all countries attempted to tap such sympathies for their own spy networks, Stone admitted, each country properly sought to prevent espionage.[91]

Up to this time, Izzy acknowledged, he had refused to write about the Rosenbergs because he had doubts about their innocence. But the campaign on their behalf, he suggested, playing as it did upon sentiment, distortion of facts, and irresponsible charges of anti-Semitism, had, in certain ways, done greater harm than good. Izzy, for his part, having joined with Ted Thackery in scouring through the appellate briefs, was less convinced than ever that the Rosenbergs had been framed. But he believed, nevertheless, like Arthur Garfield Hays of the ACLU, that the death sentence meted out to them was "barbaric, savage and way out of line with justice."[92]

Thus, even Izzy Stone had come to distance himself more and more from the shadow of its former self that the Old Left had become. It was not disillusionment with the socialist ideal that had resulted in such a move, but rather continued dismay over the practices of Communist Party members in the United States and of Communist-run governments in the Soviet Union and Eastern Europe. Coupled with the prominent role the left-wing sectarians had played—to such disastrous ends—in the Wallace campaign, the Old Left's most recent major organizational effort, the tendency of non-Communist radicals like Stone to pull back from the "movement" was perfectly understandable.

Whatever the reason, in early November, the *New York Daily Compass* printed its final edition; *Monthly Review* particularly noted the loss of "the brilliant daily column of I. F. Stone." The forty-four-year-old Stone, veteran of numerous political and journalistic wars, was now an unemployed reporter with extended family responsibilities—one child at an elite college, with two more soon to follow. He phoned and telegraphed Freda Kirchwey at *The Nation* asking for his old job back as Washington editor. But Kirchwey, recalling Izzy's sometimes intemperate dealings with colleagues and that unannounced trip to Palestine, proved unwilling to commit. Carey Mc-Williams was all in favor of Izzy's return to *The Nation*, but Kirchwey "wouldn't say yes, she wouldn't say no." As matters turned out, *The Nation*'s refusal to take back its wayward son proved fortunate for him. *The Nation*, the one mass-circulation journal that continued to forthrightly oppose the domestic Cold War, was suffering its own loss of subscribers, contributors, and stature; not until the mid-1960s would it begin to rebound and then only somewhat. A series of newspaper editors also expressed no interest in him at all, leading Izzy to wonder whether he was some kind of "ideological typhoid Mary" who happened to be butting his head against the journalistic equivalent of a blacklist.[93]

It now appeared that radical journalism was weaker than it had been over the course of the past four decades. There had been quite a collection of such publications: *The Masses* and *The Liberator* of the Lyrical Left in the World War I era; *The Nation* and *The New Republic*, the key progressive and Old Left-influenced journals from the twenties through the late forties; *PM*, the *New York Star*, and the *New York Daily Compass*, with editorial positions advancing the New Deal and the Old Left. Notwithstanding government persecution, altered political climates, or economic shortfalls, one or another of these magazines or newspapers had always kept up the good fight. True, more sectarian periodicals were still in print, including the *Daily Worker*, and *National Guardian* and *Monthly Review*, but their appeal was strictly limited and their influence on American intellectuals never akin to that of these other publications. And by this point, the little magazines or newsletters put out by the champions of personal journalism, such as Dwight Macdonald's *Politics* and George Seldes's *In Fact*, were no longer in existence.

While considering what he should do next, Izzy immediately determined to write that book he had earlier contemplated when the *Star* had gone under. Sitting in his old *Compass* office, he expressed satisfaction that he had participated in a succession of experiments in "independent liberal journalism." He thanked his publishers and editors at *PM*, the *Star*, and the *Compass*, and his readers for allowing him to make a living as he chose to. Unlike most journalists or intellectuals of his time, Izzy acknowledged, he had been able to write what he wanted to and to take on causes he believed in without "dictation, personal or political."[94]

Still very much a man whose ideals remained rooted in the decade of the 1930s, Stone urged his fellow intellectuals of an independent left cast to maintain the faith, for the socialism they believed in was sure to come. So was "the libertarian ideal" they favored, though it was threatened by authoritarians left and right, no matter whether they were true believers or disbelievers. Intellectual freedom, he insisted, remained humankind's highest ideal and something socialism required in order that the good society might someday, somehow, be constructed. "New truths" must always be allowed to do battle with established ones, he declared, no matter the "monarchs, priests, bureaucrats, . . . commissars, or that often most intolerant of despotisms, the majority itself" which stood in the way.[95]

Thus, notwithstanding the changed political climate and the dearth of employment prospects, Stone continued to foresee the eventual emergence of socialism of a nondogmatic sort. Unlike so many other left-wing intellectuals and political activists from the 1930s who had undergone a rightward shift, he maintained his identification with the radical heritage at this point. This enabled him to avoid the fate of so many of his onetime ideological fellows, of becoming a kind of celebrant or apologist for his own nation's excesses, while engaging in an odyssey from Marxist certitude to anti-Communist absolutism. Perhaps this was possible because Izzy had never been as dogmatic as many others on the left. His radicalism, although real, had almost always been more tempered. Because this was so, he was not compelled to follow the conversionary path undertaken by a good number of former Communists or Trotskyists.

Nor was he ever tempted to adopt an "objective" vantage point, which resulted in many intellectuals acting almost as wards of the state. At the same time, he was not about to do as others had done in discarding politics altogether. This was never a consideration for Izzy, who always believed that intellectuals had a general duty to serve as social critics, and that he personally was obliged to remain a political activist. The role of disinterested observer, then, was one he could not even consider.

The late forties and early fifties were a difficult time for those like I. F. Stone who saw themselves as positioned on the democratic, but not the anti-Communist, left; who in fact insisted on maintaining an anti-anti-Communist stance and not simply within the confines of an ivory tower of any kind. Not only was the number of those who did so now greatly reduced, but their influence had all but vanished as well. There remained no major progressive political organization for them to identify with; fewer people were willing to listen to their passionately reasoned arguments; and then there was the matter of lost jobs, prestige, and stature. Moreover, unlike other Old Leftists who had left behind certain of their radical ideals and moved on toward a celebration of America, Izzy was not about to be tendered an offer to work at an institution of higher learning. Individuals such as Izzy Stone and Carey Mc-Williams of *The Nation* thus appeared to be perched on an increasingly fragile intellectual limb, now withering and atrophying rapidly. Their brightest days seemed long past and the future, always so important to Americans, appeared to have little to offer. It was as though this dwindling breed threatened to become entirely extinct.

Had that been the case, the American nation itself would have been the loser. A half-century of nonsectarian radicalism would have been terminated, one that dated back to Debsian socialism and the early postwar era. Some of the country's most illustrious rebels and radicals had been included in that pantheon, such as Eugene V. Debs, Upton Sinclair, Robert La Follette, and A. J. Muste, the onetime minister, Trotskyist, and longtime pacifist. Soon to be viewed as another fixture in that camp—admittedly, to the displeasure of some—would be I. F. Stone, one of the most steadfast of the Old Leftists.

10 A
"Little Flea-Bite Publication"

On Friday, December 1, 1955, a subscription request from the Senate Internal Security Subcommittee was delivered to the home of Izzy and Esther Stone. Included was a five-dollar voucher signed by committee chairman James Eastland of Mississippi and chief counsel J. G. Sourwine. Angered by the turn of events, Izzy decided to milk this for all it was worth. That Sunday, he fired off a note to Senator Eastland, declaring that public moneys could not be used for surveillance of the press. The following day, standing as his own attorney, Izzy filed suit in U.S. District Court in Washington, D.C. Subsequently, summonses were delivered to Senator Eastland, fellow subcommittee members, research director Benjamin Mandel, and attorney Sourwine.[1]

When asked to comment on Izzy's action, an irate James Eastland dismissed it out of hand: "It's bunk."[2]

What Izzy objected to was the subcommittee's all-too-apparent determination to scour *I. F. Stone's Weekly* and other publications for material that it considered to be threatening to national security. What he feared was about to begin was another round of "intimidation, slander and guilt-by-association" that would riddle the newspaper business as government service already had been. Izzy called on publishers to demand the right to operate their enterprises free from "ideological inquiry."[3]

The *Weekly*'s suit was dismissed, as Izzy recognized it would be, on the grounds that the legislative functions of Congress could not be subject to judicial interference. By that point, he had decided that seeking an injunction would have been too much trouble anyway.[4]

But notwithstanding Izzy's run-in with Eastland and his cohorts, he never was hauled before the Senate Internal Security Subcommittee or any other during those days of the postwar witch-hunt. He could never quite figure out why that was the case, but reasoned that because he was seen as "a goddamned red," little mileage could be gained by investigating him. Dramatic exposés were what the McCarthys and Eastlands sought, and Izzy was "like Gypsy Rose Lee . . . taking it off every week." Moreover, he was his own boss so there was not much they could have done to him, or so he reasoned. Perhaps McCarthy recognized that Izzy would simply have been too much to handle. Nevertheless, the Senate Internal Security Subcommittee did see fit to name him as "one of the eighty-two most active and typical sponsors of Communist-front organizations."[5]

I n many ways, the controversy involving Senator Eastland might well have seemed like a small matter to a man who had weathered what Izzy Stone had. At the close of 1952, he had been an unemployed, middle-aged journalist and Old Leftist who appeared to be yet another victim of the temper of the times. Unlike many others who lost positions, prominence, and hope during the domestic Cold War, however, Izzy was not about to disavow political activism.

He continued to believe that the left had a role to play in the United States; that socialism remained a worthwhile goal; that the intellectual was obliged to speak out on the issues of the day, no matter how controversial; and that progressive journalism could acquire an audience. What now came in handy more than ever before was his decidedly individualistic streak, his stubborn determination to challenge icons of all types, and his faith that even a political rebel could succeed in a capitalist venture. In the process, he was about to head off on the path of a more independent brand of radicalism which lacked clear guideposts and much in the way of models yet was very much in keeping with a not ignoble American tradition.

For several years now, Izzy had considered the possibility of putting out his own newsletter. There was a model for such a journalistic enterprise, *In Fact*, published between 1940 and 1950 by George Seldes, Izzy's good friend and a fellow veteran of the Old Left. *In Fact*, thanks in part to Seldes's ties to left-wing labor unions and political organizations, had boasted a subscription total of 176,000 at one point. The changed political climate of the postwar period, however, which resulted in FBI harassment on the one hand and attacks from the sectarian left on the other, caused that newsletter to close shop.[6]

In November, the *Daily Compass* printed its last edition, and Izzy, encouraged by his brother Marc, decided to launch a four-page newsletter. Desperation, he later admitted, was what spurred him on. But for once, the Stones' financial house was in order. Intending to concentrate on the Washington scene, Izzy decided to move the family back to the capital. Awaiting them was their home in Washington, which had been rented out for the past three years and now was owned by the Stones outright, the mortage having been paid off. (Ironically, the same mover who shipped their belongings from Manhattan loaded up the possessions of the corporate lawyer from the firm of Sullivan and Cromwell who was about to take on the title of secretary of state, one John Foster Dulles.) It also proved helpful that Izzy had received a severance payment of thirty-five hundred dollars which Ted Thackrey had placed in escrow for him in the event that the *Compass* went under. In addition, an unexpected bounty came his way after he had lunch one day with Arthur Wiener, a longtime friend, at the Museum of Modern Art in New York City. Walking down the streets of the great metropolis, Izzy blurted out that he was "going to keep on fighting if I have to crank out a paper on a mimeograph machine in the cellar." Wiener promptly offered to loan him three thousand dollars, and other assistance also came his way. He had something else too—the mailing lists from *PM*, the *Star*, and the *Compass*.[7]

By the end of the month, he kicked off an extensive subscription drive. Marc later remembered Izzy as being "very timid" about the undertaking, and having to push for five thousand additional letters to be sent out, then ten thousand more. Eventually, some thirty thousand letters were mailed, while ads appeared in the *New York Times*, the *New York Post*, *The Nation*, and the *National Guardian*. In a "personal letter," Izzy promised to come through with "politically uninhibited commentary and let-the-chips-fall-where-they-may reporting." He indicated that he planned to continue the fight "for justice and civil liberties"; this was the same fight he had previously waged in his newspaper columns, he noted, "as an independent journalist." But it had never been more important, he declared, to maintain a "voice of protest."[8]

Four weeks later, Izzy admitted that he had "no access to keyholes" and would "not dish up 'hot stuff' "; but he promised "to do as sober, accurate and principled a job of reporting" as he could to defend those who had been victims of the red scare. Moreover, he sought to reach out to those whose minds were still open, no matter their political leanings. The supportive letters he had received from well-wishers gave him renewed confidence, he wrote, in both his endeavor and his country.[9]

Three thousand subscriptions arrived within the first three weeks, the *National Guardian* soon reported. Izzy continued to worry, however, that attracting a large enough group willing to brave the Cold War hysteria was like hunting "for a needle in a haystack." Day after day, the Stones checked the mail for new subscriptions. But by early February, Izzy Stone had fifty-three hundred charter subscribers, including such old friends or fans as Albert Einstein, Bertrand Russell, and Eleanor Roosevelt, willing to pay the five-dollar annual rate for the newsletter. What this demonstrated was that the good name of I. F. Stone retained its appeal for many, who saw his latest venture as a means to sustain a tradition of independent, radical journalism that now appeared to be in danger of disappearing altogether.[10]

With a weekly budget of some five hundred dollars, Izzy's salary and that of a secretary, as well as the cost of printing and mailing, were covered. Of considerable help was the second-class mailing rate granted by the U.S. Postal Service, which made it possible to ship out each copy for only one-eighth of a cent. Izzy was always grateful that in spite of his charged reputation, the "impeccable professional civil servants" tossed "no political questions" his way.[11]

However, Izzy had no way of knowing that the postmaster in Washington, D.C., had once argued for a revocation of his government subsidy. On January 25, 1954, that government official fired off three copies of *I. F. Stone's Weekly* to the solicitor of the U.S. Postal Service, along with a note indicating that its editorial stance might be "critical to such an extent as to deny the right of second-class mailing privileges." Abe McGregor Goff, the solicitor, responded that the suggestion had been carefully considered. But in Goff's estimation, no federal laws had been violated by the mailing of the newsletter.[12]

Thanks to the unknown assistance from the solicitor, *I. F. Stone's Weekly* survived a somewhat tenuous beginning and rapidly became very much of a family affair. The secretary, being a rather "fussy" sort, made Izzy feel unwelcome in his own office, so he opted to dismiss her; terribly upset by this decision, he went out and got "blind drunk," even though he was not much of a drinker. Izzy also had to deal with the hurt feelings of Marc, who believed that he was about to become a permanent staff member. Izzy, however, felt that the *Weekly* could not afford such help, and Marc departed in quite a huff. Izzy eventually turned to Esther to handle both secretarial duties and the business end of the operation. As Esther later acknowledged, Izzy never even scoured through his subscription lists. He lacked the time to attend to business matters, as she put it, and the inclination. Esther drew a weekly salary of seventy-five dollars, fifty less than that Izzy allotted to himself; her sunny disposition always seemed to match the sign perched over her desk: "Good news is on the way." For his part, Izzy took on the multiple jobs of publisher, editor, reporter, proofreader, and layout man, as he had with another newsletter three full decades earlier. Thus, the pressure he had experienced with the daily newspapers and *The Nation* only continued. He strove to write a page every day, with the lead editorial to be completed before his Tuesday-night deadline. Occasionally, he went to bed, only to toss and turn, and then return to his desk in the early morning hours to reshape that page-one story. On Wednesdays, Izzy headed downtown to the print shop, appearing to the pressmen "like a madman coming in here." This, of course, was "because Dad cared," Chris Stone recalled. The following day, he mailed out the copies of the newsletter. Consequently, the *Weekly* became what George Seldes had suggested it must become, a kind of "cottage industry."[13]

That was fortunate indeed, for Izzy had determined that the *Weekly* would necessarily grow slowly, if at all. In the tradition of early *PM*, he declined to solicit advertisements for his little publication. He refused to spend all his time and energy raising money to expand operations, believing that the current political climate would not allow for the kind of mass audience that *In Fact* had once obtained. Indeed, the subscription figures of that publication had plummeted to one-third of its peak level when its editor had called it a day.[14]

What Izzy sought from the *Weekly* was that it provide him with a forum "to make a living and speak my mind and do my best." To that end, he attempted to put out a paper that was radical in content but conservative in appearance. Consequently, he generally avoided the fiery headlines characteristic of the now defunct radical tabloids, claimed no inside tidbits as a left-wing reporter in Cold War Washington—indeed, officials and congressmen seemed to flee at his very approach—and delved into official hearings, public transcripts, and government records for necessary documentation. The sources he once had were now long gone from government service, whether because of the passing of FDR or the red-baiting frenzy, or refused to speak to Izzy any longer because of fear of being seen with someone of his political persuasion. There was all the more reason, then, for Izzy to cull through those official materials for "the significant trifle" that the establishment press tended to ignore; throughout the pages of the newsletter he sprinkled boxed material, including noteworthy facts, quotations, and analyses. This was somewhat natural for Izzy because he "really gravitated to the particular. He had a fantastic mind for the particular. Unbelievable," his son Chris later reflected. Furthermore, "his memory was capacious," Chris noted. At the same time, he "sweated blood over the writing" of the *Weekly*, Izzy admitted, in an effort "to make it like a soufflé, urbane, erudite, and witty, and a pleasure to read."[15]

On January 17, 1953, the initial edition of *I. F. Stone's Weekly* appeared, only days before the inauguration of Dwight Eisenhower as the thirty-fourth president of the United States. The *Weekly*, Izzy indicated, would attempt to pick up the mantle of independent radical journalism from the now-interred *PM-Star-Compass* triad. This quest, he believed, perhaps in Quixote-like fashion, was more necessary than ever, given the dearth of political and journalistic alternatives facing those he considered to be his intellectual fellows. He thanked well-wishers and expressed the conviction that he was about to begin working for the finest people to be found anywhere. He declared his allegiance to no person or party, and asserted his belief that a sizable number of Americans were still open to a dissident viewpoint, if it was carefully and rationally presented. To that end, Izzy continued, he promised to battle for peace and civil liberties, which he believed could not be separated.[16]

Never the modest sort, Izzy suggested that his readers might want to hold on to the first issue, for old copies, he predicted, would eventually be worth something.[17]

But in spite of the high hopes for his latest journalistic effort, Izzy did not always express such confidence in his undertaking. Now feeling like something of a pariah in Washington, the ofttimes grumpy yet gregarious Stone frequently found himself alone and something of an outcast. He especially experienced an emotional letdown whenever the *Weekly* went to press. Fortunately, Esther and the kids were as supportive as ever, and the "intense love" of his readers continually reinvigorated him.[18]

At times, the writings and actions of some of the great figures of the period did so as well. On one occasion, having dropped off the proofs of the next issue of the newsletter at the printer's, he wandered into a library, feeling somewhat despondent, and came across a book entitled *Why Men Fight*, Bertrand Russell's World War I–era pacifist tract. Russell's work suggested how difficult it was to be at odds with the general mainstream; but it also insisted that a holier-than-thou attitude had to be guarded against.[19]

Albert Einstein became another faithful reader and a friend as well. Otto Nathan, later the executor of Einstein's estate, set up a meeting at the great scientist's home in Princeton, New Jersey. Einstein, it turned out, desired to get together with the editor of the *Weekly*, and so Izzy, Esther, Jay, and Chris drove up to Princeton. Both Izzy and Chris saw Einstein in much the same light, as a saintly, Godlike figure who exuded simplicity and kindliness. Chris later recalled the first conversation between his father and Einstein, particularly the sounds which rang out thanks to Izzy's "battery of staccato" noises and his new friend's "cloudy and mellifluous sort of responses." Einstein stood as yet another and perhaps the last in a line of paternal surrogates for Izzy.[20]

While Izzy was greatly encouraged by someone such as Einstein, his own drive and hardly insubstantial ego also served to sustain him. So too did a very real sense of anger. One day, while passing through the Capitol grounds, he immodestly reflected on the domestic Cold Warriors. "You may just think I am a red Jew son-of-a-bitch," he thought to himself, "but I'm keeping Thomas Jefferson alive and you bastards are killing [him]." That conviction led Izzy to believe wholeheartedly in the fundamental importance of his journalistic experiment.[21]

Izzy saw the *Weekly* as upholding the tradition of "militant libertarian journalism" in a time when other newspapers were filled with "tidal waves of hate, poison, propaganda and misinformation." The newsletter, he believed, provided "the only breath of dissent from the cold war and the witch hunt" in many pockets, large and small, around the nation.[22]

Perhaps it was his instinctively rebellious streak that best enabled Izzy to succeed. It might even be argued that this feisty and frequently testy maverick was best suited to labor alone or with the ever-patient Esther right by his side. Because he worked out of their home, his passionate nature, frenetic work habits, and volatile temperament troubled only himself, his family of five, and his printer on occasion.

And now, subject only to his "own compulsions" and unencumbered by any political movement, Izzy Stone was able and willing to speak his mind more freely than ever before. Thus, *I. F. Stone's Weekly* became one of the handful of voices that consistently and courageously attacked Cold War machinations emanating from all sides. In the early years, only Irving Howe's *Dissent*, A. J. Muste's *Liberation*, and *The Nation* spoke out in a similar manner, adopting a critical but nondoctrinaire posture. But none did so as forthrightly and as elegantly as the *Weekly*, resulting in considerable controversy at times and fanatically loyal readers as well.[23]

Consequently, the newsletter became, as Izzy early pointed out, "something new on the Left—a success story." Within three months, the *Weekly* boasted subscribers in every state of the Union, several U.S. territories, a half-dozen Canadian provinces, Europe, Japan, and South America. By the time the third issue was printed, the subscription level shot past the six-thousand mark. By 1955, it reached ten thousand homes and offices. Others, including fellow veterans of the Old Left and members of the World War II generation alike, perhaps were encouraged by the success of the *Weekly* to begin publication of *Dissent*, the *Village Voice*, and *Liberation*. Certainly, Howe, Muste, and Norman Mailer were all familiar with Stone's work.[24]

The *Weekly* thrived as it did, it might be argued, because of its anti-ideological bent and the professionalism it exemplified. The newsletter continued to hew to the anti-anti-Communist and anti–Cold War line Izzy had adopted since the end of World War II, but it did so in a fashion that amounted to a kind of "non-partisan plague on both major political parties." What it demonstrated was that such an approach, which coupled a challenge to the powers that were—whether at home or abroad—with an independent, radical thrust, enabled Izzy's brand of investigative journalism to thrive as never before. He turned to those official documents perhaps more often than any other journalist of his generation did. Such "digging," coupled with the near-encyclopedic reading of philosophical, literary, and historical writings which Izzy engaged in, provided an unsurpassed depth and breadth to his work. Now professionalism guided Izzy more fully than ever and enabled him to carve out a niche for himself of great import in the various worlds of American journalism, radicalism, and intellectualism.

Although it remained a home-spun operation, the *Weekly* prospered enough so that Izzy and Esther were able to send Jay and Chris off to join Celia at prestigious colleges in the East. While she studied at Smith, they now went to MIT and Harvard respectively, before Jay decided to transfer to

Swarthmore. Esther's salary was set aside for educational expenses, for the Stones feared that if Celia, Jay, or Chris were to apply for scholarships, they too might suffer from some kind of blacklists.[25]

Izzy, however, refused to trouble his children about such concerns. Instead, he angrily refused to sign off on Chris's scholarship application to Harvard, huffily declaring, "I have money! I can pay!" Chris later recalled his father's reaction as being "irrational"; he also believed that Izzy, harking back to his own collegiate days, truly believed that scholarships were for commuters only and reasoned that as a good entrepreneur, he could pay his children's way. Perhaps Izzy remembered, too, that even in the worst of times, his own father had refused charity.[26]

Year one of *I. F. Stone's Weekly,* 1953, was a time when few proved willing to challenge the accepted axioms of the period, fewer still to question prevailing governmental policies. Thus, the start of the Eisenhower era hardly seemed an auspicious time for an old Popular Fronter, self-professed radical, and determined social critic to initiate such an experiment in independent political journalism. For halcyon days likely loomed ahead for government investigators, political demagogues, organization men, and a silent generation.

But as I. F. Stone had indicated, he intended that the *Weekly* serve as a voice for peace and civil liberties. As the Eisenhower administration began, Stone expressed concern because he viewed John Foster Dulles, the new secretary of state, as "a monster" with "pro-Axis sympathies." He warned that Joseph McCarthy, a Goebbels-like "master of the Big Lie," was no fool and was plotting any number of "little 'Reichstag fires.'" The circuslike atmosphere that had enveloped the nation, Stone later charged, was meant to convey the impression that only McCarthy could be trusted.[27]

But Senator McCarthy and Pat McCarran of Nevada, his Democratic Party cohort, Stone wrote, were simply "tools" of giant corporations that were engaged in a grand conspiracy to produce "a corporate State." The U.S. Chamber of Commerce, Stone had earlier pointed out, had concocted a plan for thought control. Its 1952 report on communism called for the barring of "Communists, fellow travelers, and 'dupes'" from fields that influenced public opinion, including journalism, education, publishing, and entertainment. And since 1946, the chamber had been insisting on "a Big Business iron curtain." Its annual reports had demanded—just ahead of the fact—a loyalty oath, a congressional inquiry into Communist influence in Hollywood, a Justice Department hit list of Communist-front groups, a defanging of the Wagner Labor Relations Act, and the exclusion of Communists from various occupations. The chamber's latest call for communitywide action to ferret out supposed Communist sympathizers, Stone had feared, was an attempt to intimidate radicals and pave the way for an American brand of fascism.[28]

Such scathing analyses made no friends for Izzy in certain government circles. The FBI continued to add to its extensive file on him, aided by the intelligence branch of the Department of the Army. In one confidential report, it was noted that a former American prisoner of war, during his debriefing, had acknowledged reading a book by Izzy—undoubtedly *The Hidden History of the Korean War*—while in the hands of the enemy. And in mid-March, 1954, it was reported in a memo to J. Edgar Hoover that a recommendation had been received by the chief of the Security Division of the Army that *The Hidden History* be withdrawn from its libraries.[29]

To Izzy's delight, 1954, of course, proved to be the year of Joe McCarthy's undoing. Now McCarthy went head-to-head, in a manner of speaking, with seemingly sacrosanct institutions, including the U.S. Army and President Dwight David Eisenhower. Individuals ranging from fellow Republican Ralph Flanders, the senator from Vermont, to CBS newsman Edward R. Murrow now fired back at McCarthy. The televised Army-McCarthy hearings showed the junior senator from Wisconsin at his bullying, demagogic worst and furthered his already steep loss of public support.[30]

On July 19, 1954, one month following the conclusion of the Army-McCarthy charade, I. F. Stone cautioned that the United States could not remain "just a little crazy." For "either sanity will be restored or the Fascist mentality will take power. . . . Freedom as we know it and 'security' as the paranoids preach it are incompatible. . . . This is what needs to be driven home." Three weeks later, he warned that McCarthyism could not be turned aside as long as Communists were viewed as supermen guided by a devilish Politburo which intended "to take over the world and enslave all mankind."[31]

The congressional passage of the Communist Control Act, sponsored by Senator Humphrey and other liberal Democrats, led Stone to condemn "the panic of a mob on Capitol Hill"; *The New Republic* and *The Nation* also saw liberal Democrats running for cover. The measure effectively declared membership in the Communist Party to be illegal and led Stone to affirm that the nation was edging "closer toward Fascism."[32]

While criticism that such analyses were overblown would rightfully come his way, Stone at least consistently and often courageously challenged the red-baiters, whether they appeared in Republican or Democratic guise, under conservative or liberal cover. He was one of the few who recognized that even the demise of McCarthy would not ensure an end to blind, vicious, and self-defeating anticommunism.

In a small but pointed gesture of his own directed at both the anti-Communists and the rapidly dwindling band of American sectarians, Izzy corresponded that fall with Earl Browder, former head of the national Communist Party. Presently a man without a political home, Browder had been excommunicated by his fellow American Leninists in 1946 following yet another shift in Soviet policy. Izzy now seemed to go out of the way to befriend Browder, indicating that their sons Jeremy, still at Swarthmore, and Bill, a Princeton man, were on friendly terms and offering to put up the ex-Communist Party chief and his wife during a visit to Washington.[33]

The following August, Stone chillingly related the tale of one member of the U.S. Armed Forces—which continued to follow Izzy's activities—singled out because he was said to have closely associated with a party member who just happened to be his mother. "Soldier boys," Stone advised, needed to "check on Mama before writing home." They might also look into the family history of potential spouses, he suggested, in highlighting the case of another soldier's mother-in-law, who had supposedly resurfaced from the Communist underground in order to take part in the peace movement once again. There was a problem with this report by military intelligence, however, for the woman in question had died a full decade before her daughter had even met her future husband. Consequently, the only peace activity this crypto-Communist might become involved with, Stone suggested, was "the Second Coming." Equally disturbing, he pointed out, were indications that reading could be as hazardous for "soldier boys" as "the accident of birth." It appeared that "a mindless machinery" was seeking "to grind a nation's youth into conformity."[34]

But notwithstanding such absurdities, the worst of the postwar red scare was now past. Izzy later reflected on the turn of events, particularly why his gravest fears had not been borne out. He compared what the United States had just gone through with what Germany had experienced a generation earlier. The German antifascists, he believed, had possessed no authentic liberal tradition to fall back on, unlike those who went against the grain in this country.[35]

Such a conviction served Izzy well as indicated by his response to a physician's suggestion in 1957 that he consider abandoning the newsletter. "You're so tense and jumpy, you ought to do something else," the doctor advised. "I may be tense and jumpy on the outside," Izzy admitted, but "I have a very deep sense of security. I feel that I'm really carrying on what America stands for."[36]

That same year, the Warren Court appeared to deal a fatal blow to the witch-hunt. A series of recent rulings by the High Court had abridged the power of legislative bodies to ask questions concerning political beliefs and associations and restricted the reach of the Smith Act. In Stone's estimation, the Supreme Court had demonstrated the public's increased displeasure with "that weird collection of opportunists, clowns, ex-Communist crackpots, and poor sick souls who have made America look foolish and even sinister during the last ten years with their perpetual searching under the national bed for little men who weren't there."[37]

Nevertheless, Stone remained convinced that the vestiges of hate, fear, and cowardice spawned by the red-baiters would be around for some time to come. Consequently, he was little surprised that the same devotees of personal liberty who applauded Boris Pasternak and his epic work, *Dr. Zhivago*, had never done the same for Charlie Chaplin, Howard Fast, or Paul Robeson. He condemned the unofficial blacklist still facing some of his country's cultural finest and the fact that "heretical" sorts—whose ranks included Izzy himself—could barely eke out a living, sustained only by small bands of loyal followers. Pasternak's American admirers, Stone pointed out, failed to understand just why he possessed universal significance: the Russian master represented the struggle artists and intellectuals must continually wage against the established order and the inevitable pressure to conform.[38]

Stone's warning that the shadow of the red scare would continue to fall across his own society proved prophetic. The spigot of repression could not be easily shut off once it had been opened up. The United States, as he had long predicted, paid the price for some time to come. Its foreign policy, driven by an anti-Communist fixation, continued to be afflicted with tunnel vision. The home front, too, suffered owing to the collapse of the left and the demise of vibrant liberalism and a corresponding dearth of solutions to deep-seated social, economic, and racial problems. Izzy's perspective on the costs of the anti-Communist phobia, then, had been remarkably astute throughout, even given occasionally overheated analyses.

While Stone continued to worry throughout the Eisenhower years about domestic red-baiters, he became more concerned than ever about "the gloomy thought controls" that seemed to be affixed to Soviet-styled communism. At the very beginning of the Eisenhower administration, it appeared that yet another round of purges was about to be carried out inside Soviet Russia. Nine physicians, six of them Jews, were charged with having plotted the murder of Communist Party leaders at the behest of "bourgeois" Zionists and American "imperialists." The horrific charges struck Stone as simply ludicrous. Impartial physicians and attorneys from outside the Soviet Union, he insisted, must be allowed access to those charged. The Russian government owed at least this much to its own people, to those sympathetic toward the Communist state, and to the international socialist movement.[39]

Such safeguards must be put into place, Stone pointed out, because the Soviet party leadership had "a way of erecting possibilities into actualities and then staging trials to 'prove' what they fear. Their trials were political morality plays which cynically assume an audience too unintelligent to be impressed by anything less than melodrama. It is not enough to prove a man mistaken; he must be displayed as a monster." To this end, the people of Russia during Stalin's long regime had "been fed on a heavy diet of conspiracy, treason, poisoning and murder in this political dramaturgy." That regime finally came to an end on March 5, 1953, with the death of the man Stone termed "one of the giant figures" of the contemporary period.[40]

Evidently, Stone continued to view Stalin as different from other dictators of the contemporary era; he did so in spite of the long reign of terror inside Russia, which he had repeatedly denounced, and the presence of Stalinism in the Soviet bloc, which pleased him no better. It is impossible to imagine Stone making a comparable statement about Hitler or Franco or any number of other right-wing despots. Thus, through this point, he remained far more willing to ascribe completely ignoble intentions to dictators who were positioned on the right side of the political spectrum than to their left-wing counterparts. Stalin and Mao, for all their failings, he saw as heading workers' or peasants' states.

Still, in response to letters expressing anger over his critique of the so-called Doctors' Plot, Stone blasted those who failed to heed Marx's admonition to question everything. They had been schooled to accept whatever they were told, he wrote, provided that the orders came from the Kremlin. Happily, a breath of fresh air now appeared to be sweeping through the Soviet capital; it had been acknowledged that the charges against the Moscow Nine were made up. Still, such an admission only led Stone to wonder about other "impermissible" acts of the NKVD, the Soviet secret service, and about the very composition of the Soviet government.[41]

The Soviet Union, Stone exclaimed, had too long insulted and angered those respectful of the Russian people and sympathetic to socialism. In spite of tremendous achievements which were sometimes overlooked in the face of vicious propaganda, the Soviet Union had exuded "an indifference to mass suffering and individual injustice, a sycophancy and an iron-clad conformity" which had "disgraced the socialist ideal."[42]

And yet when riots broke out later that year in East Germany, I. F. Stone, like so many others, was initially dumbfounded. How, after all, could a workers' state, no matter how imperfect, be condemned by the very workers in whose name the state supposedly operated? If such an uprising were genuine, what did that say about the very nature of the Communist state?

Perplexed by it all, Stone questioned whether this revolt involved "a spontaneous worker uprising" or was the product of "a military underground" that had played upon labor discontent. Or was the unrest intended to discredit moderates inside the new Soviet government?[43]

Two weeks later, however, Stone was readier to acknowledge that the disturbances spreading throughout Eastern Europe were based on genuine anti-Communist sentiment. He was particularly displeased with "the abject 'mea culpas' " pouring out of the mouths of the party leadership and now acknowledged that the riots were "all too real."[44]

Events in Yugoslavia—which had recently seemed so hopeful—troubled Stone as well, particularly Tito's jailing of Milovan Djilas, his former compatriot. Such a move demonstrated that fundamental paradoxes continued to beset socialism: the state refused simply to wither away; a new ruling class had appeared, composed of party cadre and government bureaucrats; and the remarkable judicial achievements of liberal capitalism seemed as far removed as ever. The Djilas case, like the one resulting in the execution of Lavrenti Beria, former chief of the Soviet secret police, Stone noted in January 1954, demanded that Marxists study Jeffersonian precepts.[45]

One year later, Stone again discussed the Djilas affair. Following Tito's break with Stalin, he acknowledged, Belgrade had stood as "a Mecca for Leftists" of all types searching "for a halfway house between capitalism and communism." Such high hopes were soon dashed, and the Yugoslav-Russian clash now appeared to resemble some kind of family quarrel. Stone underscored the admonition of Vladimir Dedijer, a Djilas defender: "A Communist should be first of all a human being, and every political movement which puts aside ethics and morals carries within it the seeds of its own destruction." Such a notion must resonate with those who believed in both socialism and democracy, Stone declared, and might well prove to be the epitaph of the Soviet-directed Communist movement.[46]

Dedijer had also insisted that socialism could not emerge without a free exchange of ideas. Stone went still farther and suggested that "free criticism . . . *which really is* directed at its very foundations" must be allowed, as Rosa Luxemburg, that sympathetic but critical supporter of the Bolsheviks, had so reasoned. It was she who had declared that "freedom for the supporters of the government only, for the members of one party only—no matter how big its membership may be—is not freedom at all. Freedom is always freedom for the man who thinks differently." Already, as Djilas recognized and Stone agreed, the ideal of communism had been besmirched and linked with totalitarianism. And terrorist rule, Luxemburg had warned, would only destroy the revolution and usher in a dictatorship of the Jacobin variety.[47]

But in May 1955, Stone argued that the Russians were at last learning to unloose the "unpleasant draconiam . . . stooge rule" they had held over much of Eastern Europe. As a consequence, he wondered if truly independent communist regimes might not be possible, which would promise a *"cordon sanitaire* in reverse" of friendly but nationalistic governments, positioned to Russia's immediate west.[48]

As of mid-November, Stone was still proclaiming the march toward socialism to be "universal and irresistible." And if war could be staved off, he reasoned, the unanticipated, distasteful features of the socialist advance might yet be overcome: draconian thought control, an absence of personal freedoms, and bureaucratic stasis.[49]

The hold of socialism on Izzy's imagination obviously remained considerable. He continued to hope that the Soviet bloc states might yet live up to the socialist vision if only the dictatorial yoke of the Communist governments could be loosened. And he believed as strongly as ever in the need to merge socialism and democracy.

Stone was pleased by recent reports which indicated that Nikita Khrushchev, the new Soviet premier, had acknowledged that in the nuclear age, the old party line on revolution should be tossed in the dustbin of history. But if the Russians truly wanted peace, Stone chimed in, they were going to have to lean on Communist parties worldwide, who continued to view Moscow as "the new Rome."[50]

With Khrushchev indicating that a parliamentary path to socialism might be possible, Stone, in a rather large leap of faith, hinted that a new Popular Front might be put together in both France and Italy—the dreams of the thirties certainly died hard; this, he declared, would help to stave off a return of fascism. But should such a front be constructed, Stone continued, it must not once again serve as "a Trojan horse" that would enable the Communists to swallow up their non-Communist partners. The frequent and startling shifts in the Communist line also had to come to an end, as did "the slavishly abject dependence of the Communists on Moscow."[51]

But in February 1956, at the Soviet Communist Party's Twentieth Congress, Khrushchev painted Stalin, that Russian Man of Steel, as a paranoid, maniacal butcher who had set the stage for the purge trials and constructed slave labor camps. Postwar red-baiting, mounting doubts about both the CPUSA and the Soviet state, and the economic boom experienced in the West had already weakened the appeal of the Communist movement. The Khrushchev revelations of 1956, like the Nazi-Soviet pact of 1939, served as the "Kronstadt"—the point of departure from the engine of the revolution, in Louis Fischer's words—for many others, including Izzy's brother Marc who had been "in and out the party over a number of years." Consequently, the dreams of the thirties now collapsed with a near absolute finality.[52]

I. F. Stone, unlike true believers, possessed no blind allegiance to either Soviet Russia or the ideal of communism. Nevertheless, he stood very much as a man of the left and thus reacted as though an electrical current had coursed through him following the unveiling of Khrushchev's speech. The admission by Lenin's latest heir that the path to communism had been strewn with broken lives and souls was as jolting for him as it was for certain of the party folk who had not shared his doubts, discontent, and disillusionment all along the way. From this point forth, his editorials on the Soviet Union were more embittered than any he had written to date; no longer was it possible for him to view that nation as any kind of progressive state. Nevertheless, Stone's analyses of Russia in no way foreshadowed the rightward drift or disillusionment with politics experienced by so many of his foes and compatriots from the heyday of the Old Left in the 1930s; among those who had headed in such a direction were individuals as disparate as Malcolm Cowley, John Dos Passos, Sidney Hook, and Reinhold Niebuhr.

On March 26, Stone asserted that the disrobing of Stalin was "Communism's self-exposure" and demonstrated that Russia, "backward" as it had proven to be, was no fit role model. Moreover, the sectarians were themselves revealed "as prize idiots abroad and prize cowards within Russia." The Communist parties in the West, for their part, represented only "a tattered scarecrow" which played into the hands of reactionary forces everywhere. It was all too apparent to Stone how their "slavish conformity" to Moscow had crippled an entire generation of radicals. It was time, he declared, for the left to recognize that the Communist movement was finished and to stop reading the law as written by Marx and Lenin. Intellectuals should still view "the great revolution of our time" sympathetically, but they must do so with a critical eye, he believed, not in the manner of party sycophants. This was something that the Communists, unfortunately, appeared incapable of understanding, he declared, for they had abandoned the practice of independent thinking.[53]

It was also time, Izzy determined, that he visit the Soviet bloc. Perhaps he had not done so previously because of the same kind of concerns that had dissuaded him from attending the 1948 Progressive Party convention. Possibly he had feared that actually witnessing the Soviet system in action would lead him away from the socialist path altogether. Whatever the reason, unlike many other leading Old Leftists, Izzy did not undertake the pilgrimage until every shred of belief in "the Soviet experiment" had disappeared.

Before he could go overseas, however, there was the little matter of getting back the passport that had been revoked five years earlier. Now he was obliged to send a handwritten note to the U.S. Passport Office which declared that he was "not and never . . . [had] been a member of the Communist Party or of the Communist Political Association."[54]

At the end of April, Izzy traveled to the former mecca of world socialism, where he stayed for six days before heading off to Poland. After departing from Russia, he filed his first report, one unencumbered by U.S. Embassy and State Department debriefings. Stone painted the picture of a somewhat schizophrenic Moscow, which attempted through "Communist Babbittry" to appear as "the best biggest and Bolshoi-est of all cities." But also present were clear signs that this was a land of peasants, of "gnarled creatures" little removed from serfdom, who retained a deep religiosity as members of the Church or the Party alike, and who remained "capable of much senseless cruelty." So this was Russia, Stone declared, "Holy Russia in a new sense to the world's intellectuals," a land that was "unmistakably backward, no model for the future, Byzantine, slavish and submissive, still enmired in the past." Nevertheless, Russia was also a great state, capable of grand accomplishments, provided that war could be avoided.[55]

His trip back home was a difficult one, owing to his awareness that a fuller accounting of his impressions of the Soviet state must come next. Stone believed at this point, as he had a quarter-century before, that "the deepest questions of history and morality" were brought to light by the Communist experience. In Russia, one could witness that very real but tragic mix of good and evil and the posing of history's eternal question, "whether-it-might-have-been-otherwise."[56]

Friends had showered Izzy with advice of all kinds, some urging him to hold his tongue in the interest of the struggle for world peace. But that way lay the very morass, Stone now declared, into which the Communist state had itself fallen; it was a morass that had ensnared Izzy himself, on more than one occasion. Now, however, in spite of the consequences, he simply had to tell it as he saw it. The Soviet Union "*is not a good society*," he charged, "*and it is not led by honest men.* No society is good in which men fear to think— much less speak—freely." For the independent thinker, the intellectual, or anyone concerned about humanistic values, Soviet Russia remained "a hermetically sealed prison, stifling in its atmosphere of complete, rigid and low-level thought control," where an entire generation of boot-lickers had been spawned.[57]

Furthermore, it was the system itself and not Stalinism alone, Stone argued, that ultimately was at fault. Although a good deal more humane and civilized than his successor, Vladimir Lenin had provided the seeds for the terror that followed. Stalinism, then, naturally evolved out of the Communist movement and was the result of party members being taught not simply blind obedience but hatred as well; they were taught, for example, to revel in the liquidation of their opponents.[58]

Almost immediately upon publication of his Moscow reports, Izzy Stone experienced something of that which he had feared, the loss of several hundred subscribers to his newsletter. As he later informed Norman Thomas, he had worried whether reader response might cripple the *Weekly*. But it was soon apparent that a whole new crop of readers was being discovered, including individuals like Thomas. Upon his return back to the States, Izzy had sent copies of the reports of his most recent trip to the old Socialist Party chieftain, indicating that they suggested "I am liable to end up as I began 'in the camp of Norman Thomas.' " Thomas responded that he had indeed read those pieces and believed that if the recent issues of the *Weekly* were any indication, "I should welcome you as heartily in 'my' camp as I did in the beginning, and, by the way, it isn't just mine."59

But Communist Party stalwarts were no more pleased by Izzy's accounts of developments in the Soviet satellites than they were by his Moscow reports. He indicated all too clearly how liberating he found Poland to be after his stay in the Soviet Union. As he noted in the *Weekly*, his initial thought upon entering Warsaw had been that he was now back in Europe. The Poles were better dressed than the Muscovites, even chic in appearance. Western European papers of the non-Communist variety, ranging from the *Times* of London to *Le Monde*, could be found in the streets of the Polish capital. And here Izzy discovered a completely different atmosphere than he had seen anywhere else in the world. Not even in Tito's Yugoslavia had he heard party members talk as they did in Warsaw, absent "Communist cliches or . . . cant"; furthermore, they were speaking considerably more openly than was presently possible in "loyalty-purge-haunted" Washington. Consequently, it was now Poland that he looked to as a model for Eastern Europe.60

European liberals and socialists, Stone declared in his editorial on June 4, 1956, should support the struggle to free Poland. Later that summer, he called for a sympathetic reading of the workers' unrest in Poznan. He warned that if socialism were to survive in Eastern Europe, leftists of all kinds in the West were going to have to stand beside the Polish workers.61

That fall, Stone's disillusionment with Russia became greater still as Soviet tanks rolled into the streets of Budapest. Shortly before the Politburo acted, Stone acknowledged that it was highly unsettling "for those us of us who all our lives regarded socialism as our ideal" to witness the depth of the workers' discontent with the workers' state. The very groups that had been most attracted to the socialist banner during Marx's lifetime—workers, students, and intellectuals—were now spearheading the revolts in Hungary and Poland; furthermore, they might be doing the same in Czechoslovakia and Russia, he suggested, in the not too distant future. Not surprisingly for those like Stone who were aware of the new ruling class arrogance, more and more anger was directed at the heavy-handed practices and the privileges of the Communist Party leaders.62

Hungary, Stone believed, threatened to become "the 1848 of communism"; it promised to ignite a series of chain reactions against a secret police that upheld party doctrine and the liturgy of "a new lay priesthood." Already, "the urban mob, the student rally, even the barricade" were appearing. Lewis Coser and Irving Howe soon delivered a similar analysis in *Dissent,* declaring the Hungarian rebels to have "vindicated man in the 20th century."[63]

The Hungarian revolt, Stone declared, was the most significant event of the postwar period, and one which was reshaping the world as a whole. It was clear now that an era was coming to an end, the era in which defense of the Russian Revolution, notwithstanding its failings and horrors, was demanded of all progressive individuals. Vanishing as well was the notion, long accepted in the East, that the Soviet Union was not an imperialistic force; Coser and Howe readily agreed. Now rising all too clearly from the wreckage that was Hungary was "the old Ivan, the bewildered peasant soldier of a bureaucratic despotism, heavy-handed, cruel in a slovenly way, and not too sure of itself, weakly reforming and brutally repressing in fits and starts."[64]

The Russian response to the Hungarian uprising, Stone wrote, demonstrated all too clearly how unbending the Soviet state was and suggested that what was now occurring in Budapest would one day take place in Moscow. Thus, the Hungarian freedom fighters had vanquished "the last illusions of an era."[65]

But still more was at stake, Stone insisted, than the image of the Soviet Union. For the good name of socialism had been marred by the very nature of Communist rule. This was unfortunate indeed, for socialism remained a necessary instrument to uplift "underdeveloped" countries. But should socialism remain associated with police-state horrors, Stone warned, reaction might triumph for a full generation. And the stain of Stalinism would not be removed, he believed, until a turn toward majority rule came about. For what was "popular democracy," he asked, "but a fraud if the people are free to discuss only one point of view, the Party's, with a capital P, like the G in God?" It was the one-party system that was at fault. Moreover, if, after four full decades, "the Revolution" remained wary of the will of the people, perhaps it was time to try something else.[66]

The tumultuous events in the Communist world in 1956 had resulted in a further loss of faith for I. F. Stone, who never again declared in an unequivocal manner that socialism was *the* answer. Thus, Russian tanks in the streets of Budapest and Nikita Khrushchev managed to accomplish that which even the collectivization campaign and other Stalinist terrors, Czechoslovakia, and the Nazi-Soviet accords had not—the journalist's movement away from certain of the ideals of the 1930s.

This was a striking development, for Stone had proudly, sometimes defiantly, considered himself to be a radical since his youth and would continue to do so. But what that translated into from this point forth was the absence of a political mooring or ideological framework to which he could turn. That in and of itself was not without benefits, compelling him as it did to continue charting his own, independent course. Nevertheless, a kind of vacuum persisted for both Izzy and the American left. Recognition of that fact led him to attempt to find another New Beginnings for the left, which could now, he believed, finally leave behind the ghosts of the 1930s. However, as matters turned out, the time was not quite ripe for a new left.

On December 14, *I. F. Stone's Weekly* hosted a public meeting held at the Community Church in New York City which was intended to discuss the possible application of the Bill of Rights to the ferment in Eastern Europe. Among the questions posed were: How might fundamental freedoms be safeguarded under socialist rule? What might the iron curtain countries learn from the American experience? What lessons might be had with regard to the erosion of basic political liberties? Izzy invited independent left and socialist editors, including the *Liberation's* A. J. Muste, the *Militant's* Daniel Roberts, the *American Socialist's* Bert Cochran, and *Labor Action's* Hal Draper, to join in a panel discussion. In advertising what he predicted would be "an ideological free-for-all," Izzy declared that as editor of the *Weekly* he would serve as "the immoderate moderator."[67]

Norman Thomas sent his regrets and warned that such a gathering of weak, left-wing groups, tainted in the minds of the public at large and even "our own," was quite possibly a fruitless undertaking. Still, demonstrating devotion to democratic principles and opposition to every conceivable strand of communism, Thomas suggested, might be worth something.[68]

His disenchantment with Soviet rule now complete, Stone continued to follow with dismay the course of events in Eastern Europe. In early 1957, he discussed the tragic case of Raoul Wallenberg, the Swedish diplomat who had valiantly struggled to keep thousands of Jews out of the Nazi death camps. When the Red Army marched into Budapest at the end of World War II, this "angel of mercy" had been arrested by the NKVD. Now the Soviets declared that a full ten years before, Wallenberg had perished in the infamous Lubianka prison. A country whose secret police meted out such treatment to a diplomat from a neutral state, Stone cried, was "a disgrace to world socialism." Indeed, only Russia, he asserted, could have treated Wallenberg "so barbarously." And following the execution of Imre Nagy, the dissident Communist who had briefly headed the Hungarian republic, Stone proclaimed the whole affair to be "sickening." The perfidy of the Russians in this case, he insisted, would not soon be forgotten.[69]

Hoping to discover how gradual movement to a less authoritarian brand of socialism might be brought about, Izzy traveled in the spring of 1959 to Poland and East Germany. In Poland, although the promise of the revolution of 1956 had ebbed, he was able to go where he chose and talk with whomever he pleased. Warsaw remained the one place in the Communist world where it was possible to communicate openly with party members, rather than simply hear Marxist-Leninist slogans tossed about. Poland, at present, appeared remarkably open, with the government containing left-wing socialists who acted not as Communists, but as men who valued freedom of thought and persuasion, rather than coercion. East Germany, by contrast, appeared ruled by Communist "Rip Van Winkles" who preferred "time-servers to honest men, obedience to zeal, submissiveness to initiative."[70]

Poland seemed genuinely freer to Izzy than did Russia or East Germany, which meant that there remained a socialist state somewhere that offered the possibility of sustaining the radical vision. Soon to appear would be another regime on the opposite side of the Atlantic, avowedly revolutionary but seemingly anti-American too.

W hile Stone believed that the Soviet Union had long ago lost its right to proclaim itself a socialist model, now, more than ever, he considered Communist parties throughout the Western world to be impediments in the fight for peace and civil liberties. In October 1956, he declared that a new progressive party could not even be put together while the American Communist Party continued to exist. For if such an organization were to emerge, he wrote, party members would necessarily move to take total control over it. What had to be recognized, he noted, was that the Communists had no faith in majority rule and believed in a double standard when it came to civil liberties for themselves or for their left-wing rivals.[71]

As the Communist Party national convention unfolded in New York the following February, Stone dismissed the "Lilliputian world" of party hacks who sought to move back to " 'hard' and 'orthodox' Muscovite policies." The largest contribution that dissident American Communists could make to the quest for justice and liberty here at home, Stone insisted, would be to call for an end of the party. This was the case, he continued, because the Soviets invariably preferred a small cadre "of submissive and obsequious fanatics," rather than honest sorts who would attempt to act as true patriots. Although there remained "good, devoted and heroic people" in the American party, he suggested, they would be of little use until liberated from the intellectual fetters that bound them. Indeed, the greatest crime of the party, he declared, was that it had led a fair number of young people and intellectuals to blindly accept Communist directives and to dismiss reports of repression in the Soviet Union.[72]

Thus, when A. J. Muste's American Forum for Socialist Education envisioned a new alliance of non-Communist leftists and their more sectarian brethren, the old Popular Fronter again warned that the Communists would move to take over; Stone, even more than Muste at this point, now seemed to appreciate what was required before an authentic new left might appear. As a consequence, his analysis had come to sound like that of the editors of *Dissent*, who went so far as to deny that the Communist Party, "an association of political enemies," should even be situated on the left. How, Stone asked, could those who truly believed in freedom line up with others for whom it was a cynical ploy alone, to be discarded when the occasion demanded? How could a new, American-based movement be constructed, which would include those who would "jump through the hoops again on signal from Moscow?" Non-Communists must defend the rights of Communists "100 percent," he declared, but they had to guard against attempts to revitalize the party.[73]

Both Stone and Muste, two members of the Old Left, were attempting to lay the foundation for a reemergence of radicalism in America. But as Old Leftists they were themselves still caught up in the sectarian wars of the thirties, still retained ideological allegiances formulated during that time, still thought in terms of movements of the past. This was perfectly natural, for their friends and associations tended to be linked to that period as well, and because the left, owing to the domestic Cold War, had lost a "generation" of political activists. Consequently, there had existed a real vacuum between the heyday of the Old Left and the end of the 1950s.

As it turned out, rather than rekindling the American left they had known, Stone and Muste were laying the foundation for another movement. When that movement did appear, they came to serve not as official spokespersons, but rather as elder statesmen.

One necessary step in the direction of a new American left was to effect a separation from the discredited vestiges of Old Left organizations. On October 28, 1957, Stone indicated that his favorite quote was one penned by the Frenchman Albert Camus, the latest recipient of the Nobel Prize for Literature. In *The Rebel*, Camus had written: "Every revolutionary ends by becoming either an oppressor or a heretic." On December 2, Stone applauded the most recent work of Howard Fast, at one time the brightest literary star of the American Communist Party. In *The Naked God*, Fast had acknowledged that no matter what the party had previously been, now "it is a prison for man's best and boldest dreams."[74]

The left-wing sectarians, whom Stone had long criticized and defended, now, like the Soviet Union, appeared to be something of a hopeless case in his estimation. They had wasted their claim to stand on the side of peace and progress, he believed, and were henceforth to be viewed as thoroughly divisive and untrustworthy. Any new American movement, he reasoned, had to distance itself from their influence.

For I. F. Stone, the discarding of all traces of sympathy for the Soviet state and American Communists proved liberating. More and more, he appeared to identify with someone like Norman Thomas, whom he grouped with Eleanor Roosevelt, Clarence Pickett, and Alexander Meiklejohn as "spiritual leaders in our barren national landscape." On the occasion of Thomas's seventy-fifth birthday, Stone proclaimed him to be "the one big man" the American left had produced in recent times and one of but a handful inside the decaying international Socialist movement. The two now corresponded somewhat frequently, with Thomas indicating how much he appreciated the newsletter.[75]

Others did so as well, as evidenced by the slow, but gradual increase in the *Weekly*'s subscription levels and by the plaudits that began to come Stone's way. His readers appeared to accept Izzy's assertion that the newsletter provided them with information not to be found elsewhere. They also seemed to go along with his notion that signing up for such a publication would help "start the process of rehabilitation" and serve to liberate those subject to "cold war brainwashing."[76]

In the pages of the *Weekly* on December 16, 1957, Izzy published a thank-you note to his readers. He expressed gratitude for having been given "five wonderful years of freedom to search, to study and to speak the truth" as he saw it. The "pet preconceptions" of each and every one of his readers, he recognized, had probably been called into question by the newsletter at one point or another. After all, the American left, like the American right, had its own sacred cows. Intellectuals, no less than anyone else, disliked having long-held tenets subjected to careful scrutiny. But what, Izzy asked, "can a man do but report what he sees?"[77]

And in the period ahead, he promised, the *Weekly* was going to focus on peace, the largest issue around. Matters appeared bleak at present, he admitted, but then that had been the case for civil liberties a mere five years earlier. Rapid changes, however, had come about, and the Supreme Court was now upholding principles that only small iconoclastic publications like the *Weekly* were then championing. "May the same happy miracle happen again in the search for peace!"[78]

In early June 1958, Izzy's rehabilitation proceeded apace as *Variety*, the entertainment bible, applauded his appearance on "The Open Mind" on WRCA-TV in New York City. The subject at hand was "All the News," and Izzy was joined by the *Hartford Courant*'s Herbert Brucker and the *New York*

Herald Tribune's William Miller. *Variety* played up Izzy as "a badgering banderillero of the American press" who "pulls no punches." While Brucker and Miller were said to be "no journalistic slouches," it was Izzy who delivered "most of the fireworks" during the half-hour show. "Stone's pyrotechnics," *Variety* reported, "put the torrid tabasco sauce into the professional shop talk."[79]

That October, Bertrand Russell felt compelled to send a note to Izzy simply to let him know "how very much I appreciate your *Weekly*. I read each number as it arrives and find always something that I am glad to know and that I do not find elsewhere." The following spring, in a letter to Professor Alexander Meiklejohn, Izzy declared himself to be "the luckiest and happiest intellectual left in the USA, able to write as I please for such good readers and at the same time make a living. What more could a man want?"[80]

As the *Weekly* neared the close of its seventh year of existence, Izzy Stone received still more accolades with the Emergency Civil Liberties Committee awarding him its Tom Paine Award for 1959. Six hundred fans showed up in New York City to watch Izzy being honored, in spite of declarations by HCUAC and the American Legion that the ECLC was a Communist-front organization. Congratulations were forthcoming from Eleanor Roosevelt, Russell, and Clarence E. Pickett, among others. The former First Lady wrote that Izzy "richly deserves the tribute," Russell saluted "his services in the causes of peace and sanity," and the longtime head of the American Friends Service Committee praised the "analytical and critical," but not embittered, tone of the newsletter.[81]

Nevertheless, the decade of the 1950s remained a troubled, even "haunted" time for Izzy Stone. Washington, D.C., in particular, remained an unfriendly, inhospitable town, with fellow members of the Fourth Estate joining government officials in avoiding him altogether. Chris Stone recalled those occasions when other journalists "sort of held their breath" as he and Izzy walked into one of the press rooms in the Capital building. "It was cold. It was really, really cold. Sometimes conversation came to a halt."[82]

At one point, an enraged I. F. Stone "just erupted." He insisted, "I don't want to be buried in this goddamned city."[83]

And, although he took great pleasure in his work, Izzy kept "an account." According to his son Chris, the "economy of his psyche was pretty positive and overflowing with energy and abundance and pleasure"; but he did make "some allowance for the snubs, a storing up of the bits of anger that understandably built up in a generalized way," which was nevertheless not directed against individuals. To Chris, his father was quite a complex figure with "a lot going on that none of us really understood."[84]

The pain and isolation that were by-products of the domestic Cold War left deep-seated scars for many who remained outside the political mainstream in the manner that Izzy Stone did. He evidently "capitalized anger," Chris noted, which "every now and then would erupt." The slights and closed doors did affect him, and even years later when the political ambience was considerably transformed, that fury could be witnessed as he spoke at colleges and universities around the land or in the capital itself. At times, the anger could seemingly overwhelm Izzy, leading him astray from his prepared text and onto tangents of which he was himself undoubtedly not fully aware.[85]

What Izzy was recalling, consciously or not, were the rebukes, the slanders, the inanities of earlier times and perhaps of the present too. Such memories must have been aplenty from the 1950s and before. And there were various shenanigans that Izzy could not even have known about such as the correspondence between James C. Hagerty, Eisenhower's press secretary, and G. W. Johnstone of the National Association of Manufacturers, which indicated how much of a controversial figure he remained to some. After Izzy's appearance on New York City's "Night Beat" in which he dismissed Hagerty as discourteous and called him "the damnedest bore we've had in the White House," NAM received a confidential memo from Radio Report, Inc. Although Johnstone declared that he nearly "jumped right through the Tube . . . and choked 'Izzy,' "Hagerty dismissed Stone as an old *PM* hand. "So don't pay any attention to anything he says," Hagerty wrote.[86]

Then there were twin episodes on the floor of the U.S. House of Representatives, about which Izzy was undoubtedly informed. On January 27, 1959, Chairman Francis E. Walter of HCUAC denounced Stone—whose real name was Isadore Feinstein, he pointed out, using the same tactic that anti-Semite John Rankin had employed in his own denunciation of Izzy during World War II—as having "publicly the worst front record of anybody that I know of." On May 5, 1960, Ohio Congressman Gordon H. Scherer, attacked in the pages of the *Weekly* as a hysterical red-baiter, declared that Stone had "regularly, consistently, yes, continuously, served the Communist cause by attacking and vilifying all those who have been in the forefront of the fight against the Communist conspiratorial apparatus." Stone, Scherer reported, had been referred to by the American Communist Party as "our good friend" and boasted "one of the longest records of service to the Communist apparatus that has ever been compiled." Scherer then proceeded to place a copy of a HCUAC report on Stone in the *Congressional Record.* Among Stone's other reputed sins were his reported sponsorship of the Friends of the Abraham Lincoln Brigade, the wartime Washington Citizens' Committee to Free Earl Browder, the Artists' Front to Win the War, and the National Committee to Defeat the Mundt Bill or Internal Security Act.[87]

Throughout this period, the FBI, now aided by the office of the secretary of defense, continued to follow Izzy and his family closely. In a letter to

J. Edgar Hoover discussing security clearance for Jeremy Stone, it was indicated that the son had dwelled in his father's home during a period when Izzy's "activities on behalf of the Communist Party were most pronounced." And Chris quite possibly was denied a Fulbright to France for which he had earlier been approved.[88]

I n certain ways, the Eisenhower years, an era of general conservatism, complacency, and conformity, proved to be particularly well suited to a natural lone actor such as Izzy Stone. It was during this period, with organized radicalism at low ebb, that a handful of independent thinkers clearly and cogently attacked prevailing attitudes and policies. Men such as the radical sociologist C. Wright Mills, the psychologist-sociologist Paul Goodman, neo-Marxist philosopher Herbert Marcuse, *Dissent* editor Irving Howe, historian William Appelman Williams, novelist and essayist Norman Mailer, peacemaker A. J. Muste, and Izzy Stone thrived during a time when no viable left-wing movements existed to dominate and possibly color their actions and perceptions. The red scare, party antics, and the Khrushchev revelations finally and perhaps fortunately dissipated whatever goodwill remained toward the American Communist Party and the Soviet Union and ensured that the Popular Frontism of the Old Left was not to return again. Such developments made it highly unlikely that any new radical movement in the United States would be dominated by home-brewed comrades, the Comintern, or the dreams and visions of the 1930s.

Thus, unfettered by any radical drive and compelled to discard or at least question as never before his own ties to the Old Left, I. F. Stone was able to chart a path of greater independence and insight which laid the foundation for his soon-to-be legendary reputation as a political and intellectual maverick. Indeed, it was during this era that he was forced to begin to come to grips with the dilemmas of independent radicalism. Perhaps the greater clarity and vision he now displayed would not have been possible were it not for his intimate involvement with the movement of the thirties, connected as it was to issues regarding sectarianism and ideological illusions. Because he had experienced something of its internecine wars, he was determined not to go that way again. And owing to the fact that he had been entangled in visions of the better society to come, he, like his Old Leftist cohorts, had given way to flights of fancy which necessarily resulted in disillusionment. Such errors—and he certainly recognized by now that they were precisely that—had to be avoided in the future by any new left, Izzy believed. As one of the few who had remained true to radical ideals throughout, he felt a sense of responsibility to ensure that new American rebels, whenever and however they might arise, discovered their own, distinctively antisectarian path. He was insistent, too, that they learn from history, not just from the failings of the Old Left but also from the radical tradition of Jefferson, Paine, Sinclair, and Thomas.

At this point in his career, the *Weekly* served as the means whereby Izzy helped to sustain that very tradition and that of independent radical journalism. And his greater—though by no means complete—respectability was one small but not insignificant sign that a thaw of sorts had come about. Another indication was the appearance of a series of political and social movements determined to challenge the norms of Cold War America, movements which Stone had long called for and immediately championed.

11 "We Have to Learn to Think in a New Way"

His curiosity was, as he later put it, piqued, to say the least. While Edward Teller and his cohorts had long claimed that underground nuclear tests could not be traced beyond a range of two hundred miles, the evidence staring Izzy in the face suggested something else again. Shirttails in the *New York Times* indicated that the very first subterranean explosion, which had been carried out beneath the Nevada desert in the fall of 1957, had been felt as far away as Toronto, Rome, and Tokyo. The *Weekly*, however, was still being run on a shoestring budget and so Izzy filed away the report in his *New York Times* file.[1]

The next spring, Izzy carefully followed the appearance by Harold Stassen, the Eisenhower administration's top disarmament negotiator, before the Humphrey Senate Disarmament Subcommittee. To his surprise, Stassen testified that listening posts 580 miles apart could pick up underground atomic tests. Two days later, the Atomic Energy Commission—which Izzy later proclaimed to be "the most mendacious agency in Washington"— reported the range of detection for the Nevada blast to be less than two hundred miles. Izzy reached back into his files, dug out the *Times* article from the previous fall, and put in a call to the AEC. "How come you guys are saying this couldn't be detected more than 200 miles away?" he asked, when the *Times* had reported it had been recorded in cities across the globe. The AEC press officer responded, "Izzy, we don't know what the answer is. We'll see what we can find out."[2]

While waiting to hear back from the AEC, Izzy began making phone calls to uncover additional information on nuclear testing. He discovered that the Coast and Geodetic Survey at the Department of Commerce contained a seismology branch. He jumped into his car, headed downtown, and came upon government seismologists who readily showed him a list of some nineteen stations that had been able to trace the Nevada test. The most remote point to the east proved to be Fayetteville, Arkansas, 1,240 miles away; the farthest point to the north, Fairbanks, Alaska, almost twice that distance from the site of the explosion.[3]

When asked why he was interested in the earlier test, Izzy explained and the government men were suddenly silent. Upon returning to his office, he received a call from the AEC's public relations man who told him, "Izzy, I hear you've been in Coast and Geodetic snooping around that story. It's too late in the day to get Nevada on the teletype. I'll let you know tomorrow." The following today, the agency informed him that a mistake had been made but failed to issue any kind of retraction. Consequently, Izzy tipped off his friend Richard Dudman at the *St. Louis Post-Dispatch*, and the story made front-page headlines. Following an investigation by the Joint Committee on Atomic Energy, the AEC admitted to an "inadvertent" mistake.[4]

Edwin A. Lahey, head of the Washington Bureau of the Knight Newspapers, proclaimed Izzy's atomic snoop to be "a good example of personal journalism at its best." Both *Science* magazine, put out by the American Association for the Advancement of Science, and the *Newsletter*, the Federation of American Scientists' publication, credited the *Weekly* with having forced the AEC's hand. So did Senator Clinton Anderson of New Mexico, in grilling Admiral Lewis L. Strauss during a hearing of the Humphrey Disarmament Subcommittee.[5]

Izzy's confrontation with the AEC demonstrated something of the possibilities of politically committed journalism and the kind of impact that the intellectual as activist could have. It highlighted as well the natural inclination of Izzy to contest established "truths" and to act as a journalistic bulldog in ferreting out a story. It was one of the premier examples of the quality of investigative reporting that Izzy and the *Weekly* were capable of. It was also the type of journalism that few others were then producing, since they were determined to display a veneer of objectivity. Finally, it indicated Izzy's determination to support the new ferment that was brewing, a ferment both connected to and disassociated from the left, particularly the Old Left, which was now all but history.

The *Weekly*'s avowed opposition to nuclear weapons served as a key component of Stone's reportorial and ideological armor. Throughout the early postwar period, he had warned that a new kind of arms race lay in store; now, with both the United States and the USSR having acquired the hydrogen bomb, he feared that another kind of holocaust might result. Within a short while, the question of thermonuclear missiles placed on a small Caribbean island threatened to erupt in a global conflagration. Just as he had once viewed the possibility of a second world war as endangering the viability of the then lone socialist nation, he now saw the threat of another international battle dooming a new revolutionary state, Cuba. Thus, nuclear warfare, in Izzy's view, imperiled not only the very existence of the human race, but the quests to shape a better world through socialism and national liberation movements.

He worried that the red-baiters in Washington and the capitalist-haters in Moscow were more than a little capable of taking the world to the brink and beyond. What was needed, I. F. Stone had long believed, was what Albert Einstein and Bertrand Russell—two personal friends of his who served as "father" figures—had recently suggested: "We have to learn to think in a new way." It was "hatred, not hydrogen" that seemed to threaten humankind. It was not generals, presidents, and commissars alone who imperiled the very fate of the world, but "our idol, that abstraction, the Common Man," who did so as well.[6]

Notwithstanding his radical perspective, Stone, unlike many on the left, never was one to view the average American as naturally or instinctively enlightened. While they portrayed that citizen as blessed with some large amount of natural wisdom, Stone saw a figure every bit as jingoistic and warlike as the self-serving politicians and professional soldiers the American left felt compelled to contest.

Nevertheless, Stone refused to consider the fight for more harmonious international relations to be hopeless and in November 1954 called for the American peace movement, no matter how weak it might be, to insist on an end to nuclear testing. He condemned the never-ending quest for the "new Ultimate Weapon," the "new Wonder-Monster," and declared the atom to be "our totem; the bomb our Moloch"; belief in overwhelming firepower, "our real national religion."[7]

At the close of the *Weekly*'s first half-decade, Stone, adopting the activist stance once more, promised to devote the next five years to the fight for peace, which he called the most important cause of the contemporary era. On February 16, 1958, Izzy delivered the weekly guest lecture at Boston's nonsectarian Community Church on "Co-existence in the Missile Age," with Scott Nearing following him to the podium. Izzy again spoke before the same congregation that spring, his topic "Nuclear Testing—Is It Dangerous? Can It Be Policed? An Answer to Dr. Edward A. Teller," his presentation coming two weeks following an appearance by Martin Luther King, Jr. Izzy delivered other addresses on behalf of the American Friends Service Committee and the Committee Against Nuclear Testing in Boston, before the Women for Legislative Action in Los Angeles and San Francisco, at the behest of the Student Council for a Sane Nuclear Policy in New York City, and alongside Socialist Party leader Norman Thomas at a Washington Square rally.[8]

In the process, he became one of the earliest and most consistent sponsors of the antinuclear campaign. He remained in that campaign for the duration of his life, fearing as he did that everything humankind had worked for could literally go up in smoke. In his view, negotiations to bring about genuine disarmament and prevent the expansion of the nuclear club were absolutely essential to the survival of the planet earth.

As matters turned out, of course, when the *Weekly*'s second five-year plan ended, nuclear holocaust had just been narrowly averted. That near disaster, of course, revolved around a tiny Caribbean island, a cigar-smoking revolutionary, the Soviet premier, and a new American president, all of whom Stone admired to one degree or another.

From the outset, Izzy championed the cause of the Cuban Revolution, often in romantic fashion, as he once had Mao Zedong's long march to power. Fidel Castro, he proclaimed on April 27, 1959, was a hero of the modern era. The young Cuban leader and his trusty band of men, he declared, had bested forces backed "by the Colossus of the North." Not surprisingly, then, no man since Bolívar, he believed, had so appealed to the young people of Latin America. In dismissing the outcry that had followed the expropriation of U.S. corporate interests, Stone claimed his own nation had long buddied up to bloody dictators in the region, demanding only that "they play ball with U.S. oil, sugar, banana and other private interests."9

As relations between the United States and the tiny Caribbean state continued to deteriorate, Stone warned that Cuba must not be turned into "our Latin American Hungary." He returned from the island in midsummer 1960, greatly impressed with the new Cuba that was in the making, so different from that which he had first seen in the midst of the Great Depression and then again in the late forties. Castro and his worthy compatriots, Stone declared, were ushering in "an admirably humane" social revolution. In Cuba, he reported, there existed grass-roots support not enjoyed by the Eastern bloc People's Republics. Despite the absence of a free press or competitive political parties, Castro's revolution in no way appeared to be one "imposed from above." In these still relatively innocent and early days of the Cuban Revolution, Stone discovered heretical writings such as Djilas's *The New Class* prominently displayed in bookstores along with busts of José Martí—who had helped to orchestrate the fight against imperial Spain—not those of Karl Marx or Vladimir Lenin.10

Stone noted that leftists from the North—who had for so long been mired "in a state atmosphere of Fifth Amendment radicalism" in the United States—found refreshing the openness with which Castro had proclaimed his intentions. This, he declared, more than anything else, indicated to those in the political know that Castro was no Communist; Carey McWilliams of *The Nation* also believed that Fidel was simply a Cuban nationalist. Indeed, Castro appeared pragmatic, Stone noted, a kind of left-wing Roosevelt, while Cuban officials seemed to exude the kind of enthusiasm that had suffused New Deal Washington. C. Wright Mills agreed that Castro's practical bent seemed to set him apart.11

Upon returning home, Izzy acknowledged that concerns about Cuba becoming a Soviet satellite were not illegitimate. But a lack of sympathy for what Cuba was facing, he predicted, would only drive the country into the camp of the Soviets. And a fight against Cuba, he wrote, would be foolish, hurtling the United States into a prolonged guerrilla confrontation. Instead, Washington needed to recognize that "Castro is our Tito." Cold War stereotypes aside, it was apparent, he indicated, that the Cuban people felt "love and devotion" toward Fidel Castro. And were he to be deposed or worse, he would remain forever etched in the hearts and minds of the people of Latin America.[12]

While Izzy had not been able to see Castro, he had spoken off the record with the other great leader of the Cuban Revolution, Ernesto "Che" Guevara, the Argentinian medical doctor turned guerrilla. The two met at the Cuban National Bank in Havana, Guevara greeting Izzy warmly "as a fellow rebel against Yanqui Imperialism." It turned out that the now Cuban economics minister had first come across Stone's work some years before upon hearing that the American Embassy in Mexico was trying to buy up every Spanish copy of *The Hidden History*. As the two met in person, Izzy was struck by Guevara's "extraordinary . . . beauty . . . simplicity and . . . sobriety." Izzy recognized as well the "apocalyptic" side of Guevara, who foresaw "a hemispheric showdown" in the making. But Guevara avoided any sectarian clichés and suggested that Cuba would become a Caribbean Yugoslavia. From his encounter with Guevara and his knowledge of Che's cohorts, Izzy believed them to be as impressive as his own country's Founding Fathers. It was "myopic folly" that led "comfortable stand-patters" to view such men, Stone declared, as "a bevy of beatniks" as the *Wall Street Journal* had depicted them.[13]

Thus, like C. Wright Mills, Saul Landau, and so many members of a New Left that was then budding in the United States, Stone appeared to be mesmerized by the initial stages and early leaders of the Cuban Revolution; but so did Waldo Frank and Scott Nearing, both of whom had also been very much a part of the Old Left of the 1930s. The novelist and essayist Norman Mailer also saw Castro as a hero of the modern era. As the sociologist and political scientist Irving Louis Horowtiz put it, "a faith in populist Marxism" seemed to explain the attraction.[14]

Still, for a time, Cuba stood as the latest socialist model for Stone, who had recently washed his hands of any kind of emotional attachment to the Soviet Union and never had identified all that fully with Mao's China. Cuba, earlier romanticized by Hemingway and now by the latest version of the American left, seemed to hold out the promise of a more hopeful revolutionary undertaking. For the left in general and for I. F. Stone in particular, there appeared to be some kind of need to believe that somewhere a socialist experiment was being carried out. The Soviet Union had been discredited, but now Cuba under Fidel Castro stood as a new kind of progressive model.

Along with the great French writer Jean-Paul Sartre and Mills, perhaps no other intellectual was as influential in spreading the gospel of Castro's Cuba as was Izzy Stone. All three helped to lay out "a bridge between the Old and New Left." The New Left was particularly drawn to the ideals and apparent makeup of the Cuban Revolution, with its supposedly freewheeling nature, flexibility, popular support, egalitarianism, and charismatic figures like Fidel Castro and Che Guevara.[15]

T he Eisenhower administration's reading, both foolish and dangerous, of the new Cuban leaders, Stone pointed out, was characteristic not only of the president but of his would-be successors. Massachusetts Senator John F. Kennedy, the Democratic Party candidate, was surrounded by a "shopworn collection of cold warriors" and appeared particularly inclined to indulge in simplistic "anti-Red rhetoric" involving Cuba; this was something that Kennedy, if elected, might later come to regret, Stone suggested. The United States should strive to keep Soviet military bases or allies from sprouting in the Western Hemisphere, he indicated, but a Good Neighbor Policy, not the Big Stick, was more likely to produce that result.[16]

The narrowness of Kennedy's victory, Stone recognized, produced nothing close to a mandate. But now, for better or worse, an activist presidency appeared certain to follow. Ahead lay crises of all sorts—in the American South, in Berlin, in Southeast Asia, and, most strikingly, in Cuba, about which Kennedy had so foolishly spoken. What was needed, Stone indicated, was a plan for peace and disarmament that might allow for a new liberal administration. But he continued to worry about "Just What Are We Cooking up in the Caribbean?"[17]

As so often proved to be the case, Stone's analysis of an American politician was on target. He acknowledged both the intelligence and verve of the incoming president, but also the fact that standard Cold War ideals and advisers seemed to be guiding him. And because of the unrest that was threatening to spill over at home and elsewhere, that presented a problem.

A t this point, one branch of the federal government, the Central Intelligence Agency, now carefully scoured *I. F. Stone's Weekly* for reports on operations related to Cuba. An in-house document, dated January 17, 1961, noted that Moscow and Peking radioteletypes, transmitted to Europe, had quoted extensively from the newsletter's coverage of U.S. policy regarding the small Caribbean nation.[18]

For a brief time, however, Stone came under the spell of Jack and Jacqueline's Camelot. Following JFK's first presidential press conference, he admittedly felt "like the prophet Jeremiah caught giving three lusty cheers." Stone, in the manner of so many others, was heartened by his belief that the United States now boasted its "first-rater in the Presidency" since Franklin Delano Roosevelt. Most important, he wrote, "the direction is clearly toward peace."[19]

Thus, Izzy, like a good number of journalists and intellectuals, was much taken with the young president. In one sense, this should not have been all that surprising for it had been well over a decade since Izzy had believed that a liberal perspective was afforded a fair hearing in the White House. Truman, owing to the poor showing of the Fair Deal and Cold War antics, had proven to be a disappointing successor to Roosevelt. Eisenhower, although no reactionary himself, had been a moderate conservative at best and had boasted John Foster Dulles as his secretary of state. Now, however, Izzy held out hope that another Democratic president might be more amenable to New Deal–flavored social programs and to calls for a shift in U.S. foreign policy. At the very least, he appeared to be relieved that the Eisenhower administration had ended, not to be replaced by Richard Milhous Nixon's.

Nevertheless, as Stone analyzed it, large problems were in store for this country. The seemingly perennial coalition of conservative Republicans and southern Democrats lay in wait in the halls of Congress for Kennedy's domestic proposals. Moreover, Kennedy himself appeared to have a propensity for viewing "an Armaggedon everywhere." But the Cold War mind-set had to be overcome so that U.S. and Soviet diplomats might iron out a nuclear test ban treaty. That would demand "a more aroused and better informed public opinion." Thus, the need for a large peace movement had never been more imperative. Fortunately, no president had ever seemed more receptive to new ideas and tactics. But the peace movement, like President Kennedy, required a large dosage of unconventionality, for its members had too long been accustomed to standing as "wailing walls" on the fringes of society. Now, more than ever, they needed to be freed from the dogmatism of both pacifists and party members and to demonstrate their independence from Moscow.[20]

For political and moral reasons, Stone hoped that the new peace forces would behave accordingly. The American Communists, he recognized, were thoroughly discredited figures whose involvement in progressive causes allowed for smear tactics and red-baiting. Just as important, they had demonstrated their inability to stand as autonomous actors.

Still, it would help matters, Stone indicated, if the public—and Kennedy himself—understood that not all international crises were the product of Soviet mischief but were often due, in fact, to CIA machinations, State Department snafus, and "melodramatic thinking at home." It was foolish, he declared, to consider Southeast Asia and Cuba as tests of Russian intentions. If Castro were, after all, really a Communist, "he could be turned on or off like a party line spigot, but he is a real revolutionary and a handful." Sweeping reform—not the Kennedy administration's Alliance for Progress, its reform package for Latin America; and not heated rhetoric—was demanded.[21]

I n February, Izzy traveled to Cuba once again, desiring to discover whether a restoration of diplomatic relations might be possible. Upon his return home, he admitted that such a mission had proven to be "a little Quixotic." The top guns of the Cuban Revolution, he had hoped, would understand that which Nagy never had: "that a revolutionary regime has to be circumspect in dealing with a big powerful neighbor." He had envisioned the Fidelistas extending an olive branch to U.S. business interests in order that the Cuban socialist experiment might be continued. He had foreseen a promise of open elections and full political freedoms in the not too distant future. But what he had discovered on the island was a "revolutionary euphoria" and "demagogy" that seemed "dangerously unrealistic." The chasm separating the United States and Cuba, he had to admit, was even wider than that which divided the superpowers. And Castro's supporters, for their part, were dwelling in their own fantasy world which revolved around Cuba and included "that big weakling to the north, the United States, and that distant but doting foster parent, the Soviet Union," poised to risk a nuclear conflagration to shield Havana "if Uncle Sam misbehaves." Thus, Cuba stood as "the Don Quixote in the world family of nations today," while the leaders of its revolution, apparently intoxicated with "a naive kind of infantile leftism," fantasized about a Cuban-orchestrated expulsion of "Yanqui imperialism."[22]

What Izzy encountered in Cuba was "a full fledged revolution, in all its creative folly and self-deceptive enthusiasm." What he saw emerging was "a Soviet-style Popular Democracy," complete with a large dosage of totalitarianism. What Izzy recognized was that he himself must appear to the Cubans as simply another sad-faced American liberal.[23]

The apparent move of Cuba toward the Soviet bloc troubled Stone, who watched as his dreams of a new and unique socialist society dissipated. He felt it necessary to defend Cuba from those who sought to undo the gains made by the revolution, but his disappointment over where the island nation appeared to be heading was readily apparent.

While disturbed by the "headlong intransigence" of the Cuban revolutionaries, Stone discovered a similar mind-set to be prevailing in Washington. Once again, he pointed out, his own country was seeking a military solution to political problems. Only now, U.S. policymakers, enthralled by Guevara's own treatise on guerrilla warfare, saw the Special Services as the answer. But one could read the book, Stone indicated, and still not get the message. Guerrillas who promised to hold back despised landlords represented one thing. An American guerrilla, championing the cause of United Fruit in demanding a return of land that had been handed over to peasants, was something else again. It was the revolutionary political program that sustained the guerrilla, he wrote, not merely the ability to engage in terrorism. And it in no way helped matters, he indicated, to view men like Che Guevara, whom he had met with once again, "as sinister puppets in some occult conspiracy."[24]

Over and over again, Stone was infuriated that U.S. policymakers acted as blindly or as rigidly as they did. He saw them as bound and determined to "lose" the Third World or to destroy it in the process. What he continued to be appalled by was the blatant contradiction between long-standing American ideals regarding self-determination and respect for the dignity of humankind and interventionist realities.

On April 10, nine days before the invasion at the Bay of Pigs, Stone warned that the Kennedy administration was moving closer and closer to intervention in the Caribbean. He appealed to American liberals to stand up and be counted, to acknowledge that U.S. policies had helped to drive Fidel into the arms of the Soviets. Now, he feared, past mistakes were to be multiplied "with the crime of war against a neighboring people." Now the American people were being asked to support that which they had condemned when Russia deposed Imre Nagy of Hungary. Now U.S. Latin American policy threatened to undo the bright promise of the new administration.[25]

Two weeks later, following the Bay of Pigs fiasco, in which Castro's forces quashed a band of CIA-backed Cuban exiles who had landed on the island, Stone wrote: "The Deed Was Done Quickly, But It's Macbeth Who's Dead." While attending a session of the United Nations General Assembly earlier in the week, he had feared that the attack on Cuban soil was damaging Ambasssador Adlai Stevenson and America morally. How, after all, could one defend, as Stevenson had, "the indefensible and deny the undeniable?" Stone hoped "this David and Goliath affair" would not lead to worse, including an attempt to restore American prestige by heading into a war in Southeast Asia or by maintaining "our vendetta" against the Cuban revolutionaries.[26]

A paid political advertisment sponsored by the Fellowship of Reconciliation which appeared in the *New York Times* on April 23 condemned intervention of any kind in Cuba. Among those who signed the letter were Erich Fromm, Robert Heilbroner, Sidney Lens, C. Wright Mills, A. J. Muste, Norman Thomas, and Izzy Stone. Another manifesto, the product of Norman Thomas's pen, insisted that any change in Castro's government must be demanded by the Cuban people. What was at stake, this "Open Letter to the President" declared, was not simply CIA "misplanning and incompetence." It was true, Thomas's document declared, that the Cuban Revolution had abandoned its initial democratic expectations. But the United States, the "Open Letter" continued, had helped to ensure that this was so. Along with Muste and Stone, the latest appeal had the support of James Baldwin, Robert M. Hutchins, Murray Kempton, Norman Podhoretz, and A. Philip Randolph. They seemed to be showing the way for intellectuals in their own land to become actively involved in the great issues of the times once again.[27]

I n a midsummer letter to Mike Blankfort, Izzy indicated he was "feeling about as depressed as I suppose I ever get." Cuba, a brewing crisis over Berlin, and most strikingly, his perception "that so few people cared" were becoming overwhelming. Nevertheless, he also acknowledged that "most of the time I'm a small boy reporter having a helluva lot of fun covering such a wonderful bunch of 10-alarm fires." And then there was Esther, who "still loves me insanely," which caused Izzy to wonder if she "must have fallen on her head as a baby to like a funny looking guy like me." But "she's an angel and I love her tenderly and we have a [wonderful] time together."[28]

A lthough the Bay of Pigs invasion had now come and gone, Stone worried more than ever that the two Mr. Ks were "ready when in doubt to reach for a gun." Kennedy appeared willing to back colonial regimes supposedly beset by subversion, while Khrushchev affirmed that his nation supported the wars of liberation that the United States so dreaded. It was in such lands, Stone indicated, that the greatest threat resided, as the United States, tragically but surely, headed toward "the side of the counter-revolution." Once again, Izzy traveled abroad, this time to Yugoslavia, where a conference for unaligned nations was being held in late summer, hoping to discover if the war machine might be somehow impeded. However, he came back more pessimistic than before, despite having spent a delightful evening with Bertrand Russell and his wife at their London townhouse. The conference itself proved to be a disappointment, and the all-too-obvious supernationalism of the nonaligned indicated they were "no better morally."[29]

Thus, Third Worlders, like the Americans and the Soviets, were capable of upsetting Stone, who continued to believe in the need for world government. But while he recognized that the superpowers contributed to international tensions, the smaller and less powerful nations at times also appeared benighted. By now, Cuba itself was already losing some of the luster it had held for him since the beginning of the revolution, although he yet hoped that a third path might still be taken by Castro, Guevera, and their followers. Such hope, however, was soon to dissipate.

In late September 1961, President Kennedy delivered an eloquent and stirring address to the UN General Assembly, proclaiming that "unconditional war can no longer lead to unconditional victory." The president required the backing of a nationwide movement, Stone wrote, to give lie to the notion "that the choice is death or surrender." It was "the No. 1 task" of the administration, he declared, to educate the American people about the real world outside their borders. The American Century was about to be cut short, while instabilities around the globe were sure to follow. But the United States still held "a proud and secure place," Stone declared; it was there that the Jeffersonian tradition was rooted, a tradition certain to inspire others, particularly in lands now under Communist tyranny.[30]

By January 1962, Izzy happily reported that a new peace movement was emerging. Along with three thousand others, he attended the demonstration in Washington called by the Women's Strike for Peace, which urged international disarmament and the shaping of a nuclear test ban treaty. Such a gathering was certainly a hopeful sign, Izzy noted, given the slanted nature of the nation's political atmosphere and the influence of an "archaic" Congress and "a Pentagon whose labyrinthine corridors lead one into a world of nightmarish military strategy." It would take just such grass-roots activism, he suggested, to free policymakers "from these frightful institutions."[31]

Izzy was still more elated by the assemblage in Washington the following month, which appeared to usher in a new student movement. "The bright young faces" and their banners that read "Neither Victims Nor Executioners," "Unjust Law Exists," and "Make the World Safe for Humanity" suggested a different crop of young people than the Silent Generation that had graced campuses throughout the nation in the 1950s. They likewise seemed far removed from the beats of the same period or Old Left sectarians. Frivolity and the party line were both absent, replaced by a new boldness and maturity and "a Third Camp" feel in their obvious rejection of "the military logic and nation state lawlessness" of both East and West. From his view at the Oval Office, Stone suggested, President Kennedy must have been moved by the pickets which employed his own rhetoric: "Neither Dead Nor Slave But Alive and Free . . . Let's Call a Truce to Terror . . . Let Us Never Fear to Negotiate . . . We Support the Peace Race. Let's Begin." Happily, the Kennedy administration responded in kind, sending out hot coffee and top advisers McGeorge Bundy, Marcus Raskin, Ted Sorenson, and Jerome Wiesner to greet the students. But talk of going slow, of not alientating Congress, was unfortunately emphasized. And as Stone saw it, such a mixture "of competence and conventionality" marked this administration.[32]

In the period just ahead, Izzy was to become intimately involved with both the peace and student movements. His early support for and encouragement of those campaigns enabled him to acquire a measure of influence among those political forces. But equally important in that regard were his own analyses of U.S. foreign and domestic policies, pertaining to Cuba and Vietnam, Jim Crow and mass poverty, in particular.

A lthough pleased by the stirrings of the peace movement in the period following the Bay of Pigs disaster, Stone continually warned that missteps could bring on a disaster. In December 1961, he condemned the possibility of another invasion of Cuba which might result in the appearance of both soldiers and military assistance from the Soviet sphere and a martial response from Washington. By early September 1962, he was urging every voice of sanity in his country to help the president "stem the drift," asserting that "we are guilty of aggression," and worrying that "Cuba Is The Spark That Could Set Off The Conflagration." Everybody, it seemed to him, was fearful "of everything but war." He saw a mood "of frustrated lunacy" sweeping over the United States when it came to its small, southern neighbor. But the presence of Soviet intermediate-range ballistic missiles on Cuban soil caused him to admit that the Politburo would not be pleased if American nuclear warheads were found to have been placed in Finland. Events were getting out of hand, he feared.[33]

If Cuba were allowed to go its own way, Stone admitted on October 1, it well might prove to be a disappointment. But if the revolution were to be crushed, there would remain "the legend of Castro the Latin American David who defied the Yankee Goliath." In an editorial in *The Nation*, his friend Carey McWilliams warned that Castroism would consequently be seen as still more of an inspiration in the Western Hemisphere.[34]

Cuba, Stone was aware, had hardly proven to be any kind of utopia. But like other small countries it deserved the chance to go its own way, he believed, regardless of the hurt feelings or paranoia of his own nation. However, the possibility of self-determination for the island state and the very fate of the planet earth now appeared more precarious than ever.

On October 22, President Kennedy ordered a naval blockade of Cuba, which was not to be removed until the Soviet missiles were. Termed a quarantine by administration officials, the action, in Stone's estimation, was an act of war pure and simple. Along with Carey McWilliams, Norman Thomas, and A. J. Muste, among others, Izzy Stone urged a lifting of the blockade. Small demonstrations against Kennedy's policy now occurred around the country, with some two thousand gathering in front of the White House on October 27. Upon hearing that Air Force reserve units had been called to active duty, many expressed the fears Izzy did in his talk to the Washington contingent that "six thousand years of human history" were about "to come to an end."[35]

By the end of the next day, the Cuban missile crisis abruptly terminated following Khrushchev's decision to remove the IRBMs in return for a no-invasion pledge. But unless "a fundamental change of behavior" occurred, Stone wrote, similar crises loomed ahead. At present, each government potentate brandishing nuclear arms possessed more of "a Divine Right" than had the kings of old. The Big Three in the Cuban affair, for example, were "all making like Joves, with their thunderbolts" threatening "to condemn mankind to hell." It was "the nation-state system," Communist or capitalist, Stone charged, that had to end "or it will end us."[36]

The United States and President Kennedy, Stone acknowledged, emerged from the missile crisis a good deal stronger than before, but now the hard part would begin. Now Kennedy had to lead Americans "to a saner view of the world, to a more sophisticated view, to a less self-righteous view." For "this may be his and our last chance." A stronger peace movement was needed, as was a move to eradicate "this monster, the bomb."[37]

A t the end of the year, Izzy undertook yet another trip to Havana to the astonishment of those he encountered along the way. Upon landing on the island shortly after midnight, along with a hundred dollars worth of medicines purchased in Mexico City, Izzy was detained at the airport and the supplies taken from him. A shouting match ensued with a fiery young militant regarding the status of the goods—brought as a gift by this friend of the Cuban Revolution. After some two hours of questioning at the hands of airport officials, Izzy headed off for Havana along with a pair of militiamen and an immigration agent. Taken to a police station in the capital, Izzy was held incommunicado until the following morning when another immigration official was scheduled to arrive for more interrogation. Not allowed to call the hotel where he was supposed to be staying, Izzy refused to sleep on the cot the Cubans set up for him alongside the jail cells.[38]

This not so quiet American dozed in a chair, awakening only in the morning to discover that the immigration official had not appeared yet. With but a few words in Spanish at his disposal, Izzy indicated to the guards that he was one of a mere handful of reporters back home sympathetic to the revolution. Furthermore, he had come bearing gifts in the form of hard-to-obtain medical supplies. In addition, Che and other revolutionary leaders could vouch for him. But finally, Izzy asked if Fidel himself had not recently attacked "*bureaucracia* and isn't this an example of bureaucracy at work?" That last point finally seemed to make some sort of impression, and one of the guards left, apparently to check out his story. Ten o'clock rolled around, however, and Izzy now determined to "raise a tantrum." He booted chairs around the station and insisted on talking with someone willing and able to converse in English. To Izzy's dismay, he was told that it was no immigration official the police were awaiting but rather a member of the Cuban security forces.[39]

Remembering that his friend Mordecai Oren, the Israeli journalist, had spent four years in jail in Communist-controlled Czechoslovakia on trumped-up charges of espionage, Izzy now became more worried still. He determined to conserve his energy for what might be in store for him and thus attempted to take a nap. After a short spell, however, he was released and back on the streets of Havana. He got through to an old friend who worked in the Foreign Ministry, vainly seeking an explanation of why the detention had taken place. His friend was every bit as perplexed as he; but it seemed "that in Cuba the vagaries of the secret police were accepted as one might accept elsewhere the vagaries of the weather."[40]

Although hotels were all booked up, Izzy turned again to his Cuban friend, who reserved a room for him at the Havana Riviera, now evidently serving as "a Foreign Ministry hostel for visiting VIPs." After cleaning up and following a short rest, Izzy headed off for Sloppy Joe's, long "the Mecca of thirsty or lonesome fellow American tourists." Only half-a-dozen patrons were in the bar, whose walls remained lined with pictures of earlier American visitors, including Joe Lewis, Joan Blondell, Willie Pep, and Carole Landis. The ninety-cent daiquiri, regardless of the change in political climate, was still the world's finest. The bartender asked Izzy if he were English. When he replied, "No, American," and asked if any of his countrymen could be found, the bartender replied warily, "No, in Cuba, Americans *feeneesh*." Izzy "felt like the last Yankee imperialist, unwelcome and no longer at home."[41]

In his reports on his most recent visit to Cuba, Stone acknowledged that the island had unquestionably become part of the Soviet sphere. No more did Havana bookstores carry heretical works of dissident Communists. No longer did the newsstands carry anything other than Soviet periodicals. And for the first time during any of his trips to Cuba, he felt "a chill" upon informing others that he was an American.[42]

Nonetheless, Stone remained hopeful about the Cuban experiment. The countryside looked richer, and "the sense of full racial equality and ease" he discovered greatly pleased this "guilt-burdened white American in Castro's Cuba." The streets of Havana were bustling and the people apparently uncowed. No Soviet soldiers and few Russian civilians could be spotted in the capital city, where everyone seemed to be armed. Although a Popular Democracy, Cuba reminded him of "a kind of continuous town meeting under a popular dictator." There appeared to be greater artistic and intellectual liberty than in any part of the Soviet bloc, other than perhaps Poland. And Cuba itself looked to be positioned between the great Communist powers, Russia and China, presently engaged in their own fierce ideological battle. Here the preachings of both Nikita Khrushchev and Mao Zedong could be discovered.[43]

While the Cuban bureaucracy was "suffocating," Stone thought of Israel when he had encountered another kind of official, one who had exchanged his gun for paperwork, and "whose sobriety and devotion" were apparent. The Cuban Revolution happily was still "in its first uncorrupted phase." Its youthful cadre, unlike so many of their counterparts elsewhere, "still believe."[44]

Admittedly, Stone noted, he had not met up with any of Castro's foes, nor had he been to the jails where political prisoners were held. "The Cuba I picture is a Cuba as it appears through friendly eyes." So this was only one part of the story. A revolution was a complex undertaking and a tragic one at that, Stone pointed out, as he had in discussing the Russian and Chinese revolutions earlier. But it was foolish to formulate policy and shape opinions, he insisted, while listening to unfriendly views alone.[45]

In late April Izzy appeared on David Susskind's "Open End" television program in New York City, where he discussed his recent visit to Cuba. A CIA report quoted Izzy as having praised Fidel, called his trip to the island "inspiring," and urged U.S. recognition of Castro's government. It also indicated that Izzy denied that Cuba threatened the United States but insisted instead that the small Caribbean state was itself imperiled by the Yankee "menace."[46]

That troubled Stone, who remained hopeful about the revolution in Cuba. For some time to come, he continued to view Castro's regime favorably, although not uncritically. Once again, he was willing to defend a dictatorial state that promised better days ahead, while it called for the appearance of "a new socialist man" and seemed more concerned with the general commonweal than with the self-interest of the rich and powerful.

S tone espied a ray of hope in the final months of the Kennedy administration. Having been abroad for a month, he was astonished to discover the very top rung of government officials speaking in terms previously used only by "fringe groups like SANE" in the midst of "a nuclear wilderness." With ratification of a limited nuclear test-ban treaty appearing imminent, he urged peace activists to underscore the absolute necessity for a new world order that could fight the spread of nuclear weapons and help to solve seemingly insoluble matters, including an ongoing crisis in Indochina. What was needed above all else, he declared, was "to think in terms of the planet and the human race as a whole if we are to secure the future for our children."[47]

But on November 22, 1963, while riding in a presidential motorcade through the streets of Dallas, Texas, John F. Kennedy—the man who oversaw the Bay of Pigs debacle and the Cuban missile crisis but the Alliance for Progress and the nuclear test-ban treaty as well—was murdered. Writing in the *Weekly,* Stone spoke of the end of America's Camelot and the passing of the witty, intelligent, and youthful presidential "Prince Charming." Perhaps, Stone acknowledged, just perhaps, JFK had "died . . . in time." This way, he would be "remembered, as ever young, still victorious, struck down undefeated." For if the truth be told, troubled times once again loomed on the horizon. The president's domestic program remained mired in congressional committee rooms while the turn toward coexistence seemed to be floundering. Nearby Cuba remained a sore spot, while rebel activity in the faraway land of Vietnam was giving the lie to "all the romantic Kennedy notions" concerning guerrilla warfare. To Stone, all of this indicated that the time for "conventional leadership" was past, and that, "when the tinsel was stripped away, [President Kennedy] was a conventional leader, no more than an enlightened conservative, cautious as an old man for all his youth, with a basic distrust of the people and an astringent view of the evangelical as a tool of leadership." Moreover, to glorify Kennedy "as an apostle of peace," Stone insisted, made little sense. For the Kennedy administration, in certain regards, had proven "warlike," ready to threaten a nuclear winter regardless of just what that might mean. What it again suggested to Stone was a willingness to risk the very fate of the planet in order that America's will should prevail and "a readiness for murder," now "become a way of life and a world menace."[48]

In the immediate aftermath of the death of the young president, bestselling tomes were produced celebrating the thousand days of the Kennedy administration. Later, revisionist studies sharply challenged those earlier interpretations, calling into question just how progressive and peace-minded JFK had actually been. I. F. Stone's immediate evaluation of Kennedy was in keeping with those far more critical studies that took him to task for his stalemated domestic agenda and ambivalent stance on civil rights, in addition to the Bay of Pigs, the Cuban missile crisis, and heightened U.S. involvement in Indochina. Indeed, Stone was not blind to JFK's faults, including his tendency to reach for military solutions and even to threaten a nuclear abyss at one point in response to what were inevitably political problems and his failure to throw the full weight of the administration behind the civil rights fight. All of this, Stone reasoned at the time, cried out for a rebirth of American radicalism. Nevertheless, his reading of Kennedy called to mind his earlier analysis of Franklin Delano Roosevelt, whom Izzy also saw as possessing great potential but as not always delivering on that promise. It was as though Stone hoped that Kennedy, like Roosevelt before him, would grow in the job and match the high hopes fueled by his eloquent inaugural. Liberal Democrats always were more of a quandry for Izzy than their conservative opponents, who could more easily be dismissed as foolish reactionaries.

Never again did I. F. Stone praise an American president with the same enthusiasm he had once showed toward John Fitzgerald Kennedy. The greater racial turmoil of the 1960s and intensified U.S. involvement in Indochina ensured that he failed to ever view Lyndon Baines Johnson, Kennedy's successor, in the same manner. Stone recognized early that Vietnam and civil rights were both becoming more and more of a quagmire, something that would have to be dealt with by Johnson's advisers, the celebrated best and brightest.

It was to the conflict in Vietnam and the struggle for civil rights in the Unites States, then, that I. F. Stone's attention increasingly turned. He watched as a civil war raged in Indochina, pitting the attempts by an American-sponsored dictatorial regime to stave off another national liberation movement; and as another civil war threatened to break out at home because of growing anger and frustration over the retention of Jim Crow barriers. These two great issues, as well as the matter of nuclear armaments, prompted Izzy to adopt once again the stance of intellectual activist, committed journalist, and critic of his own country's domestic and foreign policies. And it was Vietnam (even more than Cuba) and the civil rights struggle (to a lesser degree) that were about to make the *Weekly* a well-recognized name in broader intellectual, journalistic, and political circles.

12 Knockin' on Jim Crow's Doors

It simply did not make any sense. In the midst of a worldwide fight against Nazism, that racist brand of fascism, a black man could still be refused service in the nation's capital. How long, he wondered, was Washington, D.C., going to remain "a Jim Crow town"? And how could journalists, supposedly involved in a never-ending quest for the truth, be a party to such a practice?[1]

Wanting to get together with William H. Hastie—the first black to have sat on the federal bench—in order to discuss the judge's recent experiences in the War Department, Izzy had considered where they might go for lunch. The better sorts of eating establishments were, sadly enough, out of the question, honoring as they did "Whites Only" edicts. Izzy asked Hastie, who had just served as an aide to the secretary of war, if he were willing to chance a visit to the National Press Club which went along with the "No Negroes" policy. Izzy honestly did not believe that their appearance would cause much of a stir, for journalists, he figured, were "above that sort of thing."[2]

Elmer Davis was speaking at a special luncheon in the club's auditorium, and consequently, Stone and Hastie were quietly seated. Almost immediately, however, Izzy was paged by the manager, who declared that he and the good judge were not about to be served. As a club member he was entitled to such service, Izzy retorted, and stormed off to his table. But no waiter ever came over, and after an hour or so Izzy and Judge Hastie departed.[3]

Reporting on the incident in *The Nation*, Stone noted that the judge was not only a decent fellow but every bit "as cultivated as some of the third-rate advertising men and fourth-rate politicians who belong to the club." Hastie was, after all, a graduate of Harvard Law, dean of Howard University Law School, and a former member of the federal judiciary. Stone went on to indicate that he had attempted to convene a special meeting to discuss the club's exclusionary policy. Few of his journalistic kin, however, were so inclined; others reportedly agreed with him but were unwilling to do anything about it. Apparently, there were those, he continued, who considered "the punctilio governing a supposed 'private club' " to count for more than simple decency.[4]

Not Izzy, though. He quickly submitted his resignation.[5]

In the fight for civil rights, as in the quest to rid the planet of nuclear weapons, Izzy felt it necessary to express his opinions forcefully, even bluntly.

Here again, he believed it was incumbent upon one positioned as he was to take a stand, to display the concern of the crusading journalist, the socially conscious intellectual, and the political activist. Here too his intolerance for small-mindedness and bigotry shone loudly and clearly, as did his feeling that such practices had to come to an end. To ensure that result, he reasoned that another movement was necessary, a movement he called for and felt bound to support. Once again, he felt certain that both liberals and radicals had a role to play in such a campaign, as did progressive ideals of all types.

I F. Stone's response to the Hastie incident should not have been all that surprising, certainly to anybody who knew Izzy well enough or who was familiar with his work. In newspaper and magazine editorials, he had long railed away at the national shame that was Jim Crow. The very practice of segregation, he had earlier reported, conjured up notions of "racial inequality, mob spirit, brutal disregard for the most precious and fundamental rights, lawlessness in the guise of law." As the postwar era began, he feared that its more rabid proponents in the American Deep South were willing to usher in an American brand of fascism to defend it.[6]

He recognized that here, too, the vaunted "common man" of leftist lore had in no way lived up to his idealized image. The average voter and the unionist alike had demonstrated no more readiness to cast aside segregationist practices than did race-baiting legislators or southern "crackers." Once again, a change in spirit, a determination to live up to the high-minded ideals of both biblical injunctions and the Declaration of Independence was needed, he believed. Without such a transformation in the American psyche, Jim Crow appeared secure for some time to come. All the more need, then, for activists to lead an assault on the barriers separating black from white.

Consequently, as early as November 1947, he called for a new civil rights organization to serve as the vanguard of the struggle to further the cause of liberty and equality in this generation. His proposed "Americans in Action," Stone predicted, would invariably attract the nation's finest youth and afford that chance at heroic action quite properly demanded of them.[7]

Admittedly, a civil rights crusade would be no easy task, he acknowledged, but it would serve to sustain two key components of the American creed. The first involved "the equality of man: treat men as equals and you raise them; treat them as inferiors and you push them down into the mud." The second concerned freedom of thought, without which man remained incomplete.[8]

But as the end of the Truman era approached, Stone argued that a wholesale reexamination of "The American Dilemma" was demanded. It was time, he insisted, for America's blacks to view themselves for what they were and to act the part—"a nation within a nation . . . second class citizens in a white man's country under a white man's law." This separate nation—which brought to mind the Communist Party's earlier cry of "Self-determination for the Black Belt"—must begin to demand its own representative instruments. Furthermore, its members should refuse their labor, leave the South altogether, or even strike back when one of their own was felled by the blows of law enforcement officials. Those willing to insist on their rights, Stone reminded his readers, were the ones who would change the situation. Mass action, he insisted, could bring the promises of the Declaration of Independence to light. Who would free America's blacks? Stone asked. "They must do it themselves."[9]

Therefore, Stone reasoned that it was not simply well-intentioned white opponents of Jim Crow, whether liberal or radical, who would bring the system of segregation to its knees. Blacks, he seemed to be arguing, had to be willing to take to the streets themselves. Such a move, he recognized, was sure to be seen as provocative by segregationist diehards who were not about to allow their way of life to be overturned without resistance. What that meant was that more pain and suffering, more anguish and deaths likely were in store for those who had already had to pay such a price for so long.

The militant activism Stone envisioned as the domestic Cold War raged would not appear for some time to come. But the walls of Jim Crow soon were shaken as Thurgood Marshall and the Legal and Education Defense Fund of the National Association for the Advancement of Colored People began to triumph in the courts. On May 17, 1954, in the marbled chamber of the U.S. Supreme Court building, Izzy listened as Chief Justice Earl Warren read the decision of *Brown v. Board of Education.* Stone was among those in attendance who became teary-eyed upon realizing that the 1896 *Plessy v. Ferguson* ruling—which had placed the federal judicial stamp of approval upon Jim Crow—had at long last been overturned. Stone recognized that the NAACP attorneys had taken a great step toward felling Jim Crow, while the growing political muscle of blacks, he believed, had helped to make American democracy real. *Brown,* he wrote, would revolutionize American racial relations, but the Jim Crow system surely would not disappear overnight.[10]

Indeed, while the American form of apartheid had been dealt a legal blow, a spirit of defiance soon was evident throughout the South. A revitalized Ku Klux Klan now emerged, along with White Citizens Councils, the uptown version of the Hooded Empire. Calls for massive resistance were heard, and 101 congressmen from the old Confederate states came to sign a "Southern Manifesto" that condemned *Brown* as a stark example of judicial abuse of power.

None of this was all that surprising to I. F. Stone, who saw the southern upper crust, the middling sorts, and the "common man," that "idol of our time," express little concern about the walls separating white and black, participate in the butchering of fourteen-year-old Emmett Till, or serve on juries exonerating those who had. The battered and broken body of young Till, discovered with a bullet drilled through his right temple and a gaping wound in the back of his head, Stone cried, was the product of "a maniacal murder." His killers were "sick men, sick with race hatred," while the deed itself and the trial that followed could only have taken place "in a sick countryside." There existed a perversity in the South, he warned, that if allowed to go unchecked, might some day result in horrors every bit as terrible as Hitler's crematoria.[11]

Because this was so, Stone eerily insisted on October 3, 1955—two months before the Montgomery Bus Boycott began—that "the American Negro needs a Gandhi to lead him, and we need the American Negro to lead us." If an American Gandhi did not spring forth to do battle with all that was wrong in the South, the United States, he warned, would suffer the pains of letting "a psychopathic racist brutality" remain in place.[12]

It was in Montgomery, Alabama, of course, that the black Gandhi arose to contest Jim Crow social and legal codes that had resulted in the arrest of Rosa Parks, a forty-three-year-old seamstress and NAACP member. Parks had been taken to jail for refusing to relinquish her seat to an irate and insulting white bus driver. The then twenty-six-year-old Martin Luther King, Jr., newly arrived with Ph.D. in hand from Boston University, brought the message of nonviolent resistance to Montgomery's blacks, declaring that "the only weapon . . . we have . . . is the weapon of protest" while insisting on the need to employ instruments of both persuasion and coercion. In the face of an ever-present threat of violence, King asserted that "he who lives by the sword will perish by the sword" and that "we must meet hate with love." A year-long and ultimately successful bus boycott ensued, which Stone proclaimed to be the most moving event of 1965. Irving Howe of *Dissent* magazine went still farther, likening the Montgomery movement to the labor sit-down strikes of the depression decade.[13]

Carey McWilliams, editor of *The Nation*, saw the next step in the civil rights struggle as involving a change in the hearts of white southerners. But Izzy Stone worried about the presence of "the mob spirit" represented by the KKK and the White Citizens Councils and warned that the longer President Eisenhower failed to exert moral leadership, the greater the peril. An American volcano threatened to erupt in the South, he prophesied, and none had more cause to be angry than the region's blacks and the "freedom fighters" there, equally brave as Budapest's own.[14]

On May 17, 1957, Stone attended the Prayer's Pilgrimage in Washington, intended to draw attention to civil rights at the national level. The Reverend

King was the speaker who impressed him most; Stone indicated he would be disappointed if the young minister did not turn out to be "one of the great Americans of our time." But prayers alone, Stone insisted, would not compel white politicians to act.[15]

This was clearly the case, he believed, because southern racists were determined to uphold segregation where it stood. Consequently, Arkansas Governor Orval Faubus defied a federal court order in September 1957 that called for the desegregation of Little Rock's Central High School. As President Eisenhower ordered in federal troops in the face of mob violence, Stone proclaimed that blacks were finally being afforded their rights as American citizens.[16]

Yet troops by themselves, he recognized, also would not be enough. For greatly troubled times beckoned, which could stain American politics and possibly result in "volcanic eruptions of bloodshed."[17]

The following September, Izzy flew into Little Rock to view the post-*Brown* South for himself. Passengers who got on board in Nashville carried the local paper, the *Banner*, with headlines that roared, "Mix Now, Little Rock Told" and "Education Be Hanged!" A pair of white senior citizens spoke patronizingly of the genuine love that prevailed between white and black in the South. Tormented and inebriated southern liberals tossed around expletives like "niggers" and "coons" at a dinner party in the country, causing Izzy to appreciate playwright Tennessee Williams more fully. It appeared that the black man did not simply dwell in the South, Izzy reported—"he haunts it." At breakfast the following morning, a liberal journalist from the Arkansas state capital seemed bewildered about just what it was that blacks wanted. Lunch at the Little Rock Club saw certain members speak politely to the black waiters, while others coldly and arrogantly dealt with their "*nigra* servitors." Izzy thought to himself, "So this is the wine that goes to the white man's head in the South." In Little Rock's dilapidated Harlem district, Izzy and an English reporter got nowhere. Even Plilander Smith College, a black Methodist school, appeared to be a community "besieged." And yet Izzy saw a younger, educated generation emerging—so unlike "darkies" of stereotypical fame—whose eloquent silence spoke volumes. In a skid row bar frequented by "poor white trash," Izzy and his compatriot encountered a friendly ducktailed youth who foresaw blood as sure to flow, and his sidekick who stared "coldly, as if he weren't going to be taken in by any furriners." In another black neighborhood of well-cared-for lawns and homes, an oldest son spoke of his desires to attend Central High. He wanted to become a doctor like his father and believed that at Central High he would receive a better education and establish a precedent for others. The doctor indicated that he for one felt worried but hopeful, while his wife reported that there were no restrooms or luncheon counters for black shoppers downtown.[18]

Now Izzy headed for the Mississippi delta country along with a couple of English reporters. He was picked up at his hotel by a black lad who drove him over to the car rental office. The manager admonished the youngster, "Mandy Lee, you're getting out of your place when you come into this office." When Izzy attempted to explain that it was all his doing, the manager cut him off. "You're going down to nigger country," he was informed. "This is where they raise rice and cotton and niggers."[19]

Helena, a river town made somewhat famous by Mark Twain's *Life on the Mississippi*, boasted one shack after another where black workers resided. One young man assured the three journalists that this was all the black laborers desired. Here no school integration controversy existed as nary a black litigant arose to file suit. At the local country club, "nigger" was tossed easily and freely about. Talk of blacks being unable to control themselves sexually and of a handful of Yankees causing "all the trouble" topped off the conversation.[20]

In spite of what he had seen and heard in his trip down South, Stone remained convinced that the notion of white supremacy was fated to go the way of slavery. But black militants, he recognized, had considerable obstacles to overcome. It had taken a man like E. D. Nixon, who had helped set the stage for the Montgomery movement, nearly a decade to register to vote. Other would-be voters, "unknown heroes and obscure martyrs," faced economic reprisals, including the loss of farms and occupations. And sadly, "Jim Crowism" appeared to be gaining ground nationwide as the blackening of inner cities and public housing continued.[21]

While in Paris, Robert Silvers, then an associate editor at *Harper's*, came across a number of Izzy's pieces on civil rights. Impressed with the articles, Silvers later sought to commission an article for the journal to be written by I. F. Stone on Martin Luther King, Jr. His suggestion was turned down, the justification being that Izzy "was a man of doctrinaire views."[22]

As the new decade began, Stone continued to worry about the presence of "That 'Germany' of Our Own Below the Mason-Dixon Line." But about to arrive on the civil rights scene were the very foot soldiers and young activists he had long called for. On February 1, 1960, four black college students sat down at a Woolworth department store luncheon counter in Greensboro, North Carolina, which followed the Jim Crow line, and waited to be served. Soon to follow were scores of such sit-ins across the South as well as others that appeared from coast to coast. Thus, the era of student activisim and "the wonderful sit-downs," as Stone called them, was initiated with its pronounced emphasis on direct action. The poet Kenneth Rexroth asserted that the entire world was impressed with "those brave young faces, beautiful under the taunts and spittle." Nat Hentoff, in the pages of *Commonweal,* likened the students to "a peaceful army," while Michael Walzer, writing in *Dissent,* saw them as possessing the potential for reenergizing the American left.[23]

Stone praised just as highly the Freedom Rides, carried out in the spring of 1961 by activists from CORE, the Congress of Racial Equality, and SNCC, the Student Non-Violent Coordinating Committee, itself the product of the sit-in campaign. The Freedom Riders, with their assault on the bastions of Jim Crow, had applied Gandhian nonviolent practices, Stone exclaimed, and thereby transformed Christianity into "a revolutionary creed" once again. The South could dissemble on school desegregation, he admitted, as it long had on the black man's right to vote. But the right to sit on a bus or at a luncheon counter was something an individual with enough gumption could insist on, albeit with "insult and injury" inevitably staring him in the face.[24]

But direct action alone, Stone recognized, would not bring Jim Crow down. No, the assistance of the federal government, he pointed out, was necessary as well. A peaceful transformation of the South would only be possible if "moral leadership and ethical education" were forthcoming. Thus, Jack and Robert Kennedy had to go beyond what was politically expedient and act in the best interests of the whole nation. "Devotion to freedom should begin at home," Stone insisted.[25]

As Martin Luther King, Jr.'s nonviolent civil disobedience movement came face to face with the police dogs, fire hoses, and cattle prods of Birmingham Police Commissioner Bull Connor, Stone asked on May 27, 1963, if more blood were going to have to be shed before the president finally acted. Tragedy might well be in store, he warned, given the "savagery . . . barely below the surface among Southern whites" and the "murderous resentments" of American blacks. It would not take much, he continued, to kindle a series of racial explosions.[26]

In a nationally televised address on June 11, President Kennedy at long last urged Americans to consider the question of civil rights. "A moral issue" was at stake, the young chief executive declared, which was as ancient as the Bible "and as clear as the American Constitution." The crux of the matter was whether all citizens were to be treated equally, something which required a "peaceful and constructive" revolution.[27]

Kennedy had now exhibited moral leadership regarding the civil rights struggle, Stone acknowledged, but far more was demanded. Unless something were done about the country's "untouchables and second class citizens," blood was sure to flow. "A storm" was building against both southern apartheid and northern unions and schools with their practice of de facto segregation. The black struggle, Stone indicated, was all about humiliation, joblessness, police brutality, and conscription for "some crazy white folks' crusade for freedom far away" while a greater one needed to be waged at home. But this, Stone admitted, was a situation only blacks could really understand.[28]

As Izzy had forewarned, the burning of American cities would continue for several summers in succession. Embittered blacks, often set off by charges of police brutality and by anger over the perceived go-slow approach of even professedly liberal municipal, state, and federal administrations, exploded in the rage predicted by Stone and other observers of the times, such as James Baldwin. Hardly helping to cool tensions was the fact that the government in Washington, D.C., did not seem willing to do much to aid a moral crusade at home, yet insisted on waging an anti-Communist fight abroad, which expended valuable American material resources and the lives of both whites and blacks.

While Kennedy urged blacks "out of the streets and into the courts," Stone suggested that the president had failed to make civil rights much of a priority "until the Negro had moved out of the courts and into the streets." And for the immediate future, the streets were where the action was certain to take place. Pressure of a systematic nature must be maintained, Stone argued, to compel Congress to move, to make Jim Crow ever more costly, and to keep up the spirits of black citizens. Revolutions, after all, did not simply unfold cleanly and unchallenged in courthouses.[29]

On August 28, 1963, as over two hundred thousand people headed down the Mall on the Capitol grounds toward the Lincoln Memorial, it seemed as though a revolution of some sort had taken place. Suddenly, Izzy reported, he no longer felt quite so alone. Those who participated in the march, including the "gnarled old colored ladies on tired feet and comfortably broken shoes," greatly impressed him. Their faces might be lined with the oppression that was their lot, he wrote, but they exuded a "gentle sweetness" as they sang, "We shall not be moved." Pleasing as well was the presence of so many radicals of old, the indomitables of movements past who had lost jobs and livelihoods in days gone by but now were finally "part of a mass upsurge, no longer lonely relics."[30]

The speeches, even Martin Luther King, Jr.'s "I Have a Dream" address—which so enthralled Izzy's friend and fellow journalist Murray Kempton—moved him less. King, Izzy now remarked, seemed "a little too saccharine" to him. A civil rights gathering the following day, orchestrated by the Socialist Party and featuring A. Philip Randolph and Bayard Rustin, appeared a good deal more appealing. He listened as Randolph, longtime head of the Brotherhood of Sleeping Car Porters and the man who had first called for a March on Washington during the Second World War, spoke eloquently and poignantly about the civil rights fight. This "great American," who had finally pulled off his cherished march, chided black nationalists that white men and women had helped initiate the civil rights drive at a time when that was hardly the most popular or politic action to undertake. He reminded moderates that the vote by itself would not be enough, that the previous day's march had been for both jobs and freedom. The pacifist Rustin, a former Communist and onetime top adviser of Dr. King, called for "an economic Master Plan" to root out the technologically induced unemployment that seemed to have resulted in a permanent subproletariat, part white and part black. And in the hall where Randolph and Rustin spoke, socialism acquired new meaning for Izzy Stone. For the dispossessed of all races, he declared, the road must lead toward socialism.[31]

Thus, just as the struggle to rid the world of nuclear arms was connected in Stone's mind with the possibility of revolutionary change outside the United States, the attack on Jim Crow and the chance for a war on poverty at home again conjured up the vision of socialism. This was a democratic socialism which Stone hoped would come someday, for it could help to still the voices of racial discord and the drumbeats of war, if only given the chance. It could also prevent the continued exploitation of an American underclass.

For now, the march gave Stone renewed hope. He saw "enduring vitality and idealism" in "the racial convulsion" sweeping across the nation. He appreciated the respectful tone displayed from Kennedy on down; this indicated moral well-being and suggested that this generation would bring about full equality for black Americans. But the path ahead, he warned, would not be a smooth one. Considerable racial strife lay in wait for the North, and "this revolution, like every other, will have its follies and its crimes." In this instance, as so often during this period, Izzy spoke prophetically.[32]

The civil rights movement thus meant many things to Izzy Stone. It offered a means for the United States to right its greatest domestic wrong, to prevent the appearance of a potent fascist movement in the South, to reorder priorities at home, to serve as a model of racial harmony for other peoples around the globe. It was, as Izzy recognized, a profoundly radical effort, and one that would not proceed easily, given the obstacles to be confronted, the historical legacies to be overcome, the hatreds and hostilities that slavery, racisim, and Jim Crow had spawned. Nevertheless, like the activists who had appeared in the very movement he had long called for, Stone believed that the American Dilemma simply had to be confronted head-on. He appeared grateful that Martin Luther King, Jr., and the early

SNCC cadre had emerged to do battle with that legal, social, and ethical blight on the American republic, and for the fact that they were determined to do so in nonviolent fashion.

Stone understood that moral suasion alone would not be enough to overcome racial attitudes held for generations and that the power of the federal government, as evidenced by *Brown* and Little Rock, must be turned to again and again. Like civil rights activists, he too believed that the Kennedy administration could do more than it had. And he recognized that with frustration and resentment mounting, the day of reckoning was approaching and Gandhian tactics were not likely to be the only ones civil rights proponents turned to.

At times, his commitment to the campaign to batter down the walls of Jim Crow was such that he seemed to be willing to use "any means necessary." This was due to the fact that he continued to view Jim Crow as incipient fascism, which could lead to something still worse again. But it was also owing to the demands of simple, common decency, Izzy believed, that racial inequality simply had to come to an end. His strong stance on one of the great issues of the modern era was a position he thought fellow journalists, intellectuals, and leftists—as well as the American president—had to be willing to take.

13 "The Steve Canyon Comic Strip Mentality"

T he July 23, 1962, issue of *I. F. Stone's Weekly* contained a brief admonition to the American peace movement, small though it then still was. What was needed, the newsletter indicated, was an independent commission to investigate the Second Indochina War, set the stage for negotiations, and bring about the removal of U.S. forces. Now was the time, the *Weekly* charged, for the full story about the war and the insurgent movement doing battle with Ngo Dinh Diem's "Fascist regime" in the south to be revealed. More than enough observers, soldiers and civilians alike, were available to tell all. For one thing, they might be able to answer questions concerning Diem's hold on the south, which by every indication seemed precarious at best; three convoys had recently been battered by guerrillas just a short way outside of Saigon itself.[1]

Above all else, the *Weekly* observed, it seemed ridiculous for there to be "a growing peace movement" that failed to condemn war where it was being fought. It was time for this movement to demand a cessation of hostilities in Vietnam, the newsletter asserted.[2]

Thus, just as he had called for grass-roots movements to challenge the barriers posed by Jim Crow and the threat presented by nuclear weapons, Izzy now exhorted citizen activists to turn their attention to Indochina. For the next decade and longer, he continued to demand opposition to his country's longest, although always undeclared, war.

It was regarding the Vietnam War, more than any other issue, that I. F. Stone's legendary reputation as an investigative reporter, committed journalist, political activist, and intellectual scribe for the New Left would evolve. His refusal to accept established "truths," whether articulated by the White House, the Pentagon, or the mass media, now enabled him to view U.S. involvement in the war far more critically and incisively than did his journalistic colleagues or fellow intellectuals. His qualities as a maverick served him well, too, particularly his great determination to probe, to question, to challenge even those whose political beliefs were much like his own. All of this resulted in the *Weekly* analyzing the war perhaps more clearly than any other American publication, which in turn enabled its subscription figures to escalate side by side with the conflict.

It was not surprising that Izzy Stone, by mid-1962, felt compelled to urge that peace activists follow his lead and examine the course of events in Vietnam. His prescience in this regard was certainly rare; very few American journalists or intellectuals paid much attention at all to the goings on in Southeast Asia throughout the fifties and the early sixties. Perhaps this was part of the price both groups paid for the red scare antics and Cold War fervor of the immediate postwar period. Owing to pervasive anti-Communist hysteria and the fact that some felt obliged to display their patriotic stripes, fewer and fewer journalists or intellectuals were willing to ask hard questions about U.S. foreign policy. This disinclination was the product, in part, of genuine concerns about Soviet designs and the threat of a new totalitarian power. Such concerns led many members of the American press to view themselves as a virtual fourth branch of the federal government. Most intellectuals, including many former radicals, came to agree that in their own way they too had to serve the needs of the government. Still, it might be argued that at work as well was some considerable degree of intellectual cowardice, a failure to own up to their responsibility, as journalists and intellectuals in a democratic society, to examine the failings of their own nation. What it ensured was that simple-minded and wrongheaded policies went largely unchecked and unchallenged for nearly a full generation. By contrast, I. F. Stone was one of the few who steadily and consistently examined the very same policies throughout a good portion of the French-Indochina War and thereafter.

This was not an individual, then, who experienced "cycles of engagement" in the manner of so many American intellectuals during the postwar era, but rather one who was "engaged" all along. While it is generally acknowledged that intellectual opposition to the Vietnam War did not really brew in the United States until 1965, Izzy stood out as a lonely voice from the earliest stages of deepening American involvement.[3]

As early as February 24, 1950, a mere two weeks after Joseph McCarthy became a political figure of some notoriety and several months before U.S. military aid was specifically allocated to assist the French war effort, Stone had warned that American policy might be shaped by attempts to deflect charges that Communists had infiltrated their way into the ranks of the administration. In an editorial that proved to be startlingly perceptive, he focused on the refusal of a cowed State Department to do as the Yugoslavs had done—recognize the legitimacy of Ho Chi Minh's government. State could use "a few Reds or pinks," Stone suggested, to overcome the "political illiteracy" that was leading it to throw "another one away." Now lacking the loyalty purge victims who had possessed some appreciation of what was taking place in Southeast Asia, the American government was about to embark upon a "costly failure." This, Stone declared, in the wake of the U.S. recognition of Bao Dai's puppet regime.[4]

The United States, in Stone's estimation, tragically appeared to be linking up with the agents of colonialism. A more diplomatic move, he believed, would have the nation siding with the forces of anti-imperialism.

The decision to place the good name of America on the side of Bao Dai and his French supporters, Stone insisted, was foolish. Indeed the same cast of characters, he declared, discredited the notion that the United States was the champion of freedom in the region. The former emperor, after all, had been a Japanese puppet during World War II, the very time when Ho had battled both European and Asian occupation forces. Lacking support from the Vietnamese people, the French attempt at recolonization was beset by bribery, blackmarketeering, and the trading of military information to the Vietminh. Yet this "rathole operation" was intended to serve as America's bulwark against communism in Vietnam. Stone likened the determination to use force in Indochina to the disastrous attempt to do the same in China and asserted that here too the "y'gotta get tough" approach would simply prove unavailing.[5]

It didn't help matters, Stone declared, that the fight against Ho was perceived throughout the region as simply "old-fashioned colonial aggression." And it was Ho's outmanned and ill-equipped guerrillas, he pointed out, who controlled the countryside, not their French antagonists.[6]

Ho, Stone informed his readers, had declared his determination to stay out of the Cold War fight, suggesting that perhaps a Southeast Asian version of Titoism could flower; Andrew Roth, *The Nation*'s Asian correspondent, agreed that Ho was not simply a "Moscow agent." True, Ho, like Tito, was a "Moscow-trained Communist." But it should be obvious by now, Stone indicated, that communism and nationalism were not necessarily contradictory; indeed, an editorial in *The New Republic* pointed out that many non-Communist Vietnamese had thrown in with Ho because of their disdain for French colonialism. Furthermore, it was clear, Stone noted, that Southeast Asians viewed China much as Eastern Europeans did Russia and desired to keep that great nation at arm's length. Thus, an intelligent U.S. policy could avoid driving new revolutionary regimes into the Soviet camp. Indeed, Ho's very seeking of recognition by Yugoslavia, coming on the heels of China's, demonstrated either a similar desire for national autonomy or Mao's willingness to open a door to the West. But "the more politically antiseptic the State Dept. becomes, the bigger a help it is to the Kremlin."[7]

That December, Stone warned that the United States could suffer grievously by attempting to act beyond its means. If the country would not disengage from the Far East, and would not effect a détente with China, a new disaster, even greater than the Korean conflict, appeared likely.[8]

The first essays Stone wrote on Indochina thus articulated many of the themes he would highlight over the next quarter-century. In them, he focused on the self-defeating nature of the growing American tendency to back unpopular dictatorial elements in Asia, Latin America, the Middle East, and Africa. Such a policy precluded the very possibility of a neutralist or Third Camp approach, foolishly called for a military solution to political problems, threatened to ensnare the United States in guerrilla wars, and, ultimately, had little chance to succeed.

No other American writer so persistently and prophetically criticized the actions of U.S. adminstrations from Truman to Reagan regarding Southeast Asia. Among Western intellectuals, only the analyses of Graham Greene and Bernard Fall could compare with those of I. F. Stone in underscoring the fallacies, hypocrisies, and inanities of first French and then U.S. policy in Indochina. But none did so more tellingly, more consistently, and over a longer period than did Stone.

As the French-Indochinese War approached its denouement at Dienbienphu in early 1954, the *New York Times* declared that "a question of survival in a free world" was at stake. Stone, by contrast, again warned that the domestic red scare, along with the China Lobby, made it impossible to devise a rational Far Eastern policy. Secretary of State Dulles's part in the harassment of John P. Davies, a young diplomat and Asian expert, indicated as much; Davies was about to undergo a ninth trial on charges of subversion. The treatment of Davies, Stone believed, demonstrated all too clearly what was in store for policymakers who viewed Chiang Kai-shek critically or who soberly examined "the great convulsion in the Far East." And unfortunately, Stone noted, there presently existed no peace movement to oppose greater U.S. involvement.[9]

The ferreting out of leftists or even critical liberals from the ranks of government services eventually proved to be disastrous for U.S. policy in Vietnam. Only those who accepted the hard-line anti-Communist position, such as Dean Rusk, could hope for continued government employment, let alone future appointment to positions of greater power and prominence. U.S. policymaking concerning Southeast Asia hardened and rigidified, until Ho was depicted as just a Soviet puppet and a would-be mandarin by the name of Ngo Dinh Diem was presented as the carrier of democracy and freedom to Vietnam.

On April 5, Stone analyzed the "delusions" that he considered to be characteristic of the new secretary of state, John Foster Dulles. The growth of communism in Southeast Asia, however it came about, Dulles had indicated, had to be terminated. Such a position seemed to preclude not only revolution but even a peaceful agreement to establish a coalition government; it also suggested that a Communist victory at the ballot box would not be accepted. How did the latter square with America's usual demand for democratic elections? Stone asked. Dulles appeared to be endorsing not an addendum to the Monroe Doctrine as he liked to call it, but rather a reversion to the old Holy Alliance that John Quincy Adams had attempted to fight against. Thus, the net of the Truman Doctrine was being cast wider still.[10]

But such a commitment, Stone warned, was fraught with considerable peril. For one thing, China might not take kindly to American antirevolutionary crusading. For another, the greatest power in Asia might "behave" and Indochina could still opt to go its own way, far removed from any kind of proper anti-Communist behavior. How would the United States react then? True, Indochina could be leveled with U.S. nuclear weapons. Its people, both Communist and non-Communist, could be hit "impartially with lesser bombs and napalm," as Koreans had been. American soldiers could be sent in to fight guerrillas on their own turf, even though earlier excursions into Mexico and Nicaragua did not promise any greater success than the French were presently experiencing. However, none of these approaches, Stone warned, would win the United States any popularity contests.[11]

Turning to the gun made some sense, he had to admit, if that could make a difference. But nothing was more odious than a meting out of force simply to cause death and destruction. Dulles's call for thwarting communism in Southeast Asia suggested just such a policy, no matter the pretense that the United States was backing "a great popular movement in Indo-China." Even a congressional report directed by Walter H. Judd, Izzy's old antagonist, acknowledged as much, although it too demanded that there be no Eastern Munich. It recognized that Vietnam was sick of war and demanded to be liberated. Ho's stranglehold on Vietnamese nationalism, the report affirmed, would be broken by an end of the conflict; but it also admitted that members of Bao Dai's government, tied as they were to "anti-popular movements," lacked such support.[12]

Consequently, the Bao Dai regime could not be propped up even by force, Stone argued. Only a right-wing, authoritarian government, such as that of Syngman Rhee in South Korea, could operate in such a fashion. Nevertheless, it seemed as though the United States was poised to do battle with communism throughout the region, provided "others carry the guns, and especially if only Asians (whom we regard as bargain basement warriors) will fight Asians."[13]

Moreover, in moving "to police East Asia against 'dangerous thoughts' and Communism," Stone believed, the United States was "picking up where the Axis left off." What brand of independence was his country offering, he wondered, if the Vietnamese had to follow the American line, even if that precluded peace, diplomacy, and genuine elections.[14]

Once again, Stone had simply and eloquently pointed out the foolhardiness and the contradictions of U.S. policy in Indochina. Under the guise of opposing Communist totalitarianism, he believed, his own government was supporting a brand of right-wing authoritarianism with an odious and all-too-familiar smell. It was also threatening to produce a still wider war that could cost the United States in terms of material resources, lives, and reputation.

As the battle of Dienbienphu concluded with a French debacle, Stone worried about what would-be interventionists were up to. Every war the United States waged, liberals particularly insisted, had to be portrayed as a crusade, he noted. The French withdrawal, he worried, might lead conservatives and liberals alike to believe that a new " 'good' war," directed from the United States, was now in order. But what kind of independence, he again asked, was being considered for Indochina? What if a coalition government were constructed or an election held and Ho—viewed by his own people as a great nationalistic leader—came out on top?[15]

At a press conference Izzy attended, Secretary of State Dulles indicated that in such a "politically immature" land, an election was not warranted. This was familiar Kiplingesque language, the words of white supremacy, the inevitable response of Westerners to demands that colonialism come to an end, Stone insisted.[16]

Such an approach appalled and disgusted him, and would continue to do so through the duration of U.S. involvement in Indochina. The old-style colonialism his country had first backed and now seemed to be duplicating in Vietnam contradicted its claim to stand as a beacon of freedom and as a supporter of self-determination, two of the oldest and most sacred ideals in the United States.

At this stage in the continuing Cold War, liberals remained cowed and the peace movement "gagged." Consequently, it was men such as Army Chief of Staff Matthew Ridgway, former Army man Eisenhower, and Secretary of Defense Charles Wilson, Stone pointed out, who opposed intervention in Indochina. Notwithstanding leftist stereotypes, Stone declared, it was the Army that recognized that after the flyboys completed their air strikes, the foot soldiers would be called upon "to do the dirty work and take the terrain." Secretary of Defense Wilson, in decidedly Henry Wallace–like fashion, had warned against any attempts to serve as world policeman and asked if the American people would support the sending in of ground forces.[17]

Here, as he did throughout the Eisenhower administration, Stone appreciated the tendency of the president to shy away from calls for large-scale military incursions. This, he happily attributed to Eisenhower's genuine conservatism and his experiences as the wartime commander of Allied forces. On more than one occasion, Stone urged others on the left to "back Ike for peace," to support administration efforts to diminish Cold War tensions.

By contrast, upon the official close of the French-Indochina War on July

21, 1954, Stone criticized "our armchair generals of the press" for never having taken into account the bombed Vietnamese villages. In Vietnam as in Korea, he bristled, Westerners were accustomed to meting out murder with litte concern for the natives. Indeed, a commonly held view suggested "that the man burned out by napalm prefers incineration by the 'free world' to Communist 'enslavement.' "[18]

This was a theme Stone returned to again and again—that his fellow journalists were not performing the critical function they were obliged to carry out. Their tendency to cheerlead in the midst of international crises and their depiction of the early American role in Vietnam angered and appalled him. They, in turn, were inclined to dismiss his caustic barbs and biting analyses as the product of an out-of-favor, still fellow-traveling Old Leftist.

He was no more pleased with the policies of the John Foster Dulles–directed State Department. With peace at hand, he indicated that the reunification elections called for in Geneva would not come off if State had its way. Military solutions were preferred instead, for victory by Ho Chi Minh appeared certain.[19]

When results of a referendum were announced the following year, Stone suggested that Diem, the new premier of the American-sponsored Republic of South Vietnam, must have taken lessons from Frank Hague of Jersey City. But then even Boss Hague had never posted the numbers Diem had, more than ninety-eight percent of the votes counted.[20]

The elections designed to reunify Vietnam were never held, to Izzy's considerable dismay. The flagrant contradiction between rhetoric and action, between high-minded ideals and government policies, which characterized U.S. policy in Indochina, continued to enrage him.

By the end of the 1950s, CIA operatives along with U.S. military advisers and assistance had supplanted the earlier French connection. Diem, the Catholic nationalist and would-be mandarin, buttressed by his American backers, came to rule the southern half of Vietnam like a family fiefdom, ruthlessly crushing pockets of Vietminh resistance. Nonetheless, reports from American journalists and politicians proclaimed Vietnam to be a model for both democracy and capitalistic development. The *New York Times* edition of May 10, 1957, portrayed Diem as "An Asian Liberator." In his column in *Newsweek* on June 29, 1959, Ernest K. Lindley of *Newsweek* declared Diem to be "An Ally Worth Having." Lindley praised Diem as a "dedicated, canny, indefatigable, invincible man" who had long been seen as "the authentic symbol of nationalism."[21]

But by late 1959, in spite of U.S. backing, it was clear that all was not well in South Vietnam. The number of assassinations of government officials had increased dramatically, large-scale military operations were being carried out by Vietminh-like insurgents, and political propaganda campaigns flourished in the countryside.

For a time, however, it was Laos and not Vietnam that I. F. Stone, like President Eisenhower, feared might turn into another Korea. A coalition government, which included members of the Communist-led Pathet Lao guerrillas, had come to power the previous year, temporarily bringing a civil war to a halt. But U.S. officials supported a purge of Communist officials, and a right-wing coup followed. In September 1959, Stone warned that Americans must either accept the results of free elections or be willing to pay the price. That included watching the countrysides of other nations slide deeper toward war and despotism. And in a jungle-riddled land like Laos, guerrilla activity could go on and on. Nuclear arms and reputedly more benign chemical and biological agents, Stone declared, would be equally without effect upon such terrain. Rather, political and not military concerns remained most important, but absent a political resolution, war was certain to resume.[22]

Stone was particularly troubled that the United States, which had already expended some 250 million dollars in military assistance to Laos, was starting to toss still more money "down this same rathole." With the rebel contingent estimated at no more than five thousand, "there must be something rotten in the state of Laos," he declared, if the guerrilla insurgency there could not be halted. And it did not help matters, he suggested, that fake, foolish, and hysterical news reports were proclaiming southern Laos to be "seething" with pro-Communist Pathet Lao rebels. As it turned out, approximately five hundred to six hundred guerrillas were roaming in an area patrolled by ten times that number of government soldiers. As Stone put it, "Laos seems to seethe very easily."[23]

T he determination of the United States to reach for the gun, whether wielded by Southeast Asian government units, American combat troops, or paramilitary forces, continued to appall him. So too did the absence of a challenge to his nation's apparent "light-headed readiness for war" in a land as sparsely populated as Laos. No one seemed willing to ask if still greater sums should be expended on a hopeless jungle battle that could only lead to frustration or a wider conflagration. Few recognized why viable governments had not been constructed in Laos or South Vietnam, or questioned the disdain accorded the neutralist stance of Prince Norodom Sihanouk of Cambodia; in that Southeast Asian country, the American military and the CIA seemingly had carte blanche to act as they chose to.[24]

Just why, Stone wondered, was this so? And why, he asked in early 1961, the new Kennedy administration's fascination with counterinsurgency? He suggested that greater attention had better be paid to the failed coup in Algeria; that revolt had been conducted by the same strange band of French colonels who had begun the fad of reading Chairman Mao. Not so very long ago, those very officers had paved the way for Charles de Gaulle to become president of the French republic; however, the old general promptly and unceremoniously removed them from the French colony. De Gaulle understood all too clearly, Stone continued, something President Kennedy evidently did not. The fixation upon using guerrilla tactics for counterrevolutionary ends unknowingly transformed the French officers "into Communists-in-reverse, i.e. . . . into fascists" ready to bring back home the same dirty tricks—"the psychological warfare, the brainwashing, the cloak-and-dagger methods"—they so freely employed in northern Africa. Now it was Washington itself that was abuzz with talk of paramilitary or guerrilla warfare—all to be used against Communists, of course, in the heat of battle.[25]

The French colonels, like many of their American counterparts, Stone suggested, held on to a "comic strip concept of history," detecting Communist conspirators at the head of each and every liberation movement. "The Steve Canyon comic strip mentality" was still stronger at the Pentagon. But the military theoreticians there appeared incapable of appreciating "the injured racial feelings, the misery, the rankling slights, the hatred, the devotion, the inspiration and the desperation. So they do not really understand what leads men to abandon wife, children, home, career and friends; to take to the bush and live gun in hand like a hunted animal; to challenge overwhelming military odds rather than acquiesce any longer in humiliation, injustice and poverty."[26]

Counterinsurgency, then, was simply "the dazzling latest military toothpaste for social decay." And no one seemed to recognize that the same tactics favored by the Joint Chiefs of Staff had so recently come a cropper in Fidel Castro's Cuba. How could they be expected to succeed any better, Stone asked, in faraway Southeast Asia?[27]

At a time when the vogue of counterinsurgency and the Green Berets was in full swing, Stone's criticisms were somewhat lonely and not well received. The Kennedy brothers, Jack and Bobby, as he feared, were enamored with such practices and forces in spite of the Bay of Pigs, which had been such a disaster. The romanticism associated with these operations appealed to the president, the attorney general, and the Pentagon, something which troubled Stone greatly.

He saw more disasters as lying in store should American officials continue to believe that coups and counterconspiracies, rather than genuine reform, could thwart popularly based uprisings that demanded more than brutal repression and meaningless platitudes for an oppressed people. His own countrymen, Stone suggested, had better come to terms with the fact "that the brutal surgery of military and para-military methods" was not the answer to complicated social and economic problems.[28]

By late July 1961, Stone was indicating that the warnings of an old American general and Asia Firster had better be heeded. He discussed Douglas MacArthur's recent visit to the White House and the Korean War commander's admonition to keep American troops out of a land war in the region. For conventional soldiers in the United States, including John Fitzgerald Kennedy, Stone wrote, there loomed a possible "quicksand which could absorb a major share of our youth in endless 'limited' war."[29]

He delivered such an analysis at the very time when Lyndon Johnson was portraying Diem as the Winston Churchill of Southeast Asia, when few Americans had even heard of Vietnam, and when most reporters, young and not-so-young alike, backed administration policies wholeheartedly and unreservedly.

Unlike most of his journalistic counterparts in the early sixties, Stone saw the United States as continuing to attempt to impose American ideals "by blood and fire on a distant peaceful people." And thanks to a big boost in military spending, his country now appeared capable of waging any type of war, ranging from full-scale nuclear conflict to guerrilla struggles. No matter; in Southeast Asia, he warned, "super power becomes super impotence." A CIA-directed army in Laos was getting nowhere, while American intervention in Vietnam only resulted in the latest in U.S. military hardware ending up in the hands of VC guerrillas. The United States, then, was "a giant, but muscle-bound."[30]

As of early 1962, there were few who expressed the concerns of *The Nation* magazine that the United States was imposing an "absurd mandarin and his rotten regime" on the Vietnamese people. One who was delivering still more biting analyses was Izzy Stone, who continued to warn as he had some time earlier that Asia appeared to be "a vast marsh where swarming gnats can devour a giant." It did not help matters, he indicated, that the United States had cast its lot with "four of the queerest figures ever smuggled under the Jeffersonian mantle"—South Korea's Chung Hee Park, Formosa's Chiang Kai-shek, South Vietnam's Ngo Dinh Diem, and Thailand's Sarit Thanarat. Why, Stone wondered, did America prefer such "corrupt clowns" to Cambodia's Prince Sihanouk, an "enlightened" ruler who was treated like some kind of illegitimate child?[31]

But most significantly, Stone asked, by what right was the United States acting as it did? On September 30, 1963, in dismissing a succession of fact-finding missions to Vietnam, he indicated that the facts were crystal clear. Wealthy Catholic mandarins could not lord it over a population that was largely Buddhist. Southeast Asia could not be stabilized so long as China was treated as an outlaw state. And in words much like those expressed by William H. Hunter of *The New Republic,* Stone charged: "You can't go on pouring napalm on villages and poisons on crops, uprooting people and putting them in prison-like compounds, and expect to be liked."[32]

It all seemed simple enough to Stone—throwing in with despots would not strengthen the U.S. position in Southeast Asia. Nor would wreaking havoc on the native landscape and its people.

As Stone pointed out on October 28, the Diem regime was becoming more of an embarrassment than ever. But "the inhumanity" of Ngo Dinh Diem, he suggested, was just as rooted in American practices as in palace intrigue in Indochina. For in Washington, the following program had been concocted: "the uprooting of the rural population and its incarceration in stockaded villages, the spraying of poisons from the air on crops and cattle in violation of the Geneva convention, the use of napalm for attack on villages suspected of harboring rebels." Thus, what prevailed was the old notion that the end justifies the means whenever Communists were involved. The key priority remained the winning of the war and thus the reliance on military and covert solutions. But "the type of men, mentality and institution brought into play," Stone wrote, influenced both present and future courses of action. Like the French generals earlier, Paul D. Harkins, the American commander of U.S. forces in Vietnam, was forever espying victory just around the corner.[33]

However, such victory, Stone believed, was surely as elusive as ever. The United States was playing what promised to be a losing hand in Southeast Asia. This was something the American public had to be forewarned about.

But the New Frontiersmen, following in the footsteps of the Eisenhower and Truman administrations, was operating in Indochina "behind a thick smokescreen of official falsification." Public pronouncements often were at odds with concerns privately voiced by top government officials, such as Ike's revelation that had elections ever been held, Ho Chi Minh would have won in a landslide. One reality was that the United States had long been footing the bill for a war to force upon the people of Vietnam first one government, then another, which they never much cared for. Another reality was that South Vietnam, no matter how it had been painted until most recently by the Kennedy administration, appeared more and more like a poor version "of a Communist totalitarian regime," no democratic mecca in a sea where a red storm was rising. The Kennedy State Department was simply attempting to veil "the truth about this hopeless but savage war" from the American people.[34]

Thus, at this relatively early stage, Stone was well aware of the duplicity, the lies, and the deceit that later resulted in the infamous credibility gap that cost the Johnson and Nixon administrations so dearly. He was one of the few who saw the emergence of that divide which increasingly separated the general public and the U.S. government, starting with Truman and Eisenhower, before gathering momentum during the days of the Kennedy administration.

Stone's analysis of U.S. policy in Vietnam was far removed from that of his none-too-critical journalistic brethren and intellectuals in general. Newspapers across the land, including the reputedly liberal *New York Times,* backed the administration's position. So too did newspaper columnist Joseph Alsop and Otto Fuerbringer, *Time* managing editor. Although young turks such as David Halberstam of the *Times* and Neil Sheehan of UPI questioned the way the war was being fought, they too did not oppose American involvement. And few intellectuals, at this point, paid much attention at all to the war in Vietnam.[35]

Thus, this remained a period of "lonely dissent" regarding U.S. policy in Southeast Asia. Such was no novelty to Izzy Stone, accustomed as he was to staking a position considerably outside the political and intellectual mainstream. Even most other radical intellectuals, one scholar has noted, failed to pay heed at this time to developments in Indochina.[36]

To Stone, U.S. involvement in Vietnam promised all sorts of disasters. Following the generals' coup on November 1 that culminated in the assassinations of a president and his brother, Stone warned that the United States would prop up yet another dictatorship if the people of Vietnam did not desire more strategic hamlets, napalm, and prison sentences for those who opposed the conflict. What his own land cried out for, Stone declared in the manner he had for some time now, was a movement to demand "a truly democratic foreign policy," including an end to both the Indochinese war and the economic embargo that was directed at Cuba. Could the conscience of America be aroused? Stone asked, a question he posed at least implicitly as he began delivering a series of addresses on Vietnam in the fall of 1963.[37]

A full decade passed before Izzy ceased making such queries and speeches, and during this time his perspective on Southeast Asia acquired greater and greater respectability. As a consequence, both he and the *Weekly* lost a bit of their outlaw status and Izzy was welcomed back into the arms of at least a portion of the establishment once again. He came to be viewed—by many at least—as a responsible spokesperson for an anti-interventionist perspective.

N o other American intellectual and no other journalist more consistently or more forthrightly called into question his nation's policies toward Vietnam than did Izzy Stone. For a full decade and a half before the Vietnam War became his country's own, he persistently argued that the United States was backing the wrong side, throwing in as it was with

French colonialists and Western-sponsored mandarins or puppets, and opposing the nationalist movement spearheaded by Ho Chi Minh. He warned that the United States was heading toward a quagmire of sorts, with large-scale losses of men, materials, goodwill, and national spirit sure to follow. And regardless of the "sacrifices" that would be made, he saw the bid to further the Pax Americana necessarily coming to nought in the jungles of Indochina, well before the number of soldiers and body bags escalated so dramatically.

Not even Bernard Fall, the great French journalist and historian of the Indochina wars, and a personal friend of Izzy's, so presciently painted the picture of what lay ahead. And although Fall's coverage of first French and then later U.S. involvement was insightful, even brilliant, it lacked the radical edge Stone's possessed. Fall, notwithstanding his own anticolonialist and anti-interventionist stance, did not damn French and U.S. policies toward Vietnam in quite the some manner Stone did, perhaps because of his greater store of anticommunism.

Both Fall and Stone, as a result of their writings on Vietnam, were about to possess greater and greater influence with an American New Left. Indeed, it is difficult to conceive of any individuals, intellectuals or not, who carried more weight in antiwar circles through the middle part of the 1960s than did Bernard Fall and Izzy Stone, other than A. J. Muste, perhaps.

Furthermore, given the dearth of strong progressive labor unions and political organizations in existence at the time, the impact of individuals like Fall, Muste, and Stone on thoughtful young people of the period is hard to dispute. Along with Herbert Marcuse, C. Wright Mills, and William Appelman Williams, they had helped to keep alive critical ideals during a time of conformity. Now, for the generation coming of age in the 1960s, such intellectuals provided a framework for attacking the ills to be contested, ranging from the arms race to the continued presence of Jim Crow in the American South to U.S. policy in Indochina. They also served as models of the activist intellectual who believed it was one's duty as both intellectual and concerned citizen to speak out.

14 Telling Truth to Power: The Emperor Has No Clothes

Paul Booth and Todd Gitlin, two key figures in Students for a Democratic Society, the leading New Left organization of the period, were trying to decide which projects to push at the organization's impending national convention. The two were particularly interested in orchestrating a sit-in against Chase Manhattan Bank, which continued to provide loans for South Africa's apartheid regime. At the same time, however, as coordinators of SDS's Peace Research and Education Project, they were interested in doing "*something*" regarding Vietnam. Consequently, Booth and Gitlin decided to invite Izzy Stone to speak to the national council about the war going on there. Stone was seen as one who had "proved you *could* expose 'the system' " and the *Weekly* as "the best source of material which doesn't seem to be fit to print in major newspapers."[1]

On the evening of December 30, 1964, Izzy delivered the keynote address on "America and the Third World" at New York City's Cloakmakers' Hall—an Old Left hangout—to a rapt audience of SDS cadre. His emphasis was on the growing U.S. involvement in Vietnam, his argument "a ringing declaration" that the United States should pull out.[2]

The following day, the national council readily approved the Booth-Gitlin proposal for a March sit-in against Chase, then began to debate just what to do about Vietnam. Stone's "eloquent and stirring" talk had moved many, and the war suddenly became a topic of greater and greater concern. Discussion ensued, far more prolonged and heated than anyone would have anticipated earlier. Eventually, it was decided to sponsor a springtime mass rally to be held in Washington, which would call for the withdrawal of American forces from Vietnam.[3]

On January 7, Gitlin asked Izzy to speak at the gathering, believing he would articulate matters precisely and forcefully and serve as something of a drawing card. Izzy agreed to talk, and so too, at his prompting, did his friend and former colleague at the *New York Post*, Ernest Gruening, the senior senator from the state of Alaska and a critic of administration policy in Vietnam. At the time, only a small turnout was anticipated, at most a few thousand of the already committed.[4]

Forthcoming U.S. actions in Vietnam, however, came to dramatically alter earlier expectations. On February 8, in supposed retaliation for a Vietcong attack on the American air base in Pleiku, President Johnson ordered air strikes against purported guerrilla strongholds in North Vietnam. Three days later, the American barracks at Qui Nhon were hit, and the following day another round of reprisal raids was carried out. The United States had begun the Rolling Thunder campaign, a policy of intensified air strikes long sought by top officials in the Johnson administration. Nevertheless, a denial was issued that a watershed of any kind had been reached.

On February 27, the U.S. State Department, in an attempt to justify the escalation it continued to deny was taking place, issued a sixty-four-page White Paper on Vietnam, *Aggression from the North—the Record of North Vietnam's Campaign to Conquer South Vietnam*. On March 8—the same day the first U.S. ground forces landed in Vietnam—I. F. Stone dissected the White Paper, systematically refuting it point by point. Using the Pentagon's own figures, he noted that the guerrillas were acquiring the vast bulk of their weapons not from Communist nations, but from the United States. The State Department document also failed to acknowledge the roots of the insurgency, including American–South Vietnamese violations of the Geneva accords, the repression that had been commonplace under Diem, and the absence of authentic land reform of any sort.[5]

Those who were drawn to what had become an antiwar movement by the spring of 1965 proved to be a diverse lot, divided by a sense of history, ideological differences, and contrasting perspectives on both American domestic and foreign policies. More and more people had been attracted to the idea of a mass march in Washington, but unhappiness about SDS control was evident as well. While tiny sectarian groups quickly signed on, individuals and organizations long associated with peace activism expressed reservations. What groups such as SANE and individuals like Harvard professor H. Stuart Hughes, A. J. Muste, and Norman Thomas were troubled by was SDS's nonexclusionary policy; they were also displeased with its increasingly scathing portrayal of President Johnson and his Vietnam strategy. On April 15, both Ernest Gruening and Stone phoned SDS staffers, the senator expressing concerns that Communists might attempt to disrupt the march, Izzy warning that his friend might become a no-show. Assured that SDS remained in control, Gruening agreed to participate. Muste and Thomas, for their part, were willing to indicate general support for the march, while disavowing certain positions held by some of the participants.[6]

Owing to the escalation of the war, the size of the march far surpassed earlier expectations, with some twenty thousand arriving in Washington. Consequently, this "was no small circle of friends," as one chronicler has eloquently written, "this was the germ of a mass movement." The crowd gathered round the White House, then proceeded to the Washington Monument to listen to speeches from Staughton Lynd, Robert Parris Moses, Paul Potter, and Izzy Stone, among others. At the top of his address—which, in Paul Booth's words, "dissected and disposed of the official rationale of the fighting"—Izzy alluded to the lone sour note that threatened first the very holding of and then the success of the gathering. At the Washington Monument, a sectarian attack had been leveled at liberals such as Senator Gruening. When it was his turn to speak, Izzy fired back: "I've seen snot-nosed Marxist-Leninists come and go." He proceeded to defend his old friend and to proclaim himself one of the despised liberals.[7]

In preparing for his own talk, Izzy had studied up on the history of Indochina and the Vietnam War, reading in particular Jean Lacouture and Jean Sainteny. He termed U.S. policymakers "decent" men who happened to be ensnared in "monstrous," self-perpetuating institutions. He advised those in attendance to return home and discuss these matters, "but not in tones of hatred and self-righteousness. We have to get out of this reign of hatred." And he reflected on Vietnam's imperialistic tendencies.[8]

For the duration of the Vietnam War, Izzy served as one of the leading spokespersons for the peace movement. As U.S. involvement in Southeast Asia continued and as the antiwar forces grew in strength, his perspectives on the conflict and regarding the general direction of American foreign policy ensured a larger and larger audience for the *Weekly* and continued requests for its editor to appear at rallies and demonstrations. All along the way, Izzy demonstrated once again how journalists could use anger and outrage, how intellectuals did not simply have to stand on the sidelines, how radical ideals still had something to say to late twentieth-century America.

Those developments, coupled with the fact that other journalists and intellectuals as well as certain leading political figures were now more receptive to his ideas, made Izzy someone to be reckoned with. This, he considered, in his indomitable manner, was only fitting.

To such key figures in the early New Left as Paul Booth, Dick Flacks, Todd Gitlin, Lee Webb, and Tom Hayden, Izzy Stone was always "an exemplar" of sorts, a man of "intellectual and political integrity," and one of a very few of his generation who had not been mortally compromised by either Stalinism or dogmatic anticommunism. Unlike so many other radicals from the 1930s, he did not appear to have been permanently scarred, intellectually or morally, by his Old Left involvement. While embitteredness and disillusionment characterized so many Old Leftists, Izzy had retained his earlier radicalism, seemingly having only tempered it with a wealth of experience, which caused him to question all varieties of established truths. He retained as well his determination to serve as both intellectual critic and political activist, something the New Leftists well appreciated and attempted to emulate. And they seemed to recognize that Izzy hoped every bit as much as they did that their left would deliberately seek to avoid the dogmatism, excesses, and fate of the earlier movement. New Left leaders came to "devotedly" scour the newsletter and encouraged the SDS membership to follow suit, highlighting well-documented articles on Cuba, nuclear arms, and Southeast Asia which provided a point of view not found in establishment publications. Izzy, Gitlin later recalled, was "a spiritual eminence on early SDS." In fact, "the only others of his generation who played similar parts—respectful, admirable, and critical at the same time—were A. J. Muste and perhaps David Dellinger." Indeed, as Gitlin later recalled, the *Weekly* taught him and others "that the government lied." Flacks, for his part, likened Izzy to C. Wright Mills, writer James Agee, fellow journalist Carey McWilliams, Paul Goodman, and Muste, as one of a handful of models for the New Left, still just emerging. Hayden considered him "the voice in the wilderness" who had seemed to demonstrate that "a single individual could make a difference," a matter of tremendous importance to the early New Left with its somewhat anarchistic slant. Because of the way they saw him, Izzy, in Hayden's estimation, carried considerable weight with the SDS founders. Or as Booth later put it, "we depended on him to interpret the events of the world for us. The moment his *Weekly* arrived, we devoured it," rather than the *New York Times* or *Newsweek*, the *Daily Worker*, or even *The Nation*.[9]

This made perfect sense for Izzy, like Muste and a small number of others, provided a needed sense of continuity with a seemingly heroic past, with those who had fought the good fight against fascism and on behalf of the dispossessed, and who were themselves linked with the early twentieth-century left of Sinclair and Reed, Debs and Haywood. Lacking the kinds of heroes most American revered, from Dwight Eisenhower or Harry Truman to John Wayne or General George Patton, the early New Leftists developed their own icons, and they included the small number of intellectuals and activists who had remained true to the radical heritage during the dark days of the red scare and the age of the organization man.

Consequently, SDSers were elated when W. H. Ferry of the Center for the Study of Democratic Institutions, A. J. Muste, and Stone fired off a letter to a number of left-of-center publications urging "moral, intellectual, and financial support" for SDS's Economic Research and Action Project (ERAP), which focused on bettering the lot of the "other Americans" residing in the inner cities. In June 1963, the pro-ERAP note referred to what it called a vitally important political development, the appearance of a group of young people devoted to constructing "a new American left." The left elders praised SDS for having attracted "some of the best and angriest young minds now functioning."[10]

Like the SDS originators, Izzy was drawn to those who themselves served as models for New Leftists, SNCC activists such as Bob Moses and John Lewis. Having attended the organization's fourth annual conference, which was held at Washington's Howard University, Izzy sang their praises. "They are an impressive lot. Purity is the only word for their intrinsic quality—the absence of self-seeking or of vanity. They are the stuff of saints. They are determined to change our country . . . by non-violent means, to answer hate with love. They stand in a line that runs back from Gandhi to Tolstoy to Thoreau to St. Francis to Jesus. I regard them with reverence." Never before, he declared, had so few accomplished so much in such a brief period of time. And this "unarmed few" promised to march "through the heart" of Dixie as General Sherman once had.[11]

The activists of SNCC and SDS, Stone believed, were that youthful cadre he had hoped might be capable of instilling the American body politic with a sense of the concern, the compassion, and the commitment that had largely been absent since the heyday of the New Deal and the Old Left. Now Izzy could stand for them as that type of surrogate father he had himself long required. Certainly, in the first years of the New Left, considerable respect for each other's ideological perspective was shared by the young rebels and this now elder statesman of American radicalism.

Both Stone and the SDS leadership at this point were less enamored with hard-line young leftists, including members of the Maoist Progressive Labor Party, which in 1962 had broken away from the American Communist Party. He had intended to act as moderator at a Town Hall gathering in New York City welcoming students just returned from Cuba. He withdrew, after having listened to a number of PLers speak in the nation's capital. Their line seemed to be "a mixture of naivete, Negro nationalist distortions (understandable enough in light of the Negro's anguish, but still distortions) and out-of-the-world leftism." Figuring that he would be forced to engage in verbal fisticuffs with the PLers or stand aside in seeming agreement with their views, he subsequently declined to participate. He defended their right to speak their mind and believed that they were performing a service to the nation. But he did not care to be a party to their "hysterical exaggerations."[12]

Following the appearance before HCUAC by leaders of the Student Committee for Travel to Cuba, Stone indicated that they had made a serious error in judgment. With the opportunity to show the committee for what it was, "an abomination" and nothing else, they had decided instead to carry out "an old-fashioned *agitprop* demonstration." They seemed to believe that improved relations with Cuba would not be possible until capitalism withered away in the United States. With new trips to Cuba in the offing, Stone hoped more sensible sorts would rise to the forefront.[13]

Stone likened such youthful militants to the sectarians who had done grievous injury to the Popular Front and Old Left radicalism. He welcomed the nondogmatic orientation of the New Leftists, but saw PLers as planting the seeds of the divisiveness the movement was soon to experience.

S tone's determination to call things as he saw them appealed to his New Left friends and admirers and to his subscribers, now nearly twenty thousand strong, for whom the *Weekly* had acquired something of a cult status. Reviewers of *The Haunted Fifties*, the first collection of essays culled from the newsletter, praised him as "controversial in a day when controversy is equated with sin . . . bold, when courage is next door to treason." One unofficial reviewer, working for the CIA, by contrast, fired off a note dated November 19, 1963, indicating "this is not the kind of book you would presumably want to keep (per our discussion)."[14]

For now, however, members of SDS and SNCC gave Stone renewed hope, while the SDSers in particular turned to him for support. As early as November 1963, the *SDS Bulletin*, which had praised the *Weekly*'s highlighting of the "hard realities and internal contradictions" of U.S. foreign policy, discussed recent appearances by Paul Booth, Norman Thomas, and Izzy Stone at a rally in Washington that condemned American support for Ngo Dinh Diem's regime. The United States continued to appease dictators in the Orient, Izzy was quoted as charging. But Saigon, like Birmingham and Atlanta, was said to have despoiled his country's reputation as a land of liberty.[15]

On February 3, 1964, Stone reported that American officers in the field were referring to South Vietnam as "the laboratory"; one such officer, recently retired, charged that U.S. planes had chalked up more civilians killed in action than had the guerrillas they were supposedly targeting. Three weeks later, Stone quoted from Hanson W. Baldwin, whose report in the *New York Times* told of how high the stakes really were in Indochina. There, for the first time, the United States was trying out its theories of counterinsurgency. Fearing a setback in South Vietnam would have global repercussions, officials in Washington had come to believe that even American combat forces might be required. At the very least, it was readily apparent that there was little light at the end of the tunnel. The headline in the *Weekly* appearing above the Baldwin quote cried out, "A Warning Signal the Peace Movement Ought to Heed While There's Still Time." On April 20, declaring the choice to be between wholesale U.S. involvement in the war and negotiations with the other side, Stone insisted that "now's the time to speak up."[16]

Once again, Stone's warnings at this point remained astute and sadly unique. He seemed to understand exactly what Vietnam could mean for the generation of Americans coming of age in the 1960s and for their nation. He saw American activities in Southeast Asia as the logical and disastrous conclusion of postwar U.S. foreign policy, which well might fatally damage both the morale and the morals of his countrymen.

The war in Vietnam, he warned at this early point, was "a blind alley which is destroying faith in our government not only there but at home." He recognized that the credibility gap was worsening. And he was aware that without a major American military force, which guerrillas could encircle, negotiations simply had to be carried out.[17]

The March 30 issue of the *Weekly* included a print of a Vietnamese child covered with napalm-induced burns, a print Izzy had not been allowed to purchase as per custom from the Associated Press. Having obtained a copy on his own, he believed that the picture indicated how the United States was treating innocent villagers in Vietnam.[18]

On April 6, Stone once more insisted that the United States was in no way protecting South Vietnam against the forces of outside aggression. Rather, American policy was following the path staked out by the French; it was forcing a military regime, backed by foreign muscle, down the throats of a proud and nationalistic people who possessed a strong desire for democracy. On May 4, he warned too that "our puppet forces" were little inclined to fight. Consequently, President Johnson might soon have to decide if American troops were to be sent in. Shortly thereafter, he proclaimed this to be "Johnson's War," not Secretary of Defense Robert McNamara's, and insisted it was "the LBJ pipeline" that kept the fighting going. It seemed, Stone reported on June 29, that some ninety percent of the weapons held by the guerrillas came their way courtesy of their South Vietnamese countrymen.[19]

In early August, a series of incidents took place along the North Vietnamese coast in the Gulf of Tonkin which Stone all but uniquely recognized as a major turning point in the war. In a span of two days, the destroyer the *USS Maddox* was purportedly on the receiving end of a pair of assaults from North Vietnamese patrol boats. After the second reported attack, President Johnson ordered retaliatory air strikes.

On August 4, just prior to the American action, Stone warned that the war was being carried on "behind our backs." It appeared that boats flying the flag of the Republic of South Vietnam had staged a number of raids along the shores of North Vietnam. It was also apparent that American destroyers had, at times, joined in those very same missions.[20]

In establishment circles in Washington, however, a different story was being told. Reports of North Vietnamese attacks on American ships were played up and a congressional resolution passed, which authorized the president to take whatever means he considered necessary to protect U.S. forces and stave off aggression. Not a single vote was cast against the Tonkin Gulf

Resolution in the House, and only Oregon's Wayne Morse and Alaska's Ernest Gruening dissented in the Senate.

The U.S. government and the press, Stone charged on August 24, had hidden all there was to know about Tonkin Gulf from the American people. He attended the UN Security Council debate on the affair and heard correspondents cynically recall an earlier insistence by Ambassador Stevenson that the United States opposed retaliatory raids of any kind. However, none of these reporters were now willing to remind their readers of what Stevenson had previously said. Nor did they mention that peacetime reprisals had supposedly been placed out of bounds by the rule of international law and by the charters of the League of Nations and United Nations. Reprisals, Stone declared, were "lynch law" only.[21]

The United States, he wrote, appeared to subscribe to the doctrine of "pure 'might is right.'" Moreover, all evidence suggested that American destroyers had been spoiling for a fight with the North. And a series of raids conducted in late July by South Vietnamese boats was apparently part of an intensified campaign of operations conducted above the seventeenth parallel. Consequently, the actual attacks on the *Maddox* could well have been provoked, Stone indicated, a possibility few were even willing to consider. He also questioned whether the second strike had even taken place, for no ship had suffered any damage at all. In addition, he worried that Lyndon Johnson might have been afforded a "blank check" with which to wage the war in Vietnam.[22]

Most reports of Tonkin Gulf, such as those in *Life* and *Newsweek*, as Izzy indicated, bought into the administration's version of events. Interestingly enough, both Richard Rovere of *The New Yorker* and an unsigned editorial in William Buckley's *National Review* did call certain matters into question. Rovere dismissed Morse and Gruening as "chronic dissenters," denied that the North had been provoked in any way, but acknowledged that raids by the Army of the Republic of South Vietnam had taken place prior to the North Vietnamese action. Still, Rovere indicated that Tonkin Gulf was likely to become little more than a historical footnote. The *National Review* wondered why there had been no follow-up to the pair of reported attacks, while acknowledging that Johnson had benefited politically because of the incidents.[23]

The Nation and *The New Republic* also worried about the provocative nature of the administration's response, fearing that now escalation of the war was inevitable. *The Nation* did wonder about threatening actions by the United States and its South Vietnamese ally, but accepted official reports about the second round of attacks and acknowledged the right of American ships to defend themselves.[24]

The Gulf of Tonkin affair, along with the ouster of Ngo Dinh Diem, finally compelled more and more left-wing intellectuals to direct their attention to the war in Indochina. But among those radical intellectuals and among the reporters who covered the Washington beat, none probed official reports about Tonkin Gulf more completely than did Izzy. None argued more critically, even scathingly, than did Izzy, who maintained that U.S. actions surrounding the affair, both in Vietnam and in Washington, called into question the core assumptions taken for granted by both the administration and reporters.[25]

Perhaps this was because unlike those who worked for the major print and television media, such as the *New York Times*'s Tom Wicker, Izzy operated under a different set of assumptions. Whereas Wicker "had not yet been taught to question the President . . . had not been taught by bitter experience that our government like any other *in extremis* will lie and cheat to protect itself," Izzy believed that every reporter should begin with the belief "that every government is run by liars." Taking their cue from Izzy's reading of events in Vietnam and from speeches on the Senate floor by Wayne Morse and Ernest Gruening, SDS's Peace Research and Education Project began to give more attention to events in Indochina. Twenty-five thousand copies of a Morse speech were run off, and the fall PREP newsletter warned that "a full-scale war in Vietnam" lay ahead, which would foreclose the possibility of greater reform in the United States. The SDS paper called for the creation of "a forceful community of protest," but little action was taken prior to the organization's national convention.[26]

At this point, when American intellectuals as a whole had still displayed only sporadic interest in the Vietnam War, Izzy Stone, by contrast, had already written over two score articles and editorials condemning U.S. involvement. The *Weekly* was viewed as perhaps the best source through which one could acquire a critical, yet historically sound, perspective on the conflict.

To the further delight of the SDS leadership, Stone invited "real opposition to the left" of the Johnson administration; indeed, as Sandy Vogelgesang has noted, Izzy was one of "the few on the Intellectual Left" who had not succumbed to the president's early efforts to assuage American intellectuals in the aftermath of Kennedy's assassination. At this stage, Stone's reading of the man who had promised to conduct a war against poverty but was instead waging war, albeit often covertly, in Vietnam was mixed, admittedly. As Lyndon Johnson took over the mantle of government, Stone had proclaimed this vain, thin-skinned, and vindictive "Babbitt" to be "far below JFK in sophisticated breadth and taste"; in contrast, T. R. B.

of *The New Republic* soon remarked, "LBJ isn't JFK. So what?" But Stone also termed the new president a political master who recognized that he had to shift leftward and play up the issue of civil rights. During the debate on the Civil Rights Act of 1964, Stone praised Johnson's stewardship of the legislation and his eloquent call for Americans to leave racial hatred behind them. He spoke of the president's great energy, while proclaiming him to be a "crafty moderate conservative." It was fortunate, Stone wrote in his initial essay in the *New York Review of Books*—the first of his works to get published in a major journal since the early Cold War era—that such an "able and persuasive" southerner was in the White House at this epochal time. As Stone saw it, this "flim-flam" man—a characterization which simply "staggered" coeditor Bob Silvers—just might be able to bring the South around.[27]

Still, Izzy never saw in Johnson the promise of greatness he had once seen in John Kennedy. For one brief shining moment, Kennedy had appeared to him to possess the potential to become a chief executive of the caliber of Franklin Delano Roosevelt. But Stone did not view Lyndon Johnson as being in the same league as his predecessor.

Nevertheless, believing as he did that the candidacy of Arizona Senator Barry Goldwater would "test the country's sanity," Stone opted, like SDS, to go at least "Part of the way with LBJ." He saw the GOP presidential nominee as a reactionary throwback who simplistically viewed communism as a monolithic force and extolled rugged individualism in the manner of the depression-era Liberty Leaguers. Once again, Izzy's essay appeared in the *New York Review*, this time appearing on the front cover.[28]

Johnson's landslide victory Stone saw as a ringing affirmation for racial justice, a considered foreign policy, and the welfare state. And the American people now seemed ready to follow the president's lead, Stone believed, if he but owned up to campaign promises concerning peace and restraint and applied them to Vietnam, China, and Cuba.[29]

In the very same issue of the newsletter that cheered Johnson's electoral triumph, however, a headline read "The Worse the War in Vietnam the Finer the Double-Talk in Washington."[30]

By the end of election month, Stone was again warning that in the eyes of Vietnamese peasants, the United States, not the Vietcong, seemed to be backing "the totalitarian side." On December 7, he declared that Johnson had to decide precisely what his country's objectives were. Did the United States desire a stable world order or a global Pax Americana?[31]

In the December 17 issue of the *New York Review*, Izzy contributed perhaps the first important article on the Southeast Asian crisis, entitled "The Wrong War," to appear in the journal. Izzy's piece was soon reprinted. The following year, the *New York Review* contained additional writings on the Vietnam War by Bernard Fall, Joseph Kraft, Jean Lacouture, Hans Morgenthau, Marcus

Raskin, and Izzy. As *Dissent* later noted, the *New York Review*, at an early stage, provided such individuals with an important forum from which to challenge U.S. policy on the war. Soon it was said that the journal—long seen as colored with "unabated Anglophilia"—should be proclaimed the *London Review of Vietnam*. As American involvement escalated, the *New York Review* often printed scathing pieces on the conflict, a fair number by Stone himself, the man whose writings are credited with having helped to politicize the journal. That was a matter of no small import, given the growing influence of the *New York Review* and its left-directed perspective among the American intelligentsia as the 1960s unfolded. Indeed, Susan Sontag was heard to say at one point that Izzy's writings in the *New York Review* and the *Weekly* were "probably worth more than all the statements put together."[32]

Eventually, Stone would produce scores of articles for the *New York Review*, to the evident delight and occasional chagrin of Bob Silvers, who found editing his work to be "a nightmare" but "great fun" also. Silvers was struck by Izzy's "literary imagination" and by his "ferocious independence," as well as by the inevitable request, "You got some more space, eh?" Izzy, in turn, both valued Silvers's friendship and well appreciated his editorial acumen.[33]

The "literate, witty and often savage criticism" that filled the pages of the *New York Review* suited Izzy well. So too did the circulation of the journal, which reached fifty-four thousand by the middle of the decade; the vast bulk of those readers boasted addresses outside Manhattan, including a good number in academic communities.[34]

The growth of the *New York Review*, like that of the *Weekly*, came to parallel that of the antiwar movement, soon to become a major force in U.S. politics. It also demonstrated a kind of reawakening of at least a portion of the American intelligentsia after the hibernation of the early Cold War years. This was not pleasing to all, particularly those who had championed the disappearance of the left, the intellectuals' accommodation with the National Security State, and U.S. involvement in Third World lands such as Indochina.

I n a holiday season greeting to the readers of his newsletter dated December 21, 1964, Stone proclaimed the battle for peace to be reaching "a crucial stage—Vietnam today." Even he had no idea how telling this statement would prove to be. It was important, he argued, to establish an intellectual foundation for opposition to U.S. policy in Southeast Asia. Consequently, he traveled to New York to deliver his "America and the Third World" address before the national council of SDS, the same talk which led to the call for a spring march on Washington.[35]

While agreeing to attend that gathering, Stone continued to provide intellectual cover for the critics of U.S. policy toward Indochina. After a VC attack on Pleiku was said to have triggered the start of the Rolling Thunder bombing campaign, he warned that in spite of the big guns on its hip, the U.S. military did not do all that well "in the test that matters." American military men were adept at covering over their errors; such incompetence and deceit, he warned, had brought down other great empires.[36]

The U.S. government, Stone asserted, should "stop lying to the people"; so too did *The New Republic,* albeit somewhat more subtly. Stone soon made the same argument in the pages of *The New Republic,* the first contribution he had made to that journal since the late forties. If the truth be told, he indicated, the government in Saigon was an unpopular one, and the Army of the Republic of Vietnam, "cowardly, fearful and incompetent." Its soldiers hoped to force the Americans to do the fighting.[37]

The reprisal strikes that followed, he suggested, seemed to suggest that the fascination with counterinsurgency had just about run its course. But after four years, he declared, the guerrillas were in better shape than they had been at the outset of the Kennedy administration.[38]

On March 1, the newsletter again carried a photograph that the Associated Press had refused to sell to Izzy. In the poignant still, a tearful peasant woman, with child in arms, was seen imploring an ARVN soldier not to torch a village said to be sympathetic to the Vietcong.[39]

Two weeks later, Stone warned, as American combat soldiers landed in Vietnam, "LBJ rushes in where Ike and Kennedy feared to tread." Thus, day by day it appeared as though President Johnson's Vietnam policy was much like that proposed by Senator Goldwater. If this continued, Stone declared, the recent presidential elections would prove to be "one of the greatest frauds" in American political history. With so much concealment and dissembling taking place, *The Nation* wondered if democracy were being safeguarded in Vietnam "by destroying it at home."[40]

Others would soon be delivering similar analyses regarding the president and U.S. actions overseas. But at this still relatively early date, few reporters were doing so, accepting instead the administration's rationale that the heightened American involvement was only a defensive measure.

On March 29, Stone, again a lonely voice among his journalistic colleagues, wondered why all the controversy about employing nonlethal gas in Vietnam. For American forces and ARVN regiments had long dropped napalm on villages, used phosphorus shells, wielded antipersonnel bombs that threw off razorlike fragments, and shot bullets that twisted upon hitting the flesh of both human beings and animals. Moreover, air strikes promised the "application of terror by bombardment." Indeed, American policy seemed to be predicated on the assumption that "fire and death" could be meted out to the whole of Vietnam.[41]

Izzy quoted from one military historian who had acknowledged that "informed civilians have an inescapable duty to speak out.... The most insidious crimes of our time have been those of indifference and silence." When would Americans awaken, Stone asked, and stop "the crimes against humanity" the United States was perpetrating in that distant Southeast Asian nation?[42]

What troubled him most about American involvement in Vietnam was the basic immorality of it all. Yes, he saw U.S. policy as misguided and impolitic, backing as it did the latest crop of third-rate thugs and dictators against a nationalistic and popular uprising. But it was the violation of the fundamental precept of self-determination, the refusal of the American government to allow the Vietnamese people to decide their own destiny, and the tactics employed to that end which disturbed him more than anything.

By the spring of 1965, as indicated by teach-ins held across the country and by the march of twenty thousand people in Washington, more and more Americans were questioning their nation's Vietnam policies. I. F. Stone's "Reply to the White Paper" was a favorite of those who attended rallies from coast to coast. After playing a starring role of sorts at the SDS-sponsored march, he attended a teach-in in Washington. The concerned young participants gave him hope, while the teach-ins seemed to be making democracy real "on the issue where it has counted least and is needed most." It also seemed that the intellectuals were finally doing their part. In late May, Izzy appeared at the University of California at Berkeley before crowds of more than ten thousand at a two-day "Vietnam Day" protest; other speakers included such stars of the antiwar movement as David Dellinger, Staughton Lynd, Norman Mailer, Paul Potter, Bertrand Russell, Mario Savio, Benjamin Spock, and Norman Thomas. Izzy condemned not only U.S. actions in Vietnam but the recent sending of twenty thousand marines to the Dominican Republic to prop up a right-wing regime, an action he likened to the Soviet invasion of Hungary. No one, it was said, received louder applause.[43]

While few took up Stone's call to challenge the administration's Latin American policy, more and more stood on the side of those condemning U.S. practices in Vietnam. But even at this relatively early date, antiwar forces found themselves divided. That had proven to be the case during the march on the Capitol, something Stone expressed concerns about in his newsletter. Shortly after the Washington gathering, he urged peace activists to come together, to cast aside their differences and move to educate the nation about "the dangers." During his lengthy talk at the Berkeley teach-in, he again proclaimed himself to be no revolutionary but rather a liberal only. Although he had read Karl Marx and fancied himself a socialist, Izzy admitted he really did not deserve to be called one. He believed above all else in freedom of thought and considered Jefferson to be a nobler figure than the patron saint of Soviet communism. He saw the nuclear arms race as requiring coexistence; it made peaceful reform necessary as well. He feared the hatred his generation had seen in the form of the concentration camps and crematoria.[44]

On June 28, he again spoke of the peace movement in the newsletter. As Izzy did so, he might have thought back to the fire the *Weekly* had drawn when it had condemned conspiratorial theories—left-wing "demonology," he had put it—regarding the Kennedy assassination. Following a storm of protest letters, Izzy had indicated to Norman Thomas and Dwight Macdonald that he understood why there was so much bloodletting in revolutionary times. "There are just a lot of people around among our own Leftwingers who are full of hate and want something to kill, a devil to murder. You're a hero when you defend them but when you try to be humanly objective about 'the others' they're furious." But this did not trouble him, Izzy declared, for he liked nothing more than a good fight. And by occasionally troubling one's own readers, a publication such as the *Weekly* avoided "becoming a sedate soporific (mixed metaphor!). . . . Otherwise you have escaped the larger prison only to land in theirs."[45]

Now he wrote of the democratic elements within the peace camp that wanted to win others over through persuasion, a second group that sought to give witness in the manner of the Christian martyrs of old, and a third bloc that desired through confrontational tactics to express solidarity with rebels in Southeast Asia and the Caribbean. Only the first, he believed, seemed capable of winning American hearts and minds. The religious sorts did not have a prayer—they could not pull off overnight "what Isaiah, Buddha, Jesus, St. Francis, Tolstoy and Gandhi could not do in 2500 years." The revolutionaries, given the present political atmosphere, could do little more than stand as "*agents provocateurs*," playing into the hands of those who sought a governmental crackdown. Only if a revolutionary situation existed would their tactics make any sense; in an affluent land such as the United States, they could not attract enough supporters "for a *putsch*." And if world peace required that which many of these revolutionaries wanted—an end to capitalism in America—then prospects were certainly not very bright. Such a vision, he insisted, was but "a recipe for holocaust, an apocalyptic Marxist-Leninist version of the old belief in a Second Coming."[46]

Only the first group, Stone repeated, could affect public opinion at home and possibly slow down the American war machine. It would not help matters, he declared, for antiwar forces to add to the hysteria. And for as long as they were able to speak out, it was their duty to do so, using persuasion, not provocation. "We must appeal to kindness and to reason. These, though slim, are our only hope."[47]

The student movement, Stone warned, must not be led off the deep end "by stunt-mongers and suicide tactics." The teach-ins by now had placed the administration on the defensive, while "the wonderful students" taking part in them had accomplished more than one would have thought possible just a short while before. But still more needed to be done and greater emphasis placed on the concept of the brotherhood of man. To that end, Stone acknowledged, religious and revolutionary zealots could join in.[48]

Again Stone recognized the divisions that already beset youthful antiwar adherents. He was impressed not at all with revolutionary or violently charged rhetoric and believed that the movement had to guard against the crazies within its own ranks. Hate-filled fanatics, he believed, would only do damage to the image of the antiwar forces, preventing them from gaining favor with a majority of the American people. He refused to mute his criticisms at this point, perhaps mindful of the mistakes he and other non-Communists radicals had made during the glory days of the Old Left. Perhaps the fact that he had experienced something of what sectarianism and ideological certainty could result in made him more determined not to pull any punches now.

James Aronson, coeditor of the *National Guardian* and an old friend of Izzy's, did not take kindly to his analysis and said as much in the pages of his paper. He dismissed Izzy's depiction of the peace movement as "simplistic" and "loaded," and affirmed that student activists had "neither the time nor the patience for his tendentious reasoning." Some in SDS, which was undergoing a generational shift of sorts, began to believe Izzy was engaging in "quasi red-baiting."[49]

Nevertheless, Izzy remained one of the strongest "resource persons" for the antiwar movement. Articles of his were included in two readers on the Vietnam War published in 1965, one edited by good friends Marcus Raskin (cofounder of the left-wing think tank, the Institute for Policy Studies) and Bernard Fall. Izzy joined in the Fifth Avenue Vietnam Peace Parade to the UN Plaza on October 16 and told a crowd of about thirty thousand—at the time the largest antiwar demonstration this country had yet witnessed—"We do our country more good than a B-52 bombing attack on the people of Vietnam." Positioned in the front row of the marchers, he was struck by an egg, while others were pelted with fists and red paint. He devoted the complete issue of October 25, 1965, to defending antiwar forces against attacks from the center and the right. The "mob-like chorus of the respectable," Stone declared, would not silence "the still small voice of conscience" which opposed this "cruel . . . barbarous . . . immoral and . . . illegal war." Which was the greater act of patriotism? he asked. "To run with the pack? Or to urge at some personal risk what one believes the wiser course for one's country?" He applauded the November 27 peace march on Washington, particularly the devoted youngsters involved in both the civil rights and antiwar struggles. But he warned that political squabbles wasted energy that could be better spent in planning for still greater demonstrations.[50]

He worried, at the same time, about governmental actions that would only further alienate the activist young. He condemned the announcement in the fall of 1965 by Attorney General Nicholas Katzenbach that an investigation of the draft resistance movement was about to begin. Given the determination of true believers to bear witness, Stone suggested facetiously, it might make sense to "get rid of Christ and Constitution."[51]

It was foolish indeed, he argued with considerable foresight, to do battle with the idealistic young, with those who could not help but see the fight for civil rights in the American South and the rebellion in Vietnam as one and the same—the battle by "colored races" to throw off the chains that had long held them down. He called for a careful reading of SDS's "Build, Not Burn" strategy and SNCC's decision to stand alongside draft resisters. The "rebel minority" that refused to burn villages and sought to build them instead, Stone proclaimed "the seed corn of a better future." It made no sense at all, he continued, for the government to antagonize "the best youngsters of our time."[52]

Those same young rebels, of course, were soon to become more and more disenchanted with the practices and policies of the Johnson administration, as Stone had suggested they inevitably would. As the degree of their alienation deepened and expanded, as proponents of reform began to call for resistance and then revolution, Izzy watched in dismay and anguish.

But as 1965, the year of the great American escalation in Vietnam, neared its end, Izzy Stone's influence among antiwar cadre was still growing. More surprisingly, establishment figures, including members of the White House inner circle itself, were coming to regard Stone as someone who could not be ignored. In late November 1965, the president's social secretary invited Izzy, along with fellow journalists James Bishop and Hobart Rowen, among others, to attend a reception to be held at the White House. On January 4, 1966, Jack Valenti of the presidential staff sent a curious memo President Johnson's way. Valenti had recently spoken with Bernard Eisman of ABC News, who, it turned out, had been informed by Stone how "very grateful" he was that Johnson was in the White House; Izzy had purportedly indicated that LBJ was "the only man who is strong enough and with enough support of all the people to get away with a truce in Vietnam."[53]

The Johnson administration, however, continued to preside over a dramatic escalation of the war in Indochina. There were 25,000 bombing sorties carried out against North Vietnam in 1965; 79,000 in 1966; 108,000 in 1967. The number of American military personnel in Vietnam stood at 184,000 at the end of the first full year of Johnson's war; 385,000 one year later; 486,000 another year down the road. U.S. combat deaths mushroomed as well, from 1,369 to 5,008 to 9,378.

The United States would pay dearly, Stone warned on December 13, 1965, in a remarkable essay, for the devastation it was wreaking overseas. The Korean War had allowed McCarthyism to flourish, he noted, setting back the quest for domestic reform for a full generation; the Vietnam War, he pointed out, would have the same results. The economic costs of the Vietnam conflict were already becoming evident with inflation appearing and a curtailing of Great Society programs certain to follow. As military spending gobbled up more and more of the budget, as less money was available for urban renewal and public housing, "race war" might well break out at home. At the very least, great new problems were being spawned, involving pollution of air and water, exhaustion of the soil, and the appearance of "a youth of desperate savagery" growing up in urban slums. The war, Stone wrote, transformed the political atmosphere at home against the forces of change. This, he stated, was "the price, the retribution, for the cruelty we impose with such complacency on a distant and helpless people."[54]

As matters turned out of course, the costs of the Vietnam War were enormous. Lyndon Johnson's War on Poverty was aborted and the Great Society stillborn; the American nation began to head rightward, leaving behind the reform impulse of the early and mid-sixties; racial strife continued to erupt; environmental decay proceeded to accelerate; and angry, embittered youth-led gangs sprang up in urban centers across the land.

For now, the great urban riots of 1966 suggested to Stone that the bill was indeed coming due; yet he found some hope in the forty-odd explosions that had erupted in the mean streets of America. The riots indicated "that the poor are no longer poor in spirit." But they also demonstrated that not much time remained. Either the promise of equality would bear fruit, or the nation would itself be torn apart.[55]

Stone viewed the call for black power in much the same light. The advent of black nationalism in the civil rights camp he considered to be inevitable; furthermore, he believed, like the latest crop of SNCC leaders, that the long-term tasks of achieving economic and social equality would have to be undertaken by blacks themselves. These were "not tasks for a summer adventure in between classes." Black civil rights activists, naturally recoiling from the latest rendition of "the White Man's Burden," recognized that they must battle for their rights.[56]

"Not black power or white," he affirmed, would save the planet. But without prodding from extremists, the reconstruction of the United States would not be carried out. Still, the rekindling of a sense of community would in no way be possible as long as this nation waged "a white man's war in Asia while a black man's revolt rises at home."[57]

In the midst of the terrible riots in Newark and Detroit the following summer, Stone worried that "a racial revolt" threatened to break out. The nation's energy and resources, he exclaimed, should be drawn to "the Negro rising," not wasted away in Vietnam. As federal troops rushed into the Motor City, he indicated that a religious sort well might recognize the presence of divine handiwork, a Godlike tit-for-tat, a bringing home of just a bit of what the United States was itself doling out on a daily basis abroad. This "seventh of our successive hot summers" appeared as "the black spiral cloud of an oncoming tornado that is beginning to tear our country apart." And yet old comfortable "self-delusions" continued to be heard at the White House and in Congress.[58]

Delusions of another sort continued to guide U.S. policymakers, who seemed to believe that upping the ante—particularly by way of bombing raids—would eventually compel Ho Chi Minh to cry "Uncle." But the delusions that had come to naught in Korea, Stone wrote, would prove no more effective in Vietnam. He found it appalling that "a once flaming faith has become a faith in napalm" and warned that the escalation of the war imperiled all of Vietnam, "North and South, including the innocent and the friendly." Washington's belief in body counts suggested that the VC were seen "not as men but as a kind of vermin to be exterminated" in a kind of "rat-killing campaign." The United States was engaged in a policy not of pacification, Stone insisted, but rather of "genocide."[59]

It was his belief that war crimes had been taking place that lent such an emotional edge to his analyses of U.S. policies in Vietnam. And it was the passionate nature of his editorials and speeches on the war that caused his critiques to resonate so fully with the growing number of Americans opposed to U.S. involvement.

Vietnam, they heard him say, was "a training ground for the Legions of the Pax Americana." If the American military did quash the Vietnamese insurgency, he warned, similar treatment was in store for subject peoples wherever U.S. interests were endangered. This was something the boys at the Pentagon seemed to fantasize about. "Like Trotskyists in reverse," they "dream of permanent revolution requiring permanent agencies of suppression."[60]

But still more was involved, Stone charged, in the American war effort. Everything the United States supposedly stood for was being called into question. "It is the Machine, it is the prestige of the machine, that is at stake in Vietnam. It is Boeing and General Electric and Goodyear and General

Dynamics. It is the electronic range-finder and the amphibious truck and the night-piercing radar. It is the defoliant, and the herbicide, and the deodorant, and the depilatory." It was the very belief that there existed a technological solution for every problem, consequently, that was being so sorely tested by "those uncouth guerrillas," clad in their black pajamas.[61]

Because American policymakers had so much invested in Vietnam, politically, psychologically, and emotionally, Stone believed that they were not about to change course easily. Therefore, a great deal more death and destruction, more damage to his country's very soul, was likely to be forthcoming, he feared.

And the guerrilla insurgency was not about to go away, Stone believed, for U.S. strategists refused to address the fundamental problem in Indochina, the large number of landless peasants. The idea of genuine land reform, he argued, seemingly never crossed the minds of U.S. officials assigned to bring about pacification in the Vietnamese countryside. It seemed as though they would "do anything for the peasant but get off his back." But as he later asked in the midst of a public talk, "How do you win a war in a peasant country on the side of the landlord?" To him it was "so goddamned obvious."[62]

As always, the lines were clearly drawn for Stone where Vietnam was involved. He saw this both as a guerrilla war and an anticolonial fight in which his nation had thrown in with unpopular elites. Thus, morally as well as pragmatically, the United States had again lined up on the wrong side.

In the late spring of 1966, I. F. Stone finally visited Vietnam for the first and only time. Much to his dismay, his initial write-up of his Vietnam venture simply was not up to par, as both he and his aide, Peter Osnos, quickly recognized. But Bob Silvers of the *New York Review of Books* viewed his finished product as "brilliant." As Stone acknowledged in a series of four reports, he had no grand revelations to make. The heat, squalor, and despair of Saigon impressed him, as did the cleanliness and tranquillity of Phnom Penh. He recognized that both the South Vietnamese government and army could collapse at any moment, while Prince Sihanouk seemed as popular as ever. He was struck by how widespread opposition to the war was, but also by the antagonism to foreign soldiers of any kind. He happily reported that only courtesy came his way from American officers or civilians, but wondered "how so many well-meaning, friendly and intelligent people" could get it all wrong. What he saw were Americans dwelling "in enclaves—not just military but psychological" ones too. Moreover, in spite of lofty platitudes, considerable animosity toward the Vietnamese was all too obvious, as was the American hubris. "We assume the right to remold them, whether they choose to be remolded or not." Moreover, out in the field, sleep deprivation and terrorism—which could result in everything from acts of incivility to the torching of villages—culminated in hatred and great resentment.[63]

It was his analysis of the full implications of the Vietnam War, of course, that helped to restore I. F. Stone to the ranks of the somewhat politically respectable. His scathing critiques of the domestic and international repercussions of U.S. policy in Vietnam made Stone a figure of some influence in intellectual, journalistic, and antiwar encampments, at the very least. And for the first time in nearly two decades, his name and his articles were considered to carry a certain weight beyond the ranks of the American left. Even those such as Senate Foreign Relations Chairman J. William Fulbright, who was on the receiving end of three biting essays by Stone that appeared in successive issues of the *New York Review of Books*, were coming to accept at least something of his perspective on the war in Indochina. Furthermore, soon Fulbright and others on Capitol Hill were sprinkling their speeches on Vietnam with references to Izzy and the newsletter.[64]

This was quite a turnaround from the times when government officials had quite consciously avoided him, so that they might escape the stigma associated with one considered to be among the journalistic and politically disreputable, although there would always be those who so viewed him. But generally, this was a period when Izzy's anti-imperialist perspective and devoted commitment to the antiwar cause enabled him to begin to acquire the kind of reputation and following he had once only dreamed about. In fact, his insightful and caustic analyses of the latest age of unreason in the United States led some to begin to compare him with the biblical prophets, in addition to his nation's own.

At the very least, he had demonstrated how commitment, ideology, and his own particular journalistic approach could fruitfully, even valiantly, intersect. He had shown how the journalist could use investigative skills; the intellectual, political activism; and the lone actor, his own maverick qualities, to challenge the supposed certainties of both governmental policies and the movement to which he belonged.

15 From Pariah to Character to National Institution

For ten months, beginning in the summer of 1965, Peter Osnos served as I. F. Stone's hundred-dollar-a-week editorial assistant. Osnos, a fledging reporter at the time, was a reader and fan of the *Weekly* but also a very green twenty-two-year-old who found himself working day and night for a throughly demanding taskmaster. Izzy, with his intolerance for incompetence, was "one of the most difficult persons" imaginable to work for. Although never uncivil in any way to young Osnos, he easily grew impatient and "would lose interest if you were no good." Osnos pushed himself, working terribly hard, trying to maintain the punishing pace set by his boss, nearly sixty years old now.[1]

By 7:30 A.M., Izzy—having already sifted through the pages of the *New York Times*, the *Washington Post*, the *Wall Street Journal*, the *New York Herald Tribune*, and the *Baltimore Sun*—would be on the phone, asking if his young aide had spotted "the item on Z-12" which proved that J. Edgar Hoover really was as big a fool as he had suspected all along. If Osnos had been fortunate enough to have come across the piece, his day was made; if not, depression was sure to set in. Regardless, he was on the go until the early morning hours; only at that point would he nod off, a stack of *Congressional Records* tucked under his chin. Indexing the *Record* was one of Osnos's assignments, but no mattter how hard he tried, he never could master it as Izzy did. His boss would rifle through those volumes, as he did stacks of newspapers, magazines, and journals, and discover "these jewels" that everyone else had overlooked. Making "ten mental notes a minute," Izzy seemed to miss nothing. Moreover, he had an incredible memory, recalling the smallest details from years back.[2]

Izzy worked out of his home in the northwest sector of the capital. Reference books, including the invaluable *Facts on File* and volumes of the *U.S. Reports*, filled room after room. He pounded away on his old typewriter in rapid-fire fashion, often composing while he typed. If the need arose, he would follow up on leads by making any number of telephone calls or by heading downtown to scour official transcripts on Capitol Hill. Washington, D.C., was the best place a journalist could possibly work, as he told Osnos on more than one occasion, for "there was a story on every leaf of every branch of every tree."[3]

Beginning in 1961, Izzy had regularly set out from his house by foot, a two-and-a-half-mile walk ahead of him; tucked safely under his arm was his ever-present accordion file, the repository of memos, scraps of papers with pertinent information, and notes to himself he would make along the way. Typically, he would stop off at the State Department and the Pentagon, obtain the daily press releases, and query the clerks, "Got anything sensational today?" Occasionally, he would drop in to attend public hearings, official briefings, or press conferences. He was able to do so because of a pair of recent operations that had restored his hearing and enabled him to get about without "my Sonotone." By midafternoon, he would stop in at Nash's Newsstand to check out periodicals from the European press. For a time during the McCarthy era, it had seemed as though the proprietor there was the only one in Washington willing to talk with him. By 1965, however, Izzy had been befriended by men such as Bernard Fall, the French journalist-scholar of the Indochina wars; Larry Fernsworth of the *New York Times*, and Larry Stern of the *Washington Post*.[4]

While impressed by Izzy's work ethic, Peter Osnos found even more revealing his continued sense of outrage. After all these years, Izzy was still horrified by the latest example of government perfidy. It was that very sense of outrage, Marcus Raskin of the Institute for Policy Studies recognized, that appealed to the generation coming of age in the decade of the 1960s. Some of the best and the brightest of that generation came to consider Izzy as "a beacon" and his use of both facts and moral outrage a means to resist, particularly the Indochinese policies of the Kennedy-Johnson administrations. Posing like the academic he had once thought of becoming, he taught that the American mission in Vietnam was only a "cover story for imperial arrogance." But he emphasized that so long as protest was possible, protest Americans must—"protest, not provoke." This he believed to be the nation's only hope.[5]

As Vietnam came to monopolize the public agenda, Stone and the *Weekly* acquired a certain stature among both critics of U.S. policy and members of the establishment itself. At last, his "genius and incredibly hard work" began to pay off, in Osnos's estimation, as the subscription totals of the *Weekly* escalated dramatically, passing the twenty-seven-thousand mark by October 1966. As Osnos later recognized, its influence was much greater still because of those who read it: the politically committed, the very best journalists, and members of the university academy. Moreover, the man and the moment now were at the cutting edge as never before. Consequently, "an urgency . . . excitement . . . and exuberance" could be felt all about him. The transformed atmosphere could be seen by the spring of 1966, when, in an act of great symbolic importance for the tightly knit Washington community, Walter Lippmann, the icon of establishment journalism, invited Izzy and Esther Stone to his annual garden party. The two old reporters had recently exchanged pleasantries at a dinner engagement given by Bernard Fall, a mutual friend.[6]

During this period, not everyone, of course, felt about Izzy as Lippmann now did. Shortly after the *New York Review* published an essay of Stone's on David Halberstam and Malcolm Browne, two of the "young Turks" critical of administration policy in Vietnam, the editors of the journal discovered Richard Goodwin to be on the line. Goodwin, a former Kennedy aide and now a top adviser to President Johnson, acknowledged that Izzy was a decent enough fellow; but why not ask someone such as Joseph Alsop, Goodwin suggested, to review the next works on Vietnam to come the journal's way? About the same time, Richard Dudman, Washington bureau chief for the *St. Louis Post-Dispatch*, attempted to get Izzy admitted to the Overseas Writers, which was made up for the most part of correspondents who covered the State Department. Marvin Kalb, the organization's president, was supportive, but a pair of reporters raised questions about Izzy's "past." Dudman informed his friend, who appeared both hurt and disgusted, about the holdup. "Dave," Izzy sighed, "I just feel as if I stepped in a great big pile of horseshit."[7]

Nevertheless, it was during this period that the strength of Izzy Stone's personality and character, like that of Upton Sinclair's and H. L. Mencken's in earlier times, came to define journalism of a particular type, as Peter Osnos has put it, journalism of the personal, investigative kind. Izzy himself began to acquire "enormous importance and influence in a period when it was important that he be there as a crusading voice on the left." Clearly recognizing the growing impact the *Weekly* was having, Izzy and his work possessed the charged energy of the era.[8]

Happily for Stone, then, his commitment to antiwar and anti-imperialistic ideals and his personal makeup combined now to make him a leading figure in journalistic, intellectual, and left-of-center circles. His voice was heeded by his fellow journalists who admired his investigative skills, reportorial acumen, and editorial genius; by other intellectuals who respected his willingness to take a stand; and by activists in the movement who appreciated his lifelong devotion to "the cause" and his scathing analyses of U.S. domestic and foreign policies which they saw as matching their own.

By early 1967, however, Izzy was feeling worn out. In response to a pair of questions posed to him and some three hundred other writers concerning their attitudes on American intervention in Vietnam and how the war might be ended, he responded only "Against" and "Negotiate with the NLF," the National Liberation Front, the guerrilla fighting force doing battle with the government in power in Saigon. His friends and colleagues Paul Goodman and Nat Hentoff replied more fully in the manner Izzy had before and would again, condemning the criminality of U.S. involvement, calling for war reparations, and demanding "an end to the killing." In April, Izzy felt compelled to suspend publication of the *Weekly* temporarily, informing his readers that he was simply exhausted. Nevertheless, he urged them to back the Spring Mobilization to End the War in Vietnam. The final gathering of the Spring Mobe, which he attended, did not lift his spirits any. Much to his dismay, he discovered "Lilliputian all-night caucuses of far-out Leftists and far-out Black Nationalists" speaking past one another. Most ominously, he witnessed the contempt of black militants for their white allies. This, Izzy charged, was a good way to destroy the antiwar movement. And this, he warned, was "how agents provocateur operate."[9]

Those opposed to the war, he argued, had to make up their minds. Did they want to reach the American people or alienate them more and more? Those advocating racial strife and revolution, he insisted, should leave the peace movement immediately. "We are not going to sell peace by spreading hate and hysteria."[10]

Increasingly, Stone noted, parallels were being drawn between the Germany of the thirties and the United States of the present day. But the clearest point of convergence was conveniently overlooked: Nazism had triumphed precisely because of left divisions. To anger middle-class moderates or cause them to feel impotent and then to fill the air "with extremist hot air and riot," Stone charged, was the surest way to bring about "a Fascist-style repression." Because of such analyses, Izzy began to be seen by some in the SDS camp as "just a wimpy liberal."[11]

But Izzy's warnings about sectarianism and hate-filled rhetoric crippling the antiwar movement were characteristically on target. As calls for resistance and revolution could be heard frequently, greater fissures could be seen among New Left and peace forces. This troubled Izzy, who unhappily recalled the internecine battles of the Old Left, which had resulted in that earlier movement first fracturing and then falling apart. Believing that the United States required dissident voices more than ever, he worried what the internal rifts might result in.

Despite his reservations, Stone continued to view the antiwar activists as "the prescient" few who foresaw what lay ahead and attempted "to raise the alarm." For that, he acknowledged, they deserved to be praised. But he felt compelled to urge them to behave more intelligently.[12]

Once again, an old friend of Izzy's immediately took him to task. Otto Nathan, the literary executor of Albert Einstein's estate, claimed Izzy's story on the Spring Mobe was "regrettably inaccurate" and one that did the peace movement a grave disservice.[13]

Nevertheless, Izzy's ties to the New Left only continued to strengthen. In one case at least, familial connections played a part. In the summer of 1967, shortly following the Six-Day War, an article of his, "The Future of Israel," appeared in *Ramparts*, the San Francisco–based magazine that was becoming ever more influential among American intellectuals in general and the movement in particular. His sister Judy had become a staff writer for *Ramparts* back in March 1965, when the publication was still something of a liberal monthly. His brother Marc presently served as promotion director and later became a member of the board of directors, associate publisher, and in January 1970, publisher—for a brief spell—of that leading New Left journal.[14]

O n August 7, Izzy underwent an operation at Manhattan's Eye, Ear, and Throat Hospital because of a detached retina in his left eye. Two days later, he appeared to suffer a mild heart attack. But for a full half-day, no cardiac team came to check on Izzy, much to the dismay of Chris Stone and his wife, Ann, the first family members to visit the ailing patriarch. Chris, by then a law professor at the University of Southern California, decided to contact the chief cardiologist at New York University Medical Center.

After being transferred to the NYU hospital, Izzy, whether afflicted with a heart ailment or not, "acted out his death." He quoted from Homer and other great artists and engaged in a kind of "dress rehearsal for his death." He felt his mortality as perhaps he had not heretofore, and seemed to come to the determination that the work he had already accomplished was lacking in some way. Recognizing that he had a limited amount of time before him, he began to consider the possibility of producing a magnum opus, a tome which might stand as his greatest accomplishment. Indeed he wanted to leave behind "a contribution to Western thought."[16]

But for now, the zeitgeist of the times continued to demand that Izzy remain involved in the movement to bring an end to the war in Vietnam and an abolition of racial injustice in the United States. For the remainder of the month, however, he was compelled to remain at NYU for rest and observation. Moreover, his doctors ordered him to temporarily suspend the operations of the newsletter. As part of his recuperation, Izzy and Esther set sail for Europe in September aboard the *SS France*. After a week in London and another in Paris, where Izzy was treated as a visiting dignitary, they boarded the ship for the voyage back to the States. On November 13, he once again started up the newsletter—soon to become a biweekly for a second and final time—and expressed appreciation for the hundreds of get-well cards he had been sent. His friend Norman Thomas was one of those who had written, insisting that Izzy was "desperately" needed. In the following week's issue, Izzy inscribed a note to his readers, declaring it to be more satisfying to have returned to Washington "at the center of the storm, and to feel that exhilaration of taking some small part," no matter that the odds remained stacked against his side. He returned more convinced than ever that the very finest young people, both white and black, were striving to remain true to America's noblest traditions. "It is for the seeing and anguished handful," he now wrote, to liberate humankind from the terrible triad of hatred, racism, and war. What "could be more wonderful than to live and do one's duty at such a time?"[17]

It was during this period that Izzy took particular interest in the Liberation News Service, which had been formed in the fall of 1967; he occasionally lunched with staff members such as Raymond Mungo and Marshall Bloom, then based in the nation's capital. They in turn viewed Stone and the *Weekly* as models for the underground publications they had established a syndicate for. They also listened to Izzy's admonition that LNS remain independent from SDS and not become anyone's "mouthpiece."[18]

The *Weekly*, in its own way, like the *New York Review*, where Izzy's longer pieces were increasingly appearing, was providing an intellectual bridge between the peace movement and "left liberalism." The *New York Review* during this period was veering ever leftward, providing a forum for ideas of a New Left flavor. The year 1967 witnessed the publication in the journal of the last of Stone's three-part study of J. William Fulbright, chairman of the Senate Foreign Relations Committee, whom Izzy painted as part of "the timid opposition." It also saw Noam Chomsky's "The Responsibility of Intellectuals," a bitter condemnation of establishment liberals, appear in print. Most notorious of all, of course, was Andrew Kopkind's "Soul Power," which declared that "morality, like politics, starts at the barrel of a gun"; Kopkind's enormously controversial essay and one by Tom Hayden, entitled "The Occupation of Newark," were advertised by a front cover complete with molotov cocktail.[19]

Within a short while, Walter Goodman was to assert that the *New York Review* had adopted the voice of the "cocktail-party revolutionary" with its Vietnam essays, hurling great blame at the feet of "the American Liberal Establishment." This was "the *Ramparts* line," Goodman declared, "hung out in a more sophisticated environment." Nevertheless, "no party line," he acknowledged, ruled the pages of the prestigious publication. Its political essayists were a diverse lot, separated by both temperament and the matter of sheer competence. The reports of Izzy Stone, for example, Goodman termed "usually informed and informative."[20]

In 1967, the subscription total of the *New York Review* moved past the 75,000 mark, while the *Weekly*, as the November 20 issue indicated, now boasted 32,053 subscribers of its own. In that same issue, Izzy also announced the publication of *In a Time of Torment*, a collection of his essays culled from the journal and from the newsletter. As critiques came in, it was apparent that Izzy was a pariah no longer, as he was lauded for his "tremendous" one-man journalistic feats, proclaimed to be "in a class by himself," called "a great essayist" and reporter, adjudged a "watchdog in a time when most of his colleagues bark rarely and bite not at all," saluted as "the master debunker of the ponderous platitude and the gilded lie," and termed an "indomitable radical" who had become "virtually indispensable." Later reviews were replete with even greater accolades. The *London Times Literary Supplement* cast him as "an American Diogenes" who had never been fooled "by the conventional wisdom" or intimidated and as "a prophet who dared to be a Jeremiah and who has never prophesied smooth things to Jew or Gentile, Black or White." Writing in the *New York Review*, Henry Steele Commager, one of the nation's most distinguished historians, went all reviewers one better in portraying Izzy as "a modern Tom Paine, celebrating Common Sense and the Rights of Man, hammering away at tyranny, injustice, exploitation, deception, and chicanery with an eloquence that appeals even to the sophisticated who are most suspicious of eloquence." Commager placed Izzy in the muckraking tradition and very much "in the American grain," along with Paine, William Lloyd Garrison, Upton Sinclair, Lincoln Steffens, and A. J. Muste—"crusaders all."[21]

By the time Commager's essay appeared in print at the end of 1968, the *Weekly*'s subscription figures approached thirty-eight thousand and the *New York Times* included a feature story on I. F. Stone, respectfully drawn, naturally. No longer was he referred to in the manner Gilbert Harrison, editor of *The New Republic*, had a short while earlier: as "poor Izzy," a not very popular journalistic lone ranger of sorts given to lost causes.[22]

Rather, more and more of his colleagues were inclined to view Izzy in the manner cartoonist David Levine did. In a sketch accompanying the Commager essay in the *New York Review*, Levine portrayed a bow-tied, dapper, dimpled, jowly, large-nosed, puffy-faced Izzy, complete with thick, horned-rimmed glasses, rolled-up sleeves, substantial ears, bushy eyebrows, and disheveled hair, towering over the Capitol dome. One hand tilting it; the other, a shovel with the imprint of the newsletter, about to unearth a treasure trove of congressionally brewed trouble.[23]

Reflecting on his increased popularity, Izzy told an interviewer that now, all of a sudden, he could boast of a retirement fund. He had proven, by the very success of the *Weekly*, that free enterprise did indeed thrive in the United States. "You can sell anything." Thanks to his newfound affluence, the Stones were soon able to move to a larger house at 4420 29th Street NW in Washington, just a matter of blocks away from their home of the past quarter-century. Three rooms upstairs served as offices for the newsletter— Izzy's own, his editorial assistant's, and one for special projects—while the basement housed yellowed newspapers along with his clipping files.[24]

The reason for Izzy's greater appeal was not hard to figure. Time after time, his scathing analyses of American policies at home and abroad seemed to be more than insightful; they appeared to have a prophetic ring to them. In his inimitable way—by turns crusty or poetic but always impassioned—he appreciated as did few others the full ramifications of U.S. governmental actions in Vietnamese towns, villages, and jungles and upon American campuses and inner cities. He continued to recognize what the Vietnam conflict and the waning of the War on Poverty were costing his own country in political, economic, psychological, and moral terms.

White House and Pentagon officials maintained, throughout this period, as they had all along, that light could be seen at the end of the tunnel in Vietnam. Then came the Tet Offensive of January 1968, as National Liberation Front and North Vietnamese regular army units poured into cities and towns across South Vietnam, including Saigon and Hue, the old imperial capital. While the Vietcong and their northern allies met with heavy casualties, Tet proved to be a public relations disaster back home. President Johnson and General William Westmoreland, commander of U.S. forces in Vietnam, had just completed a public relations campaign concerning how well the war was going. Now, on television screens in the United States came scenes of VC cadre on the grounds of the American embassy in Saigon, heavy street-fighting, and a guerrilla suspect having his brains blown out by a South Vietnamese government official.

Many of the warnings Izzy and the antiwar movement had been delivering throughout the earlier stages of heightened American involvement now had been borne out. Consequently, Tet changed hearts and minds in the United States, as disillusionment with Johnson's Vietnam policy mounted. This seemingly transformed the American political scene overnight and converted the movement and movement stalwarts like Izzy Stone into public figures.

In late 1967, he had expressed concerns that the impending campaign threatened to become "America's Tragedy." He worried that peace and civil right activists would necessarily be disappointed by what the ballot box held in store; that in turn, he feared, would only further alienate the most sensitive sorts at home and feed "fantasy and hysteria, wild talk of guerrilla war" and the division of his country "into two nations, one white one black."

Never had there existed a greater need, he suggested, for the political process to be made effective and faith in the likelihood of peaceful reform sustained; but never had this appeared less likely.[25]

Izzy's closeness to old SDSers, the Liberation News Service crowd, and others involved in the antiwar campaign enabled him to recognize what many in the peace movement were now experiencing. He saw the frustration mounting, the anger brewing, and both threatening to spill over. Increasingly, he felt some of the same himself.

Where was Robert Kennedy, now a junior senator from the state of New York? Stone asked, as he had for some time. Worrying about his political future, he answered. And what about Eugene McCarthy? Stone wondered, three days before the Minnesota senator declared his candidacy. In the meantime, he proclaimed support for the "Dump Johnson" movement and promised to back McCarthy if he but chose to run.[26]

When McCarthy tossed his hat in the political ring, Stone acknowledged misgivings about the candidate's lack of passion. While McCarthy obviously was witty and charming, the poet-politician made one feel "that he doesn't really give a damn." But to get young people out of the streets, he insisted, McCarthy was going to have to stop behaving like "a graceful patsy." So while Izzy agreed to "enlist in McCarthy's army," he promised "to keep stirring up mutiny until the General stops yawning."[27]

All the while, throughout the late fall of 1967, Stone had continued to sound Jeremiah-like warnings regarding U.S. policy in Vietnam. What was demanded of the Vietcong, he noted, was their surrender. Then, a mere month before Tet, the bloody battle in the Central Highlands for Hill 875 suggested to Stone how foolish Westmoreland's proclamation that the end of the war approached really was. It appeared that Westmoreland was simply waging a war of attrition. Yet the battle for Hill 875 was merely "attrition in reverse." Stone warned that this only played into General Vo Nguyen Giap's hands, as did the fact that U.S. combat forces in Vietnam were spread so thin and thus susceptible to guerrilla incursions.[28]

The VC-North Vietnamese Army assault that began on the morning of January 30 certainly indicated that such was the case. For Stone, the Tet Offensive proved "the mendacity of our leaders and the incompetency of our military." Two incidents in particular stood out for him as symptomatic of America's Vietnam story. The first involved the justification of the shelling of Bentre by an American military officer, amid heavy civilian casualties: "It became necessary to destroy the town to save it." Such "scorched-earth tactics," inflicted upon another people's country, Stone declared, were "brutal and cowardly."[29]

The second event occurred in Khe Sanh, where American soldiers refused to admit both civilian refugees and their South Vietnamese comrades.

The truth, Stone asserted, "is that when the chips are down we feel that the 'gooks' . . . are expendable."[30]

The seeming lack of concern for Vietnamese lives thoroughly appalled him. The hubris, the arrogance, the conceit, the ethnocentrism, and the racism that this attitude suggested sickened him and indicated to Izzy how far the United States had moved from the ideals of its founders and how desperately needed the antiwar movement was.

For it was not only Vietnam and the Vietnamese, Stone feared, that were being torn apart. A week before Tet, he worried that heightened repression at home and war overseas imperiled the social fabric of his own nation. He discussed the indictment of Benjamin Spock, William Sloane Coffin, Marcus Raskin, Mitchell Goodman, and Michael Ferber for purportedly having conspired to bring about refusal of Selective Service edicts. As time passed, Stone reported, Spock and his coconspirators would soon appear "like the true patriots." This *was*, after all, "an immoral and an unjust and a wickedly foolish war." Only hubris and concern about face kept the Big Fool in the Deep Muddy. Those who demanded the withdrawal of all U.S. forces, Stone wrote, were carrying out "a sacred duty to our country and to mankind."[31]

Like so many in the movement, Izzy had seemingly moved beyond a call for reform to a cry for resistance. The voracious military machine and imperialistic policies of the United States had to be confronted, he believed. How this was to be accomplished, he, like so many others, was uncertain of. But both the so-called New Politics represented by the McCarthy campaign and the tactics of the Resistance, he had now come to believe, were necessary.

Unless this nation followed the lead of the antidraft Resistance, Stone warned, civil war might break out here too. What was needed, he wrote on March 18—two days following Robert Kennedy's entrance into the presidential race—was a new crusade throughout the land that would appeal to white Americans and stir "the angels of their better natures."[32]

Speaking of RFK's change of mind, Izzy acknowledged that he too was not all that thrilled about Bobby's attempt to steal the political thunder from the Clean for Gene crowd. And yet, he wrote, political realities had to be considered. Kennedy might be "arrogant and power-hungry" and perhaps was advised by the same clique of "opportunist-intellectuals" who had advised his brother Jack on Vietnam. But only Bobby was wealthy enough and carried the political muscle that could prevent the renomination of Lyndon Baines Johnson.[33]

In the period ahead, as President Johnson opted to withdraw from the race and the American apostle of nonviolence was gunned down on a Memphis motel balcony, it appeared that the junior senator from New York alone might be able to prevent this nation from coming apart. Following the outbreak of riots nationwide in the wake of the murder of Martin Luther King,

Jr., Stone feared that "the fire has only just begun." Although he had on occasion been critical of King, Stone now declared that the slain minister had "stood in that line of saints which goes back from Gandhi to Jesus." But while white racists undoubtedly had a hand in his death, Stone wrote, black militants who despised his pacifism were now using the occasion to foment that which he had always fought against. "Thus all sides firmly united in paying him homage."[34]

Still, the racial unrest that resulted in tens of thousands of troops being called out suggested "the agony of a lost race speaking." If no adequate response were forthcoming, Stone indicated, the "decline and fall" of the United States was sure to follow.[35]

Stone saw the possibility of a domestic racial war as tied to the conflict in Vietnam. The expending of vital resources, energy, and political goodwill on the Indochinese affair ensured that the battle to bring about racial justice at home would be given short shrift. That in turn, he believed, could only exacerbate the tendencies within a certain section of the black community toward greater distrust, decay, and disillusionment.

The shooting of Senator Kennedy, another of the great reform leaders of the era, in the early morning of June 6 following his victory in the California presidential primary, caused Stone to express sympathy to Ethel Kennedy and her children. He also spoke once again of how organized violence in the United States was simply taken for granted. The gunning down of one man still shocked the nation, he wrote, while the ability to murder millions was a commonly accepted reality. The nation's annual military budget was now set at eighty billion dollars, the purpose of which was "to kill, maim, poison, burn and asphyxiate other human beings at will." The fittest young people, the brightest scientists, and mammoth corporations were all involved in the killing machine. "We live in a human abattoir," Stone wrote, "but our nostrils are so conditioned to the stink that we no longer notice it." Nevertheless, "that man who just fell into a ditch in South Vietnam with his guts torn out by a bullet from an American helicopter also had children, perhaps ambitions, certainly some spark of that wonder we call a soul."[36]

Stone now called for the backing of McCarthy and the antiwar movement to the hilt, to honor "Bobby's last brave stand." For if a Humphrey-Nixon contest proved to be in the cards for November, he warned, "the nihilistic anger" would undoubtedly worsen. Only McCarthy's candidacy provided an alternative; thus the senator himself might be the country's last hope for peace on the home front. And if the antiwar candidate did not prevail, Stone declared, dangerous developments might. The prosecution of the so-called Boston Five, Spock and his codefendants, could serve as the start of a move to break the peace movement.[37]

As a guilty sentence was handed down against Spock, Coffin, Goodman, and Ferber—only his friend Raskin was declared innocent—Stone argued that if their opposition to the draft were criminal, then there were hardly enough jails to house their fellow coconspirators, who by now counted Izzy among their ranks. While the presiding judge proclaimed their action to be treason, Stone declared that the treason was the government's.[38]

On August 19, one week before the start of the Democratic National Convention to be held in Chicago, Stone again called for an end to the bombing raids, the nomination of Senator McCarthy, and genuine negotiations with the other side. The only chance for a Democratic victory in November, he insisted, involved the joining of party forces, blacks, the alienated young, and peace activists. Should the Republican ticket of Richard Nixon and Spiro Agnew prevail instead, he declared, the nation would continue on the downward spiral to repression, war between the races, and a tearing apart of the political system. The Nixon-Agnew campaign plan called for an appeal to southern conservatives, white paranoia, and small-town Babbittry, in part to tap into the politics of resentment that was fueling George Wallace's third-party bid.[39]

The actual proceedings in Mayor Richard Daley's town seemed to bear out Izzy's worst fears. Some ten thousand New Leftists, Yippies, and hippies—a good number of whom turned out to be police agents—gathered in the city parks and streets of Chicago, determined to demonstrate against the war and demand a peace plank in the Democratic Party platform. They were met by about twelve thousand of Chicago's finest, another twelve thousand National Guardsmen and army troops, a chain-link and barbed-wire fence ringing the convention hall, and a fortress mentality. As Lyndon Johnson's vice-president was selected as his party's nominee, tear gas, smoke bombs, billy clubs, rocks, bricks, bottles, and expletives filled the air. While the forces of law and order felt battered and ridiculed, delegates, demonstrators, and bystanders alike were on the receiving end of what a presidential commission later acknowledged to be a police riot. With chants of "The Whole World is Watching!" coming across the airwaves, the Democratic Party's chances for victory in November disintegrated.

Having spent some time in Chicago during convention week, Izzy feared that still more had been rent in the Windy City. Wandering through Lincoln and Grant parks and the headquarters of the National Mobe, he felt that the finest of a generation, sickened by the war, "were being lost—some among the hippies to drugs, some among the radicals to an almost hysterical frenzy of alienation."[40]

The appearance of this new lost generation greatly disturbed him. This phenomenon was precisely what he had feared was taking place. And at this point, more of the same seemed to be in store for the United States. Where all of this would end he was uncertain.

With the upcoming election appearing like "a one-party rubber stamp," Izzy admitted that he, for one, did not have all the answers. Three choices loomed ahead for antiwar forces: the attempt by Allard Lowenstein, orchestrator of the Dump Johnson campaign, to win over Democratic Party regulars; Marcus Raskin's call for a new progressive party; and the New Left's charge to take to the streets. It required patience and belief in the powers of persuasion, Izzy acknowledged, to address that which troubled this land. But how, he asked, did one convey these notions to the young men who faced the draft and possible service in a war that was tearing both Vietnam and their own country asunder? "Hate and frenzy" did not provide for reasoned political thought, Izzy declared, and "the *enragés* among the youth," romanticizing guerrilla war as they were, might well lead to further polarization.⁴¹

While the United States should be grateful, Stone wrote, "to the tatterdemalion army of Yippies, hippies and peaceniks" who induced the establishment to show its true face, New Leftists and their compatriots continued to suffer from delusions of their own. The most significant one was that "the people" opposed the war. But if the truth be told, Izzy exclaimed, the people had not made up their minds. And he warned that if law and order were fully abandoned and democratic safeguards tossed aside, those in the antiwar movement and their intellectual champions would be the first to pay the price. Thus, "to play with revolutionary talk and tactics" in the manner of the New Left, when no revolutionary situation existed, was to serve "as the provocateurs for an American fascism."⁴²

The greatest tragedy that had occurred in Chicago, Stone suggested, involved the discarding of nonviolent means by both black and white dissidents. Shouting down those one disagreed with, employing obscenities rather than reason, tossing aside persuasion in favor of direct action, debasing one's foes as "pigs" and worse, he declared, was to join in a contest "rightists are better equipped to play" and to provide precedents "which American Storm Troopers may some day apply to us." Hate, Izzy reminded his readers, remained the greatest antagonist of humanity, "the fuel that heats the furnaces of genocide." How could a new and better world be constructed, he asked, by giving vent to "primitive and sanguinary habits?"⁴³

Thus, despite appreciating the anger and rage that drove a certain portion of New Leftists onward, Izzy refused to withhold strongly felt reservations about their antics. Indeed, he believed it was his responsibility, as an elder in the movement, to urge his youthful cohorts to act sensibly. Not all, of course, welcomed his criticisms.

Within a matter of weeks, Stone had made his own decision, deciding to support the fourth-party route. While admitting that the establishment of a new party and the peaceful remaking of American society would be no single campaign affair, he believed them to be necessary steps toward safeguarding the mental health of the nation. A new party, he argued, could draw the lines clearly "between unilateral interventionism and internationalism." And still more important, a new party could serve as a voice of reason and help to do battle with "Daleyism," which envisioned the meeting of protest with such ferocity that revolution would become necessary. Absent Daleyism, a minuscule number of revolutionaries, Stone reported, would in no way achieve that which they wanted—something akin to another civil war. Finally, a new party was required to humanize politics once again. A feeling that bureaucracy, whether Communist- or capitalist-driven, was dehumanizing, Stone declared, had fostered revolt by the young around the globe. Only a new, fourth party "devoted to the human" could redirect that upsurge into constructive avenues. Such a party could reorder the nation along the lines of its own finest traditions, and thus prevent it from self-destructing.[44]

By the fall of 1968, Izzy was deeply troubled by the ruptures he noticed on the political landscape. On the left, a growing number of American youth, as he saw it, appeared alienated from both the political mainstream and reality. On the right, demagogues happily played to the crowd to garner votes, attention, and political offices. Although Stone understood the anger driving New Left and antiwar activists (despite being troubled by it), the right-wingers, as always, were another matter altogether.

F ollowing the narrow victory by Richard Nixon over Hubert Humphrey, I. F. Stone warned that nothing terribly novel should be expected from the president-elect. One thing did appear certain: "happy days" awaited the Pentagon.[45]

During Johnson's tenure, Stone had condemned the fiscal policy of billions for guns, millions for butter. Now he blasted "Uncle Sam's Con Man Budget" which called for the war machine to continue to devour public resources. He was particularly concerned—as he had been for some time—about the proposal for an antiballistic missile system, which promised to become the greatest boondoggle the military-industrial complex had yet come upon. In a series of well-received articles in the *New York Review*, he attacked the ABM as simply the latest version of the military's insatiable appetite for the ultimate weapon. And he saw Nixon-flavored disarmament negotiations as only "a theater of delusions."[46]

It was not easy, he acknowledged, to follow the complexities "of megamurder-mathematics." But the truth of the matter was that this nation had already expended a trillion dollars since the end of World War II "on a gigantic hoax." Although the United States came out of that conflict as unquestionably the most powerful nation on the face of the earth, "a wicked fantasy" had been spun concerning the possibility of attack from a wartime ally turned foe, which had itself suffered the loss of twenty-five million of its citizens in the world war. And to the very present, he wrote in mid-1969, such a myth continued to play right into the hands of the American war machine. This certainly remained the case, he believed, under "little old Lyndon B. Nixon." Moreover, so long as a bipolar view of the world prevailed, diplomacy was not possible, and military spending and the power of the armed forces would continue unabated. But should another good trillion dollars be tossed after bad, the United States itself might go bankrupt, Stone warned.[47]

Nixon's proposed ABM system and his military budget suggested to Stone the machinations of a con artist, while his troop deployment figures and body counts were "typical of the J. Walter Thompson war" the administration was waging. They also lent credence to the notion that there was no new Nixon, but only the old one resurfacing. Most important, the war in Vietnam had been Nixon's, Stone wrote, for a good long while now. Back in 1954, Vice-President Nixon had called for American intervention. Upon the end of the French-Indochina War, he had urged Eisenhower to side with Diem and to avoid the elections promised in Geneva. This was a man, then, who had an emotional and ideological stake in the war in Southeast Asia.[48]

Moreover, Nixon's call for a Vietnamization of the war, which would place greater responsibilities upon the ARVN forces, was also nothing new. Support of South Vietnamese president Ngo Dinh Diem, Stone wrote, was the first American attempt at this latest panacea offered by the newest edition of Richard Nixon. But why should Vietnamization under the latest South Vietnamese dictators, Generals Nguyen Van Thieu and Nguyen Cao Ky, Stone asked, prove any more effective?[49]

To I. F. Stone, there was no new Nixon but only the same old Tricky Dicky, in slightly sanitized garb. Unlike Truman, Kennedy, and Johnson, liberal presidents all, or even Eisenhower, that moderate conservative, Nixon, in Stone's estimation, offered no hope for reform or a change in Cold War policies. No, the old red-baiter seemed to offer only a prolongation of the Vietnam War and an intensification of domestic tensions.

Though now criticized by some in the New Left for not thinking in theoretical terms, Stone increasingly focused not only on the war in Vietnam but on U.S. imperialism in general. Indeed, he had done so since the early days of the conflict, warning that humankind's greatest problem was how to contain the United States of America. In early November 1969, he spoke about the stationing of 1.2 million American military personnel overseas, the presence of U.S. military missions in some fifty countries, and the maintenance abroad of nearly twenty-three hundred military installations. The cost of such responsibilities, coupled with the U.S. bill for the Vietnam War and its NATO tab, ran to something like fifty billion dollars annually. If that amount of money were to be spent at home over the course of a decade, Stone pointed out, grave domestic ills could be attended to.[50]

However, even if the war in Vietnam were to end, Stone warned, the determination to serve as world policeman would not. Thus, unless the notion of a Pax Americana were abandoned, domestic reconstruction would not come about. Imperialism and militarism, not Vietnam alone, Stone charged, consequently were the enemies.[51]

There were structural matters that needed to be attended to, Stone thus believed. If the economy remained based on "defense" spending, if American outposts continued to be spread across the globe, and if an anti-imperialist and antimilitarist position did not garner greater support, the lessons of the present war were certain to be little heeded.

Perhaps the greatest lesson to be learned from the Vietnam fiasco, Stone suggested, was that "the bigger and more diverse a nation's military establishment the bigger and more diverse the troubles it will get that nation into." Thus, as he pointed out in mid-1970, so long as American ships patrolled every sea, America bases stood on every continent, Green Berets and C-5As were at the ready for rapid deployment, the chances of more foreign policy disasters were considerable.[52]

In the post-Vietnam era such forces would be employed again and again. Central America, the Caribbean, and the Middle East were just some of the areas where U.S. soldiers, ships, and planes would be called into action, once more to back less than genuinely democratic forces.

The chances of particularly telling disasters in the midst of U.S. misadventures, Stone had believed, remained large too. American imperialism, played out in the jungles of Vietnam, culminated in the My Lai massacre. In the village known as Pinksville, frustrated American soldiers went on a rampage, "wasting" more than two hundred unarmed civilians, including women and children. Unwittingly, this war had become, Stone wrote, "an 'Anti-People's war.'" While Mao Zedong had observed that "the guerrilla survives among the people as a fish does in the sea," an American army officer had promised to "dry up the sea." The United States had indeed attempted to adopt such a policy, Stone declared, destroying villages, crops, livestock, and people in areas seen, as My Lai had been, as sympathetic to the Vietcong. With such a policy in place, it was not surprising to Stone that massacres inevitably occurred. Such were the atrocities "Nixon condones and continues."[53]

Therefore, My Lai, Stone believed, was not merely some particularly horrific aberration. Rather, it appeared to be the all but inevitable result of the anything-goes policy directed at a people perceived as the Vietnamese were by so many American "statesmen" and soldiers, as well as by such a large portion of the general public.

While Vice-President Agnew, in the middle of a speech in Houston, Texas, attempted to dismiss the newsletter as "another strident voice of illiberalism," Izzy's continued concern about the presence within the antiwar movement of extremists, "kooks," and hate-filled "escaped lunatics" caused him to be seen in certain circles as unsympathetic to the New Left. More and more, he was dismissed as yet another liberal who "still clung to a belief in party politics, Congress, and the like."[54]

Nevertheless, Izzy refused to give in to what came to be known as "Radical Chic," preferring to talk sense to the very young people the *Weekly* had helped to shape. On one occasion, while delivering a speech at New York University, he met up with certain of his critics in the movement. If American society were torn apart, he asked, what would they replace it with? Shouts of "Cuba!" came back. Listen, this old champion of the Cuban Revolution exclaimed, communism was a means for removing "surplus capital out of the bellies of the working class." Hissing began, but Izzy went on to say that in the United States he was allowed to speak his mind. One listener cried out that in the United States, change was not possible! Wearily, Izzy retorted: "Listen, if you brought about change you'd have to put three quarters of the population in concentration camps to reconcile them to that change." That silenced the crowd for a short while.[55]

In the midst of another public address, Izzy declared that frustration did not a revolutionary movement make. Venting one's rage might be therapeutic, he admitted, but how politically wise was it? How do you carry out a revolution, he asked, when eighty percent of the people were not displeased with the system currently in place? Study history, he urged those in the audience, and recognize that if the people ever did take control, "we'd all be in jail."[56]

In May 1969, Izzy wrote an editorial both condemning much that the student rebels seemed to stand for and championing their cause. A good deal of their rhetoric and many of their deeds, he admitted, were not to his liking. He did not think much of opponents being shouted down, beaten up, or disparaged as "pigs." Indeed, "I hate, *hate*, intolerance and violence." He saw them as humanity's greatest foes and did not care "to see them welling up on my side." Nevertheless, like Erasmus, who had helped spawn the Reformation, but then was repelled by its excesses, Izzy believed that the young rebels were carrying out "God's work . . . in refusing any longer to submit to evil, and challenging society to reform or crush them."[57]

As a lifelong dissident himself, Izzy admitted, he had become accustomed to accept defeat as a matter of course. In fact, he had grown suspicious of the possibility of victory and the very notion of a movement. He saw "every insight degenerating into a dogma, and fresh thoughts freezing into lifeless party line. Those who set out nobly to be their brother's keeper sometimes end up by becoming his jailer. Every emancipation has in it the seeds of a new slavery, and every truth easily becomes a lie."[58]

Such analyses, he recognized, meant little to those who were having to contend with the draft, the war in Vietnam, or racial barriers at home. And the young radicals who refused to go gently into the not-so-good night, he admitted, remained the country's last best hope.[59]

But the very same rebels needed to appreciate the fact that war, racism, and bureaucracy were universal phenomena. The communist states, for their part, had not cast aside war and imperialism, while the new African nations were hardly exemplary models of liberty or human brotherhood. The truth of the matter was that "man's one real enemy is within himself," and tearing down the United States would not bring about utopia.[60]

Thus adherence to the proper ideological line, Izzy recognized, was in no way good enough by itself. As Albert Einstein and Bertrand Russell had noted some time before, humankind had to change, not simply adopt new economic or political systems. Were that not to happen, the mistakes and follies that riddled the human species would continue indefinitely.

Despite his ambivalence, Izzy saluted the spring graduating class of 1969, which contained many of the activist young within its ranks, as the finest ever. In the fall, he continued to throw his weight behind the antiwar movement. He supported both the Moratorium (a one-day national strike on October 15) and the New Mobilization Committee to End the War in Vietnam (which sponsored the March against Death—involving a reading of the names of America's war dead—and rallies across the country on November 15). Izzy insisted that the marching had to continue because the administration was refusing to respond. If the peace movement folded its tents, he warned, the war would grind on and on. He participated in the Moratorium, joining with thousands of others in a candle-lit, evening procession that had a religious feel to it. Izzy argued that both the Moratorium, which he saw as moderate, and the Mobilization, which he considered to be radical, were needed. The process of educating and persuading the country, he declared, had to continue. Screaming was not good enough and rock-throwing "only another form of childish tantrum," not in the least bit revolutionary. Alienation would only continue to deepen, he suggested, if "the frustrated and foolish in our own ranks (and the secret police provocateurs)" gave in to violence.[61]

There were those in the administration and in the streets, Stone feared, who were determined to bring about just such a confrontation. When Vice-President Agnew declared that "it is time for a positive polarization," Stone noted that similar language could be heard from extremists in the antiwar camp. He quoted from a speech delivered at the San Francisco edition of the November 15 Mobe, by David Hilliard, a leader of the Black Panther Party, an avowedly revolutionary organization which had declared that President Nixon or "any motherfucker that stands in the way of our freedom" should be "offed." Hilliard had continued, "We aint here for no goddam peace, because we know that we can't have no peace because this country was built on war." This, Stone charged, was dangerous talk. So too was the statement made by a Mobe leader that distinguished "good" from "bad" violence. Such was the rationale, Stone pointed out, of "every murderous mob in history," including those who lynched southern blacks, Hitler's Brownshirts, and the members of Mayor Daley's police force who shot up Panthers Mark Clark and Fred Hampton. That kind of rhetoric, he insisted, was particularly foolish for a minority group.[62]

Few within the ranks of the movement were then willing to deliver such critiques of the Black Panther Party, which was seen to be in the vanguard of the New American Revolution. But Izzy never hesitated in attacking Panther Hilliard as he did, for he strongly believed that radicals had to act seriously, intelligently, and humanely.

It would help to encourage such behavior, he recognized, if the U.S. government were itself operating in a similar fashion. Instead, the government was presently prosecuting the so-called Chicago Seven, indicted for having purportedly conspired to wreak havoc in the midst of the 1968 Democratic Party convention. Moreover, defendants Tom Hayden, David Dellinger, Abbie Hoffman, Jerry Rubin, et al., were being characterized as "fags," "kooks . . . demagogues . . . social misfits" by prosecuting attorney Tom Foran and Vice-President Agnew. The jailing of leaders of the student and radical movements and such careless talk, he suggested, were surefire ways to spark "blind revolutionary rage." And "only the far-out Weathermen," the SDS splinter group—which included in its ranks Izzy's niece Kathy Boudin—were as "kooky" as Agnew, Stone wrote, in believing that broken windows actually threatened the American government.[63]

While Kathy admired Izzy, despite finding his attitudes toward sex to be "pretty bourgeois," neither he nor Esther had much sympathy for her underground work. In fact, they were both "pretty horrified" by what she was doing. As Chris Stone saw it, Izzy, along with brother-in-law Leonard Boudin, "both really believed in the system. Leonard was going to do it in court and Dad was going to do it through the press." Simply put, "bombs and stuff were not the family way."[64]

On March 6, 1970, a townhouse in Greenwich Village located next door to one owned by actor Dustin Hoffman of *The Graduate* fame exploded, the result of bombs gone awry, bombs which members of the Weather Underground had been attempting to construct. Three Weathermen died in the blast, and Stone feared that his country might be witnessing the initial stages of urban guerrilla terrorism. The Weathermen, he admitted, might be dismissed "as spoiled brats" and their manifesto viewed as "a mishmash of ill-digested pseudo-Marxist rubbish." But this was a political phenomenon, Stone insisted, and should only be met by political means. Justice should be placed on the table for America's young radicals, and a setting aside of the convictions of the Chicago Seven—seemingly predetermined from the start—would help further rational discussion and belief in the possibility of change. Most important, of course, that which spawned their rage—racism at home and war in the jungles of Vietnam—had to come to an end.[65]

What had to be realized, Stone indicated, was that the Weathermen, brats though they may have been, were their generation's most sensitive souls who took to heart the pain and anguish caused by their own society. And "these wild and wonderful—yes, wonderful!—kids" performed a useful function, goading the establishment into action as they did.[66]

Still, even though he at times had an urge to hurl some rocks himself, Izzy again insisted that "salvation by holocaust" was not the way to go. "Hate and hysteria," he declared, would not bring forth a better world. And "political suicide" did not make for revolution.[67]

Arguing that "the dynamite that threatens us sizzles on a fuse that leads straight back to the White House," Stone was distressed by the U.S.-sponsored overthrow of Prince Sihanouk of Cambodia. This was the result, he wrote on April 6, of "secret government, secret armies, secret war." The CIA, he noted, had finally gotten what it had long sought, and now a greater war might be about to begin. The peace movement, Stone declared, needed to alert the nation.[68]

The invasion of Cambodia that followed resulted in a sounding of those alarms as campuses across the land responded in an outpouring of frenzied anger and rage. On May 4, at Kent State University, National Guardsmen left four dead in Ohio, and the week following, two more students were shot down at Mississippi's virtually all-black Jackson State. "The race is on," Stone cried out, "between protest and disaster." It did not help matters, he believed, to have the president go around referring to antiwar demonstrators as "bums." Fearing that terrible times might be in store, he declared that "only the bums can save the country now." He counseled students to create "a Plague for Peace" by descending on the nation's capital. He joined with faculty and students across the land in condemning the invasion and demanded an end to U.S. military operations in Vietnam. He signed a petition to that effect, along with Paul Goodman, John Hersey, Christopher Lasch, Robert Jay Lifton, Arthur Miller, and Robert Penn Warren. But appearing at Amherst, where he received his first honorary degree—an appearance boycotted by David Eisenhower, grandson of the late president—Izzy warned that the public would not be won over by damning the United States as some kind of "monolithic monster." "Slipshod analysis and metaphors" would serve no purpose, he declared. The United States was not a fascist nation, he insisted, and following Agnew's lead in polarizing the situation would lead to no good.[69]

That September, following a bomb blast at the Army Mathematics Center at the University of Wisconsin which took the life of a graduate student, Izzy indicated that he had "never felt the despair"—not even during the depths of the Great Depression—that he was starting to experience concerning the very fate of the American nation. Now, "our instant revolutionaries" seemed to be afflicted with "a blind frustrated urge to destroy." Now, it appeared, they really were determined to bring the war home. But the end result, Izzy again warned, would be no utopia, but rather "anarchy and barbarity, race war and gang war," and the heavy hand of repression. Nor would communism with a human face result; after all, "you cannot beat men into angels, nor make them better by calling them 'pigs.' " Moreover, the hysteria and hatred certain to be unleashed would not easily result in the appearance of "that New Man of whom Mao and Che dreamed."[70]

What was needed, this former champion of the New Deal suggested, was another Roosevelt determined to chart a course to eradicate the ills that blighted the American landscape. Just imagine what could be done with the fervor that now drove some of the country's finest young people to cries of revolution.[71]

But although Stone now argued once again that widespread reform could make a genuine difference, he realized that the possibility of a second new deal was unlikely.

It was incumbent on all those with any influence on the left, he insisted in mid-November, to contest both "mob tactics" and the growing fascination with the bomb. But it was also necessary, he went on to say, to appreciate the moral resolve that led some to adopt an outlaw posture. And it was unfortunate that sitting in the Oval Office was a man "who talks and thinks like an old-fashioned cop."[72]

What was clear once again was the difficulty for someone like Stone, with his iconoclastic stance regarding inherited beliefs, to fit within the framework of a movement, even one he had long called for, helped to nurture, and very much wanted to believe in. Perhaps this demonstrated that once a movement reaches the stage that the New Left and the antiwar campaign had, once it becomes a mass movement, in other words, individuals such as Stone are almost compelled to stand outside of it. During its infancy, he had exerted enormous influence over the movement, as a model of commitment, critical thought, and determined individualism for the small number of activists who knew him personally or were, at the very least, intimately familiar with his work. As its constituency grew, he was still an important figure in the movement, but perhaps as much because of his greater stature as for the example he set. For journalists and intellectuals, Izzy's impact appeared to be firmly rooted. But to many in the New Left and among the general antiwar forces, he increasingly came to be seen as one whose time had come and gone. For such a segment of the movement, Izzy could in no way be viewed as an exemplar for activists to follow; they found their models rather where he was not able to, in Vietnam, Cuba, and China.

Remaining both within and outside the antiwar movement, Stone, in the final year of the *Weekly*, continued to warn about the costs of the American empire, the greatest the world had ever seen. On January 11, 1971, he declared that the massive military and intelligence apparatuses required by that empire were harder and harder to control. As presently constituted, they were large enough to carry out secret wars of their own.[73]

As the war widened once again with the invasion of Laos in the spring of 1971, Stone argued that the military machine was running things. This suited Richard Nixon just fine, he believed, for the "generation of peace" this president called for was "a generation of arms race, tension and war." But then this was the same man, Stone argued on April 19, who had long stood as "the foremost hawk of the Indochinese adventure."[74]

Once again, Izzy's analysis proved to be prophetic. American military expenditures did in fact mushroom, while U.S. forces continued to carry out unholy operations. The result was that the American economy was riddled with structural problems of the sort not experienced since the Great Depression, while the morality of U.S. actions was called into question yet again.

Following another massive antiwar rally, held in Washington on April 24, Stone warned that Nixon remained determined to sustain American power in Southeast Asia; peace thus remained "still a long, long march away." Nevertheless, he was encouraged by the turnout of three hundred thousand protesters and by the appearance of the Vietnam Veterans Against the War, the new stars of the movement. These men, like their fellows in the Resistance in Europe, Stone wrote, would later be viewed as having preserved their nation's honor.[75]

As the People's Coalition for Peace and Justice began a massive campaign of civil disobedience, one intended to bring the war home, but to do so nonviolently, Izzy admitted to some appreciation of the May Day tactics. Both persuasion and civil disobedience, he now agreed, might be needed because of the government's seeming inflexibility. Why should roads and streets not be tied up a bit, he asked, if that is what it took "to make the sluggish conscience of the country aware of the misery and murder we continue to rain down on Indochina?" But again, he condemned those who acted in a manner alien to Thoreau and Gandhi, including movement thugs who had showed up in Barry Goldwater's and John Tower's Senate offices. How would antiwar forces feel, Izzy asked, "if pro-war goons roughed up the offices of pro-peace Senators?"[76]

One might argue that Izzy was trying to have it both ways. He attempted to act as a voice of reason in urging the New Left to behave responsibly. He also acknowledged that the depth of his own anger led him to identify with Resistance-like tactics. But such an approach did enable him to retain a measure of influence among the various factions of the antiwar movement, unlike most of his contemporaries.

The publication that June of *The Pentagon Papers* indicated to Stone precisely why the antiwar movement had to keep the pressure on. Even he was taken aback by the pattern of operations covering five administrations which those documents revealed. Even he had been taken in, not appreciating that policymakers were quite as "mendacious and unscrupulous" as they were now proven to be. But more investigation was necessary, he indicated, to uncover that which had led such different men "into the same crimes against humanity and crimes against freedom." What was all too obvious, he declared, was that empire and democracy did not mesh.[77]

In both the *Weekly* and in an interview with Bernard Kalb of CBS, Izzy continued to express astonishment over the full dimensions of government misdeeds revealed by *The Pentagon Papers*. Government leaders were simply liars, he told Kalb, and Lyndon Johnson had been the worst one of all. And yet he was also struck by the fact that the press had performed as diligently as it had. Thomas Jefferson, he declared, would have applauded the *New York Times* which had agreed to release *The Pentagon Papers*. The American press remained the world's freest, and reporters in the field such as Homer Bigart, David Halberstam, Peter Arnett, and Neil Sheehan had performed admirably.[78]

Thus, Izzy believed his journalistic colleagues had demonstrated true professionalism as well as a sense of civic responsibility. They had begun to serve as critical chroniclers of the Vietnam conflict, something Izzy had been all along. They had shown that the very best journalism tapped into an investigative, even a radical tradition.

Through all the turmoil and tumult of the sixties and early seventies, Izzy retained his joie de vivre. During the summer of 1971, in the midst of his now annual sojourn in Europe, he invited Felicity Bryan, his British literary agent, for lunch. They met at the Ritz Hotel in London, with cherry blossoms in all their glory and Izzy thoroughly entranced. Following a delightful meal, Izzy, with some difficulty, focused on the check. Misty-eyed, he then took his guest by the hand and said, "Oh, Felicity, this has been such a lovely meal. When the Revolution comes, we'll eat here every day."[79]

By this point, *I. F. Stone's Weekly* was no longer simply a cult item of sorts for Old Leftists and New Leftists alike and for journalists somewhat off the beaten path. The subscription totals for the newsletter had only continued to jump, heading from forty-four thousand at the end of 1969 to fifty-seven thousand by the close of 1970 to sixty-six thousand by October 1971, with an additional four thousand to five thousand copies sold at newsstands and the like. Forty or so subscriptions went to Capitol Hill, and the White House paid for its own copy. *Who's Who in America* returned Izzy to its pages after a twenty-year absence, the *New Yorker* and Senator J. William Fulbright both quoted from him extensively, the "Today Show" interviewed him—although the sales department had "red-dotted" and vetoed him— and Dick Cavett regularly invited him to appear on his television program. In fact, when "The Dick Cavett Show" first went off the air in September 1969, a clerk had to be hired just to see to "the wildly wildly favorable mail about Izzy." He received his "first establishment award," the George Polk Memorial Award, along with CBS broadcaster Walter Cronkite, and was declared "at the very least, singular and unique; at most, courageous, exciting, a maker of events, and, perhaps, a phenomenon." During the awards ceremony in early 1971, he was likened to Benjamin Franklin, Sam Adams, Horace Greeley, Samuel McClure, and H. L. Mencken, and was said to have "frightened men of power everywhere."[80]

A lengthy and favorable essay appeared on him in the *Wall Street Journal* ("Gadfly on the Left: I. F. Stone Achieves Success, Respectability but Keeps Raking Muck"), of all places, and a deeply respectful interview was printed in full in the *Christian Century* ("With Atheists Like Him, Who Needs Believers?"). His newest books, *The Killings at Kent State*, mostly a compilation of *Weekly* essays on the tragedy, and *Polemics and Prophecies*, which included a number of his most poignant pieces from the newsletter and the *New York Review*, received accolade after accolade; in addition, a reprint of his *Hidden History* was adjudged a prescient warning of the Vietnam disaster. *Newsweek* wrote about Izzy's "most devastating weapon . . . his ability to read" and proclaimed him to be "a wise innocent, repeatedly violated, forever bound to believe that the future will be better, furious when it is not, resolved to make it so." *Harper's* termed him "a modern John Peter Zenger . . . who takes very seriously the traditional role of Informer of the People."[81]

Reporters from Tom Wicker, the *New York Times* columnist, to Jack Newfield of the *Village Voice,* to Carl Bernstein, then with the *Washington Post,* considered Izzy to carry a good deal of weight with his fellow journalists. Izzy and his *Weekly,* along with the underground press in general, Wicker indicated, had caused the establishment press "to be less officially oriented than we once were." Wicker went on to note that "before any of us had the courage to think for ourselves, rather than take what the President said, he was doing it." Newfield indicated that he had acquired "a reverence for facts, truth, and justice" from Izzy Stone. Bernstein also expressed appreciation for Izzy's "incredible respect for knowledge and for truth."[82]

More and more, I. F. Stone was seen as occupying a place in the ranks of leading American intellectuals. In studies of the American "intellectual elite," Izzy's name and that of both the *Weekly* and the *New York Review of Books,* where more of his essays were now appearing, were invariably included. In one poll, the newsletter, along with *Public Interest* and *Foreign Affairs,* received the most write-in votes in response to a query concerning which were the most influential journals to be found. The *Weekly* was adjudged one of the top twenty journals or magazines "regularly read" by leading American intellectuals, who put the *New York Review,* the *New York Times Book Review,* and the *New York Times Magazine* at the top of the chart. A favorable notice from Izzy or other critics in the *New York Review,* the *New Yorker, Harper's,* or the *Atlantic* was said to be capable of making an author's reputation, owing to the fact that "those are the reputable journals." In another poll, Izzy was prominently placed on a list of "the 70 most prestigious contemporary American intellectuals" of the last half of the 1960s. He was located on a level just below such individuals as Noam Chomsky, John Kenneth Galbraith, Irving Howe, Dwight Macdonald, Norman Mailer, Norman Podhoretz, Bob Silvers, and Arthur Schlesinger, Jr., but above one that contained figures like Barbara Epstein, Elizabeth Hardwick, Sidney Hook, Christopher Lasch, Philip Rahv, James Reston, and Richard Rovere. The tier Izzy was placed in saw him paired with Theodore Draper, Jason Epstein, Michael Harrington, Alfred Kazin, Murray Kempton, Walter Lippmann, and Hans Morgenthau, among others. While liberals and ex-radicals made up a good percentage of the elite intellectuals, practicing radicals on the list such as Michael Harrington and I. F. Stone were few in number.[83]

Izzy himself was declared to be one of the ten "leading influencers of American intellectuals on the war in Southeast Asia." Heading that list were Bernard Fall, David Halberstam, Robert Shaplen, Draper, Mary McCarthy,

Jean Lacouture, Schlesinger, and Jonathan Schell, all of whom had written books on the conflict, a fact which was said to have influenced the rankings. But Stone, the lone individual in the top ten who had not completed a full-length monograph on the Indochina War, was placed above Harrison Salisbury, Richard Goodwin, Douglas Pike, Susan Sontag, Lippmann, Rovere, Noam Chomsky, John Kenneth Galbraith, James Reston, David Schoenbrun, Malcolm Browne, Marcus Raskin, Tom Wicker, Frances Fitzgerald, Irving Howe, Robert Scheer, and other top American intellectuals.[84]

And when asked who had been "Most Influential on the Discussion of the Vietnam Issue within the Intellectual Community, as Perceived by Peers," Izzy placed fourth, behind Chomsky by a fair margin but just behind Morgenthau and Galbraith, and ahead of McCarthy, Fall, Schlesinger, Draper, Lacouture, and Mailer.[85]

Another query directed at American intellectuals resulted in the *Weekly* being named one of the five most influential journals on the war in Vietnam. Only the *New Yorker*, the *New York Review of Books*, and the *New York Times Magazine* were said to carry more weight, while the coverage of the conflict by the newsletter and *The New Republic* was seen as equally noteworthy. The *New York Review* was considered the best medium for speaking out to other members of the American intelligentsia regarding the war and was perceived as "a kind of organ of anti-Vietnam, intellectual sentiment." All did not look favorably upon this development.[86]

Nor did they view one of the *New York Review*'s steadiest contributors any differently than they had in the past. Notwithstanding I. F. Stone's newfound respectability and greater acclaim, he continued to be regarded as outside the pale by some. In the November 1970 issue of *Commentary*, Dennis H. Wrong, a sociology professor at New York University, unhappily referred to Izzy's continued association with the *New York Review*, which he condemned for its pro–New Left perspective. Also troubling him was the fact that the circulation of the journal approached ninety thousand, with a fair number of its readers happening to be members of the professoriate. The *New York Review* was now seen as *the* single most influential publication by American intellectuals; Wrong himself admitted that no intellectual journal in the United States had ever carried the weight that the *New York Review* now did. Beginning with his essay on LBJ, published in the midst of the 1964 presidential campaign, I. F. Stone had served as one of the steadiest contributors to the journal, along with professors Edgar Z. Friedenberg, Robert Heilbroner, and Christopher Lasch; journalist Murray Kempton; and novelist and essayist Mary McCarthy. That very fact undoubtedly disturbed Wrong, who acknowledged that the *New York Review* had initially helped to provide intellectuals a rationale with which to oppose the war. But very quickly "a new tone of extravagant, querulous, self-righteous anti-Americanism" had cast a shadow over the *New York Review*'s accounts of the war, he continued, particularly as shaped by Noam Chomsky, McCarthy, and I. F. Stone. Wrong denounced Stone as "a Stalinist fellow-traveler" from days past, who had helped to tilt the journal New Leftward some time before. The end result, in Tom Wolfe's estimation, was that the *New York Review* had become "the chief theoretical organ of Radical Chic."[87]

Stone later refused to respond to Wrong's charges but did give vent to expletives and declared, "Never kick a dead skunk."[88]

In early 1971, Senator Edmund Muskie of Maine reported that Izzy had been one of several Washington residents whom the FBI had seen fit to tail during Earth Day proceedings. Izzy declared the bureau action to be "purposeless." Shortly thereafter, Jack Anderson revealed in his column that the FBI had kept Izzy *under regular surveillance.* Vice-President Agnew singled out for attack I. F. Stone of the *Weekly;* James Reston, Tom Wicker, and Anthony Lewis of the *New York Times;* and Hugh Sidey of *Life.* Joseph Kraft in the *Washington Post* insisted that the *Weekly* had parroted the Soviet line on U.S. policies all along. Izzy deflected such criticism with some wry humor: "If you live long enough the venerability factor creeps in: You get accused of things you never did and praised for virtues you never had. As respectability darkens my door, it's sort of comforting to know that someone still thinks I'm a dangerous man."[89]

Writers on opposite ends of the political spectrum certainly seemed to think so. P. J. O'Rourke, then working for an underground publication, declared that "as good-hearted and just a man" as Stone was, he "is a hot-shot eastern liberal" only. As O'Rourke saw it, Stone "knows all the facts, but he doesn't seem to know what they mean. It's like he knows every note but can't play the tune." O'Rourke asked his readers to forgive Izzy "for his liberal's faith and reformist's optimism."[90]

While criticism of that sort compelled Izzy to jokingly refer to himself as "a counter-revolutionary," Michael M. Uhlmann did not see it that way. Writing in the *National Review,* he charged that Izzy had helped to popularize "the hard-left argument" linking racism, capitalism, and imperialism. Now, in fact, Stone's reading of the military-industrial complex has "become the official Revised Standard Version of the Liberal Gospel." But Stone had gone farther, Uhlmann insisted, accusing the U.S. government of savage crimes of various sorts—of "deceit, avarice, racism, genocide and God-knows-what-else all." Nevertheless, Stone failed to carry his argument to its logic conclusion—"rebellion"—for the type of government he described simply could not hold "the allegiance of decent-minded men."[91]

A failure to acknowledge this, Uhlmann continued, suggested "either ignorance or disingenuousness." Since Stone was "anything but ignorant, one can only conclude that the latter must be the case." Uhlmann went on to proclaim Stone an "armchair revolutionary" who had reaped success by teaching liberals "how to *play* at revolution," while "absolving them (and himself) from any responsibility for their words and deeds because, after all, they are merely playing at it." In Uhlmann's estimation, the Black Panthers, who recognized that revolution was no game and were willing to put "their lives on the line," came off looking good by comparison.[92]

N otwithstanding the occasional diatribes, the response to his announcement at the tail end of 1971 that he was about to close shop indicated that Izzy had, by and large, come full circle. He remained controversial enough—and happily so in his own mind—to produce *National Review* or countercultural-style barbs. But more important, Izzy and the *Weekly* had acquired a certain real stature and influence among journalists of both the establishment and underground press, in the eyes of intellectuals drawn to the critiques of the *New York Review* variety, and with politically concerned individuals of both Old Left and New Left vintage. Indeed, the architect of the newsletter had come to be viewed as Izzy had once predicted he eventually would be, no longer as "a pariah" or simply "a character," but rather as something of "a national institution." The *Weekly* was now seen "as authoritative and intelligent."[93]

Izzy well recognized that the *Weekly* had become part of American journalistic folklore. This was a man, after all, who, according to Peter Osnos, "liked to be the center of attention" and was something of "a showoff." He was also proud of his professionalism and seemed to find the acclaim that now came the way of his "little flea-bite publication" to be perfectly fitting.[94]

After many years of feeling isolated, Izzy and Esther had at long last joined the Washington cocktail circuit. He took "great pleasure" in the invitations that now came his way and in being recognized by more and more readers upon his return to New York City and in the capital.[95]

Thus, the response to his announcement must not have been all that surprising to him or to many others. Letters and editorials poured forth, expressing profound regret that the newsletter was calling it a day. But Izzy was suffering once more from both angina pectoris and a loss of energy and worried that he might simply drop dead at any moment. So in the final issue of the *Weekly*, Izzy informed his readers that "the familiar warnings signals" demanded a lighter load for him. Eloquently, he traced his personal history and that of the newsletter, pointing out how journalism had been in his blood from early on and how the *Weekly* had managed to thrive despite all sorts of political and economic obstacles. The *Weekly* had enabled him "to give a little comfort to the oppressed, to write the truth exactly as I saw it, to make no compromises other than those of quality imposed by my own inadequacies, to be free to follow no image of what a true newspaperman should be, and still be able to make a living for my family—what more could a man ask?"[96]

Izzy had attempted, perhaps only halfheartedly, to get some committed younger journalist to take over the newsletter. But from its very inception, the *Weekly* had been Izzy's one-man show—albeit with Esther's considerable assistance—and the thought of someone else running it must have pained him. The printing of that final issue of the *Weekly* did mean that an end of an era had occurred. This experiment in personal journalism, which harked back to Sinclair and Steffens, Seldes and Macdonald, had kept alive the spirit of radical journalism through often troubling times. Other left-of-center publications—including James Weinstein's *In These Times; Mother Jones; The Nation,* soon to be revitalized under the editorship of Victor Navasky; and the *Progressive*—would of course continue to trace their own lineage back to journalistic iconoclasts such as Izzy himself. But never again would an operation run by a lone individual succeed in the manner that the *Weekly* had.

Perhaps, as Izzy later hinted, he was getting out at just the right time. The bill for mail delivery, which had remained virtually constant since the *Weekly* began, thereby allowing first for his and Esther's salaries and later for an ever-increasing profit margin, was about to skyrocket. Coupled with an increase in the cost of paper, this made publishing a more expensive enterprise than ever before. In addition, as John Tebbel, the foremost historian of American mass media publications has noted, the number of magazines and journals produced in the United States continued to proliferate, resulting in greater specialization and fierce competition for subscribers. Left-wing periodicals like *Ramparts* and *Seven Days* folded shop, along with most of the underground newspapers of the Vietnam era, leaving the playing field to old standbys like *The Nation* and the *Progressive* and newer versions like *In These Times* and *Mother Jones.*[97]

These publications, in the manner of the *Weekly* and its predecessors, sought to employ journalism as a vehicle for independent, alternative voices. This was perhaps more necessary than ever given the movement by so many intellectuals into the ranks of the respectable and the moderately comfortable. The left-of-center publications, again like the newsletter, retained something of the outsider status and reputation that a maverick journalist and intellectual like I. F. Stone had fortunately seemed to thrive on. And similar to the *Weekly*, at least until its final years, they too lived a precarious existence, both because of a dearth of official sources and owing to financial constraints. That only added to their underground image, which progressive journalism perhaps necessarily requires.

There always had been something of the subterranean quality surrounding *I. F. Stone's Weekly.* It had been founded at the height of McCarthyism because its editor suddenly found himself to be unemployable. From its inception, it had relied on uncovering government misdeeds, criticizing the Cold War mind-set of both East and West, and supporting the fight for liberation and empowerment, whether in the United States or in distant foreign lands. Its editor, a onetime well-regarded reporter and essayist, was long shunned by government officials, dismissed by his journalistic counterparts, and tailed by government agents. He was also, because of his devoted connection to the left and to radical journalism, revered by loyal followers and sustained by a dogged belief in himself.

And with the passage of time, of course, subscribers had come to turn to the *Weekly* as they might have looked in an earlier period to a political party or movement. Even the emergence and growth of the antiwar movement of the 1960s only added to the appeal of the newsletter, and a devoted readership continued to find its word often more substantial, more carefully thought out, and more precisely documented than that of the establishment press. All the while, subscribers eagerly awaited I. F. Stone's impassioned analyses which bespoke his belief in the importance of advocacy journalism. This was a man who saw the quest to ensure objective news coverage as playing into the hands of those already in positions of power, and whose example set the stage for the revival of both the left and investigative journalism.

But now, beginning on January 1, Izzy informed his readers he was moving on to the staff of the *New York Review* to serve as contributing editor; the attempt to find a successor having come to nought, he had sold his subscription list, which the *Progressive* and *Monthly Review* had also sought to purchase, to the journal as well. To interviewers, he expressed great satisfaction that the *Weekly* had been so successful. He had become "a prosperous free-enterpriser, 'a solid bourgeois,'" able to ease into his twilight years in comfort. "I'm a very successful capitalist," Izzy chortled. But the emotional satisfaction remained greatest of all. As Esther exclaimed, "What a wonderful thing to quit when you're on top" and at the same time, to have "a new life and a new career" to look forward to.[98]

It was to Esther, not surprisingly, that Izzy dedicated the final issue of the newsletter. Esther, whose "collaboration . . . unfailing understanding, and . . . sheer genius as a wife and mother," he wrote, "have made the years together joyous and fruitful." A quote from Tibullus, "Tu mihi curarum requies, tu nocte vel atra lumen, et in solis tu mihi turba locis," was positioned prominently at the top of page one. "You are the solace of my cares, light in the blackest night and company in lonely places."[99]

Editorials and essays sang Izzy's praises. *Time* declared that "the irrepressible godfather of New Left journalism" had called an "end of the Stone age." The *Washington Post* contended that Izzy was perhaps "the only Marxist ever to make good as a capitalist in the fiercely competitive jungle of American free enterprise journalism." His "qualities of thoroughness, fairness and insightfulness," the *Post* continued, "made his work almost solid, illuminating and a goad to all his competitors." Columnist Nicholas von Hoffman wrote that Izzy's "skeptical way of working" had helped to redo the coverage of national and international affairs, refuting the notion of the primacy of insider information. And Izzy, in the process, became the top investigative reporter of his era.[100]

While others became entrapped in "the Washington merry go round," which involved a seemingly endless series of briefings, off-the-record asides, embassy gatherings, and intimate encounters with capital heavyweights, Izzy had continued to rely on his voluminous reading, diligent research, and "nose-to-the-grindstone" approach. As nationally known correspondents headed off for a tennis game with a public official or dinner at the White House, Izzy had maintained his habit of making the daily rounds of Washington, seeking not the official "scoop," but official pronouncements and reports that called into question the veracity of the federal government itself. In the process, he had challenged the commonly held assumption that Washington was no place for "the lone wolf."[101]

The nineteen-year run of *I. F. Stone's Weekly* was indeed its editor's finest hour. The newsletter had carried on *PM*'s dream of an adless, independent publication that staked out a place for radical journalism of the nonsectarian variety, while avoiding its predecessor's tendency toward sloppiness and sensationalism. But most important of all had been the *Weekly*'s critical perspective in often uncongenial times and its stance as an insightful gadfly stinging away at the American establishment. To a remarkable degree, *I. F. Stone's Weekly* had proven right in its treatment of the great issues of the day, including McCarthyism and Stalinism, superpower mischief and the arms race, civil rights, and the antiwar movement.

This had been the time, then, more than at any other point during his career, when Izzy had demonstrated that integrity and commitment could be reconciled, that one could maintain critical support for a "movement," all the while remaining true to oneself. As at no other time, Izzy stood both as an exemplar of the dedicated professional and as a political activist of a radical cast. Thus, the *Weekly* had enabled Izzy to exemplify professionalism, intellectualism, and political commitment of the greatest magnitude.

Placudits and placards alike continued to come his way. Izzy Stone was the star of the initial A. J. Liebling Counter-Convention held at the Martin Luther King Labor Center in New York City in late April 1972. During the proceedings attended by Jack Anderson, David Halberstam, Nat Hentoff, Murray Kempton, Jack Newfield, Dan Rather, Studs

Terkel, and some three thousand others, Stone received the A. J. Liebling Award, named for the famed *New Yorker* columnist. He had been chosen "for his commitment, carried out single-handedly over two decades, to independent and unrelenting investigation of public and private power in America and his defense of individual liberty." In accepting the award, Izzy proclaimed the establishment to be "full of such stuffed shirts and so much crap that it really deserves to be treated disrespectfully." And he reveled in having been an outsider. "To be a pariah," he declared, "is to be left alone to see things your own way, as truthfully as you can."[102]

In the midst of his new celebrity, Izzy, in the pages of the *New York Review,* continued to rail away at the Nixon administration's handling of the Vietnam War, which he proclaimed to be "a preposterous fraud." He viewed Nixon's decisions to mine the ports of North Vietnam and to blockade that nation as "potentially the gravest" ones ever made by an American chief of state. He characterized Henry Kissinger, the architect of the administration's foreign policy, as a modern-day Metternich. How much pain and suffering, Stone wondered, was still in store before the comfortable delusions spun by Nixon and Kissinger would be no more? How many had to die "because a superpower suffers from an inferiority complex?"[103]

Unlike a fair number of his fellow journalists, Izzy was never all that taken with the diplomatic dealings of Kissinger, a former Harvard professor. As did Seymour Hersh, Stone believed that Kissinger was hardly the master of shuttle diplomacy whose seemingly sleight-of-hand operations enthralled so many of their compatriots.

Stone found hope in the presidential candidacy of Senator George McGovern. Denying that the South Dakota Democrat envisioned any radical change in the American defense program, Stone nevertheless believed that McGovern provided an opportunity to dramatically scale down Defense Department expenditures. While the American people would need a considerable education on disarmament if McGovern were to win, Stone had great faith in the Democrat's "humanity and decency" and believed that he would grow in office—as Franklin Roosevelt had—and might even support a "more radical transformation of military and foreign policy."[104]

The nominating convention that selected Senator McGovern gave Izzy cause to cheer. Now, he wrote, a real opportunity existed to end the war, rein in the military establishment, and redirect U.S. policies. He was pleased by the presence of so many women and dark-skinned faces in the convention halls, which indicated that long-standing barriers had been overcome. He was elated that activists who had marched in the streets the last time around now boasted the badges of delegates; he saw them as the harbingers of the future. But the past was there as well in the person of any number of veterans of lost causes, including Bull Moosers, La Follette supporters, and

Henry Wallace backers. Such "foolish old indomitables," Izzy asserted, never recognized when they were whipped.[105]

Buttressed by his policy of detente with both the Soviet Union and China, Richard Nixon swept to victory in November. Like many others, Stone had been startled by Nixon's playing of the China card, but congratulated him for having altered "the course of history at home and abroad," while remaining ever suspicious of his reasons for having done so. Stone saw the two great Communist states as desperate for rapprochement with the United States and thus able to offer no more than "toothless protest" against the continuing American assault on North Vietnam. He was skeptical about the moves to end the war in late 1972 or at least to bring about a cease-fire and total removal of American forces. He warned that more fighting was almost certain to follow, leading to a continuation of the death-dealing Vietnam War. He feared that Nixon sought to maintain a U.S.-backed dictatorship in South Vietnam, thereby only continuing the policy begun by the French a quarter-century before. At the same time, he argued that the proposed peace agreement did not stand up to the 1954 Geneva Accords or even to the American offer delivered the previous winter.[106]

Among those who were displeased with such an analysis was New Left leader Tom Hayden, who charged that Izzy seldom made much of an effort to understand "the revolutionary process." The Vietnamese revolutionaries knew what they were doing, Hayden declared, and did not require lecturing from someone like I. F. Stone.[107]

When the Vietnam War, in all its manifestations, finally ended, Stone again proved incapable of being politically correct. He expressed little surprise about the Vietnamese invasion in late 1978 of Cambodia, declaring "it's imperialism. . . . I don't like the big powers picking on little powers." He denounced the ensuing Chinese incursion into Vietnam, comparing the inevitable justifications with those Hitler had made following his attack on Poland. Then on May 30, 1979, he joined with Edward Asner, Daniel Berrigan, Allen Ginsberg, Nat Hentoff, and Staughton Lynd, among others, in addressing an "open letter to the Socialist Republic of Vietnam." This document proclaimed that the same commitment that had led them to oppose the Vietnam War now demanded that they condemn the imprisonment of thousands of prisoners of conscience, "the totalitarian policies of your government," the "painful nightmare" that Vietnam had become.[108]

Such opposition was not well received by other old movement activists who seemed determined to stand by the "revolutionary" regime that had taken power in Vietnam. By contrast, they commended the government in Hanoi "for its moderation and for its extraordinary effort to achieve reconciliation among all of its peoples."[109]

Thus, the American left, which had been reenergized by opposition to the war in Vietnam, before splintering once again, remained divided about what that conflict had meant and regarding the nature of its aftermath. In contrast to the divisions among American radicals, the right experienced a resurgence, capped off by the election of one of its own to the nation's top political post.

I t was during the Vietnam era that I. F. Stone acquired a very real prominence as one of the foremost intellectuals in the land. His writings in the *Weekly* and the *New York Review* resulted in this development, as did his appearances on behalf of the antiwar movement. And while the Vietnam War helped Izzy to make his mark as never before, he, in turn, provided the movement and critics of U.S. policies in Indochina with a certain degree of intellectual respectability. His legendary attention to the facts, his determination to uncover official misdeeds, his continued sense of moral outrage concerning what American practices had wrought, his "polemics and prophecies," caused Stone to be considered a voice of reason "in a time of torment" for the entire nation.

Considering the respect the newsletter and the *New York Review* were generally afforded, the reputation he now held with his fellow intellectuals, the greater and greater influence he possessed among establishment and underground journalists, and the impact his speeches and essays had on the antiwar movement, it is difficult to conceive of any American writer or political activist who had greater impact during the Vietnam period.

As Peter Osnos has suggested, this was an era when synergistic forces came into play, when the times, the issues, and Izzy all came together, enabling him to become a "terribly important" figure in many ways. For one thing, he redefined investigative journalism. For another, he was present as an inspirational crusader on the left when just such a figure was so sorely needed. And his provocative analyses undoubtedly compelled other members of the American intelligentsia to rethink certain of their own preconceptions and perspectives.[110]

The role played by I. F. Stone during the Vietnam era demonstrated the possibilities of critical journalism, intellectual activism, nonsectarian radicalism, absolutist individualism, and rebel capitalism. Whether he thereby provided a model others could follow is a good deal more questionable, for what is most striking is how unique that combination was. Others followed his lead with their own version of investigative reporting. Many intellectuals once more displayed their own sense of commitment. There were those, from Muste to Haber, who warned about the dangers of ideological fanaticism. Celebrants of individualism challenged corporate structures of all kinds. The underground press engaged in its own version of left-wing capitalism.

Still, none exuded all of these qualities to quite the same extent or in quite the same manner as did Izzy Stone. He became in the process the father of modern investigative journalism, the embodiment of the intellectual as activist, a prime proponent of a nonsectarian new left, one who really did do things his own way, and a highly successful entrepeneur—all at the same time.

Throughout the Vietnam era, Izzy was a figure of great importance to the movement, because of his writings, speeches, and the example he set, which some determined to follow and others attempted to deny in large part. Unfortunately, too few seemed to heed that which Izzy had come to believe above all else regarding the role, history, and future of the American left: the left must retain its soul, which comprised its very essence and reason for existence. To hold on to and to strengthen that very soul, he believed, required a matching of not only passion and commitment or socialism and freedom, but of humane means and ends. A failure to remember this had crippled radical movements in the past, and now was threatening to do it all over again.

16 An Old Firehorse in Semiretirement

His semiretirement began as he had indicated to the readers of the newsletter that it would, with I. F. Stone moving, in January 1972, to the staff of the *New York Review of Books*. Old friend Mike Blankfort dropped him a note, asking if it were not true that he was now working even harder than before. Blankfort also referred to a rumor going around that the journal would have adopted the name "the ROLLING STONE" but for the fact that another publication had already done so.[1]

As matters turned out, Izzy, for a time at least, proved to be "the favorite author" of the audience of the *New York Review*, which along with the *New York Times Books Review* remained the most popular among American intellectuals. The *New York Review*, as indicated by a 1974 study of "What America's Leaders Read," was also one of the magazines that economic, political, and media executives felt compelled to turn to. This was true despite the fact that the journal, with its eighty-five thousand subscribers, continued to provide a forum for critics of the war in Southeast Asia. Not all viewed this development favorably; some argued that its coverage of the Indochina War was too extensive, and others were upset by its critical, even "caustic" analyses. Then there were those who considered the *New York Review* to be "parochial, narrow, limited, and incestuous."[2]

Richard Rovere insisted that he was not attacking the ideological slant of the *New York Review*, then proceeded to condemn those such as Noam Chomsky and I. F. Stone, who he believed set the political tone for the journal. Stone's scholarship appeared to be "impeccable," Rovere declared, but it was "based on a load of crap" and Izzy himself was not "an honest controversalist" but rather one who used evidence selectively.[3]

Despite such attacks, the *New York Review*, housed in its somewhat dilapidated offices on the west side of Manhattan, continued to be acknowledged as a fount of ideas that otherwise would have lacked a national audience. And John Leonard, the esteemed editor of the *New York Times Book Review*, admitted that he had "to read it now for I. F. Stone." Although not altogether pleased with the *New York Review*'s political slant, he declared that "any magazine that gives a home to I. F. Stone is eminently worth publishing."[4]

The left-liberal political perspective characteristic of the journal from the mid-sixties through the early seventies suited Izzy, who took great pleasure in being associated with the *New York Review of Books*. As had been the case when he worked for *The Nation*, *PM* and its successors, and his own newsletter, writing for the *New York Review* was a comfortable fit because of its ideological and journalistic makeup. And the attention garnered by the *New York Review* pleased him, particularly its reception among American and European intellectuals.[5]

Beginning in early 1972, Stone wrote a series of sometimes lengthy and frequently controversial essays for the *New York Review* on a variety of subjects of great importance to him. In the process, this natural maverick demonstrated his propensity to question both liberal and radical "truths," all the while maintaining his own allegiance to Western intellectual thought. He continued to criticize certain of the practices of Israel, the Soviet Union, and the United States—the three nations he had expended so much emotional capital upon—in his own inimitable way. The first two he had once envisioned as socialist experiments, but did so no longer, although the Jewish land still maintained a special place in his heart. His own country continued to both trouble him and increasingly stand for this founder of modern investigative journalism as it had for its earlier founders, as something of a last best hope.

While Izzy never disavowed radicalism in any way, the disappointment he felt regarding both Israel and the Soviet Union and other "socialist" states caused him to return home again, intellectually and emotionally, that is. He looked to the liberal ethos as the fulcrum of the good society. The liberalism he extolled again and again was that of Jefferson, Lincoln, and Franklin Delano Roosevelt; it stood for freedom of thought and conscience, greater opportunity for all, and a generous worldview. Absent such liberalism, he now believed more firmly than ever, socialism was doomed to gulags, one-party states, and the new ruling class Djilas had warned against. The liberal ideal was the product of Western political and intellectual development, Stone reasoned, and had to be safeguarded and sustained against all foes, no matter where they proclaimed themselves to be situated on the ideological spectrum.

Izzy's championing of liberal principles provoked controversy, with some now accusing him of hypocrisy and worse. This despite the fact that he had done so all along, side by side with his support for socialism. The difference was that now, despite ever professing to be a radical and a Marxist, Izzy seemed to underscore the importance of liberal tenets perhaps more fully than before. Still, he continued to proclaim himself a radical, to consider it necessary for intellectuals to contest established thought, and to write for both leading left and liberal publications. He did so as the New Left headed the way of its predecessors and the nation experienced another rightward shift. But as the last of the three great American lefts of the twentieth century dissipated, Izzy remained determined to position himself as the intellectual activist.

In February 1972, the *New York Review* published the first of a pair of "I. F. Stone Reports" on the Soviet Union to appear in the journal. Russia under Leonid Brezhnev, Stone believed, had turned back into something of a giant prison; the crushing of the Prague Spring by Soviet tanks ensured that the possibility of peaceful change in Eastern Europe was increasingly unlikely. In reviewing the writings of Roy and Zhores Medvedev, Stone proclaimed that they had initiated a campaign to bring about a juncture of socialism and freedom and had warned of what could occur wherever secret police were allowed to operate. Five full decades had clearly shown, he continued, that socialism without freedom, no matter all the noble pronouncements, degenerated into "a suffocating nightmare."[6]

Fearing the makings of another kind of authoritarianism, Stone traced the unfolding of the Watergate scandal that brought down the president he despised more than any other. By June 1973, Stone was arguing that only the impeachment of Richard Nixon might stave off movement "toward Caesarism in the White House." By November, he warned that a presidential dictatorship threatened, which could endanger the liberties that the Founding Fathers had sought to protect. And he considered the ensuing pardon of "the biggest subversive" this nation had ever suffered to be an example of "Nixonism, pure and undefiled."[7]

But while developments in the United States and Russia deeply disturbed Stone, events in the Middle East troubled him every bit as much. And his writings on the latter subject that appeared in the *New York Review* resulted in an intellectual firestorm, one which dated back to 1967 when his controversial article on the Six-Day War had first been published. In a sense, what he had to say in the seventies was nothing different from his statements of a full decade earlier. Once again, he insisted that the treatment meted out to the Arabs would determine what type of people the Jews would become: "either oppressors and racists in our turn like those from whom we have suffered, or a nobler race able to transcend the tribal xenophobia that afflicts mankind."[8]

Izzy's increased prominence as editor of his famed newsletter and frequent contributor to the *New York Review,* as well as his growing stature within the antiwar movement, explains, at least in part, the caustic criticisms that now came his way. So too does the antagonism that poured forth from many Jewish intellectuals, particularly those based in New York City, such as Sidney Hook. "New York intellectuals" had come to wield great influence over the nation's cultural and literary life; many were now engaged in an odyssey from 1930s radicalism to postwar Cold War liberalism to neoconservatism. While Paul Goodman argued that Stone was too uncritical of the Jewish state, James

Michener termed his conclusions "palpably anti-Zionist, probably anti-Israel, and potentially anti-Jewish." *Midstream: A Monthly Jewish Review* devoted three full essays to damning Stone and his supposed historical revisionism, "disgraceful" accusations, "preposterous" equations, moral posturing, denial of Israel's right to exist as a Jewish state, and desire that the entire world be made over before Jews could rightfully be defended themselves.[9]

Younger writers such as Norman Podhoretz, who eventually ended up in the neoconservative camp, now employed *Commentary,* about to shift rightward as the *New York Review* continued its leftward course, to attack Izzy Stone. Both Martin Peretz and Robert Alter, writing in Podhoretz's journal, acknowledged the importance of "Mr. Stone's apostasy," which was said to be more influential than any other statement on the Middle East delivered by an American Jewish intellectual. Stone demanded a flawless Israel, Peretz declared, meaning one willing to relinquish its right to exist.[10]

From this point forth, Izzy and a fair number of other Jewish American intellectuals became engaged in a running battle. His declaration that Palestinian guerrillas were acting as Jewish "terrorists and saboteurs" once had in dealing with the British no doubt antagonized many. So too did his statement in the *New York Review* that both the Democratic and Republican parties had effectively delivered "a blank check for a hawkish Israeli policy," thereby placing discussion of the Arab refugees outside the bounds of standard political discourse. Moreover, Stone showed increased support for a Palestinian state.[11]

In late 1974, Izzy, still serving as a contributing editor of the *New York Review,* received an invitation for the first time in over two decades to speak in a synagogue, courtesy of Jewish peace activists in the capital. Delivering an address at Temple Sinai, he quoted from Isaiah, his favorite prophet, who had declared that "Israel shall be redeemed by justice"; this, Izzy insisted, now demanded justice for both Jews and Arabs. At the end of his talk, which was followed by a lengthy round of applause, came heated questions. One man recalled that the Jews had survived the biblical injunction to destroy the people of Canaan and still remained "a moral light in this world." Izzy retorted, "I really ought to make my answer in German." The cry came back, "Don't call me a Nazi." But others were inspired by Izzy, and Jewish peace groups such as Breira and the New Jewish Agenda soon sprang up in the Washington metropolitan area.[12]

Shortly thereafter, Stone, in another essay in the *New York Review,* troubled many others when he insisted that "the lesson of the holocaust is that to treat other human beings as less than human can lead to the furnaces. The way to honor the dead is to see the Palestinian Arab as a displaced brother, not as an expendable." Mike Blankfort wondered why Izzy failed to condemn "Arab madmen" as forcefully.[13]

On occasion, Izzy managed to rile pro-Arab forces also. In January 1976, he fired off a note to the *Washington Post* concerning a quote he had supposedly attributed to David Ben-Gurion, Israel's first prime minister. The quote, which had Ben-Gurion declaring that Israel was a country for Jews only, appeared in a full-page advertisement entitled "Zionism Is Racism . . . Anti-Zionism Is Not Anti-Semitism?" which ran in the *Post* in the middle of the month. Izzy denied that he had ever heard the Israeli founding father make such a foolish statement. The quest for peace, Izzy went on to say, was not aided "by such inflammatory falsifications." Alfred M. Lilienthal, chairman of the American Council on the Middle East, responded that Izzy was "neither a scholar nor a gentleman." He advised Izzy to refer to his own *New York Review* article of August 3, 1967, which had Ben-Gurion declare what the ad said he had. So who was the one given to "inflammatory falsification"? Lilienthal asked, before demanding a public apology.[14]

By the mid-1970s, the *New York Review*—which had published some of Stone's pieces on the Middle East that had caused such a fury—could no longer be accused of serving as the literary embodiment of radical intellectualism. Its focus was a good deal less political than had been the case during the late sixties, and what Philip Nobile had indicated in his study of the journal could occur "only over Chomsky's, Stone's, and rows of other limp bodies" had taken place. The *New York Review* no longer served as a forum for New Left ideas, whose time, admittedly, had come and passed.[15]

Stone's association with the *New York Review* appeared suddenly to weaken in mid-1976, following the publication of a review essay by Professor Allen Weinstein of Smith College attacking the defenders of Alger Hiss, which friends believed disturbed Izzy greatly. Although he did not know whether the former New Dealer was guilty of espionage or not, he considered the review to be an intemperate one. He reasoned that his name was on the masthead as a contributing editor of the *New York Review* and yet he really had no control over what was contained within its pages, notwithstanding what friends thought. Determined not to be "a dummy director" and feeling tired once more, the now sixty-eight-year-old Stone decided to resign from the journal.[16]

Nevertheless, Izzy remained on good terms with editors Bob Silvers and Barbara Epstein. Furthermore, his son Chris wondered, perhaps Izzy came to feel that "he was wrong and [had] overreacted." By 1978, his "Confessions of a Jewish Dissident," soon to be included in a reissue of *Underground to Palestine*, appeared in the *New York Review*, now more liberal than left-directed. In that article, Stone bemoaned the attacks that he was on the receiving end of whenever he happened to speak critically about Israel or in support of the Palestinians.[17]

And indeed, publication of that essay in the *New York Review* resulted in more barbs being thrown his way. Marie Syrkin, for her part, wondered if the book had been reissued simply to support this hardly "unhonored and unsung" writer's pretense of serving as an "impartial spokesman for the oppressed." She condemned his "PLO apologetics" and denied that he deserved in any way to be considered a Jewish dissident.[18]

But such criticisms were nothing compared to the latest assault on Izzy in *Midstream*, whose editorial board included Elie Wiesel. Written by Dartmouth professor Marvin Maurer, "I. F. Stone—Universalist" proclaimed Izzy's reputation as "a voice of conscience and morality" to be undeserved because of his purportedly inconsistent stand on the issue of human rights. It termed Stone "a militant in the Marxist camp" whose reading of the Middle East meshed with his longtime commitment to Marxism-Leninism. It deemed him an "open PLO-spokesman" who worked overtime to rewrite Zionist history and thereby vindicate "one of the world's most vicious murder machines." The essay ended with the admission that the journalist wanted Jews to discover "a place in the new Socialist order. But until that millennium, and until the Zionist lust for power is wiped out, Stone remains the comrade of those who call openly for the massacre of all Jews in Israel."[19]

Mike Blankfort, while declaring that those who believed as Izzy did were "blind to history and wrong from every point of view," fatally marred by belief in an outdated, bankrupt Marxism, again rose to defend him. Blankfort called Maurer's attack "a malicious libel" and compared it with charges once made by a Wisconsin senator named Joseph McCarthy.[20]

As Blankfort suggested, the good professor clearly had not done his homework. To argue as Maurer did that Stone long considered Russia as standing "in the forefront of world progress, a model for those aspiring to Socialism" was simply mistaken. To term him a militant Marxist was equally foolhardy. To proclaim him a PLO mouthpiece was absurd on the face of it. And to adjudge him a bedfellow of those who desired the destruction of Israel made no sense whatever.

Less easily dismissed was the charge that Stone and intellectuals such as Noam Chomsky focused almost wholly on Israeli sins and generally neglected to highlight the failings of the Arab states and the terrorist bent of various Palestinian factions. There was considerable truth to such an accusation, as there was to the notion that Izzy had taken greater pains to pinpoint the excesses of right-wing regimes than those of left-of-center states. And there was no doubt that reverence for universalism rather than Zionism alone did help to shape his analyses of Israeli practices.

Nevertheless, the early misgivings of Stone and Chomsky regarding Israeli policies and actions were not without significance. They foreshadowed the shaking, if not the wholesale collapse, of an ideological and emotional consensus on the state of Israel. Soon their arguments were not to be so easily dismissed as the rantings and ravings of supposedly self-hating Jews or of those inclined to an "anti-Semitic and anti-Israeli" perspective.

Stone, in spite of the invectives that continued to come his way, never stopped speaking out on Middle East tensions. As indicated by his essay that appeared in the October 26, 1978, edition of the *New York Review,* he was delighted by the Camp David accords, which called for the return of territory taken from Gamal Abdal Nasser's Egypt during the Six-Day War. He particularly applauded Menachem Begin, the right-wing Israeli prime minister, for finally admitting what Golda Meir, a Labor Socialist, never had: that a Palestinian people existed. He singled out PLO leader Yasir Arafat for criticism, calling it "political lunacy" to be speaking now of greater terrorism to come which would be targeted against the United States.[21]

As new Israeli settlements were built on the West Bank, however, Izzy began to sound less hopeful. He worried that religious fundamentalism could damage Israel irreparably and lead it down the path to self-destruction. With the Jewish state itself now riddled with turmoil, he suggested sardonically that it might become necessary for Arabs inside Israeli borders to don "special badges—perhaps—a yellow crescent" to distinguish them from their dark-hued Jewish brothers.[22]

Along with Richard Barnet, Noam Chomsky, Barry Commoner, Nat Hentoff, Jesse Jackson, Studs Terkel, and other luminaries, Izzy signed a letter which appeared in the *Washington Post* that condemned the Israeli invasion of Lebanon in June 1982. The document decried the devastation and "inhuman assault upon the civilian population" which had resulted, calling such acts "State terrorism" while defending "the national rights of the Palestinians."[23]

By now the writings of I. F. Stone—who had come to be perceived as some kind of elder statesman by at least a portion of American journalists and the intelligentsia—occasionally cropped up not only in the *New York Review of Books* but also in the editorial pages of such leading newspapers as the *Los Angeles Times,* the *Washington Post,* the *New York Times,* and the *Chicago Tribune.* In the *New York Review* and in op-ed pieces that he determined to syndicate himself, Stone blasted the Israeli handling of the Palestinian problem as well as superpower misdeeds in Central Asia and Central America. He condemned the Soviet invasion of Afghanistan as a violation of international law and as an attempt to force a puppet regime upon "an unwilling people." The move to quash the Polish Solidarity movement, he declared, suggested once again the need for both a free press and a shakeup of the Communist Party.[24]

But he was no more pleased with frantic talk of "crumbling crescents, arcs, and northern tiers," sounded as the shah of Iran was unceremoniously deposed. And as the hostage crisis at the American embassy in Tehran unfolded, he warned that war with a Moslem state would provide an opening for fundamentalists throughout the region who supported Ayatollah Ruhollah Khomeini. While fearing that the United States might be headed for "a slippery slope in Iran," he became more concerned still as "a smell of blood in the air" could be detected in Washington when the administration of Ronald Reagan came to power. He found the prophet Amos to be particularly relevant now and declared that "times are evil and prudent men are silent," the prudent sorts being "ass-kissing sons of bitches" in his eyes. He joined with Ed Asner, Harry Belafonte, Coretta King, Linus Pauling, Carl Sagan, Benjamin Spock, and some two hundred others in condemning American support for the El Salvadoran junta. He warned that the Reagan administration officials had reduced the Central American cauldron "to a spy thriller" in which a Soviet "hit list" first called for the toppling of "the benevolent Somozas in Nicaragua," to be followed by the collapse of "the sylvan elysiums of El Salvador, Guatemala, and Honduras." There, but for the work of "misguided nuns and dialectical materialism," the argument went, the poor but simple peasants would have remained forever contented.[25]

In mid-April 1982, he returned full circle, professionally speaking, as he began contributing a number of "Izzy Says . . ." notes, "I. F. Stone Reports," or "Stonegrams" to *The Nation*, which once again stood as the preeminent intellectual journal of the post–Vietnam-era American left, admittedly now in a considerably weakened state. In his writings for *The Nation*, Stone expressed his concerns about the Reagan defense buildup, the silence surrounding death squad atrocities in Central America, the possibility that the president's blusters and blunders might result in another Vietnam, the question of just what would result when the bill came due for "a profligate era."[26]

Editor Victor Navasky was quite excited about *The Nation*'s latest association with Stone, whom he saw as having a "gift for the one-liner." Navasky had visions of syndicating Stone in the manner Will Rogers once had been, in order to introduce Izzy to a whole new generation of readers. But Izzy worried about how much he could take on at this point of his life and opted to write only an occasional piece for *The Nation* instead, which itself could prove to be a fairly considerable undertaking.[27]

As matters turned out, Izzy would often call *The Nation* office regarding an idea he had for a story, with both parties agreeing that an article of two hundred and fifty words would follow. Then he would "stumble on something of a scoop" and phone once more, indicating now that five hundred words would be forthcoming. Eventually a one-thousand-word piece would come into the crowded, disheveled, and dilapidated Fifth Avenue offices of *The Nation*. Younger staff members found all this troubling, not a bit pleased that other stories had to be bumped, lacking any awareness "about the great I. F. Stone." Navasky would inform first one new staffer, then another, that they would long consider it a privilege to have dealt with "this institution."[28]

Eventually, the "old fire-horse" found even the "Izzy Says . . ." arrangement to be too much of a burden for he constantly worried about assignments, lost sleep, and just what the wire services (the *New York Times*, the *Washington Post*, the AP, the UPI, and Reuters) might have to say about the same or a related topic.[29]

Nevertheless, Izzy remained in good standing with both Victor Navasky and Bob Silvers of the *New York Review*. In the spring of 1987, *The Nation* and *The Vrej Nederlander*, a Dutch publication, were planning a conference on investigative journalism designed to attract progressive writers throughout Europe. The editors reasoned that no better draw could be found than Izzy Stone. But neither journal was well-heeled, to put it mildly, and the conference was scheduled for Amsterdam. So plans were made for discount airfare and hotel accommodations before Hamilton Fish, publisher of *The Nation*, put in a call to Izzy. "We'd love to do it," he responded. Fish asked his editor, Victor Navasky, just what the onetime staffer of *The Nation* had meant. "Oh," Navasky replied, "that must be Esther. Izzy doesn't go anywhere without Esther."[30]

The following day, Fish received a phone call from the prospective guest of honor. "Now you know," Izzy went on, "we really have found over the years that it's too much of a strain to fly going east, so we take the boat," the boat being the *Queen Elizabeth II*. The *QE-II*, after all, was the means of transit for the Stones when they made their annual summer visit to the continent. There, on the luxury liner, Izzy could partake of a secret passion of his—ballroom dancing. When Fish indicated he would check into it, Izzy informed him about a travel agent in Jacksonville, Florida, who always took care of such matters for the Stones, even to the point of requesting the specific cabin they favored.[31]

After discovering that the *QE-II* would dock in England a few days prior to the opening of the conference, Fish called Izzy, who proceeded to inform the publisher that the layover sounded just like what was in order. After all, Izzy declared, "at *our* age *we* need some time to get *our* land legs, and *we* have this little hotel in London which makes a nice base."[32]

A couple of days later, Fish heard from Izzy once more, phoning to check about lodging in the host city. "You know, Hamilton," Izzy stated, "I'm a romantic, and it's not often one gets to go to a city that has a charming little guest house along a canal. And it just so happens that Esther and I stayed at such a guest house many years ago."[33]

Both the conference and the lead speaker were a rousing success, while *The Nation* recouped a fair amount of its expenses when Izzy handed over his honorarium. The following year, The Nation Institute and the New School sponsored a series of talks delivered at the YMHA building at 92nd Street in New York City, in which Izzy spoke extemporaneously about U.S. policy toward Central America, the crisis in the Middle East, the state of the American economy, and the joys of his latest studies.[34]

During his final years, Izzy continued to contribute an occasional article to *The Nation* and to the *New York Review* as well, ranging from an attack on Reaganomics to critical analyses of Mikhail Gorbachev, the new Soviet premier. Even the ushering in of perestroika and glasnost did not satisfy this onetime friend of the Soviet state. He admitted that Gorbachev offered an opportunity to bring about a thaw in the Soviet sphere and to terminate the arms race that now threatened to become intergalactic. But he insisted that the soul of the Russian people needed to be revived after a long night of terror. It remained perilous to attempt to act the part of the good Communist in the Soviet Union, he insisted, if that resulted in a challenge to the perquisites of party apparatchiks.[35]

A number of Izzy's critical pieces on Gorbachev appeared in *The Nation* but did not go over well in the journal's New York office. Even Victor Navasky seemed to agree with the general impression that Izzy's analysis was the wrong one for the magazine, but published the articles anyway because of who had written them. But a number of younger staff members persisted in asking whether Izzy was "still in touch." Navasky recognized that Izzy could not keep up on everything, not with his failing health, his cataracts, his loss of energy, and all. When the editor expressed his feeling that Izzy's work was "a little out of context here," his old friend "felt a little . . . put off" and indicated he would see fit to publish it elsewhere. Nevertheless, Izzy continued to phone Navasky whenever he felt the need to complain about an editorial in *The Nation,* its Washington coverage, and the frittering away of precious space on graphics.[36]

In his final piece on Gorbachev, which was published in the February 16, 1989, issue of the *New York Review,* Stone warned about the cult of personality that had sprung up in the West surrounding the Soviet premier. He called attention to Gorbachev's attempt "to turn back the clock on human rights" in demanding that scrutiny of such matters was for national consumption only. Still, Stone believed that "the iceberg" might finally be melting. Once again, angry letters poured in to the offices of the journal.[37]

It was perfectly fitting that even as he reached old age and was finally forced to slow down his pace, I. F. Stone remained capable of provoking controversy, among friends and foes alike. His condemnations of Nixon were, of course, predictable. So too, by this point, were his criticisms of the Soviet Union. More surprising to some was his failure to go along with Gorbymania. Sixty plus years of attempting to grapple with what went on in Communist Russia had led him to distrust even reformers like Mikhail Gorbachev and Nikita Khrushchev, who seemed compelled to take at least one step backward for every move forward that they undertook. And his sharper and sharper analyses of Israeli policy invariably infuriated many.

Thus, no matter the great fame and acclaim that Izzy now experienced, he remained as controversial a figure in the eyes of certain individuals as he had ever been. Perhaps this too was due to the fact that he was as feisty as always and just as determined to go his own way, no matter whose sensibilities might thereby be offended. But then Izzy was not one to go gently into the good night, seemingly preferring instead to stir up something of an intellectual hornet's nest, which would necessarily have to be attended to by friends, colleagues, readers, and old antagonists.

He was fortunate that throughout this period publications of the caliber of the *New York Review of Books* and *The Nation* continued to welcome his typically pungent and provocative editorials and analyses. And in an age when many of his contemporaries from days past had died, lost their standing, or alienated readers with ideological shifts, Izzy retained a considerable following and ever remained the maverick journalist who appealed to his fellow reporters, other intellectuals, leftists, and liberals too. Perhaps they appreciated the constancy with which he had remained committed to the practice of investigative journalism and to progressive ideals.

Undoubtedly many recognized that for Izzy, as for themselves, such steadfast commitment was not all that easily accomplished by members of the American left of the late twentieth century. The New Left and the antiwar movement of the Vietnam era had withered away with something of a wimper, and the vision of socialism had badly foundered. In this time of apparent left-wing exhaustion, the presence of the intellectual as activist in the person of an individual such as I. F. Stone consequently seemed more important than ever. Quite possibly, it was that very state of the left and of the radical vision that compelled Izzy to look more and more fondly at authentic liberalism—not of the neoliberal variety, of course—and to search, in the dawn of his own life, for the roots of that tradition.

17 A Return to the Classics

Through it all, Esther had been there by his side. Their marriage, by all accounts, was "a most wonderful" one. In the eyes of fellow journalist Mary McGrory, "that's why Izzy's nature was so sweet." Esther made arrangements for all of Izzy's talks and travels, proofread his work, and handled editors who needed to be put off. She, in fact, "did it all, and loved it."[1]

Izzy, for his part, well appreciated Esther. "A good and loving wife," he wrote, "none better ever walked the earth." He credited her with constantly rekindling his zest and energy. Theirs was a real partnership, whether his journalistic work was involved or a night at a discotheque.[2]

They also shared the pleasure in knowing how successful their children had turned out. Celia was a prize-winning poet, married to Walter Gilbert of Harvard University, a Nobel laureate in molecular biology. Chris was the Roy P. Crocker Professor of Law at the University of Southern California. Jeremy, a mathematician, headed the Federation of American Scientists out of his Washington office and had become controversial enough in his own right for Joseph Alsop to denounce him as "a communist."[3]

The final chapter in Izzy Stone's life, which spanned the period from the end of the Vietnam War to his death in a hospital room in Boston on June 18, 1989, was one in which his reputation continued to grow. This popularity troubled him not in the least, for he enjoyed being the center of attention. Furthermore, age and growing frailty were not allowed to get in the way, as Izzy "maintained a really high profile." His stature became greater and greater still, until he stood as something of an icon for a certain portion of American journalists and the intelligentsia. In early 1973, Vintage Press published *The Best of I. F. Stone's Weekly*, to the delight of those called upon to review it: the newsletter was acclaimed as "increasingly legendary" by a reviewer in *Publishers Weekly* and was said to have been packed with "the most *informed*, articulate, and impassioned reportage of our time."[4]

The following year, a documentary film entitled *I. F. Stone's Weekly*, produced by a young Canadian, Jerry Bruck, Jr., was a sensation at the Cannes Film Festival and its subject "the great star" of the occasion.[5]

The *Chicago Tribune* proceeded to proclaim Izzy "America's latest folk hero." He retorted that "you can't take yourself too seriously." He, for one, had "to look into the mirror every morning and say 'You're full of it.' It's a good way to keep healthy."[6]

Kudos of all kinds continued to come his way. American University named him a distinguished scholar in residence. At a fund-raiser for the Fund for New Priorities, which had been established to champion liberal causes, held at the New York Plaza Hotel, three hundred and fifty guests, including William Sloane Coffin, Jules Feiffer, Arthur Schlesinger, Jr., and Kurt Vonnegut, each paid fifty dollars to honor I. F. Stone. When asked why he had shown up, Jack Newfield of the *Village Voice* answered that Stone was his role model: "He taught me to read the small print." The December 1978 issue of the *Saturday Review* contained a special section on contemporary heroes, including Muhammad Ali, Walter Cronkite, R. Buckminster Fuller, William Masters and Virginia Johnson, Earl Warren, and Izzy Stone. Ali was the heavyweight of the lot, Izzy quipped, and he, "the lightweight." The *Washington Post* style section contained a lengthy write-up on the occasion of the fiftieth wedding anniversary of Izzy and Esther Stone. Dick Cavett, Tom Snyder, and Hugh Downs (host of "Over Easy") all featured visits with the aging journalist on their television programs.[7]

As the Reagan era began, those semiregular "Izzy" columns began to appear in *The Nation,* much to the delight of editor Victor Navasky. Meanwhile, the establishment press continued to welcome Izzy back into its fold, with op-ed pieces of his appearing in leading newspapers across the land. And on June 19, 1981, after thirty-eight years away, the National Press Club finally readmitted its formerly wayward son. Now welcomed back with a standing ovation, Izzy declared Washington to have been "full of such cowards" in times past, then proceeded to attack the Reagan administration. He also blasted the administration during an appearance on "Sixty Minutes," the popular television show.[8]

In 1983, the Washington-based Institute for Policy Studies, the left-wing think tank, named Izzy as its first honorary fellow; he had been involved with IPS since its founding twenty years earlier. In 1987, the ACLU awarded him its Medal of Liberty. The following year, Little, Brown decided to reissue his old volumes of essays and to print a new collection as well, *The War Years: 1939–1945,* all as part of a series entitled "A Noncomformist History of Our Times." A Library of Congress exhibition, "The American Journalist: Paradox of the Press," contained a section on "Crusaders"—including Frederick Douglass, William Lloyd Garrison, Thomas Nast, Joseph Pulitzer, and I. F. Stone. The display on Stone featured a five-dollar check from Albert Einstein, one of the *Weekly*'s charter subscribers; a laudatory letter from Bertrand Russell, another friend and mentor; Izzy's scribbled and critical notes ("Delphic declaration") regarding a copy of an address delivered by Mikhail

Gorbachev to the UN General Assembly; the magnifying glasses he used for reading near the end of his life; and his Macintosh word processor, with its twenty-four-point type.[9]

Izzy's reputation had been sustained by his devoted commitment to radical and liberal ideals—indeed, to the very idea of the left itself—and to the notion that journalists and intellectuals alike must critically examine their own societies and be willing to speak their minds. It had been nurtured, too, by the near fablelike tales of the *Weekly*, his devoted individualism, and his willingness to question the true believers, even if that included himself.

B ut Izzy's greatest acclaim during his final years resulted from the completion of a project that spanned two decades of life, beginning at the time he put the *Weekly* to rest. He had conceived the idea for the project—for his "great" work—in that New York City hospital room back in the summer of 1967 when he believed that death was approaching. A self-proclaimed lifelong radical and Marxist, he affirmed at the time that he remained "a man of the left—absolutely." Yet Izzy saw himself as "an old-fashioned liberal" as well, who considered himself to be both a Jeffersonian and a socialist. In the final issue of the newsletter, dated December 1971, he declared that the most important task of the contemporary age was to discover a means to wed freedom and socialism, something he had believed for four full decades now. Feeling relieved from the stress involved in having to put out his own publication and wanting "to give the best that's in me," he intended to produce a study on how such a state of affairs might be brought about. This in turn led him to believe that an analysis of the historical roots of freedom itself must be undertaken.[10]

The proposed study appeared daunting, but Izzy reasoned he had "been practicing scales long enough" and had "learned a thing or two about the English language." Semiretirement would afford the time and opportunity, he believed, to produce something of real worth "and make it beautiful."[11]

Feeling versed in American constitutional law, Izzy began his latest intellectual odyssey with a look at the two great English revolutions of the seventeenth century. Out of the ferment in Mother England had come Milton's "Areopagitica," which he considered to be the greatest defense of freedom of the press ever written. After immersing himself for a glorious year in seventeenth-century England, he felt the need to delve back into the Renaissance, the Reformation, and the Middle Ages, where the spiritual ancestors of Voltaire were to be found. Continuing to work his way back in time, Izzy landed in ancient Athens where he believed freedom of speech and expression had begun. He viewed Athens as the place where civilization had first really flowered, and the land from which "we're all the heirs."[12]

Thus, in his effort to sustain both radical and liberal tenets, Izzy had returned to the source of them both as he saw it—classicism. All were part of the Western intellectual tradition which he believed had accomplished much, promised still more, and was of great intrinsic worth.

He soon became even more involved in his studies. He found the standard sources to be inadequate and turned to the writings of the classical Greeks themselves, which he had always revered. But he discovered that the language of the ancients and that of modern peoples were rarely perfectly matched, and consequently soon decided that reading works in the original was required. So armed with a year of Greek and six years of Latin taken back in high school and college nearly half a century before, he began to study Greek grammar and jumped right into the Gospel of St. John. He then went on to Homer and Sappho, before attempting to read Plato. It took him months, a quartet of Greek-English editions, a Greek-French copy, and hundreds of pages of notes to plow through the first volumes. He found himself overjoyed one moment and depressed the next. Learning Greek, he discovered, was "like climbing Mt. Everest on your hands and knees." But he was grateful to have lived long enough to have devoured the *Iliad,* even though occasionally he felt overwhelmed by its vast store of knowledge. He found Homer to be "to poetry what the Bible is to prose, the fountainhead, the source, the gold mine." Sappho proved to be an enchanting temptress, taking up a full month of his time. He developed "a love-hate relationship with Plato," despising the ideas of the "reactionary old aristocrat" but marveling in the alluring genius that was Socrates' *Apology.* Now Izzy understood the appeal of the sirens for Ulysses as he felt himself caught up in "the power of the Word, as it was sung and spoken by the most gifted people that ever lived." For Esther, Izzy's reaction was not all that surprising. "Everything's so real to him. He's right there."[13]

Early in his journey back into classical times, Izzy visited St. Anthony's College at Oxford University and found the academic environment to be far more enticing this second time around. Upon returning home, he began making a daily two-and-a-half-mile trek to the closest college campus. He ended up in the library stacks at American University, where he began pulling volume after volume of Plato, the pre-Socratics, Aristotle, Xenophon, Thucydides, Aristophanes, the New Testament, Philo Judaeus, the neo-Platonists, and the fathers of the Roman Catholic Church off the shelves. After a year or so of intellectual rummaging, he was discovered by university officials, who promptly offered to name him Distinguished Scholar in Residence. He readily accepted and was given an office in the literature department, which enabled "this recycled freshman" to continue with his studies. He became something of a recognizable figure on campus, often joined by "other students" as he put it, during his lunchtime saunters to the cafeteria.

He found it thrilling to have come upon "a new community of people" eager to hear of his work.[14]

As word got out that Izzy was now traveling the road he had disdained so long ago, news clippings and invitations for guest lectures came fast and furious. The *Washington Post* headlined "I. F. Stone Returns to College at 68." The *Houston Post* noted that the still "incorrigible" Izzy Stone, "his intellectual tapeworm now demanding a new delicacy (savory ancient Greek elegies)," had spoken in Berkeley on his work-in-progress—the title of his address: "A Recycled Freshman in Ancient Greece." The *New York Times Magazine* in January 1978 printed "Izzy on Izzy," a lengthy self-interview, which highlighted his classical discoveries. He found journalism and scholarship to be a good fit, for both required a careful examination of sources and a reading between the lines.[15]

Soon Izzy felt ready to reveal something about his latest scoop, which demonstrated once again how he could become immersed in the particular or how he at times lacked "patience for large ideas," as Chris Stone readily acknowledged. It involved the trial of Socrates and the decision by the ancient city of Athens to condemn the great philosopher to death. He sought to unveil why this had occurred in the city where democracy had its roots. Socrates, he discovered, had remained in Athens during the reign of the Thirty Tyrants, failed to take them to task, and later continued to foster disrespect for the ways of the city. While not defending the verdict handed down to Socrates, Stone believed that his analyses provided some insight into the complexity of Athenian political life that had been obscured by Plato's *Apology*.[16]

It took "a lot of chutzpah," Izzy admitted, to attempt to become a classicist at this point in his career, but universities such as Princeton, Georgetown, Harvard, and McGill opened their doors for him to come talk about his latest work.[17]

Perhaps all of this was an indication of how far the political and intellectual spectrum had shifted from the days when Joseph McCarthy attempted to create a dragnet over the American nation. As Chris Stone has noted, "people became less afraid to see [Izzy] and more interested to see him." Perhaps this was simply well-deserved recognition for a long and now celebrated career. And then again, the changed attitudes might have indicated that Izzy was now perceived as presenting "less of a threat."[18]

Given his original intentions, it appeared as though Izzy had taken an unexpected and uncharacteristic detour. Since his teenage years, he had been a socially conscious and politically committed individual who turned to journalism as a means through which he could combine professionalism, activism, and intellectualism. Now he allowed himself the luxury of investigating matters dear to his own heart which did not readily demonstrate either the immediate or the long-term relevance he insisted that they did. This former college dropout had returned to school again, literally and otherwise, happily playing the role of scholar and academic, all the while still serving as a chronicler of present-day events. Nevertheless, the diligence with which he approached his classical studies—certainly not the classics themselves—demonstrated an indulgence on his part which Izzy the reporter had been incapable of.

Largely released from the rigors of the journalistic trade, Izzy was now able "to return to thoughts he had dealt with earlier to some degree . . . which are a little more subterranean or undersea or not quite as rapidly shifting and [focus] a little more . . . [upon] the permanent attributes of the world," according to Chris Stone. That "fantastic breadth of knowledge" he had acquired involving theology, church history, and philosophy undoubtedly served as a spur for his latest intellectual venture.[19]

Izzy began to lecture on the virtues of classical learning whenever the opportunity arose. One Saturday afternoon in 1981, Ilene Barth, a columnist for *Newsday*, along with her husband and their not quite two-year-old son, visited the Stones at their home in Washington. Esther and the youngster, just past the breast-feeding stage, headed off to the garden, delicate china teacups in hand, his filled with milk naturally. Looking askance, Barth listened as Izzy reassured her: "He'll live up to what's expected of him." He then pointed out how appealing Greek mythology was to even the smallest would-be classicists, who would no doubt enjoy hearing the tales of *The Iliad* of Homer.[20]

Such an occasion was an indication that Izzy had indeed "mellowed quite out a bit," as Chris noted. Now he was "more accessible" than before, had "lots of time to talk," and took particular delight in the time he spent with his four grandchildren.[21]

Nevertheless, on his eightieth birthday—with his research finally complete—the *New York Times* reported that for Izzy, that old investigative reporter, "the scooping" appeared to go on and on. Wracked by failing eyesight and hearing difficulties which had returned once again, he now also lacked his legendary supply of unbounded energy. Nonetheless, the *Times* indicated, Izzy seemed to be greatly enjoying it all, surrounded as he was by the library he dearly loved. Greek, Latin, English, French, and German editions of the classics, along with biographies, bibles, plays, historical treatises, novels, and his own newspaper work, filled the two-story home of Izzy and Esther Stone. There was so much he had yet to read, he admitted, and so much to learn. But as he informed the *Times* reporter, "I'm having a wonderful old age of scholarship. I'm having a ball."[22]

Harper's published his article "When Free Speech Was First Condemned" in February 1988, the same month his long-awaited book on his studies came out. Both revolved around the trial of Socrates in his native city of Athens, which resulted in the martyrdom, Izzy indicated, the old philosopher consciously sought. Nevertheless, Stone believed, Socrates had been unfairly accused, having committed no overt acts against Athens. The sentence itself, he continued, violated free speech, which Athenians had considered to be most sacred of all. And yet Socrates could have avoided his fate, Stone insisted, had he but chosen to make this a trial "of ideas, and therefore of Athens." Had Socrates declared freedom of speech to be a basic Athenian right, he would have found a responsive chord and been acquitted.[23]

An identical argument was more fully articulated in Izzy's latest book, *The Trial of Socrates*. Stone started off with a blanket condemnation of both Socrates and Plato, whose belief in absolute rule, rejection of the polis, and demeaning of the common man, he reasoned, contained the seeds of totalitarianism. Socrates, Stone continued, sought to besmirch democracy and to entice the young into following his lead. Stone admitted that there was no evidence to suggest that the accused had called for democracy to be overthrown by force. But Socrates' antidemocratic preaching, Stone argued, led his followers to view the Athenian constitution with disdain and to act accordingly.[24]

Thus, Socrates' teaching proved threatening "when applied to the affairs of the *Polis*." Indeed, had his "negative dialectic" become commonplace, justice and democracy could not have worked. Given the anti-Athenian cast of Socrates' preachings, Stone suggested, it was not surprising that many believed that his punishment fit the crime. But Socrates also got what he wanted, Stone continued, and as a consequence became "a secular saint" whose death left a permanent blight upon democracy. The killing of Socrates amounted to the city's "tragic crime."[25]

The Trial of Socrates became a bestseller and Izzy Stone was back in the news once again. *The New Republic* heralded the book as a particularly honest account that bespoke "the passion of a highly intelligent writer." *The Nation* proclaimed it a fully appealing "do-it-yourself detective kit, philological meander and owner's manual on free speech and class animus" in classical times. The *New York Times* declared its scholarship to be "alive and engaging." The *Los Angeles Times* saw *The Trial of Socrates* as a wholly "fascinating" study that exuded "scholarship and judgement . . . balance and understanding" and exhibited the author's devoted belief in human liberty; Stone himself was adjudged "a true wise man in a sometimes unwise era" who had conducted "this labor of love" as a septagenarian.[26]

Nevertheless, the reviews, including many of these same ones, were not altogether complimentary, and some proved to be downright scathing. *The Trial of Socrates* was declared to be no work of scholarship and Stone fearfully naive about any number of philosophical matters. His "slightly glib" and present-minded attempt to evaluate the past through the eyes of the present was criticized; his depiction of Plato, called "crude"; and his suggestion that a classical civil libertarian stance would have won the day for Socrates, simply "farfetched." As a number of reviewers pointed out, the very notion of civil liberties had no place in ancient Athens. Stone's analysis was said to be off base; Athens was an imperial and religiously oriented state where public participation in the Assembly was certainly not widespread. Only some ten percent of the population—women, slaves, and foreigners not among them— could even partake of Athenian civic life. A Yale University classics professor, critiquing the book for *Commentary,* found Stone's Athens to be a "mythical" one; his analysis of the "vulgarly reductionist" sort; and his general reading of Socrates' intentions, "ludicrous."[27]

But the most damning indictments appeared in the *New York Times,* the *Chicago Tribune,* the *Christian Science Monitor,* and the *San Francisco Chronicle,* where his sister now served as a theater critic. One reviewer pointed out that Stone appeared to be "blaming the victim" in portraying Socrates as "a patron saint of reaction." The others noted that Stone underscored Socrates' guilt by association. In the process, Stone empathized with those disturbed by the ways of Socrates and excused Athens for having sentenced him to death. The end result, in the eyes of one reviewer, meant that Stone "echoes, oddly, a McCarthyism."[28]

Izzy dismissed such criticisms as the rantings of stodgy academics. But he was troubled by at least one review drawn by "that bastard" Sidney Hook who termed him "a cultural philistine" in the pages of the *Wall Street Journal.* Hook, in his own words, had indignantly witnessed Stone's growing reputation "as a great libertarian." Hook had been infuriated when "that son-of-a-bitch" took to championing Roy Medvedev and he continued to demand that Stone "come clean" about his fellow-traveling past.[29]

Unquestionably, the emphasis I. F. Stone placed on Socrates' compelling the young rabble to pick up an anti-Athenian banner was startling indeed. So too was his insistence that "what was legitimate if sometimes ponderous philosophical playfulness . . . became disruptive when applied to the affairs of the *polis.*" Then there was Izzy's underscoring of the old man's failure to deny that certain leading oligarchs—having taken his negative dialectic to heart—had actively engaged in conspiracies. Finally, *The Trial of Socrates* contained the implicit notion that because it was widely believed that Socrates had gotten his just desserts, then he had.[30]

Notwithstanding the sales figures and admittedly mixed reviews that *The Trial of Socrates* received, the book in the end did prove to be disconcerting.

For so many of the arguments worked out in *The Trial of Socrates* flew in the face of so much that I. F. Stone had long stood for. One could almost hear the same arguments being used against Stone at various points throughout his career, arguments of a disturbingly anti-civil-libertarian sort which he surely must not have intended. *His* writings had so often been painted with an anti-American smear. *His* analyses had repeatedly been declared to have led others astray. *He* had been portrayed as a left-wing Pied Piper, merrily leading the young down a primrose path far removed from more constructive avenues.

On February 5, 1988, Izzy, in order to plug his latest book, delivered the first address he had made since turning eighty before a full house at San Francisco's Herbst Theatre. Elated simply still to be "extant," Izzy carried on "a conversation at 80," as had been promised. Looking natty in Stone-like fashion—he wore a three-piece tweed suit and a red tie with a white handerchief in the top pocket—he spoke on a wide range of subjects, including the Athenians and the clash with their most famous citizen. As the two-hour presentation neared an end, a birthday cake was brought out, causing Izzy to admit he had been wondering "what the hell does 80 years mean in the life of the human race?" Michelangelo, after all, who became an octagenarian himself, had once remarked, "What a shame, I was just beginning to learn the alphabet of my art."[31]

Certainly Izzy's Greek project, no matter how it was received, was a joyous experience for him. It enabled him to play the part of academic in his waning years, a role that he must have relished. For in spite of Izzy's mixed remembrances of his years at Penn, his appearances on college campuses in the midst of the McCarthy era, during the Vietnam War, and afterward always seemed to reinvigorate him, as did the reception he invariably was accorded. In an interview conducted while his Greek studies were still going on, Izzy admitted that yes, maybe he was now taking that other path.[32]

To a degree, of course, he had been going down that road all along, at the very same time he practiced the craft of journalism. He had long prided himself on his carefully documented writings, often the product of voluminous reading, in addition to his investigative work. Not everyone saw it that way, believing that like any good polemicist, Izzy carefully selected the facts he used to support predetermined analyses.

He had in mind one final project: "a series of biographical essays on the seminal figures involved in freedom of thought." He was fully aware that extensive research and study were required but seemed to believe "he had one more book in him."[33]

That book, of course, was not to be. A recent operation to correct his vision had reinvigorated him, but only temporarily as matters turned out. Feeling weak once again, Izzy was admitted to the cardiology unit at Boston's Brigham and Women's Hospital on May 21, 1989. In the eyes of all concerned, he remained very much himself until the very end. Upon coming out of surgery, he immediately asked, "What's going on in China?" referring to the prodemocracy movement. In a way, this should have surprised no one, Izzy being Izzy and his interest in the Chinese students being as strong as it was. Two years before, conducting a lonely vigil, Izzy could be seen close by the White House, holding up a candle for the fledgling Chinese movement. But early on the morning of June 18, the heart of this generous and egotistical, ever-serious and impish, petulant and kindly man at last gave out.[34]

The celebration of I. F. Stone's life and career immediately followed. A front-page editorial in *The Nation* saluted him for having inspired a generation of journalists; it was indicated that he would remain an exemplar for a good long while to come. He was, the journal declared, "a quadruple threat. He combined the meat-and-potatoes moxie of a police reporter, the instinct for precision of a scholar, the question-phrasing skill of a Socrates . . . and the political philosophy of an anarchist." *The Nation* piece concluded with the observation that "his like" would not be seen again. On a radio talk show, Studs Terkel was asked if "anyone around today . . . could fill his shoes?" Terkel responded with a quick, "Not by a long shot. He was unique. . . . He was independent. . . . He had to get at the truth." In a cartoon sketch, Jules Feiffer portrayed a worried-looking fellow pondering about China, Gorbachev, Eastern Europe, the Supreme Court, and the American media. "Who's left to tell me what to make of all this?" he asked himself. After all, "Izzy's dead."[35]

But fittingly enough, not everybody saw Izzy in the same light. The *National Review* dismissed him as "a conformist, a lockstep leftist." *The New Republic* contained an "Izzy Stone, R.I.P." note which argued that for the first four decades of his career, he had been at odds with mainstream thought. This "terribly nice man" did oppose McCarthyism, Jim Crow, and U.S. involvement in Vietnam. But to the very end, *The New Republic* declared, Izzy viewed his own nation in a "rather uncomplicated" manner. "He thought it in the wrong, very much on the wrong side of history." And his famed objectivity and critical eye, "his insistence on norms" were all too often missing, *The New Republic* charged, when it came to revolutionary governments. He was one who "selected the facts he reported in accordance with an ideology that had no such reverence," the magazine insisted.[36]

On July 18, four hundred friends, colleagues, and loved ones appeared at Washington's Friends Meeting Hall for a second memorial tribute to Izzy Stone. (The first had taken place in New York City on July 12.) Kai Bird, Ben Bradlee, Jerry Bruck, Bill Grieder, Seymour Hersh, Haynes Johnson, Stanley

Karnow, Charles Krauthammer, Sally Quinn, and Strobe Talbott, among others, came to pay their respects.[37]

Peter Osnos acted as moderator, as he had done at the New York service. After remarking that "it looks like Izzy had a lot of friends," Osnos spoke of working for him back in the summer of 1965 as that hundred-dollar-a-week research assistant. He remembered Izzy as a tough taskmaster but also as a "world-class talker" and one who "listened as intently as he did everything else." Osnos concluded his own observations by acknowledging, "Working for Izzy was not for sissies. But being his friend, now that was a joy."[38]

Izzy, Osnos declared, was a "reporter, writer, scholar, humanist . . . radical, entrepeneur, raconteur . . . and mensch." Marcus Raskin, cofounder of the Institute for Policy Studies, referred to Izzy as a "child of the enlightenment," for whom there was "no question that should not be asked and no place where one should not look for an answer." Eloquently and as an obvious retort to those who had long claimed otherwise, Raskin drew the picture of the I. F. Stone he knew and chose to remember. "As an American, he expected the best from his country. He loved the nation like Tom Paine or Thomas Jefferson must have loved it, as an unfinished vision, as a place to pursue happiness, as a community where opportunity and opportunism were not synonymous, as a revolutionary experiment that would always have to see to it that its social contract included all of its citizens."[39]

Controversy therefore continued to swirl about Izzy Stone, with some refusing to forgive him for purportedly having supported Stalinism in the past and both neo-Stalinism and anti-Zionism in more recent times. Others considered him to be one of the authentic heroes of the American left, an exemplar of commitment, intellectual integrity, and professionalism. They saluted his devotion to the craft of journalism, particularly his investigative work, biting editorials, and eloquent pensmanship. They respected his reverence for the loftiest ideals the West had to offer, his attempts to rekindle interest in classicism, and his lifelong quest to find a means to join liberalism and socialism. They found it noteworthy that he had sought to combine intellectual pursuits and political activism. They applauded his willingness to question both government abuses in countries as disparate as the United States, the Soviet Union, and Israel, and the failings of left-wing movements too. They admired his early support for European Jewry and his concern for the Palestinian refugees. They appreciated how this critic of American capitalism gloated in his own entrepreneurial accomplishments.

But most of all, they saw him as a man who had proven true to himself and who sought to share with a broader public his vision of the truth. They viewed him as an instinctive maverick who had nevertheless managed to become a leading figure in American left-of-center, journalistic, and intellectual circles. And they recognized that his kind would not soon come again.

His passing seemed to close a chapter in the history of the American left, at least as it had been constituted from the 1920s to the present. Now the already greatly weakened left in the United States was to be lacking not only one of its own, but a moral and intellectual touchstone, for better or worse.

18 The Rock of Stone

D id he consider himself "a happy rebel?" he was asked in the course of a pair of day-long interviews conducted sometime in the winter of his life.[1]

He—a veteran of La Follette-style progressivism, Norman Thomas socialism, early 1930s communism, the Popular Front, the New Left, and investigative journalism—pondered for a moment and then answered thoughtfully. "Yeah. Yeah, that's true. I never thought of that. I guess a lot of rebels are unhappy. I think if you're not happy, it's very bad. Because unless you enjoy bucking your head against a stone wall, you're going to be so damned unhappy. If you expect to bring paradise and utopia by tomorrow morning, you don't understand the difficulties or history. . . . See, you have to enjoy the battle for itself." He then referred to Shaemas O'Sheel's poem, "They Went Forth to Battle but They Always Fell," and declared that the only battles worth waging were the ones you were sure to lose. But fighting the good fight, no matter the outcome, enabled others to carry on.[2]

In his own lifetime, Izzy had certainly seen that happen. The antiwar movement had succeeded, he believed. J. Edgar Hoover had been disgraced. Exposés of the FBI and the CIA had taken place in the halls of Congress.[3]

He was pleased that the left, virtually obliterated during the most virulent times of the red scare, had resurfaced during the Vietnam era, before stumbling once again. This was due in part to the failure of New Leftists to study and learn from the past as Izzy felt that he had done, in order to avoid the suicidal sectarianism of the Old Left and other radical movements. Left-wing dogma, every bit as much as that of the religious variety, had to be guarded against.

He was not always optimistic, Izzy admitted, but believed that "you have to take the long view." And he recalled something a friend had once told this self-driven and ever-committed activist and intellectual, which now seemed so appropriate. "Izzy, what you do is like pissin' against a boulder. It doesn't seem to make any difference, but then the rock begins to wear away."[4]

That Sisyphean struggle had appeared to be the twentieth-century American left's as well.

Notes

Throughout the Notes section, "Stone" denotes I. F. Stone; full names are used with family members and other relatives.

Abbreviations

Compass	*New York Daily Compass*
NYRB	*New York Review of Books*
Post	*New York Post*
Record	*Philadelphia Record*
Weekly	*I. F. Stone's Weekly*

1. Izzy, the Icon

1 Interview with Stone, October 16, 1981; Jerry Bruck, Jr., director, *I. F. Stone's Weekly,* narrated by Tom Wicker, I. F. Stone Project, 1973.

2 Memorial service for Stone, New York Society for Ethical Culture, New York City, July 12, 1989; interview with Peter Osnos, July 25, 1989; *Guests,* in the possession of Esther Stone, Washington, D.C.

3 Memorial service, July 12, 1989; memorial service for Stone, Friends Meeting Hall, Washington, D.C., July 18, 1989.

4 Memorial service, July 12, 1989.

5 Ibid.

6 Mary McGrory, "The Outside Was Where He Wanted to Be," *Washington Post,* June 20, 1989, p. A2; Anthony Lewis, "The Lure of Power," *NY Times,* June 22, 1989, p. A23; Larry Josephson interview with Studs Terkel, "Modern Times" radio program, transcript, pp. 13–16.

7 Memorial service, July 12, 1989; interviews with Peter Osnos, July 24, 1989, July 25, 1989.

8 "I. F. Stone, RIP," *National Review* 41 (July 14, 1989): 19.

9 Memorial service, July 18, 1989.

2. Early Progress

1 Interview with Stone, October 15, 1981; John P. Diggins, *Mussolini and Fascism: The View from America* (Princeton: Princeton University Press, 1975), pp.

140–143; Gaetano Salvemini, "Murder by Persons Unknown," *Nation* 125 (July 13, 1927): 34–35.

2 Interview with Stone, October 15, 1981; Diggins, *Mussolini and Fascism*, pp. 213–214.

3 Interview with Stone, October 15, 1981.

4 Ibid.

5 Lou Stone, "The Family," 1987, pp. 1–2, 13; interviews with Lou Stone, July 16, 1989, September 24, 1987; interview with Christopher Stone, January 6, 1992; Stone, Passport Application, October 5, 1945, p. 1, State Department Files (SDF), PO37; "Record of a Birth in Philadelphia," Department of Public Health, Division of Communicable Diseases—Vital Statistics Section, Office of Passport Services, SDF, PO38.

6 Interviews with Lou Stone, July 16, 1989, September 24, 1987; Lou Stone, "The Family," pp. 2–3; interview with Stone, September 3, 1983; Stone, Passport Application, October 5, 1945, p. 1.

7 Lou Stone, "The Family," p. 3; Marc Stone, "Max," April 23, 1988, p. 3; interview with Stone, September 3, 1983; interview with Lou Stone, July 16, 1989.

8 Interview with Lou Stone, July 16, 1989; Lou Stone, "The Family," p. 5; Douglas B. Rauschenberger and Katherine Mansfield Tassini, *Lost Haddonfield* (Haddonfield: Historical Society of Haddonfield, 1989), p. 53.

9 Interview with Lou Stone, July 16, 1989; Lou Stone, "The Family," pp. 5–6.

10 Interviews with Lou Stone, September 24, 1987, July 16, 1989; Stone, "Books That Changed Our Minds," *New Republic* 95 (December 21, 1938): 205.

11 Interviews with Lou Stone, July 16, 1989, September 24, 1987.

12 Ibid.

13 Interview with Marc Stone, September 27, 1987; interviews with Lou Stone, July 16, 1989, September 24, 1987.

14 Interview with Lou Stone, September 24, 1987.

15 Letter to author from Lou Stone, January 26, 1992; Marc Stone, "Max," p. 4.

16 Interview with Lou Stone, July 16, 1989; interview with Judy Stone, February 23, 1992.

17 Ibid.; letter by Stone, 1934.

18 Letter by Stone, 1934.

19 Lou Stone, "The Family," pp. 7–8; interviews with Stone, September 3, 1983, October 15, 1981; Stone, "I. F. Stone on Bertrand Russell on Bertrand Russell," *Ramparts* 7 (August 10, 1968): 72; Stone, "Books That Changed Our Minds," pp. 205–206; Stone, "Notes on Closing, but Not on Farewell," *Weekly* 19 (December 14, 1971): 1; Leonard Downie, Jr., *The New Muckrakers* (New York: New American Library, 1976), p. 198.

20 Lou Stone, "The Family," pp. 7–8; interviews with Stone, September 3, 1983, October 15, 1981; Stone, "Books That Changed Our Minds," pp. 205–206; Stone, "Notes on Closing," p. 1; Downie, *The New Muckrakers*, p. 198; John Tebbel and Mary Ellen Zuckerman, *The Magazine in America, 1741–1990* (New York: Oxford University Press, 1991), pp. 203–207.

21 Stone, "Books That Changed Our Minds," p. 205; interview with Stone, October 15, 1981; Stone, "Notes on Closing," p. 1; Lou Stone, "The Family," p. 10.

22 Interview with Stone, October 16, 1981; Stone, "Notes on Closing," p. 1; Stone, "Editorials," March 1922, p. 1.

23 Stone, "Bigotry Defeated Again!" *The Progress*, April 1922, p. 1.

24 Stone, "Editorial Note," *American Mercury* 29 (May 1933): xxiv; interview with Stone, October 16, 1981; interview with Lou Stone, July 16, 1989.

25 Interview with Lou Stone, July 16, 1989; interview with Stone, October 16, 1981.

26 Ibid.

27 Interview with Stone, October 16, 1981.

28 Ibid.; Alberta Rockhill Black, note on Stone; "Isadore Feinstein," *The Shield* (Haddonfield High School Senior Yearbook), 1924.

29 E. Digby Baltzell et al., "The Jewish Communities of Philadelphia and Boston," in *Jewish Life in Philadelphia, 1830–1940,* ed. Murray Friedman (Philadelphia: Ishi Publications, 1983), pp. 309–310; Michael Blankfort, unpublished autobiography, Michael Blankfort Collection, Mugar Memorial Library, Boston University.

30 Blankfort, unpublished autobiography.

31 Ibid.

32 Ibid.

33 Ibid.; Murray Friedman, "Introduction: The Making of a National Jewish Community," in *Jewish Life,* pp. 21–22.

34 Blankfort, unpublished autobiography; Michael Blankfort, "Diary," February 28, 1929, Blankfort Collection; Michael Blankfort to Walter Hart, August 1, 1932, p. 3, Blankfort Collection; Michael Blankfort to Mr. Lyle, June 24, 1972, September 9, 1972, pp. 1–2, Blankfort Collection.

35 Interview with Stone, October 16, 1981; interview with Marc Stone, September 27, 1987; interview with Lou Stone, July 16, 1989; Blankfort, unpublished autobiography.

36 Blankfort, unpublished autobiography.

37 Interview with Stone, October 15, 1981; Stone, "Books That Changed Our Minds," p. 206; Stone, "Notes on Closing," p. 2.

38 Terry A. Cooney, *The Rise of the New York Intellectuals: Partisan Review and Its Circle, 1934–1945* (Madison: University of Wisconsin Press, 1986), p. 32.

39 Stone to Michael Blankfort, July 21, 1925, pp. 1–2 (sic), 4, Blankfort Collection; Diggins, *Mussolini and Fascism,* pp. 44, 53–55, 213–214.

40 Stone to Blankfort, July 21, 1925, pp. 1, 4.

41 Ibid., p. 3.

42 Stone to Blankfort, June 14, 1926, Blankfort Collection.

43 Interview with Stone, October 16, 1981.

44 Ibid.; Stone, "Notes in Closing," p. 1.

45 Interview with Stone, October 16, 1981.

46 Interviews with Lou Stone, September 24, 1987, July 16, 1989; interview with Stone, October 16, 1981.

47 Interview with Stone, October 16, 1981.

48 Ibid.; photograph of Stone, courtesy Lou Stone; photograph of Esther Stone, *Washington Post,* July 9, 1979, p. B1.

49 Interview with Marc Stone, September 27, 1989.

50 Myra MacPherson, "Gathering No Moss," *Washington Post,* July 9, 1979, pp. B1–2.

51 Interview with Marc Stone, September 27, 1989.

52 Interview with Lou Stone, July 16, 1989.

53 Ibid.; Lou Stone, "The Family," p. 12; Bonnie Fox Schwartz, "Unemployment Relief in Philadelphia, 1930–1932: A Study of the Depression's Impact on

Voluntarism," in *Hitting Home: The Great Depression in Town and Country,* ed. Bernard Sternsher (Chicago: Quadrangle Books, 1970), pp. 60–80.

54 Lou Stone, "The Family," p. 12; interview with Christopher Stone, January 6, 1992.

55 Interview with Christopher Stone, January 6, 1992; Lou Stone, "The Family," p. 13.

56 Letter to author from Lou Stone, January 26, 1992.

3. On the Record

1 Interview with Stone, October 16, 1981.

2 Ibid.

3 Ibid.

4 Ibid.

5 Ibid.; Daniel J. Leab, *A Union of Individuals: The Formation of the American Newspaper Guild, 1933–1936* (New York: Columbia University Press, 1970).

6 Interviews with Stone, September 10, 1983, October 15, 1981.

7 "The Hopelessness of Hoover," *Record,* December 9, 1931, p. 8; "Wanted a National Leader," *Record,* December 22, 1931, p. 6; "10,000,000 Hungry as the Administration Congratulates Itself on Relief," *Record,* December 31, 1931, p. 6.

8 "10,000,000 Hungry," p. 6; "Senators Dress the Dole in a Flour Sack, and Call It Something Else," *Record,* January 7, 1932, p. 6; "No One Thinks of Balancing Budgets in War Times," *Record,* May 7, 1932, p. 6.

9 Interview with Stone, September 10, 1983; J. David Stern, *Memoirs of a Maverick Publisher* (New York: Simon and Schuster, 1962), pp. 189–190.

10 "Roosevelt Draws the Line Separating Him from Other Candidates," *Record,* April 20, 1932, p. 6; "Roosevelt-Hating Newspapers Display Their Fear of Liberalism," *Record,* April 29, 1932, p. 6.

11 Interview with Stone, September 10, 1983; "A Platform Pointed Toward Liberalism," *Record,* July 1, 1932, p. 6.

12 "Roosevelt Wins," *Nation* 135 (July 13, 1932): 22; "The Democratic Bid," *New Republic* 71 (July 13, 1932): 219; "Roosevelt Steps Left and Right," *New Republic* 72 (September 28, 1932): 164–165; "How Shall We Vote?" *New Republic* 72 (August 17, 1932): 4–6; "Governor Roosevelt's Campaign," *Nation* 135 (November 2, 1932): 414; Malcolm Cowley, *The Dream of the Golden Mountains: Remembering the 1930s* (New York: Penguin, 1981), pp. 110–111; interview with Stone, September 3, 1983.

13 Interview with Stone, September 10, 1983; "Meet Our Next President: Franklin D. Roosevelt," *Record,* July 3, 1932, p. 4; "A New Chapter Opens," *Record,* November 8, 1932, p. 8; "Victory for All of Us," *Record,* November 9, 1932, p. 8; "The End of Herbert Hoover," *Nation* 135 (November 16, 1933): 470–471; "Roosevelt's Revolution," *New Republic* 72 (November 9, 1932): 340–341.

14 William E. Leuchtenburg, *Franklin D. Roosevelt and the New Deal, 1932–1940* (New York: Harper and Row, 1963), pp. 18–40.

15 Stone, "The Story of a Man Who Hesitated Too Long," *Record,* January 3, 1933, p. 1.

16 Ibid., pp. 1, 6.

17 Interview with Stone, September 3, 1983; "A Revolutionary Document," *Nation* 136 (January 18, 1933): 53; "Social Science Looks at Revolution," *New Republic* 73 (January 11, 1933): 228–230.

18 Interviews with Stone, April 22, 1984, October 8, 1983; Stone, note in *Writers*

Take Sides: Letters about the War in Spain from 418 American Authors (New York: League of American Writers, 1938), p. 58.

19 "Trouble Brews within the Reich," *Record,* July 4, 1932, p. 6; "Hitler's Hour," *Record,* August 12, 1932, p. 6.

20 "The Twilight of Capitalism and Democracy in Germany," *Record,* January 31, 1933, p. 8; "Hitler's Role," *Nation* 136 (February 15, 1933): 164; "There Is at Last," editorial paragraph, *New Republic* 74 (March 29, 1933): 171.

21 Interviews with Stone, September 10, 1983, October 8, 1983, October 15, 1981.

22 Interview with Leonard Boudin, July 14, 1989; Margaret Brenman-Gibson, *Clifford Odets: American Playwright* (New York: Atheneum, 1981), pp. 122–124.

23 Interview with Stone, September 3, 1983; "Social Democracy Surrenders," *Record,* April 4, 1933, p. 8; Stone, book review of *The German Phoenix* and *Germany Puts Back the Clock, Modern Monthly* 7 (April 1933): 189.

24 Ibid.

25 Stone, "Industry Cannot Profit until the Masses Can Buy," *Record,* April 15, 1933, p. 8; Stone, "Who Pays for Inflation?" *Modern Monthly* 7 (April 1933): 136–137.

26 "Franklin Roosevelt," *Nation* 136 (March 22, 1933): 301; "The New Deal Begins," *New Republic* 74 (March 15, 1933): 118; "The Industrial Recovery Act," *New Republic* 74 (May 31, 1933): 58; "The Speed," *New Republic* 74 (April 12, 1933): 225; interview with Stone, October 8, 1983.

27 Interviews with Stone, October 8, 1983, September 10, 1983.

28 V. F. Calverton to Stone, V. F. Calverton Papers, New York Public Library; SAC, Los Angeles to J. Edgar Hoover, March 23, 1953, p. 6, FBI file on Michael Blankfort, LA 100-23172, Michael Blankfort Collection, Mugar Memorial Library, Boston University; Michael Blankfort, unpublished autobiography, p. 61, Blankfort Collection; interviews with Stone, September 10, 1983; October 17, 1983.

29 Daniel Aaron, *Writers on the Left* (New York: Avon, 1969), pp. 340–342.

30 Stone, "A Gentleman in Politics," *Modern Monthly* 7 (May 1933): 84.

31 Townsend Ludington, *John Dos Passos: A Twentieth Century Odyssey* (New York: Dutton, 1980), p. 313; Aaron, *Writers on the Left,* pp. 213, 437.

32 Stone, "Roosevelt Moves Toward Fascism," *Modern Monthly* 7 (June 1933): 261.

33 Ibid., pp. 263–264.

34 Ibid., pp. 265, 274; Frank A. Warren, *Liberals and Communism: The "Red Decade" Revisited* (Westport, Conn.: Greenwood, 1976), p. 44.

35 Stone, "Morgan & Co.: A House of Ill Fame," *Modern Monthly* 7 (July 1933): 342–343.

36 Ibid., p. 344.

37 Bruce Bliven, "Roosevelt and the Radicals," *New Republic* 75 (July 12, 1933): 228–230.

38 Aaron, *Writers on the Left,* pp. 341–343; Michael Blankfort to Leonard Wilcox, August 27, 1973, Blankfort Collection.

39 Stone, "Human Nature: Still Incorrigible," *Record,* January 2, 1933, p. 6; Aaron, *Writers on the Left,* pp. 145–146, 348; Cowley, *The Dream of the Golden Mountains,* pp. 43–44.

40 Ibid.

41 Bliven, "Roosevelt and the Radicals," p. 229.

42 "The Red Menace," *Record,* June 25, 1933, p. 6.

43 Interview with Stone, October 15, 1981.

44 Letter to author from Jeremy Stone, February 25, 1990; interview with Stone, October 16, 1981.

45 Ibid.

46 "Grim Joke," *Record,* June 26, 1933, p. 6.

47 "Relativity—Even in Pacifism," *Record,* September 13, 1933, p. 8; "Meeting the Nazi Threat," *Nation* 137 (July 26, 1933): 89.

48 "Caveat Vendor," *Record,* September 14, 1933, p. 8.

49 "Germany Must Not Rearm," *Record,* October 8, 1933, p. 6.

50 Interviews with Stone, September 10, 1983, October 8, 1983; Oswald Garrison Villard, "Issues and Men: The Roosevelt Revolution," *Nation* 137 (July 26, 1933): 91; Bliven, "Roosevelt and the Radicals," p. 229.

4. A New Deal

1 Interviews with Stone, September 10, 1983, October 16, 1981.

2 Ibid.

3 Interviews with Stone, October 8, 1983, September 10, 1983; Oswald Garrison Villard, "Issues and Men: The Gifts of the New Deal," *Nation* 138 (January 3, 1934): 8.

4 Interviews with Stone, October 16, 1981, September 3, 1983; Stone, "New York Loyal to Its Own," *New York Post,* December 11, 1933, p. 1; "Newspaper Reborn," *Literary Digest* 116 (December 23, 1933): 6.

5 Interviews with Stone, October 16, 1981, September 10, 1983; Asher Lans, letter to the editors, "More Names for the Honor Roll," *The Nation* 142 (January 15, 1936): 73.

6 "The No-Man Says Yes," *Post,* December 21, 1933, p. 8; "The President Goes to Bat for a Permanent New Deal," *Post,* January 4, 1934, p. 8; "The Rich Get Richer—," *Post,* April 6, 1934, p. 8; "Self-Government—for One in Every Thousand," *Post,* May 1, 1934, p. 6; "Strike at the Root," *Post,* May 19, 1934, p. 4; "A Radical to Tories; a Tory to Reds," *Post,* July 3, 1934, p. 6.

7 "Mr. Roosevelt's First Year: A Primer for Critics," *Nation* 138 (March 7, 1934): 262–263; "Mr. Roosevelt's First Year," *New Republic* 78 (March 14, 1934): 116–117.

8 Interview with Leonard Boudin, July 14, 1989; interview with Marc Stone, September 27, 1987; interview with Stone, October 16, 1981.

9 Ibid.

10 Interview with Marc Stone, September 27, 1987; interview with Stone, October 15, 1981; interview with Lou Stone, February 15, 1989.

11 David E. Shi, *Matthew Josephson: Bourgeois Bohemian* (New Haven: Yale University Press, 1981), pp. 169–170; interview with Stone, October 15, 1981.

12 *New Republic* 81 (December 12, 1934): 114.

13 Stone, "Bedtime Story for Liberty Leaguers," *Post,* February 4, 1936, p. 10; George Wolfskill and John Hudson, *All But the People: Franklin Roosevelt and His Critics, 1933–1939* (Toronto: Macmillan, 1969), pp. 164–166; Stone, "Bedtime Story for Radicals," *Post,* February 5, 1936, p. 10.

14 Stone, "Bedtime Story for Radicals," p. 10.

15 Richard H. Pells, *Radical Visions and American Dreams: Culture and Social Thought in the Depression Years* (New York: Harper and Row, 1974), p. 300.

16 "Democracy Triumphs," *Post,* November 4, 1936, p. 18; T.R.B., "Washington

Notes," *New Republic* 92 (September 8, 1937): 130; " Wanted—a New Party," *Post,* November 5, 1936, p. 8.

17 "Wanted—a New Party," p. 8; Arthur M Schlesinger, Jr., *The Age of Roosevelt: The Crisis of the Old Order, 1919–1933* (Boston: Houghton Mifflin, 1957), pp. 447–496; Frank Freidel, *Franklin D. Roosevelt: A Rendezvous with Destiny* (Boston: Little, Brown, 1990), pp. 229–233; Leuchtenburg, *Franklin D. Roosevelt and the New Deal,* p. 235.

18 Freidel, *Franklin D. Roosevelt,* pp. 229, 231; J. David Stern, "The Question of an Amendment: More Opinions," *Nation* 144 (June 17, 1936): 761; "Purging the Supreme Court," *Nation* 144 (February 13, 1937): 173–174; "The President Faces the Court," *New Republic* 90 (March 17, 1934): 153–154.

19 Interview with Stone, September 10, 1983; interview with Leonard Boudin, July 14, 1989; R. Alan Lawson, *The Failure of Independent Liberalism, 1930–1941* (New York: Putnam's, 1971), p. 156; Stone, " 'Unpacking' the Supreme Court," *Post,* February 8, 1937, p. 6.

20 Interview with Stone, September 10, 1983; interview with Leonard Boudin, July 14, 1989; Stone to Hannah and Matthew Josephson, June 1, 1937, Matthew Josephson Papers, Beinecke Rare Book and Manuscript Library, Yale University; Matthew Josephson, "Review and Comment," *The New Masses* 23 (June 8, 1937): 22; Charles E. Clark, "Judicial Supremacy," *Nation* 144 (June 12, 1937): 682–683; Thomas Reed Powell, "The Court, the Constitution, and the Country," *Saturday Review of Literature* 16 (June 5, 1937): 3; Mark Howe, Jr., "A Journalist Looks at the Court," *New Republic* 92 (July 21, 1937): 315.

21 Stone, *The Court Disposes* (New York: Covici Friede, 1937), pp. 70, 113, 79, 93, 98, 90, 127.

22 Interview with Stone, September 10, 1983; Stone, "A Defeat More Glorious than Victory," *Post,* August 26, 1937, p. 6.

23 T.R.B., "Washington Notes," p. 130; "The President's Fighting Speech," *New Republic* 92 (September 29, 1937): 201; Stone, "The Greatest Strike-Breaker of All," *Nation* 148 (March 25, 1939): 347.

24 Stone, "Hyde Park, Tennessee Style," *New Republic* 92 (October 20, 1937): 317–318; Stone, "Our Reigning Families," *New Republic* 93 (December 29, 1937): 233; Stone, "The Greatest Strike-Breaker of All," p. 347.

25 Stone, "1937 Is Not 1914," *Nation* 145 (November 6, 1937): 495–497.

26 "Why Fascism Means War," *Post,* April 27, 1934, p. 10; interviews with Stone, October 17, 1983, October 8, 1983, October 15, 1981; "There is at Last," editorial paragraph, *New Republic* 74 (March 29, 1933): 171; "Throughout the World," ed. par., *New Republic* 79 (August 1, 1934): 302; "In All Nations," ed. par., *New Republic* 81 (December 12, 1934): 114; "Moscow Offers an Olive Branch," *Nation* 141 (August 7, 1935): 145.

27 "Again, They Hesitate," *Post,* August 20, 1936, p. 8; interview with Stone, October 15, 1981; "The People's Front in France," *Post,* April 28, 1936, p. 12.

28 Stone, "Barricades against Brown Shirt Barbarism," *Post,* February 13, 1934, p. 8.

29 "Spain Is the Key," *Nation* 144 (February 13, 1937): 172; "Democracy Fights for Its Life in Spain," *Post,* August 1, 1936, p. 6.

30 "Democracy Fights," p. 6.

31 "The Rape of Spain," *Post,* January 9, 1937, p. 6; "Russia Refuses to Cooperate," *Post,* January 19, 1937, p. 6.

32 Warren, *Liberals and Communism*, pp. 131–142; "The Loyalist Dilemma," *Nation* 145 (August 21, 1937): 185–186; H. N. Brailsford, "Impressions of Spain," *New Republic* (June 9, 1937): 119–121.

33 Stone, "The Lines Shift in Spain," *Post*, May 21, 1937, p. 10; interview with Stone, October 15, 1981.

34 Pells, *Radical Visions*, p. 309; George Orwell, *Homage to Catalonia* (New York: Harcourt Brace, 1952); Stone to Hannah and Matthew Josephson, June 1, 1937, Josephson Papers; Aaron, *Writers on the Left*, pp. 173–174, 372; Allen Guttmann, *The Wound in the Heart: America and the Spanish Civil War* (New York: Free Press of Glencoe, 1962), pp. 126–127; James K. Libbey, "Liberal Journals and the Moscow Trials of 1931–38," *Journalism Quarterly* 52 (1975): 85–92, 137.

35 Stone, note in *Writers Take Sides*, p. 58.

36 Interview with Stone, October 15, 1981.

37 Stone, book review of *The German Phoenix*, p. 189; Stone, "The Two-Edged Sword of Terror," *Post*, December 7, 1934, p. 10; "The Murder of Sergei M. Kirov," *Nation* 139 (December 19, 1934): 696; Oswald Garrison Villard, "Issues and Men: The Russian 'Purging,' " *Nation* 139 (December 26, 1934): 729.

38 Louis Fischer, "Behind the Kirov Executions—II," *Nation* 140 (May 15, 1935): 366–368; "Something Extremely," ed. par., *New Republic* 81 (January 2, 1935): 204; "Up to," ed. par., *New Republic* 81 (January 9, 1935): 233; "The Russian Executions," *New Republic* 81 (January 23, 1935): 293; "The Conditions of Civil Liberty," *New Republic* 82 (February 27, 1935): 62.

39 Stone, "Hobgoblins in Moscow," *Post*, January 19, 1935, p. 8.

40 Ibid.

41 Stone, "Jitters in the Kremlin," *Post*, August 18, 1936, p. 8.

42 "The Trial of the Trotskyites in Russia," *New Republic* 88 (September 2, 1936): 88; " 'Old Bolsheviks' on Trial," *Nation* 143 (August 22, 1936): 201.

43 Stone, "?????????," *Post*, January 26, 1937, p. 8; interview with Stone, October 15, 1981; Warren, *Liberals and Communism*, pp. 163–192.

44 Interview with Stone, October 15, 1981.

45 "Behind the Soviet Trials," *Nation* (February 6, 1937): 145; Malcolm Cowley, "The Record of a Trial," *New Republic* 90 (April 7, 1937): 269; Walter Duranty, "The Riddle of Russia," *New Republic* 91 (July 14, 1937): 270–272.

46 Ibid.; interview with Stone, September 10, 1983; "Russia and the World," *Nation* 145 (November 13, 1937): 521.

47 Stone, "1937 Is Not 1914," p. 496.

48 Ibid.; "Behind the Soviet Trials," p. 143; Cowley, "The Record of a Trial," p. 270.

49 Harold Lord Varney, "Our 'Liberal' Weeklies," *American Mercury* 42 (December 1937): 463–465.

50 Interview with Stone, October 16, 1981.

51 Interviews with Stone, October 16, 1981, September 3, 1983; letter to author from Jeremy Stone, February 25, 1990; interviews with Lou Stone, September 24, 1987, July 16, 1989; Michael Blankfort to Dick Coe, July 18, 1979, Michael Blankfort Collection, Mugar Memorial Library, Boston University.

52 Blankfort, Blankfort autobiography; Stone, Passport Application, October 4, 1945, p. 1, SDF, PO37; interview with Stone, October 16, 1981.

53 Interviews with Stone, October 16, 1981, September 3, 1983; letter to author from George Seldes, June 30, 1983; Stern, *Memoirs*, pp. 244–245; J. David Stern, *The Reminiscences of J. David Stern*, Columbia University Oral History Project, pp. 79–80;

Leo C. Rosten, *The Washington Correspondents* (New York: Harcourt, Brace, 1937), pp. 198, 214.

54 Rosten, *The Washington Correspondents*, pp. 196, 292.

55 "Stalin Takes Off His Mask," *Post*, February 15, 1938, p. 1.

56 Interviews with Stone, October 16, 1981, September 3, 1983; Stern, *The Reminiscences*, pp. 89–90.

57 Interviews with Stone, October 16, 1981, September 3, 1983, September 10, 1983; Stone to Matthew Josephson, May 17, 1937, September 24, 1938, Josephson Papers; Malcolm Cowley to Stone, n.d., Malcolm Cowley Papers, Newberry Library; Stone, letters to Max Lerner, October 31, 1938, March 27, 1941(?), Max Lerner Papers, Sterling Library, Yale University; "*The Nation*'s Future," *Nation* 144 (June 19, 1937): 695; Rosten, *The Washington Correspondents*, p. 172.

58 Stone, "How to Make a Riot," *New Republic* 79 (June 27, 1934): 178–180; Stone, "Racketeering in the A. F. of L.: I. The Poultry Racket," *Nation* 141 (September 11, 1935): 288–291; Stone, "Racketeering in the A. F. of L.: II. Skulduggery in New York," *Nation* 141 (September 18, 1935): 316–318; Stone to Michael Blankfort, September 11, 1938, pp. 1–2, Blankfort Collection.

59 Stone to Blankfort, September 11, 1938, pp. 1–2.

60 Ibid.; Blankfort, "Diary," February 29, 1929, Blankfort Collection; interview with Judy Stone, February 23, 1992.

61 Stone to Blankfort, September 11, 1938, pp. 1–4.

62 Stone to Michael Blankfort, October 15, 1939, p. 3, Blankfort Collection; Stone to Michael Blankfort, January 15, 1941, p. 2, Blankfort Collection.

63 Interview with Stone, October 16, 1981; Stone to Lerner, October 31, 1938; "*The Nation*'s Future," p. 695.

64 David Seideman, *The New Republic: A Voice of Modern Liberalism* (New York: Praeger, 1986), pp. 1135–1144; Stone, "Shuffle the Cards," *Nation* 147 (September 24, 1938): 286; Stone, "Bloody Harlan Reforms," *Nation* 147 (August 6, 1938): 121; Stone, "It Happened in Harlan," *Current History* 49 (September 1938): 31; Stone, "New Deal Crisis," *Nation* 149 (August 5, 1939): 135–136.

65 Stone, "The Horrid Word," *Nation* 147 (December 3, 1938): 581–582; Stone, "Liberals Never Learn," *Nation* 148 (March 18, 1939): 337; Stone, "Remedies for Monopoly," *Nation* 148 (April 15, 1939): 420–421.

66 Stone, "Max Lerner's Capitalist Collectivism," *Southern Review* 4 (Spring 1939): 661.

67 Ibid., pp. 662–663.

68 Stone, "Jerome Frank's Dilemma," *Southern Review* 4 (Autumn 1938): 225–226; Stone, "Max Lerner's Capitalist Collectivism," p. 664.

69 Stone, "Lift the Embargo!" *Nation* 148 (January 21, 1939): 77–78; Shi, *Matthew Josephson*, p. 179.

70 John P. Diggins, *The American Left in the Twentieth Century* (New York: Harcourt Brace, 1973), pp. 129–35; Milton Cantor, *The Divided Left: American Radicalism, 1900–1975* (New York: Hill and Wang, 1978), pp. 142–144; "Russian Tragedy, Act III," *Nation* 146 (March 12, 1938): 287; "Manifesto," *Nation* 148 (May 23, 1939): 626.

71 Matthew Josephson, *Infidel in the Temple: A Memoir of the Nineteen-Thirties* (New York: Knopf, 1967), p. 477; "To All Active Supporters of Democracy and Peace," *Nation* 149 (August 26, 1939): 228.

72 Sarah Alpern, *Freda Kirchwey: A Woman of The Nation* (Cambridge: Harvard University Press, 1987), p. 126.

73 Stone to Freda Kirchwey, 1939(?), Freda Kirchwey Papers, The Arthur and

Elizabeth Schlesinger Library on the History of Women in America, Radcliffe College; Pells, *Radical Visions*, p. 304.

74 Interview with Stone, October 15, 1981.

75 William L. O'Neill, *A Better World: The Great Schism: Stalinism and the American Intellectuals* (New York: Simon and Schuster, 1982), p. 15; interview with Sidney Hook, June 30, 1983; James T. Farrell to Freda Kirchwey, October 30, 1939, Kirchwey Papers; Philip Nobile, *Intellectual Skywriting: Literary Politics and the New York Review of Books* (New York: Charterhouse, 1974), p. 144; James A. Wechsler, *The Age of Suspicion* (New York: Random House, 1953), pp. 139–140.

76 Interview with Stone, September 10, 1983.

77 Irving Howe and Lewis Coser, *The American Communist Party: A Critical History* (New York: Praeger, 1962), pp. 387–391; Norman Holmes Pearson, "The Nazi-Soviet Pact and the End of a Dream," in *America in Crisis: Fourteen Crucial Episodes in American History*, ed. Daniel Aaron (New York: Knopf, 1952), pp. 327–348, pp. 193–215; Warren, *Liberals and Communism*, pp. 193–215; James A. Wechsler, "Stalin and Union Square," *Nation* 149 (September 30, 1939): 342–345; Shi, *Matthew Josephson*, p. 192; Peter Viereck, "Under Thirty: But—I'm a Conservative," *Atlantic Monthly* 165 (April 1940): 538; Louis Fischer et al., in *The God That Failed*, ed. Richard Crossman (New York: Bantam, 1965), pp. 200–201; Harvey Klehr, *The Heyday of American Communism: The Depression Decade* (New York: Basic, 1984): 400–404.

78 Richard Rovere, "History in the Stone Age: Hidden 'Facts' and Fiction of the War in Korea," *Post*, May 11, 1952, p. 12M; Stone to Freda Kirchwey, n.d., Kirchwey Papers; Stone, "Hitler Will Be Addressing Congress As," ed. par., *Nation* 149 (September 23, 1939): 306; Stone, "Chamberlain's Russo-German Pact," *Nation* 149 (September 23, 1939): 313.

79 Stone, "There Had Been No Fighting of Any," ed. par., *Nation* 149 (September 23, 1939): 305; Stone, "Hitler Will Be Addressing," p. 306; Stone, "Blackmailer's Peace," *Nation* 149 (October 14, 1939): 401.

80 Stone to Blankfort, October 15, 1939, p. 3.

81 Ibid., pp. 3–4.

82 Ibid., p. 4.

83 Stone to Michael Blankfort, October 21, 1939, Blankfort Colleetion.

84 Stone, "Dictators at Work," *Nation* 149 (September 30, 1939): 37–38; Stone, "Blackmailer's Peace," p. 401; Stone, "They Cry War," *Nation* 149 (November 4, 1939): 483; Stone, "When Molotov Referred to Our Policy," ed. par., *Nation* 149 (November 11, 1939): 510.

85 Stone, "The Finns at Geneva," *Nation* 149 (December 16, 1939): 667–668; "Stalin Spreads the War," *New Republic* 101 (December 13, 1939): 218–220.

5. *The American Left*

1 Aaron, *Writers on the Left*, p. 388; Granville Hicks, *Part of the Truth* (New York: Harcourt, Brace and World, 1965), pp. 187–188; Hicks, *Where We Came Out* (Westport, Conn.: Greenwood, 1973), p. 75; Richard Rovere, *Final Reports: Personal Reflections on Politics and History in Our Time* (Garden City, N.Y.: Doubleday, 1984), p. 67; Max Lerner to Malcolm Cowley, October 19, 1939, Malcolm Cowley Papers, Newberry Library; Wechsler, *The Age of Suspicion*, p. 153; letter to author from Malcolm Cowley, June 13, 1983; letter to author from Max Lerner, June 16, 1983; Wechsler, "Stalin and Union Square," pp. 343–344.

2 Aaron, *Writers on the Left*, p. 388; Wechsler, *The Age of Suspicion*, pp. 153–154;

Hicks, *Part of the Truth,* p. 188; Hicks, *Where We Came Out,* pp. 75–77; letter to author from Cowley, June 13, 1983; Shi, *Matthew Josephson,* pp. 194–195.

3 Corliss Lamont, ed., *The Trial of Elizabeth Gurley Flynn by the American Civil Liberties Union* (New York: Horizon Press, 1968); 106 *Congr. Rec.* 9650 (May 5, 1960) (information from the files of the Committee on Un-American Activities).

4 Shi, *Matthew Josephson,* p. 195; Stone, "Neutrality—a Dangerous Myth," *Nation* 145 (September 18, 1937): 283–285; "Quarantine: Gesture or Policy?" *Nation* 145 (October 16, 1937): 391–392.

5 Stone, "America and the Next War: II," *New Republic* 99 (June 21, 1939): 177–178; Warren, *Liberals and Communism,* pp. 150–162; R. Alan Lawson, *The Failure of Independent Liberalism, 1930–1941* (New York: Putnam's, 1971), pp. 235–236; Max Lerner, "America and the Next War: II," p. 177.

6 Alpern, *Freda Kirchwey,* pp. 131–141; Stone, "With Organized Minorities Deluging," ed. par., *Nation* 149 (September 30, 1939): 335; Stone, "The Chicken or the Egg?" *Nation* 149 (November 4, 1939): 500–501; Stone, "Dissenting Opinion," *Nation* 150 (March 9, 1940): 340–341; Wechsler, "Stalin and Union Square," p. 345.

7 Stone, "Dissenting Opinion," pp. 340–341.

8 Interview with Lou Stone, July 16, 1989.

9 Stone to Michael Blankfort, January 15, 1941, Michael Blankfort Collection, Mugar Memorial Library, Boston University; Stone, "Bring Them Out!" *Nation* 150 (June 29, 1940): 773.

10 Warren, *Liberals and Communism,* p. 209; W. A. Swanberg, *Norman Thomas: The Last Idealist* (New York: Scribner's, 1976), pp. 239–243; Michael Straight, *After Long Silence* (New York: Norton, 1983), pp. 158–159; Shi, *Matthew Josephson,* p. 206, Alpern, *Freda Kirchwey,* pp. 131–132.

11 Stone to Freda Kirchwey, n.d., Freda Kirchwey Papers, The Arthur and Elizabeth Schlesinger Library on the History of Women in America, Radcliffe College; Stone to Michael Blankfort, October 15, 1939, p. 2, Blankfort Collection.

12 Stone to Blankfort, October 15, 1939, pp. 2–3.

13 Interview with Stone, October 16, 1981; "The Objectives of AIU," *Your Investments* 1 (August 1940): 47; Stone, "The Worst Enemies of Labor," ed. par., *Nation* 151 (September 7, 1940): 182.

14 Interview with Stone, October 16, 1981; "Nation's 75th," *Time* 35 (February 19, 1940): 61–62; Rosten, *The Washington Correspondents,* pp. 186–187.

15 Donald A. Ritchie, *Press Gallery: Congress and the Washington Correspondents* (Cambridge: Harvard University Press, 1991), p. 221; Stephen Hess, *The Washington Reporters* (Washington, D.C.: Brookings Institution, 1981), pp. 17, 124, 127; interview with Christopher Stone, January 6, 1992.

16 Interview with Christopher Stone, January 6, 1992; Richard Rovere, "Here Comes 'PM,' " *Nation* 150 (June 8, 1940): 700–703; Roy Hoopes, *Ralph Ingersoll: A Biography* (New York: Atheneum, 1985), pp. 155–237, 401.

17 Ferdinand Lundberg, "*PM:* The Wall-Street-Popular-Front Tabloid," *Harper's* 181 (October 1940): 486–492; Hoopes, *Ralph Ingersoll,* pp. 187–212, 219, 226, 229, 232, 246; *PM* Department of Information, "*FOR IMMEDIATE RELEASE,*" 1940, pp. 1–5, Ralph Ingersoll Papers, Mugar Memorial Library, Boston University.

18 Victor Riesel, letter in "The Open Forum," *American Mercury* 51 (November 1940): 377; Eugene Lyons, "The Strange Case of *PM,*" *American Mercury* 50 (August 1940): 484–488; Lundberg, "*PM,*" pp. 486–492.

19 Rovere, "Here Come 'PM,' " p. 703; Hoopes, *Ralph Ingersoll,* p. 244; Warren, *Liberals and Communism,* p. 209.

20 Interview with Stone, October 16, 1981; letter to author from Lerner, June 16, 1983; Freda Kirchwey to Stone, August 25, 1939, Kirchwey Papers; Ritchie, *Press Gallery*, pp. 219–220.

21 David L. Protess et al., *The Journalism of Outrage: Investigative Reporting and Agenda Building in America* (New York: Guilford Press, 1991).

22 Stone to Lerner, March 27, 1941, Max Lerner Papers, Sterling Library, Yale University.

23 Freda Kirchwey to Stone, March 31, 1942, Kirchwey Papers; Freda Kirchwey to Stone, n.d., Kirchwey Papers; Freda Kirchwey to Stone, July 20, 1943, Kirchwey Papers.

24 Unsigned letter to Stone, August 24, 1943, *Nation* Collection, Houghton Library, Harvard University.

25 R. W. Flournoy to Dean Acheson, September 15, 1941, Department of State document 1940-144 (4E3), 195.7 Steel Seafarer/21, National Archives.

26 Stone to Blankfort, January 15, 1941, p. 2.

27 Interview with Christopher Stone, January 6, 1992.

28 Ibid.

29 Ibid.

30 Ibid.

31 Ibid.

32 Stone, "Aviation's Sitdown Strike," *Nation* 151 (August 17, 1940): 126–129; Stone, "Priorities and Defense," *Nation* 151 (November 9, 1940): 439–440.

33 Stone, "A Time for Candor," *Nation* 152 (January 25, 1941): 291–292.

34 "Democratic Defense," *New Republic* 104 (February 17, 1941): 227.

35 Stone, "Does FDR Want to 'Save' Il Duce?" *PM*, February 19, 1941, p. 12.

36 Stone, "Pipe Lines and Profit," *Nation* 152 (April 26, 1941): 491–492; Stone, "The Cost of Knudsenism," *Nation* 152 (May 17, 1941): 575–576; Stone, "A Tale of Two Oceans," *Nation* 152 (June 7, 1941): 659–660.

37 Hoopes, *Ralph Ingersoll*, pp. 247–249.

38 Stone, *Business as Usual: The First Year of Defense* (New York: Modern Age Books, 1941), pp. 242–245.

39 Ibid., pp. 265–266.

40 Lewis Corey, "Monopoly and Defense," *Nation* 153 (September 6, 1941): 204; Michael Straight, "The First Year and the Next," *New Republic* 105 (September 1, 1941): 284; "Business as Usual," *Management Review* (December 1941): 472; William Saroyan, "Let's Talk about Cheap Books," *New Republic* 99 (June 28, 1939): 220–221; Dwight Macdonald, "Democracy and the War Effort," *Partisan Review* 8 (September–October 1941): 438–439.

41 Stone to Freda Kirchwey, n.d., Kirchwey Papers; Freda Kirchwey to Stone, September 25, 1941, Kirchwey Papers; Philip Murray, John Brophy, James Carey, I. F. Stone, *The C.I.O. and National Defense* (Washington, D.C.: American Council on Public Affairs, 1941).

42 Stone, " 'Patriotism' and Reaction," *Record*, March 29, 1933, p. 8.

43 Stone, "Hitlerism or Americanism?" *Post*, March 31, 1934, p. 4; Stone, "The Nazi Way to Fight the Nazi Poison," *Post*, April 26, 1934, p. 6.

44 Stone, "Best News of the Week," ed. par., *Nation* 149 (August 12, 1939): 163; Stone, "Shadow Boxing in a Crisis," ed. par., *Nation* 146 (April 9, 1938): 400–401; Stone, "After What Has Happened," ed par., *Nation* 147 (October 15, 1938): 366; Stone, "Those Who Have Followed," ed. par., *Nation* 148 (March 25, 1939): 335.

45 M. J. Heale, *American Anticommunism: Combating the Enemy Within, 1830–1970* (Baltimore: Johns Hopkins University Press, 1990), p. 119.

46 Letter to author from Emil P. Moschella, October 12, 1989; Alpern, *Freda Kirchwey*, p. 155; FBI file on I. F. Stone, #100-37078, section Number 2, n.d., p. 6; see "A Note on J. Edgar Hoover," *Record*, November 24, 1936, p. 10; Herbert Mitgang, *Dangerous Dossiers: Exposing the Secret War against Ameria's Greatest Authors* (New York: Ballantine, 1989).

47 Stone, "Creel's Crusade," *Nation* 149 (December 9, 1939): 647–649; Stone, "Our Lawless G-Men," *Nation* 150 (March 2, 1940): 296.

48 Kirchwey to Stone, February 11, 1941, Kirchwey Papers; Alpern, *Freda Kirchwey*, p. 155.

49 Stone, "His Majesty—Martin Dies," *PM*, February 24, 1941, p. 13; Stone, "Why Tap Wires?" *Nation* 152 (March 8, 1941): 257–258.

50 Stone, "The G-String Conspiracy," *Nation* 153 (July 26, 1941): 66.

51 Ibid., pp. 66–67.

52 Stone, "The Case of the Trotskyites," *PM*, December 31, 1943, p. 2.

53 106 *Congr. Rec.* 9651 (May 5, 1960) (files of HCUAC).

54 Stone, "Next Steps on Bridges," *Nation* 153 (October 11, 1941): 329–330; Stone, "Washington Notes," *Nation* 154 (May 23, 1942): 591; Stone, "The Case of the Trotskyites," p. 2; Stone, "The Supreme Court and Racialism," *Nation* 159 (December 30, 1944): 788–789.

55 Alpern, *Freda Kirchwey*, pp. 147–151.

56 Stone, "Civil Rights and Wrongs," *Nation* 150 (February 10, 1940): 150.

57 Alpern, *Freda Kirchwey*, pp. 147–151; Freda Kirchwey, "Curb the Fascist Press!" *Nation* 154 (March 28, 1942): 357–358; "William Dudley Pelley," ed. par., *Nation* 154 (April 11, 1942): 154; Roger Baldwin to editors of *The Nation*, *Nation* 154 (April 11, 1942): 444; editors to Baldwin, *Nation* 154 (April 11, 1942): 444.

58 Hoopes, *Ralph Ingersoll*, pp. 260–261.

59 Alpern, *Freda Kirchwey*, p. 150.

60 Robert Justin Goldstein, *Political Repression in Modern America: From 1870 to the Present* (Cambridge: Schenkman, 1978), p. 269; Stone, "How They Kicked Maloney Upstairs," February 14, 1943, pp. 1–3, *Nation* Collection; Freda Kirchwey to Stone, February 16, 1943, *Nation* Collection; Stone, "The Real Subversives," *Nation* 159 (October 14, 1944): 424.

61 Stone, "John Rogge and the Sedition Case," *PM*, October 28, 1946, p. 2.

62 William Preston, Jr., "Shadows of War and Fear," in *The Pulse of Freedom: American Liberties: 1920–1970s*, ed. Alan Reitman (New York: Norton, 1975), pp. 113–114.

63 Stone, "The Army and the 'Reds,'" *Nation* 160 (March 3, 1945): 238–239.

6. Fighting the Good War

1 Interview with Stone, October 16, 1981; Hoopes, *Ralph Ingersoll*, pp. 257, 259, 260.

2 Richard Pells, *The Liberal Mind in a Conservative Age: American Intellectuals in the 1940s and 1950s* (New York: Harper and Row, 1985).

3 *Freda Kirchwey: On the Occasion of the Twenty-Fifth Anniversary of Her Association with the Nation* (New York: Dinner Committee, 1944).

4 Stone to Freda Kirchwey, October 2, 1941, Freda Kirchwey Papers, The

Arthur and Elizabeth Schlesinger Library on the History of Women in America, Radcliffe College; Freda Kirchwey to Stone, February 7, 1942, Kirchwey Papers; Freda Kirchwey to Stone, July 15, 1941, Kirchwey Papers.

5 Stone to Freda Kirchwey, n.d., Kirchwey Papers; Stephen Early to Freda Kirchwey, March 1, 1941, Kirchwey Papers.

6 Stone, "Washington Underground," *PM*, April 5, 1945, p. 2; Stone, "Introduction," *The Haunted Fifties* (New York: Vintage Books, 1969), p. xviii.

7 Alpern, *Freda Kirchwey*, p. 137.

8 For a Declaration of War," *New Republic* 105 (August 25, 1941): 235–236; Stone, "Oil in the Pacific," *Nation* 153 (August 9, 1941): 109; Stone, "Memo on Japan," *Nation* 153 (September 13, 1941): 217.

9 Stone, "Washington Zigzag," *Nation* 153 (October 25, 1941): 391.

10 Stone, "Fumbles for Finland," *Nation* 153 (November 15, 1941): 476.

11 Stone, "War Comes to Washington," *Nation* 153 (December 13, 1941): 604.

12 Stone, "War Comes to Washington," p. 604; Stone, "Aid and Comfort to the Enemy," *Nation* 154 (January 3, 1942): 6.

13 Stone, "Fighting the Fighting French," *Nation* 155 (November 28, 1942): 565–566.

14 Stone, "Moral Issues for Mr. Hull," *Nation* 156 (January 30, 1943): 151–152; Stone, "Hull and the Press," *Nation* 156 (February 6, 1943): 186; 89 *Cong. Rec.* 478 (February 1, 1943) (remarks of Rep. John Rankin); 89 *Cong. Rec.* 511 (February 2, 1943) (remarks of Rankin).

15 Robert Bendiner to Stone, January 28, 1943, *Nation* Collection, Houghton Library, Harvard University; Stone, "Hull and the Press," p. 186.

16 Freda Kirchwey to Stone, n.d., Kirchwey Papers; Freda Kirchwey to Stone, September 9, 1941, Kirchwey Papers; Freda Kirchwey to Stone, December 20, 1943, Kirchwey Papers; Freda Kirchwey to Stone, November 9, 1944, Kirchwey Papers.

17 Stone to Freda Kirchwey, December 20, 1942(?), p. 1, *Nation* Collection.

18 Stone, "How Washington Reacted," *Nation* 157 (August 7, 1943): 146–147; Stone, "Either-Ors in the State Dept.," *PM*, August 25, 1943, p. 2; "America and European Revolution," *New Republic* 109 (November 29, 1943): 781–782.

19 Stone, "Hard or Durable Peace?" *Nation* 159 (December 30, 1944): 789; Stone, "Stratospheric Idiocy," *PM*, January 16, 1945, p. 2.

20 Stone, "Will the Hitler Gang Escape Punishment as the Junkers Did after World War II?" *PM*, February 18, 1945, pp. 3–4; Stone, "Legalistic Loopholes for Tories," *PM*, February 20, 1945, p. 2; Stone, "The Pell Affair," *PM*, February 24, 1945, pp. 203–204.

21 Stone, "Capital Thoughts on a Second Front," *Nation* 155 (October 3, 1942): 287–288; Stone, "Washington's Forbidden Topic," *Nation* 155 (October 31, 1942): 435–436; Stone, "Russian Lives and Oil Patients," *Nation* 155 (September 26, 1942): 261–262; Stone, "General Marshall Should Explain," *Nation* 156 (May 29, 1943): 763–764.

22 Stone, "Diplomacy on the Russian Front," *PM*, March 14, 1943, p. 3.

23 Stone, "Senatorial Trouble-Maker," *Nation* 160 (March 17, 1945): 292–293; Stone, "Saluting the Red Army," *PM*, February 1, 1945, p. 2

24 Stone, "Senatorial Trouble-Maker," pp. 292–293.

25 Stone, "Anti-Russian Undertow," *Nation* 160 (May 12, 1945): 534; Alpern, *Freda Kirchwey*, p. 166.

26 O'Neill, *A Better World*, pp. 101–102; "Solution in Poland," *New Republic* 113 (July 2, 1945): 6–7.

27 Stone, "Wilson's Failure Was the People's Failure," *PM*, August 3, 1944, p. 2; Stone, "Not Utopia, but Peace," *PM*, August 22, 1944, p. 2.

28 Stone, "Pie in the 'Frisco Sky," *Nation* 160 (May 19, 1945): 561–563; Stone, "Notes before Frisco," *Nation* 160 (April 28, 1945): 478–479; Stone, "This Is the Choice," *PM*, October 20, 1943, p. 2; Stone, "Wanted: A Pacific Charter," *PM*, December 8, 1943, p. 2; Stone, "The End of War," *PM*, August 12, 1945, p. 2.

29 Stone, "Chungking and Washington," *Nation* 152 (April 5, 1941): 400–401; "A People's Warrior," *PM*, December 5, 1943, p. 2; Stone, "Wilson's Failure Was the People's Failure," p. 2; Stone, "Not Utopia, but Peace," p. 2; Stone, "Someone's Listening," *PM*, March 9, 1945, p. 2; Stone, "Trieste and San Francisco," *Nation* 160 (May 26, 1945): 589–590.

30 Stone, "Notes before 'Frisco," p. 479; Stone, "Pie in the 'Frisco Sky," p. 562.

7. Going Underground

1 Stone, "Spain's Via Dolorosa," *Nation* 162 (April 27, 1946): 498.

2 Interview with Stone, October 16, 1981.

3 Stone, *Underground to Palestine and Reflections Thirty Years Later* (New York: Pantheon, 1978), p. 9; interview with Stone, October 16, 1981.

4 Interview with Stone, October 16, 1981; Stone to Freda Kirchwey, January 9, 1947, *Nation* Collection, Houghton Library, Harvard University; Freda Kirchwey to Stone, January 11, 1947, *Nation* Collection; Harold C. Field to Stone, January 17, 1949, pp. 1–2, *Nation* Collection.

5 Interview with Stone, October 16, 1981.

6 "The Jews of Europe: How to Help Them," *New Republic* 109 (August 30, 1943): 299–315; Stone, "Murder of a People," *Nation* 155 (December 19, 1942): 668–669; Stone, "Hitler's Subtlest Poison," *Nation* 156 (February 27, 1943): 293; "The American Jewish Conference," *Nation* 157 (September 11, 1943): 282–283.

7 Interview with Stone, October 16, 1981; Stone, "The Problem of Palestine," *Post*, August 14, 1936, p. 8; Stone, "Riots in Palestine," *Post*, April 21, 1936, p. 10.

8 Stone, "Palestine Run-Around," *Nation* 158 (March 18, 1944): 326–328.

9 "No More Terrible Story," *Nation* 161 (September 1, 1945): 194–195; Stone, "The Harrison Report: A Revelation and a Challenge," *PM*, October 1, 1945, p. 2; interview with Stone, October 16, 1981.

10 Stone, "The Plight of the Jews," *Nation* 161 (October 6, 1945): 330–331; "The British Cabinet's Reported Stand," *Nation* 161 (September 29, 1945): 300–301.

11 J. King Gordon to the Passport Division, State Department, October 3, 1945, SDF, PO39; John P. Lewis to Passport Division, October 3, 1945, SDF, PO40; Stone, Passport Application, October 5, 1945, p. 2; Stone, Application for Amendment of Passport, October 20, 1945, p. 2, SDF, PO36; Stone, "Why Palestine Is 'Home' to Jews," *PM*, December 4, 1945, p. 4.

12 Stone, "Jewry in a Blind Alley," *Nation* 161 (November 24, 1945): 543–544; Swanberg, *Norman Thomas*, p. 396. See also "Some Proposed Solutions," *Nation* 164 (May 17, 1947): 610.

13 Stone, "Palestine Pilgrimage," *Nation* 161 (December 8, 1945): 615–617.

14 Ibid.

15 Stone, "Another Inquiry Begins," *Nation* 161 (December 22, 1945): 678–679; Stone, "Middle Eastern Tories," *Nation* 161 (December 29, 1945): 726–728.

16 Stone, "Gangsters or Patriots?" *Nation* 162 (January 12, 1946): 34–35.

17 Interview with Stone, October 16, 1981; John P. Lewis to Passport Division,

April 19, 1946, SDF, PO32; John J. Scanlan to John P. Lewis, April 26, 1946, SDF, PO31; Stone, Application for Amendment of Passport, May 21, 1946, pp. 1–2, SDF, PO28; Caffery telegram, "FOR PASSPORT DIVISION," May 21, 1946, SDF, PO27; annotated Caffery telegram, "FOR PASSPORT DIVISION," May 21, 1946, SDF, PO26; "File: Notified," May 22, 1946, SDF, PO25; Stone, Application for Amendment of Passport, May 24, 1946, pp. 1–2, SDF, PO24.

18 Interviews with Stone, October 15, 1981, October 16, 1981; Stone, *Underground*, pp. 23, 204, 206, 227, *passim*.

19 Stone, *Underground*, pp. 180–195, 213.

20 Interview with Christopher Stone, January 6, 1992; letter to author from Christopher Stone, January 18, 1992.

21 Ibid.

22 Ibid.

23 Ibid.; Stone, "Jews' Hopes Firm Despite Palestine Crisis," *PM*, February 28, 1947, p. 6.

24 Stone, "I. F. Stone Smuggled into Palestine by Underground; Exclusive Stories on His Experiences to Start Soon," *PM*, July 5, 1946, p. 3; Michael Blankfort to Stone, August 26, 1946, Michael Blankfort Collection, Mugar Memorial Library, Boston University.

25 Michael Blankfort to Stone, October 3, 1946, Blankfort Collection; Stone, *Underground*, p. 216.

26 Stone, *Underground*, pp. 222–224.

27 Meyer Berger, "Living Nightmares," *NY Times Book Review*, January 19, 1947, section 7, p. 7; "A Reader's List," *New Republic* 128 (December 30, 1946): 929; Bartley C. Crum, "Escape from Europe," *Nation* 164 (January 25, 1947): 104.

28 Interview with Stone, October 16, 1981.

29 Stone to Harry S. Truman, n.d., Presidential Personal File, Harry Truman Papers, Harry S. Truman Library.

30 Stone, "I. F. Stone Searched in Palestine, Papers Seized by British Agents," *PM*, February 23, 1947, p. 7; Stone, "Palestine Police Return Seized Papers," *PM*, February 26, 1947, p. 6.

31 Stone, "Round Trip to Cyprus on Deportation Ship," *PM*, March 17, 1947, p. 7; Stone, "Passover in Cyprus' Nissen Huts," *PM*, April 7, 1947, p. 7.

32 Stone, "The End of a 2000-Year Journey for the Jews," *PM*, December 1, 1947, p. 6; Freda Kirchwey, "The U.N. and Palestine," *Nation* 164 (April 26, 1947): 468–469.

33 Joseph Barnes to Ruth B. Shipley, May 3, 1948, SDF, PO29; Stone, "Tel Aviv Quiet, but You Know There's a War On," *PM*, May 12, 1948, p. 12; Stone, "Born under Fire," *New Republic* (May 31, 1948): 14; Freda Kirchwey, "America and Israel," *Nation* 166 (May 22, 1948): 565–566.

34 Interview with Stone, October 16, 1981.

35 Stone, *This Is Israel* (New York: Boni and Gaer, 1948), pp. 63, 127–128, *passim*.

36 Thomas Lask, "Israel: A Year's History," *NY Times Book Review*, November 28, 1948, section 7, p. 4; Philip S. Bernstein, "Birth of a Nation," *Nation* 168 (January 29, 1949): 132–133; *New Yorker* (December 18, 1948): 98.

37 Stone, "Time to Wipe Out the Terrorists," *NY Star*, September 20, 1948, p. 11.

38 Ibid.

39 Stone, "Histadruth Weeps," *Post*, March 1, 1949, p. 52.

40 Stone, "Are We Aroused Only by Blood and War?" *Compass*, October **23**, 1949, special section "Israel Today," p. 5; Stone, "I. F. Stone Reports from Israel," *Compass*, September 4, 1949, p. 3.

41 Stone, "The Road to Peace Lies through the Arab Refugee Camps," *Weekly* 4 (April 30, 1956): 2–3; Swanberg, *Norman Thomas*, p. 305.

42 Alexander Bloom, *Prodigal Sons: The New York Intellectuals and Their World* (New York: Oxford University Press, 1986), pp. 137–140; Terry A. Cooney, *The Rise of the New York Intellectuals: Partisan Review and Its Circle, 1934–1945* (Madison: University of Wisconsin Press, 1986), pp. 229–245; Irving Howe, *A Margin of Hope: An Intellectual Autobiography* (New York: Harcourt Brace Jovanovich, 1982), pp. 247–282.

8. The Demise of the Old Left

1 Stone, "Planning and Socialism," *Nation* 159 (October 21, 1944): 493; Stone, "What F.D.R. Forgot," *Nation* 158 (January 8, 1944): 34–35.

2 Stone, "Planning and Politics," *Nation* 156 (March 20, 1943): 405–407; Steven M. Gillon, *Politics and Vision: The ADA and American Liberalism, 1947–1985* (New York: Oxford University Press, 1987), pp. 6–7; Heale, *American Anticommunism*, p. 132; Alonzo L. Hamby, *Beyond the New Deal: Harry S. Truman and American Liberalism* (New York: Columbia University Press, 1973), pp. 34–35.

3 Stone, "Franklin Delano Roosevelt," *PM*, April 13, 1945, p. 4; T.R.B., "Washington Notes: The New President," *New Republic* 112 (April 23, 1945): 554.

4 Stone, "Will America Go Socialist?" *Nation* 161 (August 11, 1945): 124.

5 Ibid., pp. 124–125.

6 Harry Fleischman to Stone, August 9, 1945, Socialist Party Papers, 1897–1963 (microfilm) "British Labor's Program," *New Republic* 113 (August 27, 1945): 238–239.

7 Stone, "Looking Forward—from the Truman Message," *PM*, September 9, 1945, p. 2; Stone, "We Welcome the Hint," ed. par., *Nation* 161 (September 8, 1945): 213.

8 Stone, "Truman and the People," *Nation* 162 (January 12, 1946): 32; Stone, "Where There Is No Vision," *Nation* 162 (February 2, 1946): 118; Stone, "Some Notes to Cheer," *Nation* 162 (February 16, 1946): 186; T.R.B., "Washington Notes: The World Moves to Washington," *New Republic* 113 (December 10, 1945): 797.

9 Stone, "The Morning-After for British Labor," *PM*, August 21, 1945, p. 2.

10 Ibid.; Pells, *The Liberal Mind in a Conservative Age*, p. 61.

11 Stone, "U.S. and U.S.S.R.," *Nation* 162 (March 16, 1946): 306.

12 Ibid.

13 Stone, "High Principles, Naive Politics and Low Skulduggery," *PM*, March 28, 1946, p. 2; "The 'Liberal' Fifth Column," *Partisan Review* 13 (Summer 1946): 279–293.

14 Gillon, *Politics and Vision*, pp. 12–13; Schlesinger, "The U.S. Communist Party," *Life* 21 (July 29, 1946): 84–96.

15 Norman D. Markowitz, *The Rise and Fall of the People's Century: Henry A. Wallace and American Liberalism, 1941–1948* (New York: Free Press, 1973), pp. 216–223; Pells, *The Liberal Mind in a Conservative Age*, pp. 69, 108–109; Hamby, *Beyond the New Deal*, pp. 160–161.

16 Stone, "The Story of Truman versus Wallace," *PM*, September 22, 1946, p. 3; Stone, "The Cost of a War with Russia," *PM*, September 29, 1946, p. 2.

17 Mary McAuliffe, *Crisis on the Left* (Boston: University of Massachusetts Press, 1976), pp. 23–24; Gillon, *Politics and Vision*, pp. 25–27, 29; Freda Kirchwey, "Manifest

Destiny, 1947," *Nation* 164 (March 22, 1947): 317; Hamby, *Beyond the New Deal*, pp. 177–178; Freda Kirchwey, "To the Greeks Bearing Gifts," *Nation* 164 (March 29, 1947): 347–349; Henry Wallace, "The Fight for Peace," *New Republic* 116 (March 24, 1947): 12; Stone, "Reaction's Unhappy Prisoner," *Nation* 158 (March 4, 1944): 270; Stone, "What the Turks Are Afraid Of," *PM*, April 22, 1947, p. 6; Stone, "The People We're Staking in the Middle East," *PM*, April 23, 1947, p. 7; Stone, "Red Plot or Rightist Flim-Flam?" *PM*, July 11, 1947, p. 2.

18 Stone, "Is Mr. Truman Being Tempted?" *PM*, August 8, 1947, p. 2; Stone, "Is U.S. Breeding Civil War Abroad?" *PM*, July 20, 1947, p. 2.

19 Stone, "Is U.S. Breeding Civil War Abroad?" p. 2.

20 Ibid.

21 Stone, "The Report on Soviet Aims—and the American Answer," *PM*, August 22, 1947, p. 2.

22 Ibid.

23 Ibid.

24 Ibid.

25 Ibid.

26 Stone, "The ABC of an Effective Foreign Policy," *PM*, August 27, 1947, p. 2.

27 Hamby, *Beyond the New Deal*, p. 186; Stone, "Marshall Plan and Truman Program," *PM*, September 26, 1947, p. 10; McAuliffe, *Crisis on the Left*, pp. 29–32; Gillon, *Politics and Vision*, pp. 30–31; Pells, *The Liberal Mind in a Conservative Age*, p. 68; Straight, *After Long Silence*, p. 221; "The Marshall Plan," *Nation* 164 (June 21, 1947): 729–731.

28 Stone, "The Marshall Plan and Europe's Crisis," *PM*, September 29, 1947, p. 10.

29 Stone, "The Kind of 'Containment' We Need," *PM*, October 5, 1947, p. 16.

30 Ibid.

31 Stone, "What Is Going On behind the Iron Curtain?" *PM*, November 23, 1947, p. 17.

32 David Caute, *The Great Fear: The Anti-Communist Purge under Truman and Eisenhower* (New York: Simon and Schuster, 1979).

33 Stone, "Some Questions for J. Edgar Hoover," *PM*, October 6, 1946, p. 2.

34 Ibid.

35 Stone, "The Eisler Affair as Spectacle and Warning," *PM*, February 9, 1947, p. 5.

36 Ibid.

37 Ibid.

38 Hamby, *Beyond the New Deal*, p. 171; "The Communist Man-Hunt," *Commonweal* 45 (April 4, 1947): 604.

39 Stone, "Let the Screwballs Speak," *PM*, June 27, 1947, p. 2.

40 Ibid.

41 Hamby, *Beyond the New Deal*, p. 190; "Hysteria on High," *New Republic* 117 (July 14, 1947): 8–9; Stone, "It's Not the Heat, It's the Hysteria," *PM*, July 2, 1947, p. 2.

42 Stone, "Same Old but Still Explosive Firecrackers," *PM*, July 4, 1947, p. 2.

43 Stone, "The American Way—to Totalitarianism," *PM*, August 21, 1947, p. 2; Hamby, *Beyond the New Deal*, p. 185.

44 Freda Kirchwey, "Twenty Years After," *Nation* 165 (August 23, 1947): 173–175.

45 Stone, "Questions for Courts on Film Probe," *PM*, October 22, 1947, p. 2; Stone, "Message to Moscow," *PM*, October 23, 1947, p. 2.

46 "Meet the Press," October 31, 1947; Hoopes, *Ralph Ingersoll*, pp. 318–320; Schlesinger "The U.S. Communist Party," pp. 84–96.

47 Wechsler, *The Age of Suspicion*, pp. 218–221.

48 "Meet the Press," October 31, 1947.

49 Stone, "The Grand Inquisition," *Nation* 165 (November 8, 1947): 492–493.

50 Stone, "The Ultimate Disloyalty," *PM*, December 9, 1947, p. 10.

51 Ibid.

52 Markowitz, *The Rise and Fall of the People's Century*, pp. 253–259; Alpern, *Freda Kirchwey*, pp. 187–188; Allen Yarnell, *Democrats and Progressives: The 1948 Presidential Election as a Test of Postwar Liberalism* (Berkeley: University of California Press, 1974), pp. 46–47; Freda Kirchwey, "Wallace: Prophet or Politician?" *Nation* 166 (January 10, 1948): 29–31; Arthur M. Schlesinger, Jr., "Political Culture in the United States," *Nation* 166 (March 13, 1948): 306–309.

53 Stone, "The Itch to Bar the 3d Party," *PM*, January 22, 1948, p. 9; Stone, "The Wallace Plan and the Communists," *PM*, January 2, 1948, p. 10; Kirchwey, "Wallace: Prophet or Politician?" p. 31.

54 "The Crisis in Czechoslovakia," *Nation* 166 (February 28, 1948): 225; Freda Kirchwey, "Prague—a Lesson for Liberals," *Nation* 166 (March 6, 1948): 265–266; Pells, *The Liberal Mind in a Conservative Age*, pp. 104–106; Markowitz, *The Rise and Fall of the People's Century*, pp. 273–274; Stone, "What's a Desirable Newsman?" *PM*, March 31, 1948, p. 4.

55 Stone, "Count Me In, Too," *PM*, March 15, 1948, p. 11.

56 Stone, "Democrats without Faith in Democracy," *PM*, May 2, 1948, p. 16.

57 Stone, "Unraveling the Spy Mystery," *NY Star*, August 6, 1948, p. 11.

58 Stone, "Washington Perspective," *NY Star*, June 30, 1948, p. 19.

59 Ibid.

60 O'Neill, *A Better World*, pp. 157–158; Stone, "Philadelphia Perspective: Dewey or Don't We?" *NY Star*, June 23, 1948, p. 27; interview with Stone, October 16, 1981; "The Wallace Convention," *Nation* 167 (July 31, 1948): 59; Stone, "Why I Am for Henry Wallace," *NY Star*, July 26, 1948, p. 11; Stone, "Confessions of a Dupe," *NY Star*, August 25, 1948, p. 13.

61 Stone, "Confessions of a Dupe," p. 13.

62 Ibid.; Simon W. Gerson, *The Story of Peter V. Cacchione: New York's First Communist Councilman* (New York: International Publishers, 1976), pp. 202–203.

63 Markowitz, *The Rise and Fall of the People's Century*, p. 283.

64 Arthur M. Schlesinger, Jr., *The Vital Center: The Politics of Freedom* (Boston: Houghton Mifflin, 1949): Hamby, *Beyond the New Deal*, pp. 279–282.

65 Pells, *Radical Visions*, p. 361.

66 Ibid., pp. 361–362.

9. The Panic Was On

1 Interview with Stone, October 16, 1981; Cedric Belfrage and James Aronson, *Something to Guard: The Stormy Life of the National Guardian, 1948–1967* (New York: Columbia University Press, 1978), p. 93; interview with Marc Stone, September 27, 1987; interview with Lou Stone, April 10, 1990; interview with Christopher Stone, January 6, 1992.

2 Interview with Christopher Stone, January 6, 1992.

3 Ibid.; interview with Stone, October 16, 1981; interview with Marc Stone, September 27, 1987; interview with Lou Stone, April 10, 1990; interview with Judy Stone, February 23, 1992.

4 Interview with Christopher Stone, January 6, 1992.

5 Ibid.; I. F. Stone file, CIA documents, #80.

6 Interview with Christopher Stone, January 6, 1992; interview with Stone, October 16, 1981.

7 Ibid.

8 Ibid.

9 Interview with Christopher Stone, January 6, 1992.

10 Robert Lasch, " 'PM' Post-Mortem," *Atlantic Monthly* 182 (July 1948): 44–49; Lawrence Resner, "Field to Give Up Newspaper PM," *NY Times*, March 13, 1948, p. 10.

11 "To the Years Ahead," *NY Star*, June 23, 1948, p. 1; Harold C. Field to Stone, January 17, 1949, pp. 1–2, *Nation* Collection, Houghton Library, Harvard University; interview with Stone, October 16, 1981.

12 Stone, "Farewell to PM," *Post*, January 31, 1949, p. 44; A. J. Liebling, *The Press* (New York: Ballantine, 1964), p. 45.

13 Interview with Stone, October 16, 1981; interview with Marc Stone, September 27, 1987; Hamby, *Beyond the New Deal*, p. 282.

14 Celia Gilbert, "A Housewife's Right to Life," *Saturday Evening Post* 250 (May/June 1978): 56.

15 Ibid.; interview with Christopher Stone, January 6, 1992.

16 Memorial service, July 12, 1989; interview with Christopher Stone, January 6, 1992.

17 Gilbert, "A Housewife's Right to Life," p. 56.

18 Interview with Christopher Stone, January 6, 1992.

19 Ibid.

20 Interview with Judy Stone, February 23, 1992.

21 Stone, "An Extra Inning for the New Deal," *NY Star*, November 5, 1948, p. 12; Markowitz, *The Rise and Fall of the People's Century*, p. 296.

22 Stone, "New Declarations of Cold War," *Post*, January 21, 1949, p. 15; Stone, "Holy Alliance," *Post*, March 24, 1949, p. 47.

23 Stone, "Bayonets for Bread," *Post*, February 24, 1949, p. 60; Stone, "What Europe Fears," *Post*, February 23, 1949, p. 78.

24 Stone, "Bayonets for Bread," p. 60; Stone, "Atlantic Pact," *Post*, March 21, 1949, p. 43; Stone, "What of the UN?" *Post*, March 22, 1949, p. 57.

25 "The Atlantic Pact," *Monthly Review* 1 (November 1949): 3–4; Freda Kirchwey, "Signed but Not Sealed," *Nation* 168 (April 9, 1949): 403–405; "The North Atlantic Pact," *New Republic* 120 (February 14, 1949): 5–6.

26 D. L. Nicholson to Mr. Reinhardt, April 11, 1949, Division EE, Department of State, 811.00 (B)/4-749.

27 Stone, "Cold War: How It Started, Where It Leads," *Compass*, August 14, 1949, special supplement, p. S3.

28 Ibid.

29 Hamby, *Beyond the New Deal*, p. 96; Stone, "Misjudging 2 Revolutions: Russia in '19, China Today," *Compass*, August 23, 1949, p. 3; "More Bryan than Marx," *Record*, May 30, 1933, p. 6; Stone, "Chungking and Washington," *Nation* (April 5, 1941): 400; Stone, "The Answer," *Post*, April 26, 1949, p. 45; "Anna Louise Strong,"

Nation 168 (February 26, 1949): 228; "China and Socialism," *Monthly Review* 1 (November 1949): 5.

30 Stone, "Communism, Capitalism: Can They Live Together?" *Compass*, October 21, 1949, pp. 3, 21.

31 Stone, "Paging a Squirrel," *Post*, February 18, 1949, p. 76; Stone, "Lenin and Locke," *Post*, February 28, 1949, p. 48.

32 Stone, "Acheson, Hiss and Anna Louise Strong," *Compass*, January 30, 1950, p. 5.

33 Stone, "Agitprop Defense," *Post*, March 14, 1949, p. 37; Stone, "Hand-Picked Jury," *Post*, March 16, 1949, p. 73.

34 James Kutcher, *The Case of the Legless Veteran* (New York: Monad Press, 1973), pp. 76–78, 108; Stone, "The Case of the Legless Veteran," *NY Star*, October 22, 1948, p. 15; "Mr. Truman's Administration," *Nation* 167 (October 9, 1948): 386.

35 George Charney, *A Long Journey* (Chicago: Quadrangle, 1968), pp. 223–224.

36 McAuliffe, *Crisis on the Left*, pp. 49–50; Hamby, *Beyond the New Deal*, p. 387; Pells, *The Liberal Mind in a Conservative Age*, pp. 281–282; Schlesinger, *The Vital Center*, pp. 199–203.

37 Kutcher, *The Case of the Legless Veteran*, p. 152; Stone, "The Communists and Civil Liberty," *Compass*, July 1, 1949, p. 5.

38 Stone, "The Communists and Civil Liberty," p. 5.

39 Ibid.

40 "Meet the Press" interview with Glenn Taylor, July 29, 1949; Stone, "The Shadow Cast by Foley Square," *Compass*, October 14, 1949, p. 6.

41 Stone, "A Trial That Changes the Face of America," *Compass*, October 16, 1949, p. 3.

42 Stone, "The Press and the Trial—an Anthology of Fatuity," *Compass*, October 17, 1949, p. 3.

43 Stone, "Me and Marxism: Invitation—to a Dog-Fight," *Compass*, November 14, 1949, p. 5; interview with Christopher Stone, January 6, 1992.

44 Stone, "Me and Marxism," p. 5.

45 Ibid.; "Meet the Press" interview with George H. Earle, October 10, 1947; "Meet the Press" interview with Patrick Hurley, August 15, 1949.

46 "Meet the Press" interview with Sava Kosanovic, September 20, 1946; "Meet the Press" interview with Hans Freistadt, June 18, 1949; "Meet the Press" interview with Kosanovic, November 12, 1949.

47 Stone, "Me and Marxism," p. 5.

48 Ibid.

49 Ibid., p. 21.

50 Ibid., p. 5; "Meet the Press" interview with Walter Judd, November 26, 1949.

51 Stone, "Me and Marxism," p. 5.

52 Stone, "450,000,000 Chinese Can't Be Brushed Off," *Compass*, January 4, 1950, pp. 5, 21.

53 Stone, "Acheson's Bogeyman Theory of History," *Compass*, March 15, 1950, p. 5; Stone, "Washington's Farewell Address vs. Truman," *Compass*, February 23, 1950, p. 25.

54 Freda Kirchwey, "The McCarthy Blight," *Nation* 170 (June 24, 1950): 609–610; "The McCarthy Affair," *Monthly Review* 2 (June 1950): 33–34; "McCarthy's Red Scare," *New Republic* 122 (March 20, 1950): 4–5.

55 Stone, "The Sewer That Runs beneath the Capitol," *Compass*, March 22, 1950, p. 5.

56 Ibid., p. 24; Hamby, *Beyond the New Deal*, p. 392.

57 Stone, "Has the ADA Stopped Being a Truman Front?" *Compass*, April 6, 1950, p. 21.

58 Stone, "Truman's Washington and Nero's Rome," *Compass*, May 1, 1950, p. 5.

59 Stone, "An Answer to Sidney Hook," *Compass*, July 11, 1950, pp. 2, 20.

60 Straight, "The Right Way to Beat Communism," *New Republic* 122 (May 1, 1950): 10–13.

61 Ibid., p. 12; "Korea: Final Test of the UN," *New Republic* 123 (July 3, 1950): 5–6; "Gamble in Korea," *Nation* 171 (July 8, 1950): 23.

62 James Aronson, *The Press and the Cold War* (Indianapolis: Bobbs-Merrill, 1970), p. 108; Stone, "Q. and A. on Korean Crisis," *Compass*, June 27, 1950, pp. 3, 20; Stone, "The Next Move Is Up to Moscow," *Compass*, June 28, 1950, pp. 3, 20; Stone, "Has Moscow Dumped Peace Movement?" *Compass*, June 29, 1950, pp. 5, 20.

63 Stone, "U.S. War Chariot Needs Brakes," *Compass*, June 30, 1950, pp. 3, 20; Stone, "Babbitts in Congress Hurt Us in Korea," *Compass*, July 13, 1950, p. 3; Freda Kirchwey, "America's Asian Policy," *Nation* 171 (July 22, 1950): 73.

64 Stone, "U.S. Should Trade 'Face' for Time," August 1, 1950, *Compass*, p. 5.

65 Interview with Stone, October 16, 1981; Herbert Lottman, *The Left Bank: Writers, Artists, and Politics from the Popular Front to the Cold War* (San Francisco: Halo Books, 1991), pp. 277–279; Stone, "Nehru's Job Harder than Gandhi Faced," *Compass*, September 12, 1950, p. 5.

66 Stone, "Marshal Tito Grants Interview," *Compass*, October 19, 1950, p. 5; Stone, "Freedom of Speech Found in Yugoslavia," *Compass*, October 24, 1950, p. 5.

67 Stone, "Soviet-Yugoslav Row Held Family Quarrel," *Compass*, October 25, 1950, p. 5; Stone, "What's Behind Tito's Decree of Equality," *Compass*, October 27, 1950, p. 21; Stone, "Tito's Dilemma: The Bureaucracy," *Compass*, October 31, 1950, p. 4.

68 Stone, "Labor Has Real Say in Big Yugoslav Plant," *Compass*, November 8, 1950, p. 4; Stone, "Why Tito Mistrusts America's Policy," *Compass*, November 10, 1950, p. 4.

69 Stone, "Shouting into a Hurricane," *Compass*, August 13, 1950, p. 12.

70 Stone, "Looking at America from 3,000 Miles," *Compass*, October 1, 1950, p. 5; Stone, "Rip Van Winkle-ish Woes of Truman," *Compass*, October 4, 1950, p. 5.

71 "Fascism in the United States?" *Monthly Review* 2 (November 1950): 328–333.

72 Interview with Christopher Stone, January 6, 1992; Lottman, *The Left Bank*, p. 278; interview with Judy Stone, February 23, 1992.

73 Stone, "Jo Davidson, 1883–1952," *Compass*, January 6, 1952, pp. 5–6.

74 Stone, "Chinese 'Counter-Blockade' Could Be Dangerous for West," *Compass*, December 21, 1950, p. 4; Stone, "MacArthur Ravaged Korea with Methodical Destruction," *Compass*, February 14, 1951, p. 4; Stone, "Air Force Glee at Bombings Is Moral Degeneration," *Compass*, February 18, 1951, p. 4.

75 Leo Huberman and Paul Sweezy, "Publisher's Foreword," in I. F. Stone's *The Hidden History of the Korean War* (New York: Monthly Review, 1952), p. xv.

76 Stone, *The Hidden History*.

77 Aronson, *The Press and the Cold War*, p. 109; Huberman and Sweezy, "Publisher's Foreword," pp. xv, xvi, xix; the editors, note, *Monthly Review* 1 (April 1950): 379.

78 W. MacMahon Ball, "Some Questions on Korea," *Nation* 174 (July 5, 1952): 14–15; "Recent Books," *Foreign Affairs* 31 (October 1952): 167; Michael Straight, "A Fictive Report," *New Republic* 126 (June 2, 1952): 21–22; Richard Rovere, "History in

the Stone Age: Hidden 'Facts' and Fiction of the War in Korea," *Post*, May 11, 1952, p. 12M; Art Preis, "A Trotskyist Defends New I. F. Stone Book," *Compass*, May 26, 1952, pp. 5, 16.

79 Fraser Wilkins to the Department of State, Foreign Service Despatch, Circular Airgram, April 27, 1953, 511.91/5-1153 XR 911.63.

80 Interview with Stone, October 16, 1981.

81 Stone, "Room for Hope: Reason for Pride," *Compass*, July 4, 1951, p. 18.

82 Victor S. Navasky, *Naming Names* (New York: Penguin, 1981), p. 50; Carey McWilliams, *The Education of Carey McWilliams* (New York: Simon and Schuster, 1979), p. 161; Samuel Walker, *In Defense of Civil Liberties: A History of the ACLU* (New York: Oxford University Press, 1990), pp. 198–221; interview with Stone, October 16, 1981.

83 Interview with Stone, October 16, 1981.

84 Navasky, *Naming Names*, p. 56; Louis Budenz, *The Cry Is Peace* (Chicago: Henry Regnery, 1952), p. 108; Ogden R. Reid, "The Red Underground," *NY Herald Tribune*, November 4, 1951, section 2, p. 3; Stone, "Me and the Red Underground," *Compass*, November 11, 1951, p. 5.

85 "Refusal," March 28, 1951, SDF, PO28; Isidor Feinstein STONE Status Report, William P. Canfield, September 26, 1951, SDF, PO55; Stone to Willis H. Young, November 2, 1951, SDF, PO17; Willis H. Young to Stone, November 9, 1951, SDF, PO16.

86 Interview with Stone, October 16, 1981; Stone, "Comment: Fate of the Compass," *Weekly* 1 (January 17, 1953): 3; "Notes from the Editor," *Monthly Review* 4 (December 1952): inside back cover.

87 Dashiell Hammett to Stone, March 18, 1952, Victor J. Jerome Collection, Sterling Library, Yale University; Stone to Dashiell Hammett, March 1952, Jerome Collection.

88 Stone, "Why 1952 Is the Year of Great Danger," *Compass*, June 29, 1952, p. 5; Stone, "Dems Have Better Ideas, A Better Man," *Compass*, July 28, 1952, pp. 5, 15; Stone, "Memoir How to Function as a Peace Party," *Compass*, August 3, 1952, p. 5; Stone, "Why I'm for Adlai Stevenson," *Compass*, September 21, 1952, pp. 5, 25.

89 Alan Max, "I. F. Stone and Adlai Stevenson," *Daily Worker*, October 1, 1952, pp. 1, 5; Max, "Stone and the Fight against McCarthyism," *Daily Worker*, October 2, 1952, p. 5; Max, "I. F. Stone and the Old Parties," *Daily Worker*, October 3, 1952, p. 1.

90 Stone, "Lesson of Past Dictates Vote for Stevenson," *Compass*, October 2, 1952, pp. 5, 12.

91 Stone, "The Rosenberg Case," *Compass*, October 15, 1952, p. 5.

92 Ibid.; interview with Stone, October 16, 1981; Arthur Garfield Hays, "The Rosenberg Case," *Nation* 175 (November 8, 1952): 422–423.

93 "The *Daily Compass* Ends Publication," *NY Times*, November 4, 1952, p. 37; "Notes for the Editor," *Monthly Review* 4 (December 1952): inside back cover; interview with Stone, October 16, 1981; McWilliams, *The Education of Carey McWilliams*, p. 237; Robert Sherrill, "Weeklies and Weaklies," *Antioch Review* 29 (Spring 1969): 27.

94 Interview with Stone, October 16, 1981; Stone, *The Truman Era* (New York: Vintage, 1973), pp. xvii–xviii.

95 Stone, *The Truman Era*, p. xxix.

10. A "Little Flea-Bite Publication"

1 Stone, "Why the *Weekly* Rejected that $5 from Senator Eastland," *Weekly* 3 (December 12, 1955): 1, 4; interview with Stone, October 16, 1981.

2 Stone, "Why the *Weekly* Rejected That $5 from Senator Eastland," p. 1.

3 Stone, "An Open Letter to William Randolph Hearst, Jr.," *Weekly* 3 (December 19, 1955): 1.

4 Ibid.

5 Interview with Stone, October 16, 1981; Nobile, *Intellectual Skywriting,* pp. 165–166.

6 Stone, "Notes on Closing," p. 2; Robert Sobel, "In Fact: New York, 1940–1950," in *The American Radical Press, 1880–1960,* ed. Joseph R. Conlin (Westport, Conn.: Greenwood, 1974), pp. 618–621; letter to author from George Seldes, June 30, 1983.

7 Stone, "Notes on Closing," pp. 2–3; interview with Marc Stone, September 27, 1987; interview with Christopher Stone, January 6, 1992; Christopher Lydon, "I. F. Stone to Suspend 19-Year-Old Leftist Biweekly," *NY Times,* December 7, 1971, p. 43; Derek Shearer, "Izzy Stone, from Outcast to Institution," *In These Times,* June 7–13, 1978, p. 3.; Stone, "Introduction," *The Haunted Fifties,* p. xvii.

8 Interview with Marc Stone, September 27, 1987; Stone, "A Personal Letter from I. F. Stone," *National Guardian,* November 27, 1952, p. 7; "A Personal Letter from I. F. Stone," *Nation* 175 (December 6, 1952): 533.

9 Stone, "3,000 Subs in Three Wks.," *Guardian,* December 25, 1952, p. 7.

10 Ibid.; interview with Stone, October 16, 1981; interview with Christopher Stone, January 6, 1992; Sol Stern, "I. F. Stone; The Journalist as Pamphleteer," *Ramparts* (February 1968): 53; A. Kent MacDougall, "Gadfly on the Left: I. F. Stone Achieves Success, Respectability but Keeps Raking Muck," *Wall Street Journal,* July 14, 1970, p. 22; five-dollar check from Albert Einstein to Stone, January 31, 1953, in the possession of Esther Stone, on display at the "Paradox of the Press" exhibit, Library of Congress, Washington, D.C., April 5–August 12, 1990.

11 Interview with Stone, October 16, 1981; Stone, "Notes on Closing," p. 3.

12 Postmaster to Gentlemen, January 25, 1954, U.S. Post Office Department, Documents 193–194, in the Federal Bureau of Investigation files.

13 Interview with Stone, October 16, 1981; interview with Marc Stone, September 27, 1987; Bruck, *I. F. Stone's Weekly;* letter to author from Seldes, June 30, 1983; Andrew Kopkind, "The Importance of Being Izzy," *Ramparts* 12 (May 1974): 43; Peter Osnos, "I. F. Stone, a Journalist's Journalist," *NY Times,* June 20, 1989, p. A23; interview with Christopher Stone, January 6, 1992.

14 Stone, "Notes on Closing," p. 3; "To *I. F. Stone's Weekly* Readers," *Weekly* 2 (March 21, 1953): 3; letter to author from Seldes, June 30, 1983.

15 Interview with Stone, October 16, 1981; Stone, "Notes on Closing," p. 4; Stone, "Introduction," p. xviii; Belfrage and Aronson, *Something to Guard,* p. 182; interview with Christopher Stone, January 6, 1992.

16 Stone, "Comment: Fate of the *Compass:* Best People in the U.S.A.," *Weekly* 1 (January 17, 1953): 3.

17 Stone, "Please Excuse," *Weekly* 1 (January 17, 1953): 3.

18 Interview with Stone, October 16, 1981.

19 Ibid.

20 Interview with Christopher Stone, January 6, 1992; Stone, "Professor Albert Einstein," *Weekly* 3 (April 25, 1955): 4.

21 Ibid.; Kopkind, "The Importance of Being Izzy," p. 43.

22 Stone, "Our Zero Hour Approaches," *Weekly* 1 (October 10, 1953): 3; letter from Stone to friends and readers, 1954, p. 1; Stone, "Don't Forget about That Renewal—and Add a Gift Sub, Too," *Weekly* 1 (October 17, 1953): 3.

23 Interview with Stone, October 16, 1981.

24 Letter from Stone to friends and readers, 1954, p. 1; Stone, "Vital Statistics," *Weekly* 1 (March 28, 1953): 3; Stone, "Thank You, Daniel Webster," *Weekly* 1 (February 7, 1953): 3; Stone, "Notes on Closing," p. 3.

25 Interview with Stone, October 16, 1981; interview with Christopher Stone, January 6, 1992.

26 Interview with Christopher Stone, January 6, 1992.

27 Stone, "Comment: Best People in the U.S.A.," p. 3; Stone, "John Foster Dulles: Portrait of a Liberator," *Weekly* 1 (January 24, 1953): 2; Stone, "Another of McCarthy's Little Reichstag Fires," *Weekly* 1 (February 28, 1953): 4; Stone, "Time for a Deportation—to Wisconsin," *Weekly* 1 (April 4, 1953): 4; Stone, "McCarthy's Hoax and the Real Radar Scandal," *Weekly* 1 (October 24, 1953): 1.

28 Stone, "Making America a Police State," *Weekly* 1 (May 2, 1953): 1; Stone, "The Master Plan for American Thought Control," *Compass*, March 13, 1952, pp. 5, 6.

29 "Confidential," n.d., document 227, Department of the Army (DOA), U.S. Army Intelligence (USAI); W. A. Perry to the Director, FBI, March 12, 1954, document 201, DOA, USAI.

30 William L. O'Neill, *American High: The Years of Confidence, 1945–1960* (New York: Free Press, 1986), pp. 200–203.

31 Stone, "McCarthy's Advantage," *Weekly* 2 (July 19, 1954): 3; Stone, "The High Cost of Anti-Communist Mania," *Weekly* 2 (August 9, 1954): 1.

32 Stone, "The Panic of a Mob on Capitol Hill," *Weekly* 2 (September 6, 1954): 1–4; Gillon, *Politics and Vision*, pp. 107–109.

33 Stone to Earl Browder, October 29, 1954, November 14, 1954, December 20, 1954, Earl Browder Papers, Syracuse University.

34 Stone, "How the Army Controls the Minds of Our Youth," *Weekly* 3 (August 15, 1955): 1.

35 Interview with Stone, October 16, 1981.

36 Ibid.

37 Stone, "The Congressional Witch Hunt Is Over," *Weekly* 5 (June 24, 1957): 1, 4.

38 Stone, "The Test of Our Society's Freedom Is How We Treat Our Own Pasternaks," *Weekly* 6 (November 3, 1958): 4.

39 Stone, "British Socialism Can Live Only in Atmosphere of Peace," *Compass*, April 29, 1951, p. 4; Stone, "Those Diabolic Doctors," *Weekly* 1 (February 7, 1953): 4.

40 Stone, "Anti-Zionism or Anti-Semitism?" *Weekly* 1 (February 21, 1953): 1; Stone, "Washington after Stalin," *Weekly* 1 (March 14, 1953): 1.

41 Stone, "The Greatest Confession of Them All," *Weekly* 1 (April 11, 1953): 1.

42 Ibid.

43 Stone, "Only Rhee's Removal Can Save Peace," *Weekly* 1 (June 27, 1953): 1.

44 Stone, "Eisenhower's Air-Conditioned Answer," *Weekly* 1 (July 11, 1953): 1.

45 Stone, "The Djilas Affair," *Weekly* 2 (January 25, 1954): 3.

46 Stone, "The Meaning of the Djilas-Dedijer Affair in Yugoslavia," *Weekly* 3 (January 10, 1955): 7.

47 Ibid.

48 Stone, "The Liberation of Europe Has Begun," *Weekly* 3 (May 23, 1955): 1.

49 Stone, "How Washington 'Celebrated' the October Revolution," *Weekly* 3 (November 14, 1955): 3.

50 Stone, "The Meaning of Khrushchev's Revisions in Communist Doctrine," *Weekly* 4 (February 20, 1956): 2.

51 Ibid.

52 Interview with Marc Stone, September 27, 1987.

53 Stone, "In the Muddy Wake of the Moscow Melodrama," *Weekly* 4 (March 26, 1956): 1, 4.

54 Stone, "Department of State Passport Application," March 23, 1956, pp. 1–2 and attachment, SDF, PO14.

55 Stone, "A Visit to Moscow: Part One," *Weekly* 4 (May 7, 1956): 3–4.

56 Stone, "Stalinism Is Far from Liquidated," *Weekly* 4 (May 28, 1956): 1.

57 Ibid.

58 Ibid.

59 MacDougall, "Gadfly on the Left," p. 22; Stone to Norman Thomas, November 27, 1956, Norman Thomas Papers, New York Public Library; Stone to Norman Thomas, June 8, 1956, Thomas Papers; Norman Thomas to Stone, June 14, 1956, Thomas Papers.

60 Stone, "Poland Has Begun to Liberate Itself," *Weekly* 4 (June 4, 1956): 1–3.

61 Ibid., p. 3; Stone, "Still Speaking Stalin's Language," *Weekly* 4 (July 9, 1956): 4.

62 Stone, "Why the Workers Rise against the Workers' State," *Weekly* 4 (October 29, 1956): 1.

63 Ibid., p. 4; Irving Howe and Lewis Coser, "Revolution in Eastern Europe," *Dissent* 3 (November 6, 1956): 3.

64 Stone, "The Hungarian Rebels Have Destroyed the Last Illusions of an Era," *Weekly* 4 (November 19, 1956): 4; Howe and Coser, "Revolution in Eastern Europe," p. 13.

65 Ibid.

66 Stone, "Hungary," *Weekly* 4 (November 12, 1956): 3; Stone, "When Tito Jailed Djilas, He Destroyed Titoism," *Weekly* 4 (November 26, 1956): 1, 4.

67 Stone, "It Will Be a Memorable Evening," *Weekly* 4 (December 3, 1956): 3; Stone, "Don't Forget Our Get Together on Dec. 14," *Weekly* 4 (December 10, 1956): 4.

68 Norman Thomas to Stone, November 26, 1956, p. 1, Socialist Party Papers.

69 Stone, "Another Murder in the Lubianka," *Weekly* 5 (March 11, 1957): 4; Stone, "Nagy Execution May Signal General Return to Stalinist Policy," *Weekly* 6 (June 23, 1958): 2.

70 Stone, "From the Other Side of the Oder-Neisse Frontier," *Weekly* 7 (April 13, 1959): 1–4; Stone, "After Warsaw, A Visit to East Berlin is Like a Return to Stalinism . . . The East German Regime Has the Old Iron Curtain Mentality," *Weekly* 7 (April 20, 1959): 2–3.

71 Stone, "It's More than 'Sectarianism' That Ails American Communists," *Weekly* 4 (October 1, 1956): 4.

72 Stone, "Why the American Communist Party Ought to Dissolve," *Weekly* 5 (February 11, 1957): 3; Alan M. Wald, *The New York Intellectuals: The Rise and Decline of the Anti-Stalinist Left from the 1930s to the 1980s* (Chapel Hill: University of North Carolina Press, 1987), pp. 325–326.

73 Stone, "The New Forum for Socialist Education before the Internal Security Committee," *Weekly* 5 (May 27, 1957): 3; Lewis Coser and Irving Howe, "The Choice of 'Comrades,' " *Dissent* 4 (Summer 1957): 332–335.

74 Stone, "Our Favorite Quote . . . ," *Weekly* 5 (October 28, 1957): 4; Stone, "Recommended," *Weekly* 5 (December 2, 1957): 3.

75 Stone to Norman Thomas, December 18, 1953, Thomas Papers; Stone, "For Norman Thomas at 75," *Weekly* 7 (November 16, 1959): 1; Norman Thomas to Stone, December 23, 1958, Thomas Papers.

76 Stone, "How Can I Help?" *Weekly* 5 (December 16, 1957): 1+.

77 Stone, "Thank You," *Weekly* 5 (December 16, 1957): 1.

78 Ibid.

79 *"Variety* on IFS," *Weekly* 6 (June 23, 1958): 2.

80 Bertrand Russell to Stone, October 30, 1958, letter in the possession of Esther Stone, on display at the "Paradox of the Press" exhibit; Stone to Alexander Meiklejohn, March 5, 1959, Alexander Meiklejohn Papers, State Historical Society of Wisconsin.

81 Stone, "Personal Bows (and Blushes) Dept.," *Weekly* 7 (December 21, 1959): 4; Foster Hailey, "Senator Defends Right to Dissent," *NY Times,* December 16, 1959, p. 6; Bertrand Russell to Clark Foreman, November 30, 1959, letter in the possession of Esther Stone.

82 Interview with Christopher Stone, January 6, 1992.

83 Ibid.

84 Ibid.

85 Ibid.

86 Radio Reports, Inc., "I. F. Stone Thinks Jim Hagerty a Bore," July 18, 1957, Presidential General File, Dwight D. Eisenhower Library; G. W. Johnstone to James C. Hagerty, July 23, 1957, Presidential General File, Eisenhower Library; James C. Hagerty to G. W. Johnstone, July 25, 1957, Presidential General File, Eisenhower Library.

87 105 *Congr. Rec.* 1222 (January 27, 1959) (remarks of Francis Walter); 106 *Congr. Rec.* 9651-9652 (May 5, 1960) (remarks of Gordon Scherer, HCUAC file).

88 Herbert Lewis to J. Edgar Hoover, September 23, 1959, document 263, DOA, USAI; interview with Christopher Stone, January 6, 1992.

11. "To Learn to Think in a New Way"

1 Stone, "Introduction," p. xix; Nat Hentoff, "I. F. Stone: The Measure of a Man," *Village Voice,* December 23, 1971, p. 14.

2 Stone, "Why the AEC Retracted That Falsehood on Nuclear Testing," *Weekly* 6 (March 17, 1958): 1; Stone, "Introduction," pp. xix–xx; Downie, *The New Muckrakers,* p. 202; Hentoff, "I. F. Stone," pp. 14, 20.

3 Hentoff, "I. F. Stone," p. 20; Downie, *The New Muckrakers,* p. 202; Stone, "Introduction," p. xx; Stone, "Why the AEC Retracted That Falsehood on Nuclear Testing," p. 1.

4 Hentoff, "I. F. Stone," p. 20; Stone, "Introduction," p. xx; Stone, "Why the AEC Retracted That Falsehood on Nuclear Testing," p. 1.

5 Stone, "David-and-Goliath Journalism," *Weekly* 6 (May 19, 1958): 1+.

6 Stone, "We Have to Learn to Think in a New Way," *Weekly* 3 (July 18, 1955): 1; Stone, "Hatred, Not Hydrogen, Is the Fatal Explosion," *Weekly* 3 (March 14, 1955): 1; Stone, "The Common Man in His Undershirt," *PM,* August 4, 1944, p. 2.

7 Stone, "The Fatal Decisions Have Already Been Made," *Weekly* 2 (November 1, 1954): 1; Stone, "The Ultimate Weapon Illusion and the Ultimate Weapon," *Weekly* 6 (January 13, 1958): 1; Stone, "Is National Suicide a Sensible Form of Defense?" *Weekly* 3 (November 28, 1955): 1; Stone, "Back to the Arms Race," *Weekly* 3 (December 19, 1955): 3; Stone, "The Magic of Disarmament," *Weekly* 3 (October 3, 1955): 3.

8 Stone, "Thank You," December 16, 1957, p. 1+; The Community Church of Boston, Sunday program, "Future Speakers," February 2, 1958, April 20, 1958, p. 2, Martin Luther King, Jr., Collection, Mugar Memorial Library, Boston University;

Stone, "IFS to Speak in Mass. and Calif.," *Weekly* 5 (November 25, 1957): 4; Stone, "Stone to Talk on Nuclear Testing," *Weekly* 6 (September 1, 1958): 2; Stone, "Norman Thomas and IFS to Speak at Nuclear Rally," *Weekly* 6 (September 8, 1958): 4.

9 Stone, "Castro's Queasy Welcome: All We Care about Is Anti-Communism," *Weekly* 7 (April 27, 1959): 3; Stone, "The Colonialism We Oppose Elsewhere and Practice Still in Cuba," *Weekly* 7 (November 23, 1959): 4.

10 Stone, "How Eastland and Dodd Help Anti-American Propaganda in Castro's Cuba," *Weekly* 8 (February 8, 1960): 4; Stone, "Not a Revolution Imposed from Above," *Weekly* 8 (August 1, 1960): 1–2.

11 "Go Slow, Goliath," *Nation* 191 (July 23, 1960): 41–42; Irving Louis Horowitz, *C. Wright Mills: An American Utopian* (New York: Free Press, 1983), pp. 141–142.

12 Stone, "Both Parties for Welfare State at Home—Why Not in Cuba?" *Weekly* 8 (August 8, 1960): 1–3.

13 Ibid., p. 3; Stone, "The Spirit of Che Guevara," *New Statesman*, October 20, 1967, p. 501.

14 Horowitz, *C. Wright Mills*, pp. 295–296; Paul Hollander, *Political Pilgrims: Travels of Western Intellectuals to the Soviet Union, China, and Cuba, 1928–1978* (New York: Harper Colophon Books, 1983), pp. 223–267, 477.

15 David Caute, *The Fellow-Travellers: A Postcript to the Enlightenment* (New Haven: Yale University Press, 1988), pp. 405–410; Hollander, *Political Pilgrims*, pp. 223–263.

16 Stone, "After Our Failure on Cuba at San Jose," *Weekly* 8 (September 5, 1960): 1; Stone, "Why We Cannot Recommend Either Candidate," *Weekly* 8 (November 7, 1960): 1.

17 Stone, "No Firm Majority, No Clear Mandate, No Real Verdict," *Weekly* 8 (November 14, 1960): 1; Stone, "Just What Are We Cooking Up in the Caribbean?" *Weekly* 8 (November 28, 1960): 1.

18 "Foreign Broadcast," January 16, 1961, I. F. Stone File, CIA documents, b3, #57; "Foreign Broadcast," January 17, 1961, I. F. Stone File, CIA documents, b3, #56.

19 Stone, "As If the Prophet Jeremiah Were Caught Cheering," *Weekly* 9 (February 6, 1961): 1.

20 Ibid., pp. 1, 4; Stone, "Peace Groups Must Prepare Now to Support JFK on Nuclear Test Treaty," *Weekly* 9 (March 27, 1961): 2.

21 Stone, "As If the Prophet Jeremiah Were Caught Cheering," p. 4; Stone, "How We Can Defeat the Russians in Latin America," *Weekly* 9 (March 27, 1961): 1, 4.

22 Stone to Passport Office, State Department, January 27, 1961, SDF, PO07; Stone, "No Painless Diplomacy for the Ache of Castroism," *Weekly* 9 (February 27, 1961): 1–2.

23 Ibid., pp. 2–3.

24 Stone, "What Kennedy Ought to Do about Cuba Is to Reverse Eisenhower's Policies . . . ," *Weekly* 9 (March 13, 1961): 2–3; Stone, "The Spirit of Che Guevara," p. 501.

25 Stone, "Only a Smoother Sales Talk for Intervention in Cuba," *Weekly* 9 (April 10, 1961): 1–2.

26 Stone, "The Deed Was Done Quickly, but It's Macbeth Who's Dead," *Weekly* 9 (April 24, 1961): 1, 4.

27 Stone, "Appeal against War with Cuba," *Weekly* 9 (May 1, 1961): 4; "Open Letter to the President," *Weekly* 9 (May 15, 1961): 4.

28 Stone to Michael Blankfort, July 3, 1961, Michael Blankfort Collection, Mugar Memorial Library, Boston University.

29 Stone, "Why a Summit Now Seems a Dubious Proposition," *Weekly* 9 (May 22, 1961): 1; Stone, "Mr. K's New Communist Manifesto," *Weekly* 9 (August 7, 1961): 1, 4; Stone, "Observations to and from Belgrade," *Weekly* 9 (September 11–18, 1961): 1–6.

30 Stone, "Bertrand Russell's Solution for the Berlin Crisis," *Weekly* 9 (October 2, 1961): 1, 4; Stone, "The Bomb the President Must De-fuse," *Weekly* 9 (October 23, 1961): 1, 4.

31 Stone, "How You, Too, Can Strike for Peace," *Weekly* 10 (January 22, 1962): 1; Nancy Zaroulis and Gerald Sullivan, *Who Spoke Up?: American Protest against the War in Vietnam, 1963–1975* (Garden City, N.Y.: Doubleday, 1984), pp. 10–11.

32 Stone, "A Triumph of Youth, Not of Electronic Hardware," *Weekly* 10 (February 26, 1962): 1, 4.

33 Stone, "Questions on the Eve of JFK's Latin American Visit," *Weekly* 9 (December 18, 1961): 1; Stone, "Cuba Is the Spark That Could Set Off the Conflagration," *Weekly* 10 (September 10, 1962): 1; Stone, "Afraid of Everything But War," *Weekly* 10 (September 17, 1962): 1; Stone, "Cuba Offers Peace, but We're Intent on War," *Weekly* 10 (October 15, 1962): 1.

34 Stone, "How *Do* You Crush an Inspiration?" *Weekly* 10 (October 1, 1962): 1; " 'We Are a Great Country,' " *Nation* 195 (September 22, 1962): 141.

35 Stone, "An Appeal to the President to Lift the Blockade and Neutralize Cuba," *Weekly* 10 (October 29, 1962): 1–2, 4; James Miller, *"Democracy Is in the Streets": From Port Huron to the Siege of Chicago* (New York: Simon and Schuster, 1987), pp. 163–164.

36 Stone, "The Reprieve and What Needs to Be Done with It," *Weekly* 10 (November 5, 1962): 1–2.

37 Ibid., pp. 2–3.

38 Stone, "Not Easy to Be a Reporter—at Large—in Havana," *Weekly* 11 (January 7, 1963): 1–2.

39 Ibid., p. 3.

40 Ibid., pp. 3–4.

41 Ibid., p. 4.

42 Stone, "Castro's Own Brand of Marxism-Leninism," *Weekly* 11 (January 14, 1963): 1.

43 Stone, "Fresh Light on the Mystery of the Missiles," *Weekly* 11 (January 21, 1963): 4; Stone, "Castro's Own Brand of Marxism-Leninism," pp. 1–4.

44 Stone, "Fresh Light on the Mystery of the Missiles," p. 3.

45 Ibid., p. 4.

46 "Info," April 28, 1963, I. F. Stone file, CIA documents, b3, #61.

47 Stone, "Why and How Did Peace Suddenly Break Out?" *Weekly* 11 (September 2, 1963): 1, 4.

48 Stone, "We All Had a Finger on That Trigger," *Weekly* 11 (December 9, 1963): 1, 8.

12. Knockin' on Jim Crow's Doors

1 Stone, "Capital Notes," *Nation* 156 (April 10, 1943): 512–513.

2 Ibid.; Stone, "Challenge to the Press Corps," *NY Star*, December 20, 1948, p. 13.

3 Ibid.

4 Stone, "Capital Notes," p. 513.

5 Ibid.

6 Stone, "Four Negroes," *Nation* 150 (February 24, 1940): 270.

7 Stone, "Proposing: Americans in Action," *PM*, November 2, 1947, p. 16.

8 Ibid.

9 Stone, "Who'll Free the Negroes? They Must Do It Themselves," *Compass*, February 17, 1952, p. 3.

10 Stone, "The Negro Strides Toward Full Emancipation," *Weekly* 2 (May 24, 1954): 1.

11 Stone, "The Sickness of the South," *Weekly* 3 (October 3, 1955): 2; Stone, "Will the South Fire on Fort Sumter Again?" *Weekly* 3 (June 6, 1955): 1. See also Stone, "A One-Man Battle for Decency," *Compass*, July 20, 1952, p. 5.

12 Stone, "The Sickness of the South," p. 2.

13 Stone, "Toting Up Some Strong Accounts from the Old Year to the New," *Weekly* 5 (January 7, 1957): 6; Irving Howe, "Reverberations in the North," *Dissent* 3 (Spring 1956): 121–123.

14 "The Bill of Rights: 1791–1956," *Nation* 183 (December 15, 1956): 509; Stone, "The Volcanoes We Ignore—East West (and *South*)," *Weekly* 5 (January 21, 1957): 1.

15 Stone, "The Prayer Pilgrimage Must Be Counted Politically a Failure," *Weekly* 5 (May 27, 1957): 2.

16 Stone, "Toting Up Some Strong Accounts from the Old Year to the New," p. 6; Stone, "The United States as Three Nations, Not One," *Weekly* 5 (October 7, 1957): 1.

17 Ibid.

18 Stone, "Journal of a Flying Trip to Little Rock," *Weekly* 6 (September 22, 1958): 1–3.

19 Ibid., p. 4.

20 Stone, "The Upper Class White South in a Mississippi River Town," *Weekly* 6 (September 29, 1958): 3–4.

21 Stone, "The Days When Northern Mobs Rioted against Federal Court Orders," *Weekly* 6 (October 6, 1958): 2; Stone, "Report on the Negro's Slow Uphill Battle for the Vote in the South," *Weekly* 6 (May 5, 1958): 3.

22 Memorial service, July 12, 1989.

23 Stone, "That 'Germany' of Our Own below the Mason-Dixon Line," *Weekly* 8 (January 25, 1960): 1; Stone, "There, in South Africa, But for the Grace of God," *Weekly* 8 (April 11, 1960): 1; Kenneth Rexroth, "The Students Take Over," *Nation* 191 (July 2, 1960): 7; Nat Hentoff, "A Peaceful Army," *Commonweal* 72 (June 10, 1960): 275–278; Maurice Isserman, *If I Had a Hammer . . . : The Death of the Old Left and the Birth of the New Left* (New York: Basic, 1987), pp. 110–111.

24 Stone, "On a Certain Blindness to the Peril of Racism," *Weekly* 9 (May 29, 1961): 1.

25 Stone, "When's the President Going to Mention Racism?" *Weekly* 10 (October 8, 1962): 1, 4.

26 Stone, "Must We Wait for Blood to Be Shed?" *Weekly* 11 (May 27, 1963): 1.

27 Taylor Branch, *Parting the Waters: America in the King Years, 1954–1963* (New York: Simon and Schuster, 1988), pp. 823–824.

28 Stone, "Destiny May Soon Call, but Will Mr. Kennedy Be at Home?" *Weekly* 11 (June 24, 1963): 1–2.

29 Stone, "When the Streets Are Better than the Courts," *Weekly* 11 (July 8, 1963): 1, 4.

30 Stone, "The March on Washington," *Weekly* 11 (September 16, 1963): 2.

31 Ibid; Murray Kempton, "The March on Washington," *New Republic* 149 (September 14, 1963): 19–20.

32 Stone, "The March," *Weekly* 11 (September 2, 1963): 1.

13. "The Steve Canyon Mentality"

1 Stone, "Time for the Peace Movement to Call for an End of War in Viet Nam," *Weekly* 10 (July 23, 1962): 3.

2 Ibid.

3 David L. Schalk, *War and the Ivory Tower: Algeria and Vietnam* (New York: Oxford University Press, 1991), pp. 38–60.

4 Stone, "Our State Department Throws Another One Away," *Compass*, February 24, 1950, p. 5.

5 Ibid., pp. 5, 24.

6 Ibid., p. 5.

7 Ibid., p. 24; Andrew Roth, "Asia's Tito?" *Nation* 169 (September 10, 1949): 244; "Struggle in Indo-China," *New Republic* 122 (February 13, 1950): 9.

8 Stone, "U.S. Seen Dangerously Hypnotized by A-Bomb," *Compass*, December 13, 1950, p. 4.

9 Lloyd C. Gardner, *Approaching Vietnam: From World War II through Dienbienphu, 1941–1954* (New York: Norton, 1988), pp. 231–232; Stone, "Eisenhower (Like Bao Dai) Could Use Some Outside Help," *Weekly* 2 (March 29, 1954): 1.

10 Stone, "The Delusions of Mr. Dulles," *Weekly* 2 (April 5, 1954): 1.

11 Ibid.

12 Ibid.

13 Ibid., p. 2; Stone, "Talking Tough, while Brandishing a Twig," *Weekly* 2 (May 3, 1954): 1.

14 Stone, "Free to Do Anything But Make Peace," *Weekly* 2 (April 26, 1954): 1.

15 Stone, "Free Elections in Indochina Now? Mr. Dulles Says 'No,' " *Weekly* 2 (May 17, 1954): 1.

16 Ibid., p. 4.

17 Stone, "The Split Is over World War III, Not Indo-China," *Weekly* 2 (June 14, 1954): 1.

18 Stone, "The Enemy Mendes-France Defeated," *Weekly* 2 (July 26, 1954): 1.

19 Stone, "Indochina," *Weekly* 2 (November 1, 1954): 2.

20 Stone, "Democracy, Jersey City Variety," *Weekly* 2 (October 31, 1955): 4.

21 Marilyn B. Young, *The Vietnam Wars, 1945–1990* (New York: Harper Collins, 1991), p. 58; Ernest K. Lindley, "An Ally Worth Having," *Newsweek* 53 (June 29, 1959): 31.

22 Stone, "Before We Turn Laos into Another Korea," *Weekly* 7 (September 14, 1959): 1, 4.

23 Stone, "Pity That UN Investigating Committee Can't Come to Washington . . . ," *Weekly* 7 (September 21, 1959): 3; Stone, "Moscow May Make Peking 'Behave' but Who'll Sober Down Washington?" *Weekly* 7 (October 26, 1959): 3.

24 Stone, "On Our Light-Headed Readiness for War in Laos," *Weekly* 9 (April 3, 1961): 1, 4; Stone, "Putting the Spotlight on the Trouble Brewing over Cambodia," *Weekly* 7 (October 12, 1959): 2.

25 Stone, "When Brass Hats Begin to Read Mao Tse-Tung, Beware!" *Weekly* 9 (May 15, 1961): 1.

26 Ibid.

27 Stone, "Anti-Guerrilla War—the Dazzling New Military Toothpaste for Social Decay," *Weekly* 9 (May 22, 1961): 2.

28 Ibid.

29 Stone, "There Will Always Be a Berlin," *Weekly* 9 (July 31, 1961): 4.

30 Stone, "How Super Power Becomes Super Impotence," *Weekly* 11 (May 13, 1963): 1.

31 "Mandarins vs. Communists," *Nation* 194 (January 6, 1962): 1; Stone, "Where Swarming Gnats Can Devour a Giant," *Weekly* 10 (May 21, 1962): 1.

32 William H. Hunter, "The War in Vietnam, Luce Version," *New Republic* 148 (March 23, 1963): 17; Stone, "On Our Light-Headed Readiness for War in Laos," p. 4; Stone, "Another Fact-Evading Mission," *Weekly* 11 (September 30, 1963): 1.

33 Stone, "Will New Chances for Peace Be Another Lost Opportunity?" *Weekly* 11 (October 28, 1963): 3–4.

34 Ibid., pp. 4–6, 8.

35 Stanley Karnow, *Vietnam: A History* (New York: Penguin, 1984), pp. 255, 296–297; Neil Sheehan, *A Bright Shining Lie: John Paul Vann and America in Vietnam* (New York: Random House, 1988), pp. 347–350; David Halberstam, *The Making of a Quagmire* (New York: Random House, 1965); Sandy Vogelgesang, *The Long Dark Night of the Soul: The American Intellectual Left and the Vietnam War* (New York: Harper and Row, 1974), pp. 43–45.

36 Robert R. Tomes, "American Intellectuals and the Vietnam War, 1954–1975," Ph.D. dissertation, New York University, 1987, pp. 197–198.

37 Stone, "What If the People, after Diem's Overthrow, Vote for Peace?" *Weekly* 11 (November 11, 1963): 2; "I. F. Stone Will Speak on Vietnam," *Weekly* 11 (September 16, 1963): 8; Stone, "IFS Speaks on Vietnam in San Francisco," *Weekly* 11 (October 14, 1963): 4; Stone, "IFS to Speak for Peace in Vietnam," *Weekly* 11 (November 25, 1963): 7.

14. Telling Truth to Power

1 Letter to author from Todd Gitlin, February 9, 1982; letter to author from Kirkpatrick Sale, July 27, 1983; Todd Gitlin, *The Sixties: Years of Hope, Days of Rage* (New York: Bantam, 1987), p. 179; Miller, "*Democracy*," pp. 222; Kirkpatrick Sale, *SDS* (New York: Vintage, 1974), p. 170; Zaroulis and Sullivan, *Who Spoke Up?* p. 32; "Membership Bulletin," Students for a Democratic Society Papers, #2, 1962–63, p. 10 (microfilm).

2 Zaroulis and Sullivan, *Who Spoke Up?* p. 32; Sale, *SDS*, p. 170; Miller, "*Democracy*," p. 226.

3 Miller, "*Democracy*," pp. 226–227, Sale, *SDS*, p. 170; letter to author from Todd Gitlin, February 9, 1982.

4 Todd Gitlin to Stone, January 7, 1965, SDS Papers; Miller, "*Democracy*," p. 227; Sale, *SDS*, p. 170.

5 Zaroulis and Sullivan, *Who Spoke Up?* p. 35; Stone, "A Reply to the White Paper," *Weekly* 13 (March 8, 1965): 1–4.

6 Zaroulis and Sullivan, *Who Spoke Up?* pp. 39–40; Miller, "*Democracy*," pp. 227–230; Gitlin, *The Sixties*, p. 182; interview with Stone, October 16, 1981.

7 Miller, "*Democracy*," pp. 231–233; Paul Booth, "March on Washington," *SDS Bulletin* 3 (May 1965): 10; Gitlin, *The Sixties*, p. 183; interview with Stone, October 16, 1981.

8 Interview with Stone, October 16, 1981; Miller, "*Democracy*," p. 231.

9 Letter to author from Gitlin, February 9, 1982; Gitlin, *The Sixties*, p. 90; letter

to author from Tom Hayden, June 30, 1983; interview with Lee Webb, June 27, 1983; Zaroulis and Sullivan, *Who Spoke Up?* p. 32; Richard Flacks, *Making History: The Radical Tradition in American Life* (New York: Columbia University Press, 1988), p. 135; Miller, "*Democracy,*" p. 221.

10 Sale, *SDS*, p. 115.

11 Stone, "Where Caesar's Lions Failed, Can the South's Cattle Prods Win?" *Weekly* 11 (December 9, 1963): 3.

12 Stone, "IFS Will Speak on . . . Sept. 15 at New York City Town Hall Welcome for Students from Cuba," *Weekly* 11 (September 2, 1963): 4; C. P. Trussel, "16 More Ejected at House Hearing on Travel to Cuba," *NY Times*, September 14, 1963, p. 1; Stone, "Why I Withdrew from the New York Meeting," *Weekly* 11 (September 30, 1963): 7.

13 Stone, "On Students, the Right to Travel and the Right to Disagree," *Weekly* 11 (September 30, 1963): 7.

14 Stone, "Ownership, Management and Circulation," *Weekly* 11 (October 14, 1963): 3; Gerald W. Johnson, "Gadflying with I. F. Stone," *New Republic* 149 (December 14, 1963): 21–22; transmittal slip, November 19, 1963, I. F. Stone File, CIA Documents, b3, #59.

15 Doug Ireland, "Arrests Highlight Vietnam Demonstrations," *SDS Bulletin* 2 (November 1963): 6; Don McKelvey, "Random Thoughts after Cuba," *SDS Bulletin* 1 (January–February 1963): 1.

16 Gitlin, *The Sixties*, p. 90; Stone, "The Other War in Vietnam," *Weekly* 12 (February 3, 1964): 3; Stone, "A Warning Signal the Peace Movement Ought to Heed while There's Still Time," *Weekly* 12 (February 24, 1964): 1; Stone, "Better Speak Up Now," *Weekly* 12 (April 20, 1964): 3.

17 Stone, "Untested in War but Already a Genius at Finance," *Weekly* 12 (February 10, 1964): 1.

18 Stone, "What We Are Doing to Innocent Villagers in Vietnam and Cambodia," *Weekly* 11 (March 30, 1964): 3.

19 Stone, "What Fulbright, Too, Does Not Dare to Think," *Weekly* 12 (April 6, 1964): 4; Stone, "How to Make Peace in Cuba, Vietnam and the World," *Weekly* 12 (May 4, 1964): 4; Stone, "Time to Hit a Sensitive Nerve by Calling It 'Johnson's War,' " *Weekly* 12 (June 15, 1964): 3; Stone, "Those Parallels between Vietnam and Cuba—or Berlin—Are Delusions," *Weekly* 12 (June 29, 1964): 4.

20 Stone, "War behind Our Backs," *Weekly* 12 (August 10, 1964): 1.

21 Stone, "What Few Know about the Tonkin Bay Incidents," *Weekly* 12 (August 24, 1964): 1–4.

22 Ibid.; Stone, "Everybody's Guide to Liberalism," *NYRB* 3 (September 24, 1964): 7.

23 Bill Wise, *Life* 57 (August 14, 1964): 21; "Vietnam: We Seek No Wider War," *Newsweek* 64 (August 17, 1964): 17–18; Richard Rovere, "Letter from Washington," *New Yorker* 40 (August 22, 1964): 101–107, 111; William Buckley, "From Washington Straight," *National Review* 16 (September 22, 1964): 799.

24 "Shortening the Fuse," *Nation* 199 (August 24, 1964): 61; "Unmeasured Response," *New Republic* 151 (August 22, 1964): 3–4.

25 Tomes, "American Intellectuals and the Vietnam War, 1954–1975," pp. 198, 215–216.

26 Daniel C. Hallin, *The 'Uncensored War': The Media and Vietnam* (New York: Oxford University Press, 1986), p. 63; Bruck, *I. F. Stone's Weekly;* Miller, "*Democracy,*" pp. 220–221.

27 Stone, "What LBJ and the Country Need Is a Left Opposition," *Weekly* 12 (January 20, 1964): 1–2; Vogelgesang, *The Long Dark Night of the Soul*, p. 58; Dick Flacks, "The Unemployed," *SDS Bulletin* 3 (November–December 1964): 6; Stone, "Johnson Far Below JFK in Sophistication, Breadth and Taste," *Weekly* 11 (December 9, 1963): 2; T.R.B., "LBJ's Triumph," *New Republic* 150 (May 2, 1964): 2; Stone, "A Noble Task for This Generation in America," *Weekly* 12 (June 22, 1964): 1; Stone, " 'Let Us Close the Springs of Racial Poison,' " *Weekly* 12 (July 13, 1964): 1; Stone, "The Making of a President," *NYRB* 2 (July 30, 1964): 3–4; Nobile, *Intellectual Skywriting*, p. 33; Memorial service, July 12, 1989.

28 Stone, "The Collected Works of Barry Goldwater," *NYRB* 3 (August 20, 1964): 3.

29 Stone, "An Election to Make Us Proud of Our Country," *Weekly* 12 (November 9, 1964): 1, 4.

30 Stone, "The Worse the War in Vietnam the Finer the Double-Talk in Washington," *Weekly* 12 (November 9, 1964): 1.

31 Stone, "Gen. Taylor and His Chief Aides Make Some Revealing Admissions in Saigon," *Weekly* 12 (November 30, 1964): 3; Stone, "L.B.J.'s Historic Opportunity for Peace," *Weekly* 12 (December 7, 1964): 1, 4.

32 Stone, "The Wrong War," *NYRB* 3 (December 17, 1964): 11–14; Nobile, *Intellectual Skywriting*, pp. 33, 35; Schalk, *War and the Ivory Tower*, pp. 137–138; Eugene Goodheart, "The *New York Review:* A Close Look," *Dissent* 17 (March–April 1970): 135; Vogelgesang, *The Long Dark Night of the Soul*, pp. 101–102.

33 Memorial service, July 12, 1989; interview with Christopher Stone, January 6, 1992.

34 "The Book Biters," *Newsweek* 66 (December 27, 1965): 64; Charles Kadushin, *The American Intellectual Elite* (Boston: Little, Brown, 1974), p. 60.

35 Stone, note to readers, *Weekly* 12 (December 12, 1964): 1+; Miller, *"Democracy,"* pp. 222, 226–227.

36 Stone, "There Should Have Been a Court Martial, Not a Reprisal," *Weekly* 13 (February 15, 1965): 1, 4.

37 Ibid., p. 4; Vogelgesang, *The Long Dark Night of the Soul*, pp. 63–64; Stone, "An Official Turns State's Evidence," *New Republic* 152 (May 29, 1965): 24–26.

38 Stone, "A Word of Good Advice from Mao Tse-Tung," *Weekly* 13 (February 22, 1965): 1.

39 Stone, "Will No One Hear Her Plea?" *Weekly* 13 (March 1, 1965): 1.

40 Stone, "LBJ Rushes in Where Ike and Kennedy Feared to Tread," *Weekly* 13 (March 15, 1965): 1; Stone, "News Censorship and Nuclear Bombing Now Planned for Vietnam . . . ," *Weekly* 13 (March 22, 1965): 2; "The Message," *Nation* 200 (February 22, 1965): 181.

41 Stone, "Straining at the Gnat of a Little 'Non-Lethal' Gas," *Weekly* 13 (March 29, 1965): 1, 4.

42 Ibid., p. 4.

43 Thomas Powers, *The War at Home: Vietnam and the American People, 1964–1968* (New York: Grossman, 1973), pp. 54–55; Stone, "The White House Outsmarted Itself and Put the Spotlight on the Teach-in . . . ," *Weekly* 13 (May 24, 1965): 3; Stone, "Bulletin Board," *Weekly* 12 (December 14, 1964): 4; Norman Mailer et al., *We Accuse* (Berkeley: Diablo Press, 1965).

44 Stone, "A Great Storm Is Gathering," *Weekly* 13 (April 26, 1965): 2; Stone, speech at University of California teach-in, May 21, 1965, reprinted in *We Accuse*, p. 88.

45 Stone, "What Should the Peace Movement Do?" *Weekly* 13 (June 28, 1965): 1; Stone, "The Left and the Warren Commission Report," *Weekly* 12 (October 5, 1964): 1–3; Stone to Norman Thomas, October 9, 1964, p. 1, Norman Thomas Papers, New York Public Library; Stone to Dwight Macdonald, November 15, 1964, Dwight Macdonald Papers, Manuscripts and Archives, Yale University Library.

46 Stone, "What Should the Peace Movement Do?" pp. 1, 4.

47 Ibid., p. 4.

48 Ibid.

49 Aronson, *Something to Guard*, pp. 307–309; letter to author from Sale, July 27, 1983.

50 Marcus G. Raskin and Bernard B. Fall, ed., *The Viet-Nam Reader* (New York: Vintage Books, 1967); Marvin E. Gettleman, ed., *Vietnam* (New York: Fawcett World Library, 1966); Jack A. Smith, "New York: Biggest Anti-War Rally Ever in U.S.," *National Guardian*, October 23, 1965, p. 6; interview with Lou Stone, October 2, 1990; Stone, "New York's Pro-War Parade Was a Rightist Pro-Buckley Demonstration," *Weekly* 13 (November 8, 1965): 3; Stone, "Why We Welcome and Support the Nov. 27 Peace March on Washington," *Weekly* 13 (October 25, 1965): 2–3; Stone, "The Biggest Peace Demonstration in the History of Washington," *Weekly* 13 (December 6, 1965): 2.

51 Stone, "If We Could Only Get Rid of Christ and Constitution," *Weekly* 13 (October 25, 1965): 1.

52 Stone, "The South's Rebel Klansmen and the Student Rebel Left," *Weekly* 13 (November 1, 1965): 4; Stone, "What SNCC Said about the War and Why Negroes Feel the Way They Do," *Weekly* 14 (January 17, 1966): 3.

53 Executive memo SO 5 FO/MC, November 30, 1965, White House Central Name File, Lyndon Baines Johnson Library; Jack Valenti to Lyndon Johnson, January 4, 1966, MC/CO FG11-8-1/Valenti, Jack CO62 PR 18 ND19/CO312, White House Central Name File, LBJ Library.

54 Stone, "The Price at Home of the Destruction We Wreak Abroad," *Weekly* 13 (December 13, 1965): 1, 4; Stone, "Guns and Butter: Billions for One, Millions for the Other," *Weekly* 14 (January 31, 1966): 1; Stone, "A Great Society for the Military-Industrial Complex," *Weekly* 15 (February 6, 1967): 1, 4.

55 Stone, "Why They Cry Black Power," *Weekly* 14 (September 19, 1966): 1.

56 Stone, "SNCC Does Not Wish to Become a New Version of the White Man's Burden," *Weekly* 14 (June 6, 1966): 3.

57 Ibid.

58 Stone, "Proposing an American Negro Congress," *Weekly* 15 (July 17, 1967): 1; Stone, "Second Secession and Second Civil War?" *Weekly* 15 (July 31, 1967): 1, 4.

59 Stone, "Delusions That Failed in Korea Won't Work in Vietnam," *Weekly* 13 (November 29, 1965): 1, 4; Stone, "LBJ Scuttles Another Chance for Peace," *Weekly* 14 (June 27, 1966): 1; Stone, "No Way to Celebrate Christmas," *Weekly* 13 (December 20, 1965): 1; Stone, "Slow-Fuse Sarajevo," *Weekly* 14 (February 7, 1966): 4.

60 Stone, "Bobby Bakerism on a World Scale," *Weekly* 14 (October 17, 1966): 4; Stone, "Why *Not* Bring Christmas Up to Date?" *Weekly* 14 (December 19, 1966): 1.

61 Stone, "More than Steel and Chrome Can Bear," *Weekly* 15 (February 13, 1967): 1.

62 Stone, "What 'Pacification' Really Means to Vietnam's Landless Peasantry," *Weekly* 15 (March 20, 1967): 3; Stone, "They'd Do Anything for the Peasant But Get Off His Back," *Weekly* 15 (March 27, 1967): 1, 4; Bruck, *I. F. Stone's Weekly*.

63 Memorial service, July 18, 1989; Stone, "What It's Like to Be in Saigon," *Weekly* 14 (May 9, 1966): 1–4; Stone, "What Vietnamese Say Privately in Saigon," *Weekly* 14 (May 16, 1966): 1–4; Stone, "Behind the Fighting in Hue and Danang," *Weekly* 14 (May 23, 1966): 1–4; Stone, "Where Communism Has Really Been Contained," *Weekly* 14 (May 30, 1966): 1–4.

64 Stone, "An American Anthony Eden," *NYRB* 7 (December 29, 1966): 5–6; Stone, "From Hawk to Dove," *NYRB* 7 (January 12, 1967): 8, 10, 12; Stone, "Fulbright: The Timid Opposition," *NYRB* 8 (January 26, 1967): 10, 12–13.

15. From Pariah to Character

1 Interview with Peter Osnos, July 25, 1989.

2 Ibid.; Bruck, *I. F. Stone's Weekly;* Stern, "I. F. Stone," p. 54.

3 Bruck, *I. F. Stone's Weekly;* Stern, "I. F. Stone," p. 54; Jim Naughton, "I. F. Stone and the Ancient Mystery," *Sacramento Bee*, March 22, 1988, p. B6; memorial service, July 18, 1989.

4 Stone to Michael Blankfort, July 3, 1961, Michael Blankfort Collection, Mugar Memorial Library, Boston University; Bruck, *I. F. Stone's Weekly;* memorial service, July 18, 1989; Stone to Norman Thomas, February 18, 1965, Norman Thomas Papers, New York Public Library.

5 Interview with Osnos, July 25, 1989; memorial service, July 18, 1989.

6 Stone, "Ownership, Management and Circulation," *Weekly* 14 (October 10, 1966): 2; interview with Osnos, July 25, 1989; Peter Osnos, "I. F. Stone, a Journalist's Journalist," *NY Times*, June 20, 1989, p. A23; memorial service, July 18, 1989; Ronald Steel, *Walter Lippmann and the American Century* (Boston: Little, Brown, 1980), p. 576.

7 Aronson, *The Press and the Cold War*, pp. 236–237; memorial service, July 18, 1989.

8 Interview with Osnos, July 25, 1989; memorial service, July 18, 1989; Stone to Thomas, February 18, 1965, Thomas Papers.

9 Stone, "Ownership, Management and Circulation," *Weekly* 15 (April 10, 1967): 4; Cecil Woolf and John Bagguley, *Authors Take Sides on Vietnam: Two Questions on the War in Vietnam Answered by the Authors of Several Nations* (New York: Simon and Schuster, 1967), pp. 37–38; Stone, "On the Spring Mobilization Meeting," *Weekly* 15 (May 29, 1967): 1.

10 Ibid.

11 Ibid., pp. 1, 4; letter to author from Kirkpatrick Sale, July 27, 1983.

12 Stone, "On the Spring Mobilization Meeting," p. 4.

13 Otto Nathan to Stone, published in *Weekly* 15 (June 12, 1967): 4; Stone, "Our Comment," *Weekly* 15 (June 12, 1967): 4.

14 Stone, "The Future of Israel," *Ramparts* 6 (July 1967): 41–42, 44.

15 Stone to readers, September 4, 1967, Thomas Papers; interview with Christopher Stone, January 6, 1992.

16 Interview with Christopher Stone, January 6, 1992.

17 Stone to readers, September 4, 1967, Thomas Papers; interview with Stone, October 16, 1981; MacDougall, "Gadfly on the Left," p. 22; Passport Application, September 22, 1967, SDF, P001; FBI Liaison, November 1, 1967, SDF, P009; Stone, "Personal Note," *Weekly* 15 (November 13, 1967): 4; Stone, "Announcement," *Weekly* 11 (January 21, 1963): 4; Stone, "Important Announcement," *Weekly* 16 (January 22, 1968): 4; Stone, "A Joyous Despair," *Weekly* 15 (November 20, 1967): 3+; Norman

Thomas to Stone, September 18, 1967, Thomas Papers; Kopkind, "The Importance of Being Izzy," p. 41.

18 David Armstrong, *A Trumpet to Arms: Alternative Media in America* (Los Angeles: J. P. Tarcher, 1981), pp. 41, 106; Abe Peck, *Uncovering the Sixties: The Life and Times of the Underground Press* (New York: Pantheon, 1985), pp. 288–289; Raymond Mungo, *Famous Long Ago: My Life and Hard Times with Liberation News Service* (Boston: Beacon Press, 1970), p. 31.

19 Frank S. Meyer, "Struggle over the Liberal Heritage," *National Review* 22 (February 24, 1970): 270; Nobile, *Intellectual Skywriting*, pp. 40–54.

20 Walter Goodman, "On the (N.Y.) Literary Left," *Antioch Review* 29 (Spring 1969): 71, 73.

21 "Magazines: Sharpening the Knives," *Newsweek* 90 (December 8, 1967); 84; Stone, "A Joyous Despair," p. 3+; Stone, "Ownership, Management and Circulation," *Weekly* 15 (November 20, 1967): 4; Stuart W. Little, "One Man in Time," *Saturday Review* 51 (January 13, 1968): 117; " 'Izzy'," *Newsweek* 71 (January 22, 1968): 52; Robert Sherrill, "Washington's Exquisitely Unforgiving Reporter," *Commonweal* 87 (January 26, 1968): 506–507; Patrick MacFadden, "More than Stone Can Bear," *Nation* 206 (February 12, 1968): 214–215; Stern, "I. F. Stone," pp. 53–55; Ronald Steel, "Eternal Hostility to Bunk," *Book World* 2 (March 17, 1968): 6–7; "Big Fly, Small Spider," *Times Literary Supplement,* June 13, 1968, pp. 609–610; "A Prophet, Not a Gadfly," *Times Literary Supplement,* October 3, 1968, p. 1099; Henry Steele Commager, "Common Sense," *NYRB* 11 (December 5, 1968): 3–4.

22 Israel Shenker, "I. F. Stone: Gadfly Likes Peoples and Sometimes Angers Readers," *NY Times,* November 19, 1968, p. 33; Kopkind, "The Importance of Being Izzy," p. 39.

23 David Levine, cartoon, *NYRB* 11 (December 5, 1968): 3.

24 Shenker, "I. F. Stone," p. 33.

25 Stone, "The Coming Campaign as America's Tragedy," *Weekly* 15 (November 27, 1967): 1.

26 Ibid., pp. 1, 4; Stone, "When Will RFK Attack Conflict between Vietnam and War on Poverty?" *Weekly* 14 (September 5, 1966): 3.

27 Stone, "A Graceful Patsy against a Dirty Fighter?" *Weekly* 15 (December 11, 1967): 1–2.

28 Stone, "All We Ask of the Viet Cong Is Their Surrender," *Weekly* 15 (November 20, 1967): 1–4; Stone, "Westmoreland's Bloody Folly—on Hill 875," *Weekly* 15 (December 4, 1967): 1–2.

29 Stone, "Saigon Afire Now—Will It Be Washington in April?" *Weekly* 16 (February 19, 1968): 1, 5.

30 Ibid., p. 5.

31 Stone, "None So Blind as Those Who Will Not See," *Weekly* 16 (January 22, 1968): 1–3.

32 Stone, "Can 36 Saints Save America?" *Weekly* 16 (March 18, 1968): 1–3.

33 Stone, "That Latest Domino to Topple Was LBJ's Pet General," *Weekly* 16 (April 1, 1968): 3.

34 Stone, "The Fire Has Only Just Begun," *Weekly* 16 (April 15, 1968): 1, 4.

35 Ibid., p. 4.

36 Stone, "It's Only Unorganized Violence That Still Shocks Us," *Weekly* 16 (June 10, 1968): 2.

37 Ibid., pp. 2–3.

38 Stone, "When It's Dangerous to Oppose Arson," *Weekly* 16 (July 22, 1968): 1.

39 Stone, "Only McCarthy and an End to the Bombing," *Weekly* 16 (August 19, 1968): 1.

40 Stone, "When a Two-Party System Becomes a One-Party Rubber Stamp," *Weekly* 16 (September 9, 1968): 2.

41 Ibid., pp. 1, 3.

42 Ibid., pp. 1, 3.

43 Ibid., p. 3.

44 Stone, "Speech for a New (4th) Party Candidate," *Weekly* 16 (September 23, 1969): 1, 4.

45 Stone, "No Magic or Miracles in Nixon," *Weekly* 16 (November 18, 1968): 1–2; Stone, "Happy Days Ahead for the Pentagon," *Weekly* 16 (December 16, 1968): 1, 4.

46 Stone, "Guns and Butter: Billions for One, Millions for the Other," 1; Stone, "Uncle Sam's Con Man Budget," *Weekly* 17 (May 5, 1969): 1–4; Stone, "More Urgent than the Space Pact: To Stop the Anti-Ballistic Missile Race," *Weekly* 14 (December 19, 1966): 2; Stone, "The War Machine under Nixon," *NYRB* 12 (June 5, 1969): 5; Stone, "Theater of Delusion," *NYRB* 14 (April 23, 1970): 14.

47 Stone, "Well, If It Ain't Little Old Lyndon B. Nixon," *Weekly* 17 (April 7, 1969): 1–4; Stone, "The Hoax That Cost a Trillion Dollars in 25 Years," *Weekly* 17 (July 28, 1969): 1, 4; Stone, "Can Nixon Make the Hard Choices?" *Weekly* 17 (March 10, 1969): 4.

48 Stone, "It is a Pity the Whole Country," *Weekly* 18 (June 15, 1970): 2; Stone, "It Won't Be Long Now," *Weekly* 17 (October 20, 1969): 4; Stone, "The Old Nixon Surfaces Again," *Weekly* 17 (November 17, 1969): 1.

49 Stone, "The Old Nixon Surfaces Again," p. 2.

50 Stone, "Policing the 'Free World' Now Costs Us Some $50 Billion a Year," *Weekly* 17 (November 3, 1969): 1.

51 Ibid., p. 3.

52 Stone, "Lessons for Nixon," *NYRB* 13 (December 4, 1969): 4; Stone, "Nixon in the Footsteps of Popeye's Elder Statesman," *Weekly* 18 (July 13, 1970): 1, 4.

53 Stone, "The Atrocities Nixon Condones and Continues," *Weekly* 17 (December 15, 1969): 1, 4.

54 Martin Wald, "Agnew Attacks His Press Critics," *NY Times*, May 23, 1970, p. 1; Stone, "Nixon, Agnew and Freedom of the Press," *Weekly* 18 (June 1, 1970): 1, 4; Stone, "A Self-Satire of the Peace Movement," *Weekly* 17 (January 27, 1969): 1; letter to author from Kirkpatrick Sale, July 27, 1983.

55 Kevin Michael McAuliffe, *The Great American Newspaper* (New York: Scribner's, 1978), p. 238.

56 Bruck, *I. F. Stone's Weekly*.

57 Stone, "In Defense of Campus Rebels," *Weekly* 17 (May 19, 1969): 1.

58 Ibid., pp. 1, 4.

59 Ibid., p. 4.

60 Ibid., p. 4.

61 Stone, "We Salute the Finest Graduating Class in America's History," *Weekly* 17 (June 30, 1969): 1; Stone, "Policing the 'Free World' Now Costs Us Some $50 Billion a Year," p. 2; Stone, "He Couldn't Care Less," *Weekly* 17 (November 3, 1969): 1.

62 Stone, "The Old Nixon Surfaces Again," p. 4; Stone, "The Peace Movement and the Black Panther," *Weekly* 18 (January 26, 1970): 2.

63 Stone, "Who Are the Real Kooks in Our Society?" *Weekly* 18 (March 9, 1970): 1, 4.

64 Interview with Christopher Stone, January 6, 1992.

65 Stone, "Where the Fuse on That Dynamite Leads," *Weekly* 18 (March 23, 1970): 1, 4; Stone, "The Culprit Was on the Bench," *Weekly* 18 (February 23, 1970): 1.

66 Stone, "Where the Fuse on That Dynamite Leads," p. 4.

67 Ibid.

68 Ibid.; Stone, "Sihanouk Alone in Southeast Asia Cost Us Neither Lives Nor Dollars," *Weekly* 18 (April 6, 1970): 2.

69 Stone, "Only the Bums Can Save the Country Now," *Weekly* 18 (May 18, 1970): 1; The National Petition Committee, "To the Editors," *NYRB* 14 (June 4, 1970): 59; "David Eisenhower Wary of Commencement Talks," *NY Times*, April 6, 1970, p. 24; "I. F. Stone, at Amherst, Praises Youth," *NY Times*, June 6, 1970, p. 17.

70 Stone, "The Only Way to End Terrorism," *Weekly* 18 (September 21, 1970): 1.

71 Ibid., p. 2.

72 Stone, "When Sin, Smut and Students Failed," *Weekly* 18 (November 16, 1970): 4.

73 Stone, "The Price We Pay for Empire," *Weekly* 19 (January 11, 1971): 1, 4; Stone, "The Dollars and Sense of the Nixon Doctrine," *Weekly* 19 (January 25, 1971): 1, 4; Stone, "Power to the People—from Madison Avenue," *Weekly* 19 (February 8, 1971): 1–4.

74 Stone, "The Military Machine Is in Command," *Weekly* 19 (March 8, 1971): 1, 4; Stone, "Imperialism Is Not Internationalism," *Weekly* 19 (March 22, 1971): 1, 4; Stone, "What Nixon Hopes We Won't Remember," *Weekly* 19 (April 19, 1971): 1, 4.

75 Stone, "Peace Is Still a Long, Long March Away," *Weekly* 19 (May 3, 1971): 1, 4.

76 Ibid., p. 4; Stone, "The Kooks Nobody Noticed," *Weekly* 19 (May 17, 1971): 4.

77 Stone, "The Real Secret—Empire and Democracy Don't Mix," *Weekly* 19 (June 28, 1971): 1, 4.

78 Stone, "The Crisis Coming for a Free Press," *Weekly* 19 (July 12, 1971): 1–4; "American Journalism: Vietnam," interview of Stone by Bernard Kalb, June 30, 1971, Vital History Cassette (Encyclopedia Americana/CBS News Resource Library, 1972).

79 Memorial service, July 18, 1989.

80 Stone, "Ownership, Management and Circulation," *Weekly* 17 (October 6, 1969): 4; Stone, "Ownership, Management and Circulation," *Weekly* 18 (October 5, 1970): 4; Stone, "Ownership, Management and Circulation," *Weekly* 19 (October 4, 1971): 4; Bob Cunniff to B. J. Stone, "I. F. Stone Memories"; Stone, note, *Weekly* 17 (July 28, 1969): 4; Bruck, *I. F. Stone's Weekly;* "Personal Note," *Weekly* 19 (April 5, 1971): 3p; "A Times Reporter in Viet Wins a Polk Award," *NY Times*, February 17, 1971, p. 35; "Polk Awards Given at Luncheon Here," *NY Times*, March 25, 1971, p. 36.

81 MacDougall, "Gadfly on the Left," pp. 1, 22; Charles Fager, "With Atheists Like Him, Who Needs Believers?" *Christian Century* 87 (November 4, 1970): 1313–1317; Stephen E. Ambrose, reprinted review from the *Baltimore Sun* in *The Hidden History*, pp. ix–xii; Bernhardt J. Hurwood, n.t., *Saturday Review* 52 (November 1, 1969): 35–36; Geoffrey Wolf, "The Investigator," *Newsweek* 77 (February 8, 1971): 92; Jean M. Halloran, "Nonfiction," *Harper's* 242 (March 1971): 102.

82 MacDougall, "Gadfly on the Left," p. 22; Jack Newfield, "Is There a 'New Journalism'?" in *The Reporter as Artist: A Look at the New Journalism Controversy* (New York: Hastings House, 1974): 301; Bruck, *I. F. Stone's Weekly.*

83 Charles Kadushin, Julie Hover, and Monique Tichy, "How and Where to Find Intellectual Elite in the United States," *Public Opinion Quarterly* 35 (Spring 1971): 1–18; Charles Kadushin, *The American Intellectual Elite* (Boston: Little, Brown, 1974), p. 54; Charles Kadushin, "Who Are the Elite Intellectuals?" *Public Interest* 29 (Fall 1972): 109–125.

84 Kadushin, *The American Intellectual Elite*, pp. 184–185.

85 Ibid., p. 188.

86 Ibid., pp. 178, 43–44, 49, 56–57.

87 Dennis H. Wrong, "The Case of the 'New York Review,' " *Commentary* 50 (November 1970): 49–61; Kadushin, Hover, and Tichy, "How and Where to Find Intellectual Elite in the United States," pp. 1–18.

88 Nobile, *Intellectual Skywriting*, p. 165.

89 Robert Levey and Philip A. McCombs, "Subjects of 'Surveillance' Assail FBI," *Washington Post*, April 15, 1971, p. 8; Jack Anderson, "FBI Checks on Citizens, but Not Drugs," *Washington Post*, May 1, 1972; Martin Wald, "Agnew Attacks His Press Critics," *NY Times*, May 23, 1970, p. 1; Stone, "Nixon, Agnew and Freedom of the Press," *Weekly* 18 (June 1, 1970): 1, 4; McBee, "Washington's Venerable Rebel," p. 43; Meyer, "The Rolling Stone," p. 931.

90 P. J. O'Rourke, "P. J. Goes Homes [sic]," *Harry* 2 (March 12–25, 1971): 1, 3.

91 Michael M. Uhlmann, "Armchair Revolutionary," *National Review* 23 (April 20, 1971): 437–439.

92 Ibid., p. 439.

93 Bruck, *I. F. Stone's Weekly;* Kopkind, "The Importance of Being Izzy," p. 39.

94 Interview with Peter Osnos, July 25, 1989.

95 Interview with Christopher Stone, January 6, 1992.

96 Stone, "Notes on Closing," 1–4; interview with Stone, October 16, 1981.

97 Tebbel and Zuckerman, *The Magazine in America, 1741–1990*, pp. 365–366, 371–374.

98 Stone, "Notes on Closing," p. 1; John Neary, "I. F. Stone Retires to a Tough New Job," *Life* 72 (January 21, 1972): 68A; Nobile, *Intellectual Skywriting*, p. 165; Christopher Lydon, "I. F. Stone to Suspend," *NY Times*, December 7, 1971, p. 43; McBee, "Washington's Venerable Rebel," p. 43.

99 Stone, "Notes on Closing," p. 1.

100 "End of the Stone Age," *Time* 98 (December 20, 1971): 52; "I. F. Stone, Publisher," *Washington Post*, December 29, 1971, p. A14; Nicholas von Hoffman, "Izzy Stone: Premier Investigative Reporter of His Time," *Washington Post*, December 10, 1971, p. DO1.

101 Ritchie, *Press Gallery*, pp. 1, 221–228.

102 "Program for A. J. Liebling Counter-Convention," *MORE* 2 (April 1972): 23; Richard Pollack, "After the Counter-Convention," *MORE* 2 (June 1972): 3; Stone, speech at A. J. Liebling Counter-Convention, New York, April 24, 1972, quoted in "As Soon as You Want Something," *MORE* 2 (June 1972): 4.

103 Stone, "The Hidden Traps in Nixon's Peace Plan," *NYRB* 18 (March 9, 1972): 17; Stone, "Nixon's War Gamble and Why It Won't Work," *NYRB* 18 (June 1, 1972): 11; Stone, "The Education of Henry Kissinger," *NYRB* 19 (October 19, 1972): 12, 14, 16–17; Stone, "The Flowering of Henry Kissinger," *NYRB* 19 (November 2, 1972): 21–27; Stone, "Machismo in Washington," *NYRB* 18 (May 18, 1972): 13–14.

104 Stone, "McGovern vs. Nixon on the Arms Race," *NYRB* 19 (July 20, 1972): 8–11.

105 Stone, "The Morning After," *NYRB* 19 (August 10, 1972): 27–28.

106 Stone, "What's Nixon Up To?" *Weekly* 19 (September 6, 1971): 1–4; Stone, "Why Nixon Won His Moscow Gamble," *NYRB* 18 (June 15, 1972): 9–1; Stone, "A Bad Deal That May Not Work," *NYRB* 19 (November 30, 1972): 6–8.

107 Tom Hayden, "Not a Bad Deal," *NYRB* 20 (January 25, 1973): 44–45.

108 Stone, "The Fire at the End of the Tunnel," *Mother Jones* 4 (April 1979): 33–34; " 'Hawks' and 'Doves' of Viet War Days Comment on Invasion of China," *NY Times*, February 22, 1979, p. A6; Stone et al., "Open Letter to the Socialist Republic of Vietnam," *NY Times*, May 30, 1979, p. A15.

109 Peter Collier and David Horowitz, *Destructive Generation: Second Thoughts about the Sixties* (New York: Summit Books, 1990), p. 175.

110 Interview with Osnos, July 25, 1989.

16. An Old Firehorse

1 Stone, "Notes on Closing," p. 1; Michael Blankfort to Stone, July 9, 1972, Michael Blankfort Collection, Mugar Memorial Library, Boston University.

2 Kadushin, *The American Intellectual Elite*, pp. 61, 44, 48–49, 59, 52; Carol H. Weiss, "What America's Leaders Read," *Public Opinion Quarterly* 38 (Spring 1974): 1–13; Merle Miller, "Why Norman and Jason Aren't Talking," *NY Times Magazine*, March 26, 1972, p. 111.

3 Nobile, *Intellectual Skywriting*, pp. 143–145.

4 "The *New York Review of Books*: 10th Anniversary," *Newsweek* 82 (October 29, 1973): 70; Nobile, *Intellectual Skywriting*, pp. 269–270; John F. Baker, "A Look Inside the *New York Review of Books*," *Publishers Weekly* 205 (March 11, 1974): 40.

5 Interview with Christopher Stone, January 6, 1992.

6 Stone, "Every Western Intellectual," *Weekly* 17 (June 16, 1969): 3; Stone, "The Price of Crushing the Czechs," *Weekly* 16 (August 5, 1968): 1; Stone, "I. F. Stone Reports: Betrayal by Psychiatry," *NYRB* 18 (February 10, 1972): 7, 14.

7 Stone, "Impeachment," *NYRB* 20 (June 28, 1973): 12; Stone, "Why Nixon Fears to Resign," *NYRB* 20 (November 29, 1973): 14; Stone, "America's Greatest Subversive," ACLU Awards Banquet; Stone, "The Fix," *NYRB* 21 (October 3, 1974): 7.

8 Stone, "Holy War," *NYRB* 9 (August 3, 1967): 6, 8–14.

9 Paul Goodman to Stone, "Paul Goodman on Israel and the Arabs," *Weekly* 15 (June 19, 1967): 2; James Michener, letter, *NYRB* 9 (September 28, 1967): 35–37; Marie Syrkin, Joel Carmichael, Lionel Abel, "I. F. Stone Reconsiders Israel," *Midstream* 13 (October 1967): 3–17.

10 Martin Peretz, "The American Left and Israel," *Commentary* 44 (November 1967): 30–33; Robert Alter, "Israel and the Intellectuals," *Commentary* 44 (October 1967): 49–51.

11 Stone, "The Need for Double Vision in the Middle East," *Weekly* 17 (January 13, 1969): 2; Stone, "Where Was Nixon When Sadat Gave the Russians the Boot?" *NYRB* 19 (August 31, 1972): 11; Stone et al., "Appeal for Peace in the Middle East," *NYRB* 20 (June 14, 1973): 37.

12 Jay Mathews, "Jews Hear Argument for Palestinian State," *Washington Post*, November 11, 1974, p. CO1; Ken Giles, July 18, 1989, I. F. Stone Memories.

13 Stone, "War for Oil?" *NYRB* 22 (February 6, 1975): 10; Michael Blankfort, letter, *NYRB* 22 (February 6, 1975): 32–33.

14 Stone, "Inflammatory Falsification," *Washington Post,* January 30, 1976, p. A22; Alfred M. Lilienthal, "Responding to I. F. Stone," *Washington Post,* February 22, 1976, p. F6.

15 Nobile, *Intellectual Skywriting,* p. 283.

16 Interview with Stone, October 16, 1981; "Notes on People," *NY Times,* June 19, 1976, p. 13.

17 Interview with Christopher Stone, January 6, 1992; Stone, *Underground;* Larry van Dyne, "The Adventures of I. F. Stone: An Iconoclastic Journalist's Progress from the Jewish Underground to the Joys of Greek," *Chronicle Review,* February 5, 1979, p. 5.

18 Marie Syrkin, "Underground to Palestine and Reflections Thirty Years Later," *New Republic* 180 (January 27, 1979): 28–30.

19 Marvin Maurer, "I. F. Stone—Universalist," *Midstream* 25 (February 1979): 2–12.

20 Blankfort to the editor of *Midstream,* February 27, 1979, Blankfort Collection.

21 Stone, "The Hope," *NYRB* 25 (October 26, 1978): 11.

22 Stone, "Begin Could Lead Israel Down the Road to Self-Destruction," *LA Times,* March 27, 1980, part 2, p. 7; Stone, "Footnotes from the Capital," *Nation* 234 (April 10, 1982): 419.

23 Stone et al., "Death and Destruction in Lebanon," *Washington Post,* June 23, 1982, p. A11.

24 Stone, "Are We Pushing Pahlavis Back on Iran?" *LA Times,* February 20, 1980, part 2, p. 7; Stone, "On Rosa Luxembourg," *NY Times,* section 4, p. 21.

25 Stone, "A Shah Lobby Next?" *NYRB* 26 (February 22, 1979): 29; Stone, "A Terrifying Clock Ticks On," *LA Times,* April 23, 1980, part 2, p. 7; Bruce Nelson, "Former Pariah," *LA Times,* June 25, 1981, part 1-B, p. 5; Stone, "America's War-Prone Mood," February 18, 1981, part 2, p. 5; interview with Stone, May 13, 1981; "Echoes of Vietnam: Celebrities Want U.S. Out of El Salvador," *LA Times,* part 1, p. 4; Stone, "A Compress for Al Haig's Brow," *Chicago Tribune,* April 2, 1981, section 3, p. 4.

26 Interview with Victor Navasky, July 14, 1989; Stone, "Stonegram: Navigaton Warning," *Nation* 245 (July 18/25, 1987): 41; Stone, "I. F. Stone Reports: Flabby Words for a Crisis," *Nation* 245 (November 21, 1987): 580; Stone, "Deathly Silence," *Nation* 234 (May 1, 1982): 515; Stone, "Binge: End of a Profligate Era," *Nation* 245 (October 31, 1987): 469, 471–472.

27 Interview with Navasky, July 14, 1989.

28 Ibid.

29 Ibid.

30 Memorial service, July 12, 1989.

31 Ibid.; Henry Weinstein, "A Salute to the Elder Statesman of Radical Journalism," *LA Times,* December 6, 1981, part 7, p. 29.

32 Memorial service, July 12, 1989.

33 Ibid.

34 Ibid. See also: The Nation Institute and The New School present "A Conversation with I. F. Stone at 80."

35 Stone, "Binge: End of a Profligate Era," pp. 470–472; Stone, "Wedded by Hate," *Nation* 244 (April 18, 1987): 492–493; Stone, "Another Betrayal by Psychiatry?" *NYRB* 35 (December 22, 1988): 6–8.

36 Interview with Navasky, July 14, 1989; memorial service, July 12, 1989.

37 Stone, "The Rights of Gorbachev," *NYRB* 36 (February 16, 1989): 3–4, 6; Larry Josephson interview with Bob Silvers, "Modern Times" radio program transcript, p. 18.

17. A Return to the Classics
1 "Modern Times," radio transcript, p. 7.
2 Stone, "Izzy on Izzy: I. F. Stone Interviews I. F. Stone at Seventy," *New York Times Magazine*, January 23, 1978, p. 12.
3 Nelson, "Former Pariah," part I-B, p. 4; conversation with Jeremy Stone, December 1, 1989.
4 Interview with Osnos, July 25, 1989; interview with Victor Navasky, July 14, 1989; Albert H. Johnston, "I. F. Stone Reader," *Publishers Weekly* 204 (July 2, 1973): 75.
5 Vincent Canby, "New Cannes Festival Star: I. F. Stone," *NY Times*, May 23, 1974, p. 58.
6 Steve Neal, "Journalistic Radical Attains Folk-Hero Status," *Chicago Tribune*, February 17, 1974, section 2, p. 81.
7 Stewart McBride, "I. F. Stone: Rumpled Revolutionary in Ancient Greece," *Christian Science Monitor*, May 21, 1981, p. B24; Derek Shearer, "Izzy Stone: From Outcast to Institution," *In These Times*, June 7–13, 1978, p. 13; "A Special Section," *Saturday Review* 61 (December 1978): 29; Myra MacPherson, "Gathering No Moss: The I. F. Stones: Marking 50, Still Going Like Sixty," *Washington Post*, July 9, 1979, pp. B1–2.
8 Interview with Navasky, July 14, 1989; Francis X. Clines, "About Washington: The Press Club Re-Admits an Angry Young Man, 73," *NY Times*, June 20, 1981, p. 9.
9 John S. Friedman, ed., *First Harvest: The Institute for Policy Studies, 1963–1983* (New York: Grove Press, 1983), p. 170; "The American Journalist: Paradox of the Press," Library of Congress exhibition, April 5–August 12, 1990.
10 Christopher Lydon, "I. F. Stone to Suspend 19 Year-Old Leftist Biweekly," *NY Times*, December 7, 1971, p. 43; interview with Stone, May 29, 1984; Meyer, "The Rolling Stone," p. 930; Stone, "Notes on Closing," pp. 1, 4; Kopkind, "The Importance of Being Izzy," p. 41; Stone, "Izzy on Izzy," p. 12.
11 Meyer, "The Rolling Stone," p. 930; Neary, "I. F. Stone Retires," p. 68A.
12 McBride, "I. F. Stone," pp. B3, 26; Stone, "Izzy on Izzy," p. 15.
13 McBride, "I. F. Stone," p. B3; Stone, "Izzy on Izzy," p. 15,; Weinstein, "A Salute to the Elder Statesman of Radical Journalism," p. 28; Stephen Klaidman, "I. F. Stone Returns to College at 68," *Washington Post*, April 15, 1977, p. C4.
14 McBride, "I. F. Stone," p. B24; Stone, "Izzy on Izzy," p. 15,; Shearer, "Izzy Stone," p. 13; Klaidman, "I. F. Stone Returns to College at 68," p. C4; van Dyne, "The Adventures of I. F. Stone," p. 5.
15 Ibid.; "I. F. Stone Still Thriving on Controversy," *Houston Post*, November 26, 1978, p. 18a; Stone, "Izzy on Izzy," p. 12; van Dyne, "The Adventures of I. F. Stone," p. 5.
16 Stone, "I. F. Stone Breaks the Socrates Story," *NY Times Magazine* (April 8, 1979): section 6, pp. 22–23, 26, 34, 37, 67–68; interview with Christopher Stone, January 6, 1992.
17 Ellen Warren, "Ex-Muckraker Covers Greek Beat," *LA Times*, May 4, 1980,

part 5, p. 23; Phyllis Theroux, "Izzy Stone's 'Last Scoop,' " *Washington Post,* March 21, 1983, pp. B1–2.

18 Interview with Christopher Stone, January 6, 1992.

19 Ibid.

20 Ilene Barth to B. J. Stone, n.d., I. F. Stone Memories.

21 Interview with Christopher Stone, January 6, 1992.

22 David E. Rosenbaum, "I. F. Stone at 80: The Scooping Goes On," *New York Times,* December 24, 1987, p. A12.

23 Stone, "When Free Speech Was First Condemned," *Harper's* 276 (February 1988): 60–65.

24 Stone, *The Trial of Socrates* (Boston: Little, Brown, 1988), pp. xi, 9–51, 64, 75, 83, 92.

25 Ibid., pp. 87, 97, 178, 230.

26 G. W. Bowersock, "Athens's Dirty Secret," *New Republic* 198 (March 28, 1988): 38; John Leonard, "Putting the Case," *Nation* 246 (February 27, 1988): 274; Christopher Lehmann-Haupt, "Books of the Times," *NY Times,* January 18, 1988, p. C20; Fred S. Holley, "Goering Took Poison Too," *LA Times,* February 14, 1988, p. B2.

27 Bowersock, "Athens's Dirty Secret," p. 38; Lehmann-Haupt, "Books of the Times," p. 20; William H. Leckle, Jr., "Was Socrates a Martyr or Arrogant Holy Man?" *St. Louis Post-Dispatch,* February 21, 1988, p. 5C; Donald Kagan, "Death in Athens," *Commentary* 85 (March 1988): 73–74, 76.

28 Julia Annas, "Down with Democracy!" *NY Times,* February 7, 1988, section 7, p. 7; Gary Houston, "In Pursuit of Socrates and I. F. Stone," *Chicago Tribune,* February 14, 1988, section 14, p. 5; Thomas D'Evelyn, "When Socrates Talks . . . I. F. Stone Still Listens," *Christian Science Monitor,* January 20, 1988, p. 20; Leonard M. Evans, "Mistrial in the Cradle of Democracy," *San Francisco Chronicle,* February 7, 1988, p. 10.

29 Susan Reed, "Veteran Muckraker I. F. Stone Digs Up Dirt on Ancient Athens to Cover the Trial of Socrates," *People* 29 (April 18, 1988): 87–88; conversation with Stone, February 5, 1988; interview with Sidney Hook, June 30, 1983.

30 Stone, *The Trial,* pp. 87, 142.

31 David Armstrong, "Izzy Stone Finally Catches up to Socrates," *San Francisco Chronicle,* February 7, 1988, p. E1; conversation with Stone, February 5, 1988; Regan, "Izzy at 80," p. C3.

32 Interview with Stone, October 16, 1981.

33 David E. Rosenbaum, "Gentle Gadfly's Classic 'Scoop,' " *Chicago Tribune,* January 26, 1989, p. 3; memorial service, July 12, 1988.

34 Osnos, "I. F. Stone, a Journalist's Journalist," p. A23; memorial service, July 18, 1989; Martin Halstuk, "Journalist I. F. Stone Dies at 81," *San Francisco Chronicle,* June 19, 1989, p. A8.

35 "I. F. Stone, 1907–1989," *Nation* 249 (July 10, 1989): 37, 39–40; Larry Josephson interview with Studs Terkel, "Modern Times," radio program transcript, pp. 15–16.

36 "I. F. Stone, RIP," *National Review* 41 (July 14, 1989): 19; "Izzy Stone, R.I.P.," *New Republic* 201 (July 10, 1989): 8, 10.

37 Memorial service, July 18, 1989; *Guests.*

38 Ibid.

39 Ibid.

18. The Rock of Stone
   1 Interview with Stone, October 16, 1981.
   2 Ibid.
   3 Ibid.
   4 Interview with Stone, October 15, 1981.

Selected Bibliography

Note on Writings by I. F. Stone

Among the most valuable primary materials for this book were, quite naturally, Stone's own writings, from his first publications in 1922 until his final essays which appeared just before his death in June 1989. They include copies of his 1922 newsletter, *The Progress*, presently in the possession of Esther Stone, and of the 1925–26 editions of *Junto*, the Philomathean Society journal published at the University of Pennsylvania. Beginning in 1931, Stone served as an editorial writer on the *Philadelphia Record*, moving on to the *New York Post* in December 1933. While most of the editorials for these newspapers are unsigned, Stone did acknowledge responsibility for a handful of them (see chapters 3–4) and through careful examination it was possible to verify a small number of others. A series of editorials written by Stone and Sam Grafton, his co-worker at the *Post*, is contained in *Press Time: A Book of Post Classics* (1936), a copy of which was graciously given to me by Izzy himself. In 1933, Stone wrote a single essay for H. L. Mencken's *American Mercury* and a handful of articles for V. F. Calverton's *Modern Monthly*. From 1934 to 1948, he contributed to *The New Republic* and *The Nation*, particularly the latter from 1935 to 1946. *The Nation* pieces were of both the signed and unsigned variety. (The writers of unsigned editorials and editorial paragraphs in that journal can be ascertained with the assistance of priceless and incredibly fragile volumes held by the New York Public Library which often contain inscriptions indicating authorship.) Other Stone writings from that period can be found in *Current History* (1938), *The Southern Review* (1938–39), *Propaganda Analysis: A Bulletin to Help the Intelligent Citizen Detect and Analyze Propaganda* (1939), *Your Investments* (1940), and *The CIO and National Defense* (1941). His earliest books were *The Court Disposes* (1937) and *Business as Usual* (1941).

Beginning in 1940, Stone began writing for *PM*, an association that continued until June 1948. At that point, he joined the editorial staff of the *New York Star*, then returned to the *New York Post* from January to April 1949, at which time he moved over to the *New York Daily Compass*, where he remained until its closing in November 1952. His books during this period include *Underground to Palestine* (1946, 1978 second edition), *This Is Israel* (1948), *The Hidden History of the Korean War* (1952, 1969 second edition), and *The Truman Era* (1952), a collection of *The Nation* and *PM-Star-Compass* articles from 1946 to 1952. The recently published volume *The War Years* contains editorials and articles published in *The Nation* from 1939 to 1945.

Starting in January 1953, Stone began publication of *I. F. Stone's Weekly*, which had a nineteen-year run, through December 1971. Selections from the newsletter are contained in *The Haunted Fifties* (1963), *In a Time of Torment* (1967), *Polemics and Prophecies* (1971), and *I. F. Stone's Weekly Reader* (1973). *The Killings at Kent State* appeared in print in 1971.

In mid-1964, Stone began contributing to the *New York Review of Books*, and his final article in that journal was published a quarter of a century later. *In a Time of Torment* contains several early essays which first appeared in that publication, along with a single book review from *The New Republic*. A good number of the earlier pieces from the *New York Review* are collected in *Polemics and Prophecies*.

A smattering of Stone's later editorials can be found in the *New York Times*, the *Washington Post*, the *Chicago Tribune*, the *Los Angeles Times*, *Harper's*, *Technology Review*, and the *Progressive*. In 1982, Stone began to write once again for *The Nation*. In 1988, *The Trial of Socrates*, his final book, came out.

Secondary Sources

Aaron, Daniel. *Writers on the Left.* New York: Avon, 1969.

Abrahams, Edward. *The Lyrical Left: Randolph Bourne, Alfred Stieglitz, and the Origins of Cultural Radicalism in America.* Charlottesville: University Press of Virginia, 1988.

Adler, Leslie Kirby. "The Red Image: American Attitudes Towards Communism in the Cold War Era." Ph.D dissertation, University of California, Berkeley, 1970.

Alpern, Sarah. *Freda Kirchwey: A Woman of The Nation.* Cambridge: Harvard University Press, 1987.

Armstrong, David. *A Trumpet to Arms: Alternative Media in America.* Los Angeles: J. P. Tarcher, 1981.

Aronson, James. *Deadline for the Media: Today's Challenges to Press, TV & Radio.* Indianapolis: Bobbs-Merrill, 1972.

Belfrage, Cedric. *The American Inquisition, 1945–1960.* Indianapolis: Bobbs-Merrill, 1973.

———, and James Aronson. *Something to Guard: The Stormy Life of the National Guardian, 1948–1967.* New York: Columbia University Press, 1978.

Belknap, Michael R. *Cold War Political Justice: The Smith Act, the Communist Party, and American Civil Liberties.* Westport, Conn.: Greenwood, 1977.

Bliven, Bruce. *Five Million Words Later.* New York: John Day, 1970.

Bloom, Alexander. *Prodigal Sons: The New York Intellectuals and Their World.* New York: Oxford University Press, 1986.

Branch, Taylor. *Parting the Waters: America in the King Years, 1954–63.* New York: Simon and Schuster, 1988.

Breines, Wini. *Community and Organization in the New Left, 1962–1968.* New York: Praeger, 1982.

Brooks, Thomas R. *The Walls Come Tumbling Down.* Englewood Cliffs, N.J.: Prentice-Hall, 1974.

Buhle, Mari Jo et al. *Encyclopedia of the American Left.* New York: Garland, 1990.

Burns, James MacGregor. *Roosevelt: The Lion and the Fox.* New York: Harcourt, Brace, 1956.

Cantor, Milton. *The Divided Left: American Radicalism, 1900–1975:* New York: Hill and Wang, 1978.

Carson, Clayborne. *In Struggle: SNCC and the Black Awakening of the 1960s.* Cambridge: Harvard University Press, 1981.

Caute, David. *The Fellow-Travellers: A Postcript to the Enlightenment.* New Haven: Yale University Press, 1988.

———. *The Great Fear: The Anti-Communist Purge under Truman and Eisenhower.* New York: Simon and Schuster, 1979.

———. *The Year of the Barricades: A Journey Through 1968*. New York: Harper and Row, 1968.

Chafe, William H. *The Unfinished Journey: America since World War II*. New York: Oxford University Press, 1986.

Chalmers, David. *And the Crooked Places Made Straight: The Struggle for Social Change in the 1960s*. Baltimore: Johns Hopkins University Press, 1991.

Charney, George. *A Long Journey*. Chicago: Quadrangle, 1968.

Clecack, Peter. *Radical Paradoxes: Dilemmas of the American Left, 1945–1970*. New York: Harper and Row, 1973.

Conlin, Joseph R., ed. *The American Radical Press, 1880–1960*. Westport, Conn.: Greenwood, 1974.

Cook, Fred J. *The Nightmare Decade*. New York: Random House, 1971.

Cooney, Terry A. *The Rise of the New York Intellectuals: Partisan Review and Its Circle, 1934–1945*. Madison: University of Wisconsin Press, 1986.

Cowley, Malcolm. *—and I Worked at the Writer's Trade*. New York: Viking, 1978.

———. *Conversations with Malcolm Cowley*. Jackson: University Press of Mississippi, 1986.

———. *The Dream of the Golden Mountains: Remembering the 1930s*. New York: Penguin, 1981.

Crossman, Richard, ed. *The God That Failed*. New York: Bantam, 1965.

Crowl, James William. *Angels in Stalin's Paradise: Western Reporters in Soviet Russia, 1917 to 1937, a Case Study of Louis Fischer and Walter Duranty*. Washington, D.C.: University Press of America, 1982.

Daniels, Robert V. *Year of the Heroic Guerrilla: World Revolution and Counterrevolution in 1968*. New York: Basic, 1989.

DeBenedetti, Charles, and Charles Chatfield. *An American Ordeal: The Antiwar Movement of the Vietnam Era*. Syracuse: Syracuse University Press, 1990.

Diggins, John P. *The American Left in the Twentieth Century*. New York: Harcourt Brace Jovanovich, 1973.

———. *Mussolini and Fascism: The View from America*. Princeton: Princeton University Press, 1975.

———. *Up from Communism: Conservative Odysseys in American Intellectual History*. New York: Harper and Row, 1975.

Donner, Frank J. *The Age of Surveillance: The Aims and Methods of America's Political Intelligence System*. New York: Vintage, 1981.

Downie, Leonard, Jr. *The New Muckrakers*. New York: New American Library, 1976.

Draper, Theodore. *American Communism and Soviet Russia*. New York: Vintage, 1986.

Flacks, Richard. *Making History: The Radical Tradition in American Life*. New York: Columbia University Press, 1988.

Freidel, Frank. *Franklin D. Roosevelt: A Rendezvous with Destiny*. Boston: Little, Brown, 1990.

Friedman, Murray, ed. *Jewish Life in Philadelphia, 1830–1940*. Philadelphia: Ishi Publications, 1983.

Garrow, David J. *Bearing the Cross: Martin Luther King, Jr., and the Southern Christian Leadership Conference*. New York: Vintage, 1988.

Gilbert, James. *Writers and Partisans: A History of Literary Radicalism in America*. New York: Wiley, 1968.

Gillon, Steven M. *Politics and Vision: The ADA and American Liberalism, 1947–1985*. New York: Oxford University Press, 1987.

Gitlin, Todd. *The Sixties: Years of Hope, Days of Rage.* New York: Bantam, 1987.

Goldstein, Robert Justin. *Political Repression in Modern America: From 1870 to the Present.* New York: Schenkman, 1978.

Goodman, Walter. *The Committee: The Extraordinary Career of the House Committee on Un-American Activities.* New York: Farrar, Straus, 1968.

Goodwin, Richard N. *Remembering America: A Voice from the Sixties.* New York: Harper and Row, 1988.

Gornick, Vivian. *The Romance of American Communism.* New York: Basic, 1977.

Griffith, Robert. *The Politics of Fear: Joseph R. McCarthy and the Senate.* Lexington: University Press of Kentucky, 1970.

————, and Athan Theoharis. *The Specter: Original Essays on the Cold War and the Origins of McCarthyism.* New York: New Viewpoints, 1974.

Guttmann, Allen. *The Wound in the Heart: America and the Spanish Civil War.* New York: Free Press of Glencoe, 1962.

Halberstam, David. *The Powers That Be.* New York: Dell, 1979.

Hallin, Daniel C. *The 'Uncensored War': The Media and Vietnam.* New York: Oxford University Press, 1986.

Halstead, Fred. *Out Now! A Participant's Account of the American Movement against the Vietnam War.* New York: Monad Press, 1978.

Hamby, Alonzo L. *Beyond the New Deal: Harry S. Truman and American Liberalism.* New York: Columbia University Press, 1973.

Heale, M. J. *American Anticommunism: Combating the Enemy Within, 1830–1970.* Baltimore: Johns Hopkins University Press, 1990.

Hess, Stephen. *The Washington Reporters.* Washington, D.C.: Brookings Institution, 1981.

Hicks, Granville. *Part of the Truth.* New York: Harcourt, Brace and World, 1965.

————. *Where We Came Out.* Westport, Conn.: Greenwood, 1973.

Hobsbawm, Eric. *The Revolutionaries.* New York: Pantheon, 1973.

Hollander, Paul. *Anti-Americanism: Critiques at Home and Abroad, 1965–1990.* New York: Oxford University Press, 1992.

————. *Political Pilgrims: Travels of Western Intellectuals to the Soviet Union, China, and Cuba, 1928–1978.* New York: Harper Colophon Books, 1983.

Hook, Sidney. *Out of Step: An Unquiet Life in the 20th Century.* New York: Harper and Row, 1987.

Hoopes, Roy. *Ralph Ingersoll: A Biography.* New York: Atheneum, 1985.

Howe, Irving, and Lewis Coser. *The American Communist Party: A Critical History.* New York: Praeger, 1962.

Irons, Peter. *Justice at War.* New York: Oxford University Press, 1983.

Isserman, Maurice. *If I Had a Hammer . . . : The Death of the Old Left and the Birth of the New Left.* New York: Basic, 1987.

————. *Which Side Were You On?: The American Communist Party during the Second World War.* Middletown, Conn.: Wesleyan University Press, 1982.

Josephson, Matthew. *Infidel in the Temple: A Memoir of the Nineteen-Thirties.* New York: Knopf, 1967.

Kadushin, Charles. *The American Intellectual Elite.* Boston: Little, Brown, 1974.

Katz, Milton S. *Ban the Bomb: A History of SANE, the Committee for a Sane Nuclear Policy, 1957–1985.* New York: Greenwood, 1986.

Kazin, Alfred. *Starting Out in the Thirties.* New York: Vintage, 1980.

Klehr, Harvey. *The Heyday of American Communism: The Depression Decade.* New York: Basic, 1984.

Kutcher, James. *The Case of the Legless Veteran.* New York: Monad Press, 1973.

Kutler, Stanley I. *The American Inquisition: Justice and Injustice in the Cold War.* New York: Hill and Wang, 1982.

Lader, Lawrence. *Power on the Left: American Radical Movements since 1946.* New York: Norton, 1979.

Lamson, Peggy. *Roger Baldwin: Founder of the American Civil Liberties Union.* Boston: Houghton Mifflin, 1976.

Lawson, R. Alan. *The Failure of Independent Liberalism, 1930–1941:* New York: Putnam's, 1971.

Leuchtenburg, William E. *Franklin D. Roosevelt and the New Deal, 1932–1940.* New York: Harper and Row, 1963.

Levy, David W. *The Debate over Vietnam.* Baltimore: Johns Hopkins University Press, 1991.

Lewy, Guenter. *The Cause That Failed: Communism in American Political Life.* New York: Oxford University Press, 1990.

Lottman, Herbert. *The Left Bank: Writers, Artists, and Politics from the Popular Front to the Cold War.* San Francisco: Halo Books, 1991.

Ludington, Townsend. *John Dos Passos: A Twentieth Century Odyssey:* New York: Dutton, 1980.

Lyons, Eugene. *The Red Decade: The Classic Work on Communism in America during the Thirties.* Indianapolis: Bobbs-Merrill, 1941.

MacDougall, Curtis D. *Gideon's Army.* 3 vols. New York: Marzani and Munsell, 1965.

Markowitz, Norman D. *The Rise and Fall of the People's Century: Henry Wallace and American Liberalism, 1941–1948.* New York: Free Press, 1973.

Matusow, Allen J. *The Unraveling of America: A History of Liberalism in the 1960s.* New York: Harper and Row, 1984.

McAuliffe, Mary Sperling. *Crisis on the Left: Cold War Politics and American Liberalism, 1947–1954.* Amherst: University of Massachusetts Press, 1978.

McElvaine, Robert. *The Great Depression: America, 1929–1941.* New York: Times, 1984.

McKay, Kenneth Campbell. *The Progressive Movement of 1924.* New York: Columbia University Press, 1947.

McWilliams, Carey. *The Education of Carey McWilliams.* New York: Simon and Schuster, 1979.

Meier, August, and Elliot Rudwick. *CORE: A Study in the Civil Rights Movement, 1942–1968.* New York: Oxford University Press, 1973.

Miller, James. *"Democracy Is in the Streets": From Port Huron to the Siege of Chicago.* New York: Simon and Schuster, 1987.

Mitford, Jessica. *A Fine Old Conflict.* New York: Vintage, 1978.

Mitgang, Herbert. *Dangerous Dossiers: Exposing the Secret War against America's Greatest Authors.* New York: Ballantine, 1989.

Myers, Constance A. *The Prophet's Army: Trotskyists in America, 1928–1941.* Westport, Conn.: Greenwood, 1977.

Navasky, Victor S. *Naming Names.* New York: Penguin, 1981.

Nigro, Richard. "The Limits of Vision: I. F. Stone—Reluctant Progressive." Ph.D. dissertation, University of Minnesota, Minneapolis, 1980.

Nobile, Philip. *Intellectual Skywriting: Literary Politics and the New York Review of Books.* New York: Charterhouse, 1974.

O'Neill, William L. *A Better World: The Great Schism: Stalinism and the American Intellectuals.* New York: Simon and Schuster, 1982.

———. *Coming Apart: An Informal History of America in the 1960s.* New York: Times Books, 1971.

O'Reilly, Kenneth. *Hoover and the Un-Americans: The FBI, HUAC, and the Red Menace.* Philadelphia: Temple University Press, 1983.

Oshinsky, David M. *A Conspiracy So Immense: The World of Joe McCarthy.* New York: Free Press, 1983.

Paterson, Thomas G., ed. *Cold War Critics: Alternatives to American Foreign Policy in the Truman Years.* Chicago: Quadrangle, 1971.

Patner, Andrew. *I. F. Stone: A Portrait.* New York: Pantheon, 1988.

Peck, Abe. *Uncovering the Sixties: The Life and Times of the Underground Press.* New York: Pantheon, 1985.

Pells, Richard H. *The Liberal Mind in a Conservative Age: American Intellectuals in the 1940s and 1950s.* New York: Harper and Row, 1985.

———. *Radical Visions and American Dreams: Culture and Social Thought in the Depression Years.* New York: Harper and Row, 1974.

Pemberton, William E. *Harry S. Truman: Fair Dealer and Cold Warrior.* Boston: Twayne, 1989.

Pierce, Robert Clayton. "Liberals and the Cold War: Union for Democratic Action and Americans for Democratic Action, 1940–1949." Ph.D. dissertation, University of Wisconsin, Madison, 1979.

Powers, Richard Gid. *Secrecy and Power: The Life of J. Edgar Hoover.* New York: Free Press, 1987.

Powers, Thomas. *The War at Home.* New York: Grossman, 1973.

Protess, David L. et al. *The Journalism of Outrage: Investigative Reporting and Agenda Building in America.* New York: Guilford Press, 1991.

Radosh, Ronald, and Joyce Milton. *The Rosenberg File: A Search for the Truth.* New York: Holt, Rinehart and Winston, 1983.

Raines, Howell. *My Soul Is Rested. Movement Days in the Deep South Remembered.* New York: Putnam's, 1977.

Ritchie, Donald A. *Press Gallery: Congress and the Washington Correspondents.* Cambridge: Harvard University Press, 1991.

Robinson, Jo Ann. *Abraham Went Out: A Biography of A. J. Muste.* Philadelphia: Temple University Press, 1981.

Rosenstone, Robert A. *Crusade of the Left: The Lincoln Battalion in the Spanish Civil War.* New York: Pegasus, 1969.

Rosten, Leo C. *The Washington Correspondents.* New York: Harcourt, Brace, 1937.

Sale, Kirkpatrick. *SDS.* New York: Vintage, 1974.

Schalk, David L. *War and the Ivory Tower: Algeria and Vietnam.* New York: Oxford University Press, 1991.

Schlesinger, Arthur M., Jr. *The Age of Roosevelt: The Crisis of the Old Order, 1919–1933.* Boston: Houghton Mifflin, 1957.

———. *The Vital Center: The Politics of Freedom.* Boston: Houghton Mifflin, 1949.

Seideman, David. *The New Republic: A Voice of Modern Liberalism.* New York: Praeger, 1986.

Seldes, George. *Lords of the Press.* New York: Julian Messner, 1938.

Shannon, David A. *The Decline of American Communism: A History of the Communist Party of the United States since 1945.* New York: Harcourt, Brace, 1959.

Shi, David E. *Matthew Josephson: Bourgeois Bohemian.* New Haven: Yale University Press, 1981.

Simon, Rita James. *As We Saw the Thirties: Essays on Social and Political Movements of a Decade.* Urbana: University of Illinois Press, 1969.

Starobin, Joseph R. *American Communism in Crisis, 1943–1957.* Cambridge: Harvard University Press, 1972.

Steinberg, Peter. *The Great 'Red Menace': United States Prosecution of American Communists, 1947–1952.* Westport, Conn.: Greenwood, 1984.

Stern, J. David. *Memoirs of a Maverick Publisher.* New York: Simon and Schuster, 1962.

Straight, Michael. *After Long Silence.* New York: Norton, 1983.

Swanberg, W. A. *Norman Thomas: The Last Idealist.* New York: Scribner's, 1976.

Taylor, S. J. *Stalin's Apologist: Walter Duranty: The New York Times's Man in Moscow.* New York: Oxford University Press, 1990.

Tebbel, John. *The Media in America.* New York: Crowell, 1974.

———, and Mary Ellen Zuckerman. *The Magazine in America, 1741–1990.* New York: Oxford University Press, 1991.

Theoharis, Athan G. *Seeds of Repression: Harry S. Truman and the Origins of McCarthyism.* New York: Quadrangle, 1977.

———, and John Stuart Cox. *The Boss: J. Edgar Hoover and the Great American Inquisition.* New York: Bantam, 1990.

Tomes, Robert R. "American Intellectuals and the Vietnam War, 1954–1975." Ph.D. dissertation, New York University, New York, 1987.

Unger, Irwin. *The Movement: A History of the American New Left, 1959–1972.* New York: Dodd, Mead, 1974.

———, and Debi Unger. *Turning Point: 1968.* New York: Scribner's, 1988.

Viorst, Milton. *Fire in the Streets.* New York: Simon and Schuster, 1979.

Vogelgesang, Sandy. *The Long Dark Night of the Soul: The American Intellectual Left and the Vietnam War.* New York: Harper and Row, 1974.

Wald, Alan M. *The New York Intellectuals: The Rise and Decline of the Anti-Stalinist Left from the 1930s to the 1980s.* Chapel Hill: University of North Carolina Press, 1987.

Walker, Samuel. *In Defense of Civil Liberties: A History of the ACLU.* New York: Oxford University Press, 1990.

Warren, Frank A. III. *An Alternative Vision: The Socialist Party of the 1930s.* Bloomington: Indiana University Press, 1974.

———. *Liberals and Communism: The "Red Decade" Revisited.* Westport, Conn.: Greenwood, 1976.

Wechsler, James A. *The Age of Suspicion.* New York: Random House, 1953.

Weinstein, Allen. *Perjury: The Hiss-Chambers Case.* New York: Knopf, 1978.

Weinstein, James. *Ambiguous Legacy: The Left in American Politics.* New York: New View Points, 1975.

Westby, David L. *The Clouded Vision: The Student Movement in the United States in the 1960s.* Lewisburg, Pa.: Bucknell University Press, 1975.

Whitfield, Stephen J. *The Culture of the Cold War.* Baltimore: Johns Hopkins University Press, 1991.

Wilson, Edmund. *To The Finland Station: A Study in the Writing and Acting of History.* Garden City, N.Y.: Doubleday, 1953.

Wittner, Lawrence S. *Rebels against War: The American Peace Movement, 1933–1983.* Philadelphia: Temple University Press, 1984.

Wolfskill, George, and John Hudson. *All But the People: Franklin D. Roosevelt and His Critics, 1933–1939.* Toronto: Macmillan, 1969.

Yarnell, Allen. *Democrats and Progressives: The 1948 Presidential Election as a Test of Postwar Liberalism.* Berkeley: University of California Press, 1974.

Young, Nigel. *An Infantile Disorder? The Crisis and Decline of the New Left.* London: Routledge and Kegan Paul, 1977.

Zaroulis, Nancy, and Gerald Sullivan. *Who Spoke Up? American Protest against the War in Vietnam, 1963–1975.* Garden City, N.Y.: Doubleday, 1984.

Index